Surveys in Monetary Economics

Volume 1: Monetary Theory and Policy

Edited by Christopher J. Green and
David T. Llewellyn

On Behalf of the Money Study Group

BLACKWELL
Cambridge MA & Oxford UK

First published 1991

Basil Blackwell Ltd
108 Cowley Road, Oxford, OX4 1JF, UK

Basil Blackwell, Inc.
3 Cambridge Center
Cambridge, Massachusetts 02142, USA

British Library Cataloguing in Publication Data

A CIP catalogue record for this book is available from the British Library.

Library of Congress Cataloging in Publication Data

Monetary theory and policy / edited by Christopher J. Green and David
    T. Llewellyn.
        p.   cm. — (Surveys in monetary economics: v. 1)
        Includes bibliographical references.
        ISBN 0-631-17847-3
        1. Money — Great Britain.   2. Monetary policy — Great Britain.
    I. Green, Christopher J.   II. Llewellyn, David T.   III. Series.
    HG939.5.S97   vol. 1
    332.4'941   s — dc20
    [332.4'941]   90-994 CIP

Typeset in Times on 10/12pt
by Colset Private Ltd., Singapore
Printed in Great Britain by T.J. Press Ltd., Padstow, Cornwall

Contents

Notes on Contributors

David Currie is Professor of Economics, Dean of Research and Director of the Centre for Economic Forecasting at the London Business School. He was formerly Professor of Economics and Head of Department at Queen Mary College, University of London. He is currently Chairman of the Money Study Group, and a Research Fellow of the Centre for Economic Policy Research. He has published extensively in the fields of monetary economics, macroeconomics and international macroeconomics, and comments regularly on UK and international macroeconomic developments and policy issues.

Keith Cuthbertson is Professor of Money and Finance at the University of Newcastle upon Tyne. He has undertaken work in macroeconomics and applied econometrics for HM Treasury, the Bank of England, the National Institute of Economic and Social Research and various city institutions. He has published widely in the areas of monetary economics and applied econometrics. He is a member of the committee of the Money Study Group.

Charles Goodhart is the Norman Sosnow Professor of Banking and Finance at the London School of Economics (LSE). Before joining the LSE in 1985, he worked at the Bank of England for 17 years as a monetary adviser, becoming Chief Adviser in 1980. Earlier he had taught at Cambridge and LSE. He has written a couple of books on monetary history; he has just revised his graduate monetary textbook, *Money, Information and Uncertainty* (1989); he published a collection of papers on monetary policy, *Monetary Theory and Practice* (1984), and an institutional study of *The Evolution of Central Banks*, revised and republished (MIT Press) in 1988.

He was Chairman of the Money Study Group during the years 1985–9, and a committee member from 1977 until 1989.

Christopher J. Green is Sir Julian Hodge Professor of Banking and Finance at Cardiff Business School, University of Wales College of Cardiff. Educated at Oxford and Yale universities, he has been on the staff of the International Monetary Fund in the African Department and has taught at Manchester University. Prior to taking up his present appointment, in 1985, he was an assistant adviser in the Economics Division of the Bank of England. His main areas of interest are in portfolio analysis, asset price formation, and monetary policy in the industrial and developing countries, and he has published a number of articles in these areas. He was secretary of the Money Study Group from 1983 to 1986 and has been treasurer since 1986.

David Laidler is Professor of Economics at the University of Western Ontario, and was formerly Professor of Economics at the University of Manchester. He was one of the founders of the Money Study Group and served on its executive until 1975. He is the author of many works in the area of monetary economics.

Paul Levine is Professor of Economics at Leicester University and was formerly Senior Research Officer, Centre for Economic Forecasting, London Business School. His research interests include open economy macroeconomics, macroeconomic policy design, reputation and international macroeconomic policy co-ordination issues. He has many publications in leading journals in the above areas and is co-author of a forthcoming book (with David Currie), *Macroeconomic Policy Design in an Open Economy* (Cambridge University Press).

Ronald MacDonald is currently Robert Fleming Professor of Finance and Investment in the Economics Department of the University of Dundee. He is the author of *Floating Exchange Rates: Theories and Evidence*, joint author of *International Money: Theory, Evidence and Institutions*, co-editor of *Exchange Rates and Open Economy Macroeconomics* and *Recent Developments in Australian Monetary Economics*, and has also written numerous articles on international finance and macroeconomics. He has been visiting Professor of Economics at Queen's University, Canada, and the University of New South Wales, Australia.

Kent Matthews studied at the London School of Economics (LSE), Birkbeck College and Liverpool University. He has worked at the LSE, the National Institute of Economic and Social Research and Liverpool University and is currently at Cardiff Business School. While at Liverpool he was also the principal forecaster for the Liverpool Macroeconomic Research Group. His research work has mainly been in the area of macroeconomic modelling. He has held visiting appointments at the University of Leuven, the Bank of England and the University of Western Ontario.

David Miles is a lecturer in economics at Birkbeck College and a member of the Financial Markets Group at the London School of Economics. He worked for several years in the Economics Division of the Bank of England where he undertook several studies in monetary and financial issues.

A. Robert Nobay is currently the Brunner Professor of Economic Science at the University of Liverpool. He was one of the founders of the Money Study Group and served on its executive until 1975. He is the author of many works in the area of monetary economics.

Michael Parkin was an undergraduate at the University of Leicester and has held appointments at the Universities of Sheffield, Leicester, Essex, Manchester and Western Ontario. Currently, he is professor of economics at the University of Western Ontario, and formerly chairman. He has held visiting appointments at Brown University, The Reserve Bank of Australia, the Bank of Japan, and the Hoover Institution at Stanford University. He has served on the editorial boards of the *American Economic Review* and the *Journal of Monetary Economics*, and as managing editor of the *Manchester School* and the *Canadian Journal of Economics*. He is the author of *Macroeconomics* (Prentice-Hall) and *Economics* (Addison-Wesley). Michael Parkin's research on macroeconomics, monetary economics, and international economics has resulted in 160 publications in journals and edited volumes including the *American Economic Review*, the *Journal of Political Economy*, the *Review of Economic Studies*, the *Journal of Monetary Economics*, and the *Journal of Money, Credit and Banking*. His major contributions have been to the theory of portfolio choice, inflation, international finance, and business cycles.

Mark P. Taylor is Morgan Grenfell Professor of Financial Markets at the City University Business School, London, and a Fellow of the Centre for Economic Policy Research. He graduated from Oxford University in 1980 and worked as a foreign exchange dealer in the City of London while studying part-time for a Master's degree at London University. He obtained his PhD from London University in 1984. His main research interests are in international finance, financial markets, applied monetary economics and econometrics and he is the author of numerous journal articles and several books in these and related areas. Before joining the City University Business

School, he was Robert Fleming Professor of Finance and Investment at the University of Dundee and before that a research economist at the Bank of England. He has acted as an economic and financial consultant to a number of organizations, including the Ford Motor Company and, since 1987, the Bank of England, and has supplied written evidence to several House of Commons and House of Lords Select Committees on monetary affairs. He has been a member of the Money Study Group Committee since 1987 and was National Secretary during the academic year 1989–90. He is currently Visiting Scholar in the Research Department of the International Monetary Fund, Washington, DC.

Joe Wilcox is an economic adviser in the Economics Division in the Bank of England. His work includes studies of the UK building societies and of money demand.

Foreword

David Laidler, Robert Nobay and Michael Parkin

These two volumes are published to celebrate the 20 years of existence of the Money Study Group. As founding members, we are delighted to share in these celebrations and to recall something of the establishment and the early years of the Group.

The mid-1960s was a watershed in UK monetary economics. The predominant influence of Richard Sayers and Radcliffian monetary analysis was being challenged by econometric modelling efforts and post-Keynesian monetary analysis at institutions such as the London School of Economics (LSE) and the Universities of Essex, Southampton and Sheffield.

Crucially, Harry Johnson returned to take up his position at the LSE in 1967 and, not surprisingly, became the natural leader of younger academics like ourselves who were interested in contemporary macro/monetary economics. He was generous with encouragement, advice and strictures, and, above all, impressed upon us our professional responsibilities to help create and sustain an active 'state of the art' intellectual environment in the UK. The very first gathering of monetary economists in the UK took place, very much under Harry's aegis, at Hove in October 1969. The meeting was held to commemorate the tenth anniversary of the Radcliffe Report, and to take stock of the progress made by monetary economics in the UK since its publication (Croome and Johnson, 1970). One objective of that meeting, as noted in the proceedings, 'was to establish some common ground and the beginnings of a mutually understood frame of reference among economists customarily observing the monetary system from a particular institutional vantage point'. The Hove meeting highlighted the difficulties in finding a common language among participants and pointed to the need for more frequent meetings among monetary economists.

Hove whetted our appetites for some sort of regular workshop, and at one of the many informal gatherings in Harry's room at the LSE, where wide-ranging discussions and generous hospitality were the order of the day, he recalled the by then defunct joint Cambridge–Oxford–LSE seminars. Initially, we broached the idea of a joint LSE–Essex–Southampton money workshop. To Harry, this smacked a little of elitism: why not make it a national forum if we could raise finance and ensure that the meetings would be occasions for serious and productive interchange of ideas? Once an idea made sense to him, Harry wanted immediate action. Luckily, David Worswick and Cathy Cunningham at the then Social Science Research Council immediately agreed that this particular idea had merit and so was born the Money Study Group, and indeed the very concept of Study Groups. It was put to us that in seeking funding it would be politic to come up with a proposal of more than one Group; therefore we indirectly helped set up the Econometric Study Group too!

The Money Study Group had no constitution, and the executive committee (which comprised Harry and ourselves) never met formally. Nevertheless, we were clear about our objectives. These were summarized as follows in the preface to one of our publications:

> The Money Study Group was formed in 1969 with the dual objectives of bringing together people in the United Kingdom concerned with the understanding of and research into the British monetary system, whether as academic scholars, bank economists, or officials of the Bank of England and the Treasury, and promoting research into monetary economics in the United Kingdom. The Group subscribes to no particular school of monetary doctrine: its membership includes Keynesians, monetarists, empiricists and institutionalists. (Johnson and Nobay, 1974)

The early years were busy and exciting – by 1974 we had held four major conferences, a special seminar at the Bank of England in June 1971 to consider the then consultative document on competition and credit control, and special seminars in honour of John Hicks and James Meade. The latter were held at Oxford and were the forerunners of the now annual Money Study Group Conference.

The needs of students were not forgotten. Very early on, we felt that there was a serious gap in the literature readily available to students. Therefore a group of us descended upon the tranquil shores of the Hamble River in the New Forest and over two days set about selecting papers to be included in a new volume of readings. A few weeks later, we gathered again at Manchester to finalize Readings in British Monetary Economics (Johnson et al., 1972). The volume served two purposes – it was a useful text in UK monetary economics, and its royalties provided the Group with modest but much needed financial resources. We also believed that graduate students working in the relative isolation of their own institutions would benefit from the opportunity of a broader forum. Therefore a two day workshop was held in Southampton in 1975, where graduate students at an advanced stage of thesis research presented papers and senior academics acted as discussants.

Frequent one day workshop meetings were organized around research topics that were emerging as promising and important – the optimum quantity of money, open economy macroeconomics, inflation and expectations were a few of the themes for these meetings. There was a steady stream of friends and visitors from abroad, and offers of papers from the UK and elsewhere. The Group's only rule was that membership was limited to those willing to offer a paper over a two year period – this helped avoid a free-rider problem. Senior academics took the Group seriously, rarely missed sessions and gave freely of their time. The sessions quickly developed into occasions for serious intellectual and social discourse between colleagues from various backgrounds and institutions. Harry Johnson had been so right to steer us towards making the Money Study Group a truly national organization.

The very first publication by the Money Study Group was a book of readings in British monetary economics. It is fitting that the Money Study Group, now firmly established in the profession, celebrates its two decades of existence by publishing a collection of specifically commissioned survey papers by UK authors in major topics in both monetary theory and policy and financial markets and institutions.

Bibliography

Clayton, G., Gilbert, J.C. and Sedgwick, R. (eds) (1971) *Monetary Theory and Monetary Policy in the 1970s*. Oxford: Oxford University Press.

Croome, D.R. and Johnson, H.G. (eds) (1970) *Money in Britain 1959–1969*. Oxford: Oxford University Press.

Johnson, H.G. and a committee of the Money Study Group (1972) *Readings in British Monetary Economics*. Oxford: Oxford University Press.

Johnson, H.G. and Nobay, A.R. (eds) (1974) *Issues in Monetary Economics*. Oxford: Oxford University Press.

Preface to Volume I

This is the first of a two-volume collection of papers specially commissioned to celebrate the twentieth anniversary of the Money Study Group. The early days of the Group are recalled in the Foreword by three of its founder members and distinguished 'alumnae': David Laidler, Bob Nobay and Michael Parkin. The aims of the Group today remain the same as they have always been: to bring together (in the UK) academics and other professionals concerned with monetary and financial issues and thus to promote research into and better understanding of these issues.

The papers in these volumes were commissioned with the object of providing a set of major surveys covering a broad range of monetary and financial issues. Each paper aims to offer a comprehensive survey and synthesis of the subject with which it is concerned, accessible to postgraduate and advanced undergraduate students specializing in the area, and a valuable work of reference to all professionals working in the field, whether in universities or elsewhere in the public or private sector. Volume I is concerned with monetary theory and policy; volume II is concerned with financial markets and institutions, particularly in the UK.

The authors of the papers in these volumes are all based in the UK. For this reason, all the papers emphasize, to varying degrees, research results which are particularly relevant to the UK. This emphasis is somewhat more apparent in volume II than in volume I. We do not claim that the papers in these volumes cover the entire field of monetary economics. An attempt at such coverage would have produced volumes of unmanageable proportions. However, we do believe that the papers and their authors are broadly representative of monetary economists who are currently active in the UK and of their various interests. The strengths and weaknesses of the volumes reflect the strengths and weaknesses of monetary economics in the UK, and, in this respect, we hope that they will provide a spur to continued efforts in areas of strength and to improvements in areas of weakness.

Although the volumes do emphasize research which is relevant to the UK, the editors and authors have sought to avoid a narrow parochialism. Researchers working in a small open economy like the UK are constantly aware of the international implications of and constraints on domestic monetary actions. All the papers reflect this international setting in varying degrees, and some are wholly international in their emphasis. For this reason we believe that the volumes will be of interest to an international audience of professionals interested in monetary issues, as well as to other UK-based researchers.

The editors have practised division of labour with Christopher Green mainly responsible for volume I and David Llewellyn mainly responsible for volume II. Nevertheless the editors accept joint responsibility for the volumes as a whole. Thanks are due to many people who helped in the production of these volumes, particularly to the Money Study Group Committee and to the authors themselves for responding with enthusiasm to the commissions which they were invited to undertake. We also appreciate the enthusiasm with which Mark Allin of Basil Blackwell responded to this proposal and his help in producing these volumes.

Finally, we thank the Economic and Social Research Council for their continuing support of the Money Study Group over the last 20 years. This support has helped to foster a good deal of the UK-based part of the research in monetary economics which is surveyed in these volumes.

Christoper J. Green
David T. Llewellyn

1 Modelling the Demand for Money

Keith Cuthbertson

1.1 INTRODUCTION

The history of research into the demand for money is a major element in the development of monetary economics generally. There are numerous theories and voluminous applied studies. It is impossible to give an exhaustive account of work in this area; instead we concentrate on the interaction between theory and applied work without, we hope, omitting any major developments.[1] The emphasis will be on recent developments, although these will be put in their historic context.

The search for a theoretically coherent yet empirically robust model of the demand for money is central to the transmission mechanism of monetary policy. In the simple fix-price IS–LM closed economy model the size of the interest elasticity and the stability of the demand for (narrow) money determine in part the efficacy of fiscal and monetary policy. The latter applies *a fortiori* if the demand for money depends on wealth as well as income (see, for example, Cuthbertson and Taylor, 1987b). In most closed economy macroeconometric models (e.g. US models) the impact of the money supply on inflation operates via excess demand and the (often long-run vertical) price expectations augmented Phillips curve (PEAPC). In such models there

Helpful comments and suggestions from David Laidler, David Hendry, Michael Sumner, Michael Artis, Charles Goodhart, Anton Muscatelli and the editors are gratefully acknowledged. Research assistance from Pandora Stone proved invaluable. The views expressed are those of the author and not necessarily those of the Bank of England. The usual disclaimer applies. Part of this work was conducted under Economic and Social Research Council research grant BO023148.

is a clear short-run trade-off between the speed at which inflation is reduced and the temporary loss in real output caused by a contraction in the money supply.

High inflation and the move to flexible exchange rates in the early 1970s rekindled academic interest in open economy models. The Mundell–Fleming model (Mundell, 1963; Fleming, 1962) provided the basic framework here which, with the addition of a wages version of the augmented Phillips curve and a cost mark-up price equation, explains the interaction between the money supply, prices and the exchange rate, and yields 'neutrality' in the long run. In the current account monetary (CAM) model of a small open economy the demand for money function provides the main transmission mechanism between the money supply and the exchange rate. Here the exchange rate is considered as the relative price of two currencies and the latter is determined by relative money supplies. The CAM model failed to give an adequate explanation of the large swings in the *real* exchange rate experienced in the second half of the 1970s. The deficiency in the model was not considered to lie primarily in a misspecification or instability in the demand for money function but in an inadequate treatment of expectations about the exchange rate. Capital account monetary (KAM) models (Dornbusch, 1976; Frankel, 1979) demonstrate how a contractionary money supply might cause exchange rate overshooting in a model with 'smart speculators' and 'sticky' goods prices (Buiter and Miller, 1982). In all the above analytic models (and some of their large-scale econometric counterparts, particularly for the USA) the demand for money function used was for narrow money, a targeted variable in a number of industrialized nations in the 1970s and 1980s. Thus the search for a stable demand function for narrow money became paramount if vigorous monetary targeting was to have a firm empirical base. In New Classical models, credible announcements about money supply growth could have an immediate impact on (flexible) goods prices and the costs of reducing inflation in terms of lost output were therefore thought to be relatively small. Again, the policy requires a stable demand function for narrow money.

In these simple analytic models the portfolio choice is between narrow money and domestic bonds with foreign bonds and domestic bonds (usually) considered as perfect substitutes (i.e. the uncovered interest parity condition). Recognition that money may not be a perfect substitute for domestic and foreign bonds leads one to a portfolio balance model (Branson et al., 1977) in which changes in wealth (via the public sector borrowing requirement (PSBR) or current account) affect the demand for money (and other assets) and exchange rate overshooting is possible without the assumption of sticky goods prices. Some countries have adopted broad money as an intermediate target (e.g. the UK targeted sterling M3 in the first half of the 1980s), and clearly portfolio theories of the demand for money and empirical evidence on the stability of broad money are a prerequisite for the credibility and success of such targeting.

If the demand for money function contains expectations variables then policy analysis must in principle recognize potential difficulties raised by the Lucas critique. Changes in monetary policy (regime changes) cause changes in the estimated parameters of the demand for money function and render 'conventional' policy simulations redundant. Put simply, it may be the case that a stable demand for money function estimated over a period when the money supply was endogenous may not prove to be stable when monetary targeting is introduced and interest rates become more volatile (Walsh, 1984; Baba et al., 1988).

An analysis of the demand for money provides an excellent example whereby our knowledge has progressed because of the interaction between theory and evidence, and this provides the focus for this survey. We begin in section 1.2 with an account of theories based on the 'motives' approach; this is followed by the 'consumer demand' approach and finally we discuss buffer stock models. Theories of the demand for money almost invariably give rise to static equilibrium relationships some of which contain expectations variables. We therefore briefly discuss the modelling of dynamic behaviour, expectations and risk in section 1.3. In section 1.4 we provide illustrative examples of the main empirical approaches to the demand for money, and we end with a brief summary.

1.2 THEORIES OF THE DEMAND FOR MONEY

Two characteristics of money provide the starting point for a number of theories of the demand for money. Its use as a universally acceptable means of exchange (at least in the domestic economy) leads to 'transactions models', some of which assume the level of transactions to be known (i.e. inventory models) and others where net inflows are uncertain (i.e. precautionary demand models). Money acts as a store of value, and this gives rise to risk aversion models where some assets in the choice set (e.g. equities, bonds) have an uncertain nominal return because capital gains and losses may occur. Thus considering the special characteristics of money results in theories that are based on explicit motives for holding money. In the theory of consumer demand, goods are held because the individual derives utility from them, but we do not enquire into the specific motives for holding particular goods (Friedman, 1956; Laidler, 1985). The theory of consumer demand can be applied to the demand for a portfolio of assets all of which are assumed to yield utility, and for want of a better term we label this the consumer theory approach.[2] One general characteristic of nearly all the models considered is that optimization is usually over a single period.

4 K. Cuthbertson

When we approach the demand for money by considering the motives for
holding money, the theories in the main are partial models in that only one
motive is usually considered (e.g. transactions). Similarly, in the consumer
theory approach the demand for a subset of assets is usually considered
to be weakly separable from other asset decisions and decisions about consumption, leisure etc. These simplifying assumptions are made so that tractable equations ensue.

1.2.1 Early Theories of the Demand for Money

The Cambridge economist Pigou (1917) took the quantity theory identity
(Fisher, 1911) $MV = PY$ (where M is the nominal money stock in circulation, P is the aggregate price level, Y is the level of transactions and V is
the velocity of circulation) and changed the focus of interest from a model
where V is determined by the payments mechanism to one where agents
have a desired demand for money. Implicitly this was a consumer theory
approach with the model reduced to $M^d = kPY$, where M^d is the desired
demand for money. It was recognized that k may depend on other variables
in the consumer allocation problem, such as interest rates and wealth, but
the main focus of interest was the level of transactions. Broadly speaking,
Keynes (1936) accepted the Cambridge view concerning the transactions
demand but introduced two further motives for holding money: precautionary and speculative. Keynes placed most emphasis on the latter.

1.2.2 Keynes and the Demand for Money

Keynes (1936) analysed the determinants of the transactions and the precautionary demand for money. In general he envisaged these two motives
for holding money as depending primarily on income and interest rates on
alternative assets. We concentrate here on Keynes's speculative motive. The
individual is assumed to choose between a 'capital-certain' asset such as
money and a 'risky' asset such as a bond. The main predictions from Keynes's
theory are, first, that individuals do not hold a diversified portfolio of
assets: they hold either all bonds or all money. Second, a downward-sloping
demand for money function with respect to the interest rate only occurs for
the aggregate demand for money. Finally, the theory predicts that in certain
circumstances the elasticity of the demand for money with respect to the
interest rate may become infinite: this is the liquidity trap. The individual
has a fixed holding period and forms expectations about the price of the
bond at the end of the holding period with perfect certainty, i.e. he has
inelastic expectations. Clearly, if he expected the return on the bond to

exceed the known interest rate on money r_m and he holds this expectation with perfect certainty, then he will put all his wealth in bonds. The individual does not hold a diversified portfolio; he is a 'plunger'.

Keynes hypothesized that individuals have regressive expectations:

$$g^e = \alpha(r - r_N) \qquad \alpha > 0 \tag{1.1}$$

where r_N is the normal rate of interest.

There are now two ways that we can generate a smooth demand for money function in the aggregate. First, α may differ between individuals. Second, if people hold different views about what constitutes the normal rate of interest then (for any given α) a rise in the current rate of interest will induce some but not all individuals to move into bonds.

Only a brief discussion of the liquidity trap follows as this aspect has not been prominent in the empirical literature. If interest rates are very low and have been so for some time then the normal rate will be low. At the time that Keynes wrote the *General Theory* interest rates had been around 2 per cent for some considerable period. At such low stable rates of interest a small rise in the current rate above the normal rate might be expected to be reversed very quickly. (In terms of equation (1.1) we are assuming that α becomes larger as the absolute level of the normal rate becomes lower.) Under such circumstances it follows that a large number of individuals might expect a large capital gain and would substantially reduce their money holdings even though the rate on bonds had risen only slightly. In other words, at low interest rates we expect the interest elasticity of the demand for money and bonds to be large (infinite). This is the liquidity trap.

To test the liquidity trap hypothesis we could posit a non-linear relationship for the expected capital gains function (1.1). The more usual method has been to estimate the interest elasticity in a period when interest rates are low and repeat the exercise for periods with high interest rates. The relative sizes of the two elasticities are then compared. However, if the rate of inflation provides an anchor for nominal interest rates, then the liquidity trap may apply equally well in periods with high nominal interest rates. This proposition can also be tested.

1.2.3 The Transactions Demand for Money: Inventory Models

The key assumptions in the inventory theoretical approach of Baumol (1952) are as follows: (a) the individual receives a known lump sum cash payment of T per period (say per annum) and spends it all evenly over the period; (b) the individual may invest in 'bonds' paying a known interest rate r per period or hold cash (money) paying zero interest; (c) the individual sells bonds to obtain cash in equal amounts K and incurs a (fixed) brokerage fee

b per transaction. In the model all relevant information is known with certainty.[3] Agents minimize the sum of brokerage costs bT/K and interest income forgone $rK/2$. The model yields a square root relationship between the demand for money and the level of income, the brokerage fee and the bond interest rate:

$$\ln\left(\frac{M^{\mathrm{d}}}{P}\right) = 0.5\left[\ln\left(\frac{b}{2}\right) + \ln\,T - \ln\,r\right] \tag{1.2}$$

We have included a unit price elasticity in (1.2) because a doubling of the price level doubles both b and T and therefore doubles M (T and b must now be considered as real variables rather than nominal variables).

Notice that the individual will always switch into bonds immediately and will have zero money balances before switching into bonds; since receipts are perfectly foreseen any other strategy would involve a loss of interest. Equation (1.2) determines the mean holdings of money and not money holdings at a point in time, a distinction not always observed in empirical work.

The brokerage fee consists of inconvenience costs (particularly of time) as well as any direct pecuniary costs (for example stockbrokers' or bank charges). The brokerage fee may vary with the real wage rate, if the latter measures the opportunity cost of time lost, or it may decrease owing to changes in payment mechanisms. Baumol's model predicts economies of scale in holding money: a doubling in the level of transactions leads to only a 50 per cent increase in money holdings. It follows that the distribution of transactions/income influences the demand for money.

One can easily extend the simple inventory model to include interest payments i on money to obtain

$$M^{\mathrm{d}} = \frac{K}{2} = \left[\frac{bT}{2(r-i)}\right]^{\frac{1}{2}} \tag{1.3}$$

The transactions elasticity is again $\frac{1}{2}$ but the interest elasticity is now $E_r = -r/2(r-i)$. In principle, the above model can easily be estimated in log linear form with coefficients of $\frac{1}{2}$ expected on T and $r-i$: the demand for money now depends on the relative interest rate.

Sprenkle (1969) provides a damaging critique of the inventory model when applied to large firms. First, Sprenkle argues that cash holdings of large firms can be explained by the existence of multiple accounts as much as by optimal inventory behaviour. Second, it may not be profitable for firms to undertake optimal cash management if receipts of each branch of the firm are small: the firm can minimize costs by not purchasing any securities at all but keeping all their receipts in cash. Third, Sprenkle demonstrates that if firms hold some optimal and some non-optimal balances the proportion of non-optimal receipts in total receipts does not have to be very large for non-optimal balances to dominate money holdings.

If the simple inventory model, either with or without decentralized cash holdings, cannot explain the cash holdings of firms, then what does? Sprenkle believes that cash holdings of US firms are primarily determined by compensating balances. Rather than pay bank charges directly, US firms hold compensating balances, even though they earn zero interest, in order to provide an implicit payment to banks for their banking services (i.e. payments mechanism, loans, advice etc.). Thus, if we wish to determine the size of compensating balances we need greater information on the costs and demand for banking services: the level of transactions and interest rates will not influence such balances. Clearly, it would be hazardous to apply the inventory model to the demand for (transactions) money balances of large firms.

In the UK, bank charges are incurred by firms in payment for banking services and cash management is more centralized than in the USA; therefore compensating balances should be relatively small and the inventory model more applicable. However, Sprenkle (1972) suggests that even in this case the inventory model is inappropriate for large firms as they will not hold cash in excess of the minimum amount required to invest in the overnight interbank market. Thus the demand for money will vary neither with interest rates nor with the level of transactions but with any institutional changes in this 'minimum overnight trading amount'. The fact that current (sight and deposit) accounts of companies increased by much less than those of the personal sector over 1960–80 is consistent with Sprenkle's view since (nominal) sales would have also increased substantially over this period. For persons, however, the inventory model may have some relevance but the relationship between money, interest rates and transactions is likely to be more complex than in the simple Baumol (1952) model.

Extensions to the Inventory Model

There have been a number of refinements to the simple inventory model. The Baumol (1952) model neglects integer constraints on the number of sales of assets. Tobin (1956) rectified this and found that it may be worthwhile for some individuals to hold no earning assets at all (a 'corner solution'); their demand for money is then proportional to the lumpy income receipts as in Fisher's model. Barro (1976) aggregated Tobin's corner solution and square root money holders (assuming a gamma distribution for the cross-sectional distribution of income) and found, not surprisingly, that the aggregate income elasticity lay between $\frac{1}{2}$ and unity. Karni (1974) proposed that the brokerage fee depended on the value of time. If the latter rises in proportion to real income, then the Baumol model yields an income elasticity of unity ($\frac{1}{2}$ from transactions and $\frac{1}{2}$ from the brokerage fee). Feige and Parkin (1971) and Santomero (1974) introduce commodities into the choice set of the inventory framework. There are transactions costs in moving into and out of durable goods, the yield on which is the expected rate of inflation (less storage and depreciation costs). The expected rate of inflation enters the determination of the demand for money (and bonds) but, somewhat surprisingly, its sign remains ambiguous (Grossman and Policano, 1975). Barro (1970) and Santomero (1974) endogenize the period between income receipts in the money–bonds–commodity inventory model. The corner solution now depends upon interest rates and transactions costs and in Barro's model (where earnings assets are excluded) money and expected inflation are negatively related. Clearly, results vary depending on the assumptions used, and it is dangerous to generalize.

The Transactions Demand for Money: Target Threshold Model

In this section we discuss an alternative approach to the modelling of the transactions demand for money in which money holdings are only actively adjusted when they hit an upper or lower threshold level. This target threshold model (Akerlof and Milbourne, 1980) is consistent with the 'stylized facts' of empirical demand for money functions since the model predicts that the short-run income elasticity is small (i.e. around zero) and may even take a small negative value.

There are two main variants of the Akerlof–Milbourne (AM) model. In the first there is no uncertainty but in the second the timing of lump sum expenditure plans by agents is uncertain. Broadly speaking, the certainty model is an inventory model while the second is more akin to a precautionary demand model. In the AM model agents adjust their money balances only when threshold points are reached. Second, they include uncertainty in the portfolio choice problem.

In its simplest form, the model with certain net receipts assumes (a) a lump sum receipt of Y per period and (b) spending of C at a constant rate through the period. Money balances accumulate via savings: $S = Y - C$. When the money balance hits the upper threshold H^*, it is returned to C, so that money balances are exhausted by the next receipt date.

In their model with certain receipts Akerlof and Milbourne obtain

$$\frac{\partial M}{\partial Y} = -s_y \frac{Y}{4} \tag{1.4}$$

where M is the average money holding and $s_y = \partial S/\partial Y$ is the marginal propensity to save and is assumed to be positively related to income. Hence, the short-run income elasticity is negative and takes a larger negative value the higher the level of income. This result is in sharp contrast with the

Baumol result and with the classical Fisher (1911) view. The latter can be represented (following Akerlof and Milbourne) as $M^d = \lambda Y$ where Y equals the constant inflow of receipts and λ is the average time that each dollar is held. Fisher's model (λ is assumed to be constant in the short run) gives a short-run income elasticity of unity.

Akerlof and Milbourne generalize the above model to incorporate uncertainty about spending plans in the form of small stochastic lump sum purchases of durable goods. When a durable good is purchased, money balances immediately fall (but not below zero since such purchases are 'small'). After lengthy calculations and assuming that the saving ratio $s = S/Y$ is constant, Akerlof and Milbourne obtain

$$\frac{\partial M}{\partial Y} = \frac{s}{4}\left[1 + p + Yp'(Y)\right] \tag{1.5}$$

where p is the probability of a durable purchase (in any time period). Equation (1.5) reduces to the 'constant spending' case (equation (1.4)) when $p = 0$ and $p'(Y) = 0$. If the probability of a durable goods purchase increases with income $p'(Y) > 0$, then the income elasticity of the demand for money is negative. Akerlof and Milbourne show that the latter result also holds when durable purchases are large.

In summary, the essence of the inventory theoretical models of the transactions demand for money (and bonds) is the assumption of certainty: certainty concerning the timing of income receipts, the timing of the return on money and bonds, and the brokerage fee. Even in this model the demand for money only obeys the square root 'law' in the simplest case. Following Sprenkle, we have noted major reservations concerning the ability of the inventory theoretical models to explain the demand for transactions balances of firms. Extensions of the model to include commodities in the choice set, although of interest, particularly as regards the impact of the expected rate of inflation on money holdings, have not proved very tractable.

Akerlof and Milbourne have presented a transactions model of the target threshold type with lump sum receipts and payments, and this results in the demand for money having a very low (even negative) income elasticity. They extend the model to include an element of uncertainty in the timing of lump sum durables expenditures, and again a low income elasticity is a feature of the model.

1.2.4 Precautionary Models

Models of the precautionary demand are based on the transactions motive for holding money, but in contrast with most inventory models we relax the assumption that receipts and payments are known with certainty. Agents minimize the expected cost of undertaking transactions: costs again consist of brokerage fees and the interest forgone on alternative assets (bond), and there is uncertainty about the size of net cash inflows. In general, the precautionary demand for money depends on the brokerage fee and the interest rate on bonds (as in the inventory models) but in addition some measure of the variability of transactions also influences desired money holdings.

Here we consider two approaches to the precautionary demand for money. In the first, the individual does not have access to any liabilities such as bank advances and must meet his uncertain transactions needs by switching between money and a bond with a known yield. The second model allows access to bank overdrafts (loans).

Money–Bonds and Precautionary Demand

Precautionary demand models assume that net receipts are uncertain but reduce the uncertainty to one of 'risk', i.e. the probability distribution of receipts/payments is assumed to be known. The assumptions of the model are as follows. The firm incurs a brokerage cost b if net payments per period N (i.e. payments less receipts) are greater than money holdings M. The brokerage fee involves costs of selling interest-bearing assets at short notice (e.g. time, inconvenience) and is usually assumed to be constant. Holding a higher level of money balances (which for the moment we assume earn zero interest) to reduce brokerage fees involves a loss of interest on 'bonds'. The agent will therefore trade off expected brokerage fees against interest forgone, in choosing his optimal money (and bond) holdings, in much the same fashion as in the non-stochastic inventory model.

If the probability distribution of net payments is centred on zero and the probability of net payments exceeding money holdings (i.e. $N > M$) is p then total expected brokerage costs are bp. Interest payments forgone are rM (r is the yield on the alternative asset) and expected total costs TC are

$$TC = Mr + pb \qquad (1.6)$$

Precautionary demand models give different results depending upon the assumption made about the probability p of illiquidity, and the results involve fairly complex derivations. For illustrative purposes consider Whalen's (1966) precautionary demand model (which assumes very risk averse behaviour). It can be shown that the probability p of $N > M$ takes a maximum value $p = \sigma^2/M^2$ where σ is the standard deviation of net payments.[4] Substituting for p in equation (1.6) and minimizing TC with respect to M gives

$$M = \left(\frac{2\sigma^2 b}{r}\right)^{\frac{1}{3}} \qquad (1.7)$$

and the second derivative $\delta^2 TC/\delta M^2 = \delta\sigma^2 b/M^4 > 0$ indicates a minimum.

As with the inventory models we obtain the result that the individual's mean holding of money (over some finite time interval) is positively related to the brokerage fee and negatively related to the interest rate on 'bonds' (but with an interest elasticity of $\frac{1}{3}$). The demand for money also increases with the (cube root) of the variance of expected net payments.

One is tempted to enquire whether income, which has featured so prominently in estimated demand for money functions, has any precise role to play in the precautionary demand model. The answer is yes, provided that some rather restrictive assumptions are made about the distribution of net receipts which here we take to be normally distributed. If the frequency of receipts and payments increases but the value of each receipt stays the same, then it can be shown (Whalen, 1966) that $\sigma^2 = K_1 Y$ where K_1 is a constant and Y is the volume of transactions; if the converse holds, then $\sigma^2 = K_2 Y^2$. Substituting these expressions in equation (1.7) we see that the income elasticity of the demand for money will vary between $\frac{1}{3}$ (increased frequency) and $\frac{2}{3}$ (increased transactions value). If an increase in the value of receipts is accompanied by a proportionate increase in the brokerage fee b (with an elasticity of $\frac{1}{3}$), then the price level elasticity is unity (i.e. a transactions value of $\frac{2}{3}$ plus a brokerage value of $\frac{1}{3}$).

For the individual, the relationship between income and the variance of transactions is likely to be more complex than that described above. For example, as incomes rise the frequency of transactions may fall as people attempt to economize on time, since the opportunity cost of time in terms of income forgone will be higher. Over time both the transactions value and the frequency of transactions are likely to alter in such a manner that the relationship between money holdings and income is impossible to determine. Another problem in testing the theory is that actual money balances are likely to comprise inventory balances and precautionary balances simultaneously; however, actual data on money cannot be separated into these two types of 'demands'.

The Miller–Orr (1966, 1968) precautionary demand model is similar to the one described above but the individual only switches between bonds and money when upper or lower bounds for money are reached. The decision variable is then the amount transferred at these limiting points. This gives rise to a demand for money (assuming a binomial distribution for the net cash drain with a zero mean) of the form

$$M = \frac{4}{3}\left(\frac{3bm^2 t}{4r}\right)^{\frac{1}{3}} \tag{1.8}$$

where m is the amount by which the cash balance is expected to alter (with a probability of $\frac{1}{2}$) and t is the frequency of transactions. The variance of transactions is proportional to $m^3 t$ and therefore implicitly appears in the above formula. The result is almost identical with Whalen's formula with a frequency elasticity $E_t^M = \frac{1}{3}$, a value elasticity $E_m^M = \frac{2}{3}$ and an interest elasticity $E_r^M = -\frac{1}{3}$. The Miller–Orr model therefore implies homogeneity (of degree one) for nominal money balances with respect to the price level.

Milbourne (1986) has examined the impact of financial innovation on monetary aggregates within the framework of the Miller–Orr model. For example, he finds that (for US definitions) M1 should be influenced more than M2 by a fall in transactions (brokerage) cost but that M1 should be largely unaffected by the introduction of interest-bearing capital-safe assets (e.g. money market mutual funds).

The Miller–Orr model, like the AM model, is also a target threshold model and therefore incorporates the intuitively appealing idea that money balances are adjusted only when they reach a ceiling or floor. Temporary or transitory changes in money are voluntarily held. This idea will appear in a slightly different context in the section on buffer stock money.

Money, Liquid Assets and Bank Advances in a Precautionary Demand Model

Sprenkle and Miller (1980) have extended the precautionary model to include the possibility of meeting an unexpected cash drain by (automatic) overdrafts at an interest cost r_0 as well as by running down liquid assets (with an interest rate r). The model is therefore particularly useful in analysing the demand for broad money (and bank advances) by large firms who have automatic overdraft facilities.

In the model 'money' earns zero interest; there are no brokerage fees but there is a trade-off between the probable cost of overdrafts relative to the return r from investing in (alternative) liquid assets. The model predicts (for $r_0 < 2r$) that optimal cash holdings are negative, i.e. firms should usually plan to use overdraft facilities. By assuming a normal distribution for the net cash drain it is possible to show that optimal cash holding depends upon the variance of the forecast error of cash balances, but explicit demand functions are difficult to derive. Sprenkle and Miller are able to show that the demand for broad money depends on relative interest rates and demand will rise continuously (in the form of increased overdrafts which appear on the liabilities side of the bank's balance sheet as money) as r rises relative to the overdraft rate r_0, even when $r < r_0$.

This dependence of the demand for broad money on the relative interest rate $r_0 - r$ could account in part for the rapid rise in the broad money supply in the UK in some periods of the 1970s and highlights the need to use relative interest rates in the demand function for broad money.

1.2.5 Risk Aversion Models

Risk aversion models deal with the problem of choice amongst a set of assets which have uncertain capital values. As the same suggests, these models assume that individuals maximize utility by trading off risk and return subject to a wealth constraint (Markowitz, 1952, 1959; Borch, 1969; Feldstein, 1969). Holding more of the risky asset (bond) increases the return to be obtained on the whole portfolio but may also increase the riskiness of the portfolio because of the possibility of capital gains and losses on the risky assets. Under such circumstances it may be worthwhile holding a capital-safe asset such as money even if the latter does not earn interest. Risk aversion models allow the individual to hold a diversified portfolio, including money and bonds, which depends on expected returns, initial wealth and the variance–covariance matrix of returns.

The precise functional form for the asset demand functions depends on the particular parameterization for the utility function and the maximand chosen (the latter is usually assumed to depend either on the expected utility from the return on the total portfolio or end-of-period wealth).[5] The most common functional forms for the utility function are the negative exponential, a power function or the quadratic. End-of-period wealth may be nominal or real.

If all stochastic returns are regarded as normally distributed, or we disregard moments higher than second order in the distribution of W_{t+1}, then[6]

$$E[U(W_{t+1})] = U(W^e_{t+1}) + \tfrac{1}{2} U''(W^e_{t+1}) V_{t+1} \qquad (1.9)$$

If m^e is a $k \times 1$ vector of expected (proportionate) returns over the fixed holding period, m is the actual return (i.e. the known running yield plus the expected capital gain), S is the covariance matrix of returns and A is a $k \times 1$ vector of desired asset holdings at time t, then $W^e_{t+1} = (i + m^e)'A$ and $V_{t+1} = A'SA$, the variance of W_{t+1}. Maximizing (1.9) subject to a nominal wealth constraint $W_t = i'A$ yields asset demand functions of the form

$$A_t = \frac{1}{\theta} Q(i + m^e)_t + BW_t \qquad (1.10)$$

$$\theta = -\frac{U''(W^e_{t+1})}{U'(W^e_{t+1})} \qquad (1.11)$$

where i is the unit vector, Q and B are functions of the variance–covariance matrix of asset returns S and θ is the coefficient of absolute risk aversion. The set of assets in A may contain at most one capital-safe asset, money, and the asset demands satisfy the adding up constraint. Results from here on depend on the explicit form of the utility function chosen. For the negative exponential $U(W_{t+1}) = a - b \exp(-cW_{t+1})$, which exhibits constant absolute risk aversion, the asset demand functions exhibit characteristics analogous to those from neoclassical consumer demand theory,[7] namely symmetry and homogeneity with respect to expected returns and concavity $(\partial Ai/\partial m_i^e > 0)$. (Homogeneity implies that asset demands depend on relative expected nominal yields.) Symmetry and homogeneity substantially reduce the number of parameters to be estimated (note that the adding up constraint is not testable) and are a test of the basic axioms of rational choice (Deaton and Muellbauer, 1980).

Courakis (1989) contests the result of Friedman and Roley (1987) that for a power utility function (which exhibits constant relative risk aversion) asset demands are linear in expected returns and exhibit homogeneity and symmetry in expected returns. (However, Courakis agrees that these asset demands are homogeneous in initial wealth.) Dalal (1983) also provides some interesting counter-intuitive results for the expected utility approach. Clearly, different assumptions concerning the form of the utility function lead to different functional forms for the demand equations in the mean–variance approach, but the demand for assets (including the safe asset 'money') in general depends on expected returns, initial wealth, the variance–covariance matrix and the parameters of the utility function.

Although the mean–variance model has some desirable features, it is not universally applicable to all asset choices. Because assets are only distinguished according to their different variance–covariance characteristics it allows only one safe asset. In a world where a wide array of capital-certain 'short-term' assets with low transactions costs exists, these will dominate the low-interest asset narrow money for speculative purposes. The mean–variance model therefore determines the demand for short-term assets but not the demand for narrow money: the latter is not held at all in a speculative model. It can be demonstrated that with three assets–money, a short-term asset and a bond – money will be dominated in the portfolio by the short-term asset, if the return on money is less than the return on shorts and the variance on shorts is small (Sprenkle, 1974; Chang et al., 1983, 1984). However, if a wide group of assets paying competitive interest rates are included in the definition of money, the more likely it is that the mean–variance model will be applicable to explaining the demand for what will then be termed broad money or broad liquidity. In addition, it must be recognized that the model ignores the brokerage costs of switching between different assets.[8] A switch between longs and shorts involves two brokerage fees, whereas only one is required if the switch is into (narrow) money. Although the cost of switching may be small per transaction, nevertheless, if frequent switching takes place, total transactions cost may not be negligible. If switching costs are included in the mean–variance model, which realism dictates they should be, then this biases the decision away from the domination of (narrow) money by short-term assets. Hence in a more realistic mean–variance model there may be additional brokerage cost reasons for holding money (Sprenkle, 1974; Chang et al., 1984). However, the formal model presented above does not explicitly include such brokerage costs.

In the empirical implementation of the mean–variance model it is usually assumed that the variance–covariance matrix of asset returns is constant over time. If the latter assumption is incorrect then coefficient instability will result. Time-varying covariances seem a definite possibility in time series data, particularly if the authorities frequently alter their policy stance in the market for government debt. For example, a move from a policy of fixing interest rates to one of controlling the money supply by open market operations could alter the variance of returns on government long-term debt and the covariance between government debt and private sector assets. More volatile rates of inflation that are expected to be reflected in more volatile interest rate movements might also alter the variance–covariance of asset returns. (This is a form of the Lucas (1976) critique.) Modelling second moments of returns is as yet largely uncharted territory in asset demand equations (but see Baba et al., 1988). However, under the assumption of market clearing with exogenous asset supplies the demand functions of the mean–variance model can be inverted to give an equation for relative (one-period expected) yields. There has been empirical work on such asset price equations[9] where the time-varying variances and covariances have been estimated using the autoregressive conditional heteroscedasticity (ARCH) model (Engle, 1982; Bollerslev et al., 1985; Giovannini and Jorion, 1987, 1988). Space precludes discussion of this complementary strand of the literature but the general conclusion appears to be that the variance–covariance matrix is time varying.

The informational requirements in using a mean–variance approach to asset holdings might limit the applicability of the model sophisticated financial firms such as banks, insurance companies and pension funds. However, this covers the main agents who operate in risky financial markets; households comprise only a small part of this market. Alternatively, one could assume that agents apply the mean–variance analysis to broad aggregates of homogeneous assets (e.g. gilts, equities, liquid assets).

1.2.6 Asset Demands and Consumer Demand Theory

Friedman (1956), in his restatement of the quantity theory, argues that the demand for assets should be based on axioms of consumer choice. He focuses on the demand money and presents a fairly long list of possible arguments of this function (i.e. a vector of expected returns, wealth and income) with 'signs' to be determined primarily by the data. He eschews the idea of approaching the theory of demand for assets by considering explicit motives for holding money. However, Friedman did not present an explicit model of consumer choice and his model contains few *a priori* and hence potentially refutable restrictions.

Separability

To keep the decision problem tractable and, some would argue, realistic, it is usual to invoke some separability assumptions. Agents may then be viewed as acting as if they undertake some form of multistage budgeting. For example, decisions about consumption and saving may be independent of variables affecting the work–leisure choice: choice between real and financial assets may be largely independent. A variety of separability assumptions about either the utility function or the cost function can be made, but weak intertemporal substitutability and quasi-separability between blocks of assets (e.g. real assets, liquid capital certain, capital uncertain) are usually assumed when analysing the demand for financial assets.[10] The demand for a subset of assets then depends only on 'prices' within the subset and the total wealth held in the subset. Having isolated a set of n separable assets (or liabilities) one can then apply the models of consumer choice to them.

Neoclassical demand theory is usually based either on maximization of utility subject to an expenditure constraint or the equivalent 'dual' of minimizing cost to achieve a given level of utility.[11] The axioms of consumer demand theory (e.g. negativity, transitivity) are met, for example, provided that we choose a cost function that is quasi-concave and homogeneous of degree zero in prices and expenditure. Different functional forms for cost or (direct and indirect) utility functions yield different functional forms for demand functions.

To motivate the application of consumer demand theory to asset demands suppose that we make the reasonable assumption that there exists a utility function defined over the expected (one-period-ahead)[12] value of real assets a^τ_{it+1}:

$$u = u(a^\tau_{1t+1}, a^\tau_{2t+1}, \ldots, a^\tau_{nt+1})$$ (1.12)

The budget constraint is that real assets sum to real wealth:

$$\sum_i p^\tau_{it} a^\tau_{it+1} = W^\tau_t$$ (1.13)

$$p^\tau_{it} = (1 + r_{it})^{-1}(1 + g_z)$$ (1.14)

where r_{it} is the expected proportionate nominal return on asset i between t and $t + 1$ (including any capital gains), g_z is the expected proportionate rate of goods price inflation between t and $t + 1$ and p^τ_{it} is the real price (i.e. approximately equal to the inverse of 1 plus the real interest rate $(r_{it} - g_z)$. Corresponding to (1.12) there is a cost function. Of the several flexible functional forms available, we use for illustrative purposes the PIGLOG (price-independent generalized logarithmic) and within this class we use the AIDS cost function (Deaton and Muellbauer, 1980).[13] Asset shares s_i are then given by (Barr and Cuthbertson, 1989d,e)

$$s_i = \alpha_i + \sum_j \gamma_{ij} \ln p^\tau_{jt} + \beta_i \ln\left[\left(\frac{W^\tau}{P^{*\tau}}\right)_t\right] \tag{1.15}$$

where

$$s_{it} = a_{it} / W_t \tag{1.16}$$

$$\ln P^{*\tau}_t = \sum s_i \ln p^\tau_{it} = \ln P^*_t + g_z = \sum s_i \ln p_{it} + g_z \tag{1.17}$$

and a_{it} are the nominal asset holdings, W_t is the nominal wealth and $\ln p_{it} = \ln (1 + r_{it})^{-1}$ is the nominal 'price'.[14] It can be shown that the share equation (1.15) exhibits symmetry, homogeneity and negativity, all of which are testable restrictions.

Transactions, hedging or perception of risk (i.e. variances and covariances of returns) are represented in the parameters of the cost function. Should any of the latter change, then this will be picked up empirically either by a failure of the homogeneity or symmetry or by parameter instability. In principle the AIDS cost function could be altered in the light of such empirical results to produce a more general model within this broad framework. The consumer demand approach therefore yields asset demand functions that are consistent with a maximizing theory but are somewhat more tractable than the mean–variance approach.[15]

The Demand for (Non-interest-bearing) M1

Equation (1.15) represent a system of asset demand equations and does not rule out distinct demand functions for narrow and broad money (unlike the mean–variance model). What does this approach tell us about the appropriate form for the demand for narrow money (M1), which is usually estimated as a single equation rather than as part of a system? For exposition, assume that the demand for liquid assets is weakly separable from other asset and liability choices (and from consumption and leisure). Equation (1.15) implies that the demand for (non-interest-bearing (nib)) M1 may depend on a set of real prices (yields), real wealth and a composite real interest rate ($\ln P^{*\tau}$). This appears at variance with single-equation empirical studies where M1 often depends on only a single nominal interest rate, a transactions variable and the rate of inflation.

The (expected) inflation rate appears in (1.15) in two ways: as part of the rate of return (price) and in the wealth term. Assuming that asset 1 is nib M1, we have

$$s_1 = \alpha_1 + \sum_{j \neq 1} \gamma_{1j} \ln p_{jt} + \left(\sum_{j=1}^{n} \gamma_{ij} \right) g_z + \beta_1 \ln \left[\left(\frac{W}{Z} \right)_t \right]$$

$$- \beta_1 (\ln P_t^* + g_z) \tag{1.18}$$

where W_t is nominal wealth and Z_t is the aggregate goods price level.

The sum of the coefficients on the opportunity cost of narrow money (i.e. $\ln p_{jt}$) does not equal the sum of those on the rate of inflation. Hence a 1 per cent rise in all nominal yields ($\ln p_{jt}$, $j \neq 1$) and the rate of inflation g_z will have a direct impact on the demand for narrow money. This appears to justify the inclusion of nominal rates r_{jt} and the rate of inflation in single-equation studies. However, if homogeneity holds, $\Sigma \gamma_{ij} = 0$, the separate inflation term disappears and only nominal rates appear to be required (we ignore the wealth term for the moment). Clearly it is incorrect to test for homogeneity by imposing relative nominal interest rates, i.e. $\sum_{j \neq 1} \gamma_{ij} = 0$, or by running an equation of the form

$$s_1 = \alpha_1 + \delta_{11} g_z + \sum_{j \neq 1} \delta_{1j} \ln p_{jt} + \text{other terms} \tag{1.19}$$

and testing $\delta_{11} - \Sigma_{j \neq 1} \delta_{1j} = 0$, i.e. imposing real prices (interest rates). Hence by considering M1 as part of a system of demand equations that obey the axioms of consumer choice, possible errors in the single-equation approach are clearly highlighted. A further reparameterization of equation (1.18) gives

$$s_1 = \alpha_1 + \sum_{j \neq 1} \delta_{1j} \ln p_{jt} + \Theta_1 g_z + \Theta_2 \ln \left[\left(\frac{W}{Z} \right)_t \right] \tag{1.20}$$

where

$$\delta_{1j} = \gamma_{1j} - \beta_1 s_j \qquad j \neq 1$$

$$\Theta_1 = \left(\sum_{j=1}^{n} \gamma_{1j} \right) - \beta_1 \qquad \Theta_2 = \beta_1$$

If in addition, we assume that real wealth and real income are highly correlated then (1.20) looks like a conventional long-run demand function for M1 obtained from a single-equation estimation. The dependent variable could then constitute the money-to-income ratio. If homogeneity holds, then the inflation effect Θ_1 comes solely from the wealth coefficient β_1. It is also worth noting that even with homogeneity and $\beta_1 = 0$ (i.e. a wealth elasticity of unity), a 1 per cent increase in all nominal interest rates and the rate of inflation would lead to a change in the demand for M1 (see Courakis (1989) who derives a similar conclusion for a version of the mean–variance model).

Barr and Cuthbertson (1989) argue that transactions can be explicitly introduced into the demand for s_1 via a modification of the cost function which results in

$$s_i = \alpha_i + \sum_j \gamma_{ij} \ln p_{jt}^{\tau} + \beta_i \left\{ \ln \left[\left(\frac{W}{Z} \right)_t \right] - \phi \ln \left(\frac{e_{t+1}}{z_{t+1}} \right) - \ln P^* - g_z \right\} \quad (1.21)$$

where e_{t+1} is the expected level of nominal transactions in period $t + 1$ and z_{t+1} is the expected price level in $t + 1$. Thus if $\phi \neq 1$ we expect the demand for M1 to depend on the level of transactions and the wealth-to-income ratio (except when $\beta_i = 0$, i.e. $E_w = 1$). But if $\phi = 1$ (i.e. the cost function is homogeneous with respect to the level of transactions), the demand for money depends on the current period wealth-to-income ratio $n(W_t/e_{t+1}P_t^*)$. Recent evidence suggests that the demand for narrow and broad money may depend on wealth and income (see below).

The consumer demand approach can also be used to model capital-uncertain assets, where prices $\ln p_{jt}^{\tau}$ will include expected capital gains and tests of homogeneity and symmetry are straightforward. If homogeneity holds, then inflation only appears in the wealth term and we expect the term $\Sigma \gamma_{ij} \ln p_j$ to have $\Sigma \gamma_{ij} = 0$.

The application of consumer demand theory to the demand for financial assets provides a tractable approach which allows testing of the key axioms of choice theory and should therefore be considered as useful as the motives approaches to the demand for money discussed earlier.

1.2.7 Buffer Stock Money

In the recent literature there has been a revival of interest in the role of money as a buffer stock, i.e. as an asset that acts as a 'shock absorber' enabling agents temporarily to postpone otherwise costly adjustments (to alternative economic variables such as employment, investment and output) and to economize on 'information'. In broad terms this approach has been prompted by problems encountered in trying to estimate stable 'conventional' demand for money functions, in understanding the 'long and variable lags' of monetary policy (Laidler, 1984), in the phenomenon of interest rate (and hence exchange rate) overshooting under monetary targets and in the general analysis of why people hold 'money' when it is dominated by other assets (Laidler, 1988). Running in tandem with the buffer stock notion has been the wide application in macroeconomics generally of the rational expectations hypothesis and 'market-clearing' rational expectations models of the New Classical School, where a key distinction is drawn between anticipated and unanticipated events. The latter concepts have been used in some buffer stock models. Although the buffer stock approach is often dubbed 'disequilibrium money', in some buffer stock models money holdings are voluntarily held.

There is also a recurring debate in the literature (Laidler, 1982) concerning the interpretation of estimated demand for money functions: are they demand functions, or do they represent reparameterized real balance equations (where causation runs from money to the arguments of the demand for money function)? The notion that buffer holdings of money are voluntarily held in the short run and then dissipated in a slow real balance effect clearly has attractions both as an explanation of 'temporal instability' in demand for money functions and in contributing to an explanation of the 'long and variable lags' of monetary policy.

To illustrate the intuitive ideas behind the buffer stock notion, consider the probable behaviour of firms in an uncertain environment. The costs of marginal adjustments to prices, wages, production and real stock levels may be very substantial relative to the interest forgone by holding excess money balances. Shocks to the firm's production and employment plans are likely to result in a change in cash balances which will be willingly held in the short run until the shocks are perceived as either permanent or temporary. Similarly, shocks to the money supply, for example, caused by an increase in the supply of bank advances may lead to unexpected changes in money holdings by other agents when the advances are spent. In the buffer stock approach, disequilibria originating in either demand or supply are explicitly considered. The speed with which firms adjust their excess holdings of money may depend upon (a) their initial holdings, (b) the width of the band within which money balances are allowed to fluctuate, (c) the review period for decisions, (d) the transactions and information costs of moving into other assets or goods, or in altering the production process, and (e) the source of the change in money balances and a view as to whether they are permanent or transitory (Goodhart, 1984). Taking up the last point, if the source of the change in 'buffer money' is concentrated rather narrowly, then even though each individual agent may adjust fairly quickly, the system as a whole may take considerable time to adjust as 'buffer money' is passed on to different agents.

If the money transactions technology is highly efficient and it is relatively costless to transfer between 'money' and 'near money', then buffer assets are likely to consist of a wider set of assets than transaction balances. For large firms in the UK, the automatic overdraft system can also be used as a buffer stock. Excess money can be used to reduce overdrafts. Cash shortages may also lead to increased overdrafts as the spread between money rates and the cost of overdrafts is relatively small for large firms. Thus it may be liquidity rather than simply 'money' that acts as the buffer stock for large firms.

For people, the relevant interest spread between liquid assets and credit in the UK is rather large and automatic overdrafts were, until recently, somewhat uncommon. Therefore buffer assets are likely to consist of gross liquid assets, particularly money, and perhaps building society deposits. However, in countries where short-term credit is widely and easily available – for example, in the USA and increasingly so in the UK (bank credit cards) – liabilities may also perform a buffer role.

At a more theoretical level, models of the precautionary demand for money (Miller and Orr, 1966; Akerlof and Milbourne, 1980; Milbourne, 1983, 1987; Milbourne et al., 1983; Smith, 1986) provide a useful framework in which to analyse certain aspects of the buffer stock approach. In these models buffer money, in the short run, is willingly held at unchanged interest rates. What happens in such a model when there is an unanticipated increase in net receipts in the aggregate (consequent on, for example, an increase in government expenditure)? Some agents will hit their upper threshold and reduce their money balances to their 'return point holding' while others will accommodate an increase in buffer holdings. The net effect depends on the initial distribution of money balances across agents (since the shock is unanticipated, the upper and lower thresholds will remain unaltered for the moment) but there is a presumption that aggregate buffer holdings increase, particularly if money balances are not continuously monitored.[16] However, in the empirical implementation of the buffer stock notion, the precautionary demand model provides an intuitively appealing framework rather than an explicit equation suitable for estimation. There are several types of model that can be given the generic title of 'buffer stock money'; we discuss these and their empirical results in section 1.4.4.

1.3 DYNAMICS, EXPECTATIONS AND RISK

In this section we discuss the modelling of lag responses, expectations and risk. The first two aspects have been widely used in the applied literature. The modelling of risk is relatively new in the area of applied work. It has been rather widely adopted in models of asset pricing but not in the closely related area of modelling the demand for money. However, because it is likely to be increasing importance, we briefly discuss one potentially important approach, namely the ARCH procedure.

1.3.1 Lag Responses

In general, if any static theory models are fitted to quarterly time series data on money balances they do not perform well statistically. However, the addition of lagged values of money as independent variables improves their statistical performance considerably. It is probably correct to say that the latter empirical fact led to a search for theories to explain this phenomenon.

Ideally one would like a theory of the demand for money (and other assets) in which all the costs of adjustment are included in a single constrained optimization problem. However, such complete theories quickly become analytically intractable.[17] As a result we are virtually forced to assume that the individual undertakes a two-stage decision process. First he decides on the long-run optimal amount of assets to hold in accordance with the theories set out in section 2. Second, he solves a completely separate optimization problem concerning the speed at which he wishes to adjust towards this equilibrium. Thus it is assumed that the adjustment path chosen does not influence the desired (optimal) long-run level of demand for the asset.

The partial adjustment model can be derived from minimizing (one-period) quadratic costs[18] of adjustment $(m_t - m_{t-1})^2$ and costs of disequilibrium $(m_t - m_t^*)^2$ (where m_t^* is the long-run money demand). This results in

$$m = \gamma m_t^* + (1 - \gamma)m_{t-1} \tag{1.22}$$

(Without loss of generality, we can take m to be the logarithm of money balances, either real or nominal.) A defect of the first-order partial adjustment mechanism is that short-run money balances continually differ from long-run balances if m_t^* is rising as a result, say, of a continuous rise in real income. However, including additional higher-order lagged dependent variables may remove this problem. The first-order partial adjustment mechanism imposes a similar geometric lag response of m_t on a change in *any* of the independent variables; this is highly restrictive. Casual introspection might suggest that the profile over time in m_t may be different if the change in m_t is triggered by a change in income rather than in the interest rate.

We can also derive the basic *error feedback equation* (EFE) from minimizing quadratic costs (Nickell, 1985):

$$\Delta m_t = \mu_1(m_t^* - m_{t-1}) + \Psi \Delta m_t^* \tag{1.23}$$

The simple EFE suffers from the underprediction problem if m_t^* is continually rising or falling. This can be solved by introducing an integral control term

$$\Psi_1 \sum_{j=2}^{k} \left(m_{t-j}^* - m_{t-j} \right) \tag{1.24}$$

The change in m_t now depends upon past disequilibria (Hendry and von Ungern Sternberg, 1981) and therefore on higher-order lags in m_t.

Interdependent Asset Adjustment

In the simple partial adjustment model the change in the short-run desired demand for money depends only on the disequilibrium in (long-run) money holdings, i.e. on $m_t^* - m_{t-1}$. However, disequilibrium in money holdings must imply that at least one other asset is also in disequilibrium. In principle, the speed of adjustment in money holdings might depend on the disequilibrium in other asset stocks (Brainard and Tobin, 1968; Smith, 1975) such as building society deposits. This is the basis of the interdependent asset adjustment model. Here individuals face (a) a wealth (budget) constraint $\Sigma A_i = W$ (where A_i are the actual holdings of the ith asset and W is wealth) and (b) the rational desires hypothesis $\Sigma A_i^* = W$ (where A_i^* is the desired long-run stock of the ith asset).

In this framework the simple first-order partial adjustment mechanism, if applied to *all* assets, implies that all assets are always in equilibrium! Also, if simple partial adjustment is applied to a subset of explicit assets in the portfolio and the residual assets are not explicitly modelled, the residual set of assets fully adjust to their own disequilibria and passively absorb any funds that are not fully adjusted in the set of explicit assets. Therefore, for example, models that use simple partial adjustment for liquid assets only implicitly assume that illiquid assets (such as equities or long-term government stocks) adjust completely to equilibrium in the current period, which is a somewhat implausible result. In the Brainard–Tobin (Backus et al., 1980) approach the adjustment of the ith asset A_i depends upon disequilibria in other asset stocks as well as that in the own asset stock:

$$A_t = GA_{t-1} + (I - G)A_t^* \tag{1.25}$$

where A_t is a vector of assets. Christophides (1976) has demonstrated that equations such as (1.25) can be derived by minimizing the (quadratic) costs of *all* assets subject to the rational desires hypothesis $\Sigma A_i^* = W$. The dynamic response of a change in A to a change in an exogenous variable depends upon all the coefficients in G and may allow a more varied dynamic response than simple partial adjustment. (Stability in the lag response requires all the eigenvalues of G to have modulus less than 1 or, equivalently, for $G^n \to 0$ as $n \to \infty$.)

Equation (1.25) is easily generalized to produce an interdependent error feedback adjustment process (Anderson and Blundell, 1982; Barr and Cuthbertson, 1989):

$$\Delta A_t = C \, \Delta A_t^* + D(A_{t-1} - A_{t-1}^*) \qquad (1.26)$$

where C is a conformable matrix of short-run adjustment parameters and the parameters in the D matrix determine the path to long-run equilibrium.[19] Equation (1.26) can also be used to model changes in asset shares (or more generally asset ratios, for example, the money-to-income ratio).

The interdependent asset demand approach has frequently been applied to the demand for assets for a wide variety of economic agents such as banks, insurance companies and persons. While one can invoke quadratic cost minimization as a basis for the above adjustment mechanisms, the addition of lagged dependent variables to a static model is often simply viewed by applied economists as an *ad hoc* yet parsimonious method of capturing lag responses.

1.3.2 Estimation Issues

One cannot adequately analyse empirical demand for money functions without knowledge of the impact of three major areas of applied research which have become prominent over the last ten years. These are the general to specific methodology (Hendry et al., 1984), cointegration (Granger, 1986; Hendry, 1986) and the estimation of equations containing expectations terms (Wallis, 1980; Wickens, 1982; Pagan, 1984; Pesaran, 1987). However, we can only give a brief résumé of the main elements of these ideas.

Hendry (1989) argues that preferred models should be designed to meet certain criteria which, broadly speaking, include theory consistency and data coherency. The latter criteria include an error term that is white noise (i.e. no serial correlation or heteroscedasticity) and an innovation with respect to the information set used, and the model should have constant parameters. Hendry argues that since a theory tells us little about dynamics we should begin our specification search with a very general autoregressive distributed lag (ADL) model in the levels of the variables:

$$m_t = \alpha_1(L)m_{t-1} + \alpha_2(L)x_t + u_t \qquad (1.27)$$

where m_t are money balances and x_t are independent variables of the long-run money demand function, and $\alpha(L)$ and $\beta(L)$ are lag polynomials of sufficient order to ensure that u_t is white noise. Equation (1.27) is over-parameterized, and a parsimonious model which is data acceptable with sensible decision variables and theoretically consistent long-run parameters is obtained via a creative search procedure. This is the general to specific modelling strategy (Gilbert, 1986). The preferred equation is often an error correction model (ECM), for example

$$\Delta m_t = \gamma_1(L)\,\Delta m_{t-1} + \gamma_2(L)\,\Delta x_t + \gamma_3(m - \beta'x)_{t-j} + v_t \tag{1.28}$$

with static equilibrium

$$m_t = \beta'x_t \tag{1.29}$$

An alternative reparameterization of (1.28) is to search for common factors (Hendry and Mizon, 1978) in the lag polynomials $\gamma_i(L)$, $i = 1, 2$, which may result in a lower-order polynomial in the distributed lag terms plus an autoregressive error. Note therefore that it is possible to discriminate statistically between lagged adjustment and an autoregressive (AR) error using the common factor test,[20] a factor ignored in much of the US applied literature as we shall see below. The previous point does not apply to moving-average errors (or indeed to complex non-linear error structures) as these do not imply common factors.

Practitioners of the general to specific methodology, finding serial correlation in the residuals (but no common factors), will often include additional lagged variables to remove it. Critics argue that such additional lagged difference terms are not modelling a true lagged response but may be proxy variables for a complex error structure (e.g. autoregressive moving average (ARMA)). Our ignorance is then merely represented by uninterpretable lagged variables rather than an (uninterpretable) error process. At a purely empirical level this argument can be resolved by testing the complex lag coefficients and the error parameters of the complex error process for temporal stability.

Under constant growth rates for the x variables, ECMs like (1.28) yield dynamic equilibrium solutions: $m - \beta x = \psi g_x$ (Currie, 1981; Cuthbertson, 1986a). There is often little economic rationale in assuming $\psi \neq 0$; however, constraining ψ to be zero (even if accepted by the data) may radically alter the lag profile (Patterson and Ryding, 1984). Notwithstanding these problems, the general to specific methodology has been widely applied in empirical work on the demand for money, particularly outside the USA.

Cointegration (Granger, 1986; Hendry, 1986) has provided a sound statistical basis for the error feedback formulation. To simplify matters let us assume that m_t and all the variables in x_t have a stochastic trend and must be differenced once to obtain a stationary series (i.e. broadly speaking one with no trend in mean and a finite variance). These variables are then said to be integrated of order 1 (I(1) variables) and their first differences are stationary variables (I(0) variables). For a set of I(1) variables, it may be possible to find a constant vector β which yields a stationary I(0) error ϵ_t:

$$m_t - \beta'x_t = \epsilon_t \tag{1.30}$$

Since ϵ_t has no trend in mean, intuitively (1.30) implies that the trended set of I(1) variables (m_t, x_t) do not diverge over time. They are said to be cointegrated with cointegrating vector β, which may not be unique and which can be obtained from an ordinary least squares (OLS) regression on (1.30) (Stock, 1984). It follows that all the variables in (1.30) are I(0); ϵ_t is stationary and hence all statistical tests based on ϵ_t have the usual distributional properties. In fact, if a cointegrating vector β can be found (and tests are available), then this implies the existence of an ECM of the form of (1.30) (Engle and Granger, 1987).

Based on the idea of cointegrated series, two-step procedures have been used to discover a valid ECM (Engle and Granger, 1987). A set of variables (e.g. income, wealth) of the same order of integration that could potentially be related to money are permuted until a cointegrating set of variables ensues (Johansen, 1988). OLS on (1.30) then yields an estimate of $\hat{\beta}$ from this first-stage cointegrating regression. The lagged residuals from (1.30) then constitute the ECM term $(m - \hat{\beta}x)_{t-j}$ in (1.28). Searches over the lag polynomials $\gamma_j(L)$, $i = 1, 2$, then determine the most parsimonious representation of the short-run dynamics independently of the fixed long-run value of $\hat{\beta}$. This reduces the dimension of the second-stage search procedure, which is a useful practical outcome.

Direct estimation of (1.30) after applying the general to specific methodology will produce an alternative value for β, say $\hat{\beta}^*$. We should then check that $m_t - \hat{\beta}^*x_t$ is stationary. On practical grounds we would hope that $\hat{\beta}$ from the two-step method and $\hat{\beta}$ using the general to specific strategy are not too far apart. In practice, finite-sample bias exists for both techniques and there is continuing debate as to the most useful method to adopt (Banerjee et al., 1986).[21]

1.3.3 Modelling Expectations

Expectations about the rate of inflation, the level of income and the yield on assets appear in our theories of the demand for assets. Survey data on expectations and publicly available forecasts of economic variables can both be used directly in the asset demand functions. However, the most popular approaches used in the empirical literature for modelling expectations have been some variant of the adaptive expectations hypothesis and more recently the rational expectations hypothesis. Regressive and extrapolative expectations formation have not been widely used in empirical work. As far as estimation is concerned, the main feature of the adaptive expectations framework is that it introduces lagged dependent variables into asset demand functions.[22] The subjective expectations of Muth-rational expectations agents (Muth, 1961) are assumed to be identical with conditional mathematical expectations. The basic idea behind Muth-rational expectations is that, in forming his expectations, the agent uses all the available information about the economy that he finds it worthwhile to collect. Stated thus the hypothesis appears innocuous enough, and indeed it is the substantial informational requirements and the assumption of zero learning costs that make Muth-rational expectations contentious. It is assumed that the individual has complete information on the true structure of the economy and immediately (and costlessly) learns about any changes in structure that occur. Agents do not persistently over- or under-predict a particular variable over several periods.

The use of the rational expectations hypothesis in empirical work on asset demands is relatively recent. Two broad approaches have been adopted. The first invokes the unbiasedness property of rational expectations whereby the actual future value of the variable provides an unbiased predictor of the expected value and an errors in variables problem arises (e.g. McCallum, 1976; Hansen, 1982; Wickens, 1982; Cumby et al., 1983). The second approach uses the fact that the rational expectations hypothesis predicts that the expected value of a variable is formed by the individual using forecasts from the economic model that is thought to generate the variable in question. A regression of the variable in question on the exogenous and predetermined variables from the whole model provides an equation for generating future expected values (Nelson, 1975). This is known as weakly rational expectations. (Full Muth-rational expectations (Muth, 1961) requires the imposition of cross-equation parameter restrictions (Wallis, 1980).)

Expectations variables in money demand functions result in rather subtle estimation problems and we only deal with a subset of these here. Consider estimating the following demand function (a simplified version of Cuthbertson (1988b)):

$$m_t = \Theta\, m_{t-1} + \Theta_2 n_t + \Theta_3({}_t x^e_{t+1}) + \Theta_4({}_t x^e_{t+2}) + u_t \qquad (1.31)$$

where n_t are the non-expectational variables in the demand for money function. A two-step procedure might involve regressing ${}_t x_{t+j}, j = 1, 2$, on a subset Λ_t of the complete information set Ω_t. The predictions $\hat{x}_{t+j}, j = 1, 2$, then replace x^e_{t+j} in (1.31) and OLS is applied to

$$m_t = \Theta_1 m_{t-1} + \Theta_2 n_t + \Theta_3 \hat{x}_{t+1} + \Theta_4 \hat{x}_{t+2} + q_t \qquad (1.32)$$

$$q_t = u_t + \Theta_3(x^e_{t+1} - \hat{x}_{t+1}) + \Theta_4(x^e_{t+2} - \hat{x}_{t+2}) \qquad (1.33)$$

There are several problems with this commonly used procedure. If m_{t-1} or n_t are excluded from Λ_t (e.g. $\hat{x}_{t+j}$ is an extrapolative predictor based solely on $x_{t-j}, j = 1, 2, \ldots$) but they influence x^e_{t+j}, then OLS estimates of $\Theta_i(i = 1, 2, \ldots, 4)$ are inconsistent (Nelson, 1975). Regardless of the latter point, the 'usual' standard errors from OLS on (1.32) are incorrect (Pagan, 1984).

The inconsistency problem can be eliminated by using Λ_t and (m_{t-1}, n_t) in the instrument matrix and applying the errors in variables method. However, the error term q_t then contains a moving-average error due to the expectations forecasting error $(x_{t+j} - {}_t x^e_{t+j})$ and conventional corrections for serial correlation yield inconsistent estimators. Special corrections for serial correlation are required (see Hansen, 1982; Hayashi and Sims, 1983) which we do not pursue here. Thus there are some acute estimation problems when expectations terms enter the demand for money function. Pesaran (1987) argues that the conditions for identification in rational expectations models are in general very stringent and perhaps are unlikely to be met in practice; this has not prevented applications in the money demand literature.

Learning and Expectations Formation

An alternative to the rational expectations and (fixed coefficient) adaptive expectations schemes is to assume some updating or learning process by agents. The fixed coefficient approaches have a logical defect. Usually all the data are used to estimate the parameters of the expectations generating equation, and these values are then used in forecasting the expectations variable in the early periods of the sample. But at the time forecasts are made agents would not know the parameter values obtained using all the sample data (B.M. Friedman, 1979a). A simple form of updating is to estimate the expectations equation by recursive least squares and to use parameter estimates and forecasts based only on information actually available to the agent. Models with unobservable components and models with time-varying parameters (Harvey, 1981a; Cuthbertson, 1988a) have also been used to mimic optimal learning by agents (see Cuthbertson and Taylor, 1988a).

If data are highly trended then expectations proxy variables are likely to be highly correlated with current and lagged values. Hence forward-looking expectations models and backward-looking error feedback models are likely to be difficult to distinguish empirically. Cross-equation rationality restrictions (Abel and Mishkin, 1983; Mishkin, 1983; Cuthbertson and Taylor, 1987c) provide a further discriminating test, but again these may lack power in small samples. Hendry (1988) has recently proposed a rather ingenious test of a backward-looking versus forward-looking model based on parameter constancy tests. In short, Hendry (1988) argues that if we have a constant-parameter backward-looking model and an auxiliary equation to generate expectations which is non-stable (based on any subset of information used by agents), then this rules out the structural expectations model (such as equation (1.31)). Cuthbertson (1991) argues that the test is useful against any *specific* expectations generation equation but lacks the universality claimed by Hendry. This is an important area of debate but definitive results are not yet available.

1.3.4 Modelling Risk

The precautionary and risk aversion models suggest that risk is an important determinant of the demand for money. Riskiness is often measured by a moving-sample variance (e.g. see Baba et al., 1988), although there are econometric problems with this approach (Pagan, 1984; Pagan and Ullah, 1988). Recently, Engle et al. (1987) have suggested that risk showed be modelled using an ARCH process. To illustrate this approach assume that bond prices z_t depend on a set of variables Q_t (this could constitute an inverted mean–variance asset demand system):

$$z_t = Q_t \gamma + \epsilon_t \qquad \epsilon_t \sim N(0, h_t) \tag{1.34}$$

The variance of the prediction errors from equation (1.34), namely h_t, is assumed to influence the demand for money

$$m_t = f(x) + \beta h_t + u_t \tag{1.35}$$

We assume that h_t respond slowly to past forecast errors (GARCH model (Bollerslev et al., 1988)):

$$h_t = \alpha_0 h_{t-1} + (1 - \alpha_0) \epsilon_{t-1}^2 \tag{1.36}$$

The set of equations (1.34)–(1.36) can be jointly estimated using maximum likelihood techniques. To date, ARCH (and generalized ARCH (GARCH)) models have been mainly used in modelling time-varying risk premia in the foreign exchange, bond and stock markets (e.g. Engel and Rodrigues, 1987; Giovannini and Jorion, 1988), but the approach is likely to provide a focus for future work on the demand for assets as the above studies indicate that risk premia may be time varying.

1.4 EMPIRICAL EVIDENCE

The empirical literature on the demand for money is vast. We do not attempt to give an exhaustive account of the empirical evidence nor do we present a detailed econometric evaluation of specific equations. Rather, our aim is to provide illustrative examples of the different approaches adopted, concentrating on recent empirical work. Early empirical work provides illustrative examples of the partial adjustment and adaptive expectations approach.

Recent work has utilized the error feedback and interdependent asset adjustment framework to model lag responses. There has been a revival of interest in modelling buffer stock money, and this provides the final approach discussed.

1.4.1 Early Empirical Work

We begin this section with a discussion of some definitional problems and a brief overview of some early studies of the demand for money. We have chosen to be brief for a number of reasons. First, studies of the demand for money for the period from 1880 to around 1970 can be no more than indicative of what might pertain in the 1990s, particularly given the recent pace of innovation in financial markets. Second, over the data period considered the money supply may well have been endogenous and therefore these results may not be of relevance for periods when the authorities choose to target monetary aggregates. Third, later studies are likely to incorporate better statistical techniques. A survey, even a detailed one, can only provide a summary of a set of fairly disparate results, but references cited allow the reader to analyse the issues raised further.

Data and Definitional Problems

Our theories of the demand for money do not give an unambiguous indication of what constitutes 'money'. The transactions and precautionary models perhaps give the clearest indication suggesting the use of 'cash plus demand deposits' as the appropriate definition since these are universally recognized as the means of exchange in most industrialized nations. However, even here recent innovations in financial markets have rendered this distinction less clear cut than previously. The risk aversion model gives no clear indication of the appropriate definition of money since a wide variety of capital-certain assets could be defined as acting as a store of value, in nominal terms. The inventory and precautionary models yield demand functions for average money balances, and therefore some form of time-average data is appropriate, while the consumer theory and mean–variance models determine money balances at a point in time. However, this distinction is often arbitrarily treated in empirical work.

Empirical work, in the main, has treated money as consisting of various elements of the liabilities of the banking system. M0 in the UK consists mainly of cash held by the non-bank private sector but also includes bankers' balances at the Bank of England. Although it is currently a targeted aggregate, it is of little operational significance for the UK (see Trundle (1982), Johnston (1984) and Hall et al. (1989) for estimated M0 equations). These studies provide no evidence to support the assertion that M0 is an advance indicator of money gross domestic product (GDP) (Lawson, 1986, p. 12). For the demand for currency in the USA see the recent study by Dotsey (1988).

The narrow definition of M1 usually consists of cash and current (chequing) accounts held by the non-bank private sector (NBPS) and may often be further subdivided into interest-bearing and non-interest-bearing chequing accounts (e.g. nib M1 in the UK). M2 consists of M1 and usually also includes certain interest-bearing bank deposits of small denomination that are not marketable (e.g. seven day time deposits), although in the UK it includes retail deposits held in building societies as well as banks. In the USA, M2 is often referred to as broad money, but in the UK (and some other European countries) the latter usually refers to a wider set of assets held by the NBPS. In the UK, sterling M3 was the most widely discussed of the broad monetary aggregates until quite recently and consists of M1 plus sterling time deposits plus certain large denomination fixed term deposits (wholesale deposits), some of which are marketable (e.g. certificates of deposit).[23] Prior to the 1970s it was generally the cast that the various definitions of money gave similar conclusions concerning the appropriate form for the demand for money function, including the stability of such relationships. In the post-1970 period the latter view became problematic, and the appropriate definition of money became an empirical matter, i.e. money was to be defined as that financial asset which had a stable demand function and which could be controlled by the authorities.

Many of the early empirical studies use annual data and therefore the issue of adjustment lags tends to play a minor role. Laidler (1985) provides a useful summary of this work, particularly for the USA and the UK. The basic equation used is the static demand for money function

$$M = \alpha_0 + \alpha_1 X + \alpha_2 r + \alpha_3 P \tag{1.37}$$

where M is nominal money balances, P is the price level and X is the scale variable, usually taken to be current income, financial wealth or permanent income. r is the opportunity cost of holding money (either a rate on short-term assets or a rate of interest on long-term bonds); later studies included the own rate on money. The variables are in logarithms (except on occasions for r which might appear as its absolute value).

Some early studies impose untested unit income and price elasticities which render their results somewhat suspect. One of the first studies to avoid these pitfalls is that of Meltzer (1963) who used US data for the period 1900–58 for various definitions of money and of the scale variable. Brunner and Meltzer (1963) and Laidler (1966) refined this work for the USA, and Barratt and Walters (1966) and Laidler (1971) repeated this kind of analysis for the UK with broadly similar results. In these studies it is generally found that the results obtained are fairly invariant to the definition of money chosen. The demand for money appears to be related to a representative interest rate (and again the fit of the equation is fairly invariant to the choice of a short or long rate) and to permanent (expected) income which was usually proxied using the adaptive expectations mechanism. Permanent income performed better than current income but only marginally better than financial wealth (of which there was a paucity of accurate data). The evidence favoured a unit price level elasticity and hence α_3 could be constrained to be unity in annual data. Some outside sample forecast tests and Chow tests for parameter stability were conducted by a minority of investigators and in general indicated stability in the relationship over subperiods. For example, Laidler (1966) finds that the interest elasticity of the short rate with respect to M2 over the period 1892–1960 in the USA varies roughly between -0.12 and -0.15, and with respect to the long rate varies between -0.2 and -0.6.

Some early studies include a wide variety of interest rates in the demand for money. For example, for broad money in the USA, Hamberger (1966) and Lee (1967, 1969) find evidence in favour of the inclusion of the return on savings and loan association deposits and the return on equity, as well as the time deposit rate. Klein (1974a, b) and Barro and Santomero (1972) find evidence that the implicit service return on money (i.e. a form of own rate on demand deposits) is a significan determinant of narrow money holdings.

Evidence supporting the liquidity trap is mixed. Studies that test for a higher interest elasticity in periods of low interest rates (and vice versa) do not generally find any change in the elasticity (Bronfenbrenner and Mayer, 1960; Laidler, 1966). Direct tests of the liquidity trap replace r in equation (1.37) by $r - r_m$, where r_m is the minimum level of interest rates (to be chosen by the data in some way, for example by assuming adaptive expectations or a 'grid search' over alternative values for r_m (e.g. Starleaf and Reimer, 1967; Pifer, 1969)). Laidler (1985) in his survey, takes the view that 'on the whole, the evidence goes against the hypothesis'.

Studies that explicitly consider the supply and demand for money, and hence the identification and simultaneous equations problems (e.g. Brunner and Meltzer, 1964; Teigen, 1964) find that the results are little different from the single-equation studies when annual data for the USA is used. (Note that some single-equation studies use simultaneous equations estimators even though they do not explicitly consider the form of the supply function for money.)

In summary, we note that studies for this early data period using annual data suggest a well-determined fairly stable demand for money function. Broadly speaking, stability applies under different definitions of money, for different interest rates and over different data periods. As we shall see in subsequent sections it appears to be the case that in recent years economists have become more circumspect concerning our knowledge of the demand for money.

Partial Adjustment and Adaptive Expectations: US and UK Studies

Prior to Feige's (1967) study of the demand for narrow money in the USA, researchers had assumed that either partial adjustment or the adaptive expectations hypothesis (usually on income) were responsible for the lags in the demand for money. Feige considered both hypotheses simultaneously, with permanent income providing the expectations variable. The equation is estimated on annual data over the period 1915–63. Feige found the results satisfactory (for M1 and M2) on *a priori* grounds and, in particular, instantaneous adjustment (on annual data) and adaptive expectations on income are indicated. On quarterly US data Goldfeld (1973) finds less than instantaneous adjustment. Meyer and Neri (1975), using annual data for the USA, find that both narrow and broad money depend on a measure of expected income.

Laidler and Parkin (1970) apply Feige's model to UK quarterly per capita data on M2 for 1956(2)–1967(4) and obtain ambiguous results concerning adjustment and expectations lags. They interpret the results in terms of permanent income rather than adjustment lags. The interest rate is statistically insignificant, and Laidler and Parkin argue that this arises because the treasury bill rate does not provide a satisfactory proxy variable for the relative return on money: the omitted variable is the own rate on money. (For evidence on other Organization for Economic Co-operation and Development (OECD) countries see Blundell-Wignall et al. (1984).)

In hyperinflations (e.g. South American countries in the post-1945 period) the expected rate of inflation (often modelled by an adaptive expectations mechanism or rational expectations) is found to be significant (see, for example, Blejer, 1978; Viñals and van Beek, 1979; Cardoso, 1983; Calomiris and Domowitz, 1989).

UK Studies

For the UK, for various definitions of money, Artis and Lewis (1976) look at the stability of coefficient estimates as the sample period which begins in 1963(2) is extended from 1970(4) to 1973(1). For broad money, they include the interest differential between the own rate on money and the rate on long-term government debt; the variance of bond prices (measured as a moving average) is included in all equations to measure riskiness. Equations are presented with nominal and real balances as the dependent variable and first-order partial adjustment is invoked. In all cases, the equations fail the

Chow test for parameter stability over the period 1971(1)–1973(1), and for broad money the equation is dynamically unstable over the long data period (as the lagged dependent variable exceeds unity). Obviously, parameter instability is not due to the erroneous exclusion of the own rate and the riskiness of bonds, and Artis and Lewis reject the view that it is caused by a large change in the non-interest service flow on current accounts (sight deposits). They favour the view that the apparent instability in the demand for broad money is due to disequilibrium in the money market and we discuss this evidence in section 1.4.4.

A further investigation into the instability in the demand for broad money in the UK considers disaggregated functions for companies and the personal sector where nominal partial adjustment is assumed. Goodhart (1984) finds that the nominal demand for M3 (i.e. sterling M3 plus certain foreign currency deposits) is reasonably stable over the period 1963(4)–1973(4). Nominal M3 is regressed on itself lagged, a real current income variable, the current price level, an alternative interest rate (local authority rate) and the own rate (i.e. the certificate of deposit (CD) rate), together with the differential between the CD rate and the rate on bank lending. The latter picks up the effects of 'round-tripping' out of bank advances into CDs[24]; the latter are a component of broad money. Somewhat surprisingly, it is the demand for broad money by households (where the rate on long-term government debt is the only interest rate) which appears to be unstable. (However, more recent work (Lubrano et al., 1986) suggests instability in company sector demand for M3 and stability for households.)

US Studies

It is probably fair to say that most work in the USA using quarterly data on the demand for money has used and continues to use a conventional long-run function of the form (1.37) with $\alpha_3 = 1$ and the addition of a lagged dependent variable. The latter is taken to represent either (first-order) partial adjustment in real or nominal terms or, perhaps less frequently, the result of the adaptive expectations hypothesis. There are few new analytical points to emerge from this work and, as recent empirical results are well documented elsewhere (Laidler, 1980; Judd and Scadding, 1982; Roley, 1985), we content ourselves here with an overview of the main conclusions.

Over the period 1952(2)–1973(4) Goldfeld (1976) found a stable demand function for narrow money (M1) which was positively related to real GNP, negatively related to a representative market short rate (e.g. the commercial bill rate) and the rate on time deposits and incorporating first-order partial adjustment in nominal terms. However, this function seriously over-predicted money balances (in a dynamic simulation) over the period 1974–6 ('the case of the missing money') and is also found to be unstable over the period 1979–81.

Attempts to account for the temporal instability by permutations of different interest rate and transactions variables have not proved wholly successful. Admittedly the use of bank debits as an additional transactions variable alongside gross national product (GNP) (which excludes intermediate transactions and transactions in financial assets, but includes some input items for which no transactions take place) does improve matters somewhat (Judd and Scadding, 1982). Also, the use of the dividend price ratio (Hamberger, 1977) improves the performance of the M1 equation (but other criticisms of this equation have been raised – see Hafer and Hein (1979) and Laidler (1980)).

The main candidates for the observed instability in the demand for money in the USA post-1973 appear to be financial innovation, measurement problems, misspecified dynamics and the role of money as a buffer stock. We deal with the first two items in this section.

There has been a recent revival of interest in explaining secular changes in the velocity by 'structural' variables as well as by 'conventional' variables (e.g. income, interest rates) using both cross-country and time series data. Bordo and Jonung (1987) provide an excellent source (for the USA, see also Mayor and Pearl (1984)) and they find evidence that such variables as the share of labour force in non-agricultural pursuits (a measure of the monetization process) and the currency-to-money ratio (as a measure of the spread of commercial banking) influence long-run velocity for M2 in five countries (USA, Canada, UK, Sweden and Norway) for the period from 1880 to the mid-1970s. It should be noted, however, that cointegration techniques were not used and the estimated equations have severe first-order serial correlation with no common-factor tests undertaken. The results must therefore be interpreted with caution.

Recently financial innovation has involved banks offering interest-bearing accounts that are easily transferable to chequing accounts and allowing the centralization of accounts (of different branches of the firm – cash concentration accounts). Ideally, one would like direct measures of the change in brokerage fees (see Offenbacher and Porter, 1982) and of the reduction in the variance of net cash flows facilitated by these innovations. These variables could then be used directly in the inventory and precautionary models of the demand for money. Unfortunately such direct measures are not readily available and the most successful variables include the number of wire transfers and previous peak interest rates. The former reflects the increased use of cash management techniques by firms and the latter represents the increased incentive to begin using these services more frequently. When either of these variables is added to the demand for M1 they are statistically significant and the (outside sample) forecast errors of the equation (post-1973) are reduced (Judd and Scadding, 1982). In contrast with the above, the demand for narrow money in other industrialized countries does not appear to have been affected by financial innovation variables even though they also experienced high interest rates in the 1970s (Arango and Nadiri, 1981; Boughton, 1981). The pace of financial innovation appears to be accelerating in other industrialized nations and we may see similar problems with instability in the demand for M1 in these countries in the near future. (There is already some evidence for this in the demand for M1 in the UK in 1983–4 (e.g. Hall et al., 1989).)

Although there have been acute problems in finding a stable demand function for M1 in the USA post-1973, the difficulties with M2 (which consists of M1 plus small savings accounts at commercial banks) have been far less severe. Laidler (1980) reports that the conventional demand function for M2 exhibits much greater outside sample temporal stability than does M1 and is less sensitive to alternative specifications of the arguments in the function (for a counter-argument, see Hamberger (1980)). Interest, however, tends to centre on M1 as this is the targeted aggregate in the USA.

There has been an interesting attempt in the USA to measure 'money' and the return on money correctly using Divisia aggregates and to use these measures to test the stability of the partial adjustment model (Barnett et al., 1984). The approach recognizes that the components of the money supply (e.g. currency, demand and time deposits) may not be perfect substitutes for each other and should not be given equal weight as in official statistics on monetary aggregates. In the Divisia approach the separate components are weighted together, according to their contribution to money services, to form a consistent series for money. User costs measure the marginal money services yielded by each component and are porportional to the difference between the yield on a benchmark asset and the component's own yield. The share of each component's user cost in total user cost is used to weight each component in forming the Divisia aggregate.

In the demand for money function conventional aggregates are replaced by their Divisia counterparts and interest rates are replaced by the user cost indexes. On US data for narrow money there is no major improvement in the performance of the Divisia equation over the conventional function; however, for broad aggregates, where we expect conventional measures to measure money services incorrectly, the Divisia measures do produce a more stable demand function (e.g. Barnett et al. (1984); see Mills (1983) for some UK evidence). The approach is probably most useful where interest rates (which make up the user cost variables) are market determined rather than subject to regulation and hence may prove useful in an increasingly competitive financial environment. However, use of Divisia aggregates does not appear to solve the problem of the missing money and the great velocity decline of the 1980s (Lindsey and Spindt, 1986).

1.4.2 The Autoregressive Distributed Lag–Error Correction Model approach

In this section we illustrate the ADL–ECM approach with respect to the demand for narrow and broad money for both the UK and the USA. The levels and ratio terms determine the long-run static equilibrium parameters of the asset demand function, while differenced variables model the short-run dynamics around this static equilibrium position. Broadly speaking, the aim of this approach is to obtain a well-fitting (data-coherent) equation that has good statistical properties, forecasts well outside its sample period of estimation and conforms to the *a priori* notions given by the static equilibrium model. (These issues are discussed in more detail by Hendry (1983).)

The Demand for Narrow Money

Coghlan (1978) uses an unrestricted ADL model for narrow money but Hendry (1979, 1985) provides a more recent econometric study of the demand in the UK for transactions balances M1 by the NBPS. In long-run equilibrium, the real demand for M1 is assumed to depend upon real income Y (i.e. GNP), and the expected yield is assumed to depend on alternative assets r (i.e. local authority three month rate) and the rate of inflation π. A long-run unit income elasticity is proposed. In obvious notation, the static long-run equilibrium is

$$\frac{M}{PY} = Kr^{\alpha}\pi^{\beta} \qquad \alpha, \beta < 0 \tag{1.38}$$

A general unrestricted ADL equation in the logarithms of the levels of Y_{t-j}, r_{t-j}, and M_{t-j-1}, $j = 0, \ldots, 4$, is reparameterized and simplified to produce the following data-coherent dynamic ECM:

$$\Delta(m - p)_t = (0.4\Delta y_{t-1} - 0.52R_t - 0.86\Delta P_t - 0.11(m - p - y)_{t-2} -$$
$$\qquad\qquad\;\; (0.16) \qquad (0.11) \qquad (0.17) \qquad (0.02)$$

$$\qquad 0.26\Delta(m - p)_{t-1} + \; 0.04$$
$$\qquad (0.09) \qquad\qquad\qquad (0.006) \tag{1.39}$$

1961(1)–1977(1)   OLS   SE = 1.5 per cent   LM $F(3, 43) = 0.4$

where SE indicates standard error of the equation and LM is the Lagrange multiplier statistic. The long-run static equilibrium is

$$(m - p - y) = 4.2 - 5.6 \ln(1 + R) - 1.9 \ln(1 + \pi) \qquad (1.40)$$

giving a unit income elasticity, and interest rate and annual inflation semi-elasticities of -5.6 and -1.9 respectively. The median lags for y and R are less than four quarters, the equation shows no sign of serial correlation of up to order 3 (i.e. the LM statistic is distributed as F under the null) and, most important, the equation exhibits parameter constancy when the data period is extended to 1982(4) and when estimated recursively over the period 1965(3)–1982(4).

The inflation effect should probably not be interpreted as a switch from money into goods but rather as a lag response to a change in the price level (Milbourne, 1983; Cuthbertson, 1986a). In the spirit of the bounds model of Miller and Orr (1966) agents adjust money balances only when they hit an upper (or lower) threshold and this occurs after a lag.

The demand for M1 in the UK appears to be undergoing some structural change in the second half of the 1980s. Cuthbertson and Taylor (1991) note that over the period 1968(4)–1983(4) there appears to be some instability in the long-run income elasticity, and Hall et al. (1989) find evidence that the conventional variables in the demand for M1 do not form a cointegrating vector (although the addition of real financial wealth and a measure of stock market turnover tends to improve matters here).

Post-1982 real M1 grows substantially because of the growth in the interest-bearing component of M1. During the 1970s less than 10 per cent of M1 was interest bearing; by the end of 1982 this rose to 30 per cent and by the middle of 1987 the figure reached 65 per cent. Clearly, in principle we need data on the return from high interest chequing accounts (which are not readily available) and a measure of the growth in awareness of the existence of such accounts (see Baba et al. (1988) below for an attempt at modelling such learning behaviour). The latter will have to await further research to see if such additional variables can produce a cointegrating vector.

Longer Data Set

Hendry and Ericsson (1983, 1988) examine the demand for broad money in the UK using annual data over the period 1867–1975. They conclusively demonstrate the inadequacy of the statistical procedures and therefore the claims of a stable demand for money function made by Friedman and Schwartz (1982) using the same data set. Hendry and Ericsson use a general to specific modelling strategy to yield a preferred ECM equation:

$$\Delta_1(m - p - g)_t = -0.48 \Delta_1^2 p_t + 0.44_1 \Delta^2 (m - p)_{t-1} - 1.27 RS_t$$
$$ (10.5) \qquad\quad (8.3) \qquad\qquad\quad (8.5)$$

$$- 0.26(m - p - y)_{t-4} + 0.013(D_1)_t + 0.051(D_2)_t$$
$$(11.5) \qquad\qquad\qquad (1.4) \qquad\quad (8.1)$$

$$- 0.007(D_3)_t - 0.118 \qquad\qquad\qquad\qquad (1.41)$$
$$(0.8) \qquad\quad (9.9)$$

OLS   1961-70   SE = 1.95 per cent   LM(3) = 4.7   ARCH(6) = 16.2
CH(5, 85) = 7.6

where $g_t = \Delta_4 y_t / 4$, D_1 is a dummy variable for the First World War, D_2 is a dummy variable for 1921-55, D_3 is a dummy variable for the Second World War and CH is the Chow statistic. It therefore appears as if there is an unexplained shift in the money demand over the period 1921-55 (as well as in the two World War periods) and the equation also exhibits parameter instability over the period 1971-5.

Longbottom and Holly (1985) subject the Hendry–Ericsson model to further detailed tests and find that they can legitimately exclude the D_2 dummy provided that the unit effect of g_t on real balances is relaxed and the (implicit) own rate on money is introduced. The latter variable is based on Klein (1974a, b) and assumes that banks pass on to customers the net income that they receive from their earning assets. However, this results in a demand for money where statistically we can only just accept that the level of interest rates (i.e. the logarithm of the short rate relative to the own rate on money) plays a role in the long run (the t statistic on the appropriate interest rate variable is 1.7). In contrast, in the Hendry-Ericsson equation (1.41) the short rate appears statistically well determined. Although the Longbottom–Holly re-specification performs better overall is statistical terms than the Hendry–Ericsson model and indicates parameter stability over the period 1921-55, the choice between the two formulations clearly depends on one's priors versus the statistical evidence. This reviewer finds it hard to believe that the demand for narrow money is independent of the level of interest rate(s) in the long run. In a subsequent paper Hendry and Ericsson (1988) utilize the Engle–Granger (1987) two-step procedure with a non-linear error correction term, and this yields an equation with a long-run interest rate semi-elasticity of -7 and a unit nominal income elasticity. Note that all the above specifications fail parameter constancy tests over the period 1971-5, an issue we return to in a later section.

Artis and Lewis (1981) report studies on UK data on 'old' M2 (excluding building society deposits) over the period 1880-1960 giving an income elasticity of unity and an interest elasticity with respect to the long rate between -0.3 and -0.8. Extending the data period to 1981, they uncover a 'rather jolly little nut' (Artis and Lewis, 1984) whereby a very simple specification of the form

$$m - y = a + br + u_t \qquad\qquad\qquad\qquad (1.42)$$

(where r is the consol rate and all variables are in logarithms) fits rather well and suggests a fairly stable function except for 1973–6. Patterson (1987) demonstrates that in statistical terms we can improve on the Artis–Lewis equation by using an ADL–ECM model. However, broadly speaking the long-run results of Artis and Lewis remain intact. (Again, this is not surprising given knowledge of cointegration techniques.)

Patterson's (1987) ECM equation for narrow money over the period 1920–81 uses recursive estimation and recursive stability tests (Dufour, 1982). The equation has a data-acceptable unit price level and real income elasticity and the consol rate is the opportunity cost variable. Again, the evidence of instability over the period 1971–5 is clear and there appears to be some instability over the period 1920–55 which is probably a consequence of instability in the interest rate coefficient. These results are consistent with the Hendry–Ericsson findings of the need for a dummy variable for some or all of the period 1920–55 if one is to have an equation with a well-determined opportunity cost variable (whether long or short rates).

US Demand for Narrow Money

Gordon (1984) applies the ADL–ECM approach to the demand for narrow money in the USA but finds considerable instability in the equations estimated. Rose (1985) directly confronts the missing money problem for narrow money in terms of the restrictive (partial adjustment) lag structure used by previous investigators. By allowing the data to determine the appropriate lag structure within the ADL–ECM format, Rose finds a stable demand function for the missing money period (on seasonally adjusted and unadjusted data):

$$
\begin{aligned}
\Delta(m-p)_t = &- \underset{(0.02)}{0.06}(m-p-y)_{t-1} + \underset{(0.07)}{0.26}\Delta(m-p)_{t-4} - \underset{(0.16)}{0.44}\Delta p_t \\
&- \underset{(0.0001)}{0.0002}\Delta r - \underset{(0.004)}{0.026}\Delta_2 r_{t-1} - \underset{(0.004)}{0.007}r_{t-3} \\
&+ \underset{(0.01)}{0.09}(2\Delta y_t + \Delta y_{t-1}) + \underset{(0.015)}{0.03}y_{t-2}
\end{aligned}
\tag{1.43}
$$

OLS 1952(2)–1973(4)   SE = 0.5 per cent   LM $F(5, 67)$ = 0.93
ARCH (1) = 0.8   CH(20,77) = 1.07   HF(20) = 27.4

where HF stands for the Hendry (1989) forecast test for numerical parameter constancy.

The dynamic long-run equilibrium (with constant inflation $g_p = \Delta p$) is

$$
(m-p-y) = k + \underset{(0.05)}{0.57}y - \underset{(0.05)}{0.12}r - \underset{(4.5)}{7.6}g_p
\tag{1.44}
$$

$$
k = -12(g_m - g_p) + 5_g
$$

The income elasticity at 1.57 is higher than earlier representative results reported by Judd and Scadding (1982) but is only just statistically significant different from unity. However, an equation of the form (1.43) when estimated to 1977(4) exhibits parameter instability (and poor diagnostics) over the period 1978(1)–1981(4) which Rose conjectures may be caused by the change in monetary policy regime (to monetary targeting) post-1979 and general financial innovation.

Within the ADL–ECM framework Baba et al. (1988) provide the definitive empirical account of the behaviour of narrow money M1B in the USA between 1960(2) and 1984(2) covering the periods of missing money (1974(1)–1976(2)) and the great velocity decline (1982(1)–1983(2)). In the missing money episode previous models had over-predicted the demand for money by some 8–12 per cent while similar models had in the main substantially under-predicted the growth in narrow money. Building on the basic ECM of Rose (1985), Baba et al. find that both the increase in the volatility of bond yields and use of the appropriate learning-adjusted after-tax own yield on M1 instruments provide an empirical explanation for the rapid decline in velocity in the early 1980s. Volatility in bond yields has a local peak in 1971(3) and descends to a trough in 1974(1), and this accounts for the fall in the demand for money in the missing money period. (Note, however, that a $(-1, +1)$ dummy variable for 1980(2) and 1980(3) to capture credit controls is needed for parameter stability post-1980.)

If money were the only capital-safe asset and we have a money–bonds portfolio, then the static demand for money in the mean–variance model depends on the relative expected yields between bonds (including capital gains) and the own rate on money and on the variance of bond returns. However, we noted that narrow money (particularly in periods prior to the 1980s before explicit competitive interest rates were paid on narrow money) is dominated by other capital-safe assets. In a perfect capital market with a money–bills–bonds choice, Ando and Shell (1979) note that the demand for money is independent of bond risk. However, Baba et al. (1988) rationalize the inclusion of bond risk by assuming that there is a capital market imperfection. If an individual can borrow only at a higher interest rate than that at which he can lend, then the demand for money is not independent of bond risk.

The volatility measure AVA is based on a yearly standard deviation of the monthly holding period yield. Financial innovation in the form of the introduction of new interest-bearing accounts is modelled by using a weighting system based on a (20-quarter) learning ogive applied to the return on new financial instruments (e.g. NOW (Negotiable Order of Withdrawal) accounts from 1981(1), Super NOW accounts post-1983(1)). The actual return used is then the maximum of the previously available instrument (the passbook rate) and the learning-adjusted yield on new accounts. Also, after-tax yields are used. Compared with Rose (1985), these are the main innovations in the Baba et al. model and their parsimonious equation is

$$\Delta(m - p)_t = -\; 0.337 \; - \; 0.243\Delta(m - p)_{t-4} \; - \; 0.141(m - p - 0.5y)_{t-2}$$
$$\qquad\quad (0.035) \quad (0.049) \qquad\qquad\qquad (0.014)$$

$$\qquad - \; 1.74\text{AS}_t \; - \; 0.66\text{Asz}_t \; - \; 0.889\text{rmz}_t \; - \; 0.74\Delta p_t$$
$$\qquad\quad (0.17) \qquad (0.11) \qquad\;\; (0.086) \qquad\quad (0.52)$$

$$\qquad + \; 0.34\Delta\text{Ay}_t \; + \; 0.0044(\text{AVA})_{t-3} \; + \; 0.155(\text{SAVA})_{t-1}$$
$$\qquad\quad (0.05) \qquad\quad (0.0007) \qquad\qquad\quad (0.02)$$

$$\qquad + \; 0.27\text{rmocz}_t \; + \; 0.46\Delta\text{rmoc}_t \; + \; 0.013D_t$$
$$\qquad\quad (0.10) \qquad\qquad (0.12) \qquad\qquad (0.003) \qquad\qquad\qquad (1.45)$$

OLS   1960(2)–1984(2)   SE = 0.38 per cent   LMF(4, 76) = 0.57
CH_m = 1.3, CH_v = 0.81

This has a static equilibrium solution

$$(m - p) = -2.4 + 0.5y - 12.4s - 4.7sz - 6.3\text{rmz} + 1.96\text{rmocz}$$
$$\qquad\qquad - 1.3g_p + 0.03\text{AVA} + 1.1\text{SAVA} \qquad\qquad\qquad (1.46)$$

where m is the (logarithm of) nominal money (MIB), y is the (logarithm of) real GNP, P is the (logarithm of) the GNP deflator, $\text{Ay} = 0.66y_t + 0.34y_{t-1}$, S is the bond–bill spread, $\text{AS} = 0.33(s_t + s_{t-1} + s_{t-2})$, sz is the bill-learning-adjusted M2 spread, $\text{Asz} = 0.5(sz_t + sz_{t-1})$, rmz is the learning-adjusted highest prevailing yield on M2 accounts, rmocz is the learning-adjusted yield on checkable accounts, AVA is the moving standard deviation of holding period yield on long-term bonds, $SAVA = \max[0, (R_t - r_t)\text{AVA}]$ where R is the yield on 20 year treasury bonds, r_t is the yield on one month treasury bills, g_p is the annual inflation rate, D is the credit dummy variable (-1 in 1980(2), $+1$ in 1980(3), zero otherwise), LMF is the LM statistic for serial correlation of orders 1–4, with an F distribution (approximately) under the null of no serial correlation in the errors, CH_m is the Chow test over the missing money period 1975(1)–1976(2), with critical value 2.0, and CH_v is the Chow test over the period of great velocity decline 1982(1)–1983(2) with critical value 2.2.

In the long run the demand for real money balances has a real income elasticity of 0.5 and an inflation elasticity of -1.3, and exhibits a negative relationship with the yield on alternative M2 instruments (rmz and rmocz). The bond volatility measure has a direct positive effect on the demand for M1 (i.e. AVA) and an additional effect the higher the (positive) bond–bill spread (i.e. SAVA).

The policy implications, admittedly with hindsight, of the Baba et al. demand function are that the change in the Federal Reserve Bank's operating procedures in late 1979 caused an increase in the volatility of interest rates, which then led to a rise in the demand for M1 in the early 1980s (i.e. the great velocity decline). The increase in monetary growth was therefore not indicative of excess money which might lead one to advocate a tightening of monetary policy, but merely a change in desired money holdings by agents.

While one might not embrace all asspects of the results from Rose and Baba et al., one cannot avoid the inference that the ADL–ECM approach tells us more about the demand for narrow money in the USA than would be obtained by working within the partial adjustment framework (but see Slovin and Suskha, 1983; Goodfriend, 1985). Roley (1985) restricts himself to partial adjustment (and first-difference) equations for M1, and although he introduces a wide variety of other variables he is unable to make any positive inroads into the missing money and great velocity decline episodes.

Other Countries

Taylor (1986) applies the ADL–ECM methodology to a consistent set of data for M2 (den Butter and Fase, 1981) for three European countries (the FRG, the Netherlands and France) over the period 1960(1)–1976(4). The equations pass most of the diagnostic tests although there is some evidence of parameter instability over the post-sample period 1977(1)–1978(4). The long-run solutions yield unit income elasticities for Netherlands and the FRG, while that for France is 1.6, and interest rate effects are correctly signed. Milbourne (1985) provides a useful summary of empirical results for Australia. Muscatelli and Papi (1989) examine the demand for M2 for Italy, 1963(1)–1987(4), using the Engle–Granger two-step procedure and a learning-adjusted (logistic) curve on the interest rate on new financial assets (as in Baba et al., 1988). The resulting ECMs give reasonable statistical and economic results. Thus, overall, the error feedback approach has yielded reasonable results for the demand for M2 in European countries.

The Demand for Broad Money

Hendry and Mizon (1978) criticize the earlier work of Haache (1974) on the demand for M3 (i.e. sight and interest-bearing deposits) by the UK personal sector. Hendry and Mizon's criticism is that Haache began his study with an unduly restrictive model, namely one that had only first differences in the variables. If we start from an unrestricted ADL equation in the levels of the variables, a model that contains only first differences can be tested in two equivalent ways. First, we can test the common-factor restriction (autocorrelation) and then test to see whether the common factor has a root of unity (i.e. $\rho = 1$). Second, we can reparameterize the equation into difference and levels terms and test the statistical significance of the latter. Mizon and Hendry demonstrate that the implicit common-factor restrictions in the Haache model are statistically invalid, and present the following ECM of the demand for M3:

$$\Delta(m - p)_t = \quad \begin{matrix} 1.6 \\ (0.6) \end{matrix} + \begin{matrix} 0.21\Delta y_t \\ (0.1) \end{matrix} + \begin{matrix} 0.81\Delta \ln(1 + r_t) \\ (0.3) \end{matrix} + \begin{matrix} 0.26\Delta(m - p)_{t-1} \\ (0.1) \end{matrix}$$

$$\begin{matrix} - 0.40\Delta p_t \\ (0.1) \end{matrix} - \begin{matrix} 0.23(m - p - y)_{t-1} \\ (0.05) \end{matrix} - \begin{matrix} 0.61 \ln(1 + r_{t-4}) \\ (0.2) \end{matrix}$$

$$\begin{matrix} + 0.14 y_{t-4} \\ (0.04) \end{matrix}$$

$$(1.47)$$

OLS 1963(1)–1975(3)   SE = 1.0 per cent $R^2 = 0.69$ BP(12) = 6.4

where the standard errors are in parentheses, y is (the logarithm of) real personal disposable income, r_t is the yield on long-term government debt, p is the (logarithm of the) consumer price index (and the data are seasonally adjusted) and BP is the Box–Pierce statistic for serial correlation. The statistically significant level terms $(m - p - y)_{t-1}$, $\ln(1 + r_{t-4})$ and y_{t-4} reject the hypothesis that the equation should only contain first differences in the variables. The long-run dynamic equilibrium solution, where g is the constant growth rate in an independent variable is

$$(M/P) = K(1 + r)^{-2.6}(1 + g_p)^{-1.7} Y^{1.6} \tag{1.48}$$

where $K = \exp(7-4.2g_y)$.

The static elasticities are all of the expected sign and of a plausible magnitude. The growth affects, although large, may not be statistically different from zero and ideally one should test this proposition.

Wealth and Capital Gains

Grice and Bennett (1984), in a study of the demand for sterling M3 by the UK NBPS over the data for the 1960s and 1970s, introduce a dummy variable to proxy the large shift in demand after the introduction of competition and credit control (CCC) (Goodhart, 1984). Gross financial wealth as well as a transactions variable (i.e. total final expenditure) is included and the relative return on money is used in preference to using only the return on alternative assets. The relative return is measured by the own rate on money less the return to holding gilts which includes the one-period-ahead expected capital gain. This relative expected return is proxied by a weakly rational predictor. A general ADL equation is reparameterized and the resulting long-run effects are acceptable on *a priori* grounds, and the step response functions are relatively smooth. However, the reparameterized variables are not readily interpreted as behavioural, since the lags in a particular variable frequently change sign. The ADL model in this case becomes a convenient parsimonious method of approximating lag responses rather than being interpreted as an ECM. Wealth plays a more important role than income/transactions, with the former having a long-run elasticity of 1.4 and the latter a long-run elasticity of 0.3. The semi-elasticity of sterling M3 with respect to the relative yield on money and long-term government debt is 0.3. However, because expected capital gains can be substantial, the impact of the latter on the demand for money may be large. CCC has a substantial long-run effect of about 13 per cent on the demand for sterling M3. The within-sample statistical properties of the equation are good, as one might expect from the ADL approach. The outside-sample, one-step-ahead (static) forecasting performance of the equation is tolerable. Grice and Bennett provide an interesting Monte Carlo study of the effect of errors in variables on estimated lagged responses (Grether and Maddala, 1973). The wealth variable causes potential estimation problems because it may be measured with error. The experiments indicate that there is considerable elongation of the 'true' lag structure and bias in the OLS estimate of the long-run wealth elasticity of the demand for money.

Taylor (1987), in an otherwise conventional ECM demand for sterling M3, models financial innovation post-1984 by using the return on high interest chequing accounts (for deposits of between £2000 and £10,000). Prior to 1984 this own rate RM is the seven day deposit rate. The preferred equation is

$$\Delta(m - p)_t = \begin{array}{l} 0.287\Delta(m - p)_{t-2} - 0.019(m - p - y)_{t-4} \\ (0.102) \qquad\qquad (0.006) \end{array}$$

$$- 0.005(RTB_{t-1} - RM_t) - 0.003\Delta^2 RLB_{t-2} - 0.415\Delta p_t$$
$$(0.002) \qquad\qquad (0.001) \qquad\qquad (0.183)$$

$$+ 0.03$$
$$(0.007) \tag{1.49}$$

1964(2)–1985(4)   SE = 1.56 per cent   LM $F(5, 73)$ = 1.24
HF(20) = 15.60

RTB is the three month treasury bill rate, RLB is the rate on long bonds (i.e. gilt-edged stocks) and y is the total final expenditure. The equation is homogeneous in the price level and real income, and is stable over the period 1979(4)–1985(4) (HF(20)) and over the post-CCC period. The term $\Delta^2 RLB$ is probably proxying a risk term on alternative capital-uncertain assets.

Studies of gross liquidity (usually of the personal sector) are less numerous and results are more mixed than those for narrow money or even sterling M3. Official liquidity aggregates for the UK include building society deposits. On UK data, gross liquidity depends on some measure of expenditure and wealth, but long-run interest rate effects are often not well determined (Spanos, 1984; Currie and Kenally, 1985; Johnston, 1985). Cuthbertson and Barlow (1990) find evidence for a set of interest rates influencing UK personal sector gross liquidity, but Hall et al. (1989) demonstrate the difficulties of obtaining a satisfactory (cointegration) equation for liquidity of the UK private sector when data to 1989 are included.

We conclude that the ADL–ECM approach in a single-equation context has proved most useful in advancing our knowledge of the behaviour of the demand for narrow money for a number of industrialized countries (but see Cover and Keeler (1987) who favour the first-difference model for US M1 but ignore the cointegration and ECM literature). Success with broader monetary aggregates has proved more elusive.

1.4.3 Systems Approach

Estimating the demand for money as part of a system of asset demand equations has not proved as popular as single-equation studies, although this approach has proved successful in modelling asset demands other than money. Weale (1986), Hood (1987) and Barr and Cuthbertson (1990, 1991b) consider the demand for UK personal sector liquid assets in a systems framework, while Barr and Cuthbertson (1989a, b, 1991a) extend this approach to the company, other financial intermediaries (OFIs) and overseas sectors.

Weale (1986) estimates a dynamic 'partial adjustment' AIDS model over the period 1967(2)–1981(3):

$$s_t = Ls_{t-1} + \Gamma \ln p_t + \beta \left\{ \ln \left[\left(\frac{w}{p^*} \right)_t \right] - \ln e_t \right\} \tag{1.50}$$

where s_t are asset shares, $\ln p_t$ are nominal (AIDS) prices, w is wealth, e_t is expenditure and $\ln p_t^*$ is the composite (AIDS) price. Personal sector holdings of notes and coin, sterling sight deposits, sterling time deposits, savings bank deposits, building society deposits and local authority temporary deposits are modelled. The matrix of adjustment parameters L is not diagonal, indicating interdependent adjustment, and short-run symmetry of interest rate coefficients is accepted. The components of narrow money (notes and coin and sight deposits) are strong substitutes with bank deposits, while sight deposits and building society deposits are also substitutes. The β_i coefficients indicate that holdings of notes and coin and sight deposits increase with the level of expenditure and hence perform the role of transactions assets. However, the results, are not uniformly good and the local authority deposits equation yields rather implausible point estimates of long-run interest elasticities.

Hood (1987) utilizes a more aggregative asset structure comprising money, building society deposits and three separate categories of national savings. He utilizes a general ADL model in the asset shares:

$$\Delta s_t = \alpha_0 \Delta x_t + \alpha_1 x_{t-1} + \alpha_2 s_{t-1} + u_t \tag{1.51}$$

where x is the vector of asset returns and wealth held in liquid assets. Symmetry and sensible short-run interest rate effects are obtained, although there is some evidence that the assumption of weak separability from other assets (e.g. gilts, equities) is invalid and the approach to the long-run solution has rather long median lags.

Barr and Cuthbertson (1991b) utilize an interdependent error feedback AIDS model for asset shares s_t. For the UK personal sector

$$\Delta s_t = C \, \Delta X_t + L(s - s^*)_{t-1} \tag{1.52}$$

$$s_t^* = \Pi X_t \tag{1.53}$$

where s_t is the $k \times 1$ vector of asset shares, s_t^* is the long-run desired asset shares, x_t is the $q \times 1$ vector of independent variables (see equation (1.39)) Π is the $k \times q$ matrix of long-run parameters, C is the $k \times q$ matrix of short-run parameters and L is the $(k - 1) \times k$ matrix of adjustment parameters.

Barr and Cuthbertson estimate the system using the Engle–Granger two-step procedure and conventional non-linear least squares. Although the estimated equations are highly disaggregated (e.g. notes and coin, sight deposits, time deposits etc.), nevertheless one can derive demand functions that are close to the conventional aggregates (M1, M2, sterling M3 etc.). In general, they find that the system EFEs perform well statistically, and long-run homogeneity, symmetry and negativity restrictions are frequently accepted by the data. The above empirical results indicate that the demand for narrow and broad money depends on a vector of interest rates, wealth and expenditure, and the set of liquid asets are usually net substitutes. Keating (1985) used a highly restricted variant of the mean–variance model (e.g. diagonal and constant-covariance matrix) to explain disaggregated holdings of financial assets in the UK. However, this particular systems approach did not yield satisfactory results (Courakis, 1988).

Other Countries

In the USA and Canada in particular a systems approach to the demand for money has been widely utilized (see Feige and Pearce (1971) for a survey of early work). In general the evidence points to a low degree of substitutability (and sometimes even complementarity) between liquid financial assets that constitute narrow and broad money. This points to the need to model the demand for the constituent parts of M1, M2 etc., and to disaggregate by sector (e.g. people, companies) where possible. Various functional forms such as direct and indirect translog (e.g. Donovan (1978), Serletis and Robb (1986) and Serletis (1988) on Canadian data; and Ewis and Fisher (1984) and Swofford and Whitney (1986) on US data) have proved reasonably successful. Generally speaking, such studies have used rather restrictive lag structures which may account for the failure of estimated equations to satisfy the axioms of consumer theory. Some studies (e.g. Barnett, 1980; Serletis and Robb, 1986) also compare Divisia and simple sum aggregates and find in favour of the former. What the above studies indicate is that a simple demand for money function containing only one opportunity cost variable and excluding a wealth variable may involve misspecification. Evidence from systems models can be usefully complemented by non-parametric tests of the axioms of rational choice (e.g. Afriat, 1973; Varian, 1983) and separability (Swofford and Whitney, 1986) which are beginning to appear in the literature. It may also be possible to incorporate time-varying risk premiums (e.g. of bond prices) into these models (e.g. using ARCH models). The latter may also be useful in rehabilitating the mean-variance model in explaining the demand for broad money. The systems approach to the demand for money, particularly those approaches based on consumer demand theory, have provided complementary evidence to single-equation studies and suggest that aggregate (simple sum) money demand equations for broad money may be a relatively crude approximation to underlying behaviour.

1.4.4 Applied Work on Buffer Stock Money: Four Approaches

The term 'buffer stock money' covers a number of different approaches and below we classify these into four main types of model (Cuthbertson and Taylor, 1987a; Milbourne, 1988).

Single-equation Disequilibrium Money Models

Estimates of demand for money functions for almost any developed country have a sizeable autoregressive component which has frequently been interpreted as reflecting slow adjustment of short-run to long-run desired money holdings. However, when such equations are inverted to obtain the market-clearing level of, say, the interest rate, the latter will grossly overshoot its long-run equilibrium value in response to an exogenous change in the current period money supply.[25] This has led various authors (Artis and Lewis, 1976; Laidler, 1982) to interpret these estimated demand for money parameters as representing a slow real balance effect and to advocate inverting the demand for money function prior to estimation. If the supply of money is independent of demand factors, agents are temporarily forced off their long-run function because of slow adjustment in interest rates, output or the price level (e.g., Artis and Lewis, 1976; Laidler, 1980; Goodhart, 1984; Wren-Lewis, 1984).

Artis and Lewis (1976) estimate a number of inverted long-run demand for money functions assuming either slow adjustment in interest rates or nominal income. For the UK, using quarterly data up to 1973, they find more stable demand for money parameters (for narrow and broad money) than those obtained when money is taken as the dependent variable, and there is little or no implied overshooting in current period interest rates in response to a change in the current period money supply. Hendry (1985) for UK M1 and MacKinnon and Milbourne (1988) for US narrow money clearly demonstrate that inverting conventional short-run money demand function and taking the price level as the dependent variable yields exceedingly poor estimated price equations over the period 1960–85. They rightly conclude that price equations are not simply short-run 'money demand equations on their heads' (MacKinnon and Milbourne, 1988).[26] A major problem with the single-equation disequilibrium money approach is that only one argument can be chosen as the dependent variable, whereas on *a priori* grounds one might expect all the arguments of the demand function to adjust simultaneously.

Complete Disequilibrium Monetary Models

The second type of buffer stock model remedies the above defect and disequilibrium money holdings are allowed to influence a wide range of real and nominal variables. In this complete model approach the following type of equations frequently appear:

$$\Delta X_t = f(Z_t) + \gamma(L)(M_t^s - M_t^d) \tag{1.54a}$$

$$M_t^d = \alpha_0 P_t + \alpha_1 R_t + \alpha_2 Y_t \tag{1.54b}$$

X_t may be a set of real and nominal variables (e.g. output, prices, exchange rate), Z_t is a set of predetermined equilibrium variabless, M_t^d is the long-run demand for money and $\gamma(L)$ is a lag polynomial. As the money disequilibrium term appears in more than one equation, the model yields cross-equation restrictions on the parameters of the long-run demand for money function. This type of model has performed reasonably well for the USA (Laidler and Bentley, 1983), the UK (Hilliard, 1980; Laidler and O'Shea, 1980; Davidson, 1984; 1987) Australia (Jonson and Trevor, 1979) and Canada (Laidler et al., 1983). In some of these models the money supply is taken to be exogenous (e.g. Laidler and Bentley (1983) for the USA, and Laidler et al. (1983) for Canada) and hence is not explicitly modelled, whereas for the UK (Davidson, 1984) and Australia (Jonson and Trevor, 1979) the money supply is determined by the financing requirement of the PSBR. By and large, these models have been estimated using systems methods (e.g. three-stages least squares (3SLS) and full information maximum likelihood (FIML)) with a broad definition of money and have perhaps not proved as successful in explaining small open economies with flexible exchange rates as they have in the modelling of closed economies such as the USA (but see White (1981) for a critical view). In some models of this type M_t^d is estimated using cointegration techniques and the residuals are viewed as disequilibrium money. The latter is then included as an additional variable in expenditure equations such as stockbuilding (Ireland and Wren-Lewis, 1988) and non-durable consumption (Cuthbertson and Barlow, 1991).

If the coefficients of long-run money demand are the investigator's parameters of interest, then the full systems approach has the drawback that any estimates of the latter are conditional on the correct specification of the whole model. For example, if one should want to test whether the coefficients in the long-run demand for money remained stable over time, the need to estimate the whole model to obtain estimates of these parameters complicates the exercise, to say the least. (The latter criticism does not apply to the two-step cointegration procedure.) However, the complete model approach has the considerable advantage of showing the various routes whereby monetary disequilibrium affects the economy.

Shock Absorber Approaches

The third type of buffer stock model directly estimates the demand for money function, but it is assumed that shocks to the money supply are initially voluntarily held in transactions balances. The Carr and Darby (1981) version of this approach invokes the rational expectations hypothesis in that the monetary shock is the difference between actual money in circulation and the expected money supply. Some of these unanticipated balances are voluntarily held in money balances. However, anticipated changes in the money supply are immediately reflected in price expectations, and if prices are perfectly flexible, real money balances remain unchanged.

Carr and Darby test for the influence of unanticipated money on money demand using the following two-equation model:

$$(m - p)_t = \beta' x_t + \alpha(m - m^a)_t + \phi m_t^a + u_t \tag{1.55a}$$

$$m_t = \gamma' z_{t-1} + v_t \tag{1.55b}$$

where α is expected to lie in the closed interval [0, 1] and $\phi = 1 \ldots$. The first equation is a conventional demand for money function with the addition of an unanticipated and anticipated money term. m_t is the logarithm of the nominal money stock at time t, p_t is the logarithm of the price level, x_t is a vector of determining exogenous variables observed at time t, β is a suitably dimensioned coefficient vector and u_t is a random disturbance. m_t^a is the anticipated component of money supply and is determined as the predictions from equation (1.55b). z_{t-1} is a vector of variables known to agents at $t - 1$ which are considered to have a systematic influence on money supply, γ is a stable coefficient vector and v_t is the non-systematic component of the money supply process. The first two terms on the right-hand side of (1.55a) can be taken as representing planned and unplanned components of money demand respectively.

Carr and Darby use a two-step estimation procedure: OLS on equation (1.55b) yields predictions m_t^a which are then used in equation (1.55a). They report OLS estimates of equation (1.55a) which appear to support the buffer stock or shock absorber hypothesis for a number of industrialized countries. However, MacKinnon and Milbourne (1984) formally demonstrate the intuitively obvious point that $(m - m^a)_t$ and u_t are correlated, and infer that OLS estimates of α are biased towards unity. A simple reparameterization of (1.55a) allows consistent estimates to be obtained by two-step OLS which are equivalent to the maximum likelihood estimates:

$$(m - p)_t = \beta^{*'} x_t + \lambda(m^a - p)_t + \phi^* m_t^a + u_t^* \tag{1.56}$$

where $\lambda = -\alpha/(1 - \alpha)$, $\phi^* = \phi(1 - \alpha)$. We expect ϕ^* to be zero and λ to be negative. MacKinnon and Milbourne find that OLS estimates of equation (1.56) yield a statistically significant, but negative, value of α (around -4) and a statistically significant value for ϕ, thus rejecting the Carr–Darby shock absorber hypothesis. Cuthbertson (1986b) using UK data on M1, an AR(4) model for m_t^a and an ADL (or EFE) demand for money equation, finds that the shock absorber hypothesis is rejected for the MacKinnon–Milbourne formulation.

All the studies mentioned above, when determining m_t^a, assume that agents use univariate autoregressive integrated moving-average (ARIMA) fixed coefficient models. Cuthbertson and Taylor (1988a) assume that agents are likely to use a fairly simple learning model, and suggest that expectations of the money supply are based on a stochastic time trend (Harvey and Todd, 1983). Using UK data, they take an EFE (Hendry, 1979; Hendry et al., 1984) for M1 as their conventional demand for money function and use a Kalman filter to generate the m_t^a series. Assuming that money is endogenous, they utilize the MacKinnon–Milbourne formulation of the shock absorber hypothesis (equation (1.56)) and estimate $\alpha = 0.12$, whilst anticipated money has no significant effect on real money balances. Hence these results support the Carr–Darby shock absorber hypothesis even when the

MacKinnon–Milbourne critique is accepted, but demonstrate the sensitivity of the results to the expectations scheme assumed.

In a rejoinder to MacKinnon and Milbourne, Carr et al, (1985) assert that the money supply is exogenous and that equation (1.55a) must logically be considered as a price equation, thus precluding the problem of simultaneity. MacKinnon and Milbourne (1988) demonstrate that an inverted shock absorber equation with the price level as the dependent variable fails the parameter restrictions implicit in (1.55a) and performs rather poorly in statistical terms. Cuthbertson and Taylor (1986, 1988) note that, by using two-step methods, previous studies have neglected to test for the cross-equation rationality restrictions implicit in the Carr–Darby shock absorber hypothesis, and only if these are acceptable for the data can we accept the Carr et al., estimates. Cuthbertson and Taylor (1986, 1988b) are easily able to reject the implicit cross-equation rationality restrictions using US and UK data (identical with those used by Cuthbertson (1986b)). Overall, therefore, the Carr–Darby model of buffer stock money (including the rational expectations assumption) appears to be rejected by the data.

An interesting application of the shock absorber approach which eschews a role for expectations (and its associated practical problems) is provided by Browne (1989), who adds an exogenous money term to a conventional demand for money function for Ireland. For this small open economy, measures of exogenous money are provided by the UK PSBR and changes in UK high-powered money. He finds that the latter have a positive initial impact on Ireland's demand for real broad money balances (M3) with a zero long-run effect (as the price level ultimately fully adjusts to the increase in exogenous money). (See also, Artis and Lewis (1976), Santomero and Seater (1981) and Judd and Scadding (1982), who also explore this non-rational-expectations approach in a single-equation context using a variety of variables for monetary shocks.)

A Forward-looking Buffer Stock Model

On intuitive grounds it might appear somewhat bold to assume that agents who hold M1 (predominantly the personal sector in the UK, at least until very recently) form expectations of the aggregate money supply as posited by Carr and Darby. However, in determining their planned money holdings, agents may be influenced by their expected level of transactions, and in addition may temporarily hold unanticipated increases in 'money' which they will perceive as innovations in nominal income (rather than in the aggregate money supply). These intuitively plausible ideas can be formalized in a tractable way by assuming that agents determine their planned money balances by minimizing a multiperiod quadratic cost function. The solution to this problem is an exercise in the discrete-time calculus of variations (see for example Sargent, 1979) and results in a forward-looking model of the form

$$m_t = \lambda_1 m_{t-1} + (1 - \lambda_1)(1 - \lambda_1 D) \sum_0^\infty (\lambda_1 D)^s E_{t-1} m_{t+s}^* \qquad (1.57)$$

where $E_{t-1} m_{t+s}^*$ are the expected values of future long-run money balances (and λ_1 depends on the adjustment cost parameters and the discount factor D in the cost function). The buffer stock element arises because agents make decisions concerning m_t based on information in period $t - 1$ and hence surprise increases in nominal income are partly held as buffer money. Hence, if the long-run demand function is given by

$$m_t^* = c_0 p_t + c_1 y_t - c_2 r_t = c' x_t \qquad (1.58)$$

the estimating equation is (see Cuthbertson, 1988c)

$$m_t = \lambda_1 m_{t-1} + \lambda(p - p^e)_t + \beta(y - y^e)_t - \delta(r - r^e)_t$$
$$+ (1 - \lambda_1)(1 - \lambda_1 D)c' E_{t-1} \sum_0^\infty (\lambda_1 D)^s x_{t+s}^e + u_t \qquad (1.59)$$

where we assume that monetary innovations are a linear combination of innovations in prices, income and interest rates, plus a catch-all disturbance u_t. The testable predictions of the demand for money function are that the weights on the expected future variables x_{t+s}^e decline geometrically as the time horizon is extended – an intuitively plausible restriction – and that these weights are related to the coefficients on the lagged dependent variable; we refer to the latter as the backward–forward restrictions. The model subsumes (Hendry, 1983; Mizon, 1984) conventional demand for money functions. If the arguments of the demand for money function are generated by a random walk, equation (1.59) is of the ADL or EFE (Hendry et al., 1984) form.

The forward-looking buffer stock model throws some light on possible deficiencies in conventional backward-looking formulations of the demand for money function. Conventional models may omit potentially important variables, namely future values of the arguments of the demand for money. It would be paradoxical for the demand for transactions balances to depend on the past level of transactions, unless these are a proxy variable for future transactions (as in the adaptive expectations formulation of conventional functions). By explicitly modelling the expectations process, we go some way towards meeting the Lucas critique. Conentional demand functions that estimate a convolution of expectations and adjustment lags (for example, partial adjustment and error feedback equations) may exhibit instability because of instability in the expectations-generating process.

A policy implication that is immediately apparent from the model is that overshooting after an unanticipated independent change in the money supply is mitigated in the forward-looking model. If the increase in the money supply is accompanied by an unanticipated increase in nominal income, this leads to a temporary increase in holdings of buffer money. Also, to the extent that an increase in the money supply leads to a reappraisal of the expected future path of the price level and real income, the demand for money increases today, and this reduces any disequilibrium in the money market at given interest rates.

Following Kannianien and Tarkka (1986), Muscatelli (1988) provides a variant of the above model, with the main additional feature being that costs of adjustment apply to non-money asset holdings $(A_{t+s} - A_{t+s-1})^2$ rather than to money. Planned short-run money balances depend not only on expected forcing variables x^e_{t+s} as in (1.59) but also on expected future levels of saving.

Cuthbertson (1988c) uses a two-step procedure to estimate (1.59) for UK M1 with alternative AR and vector autoregression (VAR) forecasting schemes for the x variables (i.e. p, y, r). The results are encouraging: the backward–forward restrictions hold and the equation has stable parameters with long-run unit (expected price) and income elasticities accepted by the data.[27] The addition of savings to the model creates additional estimation problems and does not appear to add appreciably to the empirical performance and theoretical interpretability of the model (Muscatelli, 1988). Cuthbertson and Taylor (1987c, 1990b) test the implicit cross-equation rationality restrictions by assuming that (y_t, p_t, r_t) are generated by a VAR process; they find in favour of the rational expectations restrictions for the UK M1 and £M3 definitions of money.

Muscatelli (1989) argues that although the forward model of Cuthbertson (1988c) performs well statistically, it is variance encompassed by a backward-looking EFE. Broadly speaking, the variables in the ECM provide an additional explanatory power when added to the forward model but the reverse does not apply. (These are non-nested tests; see Davidson and MacKinnon (1981).) Cuthbertson and Taylor (1991) criticize Muscatelli's implementation of some of the test procedures but accept that, formally, the ECM does variance encompass the forward model. They note that the ECM is designed to fit the blips in the data by using complex difference variables (which may have little or no theoretical interpretation), while the forward model has an explicit dynamic structure (albeit one based on quadratic costs which, although widely used, is not particularly plausible). However, at present, the balance of the evidence is probably in favour of the feedback–ECM model for UK M1 (but see Cuthbertson and Taylor, forthcoming b).

For Italian M2 Bagliano and Favero (1989) use the stability tests proposed by Hendry (1988) and non-nested tests to exammine the relative performance of feedforward and feedback equations and find tentative evidence that an expectations model performs better than the feedback model after the change in monetary policy regime which occurred in 1969–70. Similarly, for US narrow money Cuthbertson and Taylor (1990a) find that the missing money period can be rationalized in terms of an expectations model with a shift in the expectations generation equation (see also Dutkowsky and Foote (1988) on US data).

1.5 SUMMARY AND CONCLUSIONS

A great deal of ingenuity and creativity has been applied to the study of the demand for assets, and in particular money. Let me now summarize my own general views on this vast literature – views which may not be shared by other practitioners in this area. (A wider perspective on the importance of asset demands for monetary policy can be found in Goodhart (1989) and for macrotheory in Barro and Fischer (1976) and Fischer (1988).)

On the theoretical side, the inventory and precautionary approaches have yielded useful qualitative insights into the determinants of the demand for money, but this provides only broad guidelines for applied work using aggregate time series data. The mean–variance model is only applicable to the demand for a single capital-safe asset and hence to a broad definition of money: empirically it has not proved very succesful. The consumer theory approach provides a useful framework for analysing the demand for money since it implicitly recognizes the interdependent nature of asset decisions. It also yields reasonably tractable estimating equations with testable restrictions (e.g. symmetry, homogeneity and negativity). Work on separability and (non-parametric) tests of the axioms of consumer theory also complement this approach. From the standpoint of the applied economist it has much to commend it.

A major weakness of all theories of the demand for money is a grossly inadequate treatment of dynamic adjustment. This is not a criticism of theorists, for clearly the detailed and complex transactions, information and learning costs faced by the representative agent are inherently difficult to formalize. In the econometric modelling of dynamic adjustment perhaps the main advance has been in the ECM, and it is surprising that until recently this has been largely ignored in the US applied literature. Most US applied economists appear content to work within the highly restrictive partial adjustment framework (e.g. the survey by Roley (1985)). Certainly one has to apply the general to specific and error feedback approach with due regard for theory consistency and plausible decision variables if one is to avoid the charge of data mining. However, it does appear to provide a very useful approach to dynamic modelling, with the laudable aim of yielding stable parameter estimates and testing any tentative empirical model extremely thoroughly against both the data and other competing models.

The new literature on unit roots (Dickey and Fuller, 1979; Phillips and Park, 1986) and cointegration provides a useful framework for analysing long-run relationships and can be satisfactorily combined with the ECM approach. It is bound to yield further insights concerning the demand for money (Hendry, 1986; Engle and Yoo, 1987; Johansen, 1988).

Empirical results which employ variability measures such as time-varying variances of receipts on time-varying risk premiums are in their infancy, and we might expect to see applications of, say, the ARCH model in future work. To date, evidence for time-varying risk premiums has come from inverted asset demand functions, i.e. functions with the asset price (interest rate) as the dependent variable, or more directly from reduced form asset price equations (e.g. uncovered interest parity). However, the latter evidence points strongly to the need to investigate such effects in asset demand functions.

The problem of the lagged dependent variable in estimated money demand functions is not, in my view, acute as long as one accepts the view that money has, in the past, been largely endogenous (in quarterly data) and that all agents do not react instantaneously (in, say, quarterly data). Admittedly, the lagged dependent variable could be picking up all kinds of misspecification (e.g. aggregation problems, badly measured variables, wrong functional form) and, in particular, over-restrictive lag response in the partial adjustment model. However, given limitations of the available data, empirical results from ECMs seem to me to yield plausible equations in the main, and, in particular, median lag responses are not unreasonable. However, none of the above is inconsistent with Laidler's (1982) argument that, if the money supply is rigidly controlled by the authorities, then estimated ECM type money demand functions should not be inverted to yield a solution for the interest rate, price level etc. Similarly, adopting the error correction interpretation of past behaviour does not rule out the possibility that agents use money (somehow defined) as a buffer asset which responds to unanticipated events or that some agents might not always be on their long-run demand function for (broad) money as in complete disequilibrium money models.

Whether expectations about future transactions or future bond prices play an important role in demand for money is rather an open question on which we have relatively little evidence. Our techniques for modelling expectations variables in aggregate data are rather crude. Expectations equations which incorporate learning by agents perhaps have greater intuitive appeal than fixed coefficient reduced forms, but ultimately it is difficult to distinguish models that incorporate expectations from backward-looking demand for money equations (but Hendry (1988) provides a useful test procedure notwithstanding the arguments of Cuthbertson (1991). Agents may base today's money holdings on expected transactions, but because of the highly autoregressive nature of aggregate transactions variables, this becomes largely indistinguishable from a current period trans-actions variable. Evidence that the demand for money depends on expecta-tions (of income or bond prices) is rather weak. It therefore follows that, strictly, the Lucas critique may not be an important factor in interpreting most money demand equations; structural shifts in estimated demand for money equations are likely to have been caused by factors other than changes in the way that agents form expectations.

The buffer stock notion has been implemented in a number of guises. To claim that surprises in nominal income and interest rates may result in changes in money balances seems largely uncontentious. First-difference terms in ECMs may act as proxy variables for such surprises. Modelling the impact of surprises is difficult, but as far as narrow money (M1) is concerned such effects appear to be relatively small. The Carr–Darby shock absorber model does not appear to be a sensible way of modelling buffer stock effects and certainly the rational expectations element of the hypothesis does not hold. For narrow money (e.g. M1) it is difficult to imagine agents being in prolonged disequilibrium since transactions costs in switching between M1 and other capital certain assets are relatively low. For broader monetary aggregates and given general uncertainty one can certainly entertain the possibility that disequilibrium money will lead to changes in other economic variables. Complete disequilibrium models which use broad money are therefore useful in interpreting aspects of the transmission mechanism but are not the ideal vehicle for analysing the long-run demand for money. However, cointegration in systems of equations (Davidson and Hall, 1988) may provide further insights into such models: disequilibrium in long-run money balances may lead to changes in short-run money holdings and in other variables such as prices and interest rates.

Financial innovation is clearly an important factor in influencing the demand for money. With financial innovation, the definition of what con-stitutes money becomes blurred; new financial instruments and the change in transactions and information costs (widely defined) create acute problems in finding a stable demand for money function. It is quite remarkable in the face of such changes that we can still claim to know a great deal about the past behaviour of narrow and even broad money. Prediction is more hazardous of course since it is difficult to forecast technological and institu-tional change.

Work on the demand for money has yielded reasonably satisfactory explanations of the past behaviour of the demand for narrow money for a number of industrialized nations (and in the USA for broad money, M2) despite the paucity of high quality data, major changes in economic vari-ables and the pace of financial innovation. Recent advances have been made possible by new econometric approaches rather than new theoretical models. Less success has been achieved with the broader aggregates in the UK. Over the last decade financial markets and government policy have undergone substantial changes, yet applied monetary economists have managed to utilize economic theory and best-practice econometrics to enhance our knowledge of the behaviour of the demand for money considerably. However, it must be said that our ability to forecast the probable behaviour of the demand for money (and other assets) is not sufficiently good to warrant strict control of any single monetary aggregate, particularly for an open economy such as the UK.

Notes

1   We have therefore chosen to omit discussion of the 'legal restrictions' theory of money (e.g. Hall, 1982; Sargent and Wallace, 1982; Wallace 1988) and 'cash-in-advance' models (e.g. Lucas, 1984; Hartley, 1988) because they do not feature prominently in the applied literature. For a recent clear perspective on these and other ideas in the 'new monetary economics' see Laidler (1988).
2   This distinction between the 'motives approach' and the 'consumer theory' approach is used for expositional purposes. Clearly, the underlying idea behind all these models is that money yields 'utility' in the general sense of the word, but consumer theory 'deliberately avoids any analysis of motivation and simply applies generalised notions about the determination of the demand for any good to the demand for money' (Laidler, 1985). Barnett (1980) also applies this distinction.
3   Milbourne (1983a) provides an elegant synthesis of target threshold models and demonstrates that inventory models of the Baumol–Tobin type can be viewed as a special case of the more general target threshold models (i.e. the Baumol–Tobin models have a fixed lower threshold and a non-stochastic cash inflow). However, for expositional purposes we have retained the distinction between 'inventory' and 'precautionary' models.
4   The result is based on Chebyshev's inequality. This states that the probability p that a variable x (net payments) will deviate from its mean by t times its standard deviation σ is equal to or less than $1/t^2$, i.e.

$$p(-t\sigma > x > t\sigma) \le \frac{1}{t^2}$$

Net payments are assumed to have a zero mean and so the probability of net payments equal to M, where $M/\sigma = t$ standard deviations from zero, is

$$p(N > M) \le \frac{1}{t^2} = \frac{\sigma^2}{M^2}$$

5   Aggregation over risky assets is possible for any utility function for which the marginal utility of wealth is isoelastic in a linear function of wealth (Cass and Stiglitz, 1972); the quadratic and negative exponential satisfy this property.
6   Tsiang (1972) argues that all we require for a second-order Taylor expansion

around expected wealth to be a valid approximation to an acceptable utility function is that 'risk' should remain small relative to the individual's total wealth.

7 Courakis (1988) demonstrates the issues involved in extending the mean-variance approach when the maximand involves expected terminal real wealth. For the negative exponential, asset demands are not independent of the expected rate of price inflation (even though the zero row sum condition holds) but for the power function the converse is the case.

8 Buiter and Armstrong (1978) combine the mean–variance approach with brokerage costs.

9 This model is then usually interpreted as a version of a static capital asset pricing model (CAPM).

10 Varian (1983) provides formal non-parametric tests of separability, although these have not as yet been widely applied in the asset demand literature.

11 This also raises the question of aggregation over monetary assets. Consumer theory can be used to construct appropriate Divisia monetary aggregates (rather than simple sum aggregates). Space precludes discussion of the theoretical basis of Divisia aggregates (Barnett, 1980; Barnett et al., 1984) but we do discuss empirical results using Divisia aggregates later in the chapter.

12 Merton (1973), Diewert (1974) and Barnett (1980) examine the assumptions whereby the intertemporal maximization problem can be reduced to a single-period optimization problem.

13 Other popular functional forms for the direct and indirect utility functions are the translog (Christensen et al., 1975) and the generalized constant elasticity of substitution (Chetty, 1969). Space precludes a discussion of the relative merits of the wide class of functional forms available.

14 ln $P^{*\tau}$ is an approximation in equation (1.17) (see Deaton and Muellbauer, 1980).

15 Part of the reason for illustrating the consumer theory approach with respect to the AIDS cost function is that it yields a linear system in asset shares which is amenable to comparison with 'conventional' single-equation empirical studies of the demand for money. Other flexible functional forms often yield equations that are non-linear in the parameters.

16 Milbourne (1985), utilizing the Miller–Orr model, argues that average quarterly money holdings due to an unanticipated increase in exogenous money are likely to be relatively small for a narrow definition of money (e.g. M1). This provides a strong case for abandoning the Miller–Orr model as the basis for buffer stock ideas for M1. But note that Milbourne's results are weakened if (a) we use point-in-time money stock data, (b) different agents receive additional balances sequentially, (c) agents do not continuously monitor M1 balances because of time costs of information gathering and (d) agents face generalized uncertainty and hence not a well-defined probability distribution. Assumptions (c) and (d) would of course violate the assumptions of the Miller–Orr model. See Laidler (1988) for a discussion of the importance of the precautionary demand for money in analysing the transmission mechanism and in particular that information costs and interest rates may interact to alter the distribution of cash flows in models of the Miller–Orr type.

17 For an interesting theoretically based adjustment model within the framework

of the precautionary demand for money, see Milbourne et al. (1983) and Smith (1986). In these models the adjustment speed depends on a complex function of the mean and variance of net receipts, interest rates and brokerage fees, and lagged money explicitly appears in the demand function. This approach has not been adopted in empirical work.

18   In practice, such costs are likely to be lump sum, in the main. But search and information costs concerning the terms offered on non-money assets are likely to be very complex.

19   Friedman's (1979b) optimal partial adjustment model is of the interdependent error feedback form.

20   For example, suppose that the true model is static with an AR(1) error:

$$y_t = \beta x_t + u_t \tag{1a}$$

$$u_t = \rho u_{t-1} + \epsilon_t \tag{1b}$$

These equations imply

$$y_t = \pi_0 x_t + \pi_1 x_{t-1} + \pi_2 y_{t-1} + \epsilon_t \tag{1c}$$

and

$$\pi_0 = \beta \qquad \pi_1 = -\beta_\rho \qquad \pi_2 = \rho$$

If we have an AR(1) error, then in (c) the following common-factor restriction holds: $\pi_1/\pi_0 = -\pi_2$. Hence if the π_i are statistically significant in (c) but the common-factor restriction does *not* hold we have a dynamic model; if the common-factor restriction holds we have the static model (a) (with an AR(1) error).

21   Note that in the presence of unit root I(1) series, inference may be hazardous in either the cointegration or error correction formulation. Theoretical results from the unit root literature do not yet provide definitive answers to some of these inference problems (see, for example, Banerjee at al., 1986; Phillips and Park, 1986; West, 1988).

22   First-order adaptive expectations $x_t^e - x_{t-1}^e = \lambda(x_{t-1} - x_{t-1}^e)$ is only optimal if x_t is IMA(1, 1) which is a property of numerous economic time series (Granger, 1966).

23   With the rapid pace of financial liberalization, in particular, new definitions of money frequently appear. In what follows we avoid the nuances of the various changes in definition that have occurred. In the UK major changes in definition have recently taken place, and sterling M3 and M3 are no longer to be published. (*Bank of England Quarterly Bulletin* 29(3), pp. 352–3, August 1989). However, in our discussion of the empirical work on UK broad money, the reader will not be misled if he considers M3 and sterling M3 as synonymous.

24   Round-tripping refers to the practice of borrowing on bank advances and redepositing the proceeds in wholesale deposits. The Sprenkle–Miller (1980) model indicates that this depends on the differential between wholesale deposits and bank advance rates, even when this is non-positive.

25   This argument may not be entirely watertight. If we 'mechanically' invert the partial adjustment short-run money demand function

$$m_t = \beta x_t + \gamma m_{t-1} \tag{a}$$

then we obtain $\partial x_t / \partial m_t = 1/\beta$ and a long-run effect which is smaller: $\partial x / \partial m = (1 - \gamma)/\beta, 0 > \gamma > 1$. However, as Laidler (1982) points out, if the increase in money m_t is exogenous, then agents are forced to hold it at the beginning of period t, and hence the money stock at the end of period $t - 1$ should be denoted m_t and not m_{t-1} in (a). Hence the long-run *and* short-run impact on x_t is $(1 - \gamma)/\beta$. Another argument stresses regime shifts (of which the Lucas critique (Lucas, 1976) could be viewed as a special case if (a) contains expectation terms). If (a) is estimated when m_t is endogenous and hence agents voluntarily respond to changes in x_t, then the parameters of such an equation may not remain constant when m_t is exogenous (e.g. Walsh, 1984).

26   This does not preclude the money supply's having some causal influence on the price level, but factors other than those embodied in the short-run money demand function may also influence prices (as, for example, in the complete disequilibrium money models discussed in the next section).

27   Hendry (1988) demonstrates that if (a) a feedback–ECM model for M1 is stable and (b) the AR and VAR forecasting schemes are unstable, then this implies rejection of the forward-looking model. Cuthbertson (forthcoming) argues that one can only rescue the forward model by either searching for a stable (extended) VAR or establishing that the feedback model is unstable (on the latter see Cuthbertson and Taylor (forthcoming c) and Hall et al. (1989)). Note that in the face of (a) and (b), Hendry (1988) and Cuthbertson (forthcoming) agree that the instrumental variables (IV) estimation of the structural forward model (e.g. Hansen and Sargent, 1982) is invalid. Hendry's (1988) paper also has a bearing on Goodfriend's (1985) proposition (see also Grether and Maddala, 1973) that a true static money demand function with serially correlated true income/interest rate variables which are subject to measurement error is consistent with an estimated model with measured income/interest rates and a significant lagged money variable (i.e. partial adjustment). Goodfriend's argument has not, to my knowledge, been examined empirically but can be cast in the Hendry (1988) framework since measurement error is the basis of weakly rational IV estimation procedures for expectations variables. Thus, if Hendry's point (a) holds for any (ADL) feedback model and auxiliary equations for the measurement error variables is non-constant, then this would discriminate between Goodfriend's static model with measurement errors and a dynamic model. However, unless the stochastic process of the form of the measurement error can be formulated, Goodfriend's assertion is untestable.

References

Abel, A.B. and Mishkin, F.S. (1983) An integrated view of tests of rationality, market efficiency, and the short-run neutrality of monetary policy. *Journal of Monetary Economics* 11, 3–24.

Afriat, S. (1973) On a system of inequalities on demand analysis: An extension of the classification method. *International Economic Review* 14, 460–72.

Akerlof, G.A. and Milbourne, R.D. (1980) The short-run demand for money *Economic Journal* 90 (360), 53; 885–900.

Anderson, G.J. and Blundell, R.W. (1982) Estimation and hypothesis testing in dynamic singular equation systems. *Econometrica* 50 (6), 1559–71.

Ando, A. and Shell, K. (1979) Demand for money in a general portfolio model in the presence of an asset that dominates money. In G. Fromm and L.R. Klein (eds), *The Brooking Model: Perspective and Recent Developments*. Amsterdam: North Holland.

Arango, S. and Nadiri, M.I. (1981) Demand for money in open economies. *Journal of Monetary Economics* 7 (1), 69–83.

Artis, M.J. and Lewis, M.K. (1976) The demand for money in the UK 1963–73. *Manchester School* 44, 147–81.

—— and —— (1981) *Monetary Control in the UK*. Oxford: Philip Allan.

—— and —— (1984) How unstable is the demand for money in the United Kingdom? *Economica* 51, 473–6.

Baba, Y., Hendry, D.F. and Starr, R.M. (1988) US money demand 1960–1984. Discussion Paper 27, Nuffield College, Oxford.

Backus, D., Brainard, W.C., Smith, G. and Tobin, J. (1980) A model of US financial and non-financial economic behaviour. *Journal of Money, Credit and Banking* 12, 259–93.

Bagliano, F.C. and Favero, G.A. (1989) Money demand instability, expectations and policy regimes: The case of Italy 1964–86. Mimeo, St Anthony's College, Oxford.

Banerjee, A., Dolado, J., Hendry, D. and Smith, G. (1986) Exploring equilibrium relationships in econometrics through static models: Some Monte Carlo evidence. *Oxford Bulletin of Economics and Statistics* 48 (3), 253–78.

Barnett, W.A. (1980) Economic monetary aggregates: an application of index number and aggregation theory. *Journal of Econometrics* 14 (1), 11–48.

—— Offenbacher, E.K. and Spindt, P.A. (1984) The new Divisia monetary aggregates. *Journal of Political Economy* 92 (6), 1049–85.

Barr, D.G. and Cuthbertson, K. (1988a) Econometric modelling of the financial decisions of the UK personal sector: Preliminary results. Mimeo, Bank of England, September.

—— and —— (1989a) A data based simulation model of the financial asset decisions of UK 'other' financial intermediaries. Bank of England Discussion Paper, Technical Series.

—— and —— (1989b) The demand for financial assets held in the UK by the overseas sector: An application of two-stage budgeting. Bank of England Discussion Paper, Technical Series.

—— and —— (1990) Modelling the flow of funds: with an application to the demand for liquid assets by the UK personal sector. In S.G.B. Henry and K. Patterson (eds), *Economic Modelling at The Bank of England*, Chapman and Hall.

—— and —— (1991a) An interdependent error feedback model of UK company sector asset demands. *Oxford Economic Papers*, April, forthcoming.

—— and —— (1991b) Neo-classical consumer demand theory and the demand for money. *Economic Journal*, July, forthcoming.

Barratt, C.R. and Walters, A.A. (1966) The stability of keynesian and money multipliers in the UK. *Review of Economics and Statistics* 48, 395–405.

Barro, R.J. (1970) Inflation, the payments period and the demand for money. *Journal of Political Economy* 78 (6), 1228–63.

—— (1976) Integral constraints and aggregation in an inventory model of money demand. *Journal of Finance* 31 (1), 77–88.

—— and Fischer, S. (1976) Recent developments in monetary theory. *Journal of Monetary Economics* 2 (2), 133–67.

—— and Santomero, A.M. (1972) Household money holdings and the demand deposit rates. *Journal of Money, Credit and Banking* 4, 397–413.

Baumol, W.J. (1952) The transactions demand for cash: an inventory theoretic approach. *Quarterly Journal of Economics* 66, 545–56.

Blejer, M. (1978) Black-market exchange-rate expectation and the domestic demand for money. *Journal of Monetary Economics* 4, 767–73.

Blundell-Wignall, A., Rondoni, N. and Ziegelschmidt, H. (1984) The demand for money and velocity in major OECD countries. Working Paper 13, OECD Economics and Statistics Department, February.

Bollerslev, T. Engle, R.F. and Wooldridge, J.M. (1988) A capital asset pricing model with time-varying covariances, *Journal of Political Economy* 96 (1), 116–31.

Borch, K. (1969) A note of uncertainty and indifference curves. *Review of Economic Studies* 36, 1–4.

Bordo, M.D. and Jonung, L. (1985) *The Long Run Behaviour of the Velocity of Circulation: The International Evidence*. Cambridge: Cambridge University Press.

Boughton, J.M. (1981) Recent instability of the demand for money: An international perspective. *Southern Economic Journal* 47 (3), 579–97.

Brainard, W.C. and Tobin, J. (1968) Econometric models: Their problems and usefulness: pitfalls in financial model building. *American Economic Review* 58, 2.

Branson, W.H., Halttunen, H. and Masson, P. (1977) Exchange rates in the short-run: some further results. *European Economic Review* 12, 395–402.

Bronfenbrenner, M. and Mayer, T. (1960) Liquidity functions in the American economy. *Econometrica* 28, 810–34.

Browne, F.X. (1989) A new test of the buffer stock money hypothesis. *Manchester School*, (2), 154–71.

Brunner, K. and Meltzer, A.H. (1963) Predicting velocity implications for theory and policy. *Journal of Finance* 18, 319–54.

—— and Meltzer, A.H. (1964) Some further evidence on supply and demand functions for money. *Journal of Finance* 19, 240–83.

Buiter, W.H. and Armstrong, C.A. (1978) A didatic note on the transactions demand for money and behaviour towards risk. *Journal of Money, Credit and Banking* 10 (4), 529–38.

—— and Miller, M. (1982) Real exchange rate overshooting and the output cost of bringing down inflation. *European Economic Review* 18, 83–130.

Calomiris, C.W. and Domowitz, I. (1989) Asset substitution, money demand and the inflation process in Brazil. *Journal of Money, Credit and Banking* 21 (1), 78–9.

Cardoso, E. (1983) A money demand equation for Brazil. *Journal of Development Economics* 12, 183–93.

Carr, J. and Darby, M. J. (1981) The role of money supply shocks in the short-run demand for money. *Journal of Monetary Economics* 8 (2), 183–200.

——, —— and Thornton, D. (1985) Monetary anticipations and the demand for money: Reply to MacKinnon and Milbourne. *Journal of Monetary Economics* 16, 251–7.

Cass, D. and Stiglitz, J. E. (1972) Risk aversion wealth effects on portfolios with many assets. *Review of Economic Studies* July, 331–53.

Chang, W. W., Hamberg, D. and Hirata, J. (1983) Liquidity preference as behaviour toward risk in a demand for short-term securities – not money *American Economic Review* 73, 420–7.

——, —— and —— (1984) On liquidity preference again: reply. *American Economic Review* 74 (4), 812–3.

Chetty, V. K. (1969) On measuring the nearness of near-moneys. *American Economic Review* 59, 270–81.

Christensen, L. R., Jorgenson, D. W. and Lau, L. J. (1975) Transcendental logarithmic utility functions. *American Economic Review* 65, 367–83.

Christophodes, L. N. (1976) Quadratic costs and multi-asset partial adjustment equations. *Applied Economics* 8, 4.

Coughlan, R. T. (1978) A transactions demand for money. *Bank of England Quarterly Bulletin* 18, 48–60.

Courakis, A. S. (1988) Modelling portfolio selection. *Economic Journal* 98, 619–42.

—— (1988) Anticipated inflation and portfolio selection. Discussion Paper 65, Institute of Economics and Statistics, Oxford.

—— (1989) Does constant relative risk aversion imply asset demands? Discussion Paper 78, Institute of Economics and Statistics, Oxford.

Cover, J. P. and Keeler, J. P. (1987) Estimating money demand in log-first-difference form. *Southern Economic Journal* 53 (3), 751–67.

Cumby, R. E., Huizinga, J. and Obstfeld, M. (1983) Two-step two-stage least squares estimation in models with rational expectations. *Journal of Econometrics* 21, 333–55.

Currie, D. (1981) Some long run features of dynamic time series models. *Economic Journal* 91, 704–15.

—— and Kennally, G. (1985) Personal sector demands for liquid deposits. Discussion Paper, National Institute of Economic and Social Research, January.

Cuthbertson, K. (1986a) Price expectations and lags in the demand for money. *Scottish Journal of Political Economy* 33 (4), 334–54.

—— (1986b) Monetary anticipations and the demand for money in the UK. *Bulletin of Economic Research* 38 (3), 257–70.

—— (1988a) Economics, expectations and the Kalman filter. *Manchester School* 56 (3), 223–46.

—— (1988b) Modelling the demand for M1: feedforward versus feedback mechanisms. Mimeo, Bank of England.

—— (1988c) The demand for M1: A forward looking buffer stock model. *Oxford Economic Papers* 40, 110–31.

—— (1991) The encompassing implications of feedforward versus feedback mechanisms: a reply to Hendry. *Oxford Economic Papers*.

—— and Barlow, D. (1990) The determination of liquid asset holdings of the UK personal sector. *Manchester School* 58(4), 348–60.

—— and —— (1991) Disequilibrium, buffer-stocks and consumers' expenditure on non-durables. *Review of Economics and Statistics*, forthcoming.

—— and Taylor, M. P. (1986) Monetary anticipations and the demand for money in the UK: testing rationality in the shock absorber hypothesis. *Journal of Applied Econometrics* 1 (2), 1–11.

—— and —— (1987a) Buffer stock money: an appraisal. In C. Goodhart, D. Currie and D. T. Llewellyn (eds), *The Operation and Regulation of Financial Markets*. London: Macmillan.

—— and —— (1987b) *Macroeconomic Systems*. Oxford: Basil Blackwell.

—— and —— (1987c) The demand for money: a dynamic rational expectations model. *Economic Journal (Supplement)* 97, 65–76.

—— and —— (1988a) Monetary anticipations and the demand for money: some evidence for the UK. *Weltwirtschafliches Archiv* 183, 509–20.

—— and —— (1988b) Monetary anticipations and the demand for money in the US: further tests. *Southern Economic Journal* 55 (2), 326–55.

—— and —— (1990a) On the short-run demand for money: the case of the missing money; and the Lucas critique. *Journal of Macroeconomics* 12(3), 437–52.

—— and —— (1990b) Money demand expectations and the forward looking model. *Journal of Policy Modeling* 12(2), 1–27.

—— and —— (1991) A comparison of the rational expectations and general to specific approach to modelling the demand for M1. *Manchester School*.

Dalal, A. J. (1983) Comparative statics and asset substitutability/complementarity in a portfolio model: a dual approach. *Review of Economic Studies* 50, 355–67.

Davidson, J. (1984) Monetary disequilibrium: An approach to modelling monetary phenomena in the UK. Mimeo, London School of Economics.

—— (1987) Disequilibrium money: Some further results with a monetary model of the UK. In C. A. E. Goodhart, D. Currie and D. Llewellyn (eds), *The Operation and Regulation of Financial Markets*. London: Macmillan.

—— and Hall, S. G. (1988) Cointegration in recursive systems: the structure of wage and price determination in the United Kingdom. Mimeo, Bank of England.

Davidson, R. and MacKinnon, J. G. (1981) Several tests for model specification in the presence of alternative hypotheses. *Econometrica* 49 (3), 781–93.

Deaton, A. and Muellbauer, J. (1980) *Economics and Consumer Behaviour*. Cambridge: Cambridge University Press.

den Butter, F. A. G. and Fase, M. M. G. (1981) The demand for money in EEC countries. *Journal of Monetary Economics* 8, 201–30.

Dickey, D. A. and Fuller, W. A. (1979) Distribution of the estimators for autoregressive time series with a unit root. *Journal of American Statistical Association* 74 427–31.

Diewert, W. E. (1974) Intertemporal consumer theory and the demand for durables. *Econometrica* 42 (3), 497–516.

Donovan, D. J. (1978) Modelling the demand for liquid assets: an application to Canada. *IMF Staff Papers* 25, 676–704.

Dornbusch, R. (1976) Expectations and exchange rate dynamics. *Journal of Political Economy* 84, 1161–76.

Dotsey, M. (1988) The demand for currency in the United States. *Journal of Money, Credit and Banking* 20 (1), 22–40.

Dufour, J. M. (1982) Recursive stability analysis of linear regression relationships. *Journal of Econometrics* 19 (1), 31–76.

Dutkowsky, D. H. and Foote, W. G. (1988) The demand for money: a rational expectations approach. *Review of Economics and Statistics* 70 (1), 83–92.

Engel, C. and Rodrigues, A. P. (1987) Tests of the international CAPM with time-varying covariances. NBER Working Paper 2303, National Bureau of Economic Research.

Engle, R. F. (1982) Autoregressive conditional heteroscedasticity with estimates of the variance of the UK inflation. *Econometrica* 50, 987–1008.

—— and Granger, C. W. J. (1987) Cointegration and error correction: Representation, estimation and testing. *Econometrica* 55, 251–76.

—— and Yoo, S. B. (1987) Forecasting and testing in cointegrated systems. *Journal of Econometrics* 35, 143–59.

—— Lilien, D. M. and Robbins, R. P. (1987) Estimating time-varying risk premia in the term structure. *Econometrica* 55, 391–407.

Ewis, N A. and Fisher, D. (1984) The translog utility function and the demand for money in the United States. *Journal of Money, Credit and Banking* 16 (1), 34–52.

Feige, E. (1967) Expectations and adjustments in the monetary sector. *American Economic Review* 57, 462–73.

—— and Parkin, J. M. (1971) The optimal quantity of money bonds, commodity inventories and capital. *American Economic Review* 61 (3), 335–49.

—— and Pearce, D. K. (1971) The substitutability of money and near-monies: a survey of the time series evidence. *Journal of Economic Literature* 15, 439–69.

Feldstein, M. S. (1969) Mean–variance analysis in the theory of liquidity preference and fortfolio selection. *Review of Economic Studies* 36, 5–12.

Fischer, S. (1988) Recent developments in macroeconomics. *Economic Journal* 98, 294–339.

Fisher, I. (1911) *The Purchasing Power of Money*. New York: Macmillan.

Fleming, J. M. (1962) Domestic financial policies under fixed and under floating exchange rates. *IMF Staff Papers* 9, 369–79.

Frankel, J. A. (1979) On the mark: a theory of floating exchange rates based on real interest differentials. *American Economic Review*, 69, 601–22.

Friedman, B. M. (1979a) Optimal expectations and the extreme information assumptions of 'rational expectations' macromodels. *Journal of Monetary Economics* 5, 23–41.

—— (1979b) Substitution and expectation effects on long-term borrowing behaviour and long-term interest rates. *Journal of Money, Credit and Banking* 11 (2), 131–50.

—— and Roley, V. V. (1987) Aspects of investor behaviour under risk. In G. R. Feiwel (ed.), *Arrow and the Ascent of Modern Economic Theory*. New York: New York University Press, pp. 626–53.

—— and Schwartz, A. J. (1982). *Monetary Trends in the United States and the United Kingdom: Their Relationship to Income, Prices and Interest rates 1867–1975*. Chicago, IL: University of Chicago Press.

Friedman, M. (1956) The quantity theory of money: a restatement. In M. Friedman (ed.), *Studies in the Quantity Theory of Money*. Chicago, IL: University of Chicago Press.

Gilbert, C. L. (1986) Professor Hendry's eonometric methodology. *Oxford Bulletin of Economics and Statistics* 48 (3), 283–307.

Giovannini, A. and Jorion, P. (1987) Interest rates and risk premia in the stock markets and in the foreign exchange market. *Journal of International Money and Finance* 6, 107–23.

—— and Jorion, P. (1988) The time variation of risk and return in the foreign exchange and stock markets. Discussion Paper 228, Centre for Economic Policy Research.

Goldfeld, S. M. (1973) The demand for money revisited. *Brookings Papers on Economic Activity* 3, 577–638.

—— (1976) The case of the missing money. *Brookings Papers on Economic Activity* 3, 683–730.

Goodfriend, M. (1985) Reinterpreting money demand regressions. In K. Brunner and A. H. Meltzer (eds), *Understanding Monetary Regimes*. Amsterdam: North Holland, Carnegie-Rochester Conference Series on Public Policy, vol. 22.

Goodhart, C. A. E. (1984) *Monetary Theory and Practice: The UK Experience*. London: Macmillan.

—— (1989) The conduct of monetary policy. *Economic Journal* 99, 293–316.

Gordon, R. J. (1984) The short-run demand for money: a reconsideration. *Journal of Money, Credit and Banking* 16 (4), 403–34.

Granger, C. W. J. (1966) The typical spectral shape of an economic variable. *Econometrica* 34 (1), 150–61.

—— (1986) Developments in the study of co-integrated economic variables. *Oxford Bulletin of Economics and Statistics* 48 (3), 213–28.

Grether, D. M. and Maddala, G. S. (1973) Errors in variables and serially correlated disturbances in distributed lag models. *Econometrica* 41 (2), 225–62.

Grice, J. and Bennett, A. (1984) Wealth and the demand for £M3 in the United Kingdom 1963–1978. *Manchester School* 52 (3), 239–71.

Grossman, H. I. and Policano, A. J. (1975) Money balances, commodity inventories and inflationary expectations. *Journal of Political Economy* 83 (6), 1093–112.

Haache, G. (1974) The demand for money in the UK: experience since 1971. *Bank of England Quarterly Bulletin* 14 (3), 284–305.

Hafer, R. W. and Hein, S. E. (1979) Evidence on the temporal stability of the demand for money relationship in the United States. *Federal Reserve Bank of St Louis Review* 61 (2), 3–14.

Hall, R. (1982) Monetary trends in the United States and the United Kingdom: a review from the perspective of the new developments in monetary economics. *Journal of Economic Literature* 20, 1552–5.

Hall, S. G., Henry, S. G. B. and Wilcox, J. (1989) The long run determination of the UK monetary aggregates. Mimeo, Bank of England.

Hamberger, M. J. (1966) The demand for money by households, money substitutes and monetary policy. *Journal of Political Economy* 74, 600–23.

—— (1977) The behaviour of the money stock: is there a puzzle. *Journal of Monetary Economics* 3, 265–88.

68   K. Cuthbertson

—— (1980) The demand for money in the United States: a comment. In K. Brunner and A. Meltzer (eds), *On the State of Macroeconomics*. Amsterdam: North-Holland, Carnegie Rochester Conference Series on Public Policy, vol. 12, pp. 273–85.

Hansen, L. P. (1982) Large sample properties of generalised method of moments estimators. *Econometrica* 50, 1029–54.

—— and Sargent, T. J. (1982) Instrumental variables procedures for estimating linear rational expectations models. *Journal of Monetary Economics* 9, 263–96.

Hartley, P. (1988) The liquidity services of money. *International Economic Review* 29, 1–24.

Harvey, A. C. (1981a), *Time Series Models*. Oxford: Philip Allan.

—— (1981b), *The Econometric Analysis of Time Series*. Oxford: Phillip Allan.

—— and Todd, P. H. J. (1983) Forecasting economic time series with structural and Box–Jenkins models. *Journal of Business and Economic Statistics* 1, 299–315.

Hayashi, F. and Sims, C. (1983) Nearly efficient estimation of time series models with predetermined but not exogenous instruments. *Econometrica* 51, 783–98.

Hendry, D. F. (1979) Predictive failure and econometric modelling in macro-economics: the transactions demand for money. In P. Omerod (ed.), *Economic Modelling*. London: Heinemann.

—— (1983) Econometric modelling: the consumption function in retrospect. *Scottish Journal of Political Economy* 30 (3), 193–200.

—— (1985) Monetary economic myth and econometric reality. *Oxford Review of Economic Policy*. Oxford: Oxford University Press.

—— (1986) Econometric modelling with cointegrated economic variables: An over-view. *Oxford Bulletin of Economics and Statistics* 48 (3), 201–12.

—— (1988) The encompassing implications of feedforward versus feedback mecha-nisms in econometrics. *Oxford Economic Papers* 40, 132–9.

—— (1989) *PC-GIVE: An Interactive Econometric Modelling System*. Oxford: Institute of Economics and Statistics.

—— and Ericsson, N. R. (1983) Assertion without empirical basis: an econometric appraisal of Friedman and Schwartz 'Monetary trends in . . . the United Kingdom'. Panel Paper 22, Bank of England, Panel of Academic Consultants, October 1978.

—— and —— (1988) An econometric analysis of UK money demand in *Monetary Trends in the United States and the United Kingdom* by Milton Friedman and Anna J. Schwartz. Mimeo, Nuffield College, Oxford, November.

—— and Mizon, G. E. (1978) Serial correlation as a convenient simplification, not a nuisance: A comment on a study of the demand for money by the Bank of England. *Economic Journal* 88, 549–63.

—— and von Ungern Sternberg, T. (1983) Liquidity and inflation effects on con-sumers' expenditure. In A. Deaton (ed.), *Essays in the Theory and Measurement of Consumers' Behaviour*. Cambridge: Cambridge University Press.

—— Pagan, A. R. and Sargan, J. D. (1984) Dynamic specification. In Z. Griliches and M. D. Intriligator (eds), *Handbook of Econometrics*, vol. 2. Amsterdam: North-Holland.

Hilliard, B. C. (1980) The Bank of England small monetary model: recent develop-ments and simulation properties. Discussion Paper 13, Bank of England, November.

Hood, W. (1987) The allocation of UK personal sector liquid assets. Government Economic Service Working Paper 94, HM Treasury, London.

Ireland, J. and Wren-Lewis, S. (1988) Buffer stock money and the company sector. Discussion Paper, National Institute of Economic and Social Research.

Johansen, S. (1988) Statistical analysis of cointegration vectors. *Journal of Economic Dynamics and Control* 12 (2/3), 231–54.

Johnston, R.B. (1984) The demand for non-interest bearing money in the United Kingdom. Government Economic Service Working Paper 66, HM Treasury, London.

—— (1985) The demand for liquidity aggregates by the UK personal sector. Government Economic Service Working Paper 81, HM Treasury, London.

Jonson, P.D. and Trevor, R. (1979) Monetary rules: a preliminary analysis. Discussion Paper 7903, Reserve Bank of Australia.

Judd, J.P. and Scadding, T. (1982) The search for a stable demand for money function. *Journal of Economic Literature* 20 (3), 993–1023.

—— and —— (1986) On the shock-absorber view of money: international evidence from the 1960s and 1970s. *Applied Economics* 18, 1085–101.

Karni, E. (1974) The value of time and the demand for money. *Journal of Money, Credit and Banking* 6, 45–64.

Keating, G. (1985) The financial sector of the London Business School model. In D. Currie (ed.), *Advances in Monetary Economics*. London: Croom-Helm.

Keynes, J.M. (1936) *The General Theory of Employment, Interest and Money*. London: Macmillan.

Klein, B. (1974a) The competitive supply of money. *Journal of Money, Credit and Banking* 6, 423–54.

—— (1974b) Competitive interest payments on bank deposits and the long-run demand for money. *American Economic Review* 64, 931–49.

Laidler, D.E.W. (1966) The rate of interest and the demand for money – some empirical evidence. *Journal of Political Economy* 74, 545–55.

—— (1971) The influence of money on economic activity: a survey of some current problems. In G. Clayton, J.C. Gilbert and R. Sedgwick (eds), *Monetary Theory and Policy in the 1970s*. Oxford: Oxford University Press.

—— (1980) The demand for money in the United States – yet again. In K. Brunner and A. Metzler (eds), *On the State of Macroeconomics*. Amsterdam: North-Holland, Carnegie–Rochester Conference Series on Public Policy, vol. 12.

—— (1982) *Monetarist Perspectives*. Oxford: Phillip Allan.

—— (1984) The buffer stock notion in monetary economics. *Economic Journal* (Supplement) 94, 17–34.

—— (1985) *The Demand for Money: Theories, Evidence and Problems*. New York: Harper and Row, 3rd edn.

—— (1988) Presidential Address: taking money seriously. *Canadian Journal of Economics* 21 (4), 687–713.

—— and Bentley, B. (1983) A small macro-model of the post-war United States. *Manchester School* 51 (4), 317–40.

—— and O'Shea, P. (1980) An empirical macromodel of an open economy under fixed exchange rates: the UK, 1954–70. *Economica* 47, 141–58.

—— and Parkin, J.M. (1970) The demand for money in the United Kingdom

1956-1967: some preliminary estimates. *Manchester School* 38, 187-208.

Laidler, D. E. W., Bentley, B., Johnson, D. and Johnson, S. T. (1983) A small macroeconomic model of an open economy: the case of Canada. In E. Claasen and P. Salin (eds), *Recent Issues in the Theory of Flexible Exchange Rates*. Amsterdam: North-Holland.

Lawson, N. (1986) Monetary policy. Lombard Association Speech, HM Treasury Press Release, 16 April.

Lee, T. H. (1967) Alternative interest rates and the demand for money: the empirical evidence. *American Economic Review* 57, 1168-81.

—— (1969) Alternative interest rates and the demand for money – reply. *American Economic Review* 59, 412-17.

Lindsey, D. E. and Spindt, P. (1986) An evaluation of monetary indices. Special Studies Paper 195 Federal Reserve Board, Division of Research and Statistics, March.

—— and —— (1985) Econometric methodology and monetarism: Professor Friedman and Professor Hendry on the demand for money. Discussion Paper 131, London Business School Economic Forecasting Unit.

Lubrano, M., Pierse, R. G. and Richard, J. F. (1986) Stability of a UK Money demand equation: a Bayesian approach to testing exogeneity. *Review of Economic Studies* 53, 603-34.

Lucas, R. E., Jr (1976) Econometric policy evaluation: a critique. In K. Brunner and A. H. Meltzer (eds), *The Phillips Curve and Labour Markets*. Amsterdam: North-Holland, Carnegie-Rochester Conference Series on Public Policy, vol. 1, pp. 19-46.

—— (1984) Money in a theory of finance. In K. Brunner and A. H. Meltzer (eds), *Essays on Macroeconomic Implications of Financial and Labour Markets and Political Processes*. Amsterdam: North-Holland, Carnegie-Rochester Conference Series on Public Policy, vol. 21.

MacKinnon, J. G. and Milbourne, R. D. (1984) Monetary anticipations and the demand for money. *Journal of Monetary Economics* 13, 263-74.

—— and —— (1988) Are price equations really money demand equations on their heads. *Journal of Applied Econometrics* 3, 295-305.

Markowitz, H. (1952) Portfolio selection. *Journal of Finance* 7, 77-91.

—— (1959) *Portfolio Selection: Efficient Diversification of Investment*. New York: Wiley.

Mayor, T. H. and Pearl, L. R. (1984) Life cycle effects, structural change and long-run movements in the velocity of money. *Journal of Money, Credit and Banking* 160, 175-84.

McCallum, B. T. (1976) Rational expectations and the estimation of econometric models: An alternative procedure. *International Economic Review* 17, 484-90.

Meltzer, A. H. (1963) The demand for money: The evidence from the time series. *Journal of Political Economy* 71, 219-46.

Merton, R. C. (1973) An intertemporal asset pricing model. *Econometrica* 41 (5), 867-89.

Meyer, P. A. and Neri, J. A. (1975) A Keynes–Friedman money demand function. *American Economic Review*. 65, 610-23.

Milbourne, R. (1983a), Optimal money holding under uncertainty. *International Economic Review* 24 (3), 685–98.

—— (1983b) Price expectations and the demand for money: resolution of a paradox. *Review of Economics and Statistics* 65 (4), 633–8.

—— (1985) Distinguishing between Australian demand for money models. *Australian Economic Papers* June, 154–68.

—— (1986) Financial innovation and the demand for liquid assets. *Journal of Money, Credit and Banking* 18 (4), 506–11.

—— (1987) Re-examining the buffer stock model of money. *Economic Journal (Supplement)* 97, 130–42.

—— (1988) Disequilibrium buffer stock models: a survey. *Journal of Economic Surveys* 2 (3), 187–208.

——, Buckholtz, P. and Wasan, N.T. (1983) A theoretical derivation of the functional form of short run money holdings. *Review of Economic Studies* 50, 531–41.

Miller, M. and Orr, D. (1966) A model of the demand for money by firms. *Quarterly Journal of Economics* 109, 68–72.

—— and —— (1968) The demand for money by firms: extension of analytic results. *Journal of Finance* 23, 735–59.

Mills, T.C. (1983) The information content of UK monetary components and aggregates. *Bulletin of Economic Research* 35 (1), 25–46.

Mishkin, F.S. (1983) *A Rational Expectations Approach to macroeconometrics.* Chicago, IL: Chicago University Press.

Mizon, G.E. (1984) The encompassing approach in econometrics. In D.F. Hendry and K.F. Wallis (eds), *Econometrics and Quantitative Economics*. Oxford: Basil Blackwell.

Mundell, R.A. (1963) Capital mobility and stabilisation policy under fixed and flexible exchange rates. *Canadian Journal of Economics and Political Science* 29, 475–85.

Muscatelli, V.A. (1988) Alternative models of buffer stock money: an empirical investigation. *Scottish Journal of Political Economy* 35 (1), 1–21.

—— (1989) A comparison of the rational expectations and general to specific approach to modelling the demand for M1. *Oxford Bulletin of Economics and Statistics* 51 (4), 353–75.

—— and Papi, L. (1988) Cointegration and 'General to Specific': an example of the demand for money in Italy. Mimeo, University of Glasgow.

Muth, J.F. (1961) Rational expectations and the theory of price movements. *Journal of Political Economy*, 29 (6). Reprinted in R.E. Lucas, Jr and T.J. Sargent (eds), *Rational Expectations and Econometric Practice*. London: George Allen and Unwin, 1981.

Nelson, C.R. (1975) Rational expectations and the estimation of econometric models. *International Economic Review* 16, 555–61.

Nickell, S. (1985) Error correction, partial adjustment and all that: an expository note. *Oxford Bulletin of Economics and Statistics* 47 (2), 119–30.

Offenbacher, E. and Porter, R. (1982) Update and extensions on econometric properties of selected monetary aggregates. Mimeo, Board of Governors of the Federal Reserve System.

Pagan, A. (1984) Econometric issues in the Analysis of regressions with generated regressors. *International Economic Review* 25 (1), 221-48.

—— and Ullah, A. (1988) The econometric analysis of models with risk terms. *Journal of Applied Economics* 3 (2), 87-106.

Patterson, K. (1987) The specification and stability of the demand for money in the United Kingdom. *Economica* 54, 41-55.

—— and Ryding, J. (1984) Dynamic time series models with growth effects constrained to zero. *Economic Journal* 94, 137-43.

—— (1987) *The Limits to Rational Expectations*. Oxford: Basil Blackwell.

Phillips, P.C.B. and Park, J.Y. (1986) Statistical inference in regressions with integrated processes: Part I. Paper, 811, Cowles Foundation.

Pifer, H.W. (1969) A non-linear maximum likelihood estimate of the liquidity trap. *Econometrica* 37, 324-32.

Pigou, A.C. (1917) The value of money. *Quarterly Journal of Economics* 37, 38-65.

Roley, V.V. (1985) Money demand predictability. *Journal of Money, Credit and Banking* 17 (4), 611-41.

Rose, A.K. (1985) An alternative approach to the American demand for money. *Journal of Money, Credit and Banking* 17 (4), 439-55.

Santomero, A.M. (1974) A model of the demand for money by households. *Journal of Finance* 29 (1), 89-102.

—— and Seater, J.J. (1981) Partial adjustment in the demand for money: theory and empirics. *American Economic Review* 71, 566-78.

Sargent, T.J. (1979) *Macroeconomic Theory*. New York: Academic Press.

—— and Wallace, N. (1982) The real bills doctrine and the quantity theory: a reconsideration. *Journal of Political Economy* 90, 1212-36.

Serletis, A. (1988) Translog flexible functional forms and substitutability of monetary assets. *Journal of Business and Economic Statistics* January.

—— and Robb, A.L. (1986) Divisia aggregation and substitutability among monetary assets. *Journal of Money, Credit and Banking* 18 (4), 430-46.

Slovin, M.B. and Sushka, M.E. (1983) Money interest rates and risk. *Journal of Monetary Economics* 12, 475-82.

Smith G. (1975) Pitfalls in financial model building: a clarification. *American Economic Review* 65, 510-16.

—— (1986) A dynamic Baumol-Tobin model of money demand. *Review of Economic Studies* 53, 465-9.

Spanos, A. (1984) Liquidity as a latent variable: an application of the MIMIC model. *Oxford Bulletin of Economics and Statistics* 46 (2), 125-43.

Sprenkle, C.M. (1969) The uselessness of transactions demand models. *Journal of Finance* 4, 835-47.

—— (1972) On the observed transactions demand for money. *Manchester School* 40 (3), 261-7.

—— (1974) An overdue note on some 'ancient but popular' literature. *Journal of Finance* 29, 1577-80.

—— and Miller, M.H. (1980) The precautionary demand for narrow and broad money. *Economica* 47, 407-21.

Starleaf, D.R. and Reimer, R. (1967) The Keynesian demand function for money: some statistical tests. *Journal of Finance* 22, 71-6.

Stock, J. H. (1984) Asymptotic properties of a least squares estimator of cointegrating vectors. *Econometrica* 55, 1035–56.

Swofford, J. L. and Whitney, G. A. (1986) Flexible functional forms and the utility approach to the demand for money: a non-parametric analysis. *Journal of Money, Credit and Banking* 18 (3), 383–9.

Taylor, M. P. (1986) From the general to the specific: the demand for M2 in three European countries. *Empirical Economics* 11, 243–61.

—— (1987) Financial innovation, inflation and the stability of the demand for broad money in the United Kingdom. *Bulletin of Economic Research* 39 (3), 225–33.

Teigen, R. (1964) Demand and Supply functions for money in the United States. *Econometrica* 32 (4), 477–509.

Tobin, J. (1956) The interest elasticity of transactions demand for cash. *Review of Economics and Statistics* 38, 241–7.

—— (1958) Liquidity preference as behaviour towards risk. *Review of Economic Studies* 25, 65–86.

Trundle, J. M. (1982) Recent changes in the use of cash. *Bank of England Quarterly Bulletin* 22, 519–29.

Tsiang, S. C. (1972) The rationale of the mean–standard deviation analysis, skewness preference and the demand for money. *American Economic Review* 62, 354–71.

Varian, H. R. (1983) Non-parametric tests of consumer behaviour. *Review of Economic Studies* 50, 99–110.

Vinals, J. and van Beek, F. (1979) The demand for money in Latin American countries 1964–78. IMF Working Paper, International Monetary Fund.

Wallace, N. (1988) A suggestion for oversimplifying the theory of money. *Economic Journal (Conference Papers)* 98, 267–74.

Wallis, K. F. (1980) Econometric implications of the rational expectations hypothesis. *Econometrica* 48 (1), 49–73.

Walsh, C. E. (1984) Interest rate volatility and monetary policy. *Journal of Money, Credit and Banking* 16, 133–50.

Weale, M. (1986) The structure of personal sector short-term asset holdings. *Manchester School* 54 (2), 141–61.

West, K. D. (1988) Asymptotic normality when regressors have a unit root. *Econometrica* 56 (6), 1397–417.

Whalen, E. L. (1966) A rationalisation of the precautionary demand for cash. *Quarterly Journal of Economics* May.

White, W. (1981) The case for and against 'disequilibrium' money, *IMF Staff Papers* 281 (3), 534–72.

Wickens, M. R. (1982) The efficient estimation of econometric models with rational expectations. *Review of Economic Studies* 49, 55–67.

Wren-Lewis, S. (1984) Omitted variables in equations relating prices to money. *Applied Economics* 16, 483–96.

2 The Determination of Interest Rates and Asset Prices: A Survey of Theory and Evidence

Christopher J. Green

2.1 INTRODUCTION

Interest rate and asset price formation constitutes one of the central subject areas of monetary and financial economics. References to interest and usury can be found in classical Greek literature. On the other hand, the modern theory of finance based on the principle of optimization in the face of risk can be dated from Sharpe's (1964) paper, although this had important precursors, notably Tobin (1958) and Markowitz (1959). This is a vast subject area, and one which overlaps with many other branches of economics. A compact survey of the area must therefore be highly selective.

This survey is concerned with both theoretical and empirical research. It is confined in scope mainly to the determination of freely moving market interest rates in industrial countries, and concentrates largely but not exclusively on research results reported since the establishment of the Money Study Group in 1969. Interest rate setting by financial intermediaries is not covered, nor are the particular problems of interest rate determination in developing countries. Other major omissions include the substantial literature on intertemporal asset pricing models, much of which is rather technical, and the still more voluminous literature on stock prices and returns which could fill several survey papers in its own right.[1] The focus on post-1969 research reflects the explosion of literature on interest rates and asset prices over the last two decades.

The survey is organized into two major sections which are concerned with theoretical and empirical research respectively. Within these sections a major organizing principle is the distinction between the level and structure of interest rates. In practice, this is a rather artificial distinction in that any realistic explanation of the evolution of interest rates would emphasize their simultaneous determination in a general equilibrium model of asset markets as a whole. Nevertheless, the distinction serves a useful purpose, not least because theories as diverse as liquidity preference and the capital asset pricing model have often emphasized a separation between the determination of a single key interest rate and the structure of all other interest rates relative to the key rate. Moreover, the distinction is not entirely artificial in that any closed equilibrium system of n markets can only determine $n - 1$ prices or interest rates. The nth price must serve as numeraire and has to be determined outside the system. A distinction between the level and structure of interest rates can therefore sometimes be thought of as one between the numeraire rate which sets the level and all other rates which constitute the structure.

Within the theoretical section 2.2, two subsections (2.1 and 2.2) are concerned with the level and structure respectively of interest rates studied largely from a macroeconomic perspective utilizing postulated demand and supply curves. The microfoundations of asset pricing based on individual optimization and concentrating on one-period mean–variance models are reviewed in section 2.2.3.

Within the empirical section 2.3, research on the level (section 2.3.2) and structure (section 2.3.3) of interest rates is again distinguished. These subsections are preceded by a review of methodological issues (section 2.3.1) which aims in particular to explain and comment on the single-equation and small-model-testing procedures which are prevalent in the literature.

Finally, some concluding remarks are made in section 2.4.

2.2 THE THEORY OF INTEREST RATES

2.2.1 The Level of Interest Rates

IS–LM Models

A starting point for thinking about interest rates is the ubiquitous IS–LM model (Hicks, 1937; Hansen, 1953) which can be regarded as an amalgamation of two independent theories: loanable funds and liquidity preference. According to classical loanable funds theory the rate of interest is determined by real forces, and cannot be directly influenced by monetary policy. The productivity of capital and labour determines the demand for investment goods and hence the demand for loanable funds. The savings rate in the economy provides the supply of loanable funds, and the intersection of supply and demand determines the interest rate. In contrast, liquidity preference theory (Keynes, 1936, 1937) suggests that the rate of interest is determined by the supply and demand for money and can be directly

influenced by monetary policy. While it can be argued that liquidity preference and loanable funds each constitutes a complete theory of the rate of
interest, the bowdlerized versions of these theories which have been immor-
talized in numerous textbooks are *not* complete as they neglect the influence
of income on savings and on the demand for money. Allowing for these
influences yields the IS–LM model: the IS curve gives combinations of
income and the rate of interest consistent with equilibrium in the market for
loanable funds, and the LM curve gives the money market equilibrium conditions. Simultaneous equilibrium in these markets determines the rate of
interest and the aggregate income.

Despite being subject to attack and derision,[2] IS–LM is still part of the
core of interest rate theory. Among its features are the following.

First, the interest rate is determined by a combination of the demand and
supply of a stock of assets (money) and a flow of new funds (savings investment). Tensions between stocks and flows have been the subject of a vast
literature analysing the consistency of the postulated demand schedules with
underlying budget constraints, and the relationship between stocks and
flows in the short run and the long run. These issues are considered in the
second part of section 2.2.1.

Second, IS–LM assumes fixed product prices. This forecloses on any
discussion of inflation, and hence on anything other than an elementary
treatment of nominal and real interest rates, a topic taken up in the third
part of section 2.2.1.

Third, IS–LM imposes no restriction on the interest rate to be determined.
Keynes had in mind a long-term interest rate with expectations of future
bond prices playing a key role in the determination of the demand for
money. However, in textbook expositions of IS–LM, the demand for money
is often justified in terms of the transactions motive (Tobin, 1956) where
the opportunity cost of money is thought of as a short-term rate of interest.
In principle, Tobin's (1958) liquidity preference theory justifies a more direct
focus on long-term rates. However, this theory suggests that agents form
opinions about the expectation and variance of returns on bonds, but these
opinions are treated as exogenous within IS–LM. This makes it impossible
to provide a proper analysis of policies which affect the expected value or
variance of interest rates, and there are few policies which do not have such
effects. The rational expectations literature has delivered many of the
necessary technical tools, although not always very satisfactory assumptions, for studying such issues, and these are discussed further in the fourth
part of section 2.2.1.

The fourth and final point, which is not pursued in this survey, however,
is that IS–LM monetary policy consists solely of open market operations
– an exchange of money for bonds. This offers no special role for financial

institutions in setting interest rates, which is probably one of their key functions.

IS–LM preserves the prediction of liquidity preference theory that monetary policy can change the rate of interest, with an increase in the money supply lowering the rate and vice versa. A central research theme over many years has been to establish theoretically and empirically the exact conditions under which this prediction is correct. After the publication of *The General Theory*, attention focused on the possibility of a liquidity trap and consequent horizontal LM schedule. In this event, Keynesian economists argued, the interest rate could not be driven down by an increase in the supply of money, whether brought about by an increase in the nominal quantity of money (monetary policy) or by a fall in prices which would increase the real value of the fixed quantity of nominal money balances in existence. In response, classical economists introduced the real balance effect: if expenditures depend on real cash balances as well as on income and interest rates, then a fall in prices will increase real cash balances and thus aggregate demand, even though interest rates remain constant.[3] Moreover, since this argument can be used irrespective of the slope of the LM schedule, it can equally well be asserted that changes in the nominal quantity of money will always alter aggregate demand and prices through a real balance effect, with no impact on the rate of interest. Thus it appeared that the real balance effect restored the classical invariance of interest rates with respect to monetary policy.

In a celebrated paper, Metzler (1951) pointed out that the real balance effect actually ensures that monetary policy *can* influence the rate of interest and hence it destroys the classical theory. Consider the IS–LM model augmented by a wealth effect on savings and the demand for money:

$$I(r^-) = S(Y^+, W^-) \qquad \text{IS} \qquad (2.1)$$

$$M/P = L(Y^+, r^-, W^+) \qquad \text{LM} \qquad (2.2)$$

where $W = M/P + D/r$ is private wealth, r is the rate of interest, Y is the real income, P, is the price level, M is the quantity of money and D is the number of bonds (perpetuities) in existence each paying a coupon of £1 in real terms.[4]

After substituting for the definition of wealth, (2.1) and (2.2) can be differentiated and solved for the rate of interest and either income or the price level, holding the other fixed. In the classical case, income is fixed and the solution for the rate of interest is

$$\frac{\mathrm{d}r}{\mathrm{d}M} = 0 \qquad (2.3)$$

$$\frac{dr}{dD} = \frac{S_w}{r[S_wD/r^2 + (1 - L_w)I_r - S_wL_r]} > 0 \qquad (2.4)$$

where $S_w = \partial S/\partial W$ (etc).

Metzler's point is that it makes a difference how new money is created. An increase in money accompanied by an increase in wealth (2.3) merely results in a proportionate increase in prices with no effect on the interest rate. However, an open market operation can change the rate of interest (since $dr/dD \neq 0$) because it alters portfolio balance, and hence the margin at which money and bonds are held. Moreover, it is clear from (2.4) that this only occurs if there is a real balance effect ($S_w \neq 0$).

Metzler's results depend critically on the definition of wealth which appears in the savings and money demand functions, and specifically as to whether bonds constitute net wealth. If the private sector fully capitalizes its anticipated contribution to bond interest payments through future taxation, then bonds are not net wealth and the classical result that monetary policy does not affect interest rates is reasserted. This – the 'debt neutrality' argument – was first made in this context by Mundell (1960)[5] However, the central message of Metzler's paper is that the impact of a change in the quantity of money depends on how it is brought about. This is also an important theme in *The General Theory*. Metzler was concerned with effects on interest rates; Keynes was concerned with effects on income, his point being that, in a recession, the most effective way to increase the quantity of money is by increased government spending rather than by open market operations or falling product prices.[6]

Stocks, Flows and Wealth Effects

Since IS–LM is a closed equilibrium system, postulated behavioural relationships should be consistent with underlying sectoral budget constraints, and Walras' law is applicable. This states, *inter alia*, that excess demands in all markets must sum to zero, and it implies that, if $n - 1$ of the n markets in the system are in equilibrium, the nth must also be in equilibrium. As IS–LM has three markets – for goods, money and bonds – the demands for money and for goods have implications for the unwritten demand for bonds. IS–LM models commonly exclude wealth and therefore imply that all increments to wealth are placed in bonds. However, as Metzler's model makes clear, the exclusion of wealth is an omission from specific versions of IS–LM and is not a defect of IS–LM *per se*.[7]

The exclusion of wealth from IS–LM has generally been rationalized by the supposition that portfolio decisions are taken independently of current flows, and spending decisions are taken independently of current stocks (see Tobin, 1969). In IS–LM, but not in multi-asset models, this implies that the demand for bonds must be the mirror image of the demand for money. However, this makes it difficult to provide a sensible description of the economy in disequilibrium. If either the money or bond market is in equilibrium the other must be also (because they are mirror images of one another), but then, by Walras' law, the goods market is also in equilibrium. Thus, after a shock, there must be disequilibrium in both money and bond markets. Moreover, disequilibria in money and bonds must be equal and offsetting, implying that the market for loanable funds can *never* be in disequilibrium (see Johnson, 1961)! Obviously this problem has to be solved by allowing some interaction between stocks and flows, so that in response to a shock all three markets can be out of equilibrium. When this is done, the trajectory of interest rates from one equilibrium to another depends on the exact assumptions made about the way in which funds are allocated, subject to budget constraints, out of equilibrium. The interest rate may move directly to its new equilibrium level, or it may overshoot or undershoot; few useful generalizations are possible (see Green, 1985).

A related question is that of whether asset demands should be specified at 'beginning of period' or 'end of period'. In the former specification, trading and price setting occur at the beginning of any time period and stock demands and supplies are constructed to be satisfied at this point. Flow demands and supplies are equilibrated separately during the ensuing period. End-of-period specifications call for plans to be made at the beginning of each period in anticipation of certain flows occurring during the period. Trading and price setting occur, and asset demands are satisfied at the end of each period. In response to arguments put forward by Foley (1975), Buiter (1980) showed that different results generated by the two specifications stem from non-equivalent assumptions about the existence of spot and forward markets for assets which are implied by either method. Buiter also showed that it is never conceptually correct to separate portfolio and spending decisions if the underlying model is to be properly specified. Tobin (1982) has shown how IS–LM can be adapted to an integrated approach in which portfolio and savings decisions are assumed to be taken simultaneously. Few of the major qualitative results require modification as a result of such adaptations. See also Tobin (1979) and Tobin and Braga de Macedo (1980).

These issues emerged from research aimed at studying the so-called 'intrinsic dynamics' of the economic system. The IS–LM equilibrium can be one with non-zero net investment, a government budget surplus or deficit and a balance of payments current account surplus or deficit. Over time, the flows implied by these surpluses or deficits will accumulate respectively into changes in the capital stock, changes in the outstanding amount of government debt and changes in net foreign debt. The main question addressed by this research is that of whether monetary and fiscal policy have permanent effects on the level of income, through either interest rate changes or other channels. The central features introduced by allowing for the cumulation of flows into stocks are the impact of increased wealth on aggregate demand and on the demand for money, and any increases in supply of interest-bearing assets. In general, these factors push up interest rates in the long run. Factors which reduce interest rates in the long run include any increases in the supply of money and the effect of higher wealth in increasing the demand for interest-bearing assets. The increased capital stock means that the economy can also accommodate a higher level of output and demand at lower interest rates. Indeed, in so far as interest rates are lower, production techniques which are more capital intensive can be used, thus sustaining higher output for a given level of employment. In general, given stable prices, monetized government deficits are associated with lower interest rates than non-monetized deficits (assuming that government bonds count as net private wealth). However, the main conclusion from such analyses remains the simple point that the effects of economic policy on interest rates in the short run and the long run depend on both private portfolio preferences and relative asset supplies (see *inter alia* Silber, 1970; Blinder and Solow, 1973; Tobin and Buiter, 1976; Branson, 1976; Currie, 1978; Cohen and McMenamin, 1978). When positive inflation rates are introduced into the analysis, outcomes are more complex to work out, but it remains true that changes in financing policies have permanent effects on interest rates (see G. Smith, 1979, 1982a).

A related issue concerns the interaction between interest rates and the sustainability of a budget deficit. Given the deficit, if the authorities finance with bonds, they are committed to increased future interest payments which may rise as the rate of interest rises. This in turn makes it more difficult to reduce the size of the budget deficit in the future as interest payments swallow up part of the deficit reduction effort. In the framework of Sargent and Wallace (1986), the sustainability issue arises because tight money today causes higher inflation tomorrow through the increase in debt interest payments which follow from bond financing, and because of a ceiling on the private sector's debt-to-income ratio (see also Blinder and Solow, 1973; G. Smith, 1982b). The sustainability issue can also arise because, on the one hand, money financing is inflationary and bond financing is potentially unstable, but, on the other hand, there may be limits on the rate at which government spending can be cut or taxation increased to close the deficit. Clearly, the higher is the rate of interest, the lower is the level of sustainable debt outstanding because the more government spending is swallowed up in debt interest payments (see Blanchard, 1984). All this work suggests that there are significant interactions between deficits and interest rates in the economy. However, if government bonds do not constitute net wealth, then the private sector is indifferent between a tax increase and a bond issue and sustainability is not a problem.

Nominal and Real Interest Rates

Ex ante real and nominal interest rates are connected by the identity

$$r_t = (1 + \mu_t)\,(1 + E_t\pi_{t+1}) - 1 \approx \mu_t + E_t\pi_{t+1} \tag{2.5}$$

where r_t is the nominal interest rate at time t, μ_t is the real interest rate and $E_t\pi_{t+1}$ is the expectation at time t of inflation between times t and $t + 1$. It follows that an increase in inflation expectations will increase the wedge between real and nominal interest rates by an equal amount. The interesting question is whether nominal interest rates will increase one for one with increases in expected inflation, with the real rate of interest remaining constant. This is called the Fisher effect (Fisher, 1930). Alternatively, if real interest rates change as inflation expectations change, the nominal interest rate will alter by more or less than inflation expectations, and the Fisher effect does not hold. The essential analytical point can be made using IS–LM. If inflation expectations rise, say, then both the expected nominal profit stream from investment projects and the nominal rate of interest on bonds must rise *pari passu*, thus leaving the savings–investment margin unaffected. In contrast, the margin for portfolio decisions between money and bonds is the nominal rate of interest alone, which rises with inflation expectations. Thus an exogenous rise in inflation expectations shifts the LM curve (to the left) but not the IS curve. In the IS–LM context, therefore, the Fisher effect requires a horizontal IS curve (see Tobin, 1974). If the IS curve has its usual downward slope, then higher inflation expectations reduce the real interest rate so that the nominal interest rate rises by less than the rise in inflation expectations. This phenomenon is called the Mundell–Tobin effect (Mundell, 1963; Tobin, 1965), although the exact mechanisms described by the two authors are somewhat different from one another.

In fact, the Fisher hypothesis is not well-posed since, in any realistic setting, both interest rates and inflation expectations are endogenous variables, and it does not make sense to ask questions about the impact of 'exogenous' changes in either variable. This was recognized by Tobin (1965) who posed the question of the superneutrality of money. Money is superneutral if changes in its growth rate affect only the rate of inflation and not the level and growth of real output or the real interest rate. In Tobin's model money is not superneutral because an increase, say, in the rate of money growth reduces the real rate of interest which, in turn, produces capital deepening and an increase in the full employment level of output. In other models it is possible for higher inflation to raise the real interest rate, but the Mundell–Tobin result is more common. Thus a proper examination of the Fisher hypothesis involves consideration of the impact of exogenous variables on the equilibrium real interest rate. The empirical issue concerns the transmission mechanism of monetary policy: does an increase, say, in money growth change *nominal* interest rates primarily because of the ensuing change in inflation expectations (the Fisher effect), or do the effects on nominal interest rates work more strongly through other channels, especially asset substitution effects, which also change the *real* interest rate?

Even leaving aside the Mundell–Tobin effect, the Fisher effect will not hold when account is taken of taxation, particularly differential taxation of interest income and real capital gains. In the simple case in which all assets are capital certain and only interest income is taxed, the after-tax real interest rate is given by the difference between the after-tax nominal rate and the rate of inflation. If a constant after-tax real interest rate is assumed, a rise in inflation expectations will increase the pre-tax nominal interest rate by $1/(1 - t) > 1$, where t is the tax rate on interest income. In this case therefore, taxation has the opposite impact on the inflation–interest rate relationship to that of the Mundell–Tobin effect (see Darby, 1975; Feldstein, 1976). However, depending on the exact assumptions about taxes, many different tax-adjusted Fisher relationships can be derived (see Dewald, 1986).

The Fisher hypothesis implicitly assumes risk neutral behaviour, and it ceases to hold in most settings when agents are risk averse. Risk averse agents will require a premium or discount for nominal over real assets depending on the covariances between nominal returns and the inflation rate and hence on the relative riskiness of real and nominal assets (see especially Fischer, 1975; Grauer and Litzenberger, 1980; Turnbull, 1981).

Interest Rates, Asset Prices and Forward Expectations

Although the IS–LM rate of interest is supposedly that on bonds, neither actual nor expected capital gains and losses on bonds play any role in the model. Some of the problems which result from this omission can be seen with the aid of Samuelson's (1947) dynamic IS–LM model which can be written as

$$\dot{y} = (ay - br + g) - y \qquad \text{IS} \qquad (2.6)$$

$$\dot{r} = (hy - kr) - m \qquad \text{LM} \qquad (2.7)$$

where y is income, r is interest rate, g is government spending, m is quantity of money, a, b, h, k are all positive parameters, with $a < 1$, and $\dot{y} = dy/dt$ etc. In this model, income increases in response to an excess of demand $ay - br + g$ over supply y in the product market, while the interest rate increases in response to an excess demand $hy - kr$ over supply m of money. The static IS–LM schedules are found by setting $\dot{y} = \dot{r} = 0$ and are shown in figure 2.1. This also gives the phase diagram showing possible trajectories of income and the rate of interest after a monetary expansion which shifts

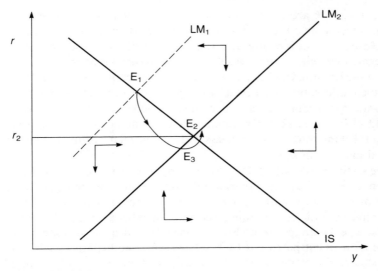

Figure 2.1 IS–LM

LM from LM_1 to LM_2. Suppose, as seems reasonable, that we identify the equilibrium interest rate with Keynes's normal rate. Following the monetary expansion, speculators will expect the rate of interest to decline towards the new normal rate r_2 and will therefore wish to buy bonds. However, along the sample trajectory in the initial segment $E_1 E_3$ the demand for money is continuously increasing, even though agents believe that interest rates will fall and capital gains can be made on bonds. This is difficult to reconcile with the speculative motive in particular and rational behaviour in general.

This issue has been addressed in the rational expectations literature which has also delivered new techniques to permit its more rigorous analysis. The Keynesian language of expectations and speculation has much in common with that of rational expectations; the main difference is that the rational expectations literature has largely jettisoned the Keynesian insistence on a profound scepticism about the extent of agents' knowledge of the true structure of the economy and about the uses to which they put this knowledge.

As Blanchard (1981) has shown, IS–LM is easily modified to allow for capital gains on bonds under the assumption of rational expectations. The modified model is:

$$\dot{y} = (ay + cq + g) - y \qquad \text{IS} \tag{2.8}$$

$$m = hy - k\frac{(1 + \dot{q})}{q} \qquad \text{LM} \tag{2.9}$$

84   C. J. Green

Here, a, c, h, k are positive parameters as before, but it is the price q of bonds which enters the model directly, rather than the interest rate.[8] IS is as before, with an increase in q (i.e. a fall in the interest rate) increasing aggregate demand. In the LM schedule, the return on bonds consists of the sum of the running yield $1/q$ and the anticipated capital gain $\dot{q}/q$. In a deterministic model rational expectations implies perfect foresight, so that actual and anticipated capital gains are identical. The key difference between (2.7) and (2.9) is that in (2.9) the money market is assumed to be continuously in equilibrium. LM is nevertheless a dynamic relationship because of the capital gains term $\dot{q}/q$.

The static IS–LM schedules are found by setting $\dot{y} = \dot{q} = 0$, and these are shown in figure 2.2. The slopes are the reverse of those in figure 2.1 as the bond price rather than the interest rate is on the vertical axis. The model determines a static equilibrium price and thus also the running yield $1/q$ on bonds. The dynamics are no longer characterized by an infinite number of stable adjustment paths but by a single stable saddlepath ZZ. In response to a shock, the economy is dynamically unstable unless it can be placed instantaneously on the saddlepath. There are two arguments to suggest that this is what could happen. First, if the underlying model is based on optimizing agents, they will recognize unstable paths which typically involve cumulative inflation or deflation (in this case in the price of bonds) and so avoid them. Second, if there exist 'free' variables in the model which are

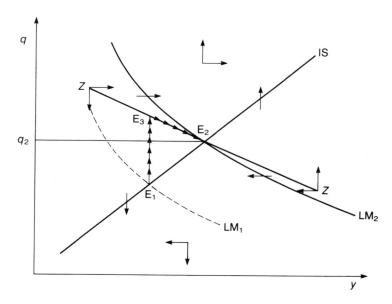

Figure 2.2 IS–LM with rational expectations

allowed to move in a discontinuous way (or to 'jump'), then such variables will adjust so as to place the economy on the saddlepath immediately after a shock. It is natural to allocate the role of jump variable to an asset price determined in continuously clearing markets. Since the price of a bond can be expressed as the discounted forward sum of the entire stream of expected future coupon payments, changes in expectations about future discount rates will cumulate into possibly sharp changes in the current price. In the IS–LM example a monetary expansion leads to a permanently higher bond price and lower yield. Discounting the fixed coupon by the lower yield implies a discrete jump in bond prices at the moment at which the monetary expansion is announced and implemented.

In figure 2.2, an unanticipated monetary expansion shifts LM from LM_1 to LM_2 and produces an immediate jump increase in the bond price. Indeed, the price overshoots its equilibrium value q_2 and then falls as income gradually rises to the new equilibrium level. Such overshooting is a characteristic though not a necessary property of models with forward expectations. Since the money market is continuously in equilibrium, agents must switch from bonds into money instantaneously as the open market operation is implemented. Agents have an incentive to do this because, at E_3 following the jump in bond prices, they correctly anticipate that, from then on, bond prices will be falling along $E_3 E_2$ and so the rate of return on bonds at E_3 is lower than at E_1. Thus, at E_3 agents realize capital gains on bonds and switch into the money created by the open market operation. Along $E_3 E_2$ the money market remains in equilibrium, so that we can infer that increasing demand for money resulting from rising incomes must be exactly offset by falling demand resulting from falling bond prices and rising interest rates.

The major difference between the Blanchard and Samuelson models is that the rational expectations approach attributes a central role to capital gains and losses which result from jumps in asset prices as they respond efficiently to new information. In practice, this is an important characteristic of asset markets even if investors do not literally possess the perfect foresight which is generally required to manipulate such models.

The implications of the idea that asset prices could be regarded as free variables were first demonstrated by Dornbusch (1976). Wilson (1979) showed how the techniques could be adapted to study the differential effects of an announced policy change which is implemented at a later date. The treatment of asset prices as free variables also has implications for empirical research. It is clear from figure 2.2 that there can be sharp discontinuities in asset price movements, with the jump from E_1 to E_3 being followed by a gradual decline to E_2. This suggests that an effective empirical research strategy must distinguish between the immediate response of asset prices to new information and their movements along stable paths. This is exceedingly difficult in practice as asset markets rarely experience even short periods without the intervention of various kinds of new information such as policy announcements, the publication of economic statistics and the like.

2.2.2 The Structure of Interest Rates

The Term Structure

Term structure theory is concerned with the relationship between the yield and term to maturity on (government) bonds. Such bonds are taken to be default free, and therefore differ only in term to maturity.[9] Thus the term structure offers an uncluttered setting for studying market interest rates and for evaluating the efficiency of financial markets.

The expectations theory is the basis from which most theorizing about the term structure begins.[10] It is based on a comparison between the return to maturity R_{nt} on an n-period discount bond and the anticipated return on a sequence of n one-period discount bonds successively purchased and redeemed, with each period's proceeds $1 + r_t$ being reinvested in a further one-period bond. As bonds are default free, these two investment opportunities are equivalent. In equilibrium, therefore, they should earn the same rate of return. Thus

$$(1 + R_{nt})^n = E_t \prod_{i=1}^{n} (1 + r_{t+i-1}) \tag{2.10}$$

or

$$1 + R_{nt} = \left[E_t \prod_{i=1}^{n} (1 + r_{t+i-1}) \right]^{\frac{1}{n}} \tag{2.11}$$

This, the main prediction of the expectations theory, is that the gross long-term interest rate is a simple (geometric) average of current and expected future short-term rates.[11]

The expectations theory can be presented in two other forms. Suppose that all the future one-period rates in (2.10) are known with certainty so that

$$(1 + R_{nt})^n = \prod_{i=1}^{n} (1 + r_{t+i-1}) \tag{2.12}$$

Shifting the maturity date n of the bond one period forward in (2.12) and dividing each side of the result by (2.12) gives

$$1 + r_{t+n} = \frac{(1 + R_{n+1t})^{n+1}}{(1 + R_{nt})^n} = 1 + f_{t+n,\,t} \tag{2.13}$$

The left-hand equality follows from the assumption that all future one-period rates are known at time t. The right-hand equality is definitional: it states that the ratio of two contiguous long rates (appropriately compounded) gives the one-period forward rate $f_{t+n,t}$ at time t applicable to time $t + n$. Abstracting from transactions costs, investors at time t can guarantee this rate for time $t + n$ by buying $(n + 1)$-period bonds and simultaneously selling short (issuing) an equal amount of n-period bonds. However, the spot rate r_{t+n} which actually materializes at time $t + n$ is not known with certainty at time t and may differ from the forward rate. Thus we can define the (one-period) term premium $\phi_{n,t}$ for any given term n and at any given time t as the difference between the forward rate and the expected future spot rate:[12]

$$\phi_{n,t} = f_{t+n,t} - E_t r_{t+n} \tag{2.14}$$

The term premium is the difference between the future spot rate implicit in the term structure (the forward rate) and the spot rate which the market actually expects. A second representation of the expectations theory simply asserts that term premiums are zero at all maturities.

To obtain the third representation from (2.12), shift time one period forward and the maturity one period back to give

$$(1 + R_{n-1, t+1})^{n-1} = \prod_{i=2}^{n}(1 + r_{t+i-1}) \tag{2.15}$$

Dividing (2.12) by (2.15) gives

$$1 + r_t = \frac{(1 + R_{nt})^n}{(1 + R_{n-1,t+1})^{n-1}} = \frac{q_{n-1, t+1}}{q_{nt}} \tag{2.16}$$

Here q_{nt} is the price of n-period discount bonds; hence $q_{n-1, t+1}/q_{nt}$ is the gross return on such bonds if they are held for exactly one period.[13] Allowing for the fact that $q_{n-1, t+1}$ is unknown at time t gives the hypothesis

$$\frac{E_t q_{n-1, t+1}}{q_{nt}} = 1 + r_t \tag{2.17}$$

The expectations theory asserts that expected one-period returns on bonds of all maturities are identical with the (certain) one-period rate.

The more familiar representation (2.11) of the expectations theory has some strong implications. If the market expects a rise, say, in interest rates, the term structure should be upward sloping (short rates stand below long rates). If a fall is expected, short rates will stand above long rates. However, this proposition is tautologous in that it can equally well be inverted to assert that an upward-sloping term structure represents the market's prediction of a rise in interest rates, and vice versa. A more problematic consequence of the theory when combined with rational expectations was demonstrated by Mishkin (1978, 1980). Returning to (2.12), shifting time t one period forward with a constant maturity n and dividing the result by (2.12) gives

$$\frac{1 + r_{t+n}}{1 + r} = \frac{(1 + R_{nt+1})^n}{(1 + R_{nt})^n} \tag{2.18}$$

We can make n arbitrarily large so that

$$\left(\frac{1 + r_{t+n}}{1 + r_t}\right)^{\frac{1}{n}} \to 1$$

and (2.18) simplifies to

$$R_{nt+1} = R_{nt} \tag{2.19}$$

Under rational expectations, (2.10) implies that the long-term rate of interest is a constant! In a stochastic setting, analogous arguments show that, under rational expectations, the long-term rate of interest must follow a random walk.[14]

A further difficulty is that many accounts of the expectations theory fail to emphasize that (2.11) and its perfect foresight equivalent (2.12) are only strictly true for discount bonds. As Begg (1984) explains, if bonds pay a periodic coupon then, even if all future one-period rates are known with certainty, (2.12) is true only if the one-period rate remains constant throughout all n future periods. This is because, if one-period rates change after time t, it will no longer be possible for the holder of the long-term bond to reinvest the coupon at the interest rates ruling at time t. Allowing for this effect in the expectations theory yields, to a linear approximation, an expression for the long rate which is a weighted average of future short rates, with the weights declining geometrically (see Shiller, 1972). It is therefore preferable to represent term structure theories as hypotheses about term premiums or one-period rates.[15] Thus, if n-period bonds pay a coupon c_{nt}, the expectations theory asserts that

$$\frac{E_t q_{n-1,\,t+1} - q_{nt} + c_{nt}}{q_{nt}} = r_t \tag{2.20}$$

An important implication of the expectations theory is that changes in the supplies of bonds of differing maturities have no effect on the term structure unless they have a direct effect on expectations about future interest rates. Thus any leverage that the authorities do enjoy over the term structure is inevitably rather tenuous in nature and, certainly, 'fine tuning' of the term structure by dealing in bonds of differing maturities is ineffectual. Blanchard's IS–LM model (fourth part of section 2.2.1) includes a term structure determined by the expectations hypothesis. Here, an unanticipated monetary expansion lowers the equilibrium level of interest rates but, at the time of intervention, interest rates jump below this level with the short rate standing below the long rate in (rational) anticipation of a subsequent rise in rates. If, however, the monetary expansion is credibly pre-announced, in the first phase of adjustment following the announcement the term structure is 'twisted' with short rates rising to maintain money market equilibrium and long rates falling in anticipation of lower interest rates in long-run equilibrium. The second phase of adjustment occurs following implementation when the term structure is untwisted by a discrete fall in the short rate, after which the interest rate trajectories are qualitatively the same as in the case of the unanticipated monetary expansion. Analogous results are reported by Turnovsky and Miller (1984) and Turnovsky (1986, 1989).

The unsatisfactory features of the expectations hypothesis stem in large part from its implicit assumption that agents are risk neutral. Risk averse agents will not, in general, be indifferent between long and short bonds paying the same expected rate of return. For an investor with a one-period time horizon one-period bonds are capital certain and n-period bonds are risky. For an investor with an n-period horizon it is the n-period bond that is capital certain and the sequence of one-period bonds that is risky because of the possibility of interest rate changes over the n periods.[16]

Modifications of the expectations theory to allow for risk have, until recently, been relatively *ad hoc*. Hicks' liquidity premium hypothesis (Hicks, 1939) conjectured that agents are prepared to pay a premium for liquidity. Hence lenders will prefer short-term and borrowers long-term debt. To compensate for the resulting 'constitutional weakness' at the long end of the market, long-term rates have to stand above short-term rates in equilibrium. This implies a positive term premium at all maturities. Market segmentation and preferred habitat theories can be regarded as extensions of this argument (see especially Modigliani and Sutch, 1967). The idea is that agents have a preferred maturity habitat determined by their preferences, and can only be persuaded out of their habitat on receipt of a premium. On this view, term premiums in general do not have a determinate sign. The term structure will also be influenced by differential taxation of income and capital gains, especially if tax rates may change over the life of a bond (see McCulloch, 1975).

Adjustments for risk and liquidity do not affect the substantive predictions of the expectations hypothesis if the liquidity or risk premium can be interpreted as constant over time, although it may differ among different maturities. Indeed, Campbell (1986) has shown that if such premiums are identically zero, the expectations hypothesis is internally inconsistent.[17] More recently, Walsh (1985) and Cox et al. (1985) have studied general equilibrium models of the term structure assuming risk aversion and rational expectations. These models suggest that term premiums will vary systematically over time and can be influenced by relatively standard policy measures such as variations in the supplies of bonds of different maturities. These influences occur primarily by altering the riskiness of a bond as measured by its covariance with market factors such as aggregate consumption. In these models the signs of the term premiums are unknown in general, although they can be predicted under any particular set of well-specified circumstances.

The main empirical questions arising from term structure theory concern the size, time variation, and predictability of term premiums. To the extent that they vary over time and are to some degree predictable, the expectations theory must be rejected.

Portfolio Balance and Asset Substitutability

Assets differ from one another in many characteristics other than term to maturity, including in particular risk and liquidity. In aggregate models, such characteristics are typically lumped together and the study of asset markets proceeds under the general assumption that all assets are less than perfect substitutes (see Tobin, 1961, 1963a, b, 1969, 1970; Tobin and Brainard, 1963, 1968; Brainard, 1964).

We can postulate that the demand for any asset i is a function of its own rate of interest r_i, the rates of interest r_j on all other competing assets, wealth W and income Y. Suppose that the economy can be aggregated into three groups of assets: high-powered money M, bonds B and equities E. The demands for these can be written

$$M = M(r_M^+, r_B^-, r_E^-, W^+, Y^+) \tag{2.21}$$

$$B = B(r_M^-, r_B^+, r_E^-, W^+, Y^-) \tag{2.22}$$

$$E = E(r_M^-, r_B^-, r_E^+, W^+, Y^-) \tag{2.23}$$

Asset holdings must sum to total wealth,

$$W = M + B + E \tag{2.24}$$

and this implies that the demand functions are subject to the (adding-up) restrictions[18]

$$M_{r_i} + B_{r_i} + E_{r_i} = 0 \qquad i = M, B, E$$

$$M_W + B_W + E_W = 1$$

$$M_Y + B_Y + E_Y = 0$$

If asset markets clear, asset demands can be set equal to the exogenous supplies, treating income as exogenous, and the resulting set of equilibrium conditions can be solved to determine the level and structure of interest rates. Since the asset demands must sum to total wealth, the three asset demand functions are not independent of one another and therefore can only be solved for two of the three interest rates, treating the other as exogenous.[19] Typically, it is the rate on money which is assumed to be exogenously fixed at zero. Solutions for interest rates and wealth, treating income as given, can then be interpreted as the LM curve of the economy.

Little can be said about the solutions of (2.21)–(2.24) unless some sign restrictions are imposed on the parameters. A common assumption is that all assets are gross substitutes, implying that a rise in the yield on any one asset will, *ceteris paribus*, increase the demand for that asset and reduce the demands for all other assets, thus giving the sign pattern shown in (2.21)–(2.23). This seems reasonable but, as Blanchard and Plantes (1977) have shown, it does not follow easily from any plausible set of theoretical assumptions about the underlying preferences of individual investors. A more plausible set of restrictions is that of symmetry of the interest rate responses together with a positive own rate response. This allows for the possibility that some assets are complements, not substitutes (see Royama and Hamada, 1967; B. Friedman, 1978). Another common assumption is homogeneity of degree one in wealth, implying that all the demand functions have a unit wealth elasticity and can be written as portfolio share equations M/W, B/W, E/W (see Tobin, 1969; Friedman and Roley, 1979a).[20] Finally, elementary considerations suggest a positive sign for income in the demand for money function and probably a negative sign elsewhere.

Adopting first the assumptions of gross substitutability and a zero return on money, we show in figure 2.3 the combinations of equity and bond yields consistent with money (MM), bond (BB) and equity (EE) market equilibrium respectively. The structure of interest rates is constant along the 45° ray through the origin (OS). Gross substitutability gives BB a smaller slope than EE as it takes smaller movements in the bond rate than in the equity rate to maintain bond market equilibrium, and smaller movements in the equity rate to maintain equity market equilibrium. Three main shocks can be analysed. First, an open market operation involving a sale of any interest-bearing asset for money raises both rates. (Figure 2.3 shows a sale of bonds.) Second, debt management – an exchange of one interest-bearing asset for another (of bonds for equity in figure 2.4) – raises the rate on the former and lowers the latter. Third, an increase in the supply of any asset (bonds in figure 2.5) accompanied by an increase in wealth raises the rate on the asset in question but may raise (figure 2.5, case 1) or lower (figure 2.5, case 2) other rates depending on the relative strengths of the substitution effect which reduces the demands for other assets and the wealth effect which

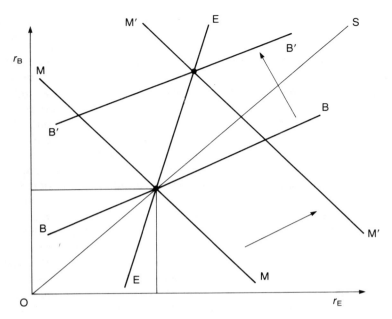

Figure 2.3   Open market sale of bonds

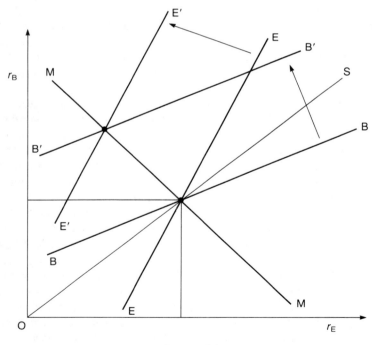

Figure 2.4   Exchange of bonds for equities

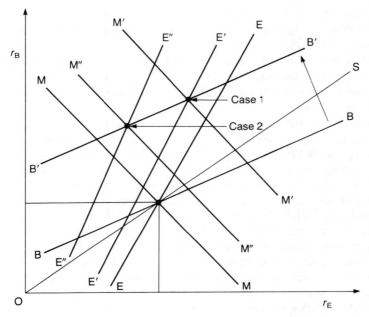

Figure 2.5   A wealth-augmenting increase in the supply of bonds

increases these demands. The extension of these results to the many-asset case is discussed elsewhere.[21]

Where some assets are complements their returns tend to move in opposite directions to one another. If bonds and equities are complements, an open market sale of bonds (for cash) raises the bond rate and lowers the equity rate. However, generalization to many assets is difficult in this case unless there are block complementarities in asset demands (see Allingham and Morishima, 1973).

Portfolio models bring out clearly the role of asset substitutability in determining the structure of interest rates. In the model above, the equity and bond rates do not adjust equally in response to a shock; their differential depends on all the parameters of the system. If bonds and equities are perfect substitutes, the EE and BB schedules in figure 2.3 merge along OS and an open market operation will simply shift MM, raising or lowering both rates proportionately to one another with the differential remaining unchanged.

Portfolio models have had a wide range of applications. B. Friedman (1978) appended an IS curve to prove that bond-financed increases in government spending only crowd out private spending if bonds and equity are close substitutes relative to bonds and money, a point originally made by Tobin (1961), and one which can also be seen from figure 2.5: case 1 gives rise to crowding out as the cost of equity capital increases, and case 2 is consistent with a rise in private spending as the cost of capital falls. Applications more specifically related to the UK include studies of competition and credit control by M. Miller (1973) and Artis et al. (1978), Spencer's (1982) analysis of the relationship between bank credit rationing and money market interest rates, and Green's (1982) survey of the main monetary policy instruments used in the 1970s.

Dynamic portfolio models could be analysed using the rational expectations approach by postulating, for example, that the short-term interest rate adjusts gradually in response to net excess demand while the long-term rate jumps in response to new information. In practice, portfolio models have not been studied in this way because it is usually more useful to think of the gradual adjustments occurring in product markets while the financial markets adjust rapidly in a forward-looking way. This necessarily gives rise to dynamic models which integrate the real and financial sides of the economy as discussed in the fourth part of section 2.2.1.

A useful strategy for dynamic econometric modelling is to begin with a flow of funds matrix in which any cell (i, j) shows net acquisitions or sales of asset i by sector j during the time period under consideration. The row sums of the matrix are zero as net purchases of an asset must equal net sales, and each column j sums to the jth sector's surplus or deficit; this is its total net acquisition of financial assets. The flow of funds matrix is transformed into a model by assuming that each cell in the matrix is a variable to be explained by an asset demand function analogous to (2.21)–(2.23). The column sums are the sector budget constraints. The row sums are reinterpreted as market-clearing conditions. They state that, in equilibrium, desired net purchases of an asset must equal desired net sales, with the desired net purchases or sales being determined by the asset demand functions. Equilibrium in the financial markets determines interest rates, asset prices and hence the flows of funds and end-of-period stocks, given the stocks at the end of the previous period and the sector surpluses or deficits. The broad qualitative characteristics of the equilibrium thus described do not differ fundamentally from those of the portfolio mode (2.21)–(2.24). The key difference is that the equilibrium in a flow of funds model is inherently temporary, for the end-of-period stocks will be carried over to the next time period and, together with a new set of sector surpluses and deficits and asset demands, will determine a new temporary equilibrium. A long-run equilibrium is one in which stocks of assets are stationary from period to period in some well-defined sense.

2.2.3 Microfoundations of Interest Rate Determination

Postulated asset demands and pricing equations can be regarded as the outcome of a myriad of optimizing decisions by individual investors. The most commonly used model of these decisions is the mean–variance model. Individual investors are postulated to maximize a one-period utility function U whose arguments are the mean M and variance V of wealth, where the latter is a measure of the riskiness of wealth.[22] Agents are assumed to be risk averse. Thus for the kth investor

$$U^k = U^k(M^k, V^k) \qquad U_M > 0, U_V < 0 \tag{2.25}$$

Investors are assumed to have common beliefs about the first and second moments which need not bear any relationship to the true moments (see Roll, 1977). However, if investor beliefs bear no relationship to the true moments then, ultimately, the theory lacks plausibility. Therefore there is a close connection between rational expectations and the mean–variance model, and it is common to assume that the moments used by investors in mean–variance optimization are indeed the true moments of wealth.

The arguments of the kth investor's utility function are

$$M^k = h^{e\prime} x^k W^k \tag{2.26}$$

$$V^k = x^{k\prime} \Omega x^k (W^k)^2 \tag{2.27}$$

where, if there are n assets available, h^e is an $n \times 1$ vector of expected gross holding period returns, with the jth element of h^e being defined by

$$h^e_j = \frac{E_t q_{jt+1} + d_{jt+1}}{q_{jt}}$$

where q_{jt} is the price of the jth asset at time t and d_{jt} is the dividend on the jth asset at time t, x^k is an $n \times 1$ vector of portfolio shares, i.e. of ratios of asset holdings to wealth, at market value, W^k is wealth at market value (a scalar), Ω is a variance–covariance matrix of gross returns defined by

$$\Omega = E_t(h - h^e)(h - h^e)\prime$$

and i is a column vector of 1s. The budget constraint states that portfolio shares must sum to unity:

$$i\prime x^k = 1 \tag{2.28}$$

Investors choose a vector of portfolio shares to maximize (2.25) subject to (2.28).[23] This yields n asset demands which are generally written as linear functions of expected returns. Linearity results from additional restrictions on the mean–variance approximation, the most common of which are constant absolute risk aversion (CARA) or constant relative risk aversion (CRRA). The former implies that $\delta_k = -2U_v^k/U_m^k$ is constant; the latter implies that $\theta_k = -2U_v^k W^k/U_m^k$ is constant, although δ_k, θ_k may differ across investors (see S. Miller, 1975). CARA implies that asset *holdings* at market value are linear functions of expected returns, whereas CRRA implies that portfolio *shares* are linear functions of expected returns (see Friedman and Roley, 1979a). Specifically, under CRRA,

$$x^k = \theta_k^{-1} A h^e + \Omega^{-1} i (i' \Omega^{-1} i)^{-1} \tag{2.29}$$

where

$$A = \Omega^{-1} - \Omega^{-1} i (i' \Omega^{-1} i)^{-1} i' \Omega^{-1} \tag{2.30}$$

The asset demands (2.29) consist of two additive components. Kouri (1977) showed that these could be interpreted respectively as a speculative portfolio, which depends on expected returns and agents' preferences, and a minimum variance portfolio, which is unique and therefore the same for all investors. If one asset is capital certain then the minimum variance portfolio is the capital-certain asset. Moreover, since individual preferences are represented solely by the scaling factor θ_k^{-1} the composition of the speculative portfolio is also unique and therefore the same for all investors. Preferences determine only the proportions of wealth placed in the speculative and minimum variance portfolios respectively. This is usually called the two-fund or separation theorem. It has been studied extensively by Merton (1972) and Roll (1977).

CRRA implies that asset demands are homogeneous of degree one in wealth. In addition, both CRRA and CARA imply that demand functions are homogeneous of degree zero in expected returns: an equal change in all expected returns leaves asset demands unaffected. This also means that asset demands can be written as functions of the differentials between any $n - 1$ expected returns and the remaining nth return.

To determine asset prices, first aggregate asset demands (2.29) across individuals:

$$x = \theta^{-1} A h^e + \Omega^{-1} i (i' \Omega^{-1} i)^{-1} \tag{2.31}$$

with

$$x = \sum_k x_k w_k \qquad \theta = \frac{1}{\Sigma_k \theta_k^{-1} w_k} \qquad w_k = \frac{W_k}{\Sigma_k W_k} \tag{2.31}$$

If asset markets clear, aggregate demands can be set equal to supplies and the system solved to give expressions for expected returns as functions of asset supplies. Since there are n markets, only $n - 1$ expected returns can be determined, with the remaining nth return acting as numeraire. This is generally taken to be the capital-certain asset where one exists. Inverting the first $n - 1$ rows of (2.31) gives

$$h_1^e - ih_n^e = \theta \hat{\Omega} x_1 + (\Omega_{1n} - iw_{nn}) \tag{2.32}$$

where vectors and matrices are partitioned between the first $n - 1$ rows and columns and the remaining nth row and column:

$$h^e = \begin{pmatrix} h_1^e \\ h_n^e \end{pmatrix} \qquad x = \begin{pmatrix} x_1 \\ x_n \end{pmatrix} \qquad \Omega = \begin{pmatrix} \Omega_{11} & \Omega_{1n} \\ \Omega_{n1} & w_{nn} \end{pmatrix}$$

and

$$\hat{\Omega} = \Omega_{11} - i\Omega_{n1} - \Omega'_{1n}i' - ii'w_{nn}$$

or

$$\hat{\Omega} = E[(h_1 - h_n) - (h_1^e - h_n^e)][(h_1 - h_n) - (h_1^e - h_n^e)]'$$

Whereas Ω is the covariance matrix of *absolute* returns, $\hat{\Omega}$ is the covariance matrix of *relative* returns (see Green and Keating (1988) and Green (1990) for details).

Equation (2.32) is the security market line (SML), one of the central theoretical results of the capital asset pricing model (CAPM) (see in particular the contributions by Sharpe (1964), Lintner (1965), Mossin (1966) and Black (1972)). This states that the excess return on any asset i over the return on the numeraire is a linear function of the covariance between the excess return on that asset and the weighted average excess return on all assets in the market (more simply termed 'the excess return on the market'). Equation (2.32) can most easily be related to the more familiar beta formulation of the SML by considering the simple case in which one asset (say the nth) is capital certain and investor preferences are all identical. If so, any row of (2.32), say the ith, can be written

$$h_i^e - h_n = \theta \sum_{j=1}^{n-1} w_{ij} x_j \tag{2.33}$$

The geometry of the separation theorem in the presence of a safe asset is given in figure 2.6 in the usual mean–standard deviation $(S = V^{1/2})$ diagram. This shows the set of mean–variance efficient portfolios EE, the capital market line CC which gives the unique risk–return trade-off available in the market to all investors and investor preferences (indifference curves II). If initial wealth is normalized at unity, investor preferences under CRRA can be represented by

$$U = M - \frac{\theta}{2} V \tag{2.34}$$

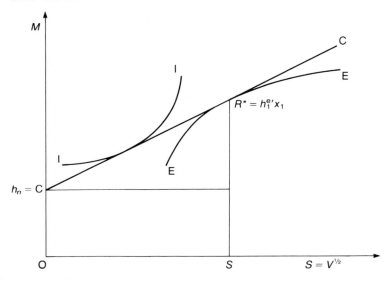

Figure 2.6 The separation theorem

Hence the slope of any mean–standard deviation indifference curve is

$$- \frac{\partial U/\partial S}{\partial U/\partial M} = \theta S \tag{2.35}$$

Figure 2.6 shows that, at equilibrium, the slope of the indifference curve must be equal to the slope of the capital market line, i.e.

$$\theta S = \frac{R^* - h_n}{S} \tag{2.36}$$

with $R^* = h_1^e{}'x_1$ (the return on the market). Hence, at equilibrium, the market price of risk, given by $(R^* - h_n)/V$, is equal to the rate of relative risk aversion θ.[24] Finally, defining

$$\beta_i = \sum_{j=1}^{n-1} \frac{w_{ij} x_j}{V}$$

and eliminating θ between (2.36) and (2.33) gives

$$h_i^e - h_n = (R^* - h_n)\beta_i \tag{2.37}$$

This is the more familiar representation of the SML in which the excess return on an asset is proportional to the excess return on the market. The factor of proportionality is the beta coefficient β_i of the asset measured as the ratio of its covariance with the market to the variance of the market.

Beta is the regression coefficient obtained by regressing the excess return on the asset on the excess return on the market. The SML gives a simple formula for the risk premium on an asset, i.e. its excess return over the safe asset. It depends on the covariance of an asset's return with the market and on the market price of risk.

The mean–variance model and the CAPM are logically equivalent and can be seen as providing microfoundations for the Tobin–Brainard portfolio approach to studying interest rates.[25] In practice, Tobin and Brainard had in mind a looser formulation than that provided by the CAPM which imposes a set of very tight restrictions on asset demands and asset pricing formulae. Moreover, the CAPM does not provide any specific role for money in determining the interest rate structure; this role is taken over by the capital-certain asset which is not necessarily money. The new monetary economics has, however, suggested some solutions to this problem. A more immediate issue is that, in the finance literature, betas were, until recently, treated as constants, implying that risk premiums on assets were also constant. In contrast, it is a central feature of the Tobin–Brainard approach that risk premiums, and hence betas, vary over time as asset supplies vary. Moreover, it is clear from (2.37) and the definition of β_i that variations in asset betas could be due either to changes in asset supplies x_j or to changes in risks w_{ij}. A key problem in empirical research is to disentangle these two factors and evaluate their relative importance.

The one-period framework of the CAPM imposes separation between portfolio and consumption decisions. The intertemporal capital asset pricing model (ICAPM) considers these decisions jointly. Agents are assumed to trade assets so as to maximize the expected utility of lifetime consumption given the anticipated path of income. Detailed consideration of the ICAPM is beyond the scope of this survey. Key contributions include those of Merton (1971, 1973), Long (1974), Breeden (1979) and Cox et al. (1981a).

2.3 EMPIRICAL RESEARCH ON INTEREST RATES

2.3.1. Methodological Issues

Empirical research on the *level* of interest rates has mostly involved either the construction of large-scale macromodels or the estimation of reduced forms. Small-scale 'structural' models have been more widely used to study the *structure* of interest rates. Here we shall concentrate on reduced form and small-model tests of interest rate hypotheses; larger models are covered in chapter 6.

The efficient markets approach provides a specific rationale for concentrating on single-equation estimation: a market is said to be weak form efficient if current prices reflect all information contained in past prices and hence cannot be predicted using these data; semi-strong form efficiency exists if prices reflect all currently published information (including past prices); strong form efficiency requires that prices reflect all information whether published or unpublished, i.e. including 'confidential' inside information (see Fama, 1970).[26] Suppose now that we are interested in explaining the return on long-term bonds. From (2.20) the preferred habitat hypothesis might be written

$$E_t^m(h_{t+1}) = r_t + \delta_t \qquad (2.38)$$

where

$$h_{t+1} = \frac{q_{n-1,\,t+1} - q_{nt} + c_{nt}}{q_{nt}}$$

E_t^m is the market's conditional expectation and δ_t is a risk or liquidity premium at the preferred habitat. According to the efficient markets hypothesis, the market's conditional expectation is identical with the true conditional expectation E_t. Hence

$$E_t(h_{t+1} - r_t - \delta_t) = 0 \qquad (2.39)$$

If the market is efficient, the excess return $y_{t+1} = h_{t+1} - r_t - \delta_t$ must be uncorrelated with past information for otherwise y_{t+1} could be predicted to some extent using such information. This would imply that the conditional expectation of y_{t+1} was not necessarily zero and that the market was inefficient as it was failing to use this information in setting bond prices.

This suggests that an appropriate test for market efficiency might be a regression of y_{t+1} on 'plausible' lagged information variables. If these variables are all insignificant this provides evidence for market efficiency. However, this is not yet a well-specified test as y_{t+1} includes the unknown and possibly time-varying risk premium δ_t. In practical applications, δ_t is often assumed to be constant, as in the expectations model of the term structure, or it is proxied by some 'plausible' variables. These additional assumptions bring out the so-called dual hypothesis problem. Regressions of y_{t+1} on information variables are simultaneously testing the hypothesis of market efficiency *and* the postulated model of market equilibrium represented by (2.38) and the assumptions on δ_t. If the model is rejected, it could be because the model of market equilibrium is invalid or the market is inefficient or both. It is impossible to discriminate among these explanations. This problem recurs frequently in the empirical literature, particularly where models of expectation formation are concerned, and it implies that empirical results should carry a health warning calling for a cautious interpretation.

Fama (1970) argued that, in financial markets, the evidence broadly favoured semi-strong efficiency and overwhelmingly supported weak form efficiency. If indeed the market is efficient, then current prices can only be influenced by new information which becomes available at the time when prices are set. It is this information that causes prices to jump. This suggests that the determinants of interest rates in an efficient market can be studied by regressions of the form

$$y_{t+1} = \sum_i \beta_i (X_{it+1} - E_t X_{it+1}) + e_{t+1} \tag{2.40}$$

where each $X_{it+1} - E_t X_{it+1}$ constitutes a stream of unanticipated shocks which influence y_{t+1}. Under certain conditions, rational expectations are equivalent to least squares predictors (see Sargent, 1987b). Hence the rational expectations of each X_{it+1} can be generated from a regression such as

$$X_{it+1} = \sum_j \sum_k \alpha_{ijk} Z_{ijt-k+1} + u_{it+1} \tag{2.41}$$

where the Z_{ij} are variables which help predict X_i. $E_t X_{it+1}$ are the one-step-ahead forecasts from (2.41). Mishkin (1981a) pointed out that efficient estimates of the α_{ijk} and β_i could be obtained by stacking (2.40) and (2.41) and estimating them simultaneously as

$$y_{t+1} = \sum_i \beta_i X_{it+1} + \sum_i \sum_j \sum_k \phi_{ijk} Z_{ijt-k} + e_t \tag{2.42a}$$

$$X_{1t+1} = \sum_j \sum_k \alpha_{1jk} Z_{1jt-k} + u_{1t} \tag{2.42b}$$

$$\vdots$$

$$X_{It+1} = \sum_j \sum_k \alpha_{Ijk} Z_{Ijt-k} + u_{It}$$

The model of y_{t+1} and the rational expectations model underlying the determination of the X_{it+1} can then be tested by imposing and testing the cross-equation restrictions implied by (2.40) and (2.41). In (2.42) these are[27]

$$\phi_{ijk} = -\beta_i \alpha_{ijk} \qquad \forall i \tag{2.43}$$

According to Sargent (1987b) such cross-equation restrictions are the hallmark of rational expectations models.

The system given by (2.42) is a special example of the widely used vector autoregression (VAR) methodology. In principle, any time series can be represented by an autoregressive moving-average (ARMA) model.

Typically, we are interested in the relationships between two time series, one of which involves an unknown expected value. The ARMA model can be used to calculate this expected value conditional on the information set used in constructing the ARMA representation. If, for example, we are interested in the relationship between nominal short-term interest rates r_t and inflation π_{t+1}, it makes sense to confine our attention to these two variables, representing them as

$$\pi_{t+1} = \sum_{j=1}^{J} a_{11j} \pi_{t+1-j} + \sum_{j=1}^{J} a_{12j} r_{t-j+1} + u_{1t+1} \tag{2.44a}$$

$$r_t = \sum_{j=1}^{J} a_{21j} \pi_{t-j} + \sum_{j=1}^{J} a_{22j} r_{t-j} + u_{2t} \tag{2.44b}$$

The system (2.44) is a VAR, hence the VAR label.

Suppose that we are interested in testing the Fisher hypothesis and, for illustration, let the VAR be

$$\pi_{t+1} = a_{10} + a_{11} \pi_t + a_{12} r_t + u_{1t+1} \tag{2.45a}$$

$$r_t = a_{20} + a_{21} \pi_{t-1} + a_{22} r_{t-1} + u_{2t} \tag{2.45b}$$

If μ_t is the real interest rate, the Fisher hypothesis states that

$$r_t = E_t \pi_{t+1} + \mu_t \tag{2.46}$$

Hence it is also true that

$$E_{t-1} r_t = E_{t-1} \pi_{t+1} + E_{t-1} \mu_t \tag{2.47}$$

However, the first two expectations in (2.47) can be calculated directly from (2.45) as

$$E_{t-1} r_t = a_{20} + a_{21} \pi_{t-1} + a_{22} r_{t-1} \tag{2.48}$$

$$\begin{aligned} E_{t-1} \pi_{t+1} &= a_{10} + a_{11} E_{t-1} \pi_t + a_{12} E_{t-1} r_t \\ &= a_{10}(1 + a_{11}) + a_{12} a_{20} + (a_{11}^2 + a_{12} a_{21}) \pi_{t-1} + a_{12}(a_{11} + a_{22}) r_{t-1} \end{aligned} \tag{2.49}$$

Under the null hypotheses that the real interest rate is constant and the Fisher effect is true (2.48) and (2.49) differ by a constant (the real interest rate). Hence the coefficients on π_{t-1} in (2.48) and (2.49) must be identical, as must be those on r_{t-1}. This implies that

$$a_{21} = \frac{a_{11}^2}{1 - a_{12}} \qquad a_{22} = \frac{a_{11} a_{12}}{1 - a_{12}} \tag{2.50}$$

and therefore, more simply, that

$$a_{11}/a_{12} = a_{21}/a_{22}$$

These are non-linear restrictions on the coefficients of (2.45).[28]

The idea of the VAR methodology is to estimate (2.45) as a system of equations without restrictions, and then to re-estimate the system imposing the restrictions (2.50). A test for the validity of these restrictions then amounts to a joint test of the rationality of expectations, the Fisher effect and the hypothesis that the real interest rate is a constant. Thus the VAR methodology involves specifying and estimating a time series model of the variables of interest, and then testing the (cross-equation) restrictions on this model implied by the joint hypotheses of rational expectations and the main hypothesis of interest.

The main advantage of the VAR methodology is that it can be employed in virtually any testing situation, although the cross-equation parameter restrictions are sometimes very complex. Of course, VARs are subject to the dual hypothesis problem. A more serious difficulty, however, is that it can be difficult to determine the appropriate order of the autoregressive scheme other than arbitrarily. If, as is likely, relevant information variables are excluded from the model, then the estimates may be rather inefficient. Hence VAR tests tend to have low power and, indeed, seem to accept restrictions rather easily.

VARs also suffer from more subtle difficulties, presuming that agents have both too much information and too little information. They presume *too much* information in the following sense. The coefficients in equations such as (2.44) are typically estimated using the entire data set for π and r, $t = 1, \ldots, T$. Clearly though, agents forecasting $\pi_{\tau+1}(\tau < T)$ could only make use of information up to time τ and may use very different estimates of the a_{ij} from those which could be obtained at future dates $t(\tau < t < T)$ using additional information as more realizations of π and r become available. Thus the more precise method of modelling expectations is to allow agents to update the regression coefficients in (2.44) each period as new information becomes available (see B. Friedman, 1979a). Very little is known about the probable magnitude of errors resulting from the direct use of (2.44) although early indications are that they may not be unduly serious (see Plosser, 1987). Forecasting with VARs is most likely to encounter problems at the time of a policy regime change, and such easily identifiable changes as exist have been a subject of particular interest in the literature.

VARs presume *too little* information in that market participants may have access to different information from econometricians, including qualitative data. In principle, agents can improve their forecasts of new statistics right up to their publication date, whereas VARs must rely on data of fixed periodicity. Thus, for example, monthly VARs neglect intramonth data. The period used in VAR estimation also fixes the interval at which a response to new information can occur. Financial markets appear to respond very rapidly to new information, and this may not show up in monthly or quarterly time series studies.

Despite these problems, VARs have been widely used in recent years for studying interest rates. Their simplicity and low demands for data give them an overwhelming advantage in generating quick, if sometimes meaningless, results.

Not all the empirical work surveyed in this chapter utilizes the efficient markets methodologies. However, these have been the predominant methodologies in the literature partly because they lend themselves to small-scale models and partly because information efficiency is a plausible characteristic of financial markets, especially in the light of Fama's (1970) survey. More recently, evidence has been accumulating to cast doubt on the validity of semi-strong form efficiency and even on weak form efficiency. These issues are considered further in the following section.

2.3.2 The Level of Interest Rates

The Fisher Effect

The source of Fisher's hypothesis about the relationship between interest rates and inflation was his investigation of the Gibson paradox, a phenomenon noticed by Keynes (1930) and named by him after the paper by Gibson (1923). Keynes argued that in long runs of US and UK data, interest rates were positively correlated with the price level. This is inconsistent with a central tenet of classical monetary theory that the level of interest rates should be independent of the price level. Fisher's (1930) explanation of the Gibson paradox was based on the distinction between real and nominal interest rates together with a hypothesis about the formation of inflation expectations. He proposed that the nominal interest rate r_t could be represented by

$$r_t = \mu + \alpha_1 E_t \pi_{t+1} + u_t \tag{2.51}$$

where μ is the average real interest rate. The expected rate of inflation $E_t \pi_{t+1}$ is modelled by

$$E_t \pi_{t+1} = \sum_{i=1}^{n} \beta^i \pi_{t-i+1} \qquad \beta < 1 \tag{2.52}$$

Substituting (2.52) into (2.51) and assuming that the real interest rate is independent of the inflation rate yields an equation which can be estimated by ordinary least squares (OLS). Fisher's estimates of this equation for several countries suggested that β was close to unity but that α_1 was considerably less than unity, implying that investors use a very long weighted average of past inflation rates in forecasting future inflation, but that nominal interest rates only adjust partially to changes in inflation expectations. Thus the Fisher effect is misnamed, as Fisher himself never claimed that the adjustment of nominal interest rates to inflation was complete. Moreover, Fisher's 'resolution' of the Gibson paradox really only involves a restatement of the problem. Since $\pi_{t+1} \approx p_{t+1} - p_t$, where p_t is the logarithm of the price level, then, if β is close to unity in (2.52), $E_t \pi_{t+1} \approx p_t$. Thus the regression of nominal interest rates on long distributed lags of inflation merely reproduces the Gibson paradox without explaining it. More recent attempts to explain the Gibson paradox have typically relied on portfolio balance arguments, but the phenomenon has proved surprisingly resistant to a full explanation.[29]

Returning to the Fisher effect *per se*, we find that research using long runs of annual data has broadly confirmed Fisher's original findings that interest rates do not adjust completely to inflation, even in the long run (see Sargent, 1973; Summers, 1983).[30] However, considerably more research has been carried out using shorter runs of higher frequency data. Initially, such research involved the estimation of models analogous to that of Fisher himself, such as

$$r_t = a_0 + a_1 E_t \pi_{t+1} + \sum_i \sum_j b_{ij} X_{it-j} + u_t \qquad (2.53)$$

Here the X_{it-j} are variables which influence interest rates independently of inflation expectations. These could include measures of monetary and fiscal policy, and variables representing exogeneous non-policy shocks. If the estimated b_{ij} are all zero and a_1 equals unity, the Fisher hypothesis is accepted. If, however, some of the b_{ij} are non-zero, the hypothesis is rejected because the X_{ij} produce variations in the nominal interest rate independently of variations in inflation expectations, and therefore generate systematic changes in the real interest rate. The Fisher hypothesis is also rejected if a_1 differs from unity. This could be because of the Mundell–Tobin effect ($a_1 < 1$) or the effects of taxation ($a_1 > 1$). Yohe and Karnosky (1969), W. Gibson (1972) and Carr and Smith (1972) utilize variants of this procedure.

A major problem with equations like (2.53) is to find a suitable measure of inflation expectations. Two such have been used. The first is direct survey evidence such as the (US) Livingstone Survey and the (UK) Carlson–Parkin index (Carlson and Parkin, 1975). Although such surveys offer direct 'objective' data on expectations, they are often criticized as being inconsistent with rationality (see Pesando (1975) and Pearce (1979) on the Livingstone Survey, and G. W. Smith (1982) on the Carlson–Parkin data). However, it is not obvious why this should be regarded as a problem, as actual expectations-generating mechanisms may not, in fact, be rational. Indeed, survey data provide a useful means of directly testing the hypothesis of rational expectations. The second method of measuring expectations follows Fisher in postulating a theory of expectation formation (typically, rational expectations) and embedding it in the main model to be tested, i.e. (2.53). Such a theory-based measure can be used to study the expectations of any variable in a model, not just those which happen to have been the subject of a survey. However, the rational expectations hypothesis imposes strong restrictions on modelling, and may itself be false.

A further problem with (2.53) is that it should not be estimated by OLS because inflation expectations are endogenous. An instrumental variable estimator may produce inefficient estimates, and may therefore tend to accept the Fisher hypothesis too frequently. Moreover, the use of instrumental variables can be regarded as equivalent to postulating a specific rational expectations scheme with the instruments constituting the information set on which expectations are conditioned (see McCallum, 1976; Wickens, 1982). It is frequently argued that survey expectations data are exogenous and they are invariably treated as such (see W. Gibson, 1972; Peek, 1982). However, if such expectations are literally exogenous they are probably a very poor measure of the true expectations. Moreover, the evidence which suggests that survey expectations data are not necessarily rational is inconsistent with their statistical exogeneity in equations such as (2.53).

Despite these problems, equations like (2.53) have been popular in practice and have typically produced estimates of a_1 for the post-war period which are significantly and sometimes substantially less than unity, rejecting both the simple and the tax-adjusted Fisher effect. However, when allowance is made for the adjustment over time of nominal interest rates to inflation, the long-run estimate of a_1 is much closer to unity.[31] As before, these results are qualitatively similar to those of Fisher, although they also suggest that changes in inflation expectations are the single most important (but not the only) determinant of nominal interest rates in both the long and the short run.

These conclusions were challenged in an ingenious and much cited paper by Fama (1975) who argued that regressions such as (2.53) were estimated the wrong way round; the correct procedure was to estimate

$$\pi_{t+1} = a_0 + a_1 r_t + u_t \tag{2.54}$$

If asset markets are efficient, asset prices and interest rates are set to utilize all available information, including in particular that which helps to predict inflation.[32] It follows that the difference between the nominal interest rate and the real rate constitutes the best prediction of inflation available, and is indeed the market prediction. Hence we can write

$$E_t \pi_{t+1} = r_t - \mu_t \tag{2.55}$$

If information is used efficiently, expectations of inflation must be formed rationally, so that

$$\pi_{t+1} = E_t \pi_{t+1} + v_{t+1} \tag{2.56}$$

where v_{t+1} is a white noise error which, by construction, is uncorrelated with $E_t \pi_{t+1}$. Substituting (2.55) into (2.56) gives

$$\pi_{t+1} = -\mu_t + r_t + v_{t+1} \tag{2.57}$$

If the real interest rate is constant, (2.57) can be written

$$\pi_{t+1} = a_0 + a_1 r_t + v_{t+1} \tag{2.58}$$

which can be estimated by OLS. The estimated value of a_0 gives (minus) the constant real interest rate, and, if $a_1 = 1$, then the Fisher hypothesis is true. The rationality of expectations can be checked by examining the residuals of (2.58) and by including additional regressors, especially π_t. Non-autocorrelated residuals and an insignificant coefficient on π_t are consistent with rational expectations.

It is worth emphasizing the way in which the rational expectations hypothesis is used by Fama (1975) as it is characteristic of a large number of subsequent papers. The central point is to set up the model in such a way that it can be estimated by OLS. This means that the actual value of the expectational variable at time $t+1$ is on the left-hand side, while the information variables dated at time t or earlier are on the right. In this set-up the part of the right-hand side which is known at time t (the explanatory variables and their coefficients) can be regarded as the expectation of the left-hand side, while the regression residuals (whose values materialize at time $t+1$) are the expectational errors. Thus the modelling process mimics the postulated rational expectation formation process.

Using US treasury bill rates and inflation over the period 1953–71, Fama found strong evidence in support of all his testable propositions: market efficiency, the predictability of inflation, the Fisher effect ($a_1 = 1$) and rational expectations.

These results generated considerable controversy and are now generally regarded as incorrect. However, this does not vitiate the methodological contribution of the paper. Attention focused first on the assumption of a constant real interest rate. Nelson and Schwert (1977) pointed out that (2.58) is a valid regression only if the real interest rate is an exact constant. It is not even sufficient to suppose that μ_t is a constant-mean white noise process. For, suppose that μ_t is given by

$$\mu_t = \mu + e_t \tag{2.59}$$

where e_t is a white noise error. Then equation (2.58) becomes

$$\pi_{t+1} = -\mu + r_t + (v_{t+1} - e_t) \tag{2.60}$$

Since $r_t (= E_t\pi_{t+1} + \mu_t)$ contains $\mu_t (= \mu + e_t)$, the composite error in (2.60) is not independent of r_t and OLS will deliver an inconsistent estimate of a_1 in (2.58). This suggests a need to model the real rate of interest more carefully. It also transpired that Fama's results were largely an artefact of his data period–a time when inflation was low and the real interest rate may have been relatively stable. Retaining the methodology but extending the data period forward from 1971 or backwards into the pre-war period leads to an immediate breakdown of Fama's results (see Nelson and Schwert (1977) and Summers (1983) respectively).

These exchanges re-established the consensus that nominal interest rates do not ajust one for one to changes in inflation expectations, with real interest rates remaining constant,[33] a result which appears to be robust across countries (see MacDonald and Murphy, 1987). However, there is less agreement on why this should be so. Summers (1983) found that inflation had led to a decline in US bond returns relative to those on equities and conjectured that this was consistent with the existence of money illusion in financial markets, a position also taken by Modigliani and Cohn (1979) in a study of post-war US equity yields. Garbade and Wachtel (1978) and Dwyer (1981) argued that the frailty of the relationship between interest rates and expected inflation was due primarily to variations in the real interest rate, and not to a failure of the Fisher effect *per se*. Whatever the explanation may be, the balance of the evidence is that changes in inflation expectations affect both real and nominal interest rates. Thus, in recent years, the focus of empirical reseach has shifted from studying the Fisher effect towards attempting to model more directly the determinants of the real interest rate.

Determinants of the Real Interest Rate

Studies of the real interest rate must also, apparently, confront the question of how to measure inflation expectations. Mishkin (1981b) pointed out that this question can, in fact, be circumvented using a variant of Fama's method. Suppose that the *ex ante* real interet rate is modelled as

$$\mu_t = \sum_i \sum_j b_{ij} X_{it-j+1} + u_k \tag{2.61}$$

Consider the regression

$$r_t - \pi_{t+1} = \sum_i \sum_j \beta_{ij} X_{it-j+1} + e_{t+1} \tag{2.62}$$

The left-hand side variable is the ex post real interest rate. This is related to the *ex ante* real interest rate by

$$\mu_t - \left(r_t - \pi_{t+1}\right) = \left(\pi_{t+1} - E_t\pi_{t+1}\right) = v_{t+1} \qquad (2.63)$$

Combining (2.61) and (2.63) gives (2.62). In (2.62), however, the error has two components: the residual u_t in the model of real interest rates and the error v_{t+1} in forming inflation expectations. Under rational expectations v_{t+1} is uncorrelated with $E_t\pi_{t+1}$ and hence with all the X_{it-j+1}. Thus (2.62) is a regression equation and, as Mishkin showed, OLS estimates of the β_{ij} are unbiased estimates of the corresponding b_{ij}. However, the β_{ij} are necessarily inefficient estimators of the b_{ij}, although under some circumstances it is possible to correct for this inefficiency.

A problem with this approach is that, in most applications, it transpires that the variance of inflation considerably exceeds the variance of the real interest rate (see Nelson and Schwert (1977) on US data and Symons (1983) on UK data). This suggests that the variance σ_{vv} of v_t may be large relative to the variance σ_{uu} of u_t so that equations like (2.62) are likely to be *very* inefficient and effectively dominated by the inflation expectation errors. Support for this point of view comes from Mills and Stephenson (1985) who use signal extraction techniques to derive direct estimates of σ_{uu} and σ_{vv}[34] and find that, for UK treasury bills (1952–85), $\sigma_{uu}/\sigma_{vv} = 0.66$. Thus the Mishkin technique has experienced mixed popularity, and many researchers have preferred to estimate equations like (2.61) using survey- or theory-based measures of inflation expectations to calculate μ_t.

Determinants of real interest rates can be divided into two main categories: shocks, from whatever source, which work solely by changing inflation expectations (the Mundell–Tobin effect) and shocks which work independently of changes in inflation expectations. The main sources of exogenous shocks are monetary and fiscal policies, portfolio (LM) shifts and shocks to aggregate demand (IS) and supply.

For short-term interest rates, it is generally agreed that there has been a significant Mundel–Tobin effect in the post-war period in both the USA (Mishkin, 1981b) and the UK (Mills and Stephenson, 1985, 1987). This is sufficiently strong that movements in the nominal interest rate are invariably a poor indicator of movements in the real interest rate. Indeed, on occasion, the two rates are negatively correlated. Moreover, these results appear robust with respect to the method of modelling inflation expectations (the Mishkin method, survey data (Makin, 1982) or VAR models (Saracoglu, 1984)).

It also seems clear that there are significant determinants of real interest rates which are independent of changes in inflation expectations. However, it is hard to summarize these determinants other than by listing the variables that proved significant in different models. Thus, in the UK, Symons

(1983) found (anticipated) M1 growth to be a significant determinant of the real treasury bill rate, whereas Mills and Stephenson (1987) found M3 growth to be significant. The latter also found a significant positive effect of unemployment. These results suggest that monetary policy shocks, tracing out the IS curve, were an important influence on UK real interest rates. For the USA, Mishkin (1981b) found that influences on the real interest rate other than those working through changes in inflation expectations were negligible. However, Huizinga and Mishkin (1986) found that, after the change in the operating procedures of the US Federal Reserve in 1979, real and nominal interest rates moved closely together with virtually no discernible Fisher effect.[35] Work which does not employ Mishkin's method has found evidence of significant effects on US real interest rates other than those arising through changes in inflation expectations. Makin (1982) and Wilcox (1983) both found that expansionary monetary or fiscal policies tend to have significant effects in respectively reducing or increasing real interest rates. Wilcox also found that negative supply shocks were an important factor behind the low real interest rates of the 1970s, while Blanchard and Summers (1984) point to positive supply shocks as a key determinant of the high real rates in the 1980s.

There has been less research on long-term real interest rates. Since the one-period real return on a long-term bond can be written as

$$\frac{E_t q_{t+1} - q_t + c_t}{q_t} - E_t \pi_{t+1}$$

studies of long-term interest rates must model asset price expectations as well as inflation expectations. Moreover, the appropriate holding period for the analysis and hence the period over which expectations are formed are both unclear. Investors in 20 year bonds do not necessarily have a 20 year holding period. It is common to assume that the holding period corresponds to the timing of a regular portfolio review, which in turn is assumed to be the point at which all transactions take place. However, the length of this holding period in real time is usually chosen in some rather arbitrary manner on the basis of data availability.

For these reasons, there is little consensus on the determinants of real long-term interest rates. For bonds, Huizinga and Mishkin (1984) find a significant Mundell–Tobin effect in the USA, but Mills and Stephenson (1986) find that, in the UK, the relationship between inflation and real returns is perverse (positive). Mills and Stephenson also find a perverse (positive) relationship between M3 money growth and interest rates, at least after 1979. For stocks, Fama (1981) documents a negative relationship between US stock returns and inflation in the post-war period. However, output and real interest rates appear to be positively rather than negatively correlated as required by the Mundell–Tobin effect. Fama's explanation for these correlations is that increases, say, in capital expenditure drive up output and real interest rates and, in a regime of monetary targets, higher output growth is associated with lower inflation. This combination gives a negative relationship between inflation and real interest rates. Fama's idea is that real interest rates are driven by IS rather than LM shifts. However, his explanation is not entirely satisfactory in that exogenous changes in capital expenditures amount to a *deus ex machina* in the story.

Monetary and Fiscal Policy and Long-term Interest Rates

Mishkin (1981a) and Plosser (1982) argued that the efficient markets methodology can be used to study the impact of monetary and fiscal policy on long-term nominal interest rates. If the bond market is efficient, the expected excess return y_{t+1} on long-term bonds should be zero:

$$E_t(y_{t+1}) = E_t(h_{t+1} - r_t - \delta_t) = 0 \qquad (2.64)$$

where $h_{t+1} = (q_{t+1} - q_t + c_t)/q_t$ is the holding period rate on bonds and δ_t is the risk or liquidity premium. In an efficient market, the only variables that can influence the price and hence the rate of interest at time $t + 1$ are those whose values could not be forecast at time t. Therefore, assuming a constant risk premium, long-term interest rates can be modelled by regressions such as

$$y_{t+1} = \delta + \sum_i \beta_i (X_{it+1} - E_t X_{it+1}) + e_{t+1} \qquad (2.65)$$

Here, the X_{it+1} are variables thought to influence long-term interest rates. The expectation of each X_{it} can be estimated from the regression

$$X_{it+1} = \sum_j \alpha_{ij} Z_{ijt} + u_{t+1} \qquad (2.66)$$

This set-up is obviously identical with (2.40) and (2.41) and, as Mishkin pointed out, more efficient estimates can be achieved by simultaneous estimation of (2.65) and (2.66). For variables likely to influence long-term interest rates Mishkin appealed to an inverted demand for money function and used the rate of money growth (M1 and M2), the rate of inflation and the rate of growth of real income. Using US quarterly data (1954–76), he found that unanticipated money growth had no significant effect on long-term interest rates, but both unanticipated output and inflation affected interest rates with the correct (positive) signs.

Plosser (1982, 1987) investigated the impact of government financing on

US long-term rates, with the policy variables being government purchases, non-monetized government debt held by the private sector and monetized debt. He found that the excess return was uncorrelated with its own past values as well as with past values of all three policy variables, suggesting that the bond market is indeed semi-strong form efficient. Estimation of (2.65)–(2.66) revealed that unanticipated money and debt had no effect on the long rate but unanticipated government spending had the orthodox positive effect.[36] However, slight evidence of a positive effect of debt on long rates was found when total debt was disaggregated to distinguish among differing maturities.

Several other studies have been carried out using this method and they have generally produced results with a similar flavour. Thus Merrick and Saunders (1986) found evidence that 'exogenous' US government (military) spending raised world interest rates in the 1980s, but no evidence that US deficits raised interest rates. Huang (1986) investigated the impact of monetized and non-monetized debt on *ex post* real returns on US corporate bonds, equities, government bonds and bills, and again could find little effect of either the debt variable or their total on these returns. Evans (1987) looked at Eurocurrency rates in Canada, Japan, France, the FRG, the UK and the USA. With few exceptions, he found that neither unanticipated government spending nor unanticipated deficits had any effect on long-term rates.

These results appear to suggest that long-term interest rates are invariant to monetary and debt policy, although not necessarily to tax-financed government spending. Mishkin's results are consistent with his finding (Mishkin, 1981b) that monetary policy effects on real interest rates work primarily through changes in inflation expectations although, as discussed earlier, this finding can itself be questioned. Plosser claims that his results 'provide little evidence that government bonds represent net wealth to the private sector' and are thus consistent with debt neutrality. Evans is even less cautious: 'My findings contradict the implications of conventional macroeconomic analysis'.

On closer inspection, however, these studies warrant no such conclusions. Equation (2.65) is unsatisfactory in many ways. If monetary policy is endogenous, with monetary and debt surprises responding to interest rate surprises, then $X_{it+1} - E_t X_{it+1}$ and e_{t+1} will be correlated and estimates of β_i will be inconsistent. Another source of inconsistency arises if the risk premium δ_t varies over time, as it would then be correlated with y_{t+1} and hence e_{t+1}. If δ_t is non-constant, it is also likely to be correlated with movements in the short-term rate so that a simple diagnostic is to test the hypothesis that $\alpha = 0$ in the regression

$$y_{t+1} = \delta + \alpha r_t + \sum_i \beta_i (X_{it+1} - E_t X_{t+1}) + u_{t+1} \tag{2.67}$$

Huizinga and Mishkin (1984) found that indeed $\alpha = 0$, but Campbell (1987) showed that this result depended on the time period chosen and was not true post-1979. In the UK, Mills and Stephenson (1986) found α to be significantly different from zero.

Since the excess return is equal to the risk premium on long-term bonds plus a noise component, if the risk premium does vary over time, then (2.65) amounts to a model of the risk premium and hence of the term structure and does not constitute a model of the long-term rate *per se*.[37] This distinction is important because it is quite possible to believe that monetary and debt policies have strong effects on the 'level' of interest rates but negligible effects on the term structure. In a portfolio balance model, this is equivalent to claiming that long and short bonds are perfect substitutes. Of course, even if assets are perfect substitutes, monetary policy can still influence the term structure as explained by Blanchard (1981). However, in his model, the term structure changes over time because unanticipated monetary policy affects variables such as output which cannot jump at a point in time. In the Mishkin–Plosser set-up, all unanticipated policies are sequences of random shocks: the model is incapable of distinguishing between shocks which do and shocks which do not affect slow-moving variables such as output. The former 'should' and the latter 'should not' affect the term structure. Thus, in addition to the usual problems of VARs, these tests have particularly low power.

The strategy underlying this research is one in which failure is described as success. The key hypothesis is that all current information is impounded in r_t, and hence y_{t+1} should be uncorrelated with anything other than new information available at time $t + 1$. In fact, it is easy to find variables which are known at time t and which are indeed correlated with y_{t+1}. Campbell (1987) documents a number of term structure variables which meet this criterion. Frankel and Dickens (1984) and Green and Na (1988) show that portfolio share data for the USA and UK respectively can be used to help explain the one-period-ahead excess returns on long-term bonds and other assets. In short, the results discussed do not warrant any strong conclusion about the impact of monetary and fiscal policy on long-term interest rates.

Monetary Announcements and Interest Rates

As discussed in the fourth part of section 2.2.1, a major implication of the rational expectations literature is the need to distinguish between the impact effect of new information and subsequent movements towards a new equilibrium. A key problem in this endeavour stems from the fact that financial markets are open almost continuously around the world and are generally believed to respond extremely rapidly to new information–within a few minutes or hours. Tests for efficiency which rely on monthly data or data of even lower frequency are likely to be biased towards acceptance. A financial market would have to be inefficient indeed if it needed a month or more to respond to new information.[38]

These considerations have led to a line of research aimed at investigating the very short term impact on market interest rates and asset prices of the announcement or publication of new data or 'news'. Particular interest has focused on the announcement of (provisional) money supply figures, especially because of the importance of monetary targets in the 1970s and 1980s in both the USA and the UK. Tests of the impact of the new information on the market can be carried out using regressions such as

$$q_t - q_{t-1} = a_0 + a_1(m_t - \mathrm{E}_{t-1}m_t) + a_2\mathrm{E}_{t-1}m_t + u_t \qquad (2.68)$$

Here, $\mathrm{E}_{t-1}m_t$ is expected money growth over the week (month) to which the current announcement refers, m_t is the rate of money growth which is announced and $q_t - q_{t-1}$ gives the change in asset price or interest rate between 'just' before and 'just' after the announcement. In practice, q_{t-1} is usually the closing price the day before the announcement and q_t is the closing price on the day of the announcement. In an efficient market q_{t-1} should incorporate all information up to but excluding the announcement. Hence a test for efficiency in (2.68) is that $a_2 = a_0 = 0$. Meanwhile, a_1 measures the effect of new information on prices. It is also easy to test more precisely the response time of the market by estimating regressions such as

$$q_{t+i} - q_{t-1} = a_{i0} + a_{i1}(m_t - \mathrm{E}_{t-1}m_t) + a_{i2}\mathrm{E}_{t-1}m_t + u_{it} \qquad i = 0,1,..$$
$$(2.69)$$

The extent to which the market's reaction to an announcement is delayed by one or more days can be traced out by examining the value and significance of a_{i1} as i is increased in successive regressions.

This line of research has largely been made possible by the activities of Money Market Services (MMS) which surveys 60 government bond dealers in the US once each week for their expectation of the weekly M1 change.[39] In the UK, a twice monthly survey is carried out among 20 money market dealers. The mean or median values of these surveys are generally able to accept standard rationality tests (see Grossman (1981) on US data and MacDonald and Torrance (1987a) on UK data). The US data also appear to contain additional information not available in a univariate time series model.

The consensus of the research on US data is that, since 1977, *anticipated* money growth (M1) has had no significant effect on short-term interest rates over the following 24 hours, whereas *unanticipated* money growth (i.e. a positive shock) tends to produce a significant increase in short-term interest rates. Urich (1982) pointed out that, if the monetary authority is following any systematic decision rule, the sign of a_1 is not known *a priori*. The market rate of interest contains information about both future interest rates and future money growth. Thus, if money growth turns out to be greater than expected, interest rates could either rise or fall.

There are four main hypotheses to account for the positive response of interest rates to unanticipated money. First, the inflation premium hypothesis asserts that the increased money is perceived to be a permanent rise in the money supply because the authorities have no counter-inflation credibility. The market expects that inflation will be higher in future; hence nominal interest rates must rise owing to the Fisher effect. Second, the liquidity or policy adjustment hypothesis asserts that the authorities do have credibility, and the unanticipated money is perceived to be caused by a shock to demand. Since the money supply will be held within its target range, interest rates will eventually have to be raised to achieve this. Third, the output hypothesis proposes that unanticipated money growth will lead to higher output and therefore higher short-term interest rates as the demand for money increases. Fourth, the portfolio shift hypothesis asserts that the demand for money could be higher because of a portfolio shift due to an increase in the risk premium on interest-bearing assets. In this event also, interest rates will rise.

Although these hypotheses have the same implications for the impact of unanticipated money on short-term interest rates, they have varying implications for its impact on other asset prices. This suggests estimating equations like (2.68) with different asset prices as the dependent variable. Hardouvelis (1984) argued that the inflation hypothesis would suggest a rise in long rates while the policy hypothesis would produce a fall or at least no change. However, while long rates may rise by less if the policy adjustment hypothesis is true, it is more difficult to see why they should actually fall and, indeed, Hardouvelis found that long rates did rise in response to a positive unanticipated money shock. More convincing is the argument that policy adjustments would imply an appreciation of the dollar, and the inflation effect a depreciation. Engel and Frankel (1984) and Hardouvelis both found that the dollar did indeed appreciate, thus providing some support for the policy adjustment hypothesis over the inflation hypothesis. Evidence against the output hypothesis was provided by Cornell (1983) who found that the stock market fell after a positive monetary shock. If such shocks were a portent of higher output, we would expect a rise in the stock market.

If the policy adjustment hypothesis is true, then we should observe activity consistent with central bank efforts to keep the money supply within the target range after a shock. In the USA there is some evidence in support of this proposition. Roley (1983b) found that where the announced values of the money figures fell outside the target range, the response of the short-term interest rate (in either direction) was considerably larger than if money was inside the target range. Girton and Nattress (1985) reported that unantici-pated money helped predict future actual and expected money with the correct negative sign. However, Cornell (1983) found that announcements of the monetary base (a policy instrument) had no effect on interest rates. Huizinga and Leiderman (1987) reported a complex pattern of interactions between M1, the base and short-term interest rates. However, the feedbacks from unanticipated money and unanticipated base to future expected and actual money and base were not wholly consistent with either the inflation or the policy adjustment hypothesis.[40]

Roley and Huizinga and Leiderman both found that the impact of mone-tary announcements on interest rates increased significantly after October 1979, following the change in the Federal Reserve's operating procedures from targeting the Federal Funds rate towards targeting the monetary base. This suggests that the response of interest rates to these announcements is connected, at least to some extent, to the operation of policy. Overall, in the USA, it is probably fair to conclude that the balance of academic opinion favours the policy adjustment hypothesis even though the balance of empirical evidence does not point quite so strongly in that direction (see Roley, 1987).

There has been less work on the impact of announcements in the UK. MacDonald and Torrance (1987a, b, 1988) have analysed the MMS forecasts of sterling M3 and M0 with mixed results. For 1981–5 both short and long rates rose in response to unanticipated sterling M3. For 1982–6 nominal and real long rates also responded positively to unanticipated sterling M3 with the differential in the magnitude of their response being suggestive of a Fisher effect.[41] These results are consistent with the inflation hypothesis. For 1984–6, however, unanticipated sterling M3 increased short rates but reduced long rates while unanticipated M0 had exactly the opposite effect. Apart from the effect of M0 on long rates, these results are consistent instead with the policy adjustment hypothesis. However, MacDonald and Torrance also found that, during 1984–6, unanticipated sterling M3 was followed by a *depreciation* of sterling against the deutschmark which is consistent with the inflation hypothesis. On the other hand, Goodhart and Smith (1985) had found that unanticipated sterling M3 produced an *appreciation* of sterling, but against the dollar. MacDonald and Torrance rationalize their own results as reflecting a shift in the market's perception of the Bank of England which, they claim, probably became more 'anti-inflation credible' over the 1980s. For M0, they argued that this aggregate is largely demand determined in the UK and if so the results are consistent with the portfolio shift hypothesis reflecting a movement out of long-dated assets into short-dated assets. Overall, however, the results of UK research do not yet justify a con-sensus view on the impact of monetary announcements. Given the uncer-tainty that has surrounded the immediate objectives of monetary policy in the 1980s, with the authorities switching between different monetary aggregates and between monetary and exchange rate targets, it is scarcely surprising that the market's response to unanticipated money is itself difficult to interpret.

In both UK and US research, it has been found that asset prices respond to announcements both on the day of the announcement and on the following day (see Smith and Goodhart (1985) on the UK and Urich (1982) on the USA). Since there is virtually no evidence of the effects of announcements persisting beyond day 2, it seems reasonable to conclude that the financial markets are rather efficient and broadly rational in their response to new information. However, the research in this area is concerned with announcements which give provisional data, virtually all of which are incorrect and sometimes differ widely from the final figures.[42] There is little econometric evidence but some anecdotal evidence to suggest that markets do not respond significantly to data revisions. It could be argued that markets which move in response to new information which is certainly incorrect, but which fail to respond to the subsequent news correcting those earlier estimates, are displaying inefficiency and irrationality of a rather fundamental nature.

2.3.3 The Structure of Interest Rates

The Term Structure

Expectations of future interest rates play a central role in term structure theory. B. Friedman (1980c) investigated the interest rate forecasts of a sample of US investment managers published in the Goldsmith–Nagan *Bond and Money Market Letter*. He found that they departed substantially from rationality and could easily be improved upon by simple regression techniques.[43] I would guess that a majority of economists would argue that observed market interest rates, as forward-looking variables, already constitute the highest quality expectational data available, and therefore that survey data which are non-rational cannot measure the market's true expectations (see Pesando, 1981). Of course, if this were true, it is hard to know what could constitute a falsification of rational expectations. Nevertheless, virtually all research on the term structure has utilized a theory-based approach to expectation formation.

The seminal empirical study is that of Meiselman (1962) who assumed the truth of the expectations theory and, conditional on this, tested a theory of expectation formation (adaptive expectations) which can be represented by

$$f_{t+k,\, t} - f_{t+k,\, t-1} = \alpha_k + \beta_k (r_t - f_{t,\, t-1}) + u_t \tag{2.70}$$

where r_t is the spot rate on one year bonds and $f_{t+k,\,t}$ is the one year forward rate at time t applicable to $t + k$. Under the expectations hypothesis

$$f_{t+k,\,t} = E_t r_{t+k} \tag{2.71}$$

Hence $r_t - f_{t,\,t-1}$ is the unanticipated part of the short-term rate at time t. Thus (2.70) states that expectations of future interest rates are revised in proportion to the error made in predicting the current spot rate. Moreover, since k can take on any (positive integer) value, Meiselman's theory is applicable to the entire structure of forward rates.[44] Meiselman estimated this model on bonds with implied forward rates k of between 1 and 30 years ahead using US data for 1901–54. He concluded that the data supported the expectations theory, and he found that the estimated values of β_k were positive and declining as k increased, implying that the current forecast error resulted in a smaller revision to expectations of spot rates in the more distant future than in the near future. Using analogous techniques on UK data, Grant (1964) and Dodds and Ford (1974) concluded against the expectations theory. However, they did find evidence for the hypothesis that there is a normal long-term rate of interest. This provides a partial reconciliation of their results with Meiselman, for, as discussed below, the pattern of Meiselman's β_k is consistent with mean-reverting behaviour of the long-term interest rate and this is also one possible characterization of the concept of a 'normal' rate.

Since Meiselman's contribution, the investigation of rational expectations and risk premiums have been the two principal research preoccupations. Expectations in Meiselman's model are rational if the coefficients of (2.70) are identical with those of the process generating the short rate itself. Sargent (1972) found that these coefficients actually differed substantially across the two equations and were therefore inconsistent with rational expectations. Modigliani and Shiller (1973) investigated rational expectations in the context of the preferred habitat model. They represented expectations of future short-term rates by least squares regressions

$$E_{t-1} r_t = \beta_0 + \sum_i \sum_j \beta_{ij} X_{it-j} \tag{2.72}$$

The X_{it-j} consisted of distributed lags of the short-term rate and inflation, thus implicitly separating real and nominal influences on r_t. Since the long rate R_t is postulated to be a weighted average of current and expected future short rates plus a variable risk premium k_t of unknown sign, it can be modelled by a regression such as

$$R_t = \delta_0 r_t + \sum_i \sum_j \delta_{ij} X_{it-j} + \alpha k_t + u_t \tag{2.73}$$

Modigliani and Shiller found that the estimated values of δ_0 decreased as the term to maturity of the long rate increased, a result which is consistent with the pattern of Meiselman's β_k. To test the hypothesis of rational expectations they used a bivariate VAR to generate inflation and nominal short-term interest rate forecasts. If it is assumed that k_t is independent of the variables that help predict inflation and short-term interest rates, the lag profiles of the VARs can be solved for the implied set of δ_{ij} in (2.73) and then compared with the δ_{ij} obtained by freely estimating (2.73). In contrast with Sargent (1972), Modigliani and Shiller found the correspondence between the two sets of estimates to be remarkably good and concluded in favour of rational expectations.

They also found evidence of a significant positive risk premium on long-term bonds which they measured by a moving standard deviation of the short rate. For the UK, Rowan and O'Brien (1970) and Burman and White (1972) found that measures of the variance of interest rates contributed to explaining the term structure. However, it has proved surprisingly difficult to discover the underlying source of such 'risk premiums'. According to most asset-pricing models, variations in asset supplies are likely to be a key determinant of risk premiums on individual assets. However, Modigliani and Sutch (1967) and Singleton (1980) could find no evidence that the US term structure was significantly influenced by the maturity composition of new or outstanding debt. Likewise, Goodhart and Gowland (1978) reported almost complete failure in their efforts to find any influences of debt supplies on UK term structure data. Meanwhile, evidence for the (risk neutral) efficient markets, rational expectations approach accumulated. Roll (1970), Phillips and Pippenger (1976) and Mishkin (1978) found evidence for the efficiency of the US bond market; Pesando (1978) found similar evidence for Canada. Goodhart and Gowland (1977) reported weaker results for the UK. While the 20 year and five year rates each approximated a random walk, the relation between the contemporaneous changes in the two rates was not consistent with the expectations theory.[45] Much of this literature focused on weak form aspects of market efficiency, i.e. the question of whether long-term bond rates follow a random walk. As Mishkin (1980) showed, even if long rates do follow a random walk, it is still possible for a systematic time-varying risk premium to exist unless, as Goodhart and Gowland found, short rates also follow a random walk.

The culmination of this line of research was a much cited paper by Sargent (1979) who tested the expectations theory by estimating a bivariate VAR model of the US long-term (five year) rate and short-term (three month treasury bill) rate. His principal contribution was to work out and explicitly test the relatively complex cross-equation restrictions implied by the theory. Over the period 1953–71 Sargent was unable to reject the restrictions implied by the expectations model. However, on closer inspection the results look suspect, as seven out of sixteen coefficients change sign between the unrestricted and restricted estimates of the model, and a further five coefficients change in magnitude by a factor of 10 or more. This strongly suggests what is now commonplace, namely that VAR tests have relatively low power. In this instance, the data would probably have accepted *any* restrictions and the results are therefore of little value. These suspicions were confirmed by Baillie and McMahon (1987), who re-examined Sargent's data using five lags of the short and long rate in estimating the initial VAR, rather than four as Sargent had done. This small difference was sufficient to reverse Sargent's results. Baillie and McMahon also examined Grant's (1964) UK data for 1922–62 and, for virtually all permutations of short and long rate, these data rejected the expectations hypothesis. Shiller (1979, 1981a) pointed out that the expectations model actually imposed more restrictions than were tested by Sargent whose specification implicitly assumed that the additional restrictions were satisfied. If the VAR is instead specified in a more general way and the additional restrictions tested, then Sargent's results are again reversed.

The VAR approach to testing the term structure typically produces rather complex non-linear restrictions. Since VARs also have low power, attention has increasingly turned to simpler tests of term structure theory. One possibility is to investigate the (one-period) excess return on long-term bonds given by

$$y_{t+1} = h_{t+1} - r_t = \frac{q_{t+1} - q_t + c_t}{q_t} - r_t \qquad (2.74)$$

Under the expectations hypothesis, $E_t y_{t+1} = 0$. Mishkin (1981a) and Plosser (1982) argued that, in the USA, y_{t+1} was indeed not predictable on the basis of information available at time t, but it is actually not difficult to find the contrary result. In addition to the studies cited in section 2.3.2, Jones and Roley (1983) investigated weekly data on three month and six month US treasury bills and found that several variables (including asset supplies and a moving average of the absolute value of past interest rate changes) were collectively significant in explaining y_{t+1}. Likewise, Campbell and Shiller (1984) and Campbell (1987) have documented term structure variables known at time t which help explain y_{t+1} in a variety of data sets of US bills and bonds. Outside the USA, Campbell and Clarida (1987) report that excess returns on short-term Euromarket paper contain predictable elements, and MacDonald and Speight (1988) report similar findings in a comparative study of the domestic markets of Belgium, Canada, the FRG, the UK and the USA. Campbell and Shiller have found that spreads between long and short rates often help predict the next period's excess return with a positive coefficient. Since q_{t+1} is inversely related to

R_{t+1}, this carries the implication that an increase in the long–short differential helps predict a decline in the long rate, whereas the expectations theory predicts exactly the opposite.[46]

A second possible strategy is to focus on the forward–spot rate differential. Under the expectations hypothesis the forward rate is equal to the expected future spot rate and the forward–spot differential should therefore help predict the direction of change of the spot rate (with a positive sign). If, however, the expectations hypothesis is false and term premiums are not zero but are dominated by (slowly moving) risk premiums, then the forward–spot differential should help predict future risk premiums rather than future interest rates *per se*. This insight was exploited in an ingenious paper by Fama (1984). Consider the regressions

$$y_{t+i+1} = \alpha_1 + \beta_{i1}\left(f_{t+i,t} - r_t\right) + e_{1t+i+1} \tag{2.75a}$$

$$r_{t+i} - r_t = \alpha_2 + \beta_{i2}\left(f_{t+i,t} - r_t\right) + e_{2t+i} \tag{2.75b}$$

If the expectations theory is true we would expect $\beta_{i2} = 1$, $\beta_{i1} = 0$. If, however, forward rates are dominated by risk premiums, then it will more nearly be true that $\beta_{i1} = 1$, $\beta_{i2} = 0$. Using 1959–82 monthly data on one to six month US treasury bills, Fama found that estimates of both β_{i1} and β_{i2} were invariably significantly positive and less than unity. Broadly similar results were obtained by Fama and Bliss (1987) for one to five year discount bonds, and by Mishkin (1988).

The single most important feature of these latter results is that forward rates contain information about both future spot rates and future risk premiums. They therefore provide further evidence against the simple expectations hypothesis. A second interesting feature is that, for bonds of more than one year's maturity, the forecasting power of forward rates (the value of β_{i2} in (2.75)) tends to increase as the time horizon i of the forecast increases, a result which was also reported by Shiller (1979). Fama and Bliss explained this seemingly counter-intuitive result with the argument that interest rates display stationary mean-reverting behaviour. Suppose that the short rate can be represented by

$$r_{t+1} = \delta r_t + (1 - \delta)r + u_{t+1} \tag{2.76}$$

where r is the mean value of r_t and $\delta < 1$. The T-steps-ahead forecast of r is given by

$$E_t r_{t+T} = \delta^T r_t + (1 - \delta^T)r \tag{2.77}$$

As T increases, δ^T approaches zero, and the constant mean value of r carries an increasing weight in the forecast.[47] Intuitively, therefore, forecasts into the more distant future can rely increasingly on the mean-reverting behaviour of the interest rate. Fama and Bliss showed that the behaviour of the one year rate was consistent with (2.76) but, for some maturities, the forward rate outperformed their estimate of (2.76) in predicting the future spot rate. Thus mean reversion does not seem to provide a complete explanation of the superior forecasting power of forward rates at longer maturities. However, the argument that interest rates display mean-reverting behaviour is important: first, because it has been a recurrent finding since Meiselman's work, and second because mean reversion is one possible characterization of the concept of a 'normal' rate of interest.

Overall, therefore, the weight of evidence decisively rejects the simple expectations hypothesis. This could be due either to the existence of time-varying risk premiums or to failure of the rational expectations assumption or to both.[48] In general, economists seem reluctant to abandon the rational expectations hypothesis. However, work aimed at characterizing the behaviour of term premiums has produced few clear-cut results. It has proved exceedingly difficult to establish firm connections between asset supplies and the term structure, although there is evidence that volatility in interest rates affects the term structure as might be expected. Moreover, the size and time variation in risk premiums needed to account fully for departures from the expectations theory are considerable (Mankiw and Summers, 1984). For these reasons, the rational expectations assumption has also been questioned. The most direct efforts to do this involve variance bounds tests which are discussed next.

Variance Bounds Tests

The expectations theory is a simple application of the present value model. These theories impose restrictions on the relationship between current and expected future returns on securities. The research summarized in this section starts from the observation that the present value model also imposes restrictions on the variances of asset returns (see Shiller, 1979, 1981b). First, define the *ex post* rational price q_t^* of a security as the present value of the *realized* future payments on the security. Clearly q_t^* is known only at some future date $t + T$ $(T > 0)$ when payments on the security are known. According to the present value model, the actual current price q_t equals the present value of *expected* future payments. Thus the actual price constitutes a forecast of the *ex post* rational price:

$$q_t = E_t q_t^* \tag{2.78}$$

Under rational expectations, therefore

$$q_t^* = q_t + e_t \tag{2.79}$$

where e_t is a white noise error which is uncorrelated with q_t. It follows that the variances σ_{xx} are related by

$$\sigma_{q^*q^*} = \sigma_{qq} + \sigma_{ee} \qquad (2.80)$$

and, since variances are strictly positive,

$$\sigma_{q^*q^*} > \sigma_{qq} \qquad (2.81)$$

Thus the variance of prices should be less than the variance of the present value of actual (*ex post*) future payments. In any time series, the *ex post* price q_t^* can be calculated using the present value formula. Hence the truth of the inequality (2.81) can easily be checked. Similar inequalities involving dividend or coupon payments can also be established (see Shiller, 1981b). Tests of inequalities such as (2.81) are generally known as variance bounds tests.

Variance bounds tests have mostly been applied to the stock market. However, they can equally well be used to test the expectations theory. This asserts that long-term interest rates R_t constitute a forecast of the average of future short rates. Writing R_t^* as the *ex post* average of future short rates, we have

$$R_t^* = R_t + e_t \qquad (2.82)$$

Hence

$$\sigma_{R^*R^*} > \sigma_{RR} \qquad (2.83)$$

This suggests than the variance of long-term interest rates should be less that the variance of average actual future short rates. As Shiller (1979) points out, exactly the reverse is true.[49]

Shiller also drew attention to a parallel argument attributed to Culbertson (1957) concerning the relationship between one-period returns on long-term and short-term bonds. Under the expectations hypothesis the expected value $y_{t+1} = h_{t+1} - r_t$ of the excess return on long-term bonds is zero. However, the one-period return h_{t+1} on long bonds is approximately equal to the change in the long-term interest rate. When compared with the short rate, *ex post* movements in h_{t+1} appear far too volatile to be consistent with the expectations hypothesis. For example, in the UK over the period 1972–85, the three month local authority rate varied between a high of 18.5 per cent per annum and a low of 4.56 per cent per annum, whereas the three month return on ten year bonds, calculated using monthly data as $(q_{t+3} - q_t + c_t)/q_t$, varied between $+36.4$ per cent per annum and -14.7 per cent per annum. The quarter-by-quarter variations in the two rates were equally disparate.

However, it transpires that the logic underlying variance bounds tests is flawed to some extent. Flavin (1983) proved that the small-sample properties of these tests differ appreciably from their asymptotic properties and could easily give rise to violations of the inequalities in a sample, even when there are no violations in the population. Kleidon (1986) attacked the stationarity assumption implicit in most variance bounds tests. If, as appears to be the case, dividends are non-stationary, then any dividend increase is perceived as permanent and will therefore have a sharp impact on stock prices. Thus variance bounds will appear to be violated even though the present value model may be true. However, this defence of the model carries less conviction in relation to term structure theory because of the evidence that short-term rates of interest may indeed be stationary as required (see the first part of section 2.3.3). Overall, the questions raised in these interchanges remain troublesome and unresolved. The most compelling argument is also the simplest. Any time series plot of a short-term rate r_t with the comparable *ex post* one-period rate h_{t+1} on a long-term bond (e.g. Shiller, 1979) immediately prompts Culbertson's question: 'What sort of expectation could possibly have produced this result?'

Evidence on Asset Substitutability

In principle, differences in asset substitutability can provide an account of movements in the structure of interest rates (including the term structure). Measures of the degree of substitutability among assets are provided by the own- and cross-elasticities of demand with respect to interest rates. However, these elasticities are essentially descriptive and do not identify the source of the imperfect substitutability, whether it be in differences in risk, liquidity or other factors. Research which aims to provide a 'deeper' explanation of interest elasticities (in terms of the CAPM) is considered in the fourth part of section 2.3.3; the present section is concerned solely with work involving the estimation of asset demand functions and in which the principal purpose is to use the estimated asset demands to determine interest rates.

Early efforts to implement the Tobin–Brainard approach such as that of Miller (1971) relied mainly on static models of asset demands, but it quickly became apparent that such models could not explain the autocorrelated behaviour of asset holdings. Indeed, Tobin and Brainard (1986) in their 'Pitfalls' paper already advocated the use of 'general disequilibrium' models. The characteristic of such models, discussed by G. Smith (1975), is that the demand for any particular asset in the short run has to be related not just to its own disequilibrium but also to the disequilibria in all other asset holdings which may 'spill over' onto the demand for the asset in question. Suppose that there are n assets $(X_{1t}, \ldots, X_{nt})$, holdings of which sum to total wealth W_t. Following the treatment in section 2.2.3, the static or long-run demand X_{it}^* for any asset can be written as a linear function of interest rates r_{it} and m other variables Z_{it}:[50]

$$\frac{X_{it}^*}{W_t} = x_{it}^* = a_{i0} + \sum_{j=1}^{n} a_{ij} r_{jt} + \sum_{j=1}^{m} b_{ij} Z_{jt} \qquad i = 1, \ldots, n \qquad (2.84)$$

The constraint that desired asset holdings must sum to wealth implies that $\Sigma x_{it}^* = 1$ and that the coefficients in (2.84) must obey the adding-up restrictions

$$\sum_i a_{ij} = 0 \qquad \sum_i b_{ij} = 0 \qquad \sum_i a_{i0} = 1 \qquad \forall j$$

In the short run, because of transactions and other costs, asset holdings may differ from their desired or long-run level. The 'pitfalls' model is a partial adjustment model and specifies that asset holdings are adjusted over time in response to deviations of previous actual from desired holdings, and other factors, i.e.

$$X_{it} - X_{it-1} = \sum_{j=1}^{n} \alpha_{ij} (X_{jt}^* - X_{jt-1}) + \sum_{j=1}^{1} \beta_{ij} Y_{jt} \qquad i = 1, \ldots, n \qquad (2.85)$$

Here, the $X_{jt}^* - X_{jt-1}$ are deviations of actual from desired holdings, and the Y_{jt} are variables which are thought to influence the adjustment process directly. The adding-up restrictions in (2.85) are

$$\sum_i \alpha_{ij} = 1 \qquad \sum_i \beta_{ij} = 0 \qquad \forall j$$

The X_{it}^* are unobservable, but substituting (2.84) into (2.85) yields equations which can be estimated directly by least squares regression.

The 'pitfalls' model was generated and solved using entirely calibrated (i.e. postulated) coefficients and artificial data. However, empirically estimated 'pitfalls' models have often proved to have rather unsatisfactory properties. In general, estimated interest elasticities and speeds of adjustment of actual to desired asset holdings are appreciably lower than intuition would suggest is plausible. Green and Kiernan (1989) show that the combination of multi-collinearity and measurement error among the interest rates can produce estimated interest rate coefficients which are substantially too small in magnitude and sometimes of the wrong sign in relation to their true value. Multicollinearity is almost inevitable if assets are close substitutes, as the interest rates on such assets will tend to move closely together. Measurement error arises in the need to utilize some proxy for the unobserved expected (real) returns on long-term assets as explanatory variables. A further problem in evaluating estimated 'pitfalls' models is that the estimated interest rate coefficients are linear combinations of the a_{ij} from (2.84) and the α_{ij} from (2.85). Theory can be used to impose constraints on the structure of the a_{ij} (section 2.2.3) and on the α_{ij} (see Hunt and Upcher, 1979). However, linear combinations of the a_{ij} and α_{ij} are unconstrained as to size and sign, and it is these linear combinations which determine the simulation properties of interest rates in the model from period to period. Even if the estimated a_{ij} and α_{ij} appear plausible, their linear combinations can still give rise to implausible interest rate movements in simulation experiments.

These considerations have led Tobin and his associates to utilize a more Bayesian approach to the estimation of such models. This resolves the problems of multicollinearity and measurement error by imposing more 'plausible' values on coefficients with large standard errors. However, it requires the prior specification of all the coefficients in the model including their covariance matrix. This is potentially a Herculean task, and one which is subject to complex consistency conditions (see G. Smith, 1981). Backus et al. (1980) report that the use of prior information was successful in removing virtually all the 'peculiar' elements in the matrices of adjustment coefficients, but still left certain anomalies in the matrices of interest rate responses. However, the overall simulation properties of their model were reasonable.

With these problems, it is not surprising that dynamic portfolio models have not proved popular in small-scale research. Hendershott's (1977) flow of funds model of the US contains considerable complexity but explains only three market-clearing interest rates. Green's (1984) model of the UK is more ambitious in attempting to explain seven market-clearing interest rates in a five-sector model, but he reports difficulty in simulating his model. Kearney and MacDonald (1986) report on a one-sector four-market model of the UK, but also find it necessary to use prior information to obtain satisfactory results. Christofides (1980) has studied the Canadian term structure utilizing the 'pitfalls' approach treating short and long bonds as less than perfect substitutes.[51] Few general conclusions can be gleaned from all these efforts, except that the wide range of coefficient values which was obtained underlines the difficulties discussed above.

Critics of the 'pitfalls' approach have drawn attention to further problems, caused in particular by the large scale of such models, the simplicity of the partial adjustment model and the treatment of expectations. Some of these issues have been addressed in a series of papers by B. Friedman and Roley. On the questions of scale and disaggregation B. Friedman (1980a) compared the estimation and simulation results of an eight-sector model of the US corporate bond market with that of a two-sector ('demand' and 'supply') model. He concluded that sectoral disaggregation was only marginally useful in improving the performance of the model, and therefore that disaggregation was not an essential feature of the pitfalls approach. B. Friedman (1977) also introduced a more general dynamic model which he described as the 'optimal marginal adjustment model' and which is based on the argument that investors find it less costly to allocate new flows of funds such as income receipts than to rearrange existing portfolio holdings.[52] This gives rise to the following adjustment equation:

$$X_{it} - X_{it-1} = \sum_{j} \delta_{ij} (x_{jt}^* W_{t-1} - X_{jt-1}) + x_{it}^* (W_t - W_{t-1}) \quad i = 1, \ldots, n$$

$$(2.86)$$

Here, x_{jt}^* is the long-run portfolio share of the jth asset given by (2.83). When (2.84) is substituted into (2.86) we obtain a set of regression equations with a series of non-linear terms in interest rates and wealth. B. Friedman (1977, 1979b, 1980b, d, 1981) and Roley (1980, 1981, 1983a) have estimated disaggregated models of the US corporate and government bond markets using different versions of (2.86). Indeed, Roley (1980, 1981) extends (2.85) to allow the speed of adjustment of asset holdings to differ as between net inflows and net outflows of funds. Judged mainly by simulation properties the Friedman–Roley approach has proved quite successful. However, it too is not without problems. First, it is extremely difficult to derive the model from a simple underlying objective function, whereas the standard partial adjustment model can be derived from the maximization of a quadratic cost function subject to the usual budget constraint (see Sharpe, 1973). Second, the optimal marginal adjustment model imposes few constraints on the estimated coefficients. Symmetry of the matrix of interest rate responses can be recovered and tested (see Roley, 1983a). However, very little can be said about many of the other coefficients.

A further criticism of the Tobin–Brainard approach in general concerns the treatment of expectations. If, as is common, redemption yields on bonds and dividend yields on equities are used as regressors, then the researcher is implicitly assuming that interest rates will remain constant indefinitely, and this will be inconsistent with the underlying dynamics of the model itself. However, this defect can also be rectified. Keating (1985) has modelled asset price expectations in an empirical portfolio model as being rational. Friedman and Roley (1979b) have compared the performance of portfolio models under three different hypotheses about asset price expectations: unitary (zero capital gains), rational and autoregressive (i.e. an autoregression of past values of interest rates). These expectations were embedded in a model of the US corporate bond market. Since unitary expectations are nested in autoregressive and rational expectations, but the two latter hypotheses cannot be nested in one another, these hypotheses can only be tested on a pairwise basis. However, since unitary expectations outperform rational expectations and autoregressive expectations outperform unitary expectations (in F tests), on the not strictly valid assumption of transitivity, we could conclude with Friedman and Roley that the evidence favours autoregressive expectations. However tentative this result, it is yet another interesting echo of the considerable amount of disparate evidence that interest rate expectations are formed in a mean-reverting (autoregressive) manner, consistent, that is, with a belief in the existence of a 'normal' rate of interest.

Inverted Portfolio Models

Conventional portfolio models have had less success than might have been expected in explaining portfolio behaviour and, by inference, interest rates. In addition to the difficulties already discussed, an important methodological problem is posed by the way in which portfolio models are invariably used to determine interest rates. When estimated asset demands are inverted and the result described as showing the effects on interest rates of exogenous shocks to asset supplies in the context of a freely clearing market, the implicit assumption is that it is *exogenous* asset supplies which determine the *endogenous* interest rates. However, this implies that the regression of an asset quantity on interest rates does not estimate a demand curve; indeed, it is not a meaningful exercise since it amounts to regressing an exogenous variable on a collection of endogenous variables. If this argument is accepted, then the appropriate way of modelling interest rates is to regress an (endogenous) interest rate on (exogenous) asset supplies rather than the other way round.

This insight was used by Frankel and Engel (1984) in an analysis of foreign currency risk premiums and has subsequently been applied to other asset returns. Their key contribution was to demonstrate the simple and intimate connection between portfolio demand functions and properly specified interest rate equations. As shown in section 2.2.3, the SML of the CAPM (2.32) can be derived by inverting a standard mean–variance portfolio demand function. Suppose that the nth asset is a safe asset; then (2.32) reduces to

$$h^e_{1t+1} - h_{nt+1} = \theta\Omega_{11}x_{1t} \tag{2.87}$$

Under rational expectations

$$h_{1t+1} = h^e_{1t+1} + u_{t+1} \tag{2.88}$$

Substituting (2.87) in (2.88) and noting that u_{t+1} is orthogonal to h^e_{1t+1}, we obtain a set of regression equations

$$y_{1t+1} = h_{1t+1} - h_{nt+1} = \theta\Omega_{11}x_{1t} + u_{t+1} \tag{2.89}$$

Equations (2.89) are $n - 1$ regressions of excess returns on portfolio shares. They constitute a model which is consistent with mean–variance asset demands and the CAPM under rational expectations. The matrix of coefficients $\theta\Omega_{11}$ in this regression is proportional to the covariance matrix Ω_{11} of asset returns with the factor of proportionality being the coefficient of relative risk aversion θ. Moreover

$$E_t(h_{1t+1} - h^e_{1t+1})\,(h_{1t+1} - h^e_{1t+1})' = \Omega_{11} \tag{2.90}$$

i.e. the residual covariance matrix of the regression model is an estimate of the conditional coveriance matrix of asset returns which, under rational expectations, is also equal to agents' perceptions of this covariance matrix. It is possible to estimate (2.89) under the constraints (2.90). This also delivers an estimate of the coefficient of relative risk aversion.

This set-up allows for time variation in conditional expected excess returns which, in turn, implies the existence of time-varying risk premiums. The latter emanate from changes in asset supplies which alter the weight x_{it} of each asset in the portfolio. This, in turn, changes asset betas and hence their risk premiums. Here, therefore, time-varying risk premiums are attributable entirely to time-varying asset supplies, with risks Ω_{11} remaining constant. Equation (2.89) also shows clearly that, even in an efficient market, if agents are risk averse, information dated at time t can help predict excess returns at time $t + 1$. One caveat concerning (2.89) is that, in practice, it assumes that the only errors are expectational. This seems rather implausible and, if there are also errors in asset demands, OLS will not produce consistent estimates of $\theta\Omega_{11}$. This issue has not yet been squarely faced in the literature.

Frankel (1985) and Frankel and Dickens (1984) estimated (2.89) on post-war US data and obtained ambiguous results. On the one hand they found significant evidence that portfolio shares helped explain asset returns, but that the CAPM restrictions (2.90) were rejected by the data. On the other hand, when thse restrictions were (invalidly) imposed, portfolio shares were found to have very little influence on interest rates. Frankel took this as evidence against the importance of portfolio effects, but since the restrictions were invalidly imposed on the data this interpretation could be questioned. Similar investigations were carried out by Green (1987, 1988, 1990) and Green and Na (1988) using UK monthly data from 1971 onwards. They obtained broadly similar results, namely that the data rejected the CAPM but that portfolio data made a significant contribution to explaining the time variation in excess returns. Green (1988, 1990) obtained the curious result that the restrictions given by (2.90) were accepted, but the estimated coefficient of relative risk aversion was significantly negative. This is inconsistent with simultaneous mean–variance optimization and portfolio diversification. Green and Na investigated variables other than portfolio shares, and found that variables such as tax rates, aggregate consumption and dividend yields all had a significant effect on excess returns, as did portfolio shares.

The next logical step in this line of research has been to relax the assumption of constant risks Ω_{11}. A key tool in this endeavour has been Engle's (1982) autoregressive conditional heteroscedasticity (ARCH) family of models for error variances. The generalized autoregressive conditional heteroscedasticity (GARCH) model starts with the linear regression model

$$Y_t = X_t\beta + e_t \tag{2.91}$$

The random variable e_t in (2.91) is said to follow a GARCH(p, q) process if

$$E_{t-1}e_t = 0$$

$$V_{t-1}e_t = h_t = \alpha_0 + \sum_{i=1}^{q}\alpha_i^2 e_{t-i} + \sum_{i=1}^{p}\beta_i h_{t-i} \tag{2.92}$$

where V_{t-1} is the variance conditional on information available at time $t - 1$ and $\alpha_0 > 0$, $\alpha_i > 0$, $\beta_i > 0$ (see Bollerslev, 1986; Engle and Bollerslev, 1986). Equation (2.92) states that the conditional variance at time $t - 1$ is equal to a weighted sum of past conditional variances and past squared errors. Put simply, the ARCH class of models is analogous to Box–Jenkins time series models. The standard ARMA model is an *ad hoc* model of the conditional mean of a time series expressing it as a function of its own past values (AR) and the new information provided by successive white noise shocks (MA). The GARCH process is just a form of ARMA model, but of the conditional variance, with the forcing variables (the white noise shocks) appropriately scaled to the correct metric (i.e. squared). Thus the h_{t-i} represent the persistence in the conditional variance while the $\alpha_i e_{t-i}^2$ represent the new information in each period's squared error about the next period's variance. As an example, the first-order ARCH process

$$h_t = \alpha_0 + \alpha_1 e_{t-1}^2 \tag{2.93}$$

postulates that observations with a relatively large variance will tend to be followed by other observations with a large variance. Theory has little guidance to offer on variables that might determine movements in the variance over time; although in principle there is no reason why ARCH models could not be extended to include more 'economic' determinants of the variance. However, since theory does predict that the variance is a suitable measure of risk, ARCH models have become increasingly popular in the analysis of asset price movements. ARCH processes provide a more systematic, even if *ad hoc*, method for modelling time variation in risks.

As this is a relatively new field, few general results are yet available. Bollerslev (1987) studied a time series model of US asset prices using the

GARCH model and found evidence of persistence in the variance of key series accompanied by a lack of autocorrelation in the mean. This has a natural and appealing interpretation as reflecting 'tranquil' and 'volatile' periods, although there still remains the question of whether there are deeper underlying causes of tranquillity and volatility. Bollerslev et al. (1988) estimated (2.89) on US aggregate data, using a GARCH model of the residual variances, and reported an average economy-wide coefficient of relative risk aversion of 0.5. Friedman and Kuttner (1988) obtained a value of 2 for this parameter. These values appear more plausible than that of 110 reported by Frankel and Dickens (1984). However, these new results still include various anomalous features. Friedman and Kuttner found that investors discount past information about risks extremely rapidly, a rather surprising result, and Bollerslev et al. found that variables such as aggregate consumption also helped predict asset returns.

ARCH models can also be applied to the term structure and early results suggest that here too there is significant time variation in the variances and covariances of the excess returns on bills and bonds (see Engle et al. 1987, 1988).

Relatively little work on ARCH models has been done in the UK. In a comprehensive but mainly descriptive study of weekly data, Dickens (1987) found significant time variation in the variance of returns on a selection of UK asset prices. Hall et al. (1989) have estimated a hybrid version of the CAPM, including both consumption and portfolio risks and a GARCH model of the error variances, in an effort to explain excess returns on selected stock market industry groups.

The CAPM and ICAPM respectively predict that *either* portfolio *or* aggregate consumption data can be used to predict asset returns. However, as is clear from the preceding summary, several empirical papers using inverted portfolio models conclude that both portfolio and aggregate consumption data are needed to explain asset returns. Theory has yet to account for these findings. Nevertheless it seems clear that the ARCH class of models will prove important in the future as a framework for studying interest rates and asset prices.

2.4 CONCLUSIONS

A survey of this kind is unlikely to be able to offer many concluding remarks which are simultaneously general and interesting. Nevertheless, there are a few points which appear to be worth making.

On the theoretical side, there is a vast body of literature on interest rate determination and, in one perspective, much of this looks like a very settled area. New theoretical results often involve the application of known techniques to new circumstances, such as the use of portfolio balance models to study the implications of the financial structure of a particular country. From another perspective, however, this is still an area of considerable original activity. If it is possible to sum up the main outstanding issue, it is to characterize the movement of interest rates over time under risk aversion and (possibly) rational expectations. This endeavour was well under way in the 1950s and 1960s but was side-tracked to some extent in the 1970s, when rational expectations prompted a long new look at risk neutral arbitrage models. In the most recent decade, new analytical tools have provided a fresh impetus to the study of rational risk averse agents in the context of stochastic intertemporal optimizing models. Much of this literature is very technical and it is too early to assess which are the most durable contributions. A closely related issue is that of the interaction between interest rates, asset stocks, and output and prices. The dynamics of interest rate movements under rational expectations and risk neutrality are now quite well understood, but it still remains to work out in full the comparable results when agents are risk averse.

On the empirical side, there is clearly more work to be done, although such work may in itself prompt new thoretical puzzles and insights. The determinants of short-term real interest rates are beginning to be understood in broad outline, but those of long-term real interest rates are much less well documented. Since it is generally reckoned that it is long-term real interest rates which play a central role in determining expenditure decisions and hence in the process of real monetary interactions, this is obviously an area of great importance. As far as the structure of interest rates is concerned, the expectations model is clearly dead if not yet decently buried. However, it is still a matter of dispute as to how far the model fails because of time-varying risk premiums and how far because of non-rational expectations. Likewise, if the existence of time varying risk premiums is accepted, as it surely must be, it is unclear as to how far such risk premiums are caused by variations in asset supplies or independent variations in risks. Promising tools for studying these issues include the ARCH class of models as well as the intertemporal optimizing models which have not been covered in this survey.

A vast quantity of recent literature has been concerned with tightly specified intertemporal optimizing models. No doubt these models do have a key role to play in understanding asset prices and returns, but at present they are being developed at a very high level of abstraction, divorced in particular from important constraints which are present in real-world capital markets. If they do not make room for such constraints, these models may end up in the same class as the expectations theory of the term structure – an invaluable expositional tool but constituting a dead end as far research aimed at understanding interest rates is concerned. Finally, research on the structure of interest rates has particularly emphasized the term structure. If agents are risk averse, as seems certain, the determinants of interest rates on different groups of assets are intimately connected. This in turn suggests the need for more research on the relationships among returns on different asset groups, such as stocks and bonds, and less on the time series properties of individual asset returns taken in isolation.

Notes

1 Edwards and Khan (1985) review the principles of interest rate determination in developing countries, Sargent (1987a) is a standard textbook reference to intertemporal monetary models and Bicksler (1979) contains major but now quite dated surveys of the literature on stock prices and returns. Other related surveys include Fischer (1988) on macroeconomics, Branson and Henderson (1984) on the specification of asset demands in open economy models, Leroy (1982) on expectations models of asset prices, Shiller (1987) on the term structure of interest rates and, of course, the other chapters in this volume.

2 See especially Clower (1965) and Leijonhufvud (1968).

3 Pigou (1943) was the architect of the real balance effect, but its logic was more fully explored by Archibald and Lipsey (1958) and Patinkin (1965). Textbooks concentrate on the role of the real balance effect in the theory of income determination, but its role in the theory of interest is equally important.

4 In Metzler's paper the interest-bearing asset was common stock. Government-indexed bonds are used here to retain conformity with IS–LM. This does not affect the argument or the ensuing discussion of the significance of Metzler's results.

5 The argument was resuscitated more recently by Barro (1974). An alternative interpretation of Metzler's analysis focusing on the inside–outside money distinction is given by Wood (1980). See Niehans (1978) for an overall assessment of Metzler's work, and Buiter and Tobin (1979) for a review of the debt neutrality debate.

6 An alternative attempt to rationalize the classical invariance proposition is Milton Friedman's (1970) suggestion of an horizontal IS curve. In this case the interest rate is held constant by perfect arbitrage between financial assets and real aasets. However, it is difficult to regard this as anything other than a special case which is not very interesting.

7 It can be argued that, even without wealth, IS-LM provides a consistent specification of asset market equilibrium; see McCaleb and Sellon (1980).

8 This is a simplified version of the model studied by Blanchard (1981). The key interest rate in Blanchard's model is the return on equities, with the term structure of interest rates being determined by arbitrage conditions. To maintain comparability with IS-LM, the exposition here assumes that bonds are the only interest-bearing asset. These bonds are defined as perpetuities each paying a coupon of £1.

9   This is not always a good assumption. Apart from the debt problems of Third World governments, there have been instances of default by the governments of major industrial countries. In general, such defaults are caused by technical problems in the transmission of payments but, if the security is a one month bill, a delay of just one or two days in repayment can impose significant costs on the lenders, and there is evidence that such delays do have an impact on subsequent interest rate movements (see Zivney and Marcus, 1989).

10   The theory has old roots. Hicks (1939) and Culbertson (1957) are frequently cited references, but Fisher (1930) and other writers also expounded some of the main ideas.

11   The notation E_t in (2.10) and (2.11) means 'the expectation conditional on information at time t', the 'gross' rate of interest is 1 plus the interest rate and the Π notation means take the product over the range of i. The formula given in (2.11) is often linearized by taking logarithms on both sides and using the approximation $\ln(1 + r_t) \approx r_t$. This gives the actual long rate as the arithmetic average of expected future short rates.

12   Analogous formulae can be developed for term premiums for two or more periods.

13   Analogous formulae can be developed for bonds held for two or more periods. The return on an asset held for a specified period is usually called 'the holding period return'.

14   The argument here is simplified to omit side conditions needed to justify making n large. See Mishkin (1978, 1980) and Begg (1984) for further discussion.

15   The exact calculation of the forward rate for non-discount bonds must also allow for coupon receipts and payments.

16   It is often said that long-term bonds suffer from capital risk and short-term bonds from income risk. This is not altogether precise as, in each case, the nature of the risk really depends on the investor's time horizon.

17   The problem can be seen by referring back to (2.12) which was derived from (2.10) assuming perfect foresight. If interest rates evolve stochastically, we cannot use (2.10) to derive a stochastic version of (2.12) because the expectation of the product $(1 + r_t) \ldots (1 + r_{t+n-1})$ is not equal to the product of the expectations $E_t(1 + r_t) \ldots E_t(1 + r_{t+n-1})$. This was pointed out by Cox et al. (1981b) among others. Campbell (1986) made clear the difference between versions of the expectations hypothesis in which term premiums are identically zero and those in which they are simply constant over time.

18   See Tobin and Brainard (1963, 1968). The notation A_x stands for the partial derivative $\partial A/\partial x$.

19   This also follows from Walras' law. Equations (2.21)–(2.24) constitute a closed system so that equilibrium in any two markets necessarily implies equilibrium in the third market.

20   Tobin has always been careful to avoid imposing a unit wealth elasticity. His asset demands are often linear homogeneous in wealth but include as an argument the income-to-wealth ratio. This is a natural variable to use in tying down long-run savings behaviour (see Tobin and Buiter, 1976, 1980).

21   In the many-asset case, an open market operation involving money raises all rates. Debt management has the same predictable effect on the two assets

involved, but its effect on the rates on other assets is ambiguous. A wealth-augmenting increase in the supply of any asset has the same qualitative effects as in the three-asset case.

22 Mean–variance utility functions can be thought of as quadratic approximations to a von Neumann–Morgenstern utility function. They can be shown to provide arbitrarily good approximations of this type (see Samuelson, 1970; Markowitz, 1987).

23 In the following developments the time subscripts are suppressed as there is only one time period in the model. The model is formulated using portfolio shares as the object of choice in order to make the subsequent exposition easier. However, asset holdings can also be treated as the object of choice (see Walsh, 1983; Green and Keating, 1988).

24 The slope of the capital market line represents the market price of risk measured in terms of the standard deviation of return. See Roll (1977) for a discussion of the differences in representation of the CAPM when risk is measured using the variance as against the standard derivation. Clearly, since $S = V^{\frac{1}{2}}$, the two representations are logically identical.

25 The mean–variance model can also be used to study the term structure (see Roley, 1979).

26 This concept of efficiency refers solely to the extent to which prices fully reflect available information. As Tobin (1984) points out, this is a rather weak concept of efficiency. However, it is widely used in the context of financial markets.

27 This presentation assumes that no Z_{ij} helps predict more than one X_i. If some Z_{ij} do help predict more than one X_i, restrictions analogous to but more complex than (2.43) are easily derived.

28 The difference between the constant terms in (2.48) and (2.49) gives the unknown constant real interest rate, i.e. $\mu = a_{20}(1 - a_{12}) - a_{10}(1 + a_{11})$. Dwyer (1981) studies a more general version of this model.

29 Sargent (1973) argued that a rise in the rate of interest increases the velocity of money, and thus increases the price level (see also Barsky and Summers, 1988). However, this presumes that price level movements are associated mainly with movements in velocity rather than with the ratio of money to real income. In fact, Shiller and Seigel (1977) showed that, for UK data (1880–1970), the reverse is true. Shiller and Seigel proposed instead an explanation based on wealth effects in asset demands, but this too has been disputed (see Lee and Petruzzi, 1987).

30 See also the comment by MacCallum (1984) and the reply by Summers (1986).

31 Pesando (1976) reviews the US and Canadian evidence; Demery and Duck (1978) is the main study of the UK.

32 Fama used the rate of change of the value of money as the left-hand side variable. This is approximately minus the rate of inflation and leads to the prediction that $a_1 = -1$ rather than $a_1 = +1$ as discussed in the text.

33 An exception is Peek (1982) who finds that US data are consistent with the tax-adjusted Fisher effect. However, he treats survey expectations as exogenous and his results are therefore suspect.

34 Note that what is at issue is the relative size of the error variances σ_{uu} and σ_{vv}.

The variances of μ_t and π_{t+1} give only limited (and possibly misleading) information about σ_{uu} and σ_{vv}.

35 A similar pattern appears to have emerged immediately after the sharp increases in the Federal Reserve discount rate (practically an equivalent regime change) in June 1920). In the post-war era Peek and Wilcox (1987), using survey-based estimates of inflation expectations, also find significant differences in the behaviour of the real interest rate across regime changes.

36 Since government spending can be financed either by tax increases or sales of monetized or non-monetized debt, an increase in government spending, holding debt constant, is equivalent to a tax-financed increase in spending.

37 Both Mishkin and Plosser acknowledge this point in their introductions but lose sight of it as the argument proceeds.

38 Reported correlations between excess returns and lagged data such as those mentioned in the third part of section 2.2.2 are consistent with efficiency as they could reflect systematic time variation in a risk premium. Inefficiency is associated with information which could be exploited for profit but which is not so exploited.

39 The survey was carried out twice weekly until February 1980; see Grossman (1981) for further details.

40 A limitation of the Huizinga–Leiderman results is that anticipated and unanticipated base money had to be constructed from a univariate time series model and may therefore not be fully comparable with the MMS anticipations data on M1.

41 MacDonald and Torrance used the return on index-linked gilts as a measure of the real interest rate. It should be noted that some of the features of index-linked gilts are such that their return does not correspond precisely to a real rate (see MacDonald and Torrance, 1987b).

42 The provisional money figures are relatively more reliable than certain other statistics. Provisional balance of payments data are notoriously unreliable and yet announcements of these data for the UK have had a (just) significant impact on the government bond yield (see Goodhart and Smith, 1985).

43 See also Taylor (1988) on the general economic forecasts of a sample of UK investment managers.

44 Thus (2.70) is a generalization of adaptive expectations, the more common version of which is the specialization of (2.70) to

$$f_{t+1,\,t} - f_{t,\,t-1} = \alpha_0 + \alpha_1(r_t - f_{t,\,t-1}) + \mu_t$$

Telser (1967) pointed out that the above equation implies an asymptotically flat yield curve, whereas Meiselman's hypothesis is consistent with a yield curve of any shape and therefore provides a more complete theory of the term structure of forward rates.

45 The paradox in the Goodhart–Gowland results is that regressions of the change in the long rate on the change in the short rate yielded a coefficient of 0.5, and not unity as required by the expectations theory. There are several possible explanations for this which are discussed in detail by Goodhart and Gowland.

46 This can be seen from the random walk implications of the expectations theory.

Since today's long rate is the best predictor of tomorrow's long rate, higher current long rates must predict higher future long rates.

47   Fama and Bliss also proved that the variance of the forecast is bounded as T increases.

48   When allowance is made for the impact of taxation the expectations theory encounters further problems for, given market interest rates, there is a different term structure for investors in different tax brackets (see Schaefer, 1981).

49   The evidence for stock prices is much the same. Stock prices look much too volatile to constitute rational forecasts of future dividends (see Shiller, 1981b).

50   See in particular equation (2.29). It is convenient but not essential to write the asset demands in the form of portfolio share equations, i.e. with X_{it}^*/W_t as the dependent variable.

51   Masson (1978) reported on a similar model. However, the dynamic structure of the asset demand functions was attributed to and modelled as a particular form of autocorrelation rather than as an explicit partial adjustment model.

52   Purvis (1978) also introduced a modified adjustment model which incorporated simultaneous adjustments in asset holdings and consumption. Green (1984) considered a partial adjustment scheme in which capital gains contribute differentially to adjustment speeds. Such partial models are all, typically, special cases of a more general dynamic specification and are therefore subject to the methodological criticisms of Hendry and his associates (see, for example, Hendry et al., 1984).

References

Allingham, M. G., and Morishima, M. (1973) Qualitative economics and comparative statics. In M. Morishima and others (eds), *The Theory of Demand: Real and Monetary*. Oxford: Oxford University Press, ch. 1, pp. 3–69.

Archbald, G. C. and Lipsey, R. G. (1958) Monetary and value theory: A critique of Lange and Patinkin. *Review of Economic Studies* 26 (1), 1–22.

Artis, M. J., Green, C. J., Miller, M. H. et al. (1978) Competition and credit control. Submission to the Committee to Review the Functioning of Financial Institutions (The Wilson Committee), August.

Backus, D., Brainard, W. C., Smith, G. and Tobin, J. (1980) A model of US financial and non-financial economic behaviour. *Journal of Money, Credit and Banking* 12 (2), 259–93.

Baillie, R. T. and McMahon, P. C. (1987) Rational forecasts in models of the term structure of interest rates. In C. Goodhart, D. Currie and D. T. Llewellyn (eds), *The Operation and Regulation of Financial Markets*, London: Macmillan, ch. 8, pp. 189–206.

Barro, R. J. (1974) Are government bonds net wealth? *Journal of Political Economy* 82 (6), 1095–117.

Barsky, R. B. and Summers, L. H. (1988) Gibson's paradox and the Gold Standard. *Journal of Political Economy* 96 (3), 528–50.

Begg, D. K. H. (1984) Rational expectations and bond pricing: modelling the term structure with and without certainty equivalence. *Economic Journal (Supplement)* 94, 45–58.

Bicksler, J. L. (ed.) (1979) *Handbook of Financial Economics.* Amsterdam: North-Holland.

Black, F. (1972) Capital market equilibrium with restricted borrowing. *Journal of Business* 45, 444–55.

Blanchard, O. J. (1981) Output, the stock market and interest rates. *American Economic Review* 71 (1), 32–43.

—— (1984) Current and anticipated deficits, interest rates and economic activity. *European Economic Review* 25, 7–27.

—— and Plantes, M. K. (1977) A note on gross substitutability of financial assets. *Econometrica* 45 (3), 769–71.

—— and Summers, L. H. (1984) Perspectives on high world real interest rates. *Brookings Papers on Economic Activity* 2, 273–324.

Blinder, A. S. and Solow, R. M. (1973) Does fiscal policy matter? *Journal of Public Economics* 2, 319–37.

Bollerslev, T. (1986) Generalized autoregressive conditional heteroskedasticity. *Journal of Econometrics* 31, 307–27.

—— (1987) A Conditionally Heteroskedastic Time Series Model for Speculative Prices and Rates of Return. *Review of Economics and Statistics* 69 (3), 542–7.

—— Engle, R. F. and Wooldridge, J. M. (1988) A capital asset pricing model with time varying covariances. *Journal of Political Economy* 96 (1), 116–31.

Brainard, W. C. (1964) Financial intermediaries and a theory of monetary control. *Yale Economic Essays* 4 (10), 431–82.

Branson, W. H. (1976) The dual roles of the government budget constraint and the balance of payments in the movement from short-run to long-run equilibrium. *Quarterly Journal of Economics* 90 (3), 345–67.

—— and Henderson, D. W. (1984) The specification and influence of asset markets. NBER Working Paper 1283, National Bureau of Economic Research.

Breeden, D. T. (1979) An intertemporal asset pricing model with stochastic consumption and investment opportunities. *Journal of Financial Economics* 7, 265–96.

Buiter, W. H. (1980) Walras law and all that: Budget constraints and balance sheet constraints in period models and continuous time models. *International Economic Review* 21 (1), 1–16.

—— and Tobin, J. (1979) Debt Neutrality: A brief review of doctrine and evidence. In G. M. Von Furstenberg (ed.), *Social Security Versus Private Saving.* Cambridge, MA: Ballinger, pp. 39–63.

Burman, J. P. and White, W. R. (1972) Yield curves for gilt-edged stocks. *Bank of England Quarterly Bulletin* 12 (4), 467–86.

Campbell, J. Y. (1986) A defense of traditional hypotheses about the term structure of interest rates. *Journal of Finance* 41 (1), 183–93.

—— (1987) Stock returns and the term structure. *Journal of Financial Economics* 18, 373–99.

—— and Clarida, R. H. (1987) The term structure of euromarket interest rates: an empirical investigation. *Journal of Monetary Economics* 19 (1), 25–44.

—— and Shiller, R. J. (1984) A simple account of the behaviour of long-term interest rates. *American Economic Review, Papers and Proceedings* 74 (2), 44–8.

Carlson, J. A. and Parkin, A. (1975) Inflation expectations. *Economica* 42, 123–38.

Carr, J. and Smith, L. B. (1972) Money supply, interest rates and the yield curve. *Journal of Money, Credit and Banking* 4, 582–94.

Christofides, L. N. (1980) An empirical analysis of bond markets and their implications for the term structure of interest rates. *Manchester School* 48 (2), 111–25.

Clower, R. W. (1965) The Keynesian counterrevolution: a theoretical appraisal. In F. H. Hahn and F. P. R. Brechling (eds), *The Theory of Interest Rates*. London: Macmillan, ch. 5.

Cohen, D. and McMenamin, J. S. (1978) The role of fiscal policy in a financially disaggregated macroeconomic model. *Journal of Money, Credit and Banking* 10 (3), 322–36.

Cornell, B. (1983) The money supply announcements puzzle. *American Economic Review* 83 (4), 644–57.

Cox, J. C., Ingersoll, J. E. Jr and Ross, S. A. (1981a) An intertemporal general equilibrium model of asset prices. *Econometrica* 53, 363–84.

——, —— and —— (1981b) A re-examination of traditional hypotheses about the term structure of interest rates. *Journal of Finance* 36, 769–99.

——, —— and —— (1985) A theory of the term structure of interest rates. *Econometrica* 53, 385–408.

Culbertson, J. M. (1957) The term structure of interest rates. *Quarterly Journal of Economics* 71, 485–517.

Currie, D. (1978) Macroeconomic policy and the government financing requirement: a survey of recent developments. In M. J. Artis and R. Nobay (eds), *Studies in Contemporary Economic Analysis*, vol. 1. London: Croom-Helm.

Darby, M. R. (1975) The financial and tax effects of monetary policy on interest rates. *Economic Inquiry* 13, 266–74.

Demery, D. and Duck, N. (1978) The behaviour of nominal interest rates in the United Kingdom 1961–1973. *Economica* 45, 23–37.

Dewald, W. G. (1986) Government deficits in a generalized Fisherian credit market: theory with an application to indexing interest taxation. *IMF Staff Papers* 33 (2), 243–75.

Dickens, R. (1987) Variability in some major UK asset markets since the mid-1960s: an application of the ARCH model. In C. A. E. Goodhart, D. Currie and D. T. Llewellyn (eds), *The Operation and Regulation of Financial Markets*. London: Macmillan, ch. 10, pp. 231–70.

Dodds, J. C. and Ford, J. L. (1974) *Expectations, Uncertainty, and the Term Structure of Interest Rates*. London: Martin Robertson.

Dornbusch, R. (1976) Expectations and exchange rate dynamics. *Journal of Political Economy* 84 (6), 1161–76.

Dwyer, G. P. (1981) Are expectations of inflation rational? or is variation of the expected real interest rate unpredictable? *Journal of Monetary Economics* 8 (1), 59–84.

Edwards, S. and Khan, M. S. (1985) Interest rate determination in developing countries: a conceptual framework. *IMF Staff Papers* 32 (3), 377–403.

Engel, C. and Frankel, J. (1984) Why interest rates react to money announcements: an explanation from the foreign exchange market. *Journal of Monetary Economics* 13 (1), 31–40.

Engle, R. F. (1982) Autoregressive conditional heteroskedasticity with estimates of the variance of UK inflation. *Econometrica* 50, 987–1008.

—— and Bollerslev, T. (1986) Modelling the persistence of conditional variances. *Econometric Reviews* 5 (1), 1–50.

—— Lilien, D. M. and Robins, R. P. (1987) Estimating time varying risk premia in the term structure: The ARCH-M model. *Econometrica* 55 (2), 391–407.

—— Ng, V. and Rothschild, M. (1988) Asset pricing with a factor ARCH covariance structure: empirical estimates for treasury bills. NBER Technical Working Paper 65, National Bureau of Economic Research, June.

Evans, P. (1987) Do budget deficits raise nominal interest rates? Evidence from six countries. *Journal of Monetary Economics* 20 (2), 281–300.

Fama, E. F. (1970) Efficient capital markets: a review of theory and empirical work. *Journal of Finance* 25, 383–417.

—— (1975) Short-term interest rates as predictors of inflation. *American Economic Review* 65, 269–82.

—— (1981) Stock returns, real activity, inflation and money. *American Economic Review* 71 (4), 545–65.

—— (1984) The information in the term structure. *Journal of Financial Economics* 13, 509–28.

—— and Bliss, R. R. (1987) The information in long-maturity forward rates. *American Economic Review* 77 (4), 680–92.

Feldstein, M. (1976) Inflation, income taxes and the rate of interest: a theoretical analysis. *American Economic Review* 66, 809–20.

Fischer, S. (1975) The demand for index bonds. *Journal of Political Economy* 83, 509–34.

—— (1988) Recent developments in macroeconomics. *Economic Journal* 98 (391), 294–339.

Fisher, I. (1930) *The Theory of Interest*. New York: Macmillan.

Flavin, M. A. (1983) Excess volatility in the financial markets: A reassessment of the empirical evidence. *Journal of Political Economy* 91 (6), 929–56.

Foley, D. K. (1975) On two specifications of asset equilibrium in macroeconomic models. *Journal of Political Economy* 83 (2), 303–24.

Frankel, J. A. (1985) Portfolio crowding out empirically estimated. *Quarterly Journal of Economics* 100 (5), 1041–65.

—— and Dickens, W. T. (1984) Are asset demand functions mean–variance efficient? NBER Working Paper 1113, National Bureau of Economic Research, June.

—— and Engel, C. M. (1984) Do asset demand functions optimize over the mean and variance of real returns? A six-currency test. *Journal of International Economics* 17, 309–23.

Friedman, B. M. (1977) Financial flow variables and the short-run determination of long-term interest rates. *Journal of Political Economy* 85 (4), 661–89.

—— (1978) Crowding-out or crowding-in? Economic consequences of financing government deficits. *Brookings Papers On Economic Activity* 3, 593–641.

—— (1979a) Optimal expectations and the extreme information assumptions of rational expectations macromodels. *Journal of Monetary Economics* 5 (1), 23–42.

—— (1979b) Substitution and expectation effects on long-term borrowing behaviour and long-term interest rates. *Journal of Money, Credit and Banking* 11 (2), 131–50.

—— (1980a) How important is disaggregation in structural models of interest rate determination. *Review of Economics and Statistics* 62 (2), 271–6.

—— (1980b) Price inflation, portfolio choice and nominal interest rates. *American Economic Review* 70 (1), 32–48.

—— (1980c) Survey evidence on the 'rationality' of interest rate expectations. *Journal of Monetary Economics* 6 (4), 453–66.

—— (1980d) The determination of long-term interest rates: implications for fiscal and monetary policies. *Journal of Money, Credit and Banking* 12 (2), 331–52.

—— (1981) Debt management policy, economic activity and interest rates. NBER Working Paper 830, National Bureau of Economic Research, December.

—— and Kuttner, K. N. (1988), Time varying risk perceptions and the pricing of risky assets. NBER Working Paper 2694, National Bureau of Economic Research, August.

—— and Roley, V. V. (1979a) A note on the derivation of linear homogeneous asset demand functions. Working Paper RWP 79–05, Federal Reserve Bank of Kansas City, June.

—— and Roley, V. V. (1979b) Investors' portfolio behaviour under alternative models of interest rate expectations: Unitary rational or autoregressive. *Econometrica* 47 (6), 1475–97.

Friedman, M. (1970) A theoretical framework for monetary analysis. *Journal of Political Economy* 78, 193–238.

Garbade, K. and Wachtel, P. (1978) Time variation in the relationship between inflation and interest rates. *Journal of Monetary Economics* 4, 755–65.

Gibson, A. H. (1923) The future course of high class investment values. *Bankers Magazine* 115, 15–34.

Gibson, W. E. (1972) Interest rates and inflationary expectations: New evidence. *American Economic Review* December, 854–65.

Girton, L. and Nattress, D. (1985) Monetary innovations and interest rates. *Journal of Money, Credit, and Banking* 17 (3), 289–97.

Goodhart, C. A. E. and Gowland, D. A. (1977) The relationship between yields on short and long-dated gilt-edged stocks. *Bulletin of Economic Research* 29 (2), 96–107.

—— and —— (1978) The relationship between long-dated gilt yields and other variables. *Bulletin of Economic Research* 30 (2), 59–70.

Goodhart, C. A. E. and Smith, R. G. (1985) The impact of news on financial markets in the United Kingdom. *Journal of Money, Credit and Banking* 17 (4), 507–11.

Grant, J. A. G. (1964) Meiselman on the term structure of interest rates: a British test. *Econometrica* February, 51–71.

Grauer, F. L. A. and Litzenberger, R. H. (1980) Monetary rules and the nominal rate of interest under uncertainty. *Journal of Monetary Economics* 6 (2), 277–88.

Green, C. J. (1982) Monetary policy and the structure of interest rates in the United Kingdom: A flow of funds model 1971–77. Ph. D. Dissertation, Yale University.

—— (1984) Preliminary results from a five-sector flow of funds model of the United Kingdom 1972–77. *Economic Modelling* 1 (3), 304–26.

—— (1985) Permanent income, budget constraints and overshooting in simple aggregate models. *Manchester School* 53, 231–40.

—— (1987) Did high-powered money rule the roost? Monetary policy, private behaviour and the structure of interest rates in the United Kingdom. In C. A. E. Goodhart, D. Currie and D. T. Llewellyn (eds), *The Operation and Regulation of Financial Markets*. London: Macmillan, ch. 9, pp. 207–30.

—— (1988) Adjustment costs and mean–variance efficiency in UK financial markets. In H. Motamen (ed.), *Economic Modelling in OECD Countries*, London: Chapman and Hall, ch. 7, pp. 119–40.

—— (1990) Asset demands and asset prices in the UK: is there a risk premium? *Manchester School* 58, 211–28.

—— and Keating, G. B. (1988) Capital asset pricing under alternative policy regimes. *Economic Modelling* 5 (2), 133–44.

—— and Kiernan, E. (1989) Multicollinearity and measurement error in econometric financial modelling. *Manchester School* 57 (4), 357–69.

—— and Na, S. (1988) Testing the capital asset pricing model on aggregate UK data: Market imperfections, portfolio and consumption effects. FIM Working Paper 9, September.

Grossman, J. (1981) The rationality of money supply expectations and the short-run response of interest rates to monetary surprises. *Journal of Money, Credit and Banking* 13 (4), 409–24.

Hall, S., Miles, D. K. and Taylor, M. P. (1989) Modelling asset prices with time-varying betas. *Manchester School* 57 (4), 340–56.

Hansen, A. H. (1953) *A Guide to Keynes*. New York: McGraw-Hill.

Hardouvelis, G. A. (1984) Market perceptions of Federal Reserve policy and the weekly monetary announcements. *Journal of Monetary Economics* 14 (2), 225–40.

Hendershott, P. H. (1977) *Understanding Capital Markets*, vol. I, *A Flow of Funds Model*. Lexington, MA: D. C. Heath.

Hendry, D. F., Pagan, A. R. and Sargan, J. D. (1984) Dynamic specification. In Z. Griliches and M. D. Intriligator (eds), *Handbook of Econometrics*, vol. 2. Amsterdam: North-Holland.

Hicks, J. R. (1937) Mr. Keynes and the 'Classics': a suggested interpretation. *Econometrica* 5, 147–59.

—— (1939) *Value and Capital*. Oxford: Oxford University Press.

Huang, R. D. (1986) Does monetization of federal debt matter? Evidence from the financial markets. *Journal of Money, Credit and Banking* 18 (3), 275–89.

Huizinga, J. and Leiderman, L. (1987) The signalling role of base and money announcements and their effects on interest rates. *Journal of Monetary Economics* 20 (3), 439–62.

—— and Mishkin, F. S. (1984) Inflation and real interest rates on assets with different risk characteristics. *Journal of Finance* 39, 669–712.

—— and —— (1986) Monetary policy regime shifts and the unusual behaviour of real interest rates. *Journal of Monetary Economics* 24, 231–74.

Hunt, B. E. and Upcher, M. R. (1979) Generalized adjustment of asset equations. *Australian Economic Papers* December, 308–21.

Johnson, H. G. (1961) The General Theory after twenty-five years. *American Economic Review* 50 (2), 1–17.

Jones, D. S. and Roley, V. V. (1983) Rational expectations and the expectations model of the term structure of interest rates: a test using weekly data. *Journal of Monetary Economics* 12 (3), 453–66.

Kearney, C. and MacDonald, R. (1986) A structural portfolio balance model of the sterling exchange rate. *Weltwirtschaftliches Archiv* 122 (3), 478–96.

Keating, G. (1985) The financial sector of the London Business School Model. In D. Currie (ed.), *Advances in Monetary Economics*. London: Croom-Helm, pp. 86–126.

Keynes, J.M. (1930) *A Treatise on Money,* vol. II. London: Macmillan.

—— (1936) *The General Theory of Employment, Interest and Money*. London: Macmillan.

—— (1937) Alternative theories of the rate of interest. *Economic Journal* 47, 241–52.

Kleidon, A.W. (1986) Variance bounds tests and stock price valuation models. *Journal of Political Economy* 94 (5), 953–1001.

Kouri, P.J.K. (1977) International investment and interest rates linkages under flexible exchange rates. In R.Z. Aliber (ed.), *The Political Economy of Monetary Reform*. London: Macmillan, pp. 74–96.

Lee, C.W.J. and Petruzzi, C.R. (1987) A test of the Shiller–Siegel hypothesis of the Gibson paradox. *Australian Economic Papers* 26 (48), 157–64.

Leijonhufvud, A. (1968) *On Keynesian Economics and the Economics of Keynes*. New York: Oxford University Press.

Leroy, S.R. (1982) Expectations models of asset prices: a survey of theory. *Journal of Finance* 37, 185–217.

Lintner, J. (1965) The valuation of risk assets and the selection of risky investments in stock portfolios and capital budgets. *Review of Economics and Statistics* 47 (1), 13–37.

Long, J.B. (1974) Stock prices, inflation and the term structure of interest rates. *Journal of Financial Economies* 1, 131–70.

MacDonald, R. and Murphy, P.D. (1987) Testing for the long-run relationship between nominal interest rates and inflation using cointegration techniques. Discussion Paper 87–06, Aberdeen University.

—— and Speight, A.E.H. (1988) The term structure of interest rates under rational expectations: some international evidence. Discussion Paper, Aberdeen University.

—— and Torrance, T.S. (1987a) Narrow and broad money surprises: their effect on asset prices compared and contrasted. Discussion Paper 87–01, Aberdeen University.

—— and —— (1987b) Monetary policy and the real interest rate: some UK evidence. Discussion Paper 87–04, Aberdeen University.

—— and —— (1988) Sterling M3 surprises and asset prices. *Economica* 55, 467–79.

Makin, J.H. (1982) Effects of inflation control programmes on expected real interest rates. *IMF Staff Papers* 29 (2), 204–32.

Mankiw, N.G. and Summers, L.H. (1984) Do long-term interest rates overreact to short-term interest rates? *Brookings Papers on Economic Activity* 1, 223–42.

Markowitz, H.M. (1959) *Portfolio Selection*. New Haven, CT: Yale University Press.

—— (1987) *Mean–Variance Analysis in Portfolio Choice and Capital Markets*. New York: Basil Blackwell.

Masson, P.R. (1978) Structural models of the demand for bonds and the term structure of interest rates. *Economica* 45, 363–77.

McCaleb, T.S. and Sellon, G.H. (1980) On the consistent specification of asset markets in macroeconomic models. *Journal of Monetary Economics* 6 (3), 401–18.

McCallum, B.T. (1976) Rational expectations and the natural rate hypothesis. *Econometrica* 44 (1), 43–52.

—— (1984) On low-frequency estimates of long-run relationships in macro-economics. *Journal of Monetary Economics* 14 (1), 3–14.

McCulloch, J.H. (1975) The tax-adjusted yield curve. *Journal of Finance* 30, 811–30.

Meiselman, D. (1962) *The Term Structure of Interest Rates*. Englewood Cliffs, NJ: Prentice-Hall.

Merrick, J.J. and Saunders, A. (1986) International expected real interest rates: new tests of the parity hypothesis and US fiscal policy effects. *Journal of Monetary Economics* 18 (3), 313–22.

Merton, R.C. (1971) Optimum consumption and portfolio rules in a continuous time model. *Journal of Economic Theory* 3, 373–413.

—— (1972) An analytic derivation of the efficient portfolio frontier. *Journal of Financial and Quantitative Analysis* September, 1851–73.

—— (1973) An intertemporal capital asset pricing model. *Econometrica* 41 (5), 867–87.

Metzler, L.A. (1951) Wealth, saving and the rate of interest. *Journal of Political Economy* 59 (2), 93–116.

Miller, M.H. (1971) An empirical analysis of monetary policy in the UK 1954–65. Ph.D. Dissertation, Yale University.

—— (1973) Competition and credit control and the open economy. *Manchester School* 41, 123–40.

Miller, S.M. (1975) Measures of risk aversion: some clarifying comments. *Journal of Financial and Qualitative Analysis* June, 299–309.

Mills, T.C. and Stephenson, M.J. (1985) An empirical analysis of the UK treasury bill market. *Applied Economics* 17, 689–703.

—— and —— (1986) Modelling real returns on UK government stock. *Bulletin of Economic Research* 38 (3), 237–56.

—— and —— (1987) The behaviour of expected short-term real interest rates in the UK. *Applied Economics* 19, 331–46.

Mishkin, F.S. (1978) Efficient markets theory: implications for monetary policy. *Brookings Papers on Economic Activity* 3, 707–52.

—— (1980) Is the preferred habitat model of the term structure inconsistent with financial market efficiency? *Journal of Political Economy* 88, 406–11.

—— (1981a) Monetary policy and long-term interest rates: an efficient markets approach. *Journal of Monetary Economics* 7 (1), 29–56.

—— (1981b) The real interest rate: An empirical investigation. In K. Brunner and A.H. Meltzer (eds), *The Costs and Consequences of Inflation*, Carnegie-Rochester Conference Series on Public Policy, vol. 15, pp. 151–200.

—— (1988) The information in the term structure: some further results. *Journal of Applied Econometrics* 3, 307–14.

Modigliani, F. and Cohn, R.A. (1979) Inflation, rational valuation and the market. *Financial Analysts' Journal* 35, 24–44.

—— and Shiller, R.J. (1973) Inflation, rational expectations and the term structure of interest rates. *Economica* 40, 12–43.

—— and Sutch, R. (1967) Debt management and the term structure of interest rates: An empirical analysis of recent experience. *Journal of Political Economy* 75, 569–89.

Mossin, J. (1966) Equilibrium in a capital market. *Econometrica* 34, 768–83.

Mundell, R. A. (1960) The public debt, corporate income taxes and the rate of interest. *Journal of Political Economy* 68, 622–6.

—— (1963) Inflation and real interest. *Journal of Political Economy* 71, 280–3.

Nelson, C. and Schwert G. W., (1977) Short-term interest rates as predictors of inflation: On testing the hypothesis that the real rate of interest is constant. *American Economic Review* 67, 478–86.

Niehans, J. (1978) Metzler, wealth and macroeconomic: a review. *Journal of Economic Literature* 16, 84–95.

Patinkin, D. (1965) *Money Interest and Prices*. New York: Harper and Row, 2nd edn.

Pearce, D. K. (1979) Comparing survey and rational measures of expected inflation forecast performance and interest rate effects. *Journal of Money, Credit and Banking* 11, 447–56.

Peek, J. (1982) Interest rates, income taxes and anticipated inflation. *American Economic Review* 72 (5), 980–91.

—— and Wilcox, J. A. (1987) Monetary policy regimes and the reduced form for interest rates. *Journal of Money, Credit and Banking* 19 (3), 273–91.

Pesando, J. E. (1975) A note on the rationality of the Livingstone price expectations. *Journal of Political Economy* 83, 849–58.

—— (1976) Alternative models of the determination of nominal interest rates. *Journal of Money, Credit and Banking* 8 (2), 209–18.

—— (1978) On the efficiency of the bond market: some Canadian evidence. *Journal of Political Economy* 86 (6), 1057–76.

—— (1981) On forecasting interest rates: an efficient markets perspective. *Journal of Monetary Economics* 8 (3), 305–18.

Phillips, L. and Pippenger, J. (1976) Preferred habitat versus efficient market: a test of alternative hypotheses. *Federal Reserve Bank of St Louis Review* 58 (5), 11–19.

Pigou, A. C. (1943) The classical stationary state. *Economic Journal* 53, 343–51.

Plosser, C. I. (1982) Government financing decisions and asset returns. *Journal of Monetary Economics* 9 (3), 325–52.

—— (1987) Fiscal policy and the term structure. *Journal of Monetary Economics* 20 (2), 343–68.

Purvis, D. D. (1978) Dynamic models of portfolio behaviour: more on pitfalls in financial model building. *American Economic Review* 68 (3), 403–9.

Roley, V. V. (1979) A theory of federal debt management. *American Economic Review* 69 (5), 915–26.

—— (1980) The role of commercial banks' portfolio behaviour in the determination of treasury security yields. *Journal of Money, Credit and Banking* 12 (2), 353–69.

—— (1981) The determinants of the treasury security yield curve. *Journal of Finance* 36 (12), 1103–26.

—— (1983a) Symmetry restrictions in a system of financial asset demands: Theoretical and empirical results. *Review of Economics and Statistics* 65 (1), 124–30.

—— (1983b) The response of short-term interest rates to weekly money announcements. *Journal of Money, Credit and Banking* 15 (3), 344–54.

—— (1987) The effects of monetary announcements under alternative monetary control procedures. *Journal of Money, Credit and Banking* 19 (3), 292–307.

Roll, R. (1970) *The Behaviour of Interest Rates: An Application of the Efficient Markets Model to US Treasury Bills.* New York: Basic Books.

—— (1977) A critique of the asset pricing theory's tests. *Journal of Financial Economics* 4, 129–76.

Rowan, D. C. and O'Brien, R. J. (1970) Expectations, the interest rate structure and debt policy. In K. Hilton and D. F. Heathfield (eds), *The Econometric Study of the United Kingdom.* London: Macmillan, ch. 11, pp. 275–316.

Royama, S. and Hamada, K. (1967) Substitution and complementarity in the choice of risky assets. In D. D. Hester and J. Tobin (eds), *Risk Aversion and Portfolio Choice.* New York: Wiley, pp. 27–40.

Samuelson, P. A. (1947) *Foundations of Economic Analysis.* Cambridge, MA: Harvard University Press.

—— (1970) The fundamental approximation theorem of portfolio analysis in terms of means, variances and higher moments. *Review of Economic Studies* 37, 537–42.

Saracoglu, R. (1984) Expectations of inflation and interest rate determination. *IMF Staff Papers* 31 (1), 141–78.

Sargent, T. J. (1972) Rational expectations and the term structure of interest rates. *Journal of Money, Credit and Banking* 4 (1), 74–87.

—— (1973) Interest rates and prices in the long-run: A study of the Gibson paradox. *Journal of Money, Credit and Banking* 5, 385–449.

—— (1979) A note on maximum likelihood estimation of the rational expectations model of the term structure. *Journal of Monetary Economics* 5 (1), 133–44.

—— (1987a) *Dynamic Macroeconomic Theory.* Cambridge, MA: Harvard University Press.

—— (1987b) *Macroeconomic Theory.* New York: Academic Press, 2nd edn.

—— and Wallace, N. (1986) Some unpleasant monetarist arithmetic. In T. J. Sargent (ed.), *Rational Expectations and Inflation.* New York: Harper & Row, ch. 5, pp. 158–90.

Schaefer, S. M. (1981) Measuring a tax-specific term structure of interest rates in the market for British government securities. *Economic Journal* 91 (2), 415–38.

Sharpe, I. G. (1973) A quarterly econometric model of portfolio choice – Part 1: Specification and estimation problems. *Economic Record* December, 518–33.

Sharpe, W. F. (1964) Capital asset prices: a theory of market equilibrium under conditions of risk. *Journal of Finance* 19 (3), 425–42.

Shiller, R. J. (1972) Rational expectations and the structure of interest rates. Ph.D. Dissertation, Massachusetts Institute of Technology.

—— (1979) The volatility of long-term interest rates and expectations models of the term structure. *Journal of Political Economy* 87 (6), 1190–219.

—— (1981a) Alternative tests of rational expectations models: the case of the term structure. *Journal of Econometrics* 16, 71–87.

—— (1981b) Do stock prices move too much to be justified by subsequent changes in dividends? *American Economic Review* 71 (3), 421–36.

—— (1987) The term structure of interest rates (with an appendix by J. H. McCulloch giving US term structure data, 1946–87). NBER Working Paper 2341, National Bureau of Economic Research.

—— and Siegel, J. J. (1977) The Gibson paradox and historical movements in real interest rates. *Journal of Political Economy* 85 (5), 891–907.

Silber, W. E. (1970) Fiscal policy in IS–LM analysis: a correction. *Journal of Money, Credit and Banking* 1, 461–72.

Singleton, K. J. (1980) Maturity-specific disturbances and the term structure of interest rates. *Journal of Money, Credit and Banking*, 12 (4), 603–14.

Smith, G. (1975) Pitfalls in financial model building: a clarification. *American Economic Review* 65 (3), 510–16.

—— (1979) The long-run consequences of monetary and fiscal policies when the government's budget is not balanced. *Journal of Public Economics* 11, 59–79.

—— (1981) The systematic specification of a full prior covariance matrix for asset demand equations. *Quarterly Journal of Economics* May, 317–39.

—— (1982a) Flexible policies and IS–LM dynamics. *Journal of Macroeconomics* 4 (2), 155–78.

—— (1982b) Monetarism, bondism and inflation. *Journal of Money, Credit and Banking* 14 (2), 278–86.

Smith, G. W. (1982) Inflation expectations: direct observations and their determinants. In M. J. Artis, C. J. Green, D. Leslie and G. Smith (eds), *Demand Management Supply Constraints, and Inflation*. Manchester: Manchester University Press, pp. 255–74.

Smith, R. G. and Goodhart, C. A. E. (1985) The relationship between exchange rate movements and monetary suprises: results for the United Kingdom and United States compared and contrasted. *Manchester School* 53 (1), 2–22.

Spencer, P. D. (1982) Bank regulation, credit rationing and the determination of money market interest rates. *Manchester School* 50, 41–60.

Summers, L. H. (1983) The non-adjustment of nominal interest rates: a study of the Fisher effect. In J. Tobin (ed.), *Macroeconomics: Prices and Quantities*. Oxford: Basil Blackwell, pp. 201–41.

—— (1986) Estimating the long-run relationship between interest rates and inflation: a response to McCallum. *Journal of Monetary Economics* 18 (1), 77–86.

Symons, J. S. (1983) Money and the real interest rate in the UK. *Manchester School* 51 (3), 250–65.

Taylor, M. P. (1988) What do investment managers know? An empirical study of practitioners' predictions. *Economica* 55, 185–202.

Telser, L. G. (1967) A critique of some recent empirical research on the term structure of interest rates. *Journal of Political Economy* (*Supplement*) 546–61.

Tobin, J. (1956) The interest elasticity of the transactions demand for cash. *Review of Economics and Statistics* 38, 241–7.

—— (1958) Liquidity preference as behaviour towards risk. *Review of Economic Studies* 25 (67), 54–86.

—— (1961) Money, capital and other stores of value. *American Economic Review, Papers and Proceedings* 51, 26–37.

—— (1963a) An essay on the principles of debt management. In Commission on Money and Credit, Fiscal and Debt Management Policies. Englewood Cliffs, NJ: Prentice-Hall, pp. 143–218.

—— (1963b) Commercial banks as creators of money. In D. Carson (ed.), *Banking and Monetary Studies*. Homewood, IL: R. D. Irwin, pp. 408-19.

—— (1965) Money and economic growth. *Econometrica* 33 (4), 671-84.

—— (1969) A general equilibrium approach to monetary theory. *Journal of Money, Credit and Banking* 1, 15-29.

—— (1970) Deposit interest ceilings as a monetary control. *Journal of Money, Credit and Banking* 2, 4-14.

—— (1974) Friedman's theoretical framework. In R. J. Gordon (ed.), *Milton Friedman's Monetary Framework: A Debate with his Critics*. Chicago, IL: University of Chicago Press, pp. 77-89.

—— (1979) Deficit spending and crowding-out in shorter and longer-runs. In H. J. Greenfield, A. M. Levenson, W. Hamovitch and E. Rotwein (eds), *Theory For Economic Efficiency: Essays in Honour of A. P. Lerner*. Cambridge, MA: MIT Press, ch. 15, pp. 217-36.

—— (1982) Money and finance in the macroeconomic process. *Journal of Money, Credit and Banking* 14 (2), 171-204.

—— (1984) On the efficiency of the financial system. *Lloyds Bank Review* July, 1-15.

—— and Brainard, W. C. (1963) Financial intermediaries and the effectiveness of monetary controls. *American Economic Review, Papers and Proceedings* 53 (2), 383-400.

—— and —— (1968) Pitfalls in financial modelbuilding. *American Economic Review, Paper and Proceedings* 58, 99-122.

—— and Braga de Macedo, J. A. (1980) The short-run macroeconomics of floating exchange rates: An exposition. In J. S. Chapman and C. P. Kindleberger (eds), *Flexible Exchange Rates and the Balance of Payments: Essays in Honour of Egon Sohmen*. Amsterdam: North-Holland, pp. 5-28.

—— and Buiter, W. H. (1976) Long-run effects of fiscal and monetary policy on aggregate demand. In J. L. Stein (ed.), *Monetarism: Studies in Monetary Economics*. Amsterdam: North-Holland, ch. 4.

—— and —— (1980) Fiscal and monetary policies, capital formation and economic activity. In G. M. Von Furstenberg (ed.), *The Government and Capital Formation*. Cambridge, MA: Ballinger, pp. 73-151.

Turnbull, S. M. (1981) The measurement of the real rate of interest and related problems in a world of uncertainty. *Journal of Money, Credit and Banking* 13 (2), 177-91.

Turnovsky, S. J. (1986) Short-term and long-term interest rates in a monetary model of a small open economy. *Journal of International Economics* 20, 291-311.

—— (1989) The term structure of interest rates and the effects of macroeconomic policy. *Journal of Money, Credit and Banking* 21 (3), 321-47.

—— and Miller, M. H. (1984) The effects of government expenditure on the term structure of interest rates. *Journal of Money, Credit and Banking,* 16 (1), 16-33.

Urich, T. J. (1982) The information content of weekly money supply announcements. *Journal of Monetary Economics* 10 (1), 723-88.

Walsh, C. E. (1983) Asset prices, stocks and rational expectations. *Journal of Monetary Economics* 11 (3), 337-50.

—— (1985) A rational expectations model of term premia with some implications for empirical asset demand functions. *Journal of Finance* 40, 63-83.

Wickens, M. R. (1982) The efficient estimation of econometric models with rational expectations. *Review of Economic Studies* 49, 55–67.

Wilcox, J. A. (1983) Why real interest rates were so low in the 1970's. *American Economic Review* 73 (1), 44–53.

Wilson, C. A. (1979) Anticipated shocks and exchange rate dynamics. *Journal of Political Economy* 87 (3), 639–47.

Wood, J. H. (1980) Metzler on classical interest theory. *American Economic Review* 70 (1), 135–48.

Yohe, W. P. and Karnosky, D. S. (1969) Interest rates and price level changes 1952–69. *Federal Reserve Bank of St. Louis Review* 51, 19–36.

Zivney, T. L. and Marcus, R. D. (1989) The day the United States defaulted on treasury bills. *Financial Review* 24 (3), 475–90.

3 Exchange Rate Economics

Ronald MacDonald and Mark P. Taylor

3.1 INTRODUCTION

The exchange rate plays a crucial role in the performance of a modern open economy. Indeed, for the majority of countries in the Organization for Economic Co-operation and Development (OECD) analysis of macro-economic policy in the context of a closed economy is probably so unrealistic as to be of interest only to the pure theorist. It is not surprising, therefore, that exchange rate economics is one of the most heavily researched areas of the discipline. The period since the advent of generalized floating exchange rates in 1973 – as well as the more recent 'controlled experiment' with the European Monetary System – has generated a wealth of data on exchange rates and on the factors which supposedly determine them, giving econometricians and applied economists an unprecedented opportunity to test a number of propositions relating to foreign exchange markets. As we shall see, however, the economics of exchange rates is also one of the least successful areas of economics in the sense that there is still virtually no consensus

Ronald MacDonald is Robert Fleming Professor of Finance and Investment at the University of Dundee. Mark P. Taylor is Morgan Grenfell Professor of Financial Markets at the City University Business School, a Fellow of the Centre for Economic Policy Research and Consultant to the Bank of England, and is currently a Visiting Scholar in the Research Department of the International Monetary Fund, Washington, DC. The authors are grateful to Christopher Green for helpful comments on an earlier draft, although responsibility for the current version rests with them. Any views expressed are those of the authors and are not necessarily those of the Bank of England or of the International Monetary Fund.

on the determinants of exchange rates and, moreover, few, if any, of the theories which have variously been proposed have withstood close empirical examination.

In this chapter we survey the literature on exchange rate economics which has developed since the early 1970s. In an attempt to optimize the subject within the given space contraints, we confine ourselves to surveying the literature on exchange rate determination and, more briefly, on foreign exchange market efficiency. In particular, in section 3.2 we examine the two main views of exchange rate determination that have evolved since the early 1970s: the monetary approach to the exchange rate (in both its flexible price and sticky price formulations) and the portfolio balance approach to the exchange rate. In section 3.3 we discuss the extant empirical evidence on the models outlined in section 3.2 and conclude by discussing how the future research startegy in the area of exchange rate determination is likely to develop. The application of the efficient markets hypothesis (EMH) to the forward market for foreign exchange is briefly reviewed in section 3.4.

3.2 THEORIES OF EXCHANGE RATE DETERMINATION

At the most fundamental level, the exchange rate is simply the price of foreign currency which clears the foreign exchange market. Theories of exchange rate determination therefore differ only in their different specifications of the supply of and demand for foreign exchange.

The insight of the classic Mundell–Fleming model of exchange rate determination (Fleming, 1962; Mundell, 1968) was that net excess demand for foreign exchange is just the overall balance of payments (current plus capital account). Under a free float, this must be equal to zero in equilibrium. Combining this equilibrium condition with standard equilibrium conditions for the goods market (the IS curve) and the money market (the LM curve) then allows us to solve for the exchange rate (and the other endogenous variables, normally real output and the interest rate) and to determine the comparative static effects of fiscal and monetary policy.

The integration of asset markets and capital mobility into open economy macroeconomics was a major innovation of the Mundell–Fleming model, but it contains a fundamental flaw: it is cast almost entirely in flow terms. In particular, the model allows current account imbalances to be offset by flows across the capital account without any requirement of eventual stock equilibrium in the holding of net foreign assets. In papers dating from the 1950s (see, for example, Johnson, 1958), Harry Johnson had stressed the distinction between stock and flow equilibria in the open economy context, and this was to become a hallmark of the monetary approach to balance of payments analysis (see, for example, Frenkel and Johnson, 1976) and subsequently the monetary approach to the exchange rate (see, for example, Frenkel and Johnson, 1978).

Indeed, since an exchange rate is, by definition, the price of one country's money in terms of that of another, it is perhaps natural to analyse the determinants of that price in terms of the outstanding stocks of and demand for the two monies. This is the basic rationale of the monetary approach to the exchange rate. A problem with the early flexible price variant of the monetary approach, however, is that it assumes continuous purchasing power parity (PPP). Under continuous PPP, the real exchange rate – i.e. the exchange rate adjusted for differences in national price levels – cannot vary, by definition. Yet, a major characteristic of the recent experience with floating has been the wide gyrations in the real rates of exchange between many of the major currencies, bringing with it the very real consequences of shifts in international competitiveness (see, for example, Dornbusch, 1987). Clearly, therefore, the simple flexible price monetary approach does not fit the facts of observation. An attempt to rehabilitate the monetary model in this respect led to the development of a second generation of monetary models, originally due to Dornbusch (1976). These sticky price monetary models allow for substantial overshooting of the nominal and real price-adjusted exchange rate above their long-run equilibrium (PPP) levels as the 'jump variables' in the system – exchange rates and interest rates – compensate for sluggishness in other variables – notably goods prices.

The sticky-price monetary model is clearly an advance over the simple (continuous PPP) monetary model in that it more closely explains the facts of observation. However, it is fundamentally monetary in that attention is focused on equilibrium conditions in the money market. Monetary models of the open economy are able to do this by assuming perfect substitutability of domestic and foreign non-money assets. These can then be aggregated into a single extra market ('bonds') and excluded from explicit analysis by application of Walras' law. This perfect substitutability assumption is relaxed in the portfolio balance model of exchange rate determination. In addition, the portfolio balance model is stock flow consistent in that it allows for current account imbalances to have a feedback effect on wealth and hence on long-run equilibrium.

We now consider the monetary and portfolio balance exchange rate models in more detail.

3.2.1 The Flexible Price Monetary Model

The flexible price monetary (FLPM) model relies on the (continuous) PPP condition and stable money demand functions. The (logarithm of the) demand for money can be assumed to depend on (the logarithm of) real income y, the (logarithm of the) price level p and the level of the interest rate r. We assume a similar foreign demand for money function (foreign variables are denoted by an asterisk). Monetary equilibria in the domestic and foreign country respectively are given by

$$m^s = p + \phi y - \lambda r \qquad (3.1)$$

$$m^{s*} = p* + \phi*y* - \lambda*r* \qquad (3.2)$$

In the FLPM model the domestic interest rate, at least in the long run, is exogenous because of the implicit assumption of perfect capital mobility – domestic interest rates are determined on world markets. Equilibrium in the traded goods market ensues when there are no further profitable incentives for trade flows to occur, i.e. when prices in a common currency are equalized and PPP holds. Again, using lower-case letters to denote logarithms, the PPP condition is

$$s = p - p* \qquad (3.3)$$

so that, if PPP holds, the logarithm of the real exchange rate, q say ($q \equiv s - p + p*$), is zero. The world price $p*$ is exogenous to the domestic economy, being determined by the world money supply. The domestic money supply determines the domestic price level and hence the exchange rate is determined by relative money supplies. Algebraically, substituting (3.1) and (3.2) into (3.3) gives, after rearranging,

$$s = (m^s - m^{s*}) - \phi y + \phi*y* + \lambda r - \lambda*r* \qquad (3.4)$$

which is the basic FLPM equation. From (3.4), we can see that an increase in the domestic money supply, relative to the foreign money stock, will lead to an exchange rate depreciation. This seems intuitive enough. On the other hand, an increase in domestic output appreciates the exchange rate – exactly the converse of what the Mundell–Fleming approach would predict (in the latter approach, higher real income worsens the trade balance as imports rise and requires a depreciation to return to equilibrium). Similarly, a rise in domestic interest rates depreciates the exchange rate (in the Mundell–Fleming model this would lead to capital inflows and hence an appreciation).

In order to resolve these apparent paradoxes, we have to remember the fundamental role of relative money demand in the FLPM model. A relative rise in domestic real income creates an excess demand for the domestic money stock. As agents try to increase their (real) money balances, they reduce expenditure and prices fall until money market equilibrium is achieved. As prices fall, PPP ensures an exchange rate appreciation. An exactly converse analysis explains the response of the exchange rate to the interest rate – an increase in interest rates reduces the demand for money and so leads to an exchange rate depreciation.

In the latter half of the 1970s, the FLPM model ceased to be an accurate description of the behaviour of exchange rates for a number of small open economies (this will be discussed in more detail in section 3.3). For example, in the UK over the period 1979–81 the sterling nominal effective exchange rate (i.e. the rate against a basket of currencies) appreciated substantially even though the UK money supply grew rapidly relative to growth in the 'world' money supply. However, more startling, the real exchange rate (i.e. 'price competitiveness' or the 'terms of trade') appreciated by about 40 per cent over this period and this was followed by an equally sharp fall over the period 1981–4. Large and volatile swings in the real exchange rate may lead to large swings in net trade with consequent multiplier effects on domestic output and employment. In the FLPM model, output is determined exogenously and unless the model is extended it is incapable of explaining changes in real output. Sticky price monetary (SPM) models provide an explanation of exchange rate overshooting together with short-run changes in real output, as for example occurred in the very severe recession of 1979–82 in the UK. The seminal paper in this context is Dornbusch (1976).

3.2.2 The Sticky Price Monetary Model

The intuition underlying the overshooting result in the SPM model is relatively straightforward. Imagine the effects of a cut in the nominal UK money supply. Since prices are sticky in the short run, this implies an initial fall in the real money supply and a consequent rise in interest rates in order to clear the money market. The rise in domestic interest rates then leads to a capital inflow and an appreciation of the nominal (and, given sticky prices, the real) exchange rate. Foreign investors are aware that they are artificially forcing up the exchange rate and that they may therefore suffer a foreign exchange loss when the proceeds of their investment are reconverted into their local currency.[1] However, as long as the expected foreign exchange loss (expected rate of depreciation) is less than the known capital market gain (i.e. the interest differential), risk neutral investors will continue to buy sterling assets. A short-run equilibrium is achieved when the expected rate of depreciation is just equal to the interest differential (uncovered interest parity holds). Since the expected rate of depreciation must then be non-zero for a non-zero interest differential, the exchange rate must have overshot its long-run equilibrium (PPP) level. In the medium run, however, domestic prices begin to fall in response to the fall in money supply. This alleviates pressure in the money market and domestic interest rates begin to decline. The exchange rate then depreciates slowly in order to converge on the long-run PPP level. This model therefore explains the paradox that countries with relatively high interest rates tend to have currencies whose exchange rate is expected to depreciate. The initial rise in interest rates leads to a step appreciation of the exchange rate after which a slow depreciation is expected in order to satisfy uncoveted interest parity (UIP). We now consider the Dornbusch (1976) model in more detail.

Since the model is set up in (log) linear form, we can apply the certainty equivalence principle, i.e. that solving the model assuming perfect foresight yields the same solution as assuming rational expectations (see, for example, Begg, 1982, p. 52). Thus, in continuous time, the actual rate of depreciation s must be equal to the interest differential, according to UIP. The full set of equations for our simplified Dornbusch model are

$$\dot{s} = r - r^* \tag{3.5}$$

$$m - p = \phi\bar{y} - \lambda r \tag{3.6}$$

$$\dot{p} = \pi\left[\alpha + \delta(s - p) - \sigma r - \bar{y}\right] \tag{3.7}$$

For simplicity, we assume that output is fixed at $\bar{y}$. Equation (3.5) is the UIP condition. Equation (3.6) is the condition for money market equilibrium (the LM curve). Equation (3.7) is a Phillips curve, which relates the rate of change of prices to the excess of demand over output supply. Demand is assumed to be a function of an autonomous component α, the real exchange rate (holding foreign prices constant and normalized so that $p^* = 0$) and interest rates.

In long-run equilibrium, the rate of depreciation will be zero (and hence $r = r^*$ by (3.5)), and the price level settles down to its long-run value $\bar{p}$. Hence the long-run money market equilibrium condition is

$$m - \bar{p} = \phi\bar{y} - \lambda r^* \tag{3.8}$$

Subtracting (3.6) from (3.8) yields

$$p - \bar{p} = \lambda(r - r^*) \tag{3.9}$$

or, using (3.5) and (3.9),

$$\dot{s} = \frac{1}{\lambda}(p - \bar{p}) \tag{3.10}$$

On the goods market side, solving (3.6) for the domestic rate of interest and substituting into (3.7) yields

$$\dot{p} = \pi\left[\alpha + \delta(s - p) + \frac{\sigma}{\lambda}(m - p) - \left(1 + \frac{\sigma\phi}{\lambda}\right)\bar{y}\right] \tag{3.11}$$

or, in long-run zero inflation equilibrium

$$0 = \pi\left[\alpha + \delta(\bar{s} - \bar{p}) + \frac{\sigma}{\lambda}(m - \bar{p}) - \left(1 + \frac{\sigma\phi}{\lambda}\right)\bar{y}\right] \tag{3.12}$$

Subtracting (3.12) from (3.11) we obtain

$$\dot{p} = \pi\delta(s - \bar{s}) - \pi\left(\delta + \frac{\sigma}{\lambda}\right)(p - \bar{p}) \tag{3.13}$$

The differential equations (3.10) and (3.13) can be expressed in matrix form as

$$\begin{bmatrix} \dot{s} \\ \dot{p} \end{bmatrix} = \begin{bmatrix} 0 & 1/\lambda \\ \pi\delta & -\pi(\delta + \sigma/\lambda) \end{bmatrix} \begin{bmatrix} s - \bar{s} \\ p - \bar{p} \end{bmatrix} \tag{3.14}$$

For this system to have a unique convergent saddlepath, the necessary and sufficient condition is that the coefficient matrix in (3.14) has a negative determinant (so that the characteristic equation has one positive and one negative root) (see, for example, Blanchard and Khan, 1980), and this is easily seen to be the case:

$$-\frac{\pi\delta}{\lambda} < 0$$

The qualitative solution to (3.14) is given in figure 3.1, where the $\dot{s} = 0$ and $\dot{p} = 0$ loci are obtained from (3.10) and (3.13). Given the arrows of motion, the qualitative shape of the saddlepath is easily inferred (see, for example, Begg, 1982, p. 52).

Now, if we assume that agents will be unwilling to participate in an unstable economy (see, for example, Shiller, 1978; Begg, 1982, ch. 3) the economy will always be located on the saddlepath and, given the stickiness

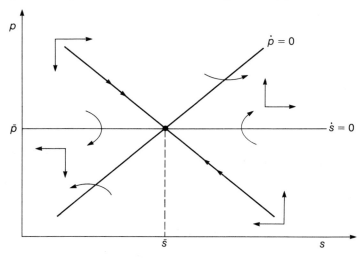

Figure 3.1   The saddlepath equilibrium for the sticky price monetary model

of prices, this means that the exchange rate has to jump in response to shocks which cause a shift in the saddlepath and then converge slowly to the equilibrium along the new saddlepath.

If $-\theta$ is the stable (negative) root of the system, then we know that the equation of motion for s must satisfy

$$\dot{s} = -\theta(s - \bar{s}) \tag{3.15}$$

Substituting (3.15) into (3.10) gives

$$s = \bar{s} - \frac{1}{\lambda\theta}(p - \bar{p})$$

and this is, in fact, the equation describing the saddlepath.

Take the example of an increase in the money supply m. From (3.8) this implies a rise in the long-run price level $\bar{p}$ (given exogenous $\bar{y}$ and r^*) and hence, from (3.12), a rise in $\bar{s}$ (long-run depreciation). Thus the saddlepath shifts up and to the right (figure 3.2) given the initial stickiness of prices, and the exchange rate initially jumps from A to B and then slowly converges to the new equilibrium C. The distance $s_{os} - \bar{s}_2$ then measures the amount of exchange rate overshooting.

The model can also be extended to allow for short-run effects on output (Dornbusch, 1976, 1980). Buiter and Miller (1981) extend the model to allow for a non-zero rate of core inflation (i.e. $\dot{p} \neq 0$ even when net excess

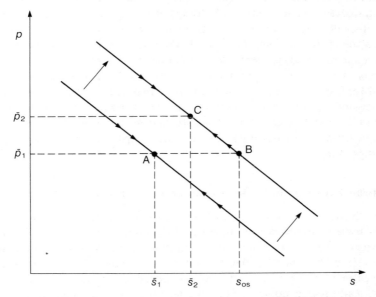

Figure 3.2   Exchange rate overshooting in the sticky price monetary model

aggregate demand is zero) and analyse the impact of a natural resource discovery (e.g. oil or gas) on the exchange rate. Since the higher income resulting from the resource discovery leads to a higher demand for non-oil output, with long-run output fixed, the long-run exchange rate must appreciate in order to worsen the terms of trade and reduce long-run demand (the so-called 'Dutch disease' (Forsyth and Kay, 1980)).

3.2.3 The Portfolio Balance Model

The FLPM and SPM models which have been the subject matter of the preceding sections make at least two important simplifying assumptions: domestic and foreign assets are perfect substitutes (so that no distinction need be made between them),[2] and the wealth effects of a current account surplus or deficit are negligible. The portfolio balance model of exchange rates explores the consequences of explicitly relaxing these assumptions (see, for example, Branson, 1977, 1983, 1984; Dornbusch and Fischer, 1980; Isard, 1980).

In common with the FLPM and SPM models, the level of the exchange rate in the portfolio balance model (PBM) is determined, at least in the short run, by supply and demand in the markets for financial assets. The exchange rate, however, is a principal determinant of the current account of the balance of payments. Now, a surplus (deficit) on the current account represents a rise (fall) in net domestic holdings of foreign assets which affects the level of wealth, which in turn affects the level of asset demand, which again affects the exchange rate. Thus the PBM is an inherently dynamic model of exchange rate adjustment which includes in its terms of reference asset markets, the current account, the price level and the rate of asset accumulation. Moreover, we can distinguish between short-run equilibrium (supply and demand equated in asset markets) and the dynamic adjustment to long-run equilibrium (a static level of wealth and no tendency of the system to move over time). We begin by analysing the short-run determination of the exchange rate.

Short-run Exchange Rate Determination in the Portfolio Balance Model

In the short run (on a day-to-day basis), the exchange rate is determined purely by the interaction of supply and demand in asset markets. During this period, the level of financial wealth (and the individual components of that level) can be treated as fixed. For simplicity, we shall treat the net financial wealth of the private sector as composed of three assets: money M, domestically issued bonds B and foreign bonds F denominated in foreign currency. B is essentially government debt held by the domestic private sector, and F is the level of net claims on foreigners held by the private sector. Since, under a free float, a current account surplus on the balance of payments must be exactly matched by a capital account deficit (i.e. capital outflow and hence increase in net foreign indebtedness to the domestic economy), the current account must give the rate of accumulation of F over time.

With foreign and domestic interest rates given by r and r^* as before, we can write down our definition of wealth and simple domestic demand functions for its components as follows:

$$W = M + B + SF \tag{3.16}$$

$$M = M(r, r^*)W \qquad M_r < 0, \ M_r^* < 0 \tag{3.17}$$

$$B = B(r, r^*)W \qquad B_r > 0, \ B_r^* < 0 \tag{3.18}$$

$$SF = F(r, r^*)W \qquad F_r < 0, \ F_r^* < 0 \tag{3.19}$$

Relation (3.16) is an identity defining wealth. The major noteworthy characteristics of equations (3.17)–(3.19) are that, as is standard in most expositions of the PBM, the scale variable is the level of wealth W and the demand functions are homogeneous in wealth; this allows them to be written in nominal terms (assuming homogeneity in prices and real wealth, prices cancel out) (see Tobin, 1969). For the moment, we shall assume that expectations are static – in particular, that the expected rate of depreciation is zero. Therefore, we need not include exchange rate expectations in the asset demand functions. This assumption is relaxed below when we consider the model under the assumption of rational expectations. Note that we are no longer working in log linear terms – S is the *level* and not the *logarithm* of the exchange rate.

Figure 3.3 shows the short-run determination of the exchange rate diagrammatically in (S, r) space. The line BE in figure 3.3 gives the locus of points in (S, r) space at which, *ceteris paribus*, the supply and demand for domestic assets are equated. Similarly, the line FE gives the equilibrium locus along which the domestic demand for foreign assets is equal to the (short-run) fixed supply, and ME describes the money market equilibrium locus.

A depreciation of the exchange rate (rise in S) raises the domestic currency value of foreign assets F and hence increases wealth W. This raises the demand for both M and B. In order to maintain equilibrium in the money market, interest rates must rise – thus the ME schedule is upward sloping in (S, r) space. Similarly, in order to maintain domestic bond market equilibrium, the domestic interest rate must fall – the BE schedule is downward sloping. As the domestic interest rate r rises, the domestic demand for foreign bonds falls as agents substitute domestic for foreign bonds in their

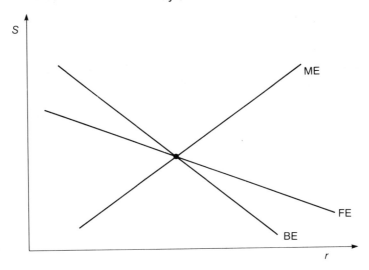

Figure 3.3 Short-run equilibrium in the portfolio balance model

portfolios. As foreign assets are sold, the foreign currency proceeds are converted into domestic currency, thus bidding up the exchange rate (S falls) – hence FE is downward sloping in (S, r) space. Since it seems reasonable to suppose that a given change in r will have a greater effect on domestic bond demand than on foreign bond demand, the FE schedule is flatter than the BE schedule.

The intersection of the ME, BE and FE schedules gives the short-run equilibrium levels of the interest rate and the exchange rate. In fact, because of the adding-up constraint (3.16) we know that equilibrium in any two markets implies equilibrium in the third (Walras' law), and so our analysis of the PBM can be conducted using any two of the three schedules.

The stability of short-run equilibrium can be established as follows. Consider any point to the right of the BE schedule. At such a point, we know that the domestic interest rate is too high, for the given level of S, for there to be domestic bond market equilibrium, i.e. there must be excess demand for the (short-run) fixed level of domestic assets. This excess demand will tend to depress r towards the BE line. A converse argument applies to any point to the left of the BE schedule, and so we can draw in the horizontal arrows of motion as in figure 3.4. Now consider any point above the FE schedule. At such a point, the level of S is too high, given r, for the domestic level of demand for foreign assets to be equal to the (short-run) fixed supply. This means that the domestic currency value SF of foreign asset holdings is too high. Thus agents will attempt to sell foreign assets and convert the

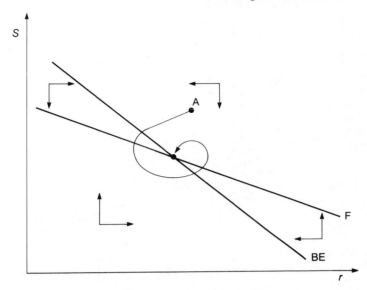

Figure 3.4   Global stability of short-run equilibrium

proceeds into domestic currency, causing the exchange rate to appreciate (S falls). Thus, at any point above FE, the vertical arrows of motion must point towards the FE schedule and, by a converse argument, at any point below FE the vertical arrows of motion must point upwards, as in figure 3.4. Combining these observations, we can see from figure 3.4 that starting from any point away from the intersection of the BE and FE schedules, such as point A, the economy will tend to move towards the equilibrium – the system is globally stable.

Before we examine the full impact effect of monetary policy in the PBM, we need to review briefly the comparative statics effects of increases in money, domestic bonds and foreign bonds.

An increase in M, *ceteris paribus*, will lead agents to attempt to rebalance their portfolios by buying domestic and foreign bonds. Thus a new equilibrium will be established after interest rates have fallen and the exchange rate has depreciated. Diagrammatically, the FE schedule shifts up and the BE schedule shifts to the left. An increase in domestic holdings of foreign assets F leads to an excess supply of foreign currency as agents try to rebalance their portfolios. As foreign bonds are sold, the exchange rate appreciates. As the exchange rate appreciates, the domestic currency value of foreign bonds falls until equilibrium is re-established with the interest rate unchanged and the domestic value of the new level of foreign bond holding, $S_1 F_1$ say, just equal to the old value $S_0 F_0$. Diagrammatically, the BE and

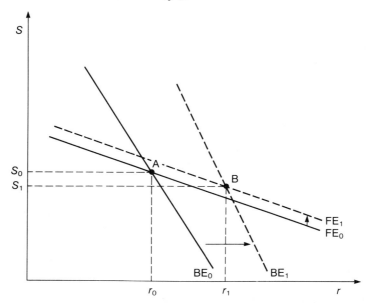

Figure 3.5 Increase in B where domestic and foreign assets are close substitutes

FE schedules both shift to the left to intersect at a point vertically below the initial equilibrium. An increase in B can be expected to lead to a rise in interest rates as the excess supply of domestic bonds depresses their market price (the BE schedule shifts to the right). Although the increase in wealth will tend to raise the demand for foreign assets (the FE schedule shifts upward), if domestic and foreign bonds are close substitutes in portfolios, this wealth effect will be swamped by the substitution effect of increased holdings of domestic bonds and there will be net sales of foreign bonds, leading to an exchange rate appreciation (figure 3.5). If, however, domestic and foreign bonds are not close substitutes, then the wealth effect will dominate and the exchange rate will depreciate as agents increase their holdings of foreign bonds (figure 3.6).

The Impact of Monetary Policy in the Portfolio Balance Model

Consider an increase in the money supply engineered by open market operations, i.e. the monetary authorities print an amount of money ΔM and use it to purchase domestic bonds. Thus domestic holdings of money rise by an amount ΔM and domestic bond holdings change by an amount ΔB such that $\Delta M + \Delta B = 0$. Since this directly affects the money and domestic bond markets, it will be convenient to use the BE and ME schedules for our

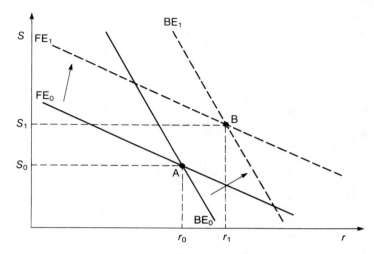

Figure 3.6   Increase in B where domestic and foreign assets are not close substitutes

analysis. The increase in private sector money holding can only be brought about by reducing the opportunity cost of money holding, i.e. r must fall for a given level of S (equivalently, the authorities drive up domestic bond prices and hence depress r in their attempts to repurchase government bonds). Thus the ME schedule must shift to the left (figure 3.7). Similarly, in order to induce wealth holders to part willingly with domestic assets, the rate of return r must fall for given S – the BE schedule also shifts to the left (figure 3.7). Now although the FE schedule is not drawn in figure 3.7, we know that the new short-run equilibrium must lie on FE. Thus, since FE is negatively sloped and flatter than BE, we know that the new short-run equilibrium B must be above and to the left of the initial equilibrium A – the interest rate falls and the exchange rate depreciates (point B).

Now consider the impact of open market operations in foreign assets ($\Delta M + S \Delta F = 0$). There will again be a tendency for r to fall because of the excess supply of money (the ME schedule shifts to the left). The government purchase of foreign assets (and hence foreign currency) will tend to depreciate the exchange rate (the FE schedule shifts upward). Since the new equilibrium must lie on the BE schedule (unchanged) the new equilibrium B must again be above and to the left of the initial equilibrium A (figure 3.8). The exchange rate has depreciated and the domestic interest rate is lower.

Thus the qualitative effects of open market operations are the same whether the government buys domestic or foreign assets. The quantitative effects are different, however. In figure 3.7 the new equilibrium must lie on

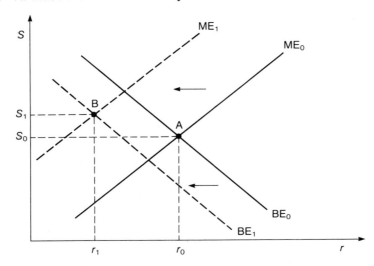

Figure 3.7   Increase in M ($\triangle M + \triangle B = 0$)

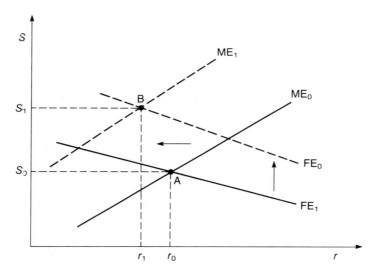

Figure 3.8   Increase in M ($\triangle M + \triangle B \neq 0$)

the unchanged FE schedule, whilst in figure 3.8 the new equilibrium must lie on the unchanged BE schedule. Since the FE schedule is flatter than the BE schedule, the change in the exchange rate $S_1 - S_0$ must be smaller in figure 3.7 than in figure 3.8, whilst the change in the interest rate must be larger. This is quite intuitive – open market purchases of domestic assets affect r directly while open market purchases of foreign assets affect S directly. Thus the real impact of monetary policy on the tradeables-producing sector (through S) and the sector producing interest-sensitive durable goods will depend upon the mix of open market operations.

We can now summarize all the impact effects of changes in the components of wealth and monetary policy on the exchange rate and the domestic interest rate, as in table 3.1, before going on to examine dynamic adjustment to long-run equilibrium in the PBM.

Dynamic Adjustment in the Portfolio Balance Model

So far we have not analysed the effect of monetary policy on the exchange rate through changes in the price level, nor have we looked at the dynamic stock flow interaction of changes in the exchange rate, the current account and the level of wealth. An increase in the money supply would be expected to lead eventually to a rise in domestic prices, but a change in prices will affect net exports and hence will have implications for the current account of the balance of payments. This in turn affects the level of wealth which, in the adjustment to long-run equilibrium, feeds back into asset market and hence affects exchange rate behaviour.

Holding the (exogenous) foreign price level constant, the current account balance (in foreign currency) can be written as

$$CA = N\left(\frac{S}{P}\right) + r^*F \tag{3.20}$$

In equation (3.20), $N(\ )$ represents the trade balance; this will improve as S rises[3] and/or P falls (competitiveness improves for a given level of foreign prices). The term r^*F represents net interest income from domestic holdings of foreign assets F. If the economy has traditionally been a net capital exporter, so that r^*F is positive, then a balance on the current account requires a trade deficit. Since a non-zero current account implies changes in F and hence in wealth, a trade deficit may be required in long-run equilibrium.

Now consider an increase in the money supply brought about by an open

Table 3.1   Impact effects in the portfolio balance model

	Changes in stocks			Open market operations	
Effect on	ΔF	ΔM	ΔB	$\Delta B + \Delta M = 0$	$\Delta M + S\Delta F = 0$
S	−	+	?	+	++
r	0	−	+	−−	−

market purchase of domestic bonds by the authorities. As we saw above, the impact effect of this will be to cause an immediate depreciation of the exchange rate. This is not the end of the story, however. Suppose that the economy was initially in equilibrium with a trade balance of zero and net foreign asset holdings of zero (and hence a current account balance of zero). This is depicted in figure 3.9 at the point corresponding to time t_0. Figure 3.9 is drawn so that the initial values (at time t_0) of the price level and the exchange rate are normalized to unity: $P_0 = S_0 = 1$. The impact effect is a jump in the exchange rate S_0 to S_1 (AC). Moreover, assuming that the Marshall–Lerner condition holds, the improvement in competitiveness will improve the trade balance from zero to a positive amount (FG).[4] This means that the current account goes into surplus and domestic residents begin to acquire net foreign assets (F accumulates). As we discussed above, an increase in F will tend to appreciate the exchange rate from C along CD, and the trade balance thus begins to worsen along GH. Meanwhile, the

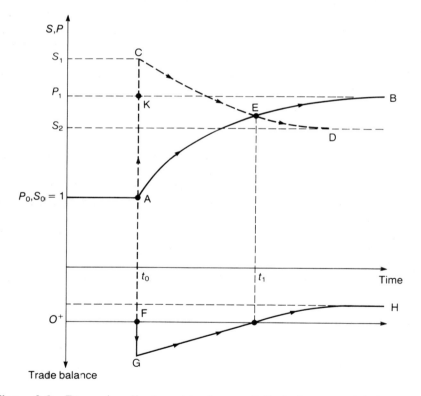

Figure 3.9 Dynamic adjustment in the portfolio balance model: increase in $M(\triangle M + \triangle B = 0)$

increase in the money supply will have begun to increase prices along the path AB towards the new long-run equilibrium price level P_1. This adds to the deterioration of competitiveness and hence the trade balance. At point E (time t_1) the exchange rate and the price level are equal in value and hence their ratio is unity ($S/P = 1$), but this is the same as the initial ratio at time t_0. Hence, the trade balance at time t must be back to its original level, i.e. zero. However, this is no longer enough to restore long-run equilibrium. Domestic wealth holders have now acquired a positive level of net foreign asset holdings and will be receiving a stream of interest income $r*F$ from abroad. Therefore, in order for the current account balance to be zero, the trade balance must actually go into deficit. This requires a further appreciation of the exchange rate (fall in S) to its long-run equilibrium level S_2, by which time the price level has reached its long-run equilibrium level P_1 and the current account just balances ($-N(S_2/P_1) = r*F$) so that there is no further net accumulation of foreign assets.

Note that the PBM gives an alternative derivation of the overshooting result described in section 3.2.2 – the exchange rate S jumps immediately above its long-run level and then falls slowly. Moreover, overshooting in the PBM does not rely solely on price level stickiness as in the Dornbusch overshooting model. Say, for example, that following the increase in the money supply the price level adjusted immediately to P_1 along AK in figure 3.9. As long as the new short-run equilibrium exchange rate S_1 exceeds P_1, competitiveness will have increased, the trade balance will have gone into surplus and a slow appreciation to the long-run exchange rate level would ensue as above.

Rational Expectations in the Portfolio Balance Model

We now extend our analysis of the PBM to consider rational expectations (Branson, 1983, 1984). In the analysis so far, the exchange rate jumps immediately in order to clear the asset markets and then adjusts slowly in response to induced current account imbalances. In the rational expectations portfolio balance model (REPBM), the essential difference is that expectations of future current account imbalance impact immediately on the exchange rate as the market looks ahead. Comparing the two versions of the model, we shall find that the long-run effects of various shocks remain the same, whilst the impact effects become magnified.

The REPBM is as follows:

$$W = M + B + SF \tag{3.21}$$

$$M = M(r, \; r* + \hat{S}) \, W \tag{3.22}$$

$$B = B(r, \; r* + \hat{S}) \, W \tag{3.23}$$

$$SF = F(r, \ r^* + \hat{S}) \ W \qquad (3.24)$$

$$\dot{F} = N(S/P, \ Z) + r^*F \qquad (3.25)$$

In fact, relations (3.22)–(3.24), which correspond to relations (3.17)–(3.19), implicitly assume that the certainty equivalence principle applies, so that the foreign rate of return is augmented by the actual rather than the expected proportional rate of depreciation of the exchange rate ($\hat{S} = \dot{S}/S = \dot{s}$). Relation (3.25) corresponds to (3.20), where we have made explicit that the current account surplus represents the rate of accumulation of foreign assets and we have included a real shift variable Z in the trade balance function ($N_z > 0$).

We shall solve the model qualitatively by sketching the phase diagram and the stable manifold in (F, S) space. Equation (3.25) already gives a dynamic equation for F. A corresponding equation for S can be derived as follows. Divide (3.22) and (3.24) by W and differentiate totally, holding the foreign yield constant:

$$\begin{bmatrix} d\,(SF/W) \\ d\,(M/W) \end{bmatrix} = \begin{bmatrix} F_r & F_s \\ M_r & M_s \end{bmatrix} \begin{bmatrix} dr \\ dS \end{bmatrix}$$

which implies

$$\begin{bmatrix} dr \\ dS \end{bmatrix} = (F_r M_s - M_r F_s)^{-1} \begin{bmatrix} M_s & -F_s \\ -M_r & F_r \end{bmatrix} \begin{bmatrix} d\,(SF/W) \\ d\,(M/W) \end{bmatrix}$$

so that dS is given by

$$dS = (F_r^{-1} M_s - M_r F_s) \left[-M_r \, d\,(SF/W) + F_r \, d\,(M/W) \right] \qquad (3.26)$$

The coefficients of SF/W and M/W in (3.26) can be interpreted as the partial derivatives of an adjustment function for $\hat{S}$:

$$\hat{S} = \phi\left[(SF/W), \ (M/W)\right] \qquad \phi_1 > 0, \ \phi_2 < 0 \qquad (3.27)$$

where the signs of the derivatives of (3.27) are inferred from (3.26).

Now consider setting $\hat{S} = 0$ (and hence $\dot{S} = 0$) in (3.27). Since S and F enter $\phi(\ )$ multiplicatively (in SF and W), changes in S and F which keep the product SF constant will keep $\hat{S}$ constant. In particular, therefore, the locus of points for which $\hat{S} = 0$ and hence $\dot{S} = 0$ must be a rectangular hyperbola

$$SF = \lambda \qquad (3.28)$$

where λ is a constant. This is sketched in figure 3.10.[5] From (3.27) we can see that an increase in S or F from a point on the $\dot{S} = 0$ locus will lead to rising, i.e. depreciating, S: $S > 0$.

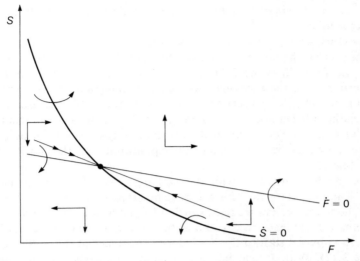

Figure 3.10   The saddlepath equilibrium for the rational expectations portfolio balance model

From (3.25) we can infer that the $\dot{F} = 0$ locus must be drawn downward sloping in (F, S) space and that increases in S or F will lead to rising F, $F > 0$; this is also sketched in figure 3.10. From figure 3.10 we can see that a saddlepath equilibrium will only exist if the $\dot{F} = 0$ locus is flatter than the $\dot{S} = 0$ locus in the neighbourhood of the intersection. From (3.28) we have

$$\left. \frac{dS}{dF} \right|_{\dot{S} = 0} = -\frac{S}{F}$$

while from (3.25) we have

$$\left. \frac{dS}{dF} \right|_{\dot{F} = 0} = -\frac{r^*}{N_s}$$

Hence, for a saddlepoint equilibrium we require

$$-\frac{S}{F} < -\frac{r^*}{N_s}$$

At equilibrium, $\dot{F} = 0$ and hence the saddlepath equilibrium condition reduces to

$$\frac{SN_s}{N} > 1$$

which is the familiar Marshall–Lerner condition for foreign exchange market stability.

Now consider a positive real shock to the current account. From (3.25), this means that the new $\dot{F} = 0$ locus must have lower values of S and F for higher Z. Thus, in figure 3.11 the $\dot{F} = 0$ locus shifts down. From initial equilibrium at A, the exchange rate therefore jumps in a step appreciation to point B and then appreciates slowly along the stable manifold, with S appreciating further and F accumulating until the new long-run equilibrium at point C is reached. Thus real disturbances lead to partial adjustment of the exchange rate to long-run equilibrium in the REPBM, i.e. undershooting.

This can be contrasted with the exchange rate effects of a monetary shock – an increase in M. This will have no effect on the $\dot{F} = 0$ locus. From (3.27), however, we can see that, starting from a position where $\hat{S} = \dot{S} = 0$, an increase in M leads to $\hat{S} < 0$ and hence $\dot{S} < 0$. Diagrammatically, this implies an upward shift of the $\dot{S} = 0$ locus and hence of the stable manifold (figure 3.12). With F held initially constant, the exchange rate therefore instantaneously depreciates from point A to point B and then slowly appreciates along BC to the new long-run equilibrium C. Thus the overshooting effect of monetary shocks is preserved in the REPBM. Note that, because the $\dot{F} = 0$ locus is downward sloping, point C must be below point A in figure 3.12 – a monetary expansion leads to a long-run appreciation of the

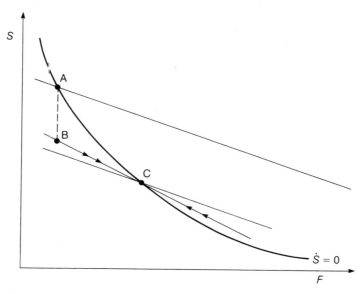

Figure 3.11 A positive real disturbance in the rational expectations portfolio balance model

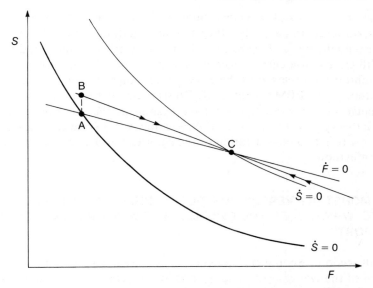

Figure 3.12 A positive monetary disturbance in the rational expectations portfolio balance model

exchange rate. Intuitively, this is because the initial large depreciation (A to B) leads to a current account surplus and hence an accumulation of foreign assets. The subsequent increase in F is then sufficient to appreciate the exchange rate to C.

3.2.4 Conclusion for Theoretical Exchange Rate Models

Monetary models of exchange rate determination were a clear advance over more traditional Mundell–Fleming models in that they took explicit account of stock equilibria in international asset markets rather than concentrating on the simpler flow equilibrium conditions as had been done in earlier analyses. However, early FLPM soon exchange rate models began to be seriously at odds with the facts of observation during the turbulent 1970s. In particular, early FLPM models assumed continuous PPP whilst large and sustained deviations from PPP were often manifestly clear. This defect was remedied by the second generation of monetary models – the SPM overshooting exchange rate models. In SPM models, differences in the speed of adjustment of goods and asset prices cause the exchange rate to act as a jump variable which can consistently overshoot long-run equilibrium levels in response to real and financial shocks.

Both these kinds of monetary model make a number of implicit assumptions, however. In particular, they assume that domestic and foreign assets are essentially perfectly substitutable in investors' portfolios, and that the wealth effects of a current account surplus or deficit are negligible. These assumptions are relaxed in the PBM of exchange rate determination.

Although the PBM (or rather REPBM) is clearly the most general of the exchange rate theories that we have examined, the question concerning which theory best fits the facts of observation is clearly an empirical matter. We now turn to a consideration of the empirical evidence on exchange rate determination.

3.3 MONETARY VERSUS PORTFOLIO MODELS OF THE EXCHANGE RATE: WHICH DOES THE EVIDENCE FROM THE RECENT FLOAT SUPPORT?

In this section we conduct a stocktaking exercise in an attempt to determine which of the two competing asset models (monetary or portfolio) are supported by the evidence for the recent floating experience. We start, in section 3.3.1, by outlining some of the relationships which underpin the asset approach. In section 3.3.2 we present a survey of the evidence relating to various formulations of the monetary approach to the exchange rate. In section 3.3.3 we discuss the more general portfolio balance approach and in section 3.3.4 we consider a synthesis of the monetary and portfolio balance approaches. In section 3.3.5 we examine the evidence on the out-of-sample predictive performance of the various exchange rate models which have been put forward. The discussion is summed up in section 3.3.6.

3.3.1 Some Modelling Relationships

At the outset it is useful to gather together some relationships which we shall refer to repeatedly throughout our survey. Equations (3.29) and (3.30) denote home and foreign semilog linear money demand functions:[6]

$$m_t^d = p_t + \phi y_t - \lambda r_t \tag{3.29}$$

$$m_t^d = p_t^* + \phi^* y_t^* - \lambda^* r_t^* \tag{3.38}$$

Assuming money market equilibrium then yields the equilibrium conditions given in equations (3.1) and (3.2).

The relationship between the home and foreign interest rate is assumed to be governed by a risk-adjusted interest parity relationship such as

$$r_t = r_t^* + \Delta s_{t+1}^e + \rho_t \tag{3.31}$$

where Δs^e_{t+1} denotes the expected change in the exchange rate, s is the natural logarithm of the home currency price of a unit of foreign exchange[7] and ρ_t denotes a risk premium.[8] Further, if covered interest parity holds, i.e.

$$r_t - r^*_t = \text{fp}_t \tag{3.32}$$

where fp_t is the forward premium $f_t - s_t$ and f_t is the logarithm of the forward exchange rate for maturity one period ahead, we can usefully write the risk premium ρ_t as

$$\rho_t = \text{fp}_t - \Delta s^e_{t+1} \tag{3.33}$$

The risk premium is that part of the expected rate of depreciation not discounted in the forward premium.

Finally, we can define the (logarithm of the) real exchange rate q_t as the deviation from PPP:

$$q_t = s_t - p_t + p^*_t \tag{3.34}$$

3.3.2 The Monetary Approach – Three Formulations

In this section we consider three empirical models of the exchange rate which we believe are representative of the monetary view. First, we consider an empirical model which purports to capture the FLPM approach. Second, we examine an empirical model derived from the Dornbusch (1976) theoretical model of exchange rate overshooting. Finally, we consider an empirical exchange rate model due to Frankel (1979a) – the real interest differential (RID) model – which purports to discriminate between the FLPM and SPM models.

Before reporting on the performance of these empirical models we discuss a number of econometric issues which arise in estimating models of this kind. We also consider what we term the first-period tests of the FLPM and RID models. Such tests, mostly conducted for the deutschmark–US dollar and sterling–US dollar exchange rates, run from 1972 to 1978 and are largely supportive of the monetary approach. The second-period tests of the FLPM and RID models are for the period from 1978 onwards and are seen to question the validity of the approach. Tests of the SPM model for the whole of the floating period are also considered.

The Flexible Price Monetary Formulation

In section 3.2.1 we derived an equation representative of the FLPM model:

equation (3.4). If the domestic and foreign money demand coefficients are equal ($\phi = \phi^*$, $\lambda = \lambda^*$), (3.4) reduces to

$$s_t = (m - m^*)_t - \phi(y - y^*)_t + \lambda(r - r^*)_t \tag{3.35}$$

A further assumption underlying the FLPM model is that the risk premium ρ_t in (3.31) is identically zero and therefore UIP holds continuously. Thus we can substitute Δs^e_{t+1} for $(r - r)^*_t$ in (3.35) to give

$$s_t = (m - m^*)_t - \phi(y - y^*)_t + \lambda\Delta s^*_{t+1} \tag{3.36}$$

Thus the expected change in the exchange rate and the interest differential, which reflects inflationary expectations, are interchangeable in this model. Some researchers relax the constraint that the income and interest rate elasticities are equal and thus specify an equation of the form (3.4) or, as a sort of hybrid,

$$s_t = (m - m^*)_t - \phi y_t + \phi^* y^*_t + \lambda\Delta s^e_{t+1} \tag{3.37}$$

Note also that (3.37) can be expressed as

$$s_t = (1 + \lambda)^{-1}(m - m^*)_t - (1 + \lambda)^{-1}\phi y_t + (1 + \lambda)^{-1}\phi^* y^*_t$$
$$+ \lambda(1 + \lambda)^{-1}s^e_{t+1} \tag{3.38}$$

If expectations are assumed to be rational,[9] then by iterating forward it is easy to show that (3.38) can be expressed in the forward solution form

$$s_t = (1 + \lambda)^{-1}\sum_{i=0}^{\infty}\left(\frac{\lambda}{1 + \lambda}\right)^i\left[(m - m^*)^e_{t+1} + \phi y^e_{t+1} + \phi^* y^{*e}_{t+1}\right]$$

where it is understood that expectations are conditioned on information at time t. Equation (3.39) makes it clear that the monetary model, with rational expectations, involves solving for the expected future path of the forcing variables, i.e. relative money and income. As is common in rational expectations models, the presence of the discount factor $\lambda/(1 + \lambda) < 1$ in (3.39) implies that expectations of the forcing variables need not, in general, be formed into the infinite future as long as the forcing variables are expected to grow at a rate less than $(1 + \lambda)/\lambda - 1$.

One immediate problem facing researchers in attempting to implement equation (3.35) for the recent floating experience is that PPP has manifestly not held continuously (see, for example, Frenkel, 1981; Taylor, 1988a, 1990b), and thus an important assumption necessary to derive (3.35) (i.e. $q = 0$) does not hold. Monetarists such as Mussa (1976) counter this by arguing that, since the exchange rate is the relative price of national monies and is thus determined in asset markets, a researcher should go directly from the relative money market equilibrium relations to equations (3.35) or (3.36).

However, even though (3.35) can be derived without imposing PPP directly, the interpretation placed on the interest differential in such equations may still be questionable. For example, and as we shall see below, proponents of (3.35) usually use short-term interest rates to capture inflationary expectations. However, we might question the validity of this assumption during periods when PPP does not hold and inflationary expectations are moderate. Under such circumstances it seems likely that the short-term interest rate differential will reflect real monetary disturbances, as in the SPM model, rather than inflationary expectations. Thus, it would be useful if equation (3.35) could be modified to allow for the separate effects of money supply changes on real interest differentials and also on inflationary expectations. Frankel (1979a) has in fact developed a monetary approach reduced form which relaxes the assumption that PPP holds continuously and splits the interest rate effect of a monetary change into real and inflationary components. We consider the Frankel (1979a) formulation below, but first we turn to an examination of empirical models of the SPM formulation.

The Sticky Price Monetary Formulation

An alternative monetary approach empirical model can be derived on the basis of the structural equations of the Dornbusch (1976) sticky price theoretical model which we discussed in section 3.2. As our starting point, we take the relative monetary equilibrium equation derived from (3.1) and (3.2) with the assumption of identical foreign and domestic money demand coefficients:

$$(m - m^*)_t = (p - p^*)_t + \phi(y - y^*)_t - \lambda(r - r^*)_t \qquad (3.40)$$

Since PPP does not hold continuously in the SPM model, we need an additional equation to describe the evolution of the price level. Driskell (1981) assumes that relative prices evolve according to a relationship of the following kind:

$$(p - p^*)_t = (p - p^*)_{t-1} + \pi[d - (y^* - y)]_{t-1} \qquad (3.41)$$

where d denotes relative aggregate demand which can be modelled as

$$d_t = \beta_1(s - p + p^*)_t + \beta_2(y - y^*)_t - \beta_3(r - r^*)_t \qquad (3.42)$$

Equation (3.41) is a relative Phillips curve, which is a discrete-time version of equation (3.7) in which variations in the foreign price level are explicitly allowed for rather than held constant. Relative aggregate demand depends upon a competitiveness term, relative income and the relative interest rate. By combining (3.40)–(3.42) the relative price equation can be obtained:

$$(p - p^*)_t = \beta_1 \pi s_{t-1} + \left(1 - \beta_1 \pi - \frac{\beta_3 \pi}{\lambda}\right)(p - p^*)_{t-1}$$

$$+ \frac{\beta_3 \pi}{\lambda}(m - m^*)_{t-1} + \left(\beta_2 \pi - \frac{\beta_3 \phi \pi}{\lambda}\lambda\right)(y - y^*)_{t-1} \qquad (3.43)$$

Driskell follows Dornbusch (1976) in assuming that exchange rate expectations are regressive and, in addition, assumes that the long-run exchange rate is proportional to the relative money supply:

$$\Delta s^e_{t+1} = -\nu(s_t - \bar{s}_t)$$

$$= -\nu(s_t - (m - m^*)_t) \qquad (3.44)$$

Using (3.40)–(3.44) plus a UIP condition, we can derive the following equation:

$$s_t = -\frac{\beta_1 \pi}{\lambda \nu} s_{t-1} + \left(1 + \frac{1}{\lambda \nu}\right)m'_t - \frac{\beta_3 \pi}{\nu \lambda^2} m'_{t-1} - (\lambda - \beta_1 \pi \lambda$$

$$- \beta_2 \pi)(\nu \lambda^2)^{-1} p'_{t-1} - \frac{\phi}{\nu \lambda} y'_t - (\beta_2 \pi \lambda - \beta_3 \phi \pi)(\nu \lambda^2)^{-1} y'_{t-1} \qquad (3.45)$$

or

$$s_t = \kappa_1 s_{t-1} + \kappa_2 m'_t + \kappa_3 m'_{t-1} + \kappa_4 p'_{t-1} + \kappa_5 y'_t + \kappa_6 y'_{t-1} \qquad (3.46)$$

where

$$x' = x - x^* \qquad \text{for } x = m, p, y$$

Comparing (3.45) and (3.46), we can infer the following coefficient restrictions on (3.46):

$$\sum_{i=1}^4 \kappa_1 = 1 \qquad \kappa_i < 0 \text{ for } i \neq 1, 3, 5 \qquad \kappa_2 > 1 \qquad (3.47)$$

The first constraint follows from the long-run neutrality of money which is implicitly assumed in (3.44). The remaining restrictions capture the overshooting characteristics of the model. It is instructive to rewrite (3.46) after imposing the first of these constraints and rearranging as

$$\Delta s'_t = (\kappa_1 - 1)(s - m')_{t-1} + \kappa_2 \Delta m'_t + \kappa_4(p' - m')_{t-1}$$

$$+ \kappa_5 y'_t + \kappa_6 y'_{t-1} \qquad (3.48)$$

If long-run stationary equilibrium obtains when $\Delta s_t = \Delta m'_t = 0$, $(r - r^*)_t = 0$ and $y'_t = y'_{t-1} = \bar{y}'_t$, then (3.48) can be interpreted as follows.[10] In the short run, the exchange rate overshoots in response to monetary shocks $\kappa_2 > 1$) and then the error correction term $(s - m')_{t-1}$ forces regression towards the long-run equilibrium exchange rate $\kappa_1 - 1 < 0$. In the long run, if relative differences in income are zero ($\bar{y}'_t = 0$), then $(\bar{m}' - \bar{p}')_t = 0$ (set $(r - r^*)_t = y'_t = 0$ in (3.40)) and the long-run equilibrium solution to (3.48) emerges as $\bar{s}_t = m'_t$.

The empirical (3.46) model can also be derived without imposing perfect capital mobility (in the sense of allowing short-run deviations from UIP). Although some of the coefficient restrictions remain under this derivation, the coefficient κ_2 on money growth need not be greater than unity (see Driskell, 1981). This restriction can therefore be interpreted as a test of perfect capital mobility in the context of the SPM model.

The Real Interest Differential Formulation

Frankel (1979a) argues that a shortcoming of the Dornbusch (1976) formulation of the SPM model is that it does not allow a role for differences in secular rates of inflation. His model is therefore an attempt to allow for this defect and the upshot is an exchange rate equation which includes the real interest rate differential as an explanatory variable – the RID variant of the monetary model.

In section 3.2.2 we showed that the rationally expected rate of depreciation in the Dornbusch model is proportional to the deviation from the long-run rate (equation (3.15)). Frankel modifies this to allow for secular rates of inflation:

$$\Delta s^e_{t+1} = -\nu(s_t - \bar{s}_t) + \pi^e_t - \pi^e_t{}^* \tag{3.49}$$

where π^e_t represents the current rate of expected long-run inflation. Combining this with the UIP condition (3.31) (with π_t set to zero) we have

$$s_t - \bar{s}_t = \nu^{-1}[(r - \pi^e)_t - (r^* - \pi^e{}^*)_t] \tag{3.50}$$

Although π^e_t and $\pi^e_t{}^*$ refer to long-run inflation expectations, (3.50) can be viewed as relating the exchange rate to real interest differentials. Given UIP and (long-run) PPP, the long-run interest differential must be equal to the long-run expected inflation differential,

$$\bar{r}_t - \bar{r}^*_t = \pi^e_t - \pi^{*e}_t \tag{3.51}$$

and so (3.50) can be alternatively expressed as

$$s_t - \bar{s}_t = -\nu^{-1}[(\bar{r}_t - r_t) - (\bar{r}^*_t - r^*_t)] \tag{3.52}$$

The exchange rate appreciates above its long-run level whenever the relative short-long nominal interest spread also does so.

Now, using (3.35) and (3.51) and denoting long-run values by a bar, as before, we have

$$\bar{s}_t = (\bar{m} - \bar{m}^*)_t - \phi\,(\bar{y}_t - \bar{y}_t^*) + \lambda(\pi_t^e - \pi_t^{*e}) \tag{3.53}$$

Substituting (3.53) into (3.50) and assuming, for simplicity, that the current equilibrium money supplies and income levels are given by their current actual levels (which amounts to assuming that they follow random walks), we derive the RID formulation:

$$s_t = (m - m^*)_t - \phi(y - y^*)_t - \nu^{-1}(r - r^*)_t + (\theta^{-1} + 1)(\pi^e - \pi^{*e})_t$$

or

$$s_t = \alpha_1(m - m^*)_t + \alpha_2(y - y^*)_t + \alpha_3(r - r^*)_t + \alpha_4(\pi^e - \pi^{*e})_t \tag{3.54}$$

Note that (3.54) is similar to the FLPM formulation (3.35), with the addition of the long-run expected inflation differential, so that a test of the significance from zero of α_4 should, in principle, allow discrimination. Since, however, the RID formulation involves only long-run PPP in its derivation, it can be viewed as a variant of the SPM model. The discriminating factor might then hinge on whether the relative inflation expectations term should appear, as here, or should not appear, as in the SPM formulation.

However, under the FLPM formulation, the nominal interest differential coefficient is expected to be positive, whilst under both the RID and SPM formulations it should be negative.[11]

Econometric Issues

Having derived equations such as (3.35), (3.45) and (3.54), it is tempting to view them as ideal candidates for estimation. However, there are important econometric issues that should be considered before any attempt is made to estimate equations such as these. For illustrative purposes only equation (3.35), rewritten here with a white noise error term, is considered in the following discussion:

$$s_t = \alpha_0(m - m^*)_t + \alpha_1(y - y^*)_t + \alpha_2(r - r^*)_t + \epsilon_t \tag{3.55}$$

First, a researcher estimating equation (3.55) for the recent floating exchange rate period faces a potential simultaneity problem – is this truly a reduced form equation? For example, it is now clear that the recent float has been one in which monetary authorities have intervened, at times substantially, in foreign exchange markets (see, for example, Artus, 1976; Mussa, 1981). If the effect of this intervention on the money supply is not sterilized, then the relative money supply term in (3.55) may be correlated with the error term as shocks to the exchange rate ϵ_t lead to intervention which changes the level of reserves which, if domestic credit expansion is not altered in order to sterilize the effect, will change the monetary base and hence the level of the money supply. Simultaneous equation bias will also be present in ordinary least squares (OLS) estimates of equation (3.55) if interest rates are set at least partly according to the current level of the exchange rate.

The above discussion indicates that, in implementing asset approach exchange rate equations in periods with foreign exchange intervention, researchers should carefully specify the reaction function for interest rates and money and use this information in estimating an equation such as (3.55) (eg by two-stage least squares (25LS)). A simpler method of accounting for the simultaneity between s and $m - m^*$ has been proposed by a number of researchers (see, for example, Frankel, 1979a) and involves constraining the coefficient on $m - m^*$ to unity and estimating an equation similar to (3.56)

$$s_t - (m - m^*)_t = \alpha_1 (y - y^*)_t + \alpha_2 (r - r^*)_t + \epsilon_t \qquad (3.56)$$

Thus the variables on the right-hand side of (3.56) reflect money demand influences which will lead to exchange rate movements under flexible rates or changes in the money supply under fixed rates as in the monetary approach to the balance of payments (see Frenkel and Johnson, 1976).

The First-period Tests of the Flexible Price Monetary and Real Interest Differential Empirical Models

One of the first tests of equation (3.36) was conducted by Frenkel (1976) for the deutschmark–US dollar exchange rate over the period 1920–3. Since this period corresponds to the German hyperinflation, Frenkel argues that domestic monetary impulses will overwhelmingly dominate dominate equation (3.36) and thus domestic income and foreign variable can be dropped, and attention focused simply on the effects of German money and the expected inflation (operating through expected depreciation). Further, Frenkel assumes that the risk premium in the UIP relationship (3.31) is zero and that covered interest rate parity holds so that the expected rate of depreciation is just the current forward premium (set $\pi_t = 0$ in (3.33)). Thus Frenkel's version of equaion (3.36) is

$$s_t = \alpha_0 + \alpha_1 m_t^G + \alpha_2 \mathrm{fp}_t + \epsilon_t \qquad (3.57)$$

where all variables are in natural logarithms and a G superscript denotes a German variable. The estimated version of (3.57) is

$$s_t = 5.135 + 0.975 m_t^G + 0.571 \,\mathrm{fp}_t$$
$$\quad (7.02) \quad (19.50) \qquad (8.10)$$

$$R^2 = 0.99 \qquad DW = 1.91 \qquad\qquad (3.58)$$

where t ratios are in parentheses, R^2 is the coefficient of determination and DW is the Durbin–Watson statistic. Since the elasticity of the exchange rate with respect to the money supply does not differ significantly from unity and the elasticity of the expected change in the exchange rate is positive, as predicted by the theory, this result clearly offers support for the FLPM model. But what happens when we consider periods in which monetary impulses do not dominate, as in the hyperinflation model?

A number of researchers have estimated FLPM equations for the more recent experience with floating exchange rates. For example, Bilson (1978a) tests equation (3.37) for the deutschmark–sterling exchange rate (with the forward premium fp_t substituted for Δs_{t+1}^e and without any restrictions on the coefficients on domestic and foreign money) over the period from January 1972 to April 1976, and his OLS results are reported in table 3.2, column 1. Although all the coefficients are correctly signed, only one coefficient differs significantly from zero. The insignificance of the coefficients combined with the high R^2 lead Bilson to conclude that multicollinearity is also a problem, and the presence of autocorrelation is suggestive of model misspecification. To account for the latter, Bilson incorporates a familiar partial adjustment scheme for the exchange rate and a first-order auto-regressive for the error term into equation (3.37) and obtains

$$s_t = \alpha_0 + \alpha_1 m_t + \alpha_2 m_t^* + \alpha_3 y_t + \alpha_4 y_t^* + \alpha_5 fp_t + \alpha_6 s_{t-1} + \epsilon_t$$

$$\epsilon_t = \rho \epsilon_{t-1} + u_t \tag{3.59}$$

Bilson's estimated version of (3.59) is reported in table 3.2, column 2. This equation appears to fit the data better than (3.37) in does terms of having a higher R^2, lower SER and DW to 2, but again only one coefficient differs significantly from zero. The second stage of Bilson's attempt to improve equation (3.37) is to account for the evident multicollinearity using the Theil–Goldberger mixed estimation procedure. Using as his priors for the procedure coefficients from closed economy money demand studies, Bilson derives an equilibrium exchange rate equation (table 3.2, column 3) which is clearly supportive of the FLPM. In a further paper Bilson (1978b) extends equation (3.37) by including a time trend to capture the 'secular decline in the demand for pounds relative to the DM' for the longer period 1970–77. Again, when the Theil–Goldberger procedure is utilized, results in accordance with the monetary approach are reported.

Hodrick's (1978) tests of equation (3.37) for the US dollar–deutschmark sterling–US dollar exchange rates over the period July 1972 to June 1975 are highly supportive of the FLPM. For example, the US dollar–deutschmark equation, reported in table 3.2, column 4 has the home and foreign money supply terms close to $+1$ and -1 (the hypothesis that they are equal to $+1$ and -1 cannot be rejected at the 5 per cent level), the income coefficients are both correctly signed but only the US term is significant (although its magnitude is too great), and the interest rate coefficients are both significant but the German interest rate has the wrong sign. Notice that in the studies by Bilson (1978a, b) and Hodrick (1978) no account is taken of the potential simultaneous equation bias that may exist in monetary approach empirical models of this kind.

In estimating equation (3.37), Bilson found it necessary to use a sophisticated econometric technique to account for the multicollinearity. An alternative, and much simpler, method that researchers have used to overcome this problem is to introduce relative money supplies, income and interest rates in a constrained fashion, and estimate equation (3.35).

Putnam and Woodbury (1979) estimate equation (3.35) for the sterling-US dollar exchange rate over the period 1972-4 and their estimated result is reported in table 3.2, column 5 (because OLS estimates of (3.35) revealed autocorrelation, the equation was estimated using the Hildreth–Lu technique). Notice that all the coefficients are significantly different from zero at the 5 per cent significance level and all are correctly signed in terms of the monetary approach; however, the money supply term is significantly different from unity. Putnam and Woodbury fail to allow for any potential simultaneity between the explanatory variables and the exchange rate in equation (3.35)

Dornbusch (1979), in his study of the deutschmark–US dollar exchange rate (March 1974 to May 1978), proposed accounting for any simultaneity between $m - m^*$ and s by estimating equation (3.56). An equation representative of Dornbusch's results is reported in table 3.2, column 6, and although both the income and interest rate terms are correctly signed, only the former is significant. Furthermore, judging by DW, the equation suffers from acute first-order autocorrelation even after estimating the equation with a first-order autoregressive process specified for the error term. This may be a consequence of the lack of dynamics in the model. For instance, most single-country money demand studies do not assume that money market equilibrium is continuously maintained and indeed find evidence of strongly significant partial adjustment terms (see, for example, Coghlan (1978) for the UK and Goldfeld (1976) for the USA). In an attempt to improve the performance of the monetary approach equation, Dornbusch assumes that the dependent variable $(s - m + m^*)_t$ follows a simple partial adjustment scheme and improves the specification of the money demand function by introducing a long-term interest rate as an additional opportunity cost variable (it is important to note that such specification changes will not be legitimate in models where regressive expectations are also assumed to be rational (see Minford and Peel (1983) for a discussion). The resulting equation is

$$s_t = (m - m^*)_t + \alpha_0 (s - m + m^*)_{t-1} + \alpha_1 (y - y^*)_t$$
$$+ \alpha_2 (r - r^*)_t + \alpha_3 (r_L - r_L^*)_t \tag{3.60}$$

Table 3.2 The first-period tests of the flexible price monetary and real interest differential reduced forms

| | DM–UK £ Jan 1972 to Apr 1976[a] | | | US$–DM Apr 1973 to Sep 1975[b] | DM–US$ 1972–7[c] | UK£–US$ Mar 1974 to May 1978[d] | |
| | OLS | OLS | Theil-Goldberger mixed | OLS | Hildreth–Lu | AR 1 | AR 1 |
Variable	1	2	3	4	5	6	7
m_t	0.417 (0.94)	0.358 (0.94)	1.001	1.520 (2.98)	–	–	–
m_t^*	−0.915 (4.32)	−0.586 (2.86)	−1.008	−1.390 (2.48)	–	–	–
$(m - m^*)_t$	–	–	–	–	0.630 (9.50)	1	1
y_t	−0.208 (0.72)	−0.408 (1.58)	−1.018	−2.230 (2.16)	–	–	–
y_t^*	−0.171 (0.56)	−0.014 (0.06)	0.999	0.070 (0.18)	–	–	–
$(y - y^*)_t$	–	–	–	–	−0.770 (6.10)	−0.410 (2.50)	−0.230 (1.35)
τ_t	–	–	–	2.530 (2.16)	–	–	–
τ_t^*	–	–	–	1.930 (2.88)	–	–	–

	(1)	(2)	(3)	(4)	(5)	(6)
$(r - r^*)_t$	—	—	—	0.140 (7.60)	0.870 (0.54)	−1.050 (0.70)
$(r_t - r_t^*)$	—	—	—	—	—	10.270 (3.93)
ρ	0.002 (0.59)	0.003 (1.39)	0.023 (1.46)	—	—	—
s_{t-1}	—	0.423 (2.95)	—	—	—	—
$s - m + m^*$	—	—	−0.014	—	—	0.67 (6.09)
Constant	4.454 (4.78)	3.097 (2.21)	7.850 (3.03)	—	1.130 (11.30)	0.46 (2.30)
R^2	0.92	0.96	0.66	0.88	n.a.	n.a.
Durbin–Watson	0.51	1.89	1.61	1.75	1.28	1.94
SER	0.047	0.031	0.37	—	0.021	0.018
$\hat{\rho}$	—	—	—	0.53	0.97	0.53

SER, standard error of regression; R^2, coefficient of determination; $\hat{\rho}$, estimated first-order autocorrelation coefficient; AR 1, first-order autoregression; n.a., not available; t ratios in parentheses.

[a] Bilson, 1978a.
[b] Hodrick, 1978.
[c] Putnam and Woodbury, 1979.
[d] Dornbusch, 1979.

where r_L is the long-term bond yield. The estimates of this equation are reported in table 3.2, column 7. This specification of the FLPM reduced form is claimed by Dornbusch to be a substantial improvement over the simple monetary approach specification. In particular, the lagged adjustment term is significant, the long interest rate differential is statistically significant and the SER is lower than that in column 6; however, in other ways the equation is somewhat disappointing (e.g. the relative income and short interest rate terms are both insignificant).

The long interest rate term in equation (3.60) was included as an empirical expedient; it was hoped that its introduction would improve the empirical fit of equation (3.35). However, an interpretation which is consistent with Frankel's RID equation can be placed on the long interest differential. Thus Frankel (1979a), in his implementation of equation (3.59) for the deutschmark–US dollar exchange rate over the period July 1974 to February 1978, uses a long bond interest differential as an instrument for the expected inflation term, on the assumption that long-term rates of interest are equalized. His estimated equation is

$$
\begin{aligned}
s_t = \ &1.39 + \underset{(0.21)}{0.97}\,(m - m^*)_t - \underset{(0.22)}{0.52}\,(y - y^*)_t - \underset{(2.04)}{5.40}\,(r - r^*)_t \\
&+ \underset{(3.33)}{29.40}\,(\pi^e - \pi^{*e})_t
\end{aligned}
\tag{3.61}
$$

$$
R^2 = 0.91 \qquad \hat{\rho} = 0.46
$$

where estimated standard errors are given in parentheses. Comparing the coefficient signs in equation (3.61) with the hypothesized signs of the RID equation (3.54), we see that all variables are correctly signed and statistically significant. Frankel argues that since the coefficients on the interest rate and expected inflation terms are both significant the extreme FLPM and SPM models are both rejected in favour of his RID model (see table 3.2). Using the coefficient on the interest differential from equation (3.61), an estimate of θ in (3.50) can be obtained as $1/5.4$ ($= 0.1854$) so that 81.5 per cent of any deviation from PPP remains after one quarter and 44.1 per cent (i.e. 0.815^4) is expected to remain after one year.

The estimated values in equation (3.61) allow a calculation of how much the deutschmark–US dollar exchange rate would have to depreciate for a once and for all increase in the US money supply of 1 per cent. The calculated fall in the RID (i.e. the SPM effect) gives a current exchange rate overshoot of 1.23 per cent. If, however, the monetary expansion signals to investors a new higher target for monetary growth, the initial overshooting will be greater. Frankel estimates that if agents' expected inflation rate is raised by 1 per cent per annum this will lead to a short-run exchange rate overshoot of 1.58 per cent. Thus, ignoring the expected inflation effect biases downwards our estimate of any short-run exchange rate overshooting.

This completes our review of the early tests of the monetary approach to the exchange rate. On balance, the results seem to lend support to the monetary approach in both its FLPM and RID versions. However, for two reasons the results should be treated with caution. First, few authors consider the simultaneity issue and, of those that do, attention is focused only on the relative money supply term with no consideration given to short-term interest rates. Second, all the researchers for the 1970s report autocorrelated residuals from their estimates of the monetary approach equation. Indeed, Dornbusch (1979) reports autocorrelated residuals after correcting for first-order autocorrelation. This suggests that the monetary model is misspecified: either (serially correlated) variables have been excluded which are important determinants of the exchange rate, or the dynamics of the equation, in terms of the lag structure, are inadequate. We shall return to these issues after discussing tests of the monetary approach equation for the second half of the floating period.

The Second Period Tests of the Flexible Price Monetary and Real Interest Differential Reduced Forms

Although the monetary approach appears reasonably well supported for the period up to 1978, the picture alters dramatically once the sample period is extended. For example, in table 3.3 we report estimates of the RID model reported by Dornbusch (1980), Haynes and Stone (1981), Frankel (1984) and Backus (1984) which cast serious doubt on its ability to track the exchange rate in-sample: few coefficients are correctly signed (many are wrongly signed), the equations have poor explanatory power as measured by the coefficient of determination and autocorrelation is a problem. One particularly disturbing feature of the equations in table 3.3, columns 1, 3 and 4 (the deutschmark–US dollar) is that the sign on the relative money supply term is negative for the period, suggesting that an increase in the home relative money supply leads to an exchange rate appreciation! The latter phenomenon, of the price of the deutschmark rising as its supply is increased, has been labelled by Frankel (1982a) as the 'mystery of the multiplying marks' (we shall return to this below).

How can we explain this poor performance of the monetary approach equations for the second half of the floating sample? Rasulo and Wilford (1980) and Haynes and Stone (1981) have suggested that the root of the problem can be traced to the constraints imposed on relative monies, incomes and interest rates. The imposition of such constraints may be justified on the grounds that, if multicollinearity is present, constraining the variables will increase the efficiency of the coefficient estimates. However,

Haynes and Stone (1981) show that the subtractive constraints used in monetary approach equations are particularly dangerous because they may lead to biased estimates and also (in contrast with additive constraints) to sign reversals, and this could explain the 'perverse' sign on the relative money supply terms reported in table 3.3. Indeed, when Haynes and Stone estimate an unconstrained version of the RID model, the sign on the relative money term is as predicted by the theory (see table 3.3, column 5). However, notice that in their estimated equation we again have a textbook example of multicollinearity: high R^2 combined with few individually statistically significant variables.

An alternative explanation for the poor performance of the monetary model in the second period has been given by Frankel (1982a). He attempts to explain the mystery of the multiplying marks by introducing wealth into the money demand equations. The justification for this inclusion is that the FRG was running a current account surplus in the late 1970s which was redistributing wealth from US residents to German residents, thus increasing the demand for deutschmarks and reducing the demand for dollars independently of the other arguments in the money demand functions. By including home and foreign wealth (defined as the sum of government debt and cumulated current account surpluses) in equation (3.54) and by not constraining the income, wealth and inflation terms to have equal and opposite signs, Frankel (1982a) reports a monetary approach equation in which all variables, apart from the income terms, are correctly signed and most are statistically significant; the explanatory power of the equation is also good.

A further explanation of the failure of the monetary approach equations can be traced to the relative instability of the money demand functions underlying reduced forms such as (3.54). Thus a number of single-country money demand studies strongly indicate that there have been shifts in velocity for the measure of money utilized by the above researchers (see Artis and Lewis (1981) for a discussion). Frankel (1984) incorporates shifts in money demand functions into equation (3.54) by introducing a relative velocity shift term $v - v^*$ which is modelled by a distributed lag of $(p + y - m) - (p^* + y^* - m^*)$. Including the term $v - v^*$ in equation (3.54) (along with a term capturing the real exchange rate – the inclusion of such a term in an asset reduced form will be considered below) for five currencies leads to most of the monetary variable coefficients becoming statistically significant and of the correct sign. However, significant first-order serial correlation remains a problem in all the reported equations.

Driskell and Sheffrin (1981) argue that the poor performance of the monetary model can be traced to the failure to account for the simultaneity bias introduced by having the expected change in the exchange rate (implicitly) on the right-hand side of the monetary equations. One potential method of circumventing such simultaneity is offered by the rational expec-

Table 3.3 The second-period tests of the flexible price monetary and real interest differential reduced forms

Variable	1	2	3	4	5	6
	US$-DM Feb 1973-9[a]		DM-US$ Feb 1974 to July 1981[b]	DM-US$ July 1974 to April 1980[c]		Can$-US$ 1971(1)-1980(4)[d]
	AR 1	OLS	AR1	AR 1	AR 1	OLS
m_t	-	-	-	-	0.24 (0.84)	-
m_t^*	-	-	-	-	-1.84 (3.95)	-
$(m-m^*)_t$	-0.03 (0.07)	1	-0.05 (0.15)	-0.57 (1.89)	-	1.097 (3.64)
y_t	-	-	-	-	0.20 (0.77)	-
y_t^*	-	-	-	-	0.56 (2.20)	-
$(y-y^*)_t$	-1.05 (0.97)	0.16 (0.17)	0.07 (0.32)	0.02 (0.08)	-	-0.453 (0.82)
r_t	-	-	-	-	0.02 (0.01)	-
r_t^*	-	-	-	-	-2.50 (1.29)	-
$(r-r^*)_t$	0.01 (1.90)	-0.01 (1.36)	-0.61 (2.26)	0.22 (0.13)	-	-0.000 (0.03)

continued

Table 3.3 *continued*

Variable	1 US$-DM Feb 1973-9[a]	2	3 DM-US$ Feb 1974 to July 1981[b]	4 DM-US$ July 1974 to April 1980[c]	5	6 Can$-US$ 1971(1)-1980(4)[d]
	AR 1	OLS	AR1	AR 1	AR 1	OLS
$\Delta p^e - \Delta p^{e*}$	0.04 (2.07)	0.01 (0.67)	1.34 (1.63)	13.33 (3.57)	–	-0.106 (3.00)
Δp^e	–	–	–	–	2.62 (0.67)	–
Δp^{e*}	–	–	–	–	3.53 (0.75)	–
$(s - m + m^*)_{t-1}$	–	0.83 (8.26)	–	–	–	–
Constant	5.76 (2.81)	0.23 (0.12)	0.80 (3.80)	-4.08 (23.40)	1.86 (1.65)	–
$\bar{R}^2$	0.33	0.88	–	0.38	0.85	0.43
Durbin–Watson	1.83	1.85	–	–	–	0.60
SER	0.05	1.85	0.33	–	–	–
$\hat{\rho}$	0.88	–	0.95	0.77	0.59	–

Definitions as in table 3.2.
[a] Dornbusch, 1980.
[b] Frankel, 1984.
[c] Haynes and Stone, 1981.
[d] Backus, 1984.

tations solution of the monetary model, which effectively gives an equation purged of the interest differential–forward exchange rate effect. Recently a number of researchers have begun to test this version of the model, with some degree of success. For example, Hoffman and Schlagenhauf (1983) implement a version of the forward solution FLPM formulation (equation (3.39)) by specifying a time series model for the stochastic evolution of the fundamentals. More specifically, the money and income variables in (3.39) are assumed to be generated by ARIMA $(1, 1, 0)$ processes:

$$\Delta z_t = \rho_z \Delta z_{t-1} + \epsilon_t \tag{3.62}$$

so that

$$\Delta z_{t+1} = \rho_z^1 \Delta z_t \tag{3.63}$$

where $z = m, m^*, y, y^*$. Rearranging (3.39) and continuously substituting from (3.63), the forward solution for the FLPM under rational expectations becomes (with $\phi^* = \phi$)

$$s_t = (m - m^*)_t - \phi(y - y^*)_t + \frac{\rho_m \lambda}{1 + \lambda - \lambda \rho_m} \Delta m_t$$
$$- \frac{\rho_m \lambda}{1 + \lambda - \lambda \rho_{m^*}} \Delta m_t^* - \frac{\phi \rho_y \lambda}{1 + \lambda - \lambda \rho_y} \Delta y_t + \frac{\phi \rho_{y^*} \lambda}{1 + \lambda - \lambda \rho_{y^*}} \Delta y_t$$

$$\tag{3.64}$$

Equation (3.64) is estimated jointly with (3.62) for France, the FRG and the UK, and likelihood ratio tests are computed for the validity of the rational expectations hypothesis and the validity of this hypothesis plus the coefficient restrictions implied by the FLPM (such as the unitary coefficient on relative money supplies), and although the expectations restrictions are not rejected for any of the countries the FLPM restrictions are rejected for the FRG. Kearney and MacDonald (1990) estimate (3.62) and (3.64) for the Australian dollar–US dollar exchange rate and cannot reject the restrictions implied by rational expectations FLPM model.

The rational expectations solution to the FLPM has spawned further empirical work which seeks to test for the presence of speculative bubbles. Thus it is well known from the rational expectations literature that equation (3.39) is only one solution from a potentially infinite sequence (see, for example, Blanchard and Walson, 1982). If we denote the exchange rate given by (3.39) as $\hat{s}$, then it is straightforward to demonstrate[12] that equation (3.38) has multiple rational expectations solutions, each of which can be written in the form

$$s_t = \hat{s} - b_t \tag{3.65}$$

where the 'rational bubble' term b_t satisfies

$$b^e_{t+1} = \lambda^{-1}(1 + \lambda)\,b_t$$

Meese (1987) attempts to test for bubbles by applying a version of the Hausman (1978) specification test suggested by West (1986) for present value models. The test involves estimating a version of (3.38) (which produces consistent coefficient estimates regardless of the presence or otherwise of rational bubbles) and a closed form version of (3.39) (which produces consistent coefficient estimates only in the absence of bubbles). Hausman's specification test is used to determine if the two sets of coefficient estimates of β are significantly different. If they are, then this is suggestive of the existence of a speculative bubble. In fact, for the US dollar–yen, US dollar–deutschmark and US dollar–sterling exchange rates Meese finds that the two estimates of β are significantly different and therefore rejects the no-bubbles hypothesis.[13] Kearney and MacDonald (1990) apply a version of this methodology to the Australian dollar–US dollar exchange rate and cannot reject the no-bubbles hypothesis.

An alternative way of testing for bubbles has been to adopt the variance bounds test methodology originally proposed by Shiller (1979) in the context of interest rates. This can be illustrated in the following way. If we define the *ex post* rational or perfect foresight exchange rate as that given by replacing expected future values of money and income in (3.39) with their actual values

$$s^*_t = (1 + \lambda)^{-1} \sum_{i=1}^{\infty} \left(\frac{\lambda}{1 + \lambda}\right)^i [(m - m^*)_{t+1} - \phi y_{t+1} + \phi^* y_{t+1}] \qquad (3.66)$$

then s^*_t will differ from $\hat{s}_t$ by a rational forecast error, u_t say (i.e. $s^*_t = \hat{s}_t + u_t$). Given that u_t is a rational forecast error, $\hat{s}_t$ and u_t must be orthogonal and so we have

$$\text{var}(s^*_t) = \text{var}(\hat{s}_t) + \text{var}(u_t)$$

which implies

$$\text{var}(s^*_t) \geq \text{var}(\hat{s}_t) \qquad (3.67)$$

In the absence of bubbles the inequality given by (3.67) should hold. However, in the presence of bubbles (3.67) is likely to be violated since, on using (3.65), we have $s^*_t = s_t - b_t + u_t$ and the relationship corresponding to (3.67) is

$$\text{var}(s^*_t) = \text{var}(s_t) + \text{var}(b_t) + \text{var}(u_t) - 2\,\text{cov}(s_t, b_t) \qquad (3.68)$$

Since, in the presence of bubbles, s_t and b_t are likely to be positively correlated, we cannot derive (3.67) from (3.68), and if we find in an empirical study that (3.67) is violated (i.e. evidence of excess volatility) this could be taken as evidence of bubbles.

Huang (1981) tests versions of (3.67) for the US dollar–deutschmark, US dollar–sterling and sterling–deutschmark exchange rates for the period March 1973 to March 1979. His results support excess volatility and by inference he finds against the no-bubbles hypothesis. Kearney and MacDonald (1990) implement (3.67) for the Australian dollar–US dollar exchange rate over the period January 1984 to December 1986 and generally find in favour of the no-bubbles hypothesis.

There are, however, a number of problems with this kind of approach. First, they are conditional on an assumed model of the exchange rate: violation could be due to the inappropriate model (we shall consider variance bounds tests for the other models below). Second, and perhaps more importantly, there may be other possible explanations for the presence of bubbles: there may be a measurement error in computing the perfect foresight exchange rate, the stationary transformations may be inappropriate or there may be small-sample bias.

Tests of the Sticky Price Monetary Reduced Form Equation

We now turn to some empirical estimates of the SPM reduced form. Driskell (1981) presents an estimate of equation (3.46) for the Swiss franc–US dollar rate for the period 1973–7 (quarterly data):

$$s_t = 2.22 + 0.43s_{t-1} + 2.37(m - m^*)_t - 2.45(m - m^*)_{t-1}$$
$$(2.82) \quad (3.65) \quad (5.73) \quad (5.60)$$

$$+ 0.93(p - p^*)_t \tag{3.69}$$
$$(2.23)$$

$$R^2 = 0.99 \qquad \text{Durbin's } h = 0.21 \qquad \hat{\rho} = 0.35$$
$$(1.37)$$

where, because of the unavailability of a quarterly income series, the y terms have been dropped and the presence of first-order residual autocorrelation necessitated estimation using the Cochrane–Orchutt procedure. Note that $\Sigma_1^4 \kappa_1 = 1.28$ and turns out to be insignificantly different from unity at the 5 per cent level, thus supporting PPP as a long-run phenomenon. Interestingly, although the coefficient on $(m - m^*)_t$ is greater than unity, which is clearly supportive of the perfect capital mobility version of the SPM model, the coefficients on s_{t-1} and $(p - p^*)_{t-1}$ are both positive, which is supportive of the imperfect capital mobility version of the SPM model (see Driskell, 1981). Driskell does not use a structural equation estimator to account for potential simultaneity between s and m' on the grounds that the Swiss franc's float was relatively clean for this period (because of currency substitution the Swizz authorities adopted a managed float in the period after 1977 (see Vaubel, 1980)).

Other tests of the SPM reduced form have been conducted by Wallace (1979), Hacche and Townend (1981) and Backus (1984). Wallace was OLS to estimate an unconstrained version of equation (3.46) for the Canadian dollar–US dollar for the period 1951(2)–1961(1). Results supportive of the SPM are presented and, interestingly, it is shown that the coefficient on the domestic money supply is significantly less than unity, which is supportive of the imperfect capital mobility version of the model. Backus (1984) tests equation (3.46) for the same exchange rate as Wallace for the recent Canadian floating experience (1971(1)–1980(4)) and, in support of the earlier results, finds no evidence of overshooting. However, Backus's OLS results differ from those of Wallace in that he finds few statistically significant coefficients.

Estimates of a more dynamic version of equation (3.46) by Hacche and Townend (1981) for the sterling effective exchange rate (May 1972 to February 1980) suggest exchange rate overshooting, but in order respects the estimated equation is unsatisfactory: many coefficients are insignificant and wrongly signed, and the equation does not exhibit sensible long-run properties.

Clearly, the problems associated with the models discussed in the previous section are equally valid here, and this may explain the mixed empirical support for equation (3.46). Indeed, Pappell (1988) argues that the price and exchange rate dynamics underlying the Dornbusch SPM cannot be captured by single-equation estimation methods. To capture such dynamics, he argues, it is necessary to use a system method of estimation which incorporates the cross-equation constraints derived from the structural equations and the assumption of rational expectations. His procedure allows domestic income and interest rates, but not the money supply, to be modelled endogenously. Effectively, what Pappell does is to reduce the structural model to a reduced form vector autoregressive moving-average (ARMA) model which has non-linear constraints on the parameters and is estimated jointly with equations for income and the interest rate. Using constrained maximum likelihood methods, the model is estimated for the effective exchange rates of the FRG, Japan, the UK and the USA with data for the period 1973(2)–1984(4). Pappell notes: 'The results of the estimation are moderately successful. Most of the structural coefficients have the expected sign, are of reasonable magnitude, and are significant . . . . Our results . . . show that Dornbusch's model and its extensions provide a solid empirical, as well as theoretical, basis for understanding the functioning of the flexible exchange rate system.'

A version of the SPM model due to Buiter and Miller (1981) has been empirically implemented by Barr (1989) and Smith and Wickens (1988, 1990) for the sterling–US dollar exchange rate and both sets of authors report favourable in-sample estimates of the model. The results reported in these papers are likely to be fairly robust since care has been taken in specifying the model dynamics and also Smith and Wickens estimated the model structurally. In simulating their model, Smith and Wickens (1988) find that the exchange rate overshoots by 21 per cent in response to a 5 per cent change in the money supply.

Wadhwani (1984) uses the SPM model to generate s^* in (3.67) and finds that the inequality is violated for the US dollar–sterling rate over the period 1973(1)–1982(3). His results are therefore supportive of those generated by Huang (1981) using the FLPM: bubbles seem to be important in foreign exchange markets.

3.3.3 The Portfolio Balance Approach

As we discussed in section 3.2, the distinctive features of the PBM are that domestic and foreign bonds are assumed to be imperfect substitutes and wealth enters asset demand equations as a scale variable. Thus the asset sector of a simple portfolio model for the home country can be described as (similar relationships are assumed to hold for the foreign country)

$$m_t - p_t = \alpha_0 y_t + \alpha_1 r_t + \alpha_2 r_t^* + \alpha_3 w_t \qquad \alpha_0, \alpha_3 > 0 \quad \alpha_1, \alpha_2 < 0$$
$$(3.70)$$

$$b_t - p_t = \beta_0 y_t + \beta_1 r_t + \beta_2 r_t^* + \beta_3 w_t \qquad \beta_0, \beta_1, \beta_3 > 0 \quad \beta_2 < 0 \quad (3.71)$$

$$fb_t + s_t - p_t = \pi_0 y_t + \pi_1 r_t + \pi_2 r_t^* + \pi_3 w_t \qquad \pi_0, \pi_2, \pi_3 > 0 \quad \pi_1 < 0$$
$$(3.72)$$

where b denotes domestic (non-traded) bonds, fb denotes foreign (traded) bonds, w denotes real wealth, money and bond demands have been set equal to their respective supplies, and home and foreign interest rates are linked via the interest parity relationship. The main implication of equations (3.70)–(3.72) is that the exchange rate is determined not just by money market conditions, as in the monetary model, but also by conditions in bond markets.

Compared with the monetary approach to the exchange rate, relatively less empirical work has been conducted on the PBM, mainly because of the limited availability of good disaggregated data on non-monetary assets. Broadly, two types of empirical test have been conducted by researchers. The first concentrates on solving the short-run portfolio model as a reduced form (assuming expectations are static) in order to determine its explanatory power.

The second indirect type of test involves solving the PBM for the risk premium in the UIP equation (3.34) in order to determine whether bonds denominated in different currencies are perfect substitutes.[14] In addition, Branson (1984) examines the time series behaviour of a number of financial variables for several countries to see whether it is consistent with the PBM.

The reduced form exchange rate equation derived from the above system can be written as follows (see Branson et al. (1977) – the assumed short-run nature of the relationship allows y and p to be assumed exogenous and constant):

$$s_t = g(m_t, m_t^*, b_t, b_t^*, \text{fb}_t, \text{fb}_t^*)$$ (3.73)

Branson et al. (1977) estimate a log linear version of equation (3.73) for the deutschmark–US dollar exchange rate for August 1971 to December 1976. The actual form of the equation estimated is

$$s_t = \alpha_0 + \alpha_1 m_t + \alpha_2 m_t^* + \alpha_3 \text{fb}_t + \alpha_4 \text{fb}_t^* + \epsilon_t$$ (3.74)

where the money supplies are defined as M1 and the foreign assets are proxied by cumulated current accounts. In moving from (3.73) to (3.74), Branson et al. drop the b and b^* terms because of the ambiguous effect that they have on the exchange rate, depending on the degree of substitutability between traded and non-traded bonds (see the first part of section 3.2.3). However, as Bisignano and Hoover (1982) point out, this rather arbitrary exclusion will generally result in biased regression coefficients. Although the OLS estimates of equation (3.74) reported by Branson et al. are deemed supportive of the PBM, once account is taken of acute first-order residual autocorrelation, only one coefficient, that on the US money supply, is statistically significant. By specifying a simple reaction function which purports to capture the simultaneity between the exchange rate and the money supply, Branson et al. re-estimate equation (3.74) using 2SLS and report more satisfactory estimates of the empirical PBM; however, autocorrelation remains a problem (the estimated first-order autocorrelation coefficient is 0.87, which suggests that unexplained shocks have persistent effects on the exchange rate and hence that this version of the PBM does not fully explain the deutschmark–US dollar exchange rate). Branson et al. (1979) estimate equation (3.74) for the deutschmark–US dollar exchange rate for the longer period August 1971 to December 1978, but the results are shown not to differ significantly from the earlier ones; again, persistent autocorrelation is a problem. In a further paper, Branson and Halttunen (1979) estimate equation (3.74) for five currencies (the yen, the French franc, the Italian lire, the Swiss franc and sterling) against the deutschmark for a variety of different sample periods over the 1970s. Although Branson and Halttunen report equations which seem supportive of the PBM, in terms of statistically significant and correctly signed coefficients, a note of caution must be sounded since the residuals in their OLS equations are all highly autocorrelated.

One problem with the Branson et al. implementation of the PBM lies in their use of cumulated current accounts for the stock of foreign assets. Such an approximation will, of course, include third-country items which are not strictly relevant to the determination of the bilateral exchange rate in question.

Bisignano and Hoover (1982) pick up this point and argue that the PBM approach should be implemented using only bilateral data for foreign assets and also, to be consistent, b and b^* should be included in the PBM reduced form (see above). Incorporating such modifications in their estimates of equation (3.74) for the Canadian dollar–US dollar exchange rate over the period March 1973 to December 1978, Bisignano and Hoover (1982) report moderately successful econometric results; in particular, they show that it is wrong to neglect domestic non-monetary asset stocks in exchange rate reduced forms.

3.3.4 The Portfolio Balance and Monetary Reduced Forms: A Synthesis

In an attempt to improve on the estimates of the reduced form monetary approach and portfolio balance equations, and in particular to overcome the model misspecification suggested by the typically high value of the first-order autocorrelation coefficient in such equations, a number of researchers have attempted to combine features of both the monetary and portfolio approaches into a reduced form exchange rate equation. Thus, if risk is important, the monetary approach reduced form will be misspecified to the extent that it ignores the imperfect substitutability of non-money assets. The portfolio balance reduced form is also likely to be misspecified because of its failure to incorporate expectations into the model (i.e. the reduced form equations in section 3.3.3 were derived by invoking static expectations rather than the more general formulation of the REPBM considered in section 3.2). However, since the PBM stresses that in long-run equilibrium the real exchange rate will be determined so as to balance the current account, we would expect, with rational expectations, that agents would revise their estimates of the expected real exchange rate as new information about the future path of the current account reaches the market: the spot exchange rate in a portfolio balance reduced form should include news about the current account as an explanatory variable. We now turn to some empirical attempts to synthesize the portfolio and monetary approaches, with emphasis being placed on the modelling of the risk premium and news about the current account.

Two developments of our basic monetary approach framework are required to derive a hybrid portfolio monetary approach equation. First, we divide the equilibrium nominal exchange rate into relative price and real components:

$$\bar{s}_t = \bar{p}_t - \bar{p}_t^* + \bar{q}_t \tag{3.75}$$

where q_t is the equilibrium real exchange rate. Following Hooper and Morton (1982) we assume that the expected change in the equilibrium real exchange rate is zero and q moves over time in response to unexpected developments, or news, about the current account c. Thus

$$q_t - q_{t-1} = \alpha(c_t - \mathrm{E}_{t-1}c_t) \qquad \alpha < 0 \tag{3.76}$$

and on integrating this expression over time we obtain

$$\bar{q}_t = \bar{q}_0 + \alpha \sum_{i=0}^{\infty}(c_{t-1} - \mathrm{E}_{t-i-1}c_t) \tag{3.77}$$

which states that the equilibrium exchange rate in period t is a function of an initial condition $\bar{q}_0$ and the cumulative sum of past (non-transitory) unexpected current account shocks. The second relationship utilized in the derivation of a hybrid monetary portfolio model is a UIP equation

$$r_t - r_t^* - \Delta s_{t+1}^e = \rho \tag{3.78}$$

which is familiar from our discussion in section 3.3.1 but where we assume that the risk premium is constant.

By substituting the regressive expectations equation (3.49) into (3.78) we obtain

$$s_t - \bar{s}_t = \vartheta^{-1}\left[(r - \pi^e)_t - (r^* - \pi^{*e})_t\right] + \vartheta^{-1}\rho \tag{3.79}$$

and by substituting (3.53), (3.75) and (3.77) into (3.79) we obtain the following hybrid model:

$$s_t = m_t' + \beta y_t' + \beta\pi_t^{e\prime} - \beta(r' - \pi^{e\prime})_t + \beta\rho + \\ \sum_{i=0}^{\infty}(c_{t-1} - \mathrm{E}_{t-i-1}c_{t-1}) + \bar{q}_0 \tag{3.80}$$

Versions of (3.80) have been estimated by a number of researchers (Isard, 1980; Hacche and Townend, 1981; Hooper and Morton, 1982; Frankel 1983, 1984). In Hooper and Morton's implementation of equation (3.80), the risk premium is assumed to be a function of the cumulated current account surplus net of the cumulation of foreign exchange market intervention. With this modification, the equation is estimated for the dollar effective exchange rate for 1973(2)–1978(4) using an instrumental variables estimator; representative variables are reported in table 3.4, column 1. Notice that all the mone-

Table 3.4 The hybrid monetary-portfolio model

Variable	1 Dollar effective 1973(1)–1978(4)[a] Instrumental	2 Sterling effective November 1977–December 1981[b] ALS	3 DM–US$ February 1974–July 1981[c] ALS	4 UK£–US$ February 1974–June 1981[c] ALS
$m - m^*$	0.770 (2.56)	0.032 (0.84)	0.150 (1.50)	-0.030 (0.6)
$y - y^*$	-1.840 (2.72)	-0.144 (1.01)	0.060 (1.20)	0.030 (0.75)
$\pi^e - \pi^{e*}$	2.410 (0.98)	-0.005 (1.66)	-0.240 (1.00)	0.000 (0)
$(i - \pi^e) - (i^* - \pi^{e*})$	-0.150 (0.27)	-0.009 (1.80)	0.050 (0.63)	0.030 (0.60)
$c - Ec$	-1.690 (3.90)	0.033 (0.47)	–	–
ρ	0.970 (0.82)	-0.095 (4.32)	–	–
Oil price	–	0.139 (5.79)	–	–
B/W	–	–	-0.060 (0.14)	-3.440 (10.75)

Table 3.4 *continued*

Variable	1 *Dollar effective* *1973(1)–1978(4)* *Instrumental*	2 *Sterling effective* *November 1977–* *December 1981*[b] *ALS*	3 *DM–US$* *February 1974–* *July 1981*[c] *ALS*	4 *UK£–US$* *February 1974–* *June 1981*[c] *ALS*
W_a/W	–	–	-2.210 (6.90)	2.260 (5.14)
W_{US}/W	–	–	1.130 (7.06)	1.670 (11.93)
Constant	4.550 (131.90)	3.733 (28.72)	-0.050 (0.22)	-2.070 (8.63)
R^2	0.78	0.97	–	–
Durbin–Watson	1.87	–	–	–
SER	–	0.014	0.008	0.007
$\hat{\rho}$	–	0.778 (6.59)	0.98 (–)	1.00 (–)

Definitions as in table 3.2.
[a] Hooper and Morton, 1982.
[b] Hacche and Townsend, 1983.
[c] Frankel, 1984.

tary approach variables enter with the correct sign and two are statistically significant, but that, of the portfolio balance variables, only the current account news term is statistically significant (and correctly signed); the risk premium is insignificant (and wrongly signed). An interesting feature of the equation is the absence of first-order autocorrelation (the authors unfortunately do not report diagnostics for higher-order autocorrelation), and thus on this criterion we would appear to have a better specified reduced form exchange rate equation than either the simple monetary or portfolio balance reduced form equation.

Another interesting feature of the Hooper–Morton reduced form is that it can be used to show that about 80 per cent of the dollar's decline in 1977–8 can be explained by the current account revision term and only 20 per cent by the monetary approach variables (see the discussion in section 3.3.2 regarding the breakdown of the monetary model for the post-1977 deutschmark–US dollar rate).

Using the Hooper–Morton specification, Hacche and Townend (1981) implement equation (3.80), with the addition of the price of oil, for the sterling effective exchange rate over the period June 1972 to December 1981. A representative result, reported in table 3.4, column 2, is clearly disappointing: few coefficients are significant and, of those that are, the risk premium is wrongly signed and the oil price rightly signed. In contrast with the Hooper–Morton estimates, this result exhibits severe first-order autocorrelation. Two factors may explain the poor performance of Hacche and Townend's implementation of equation (3.80). One is the use of monthly data which is widely regarded as being extremely noisy, resulting in a low signal-to-noise ratio. Also, in contrast with Hooper and Morton, Hacche and Townend do not use a simultaneous equation estimator and thus their results are likely to be biased and inconsistent.

In Frankel's (1984) implementation of the portfolio–monetary hybrid reduced form model, the current account news term is not considered and the risk premium is derived as the solution to the PBM. The Frankel version of equation (3.80) is estimated for five currencies against the US dollar for the period 1974–81 (monthly data, with the exact beginning and end points being currency specific). Two of Frankel's equations, for the deutschmark–US dollar and sterling–US dollar exchange rates, are reported in table 3.4, columns 3 and 4. Interestingly, although all the monetary coefficients are insignificant and some are wrongly signed, the risk premium terms are, in contrast with the estimates in the previous section, significant and correctly signed in four out of the six terms. The failure of the monetary variables to enter with significant coefficients can perhaps be traced, as in the Hacche and Townend estimates, to the use of monthly data and the failure to account for simultaneity.

3.3.5 The Out-of-sample Forecasting Performance of Some Asset Approach Reduced Forms

Hitherto, we have considered only the in-sample properties of the asset approach reduced forms. A stronger test of the validity of these models would be to determine how well they perform out of sample compared with an alternative such as the naive random walk model. Meese and Rogoff (1983) have conducted such a study for the US dollar–sterling, US dollar–deutschmark, US dollar–yen and trade-weighted US dollar exchange rates using data running from March 1973 to June 1981. The reduced form asset equations tested in their study are the FLPM model (equation (3.36)), the RID model (equation (3.54)) and the portfolio–monetary synthesis equation (3.80). The out-of-sample performance of these equations is compared with the forecasting performance of the random walk model, the forward exchange rate, a univariate autoregression of the spot rate and a vector autoregression formed using lagged values of the explanatory variables of equation (3.54) plus cumulated home and foreign trade balances. Meese and Rogoff compute their forecasts in the following way. First, the equations are estimated using data from the beginning of the sample to November 1976 and four forecasts are made for one, three, six and twelve months ahead. The data for December 1976 are then added to the original data set, the equations are re-estimated and a further set of forecasts are made for the four time horizons. This 'rolling regression' process is then continually repeated. The statistics used to gauge the out-of-sample properties of the models are the mean error (ME), mean absolute error (MAE) and the root mean square error (RMSE). A sample of the RMSE results of Meese and Rogoff (for the six month forecast and excluding the forward rate, univariate and vector autoregression forecasts) is reported in table 3.5 where the reduced forms derived from structural models have been estimated using the Fair (1970) procedure.

Table 3.5   Root mean square forecast errors for selected exchange rate equations

Exchange rate	Forecast Horizon (months)	Random walk	FLPM	RID	Monetary–portfolio Synthesis
US$–DM	6	8.71	9.64	12.03	9.95
US$–Yen	6	11.58	13.38	13.94	11.94
US$–UK£	6	6.45	8.90	8.88	9.08
Trade-weighted US$	6	6.09	7.07	6.49	7.11

Source: Meese and Rogoff, 1983.

The devastating conclusion that emerges from the Meese–Rogoff study is that none of the asset reduced forms considered outperforms the simple random walk model. This result is all the more striking when it is remembered that the reduced form forecasts have been computed using *actual* values of the various assets etc. To try to improve on the poor performance of the asset reduced forms, Meese and Rogoff alternatively attempt estimating the models in first differences, allow home and foreign magnitudes to enter unconstrained, include price levels as additional explanatory variables, use different definitions of the money supply and replace long-term interest rates with other proxies for inflationary expectations. But all to no avail: the modified reduced form equations still fail to outperform the simple random walk. In a further paper, Meese and Rogoff (1984) consider possible explanations of why the reduced form asset models fail to beat the random walk model out of sample. In particular, they show, using the vector auto-regressive methodology, that the instruments used in simultaneous estimates of asset reduced forms may not be truly exogenous and thus the estimated parameter estimates may be extremely imprecise. To overcome this problem Meese and Rogoff impose coefficient constraints, culled from the empirical literature on money demand equations, in the asset reduced forms and re-estimate the RMSEs for the same period as their 1983 paper. Interestingly, they find that, although the coefficient-constrained asset reduced forms still fail to outperform the random walk model for most horizons up to a year, in forecasting beyond a year (which was not possible, owing to degrees of freedom problems, with the unconstrained estimates in Meese and Rogoff (1983)) the asset reduced forms do outperform the random walk model in terms of RMSE. As Salemi (1984) points out, this tends to suggest that the exchange rate acts like a pure asset price in the short term (i.e. approximately a random walk (see, for example, Samuelson, 1965)) but that in the longer term its equilibrium is systematically related to other economic variables. One important point to bear in mind about the Meese–Rogoff work is that their comparison of the random walk model with the structural models is a little unfair because the random walk predictions are one step ahead and therefore use information not available to the multistep-ahead forecasts.

A fair sized literature has emerged which seeks to determine whether Meese and Rogoff's specification of the asset reduced form equations, their estimation strategy or the models themselves are at fault. Woo (1985) and Finn (1986) estimate versions of the rational expectations form of the FLPM (equation (3.39)) with the addition of a partial adjustment term in money demand and perform a Meese–Rogoff forecasting exercise. Finn reports that this model forecasts as well as the random walk model (but fails to *outperform* a random walk) whilst Woo finds that his formulation outperforms the random walk model in terms of both the MAE and RMSE for the deutschmark–US dollar exchange rate. Somanath (1986) also utilizes money demand partial adjustment terms in his formulation of various asset reduced form equations (such as FLPM, RID and hybrid) for the deutschmark–US dollar exchange rate. Interestingly, he finds, for the period studied by Meese and Rogoff, that this modification results in the structural exchange rate models outperforming the random walk model in terms of the standard criteria, and that for a sample period extending beyond that of Meese-Rogoff the basic (i.e. without any additional dynamics) FLPM, RID and hybrid equations outperform a random walk.[15]

A time-varying parameter model has been used by Wolff (1987) and Schinasi and Swamy (1987) as the preferred estimation technique for econometric implementation of the RID and FLPM equations. Both sets of authors argue that the poor forecasting performance noted by Meese and Rogoff may be due to the failure of these authors to account for parameter instabilities. There are in fact a number of reasons why the parameters in equations like (3.18) and (3.26) are unlikely to be constant for the recent floating experience. For example, instabilities in the underlying structural equations (money demand and PPP equations), policy regime changes (Lucas, 1976) and heterogeneous beliefs by agents (leading to a diversity of responses to macroeconomic developments over time) could all impart parameter instabilities over time. Using the Kalman filter methodology, Wolff (1987) reworks the Meese–Rogoff results (same currencies and time period) for the FLPM and RID reduced forms, assuming that the parameters follow a random walk process. However, Wolff reports that this strategy only results in the FLPM and RID models beating a random walk in the case of the US dollar–deutschmark exchange rate (for both the US dollar–yen and US dollar–sterling exchange rates the random walk has a better forecasting performance across all forecast horizons, and indeed if one takes the average across all currencies and forecast horizons the random walk model dominates). Schinasi and Swamy (1987) use a less restrictive time-varying model than Wolff and find that their model results in consistently better forecasts (than a random walk) for the FLPM, RID and hybrid equations (for the deutschmark–, yen– and sterling–US dollar bilateral exchange rates). However, it is not entirely clear whether the improved performance of the structural models is due to the use of time-varying parameters or simply to the fact that a multistep random walk forecast is used rather than the one-step forecast used by Meese and Rogoff. In a further experiment, Schinasi and Swamy add a lagged dependent variable to the various monetary reduced forms and compare their forecasting performance with a one-step-ahead random walk. It is demonstrated for all cases that the time-varying parameter version is always superior to the fixed coefficients version and, furthermore, outperforms the one-step-ahead random walk in almost all cases.

Finally, Boughton (1984) tests the out-of-sample forecasting performance of a preferred habitat version of the PBM (using fixed coefficient methods) against a random walk model for a variety of currencies. It is demonstrated that it outperforms the random walk model in every case. However, it seems likely that this result reflects Boughton's use of quarterly data (all the other studies use monthly data) since his estimates of the hybrid equation also generally outperform the random walk model.[16]

3.3.6 Empirical Exchange Rate Models: New Directions

In this section the econometric evidence on models of exchange rate determination has been considered in some detail. The broad conclusion that emerges is that the asset approach seems to work well for some time periods, such as the interwar period and, to some extent, the first part of the recent floating experience (i.e. 1973–8), but not so well for the second part of the recent float.

The failure of simple asset approach equations to perform satisfactorily for the latter period may be due to misspecification. Such misspecification may be of an econometric nature in so far as the dynamic properties of the asset equations, in relation to the methodology of Hendry et al. (1984), have been very poorly specified (the persistent indication of first-order autocorrelation supports this view). Simple asset approach equations may also be misspecified from an economic point of view. Thus the breakdown in the performance of the monetary model could be a consequence of the omission of important variables such as the current account, wealth and risk factors. However, when such additions are added to the simple asset models little improvement in equation performance is reported. One useful way of ensuring that the exchange rate models are correctly specified (in terms of the correct variables to include, the exogeneity assumptions made and the dynamic specifications) is to estimate the models structurally, and this seems to be a useful avenue for future research (see Kearney and MacDonald (1985) and Smith and Wickens (1988, 1990) for recent examples).

Other explanations which have variously been put forward to explain the poor empirical performance of asset approach exchange rate equations include the following.

First, some authors have stressed the idea that foreign exchange rates may have consistently deviated from their underlying 'fundamental' levels (i.e. as predicted by economic theory) because of the presence of rational bubbles, as discussed earlier (see, for example, Flood and Hodrick, 1990).

Other researchers have concentrated on the influence of foreign exchange analysts who do not base their predictions on economic theory but on the identification of supposedly recurring patterns in graphs of exchange rate movements, i.e. technical or chart analysts. Frankel and Froot (1986c, 1990), for example, suggest a model of the foreign exchange market in which traders base their expectations partly on the advice of fundamentalists (i.e. economists) and partly on the advice of non-fundamentalists (i.e. chartists). They argue that such a model would seem to explain the heavy overvaluation of the US dollar during the mid-1980s. Some support for the view that non-fundamentalist advice may be an important influence in foreign exchange markets is provided by Allen and Taylor (1989, 1990) who conducted a survey of chief foreign exchange dealers in the London foreign exchange market and found that a high proportion of them use some form of chart analysis in forming their trading decisions, particularly at the shorter horizons. At the shortest horizons (intraday to one week) Allen and Taylor find that over 90 per cent of their survey respondents reported using some form of chart analysis and around 60 per cent judged charts to be at least as important as fundamentals at this horizon. As the time horizon is lengthened, however, the weight given by dealers to fundamental analysis increases. At the longest forecast horizons considered (one year or longer), nearly 30 per cent of chief dealers reported relying on pure fundamental analysis and 85 per cent judged fundamentals to be more important than chart analysis at this horizon. In addition, Allen and Taylor (1990) analyse the accuracy of a number of individual chart analysts' one-week-ahead and four-week-ahead forecasts of the US dollar–sterling, US dollar–deutschmark and US dollar–yen exchange rates and find that some of them consistently outperform a whole range of alternative forecasting procedures, including the random walk model, vector autoregressions and univariate autoregressive integrated moving-average (ARIMA) models. Given this evidence, it is hardly surprising that empirical models based on pure 'fundamental' economic theory fail to provide an adequate explanation of short-term movements in exchange rates, although the finding that foreign exchange participants focus more on fundamentals at longer horizons suggests that more attention might fruitfully be given to modelling the fundamental determinants of *long-term* exchange rates.

Masson and Knight (1986, 1990) and Frenkel and Razin (1987) emphasize the role of shifts in fiscal policy stance among the major OECD countries as important determinants of exchange rate behaviour (see also Dornbusch, 1987). These authors argue that the large autonomous changes in national savings and investment balances – in particular those influenced by shifts in public sector fiscal positions in the largest industrial countries – must exert a very strong influence on current account positions, real interest rates and hence exchange rates.

Dooley and Isard (1987, 1989a, b) focus their attention on factors affecting the choice of where to locate tangible assets and other 'taxable' forms of wealth. In support of this view, Dooley and Isard point to the experience during the 1980s of a number of debt-burdened developing countries who experienced substantial depreciations of their real exchange rate around the time of the outbreak of the international debt crisis in 1982. Dooley and Isard (1989b) argue that '. . . these depreciations can be attributed primarily to a set of events that considerably reduced the attractiveness of owning assets located in the debt-burdened countries, thus giving rise to a "transfer problem" in which real depreciation played an important role in the adjustment to substantially smaller net capital inflows and current account deficits.'

Dornbusch (1987) stresses the importance of analysing a country's industrial structure in attempting to explain the behaviour of its exchange rate. For example, the effect of a change in exchange rate on a firm's pricing decisions (and hence on further changes in the exchange rate) will depend upon whether the industry faces competition from imports which are close substitutes for their goods, whether the market is characterized by oligopoly, imperfect competition etc., and the functional form of the specific market demand curve. After demonstrating these points with a number of concrete examples, Dornbusch concludes: 'Even though this application of industrial organization ideas to the effects of exchange rate movements does not emerge with firm results, it is quite apparent that it offers a major avenue for theoretical research and for applied studies'.

Which of these directions is likely to lead us towards a better understanding of exchange rate behaviour? In our view, the rational bubbles explanation is perhaps the least attractive, not least because a growing amount of empirical research now suggests that asset market participants may not be endowed with fully rational expectations (Frankel and Froot, 1987; Taylor, 1988c). The evidence of Allen and Taylor (1989, 1990) on the prevalence of non-fundamentalist analysis in foreign exchange markets suggests that, as a guide to the *short-run* behaviour of exchange rates, the fundamentals versus non-fundamentals approach seems promising. Unfortunately, this road is likely to be difficult to tread in terms of developing reliable models of exchange rate behaviour. For example, Allen and Taylor (1990), after analysing survey data on chartists' exchange rate forecasts, report a significant degree of heterogeneity amongst chartist forecasts – not all chartists see the same patterns (or draw the same conclusions from them) at the same points in time. They argue, moreover, that the degree of consensus is likely to shift significantly over time in a fashion which may be hard to model empirically. Thus, while this approach may help us to rationalize the *past* behaviour of exchange rates (e.g. Frankel and Froot, 1990), it may prove rather more difficult to apply it to predicting *future* short-term exchange rate behaviour.

Given Allen and Taylor's evidence that foreign exchange market participants rely more on fundamental economic analysis at longer horizons, it would seem that more attention ought to be focused on attempting to model the *long-run equilibrium* exchange rate, and it is perhaps in this area that the new approaches involving accounting for fiscal policy stance, locational decisions and industrial organization might be most fruitfully applied. In addition, the recent development of econometric techniques which aid in the identification of long-run relationships using short-run data (see, for example, Engle and Granger, 1987) is likely to provide a further impetus in this direction.

3.4 THE EFFICIENT MARKETS HYPOTHESIS AND THE FORWARD MARKET FOR FOREIGN EXCHANGE

3.4.1 Basic Relationships

In this section we present a brief review of the literature on the EMH as applied to the forward market for foreign exchange. The EMH is conventionally seen as a joint hypothesis of a view of equilibrium returns and the contention that agents are endowed with rational expectations. For our purposes, the latter proposition can be stated as

$$\Delta s_{t+k} = \Delta s_{t+k}^e + \eta_{t+k} \qquad \Delta s_{t+k}^e = \mathrm{E}(\Delta s_{t+k} \,|\, I_t) \tag{3.81}$$

where $\Delta s_{t+k} = s_{t+k} - s_t$, $\Delta s_{t+k}^e = s_{t+k}^e - s_t$, s denotes the logarithm of the spot rate (home currency price of the dollar), s_{t+k}^e denotes the expected value of s_{t+k} at time t, E is the mathematical conditional expectation operator, I_t is the information set on which agents base their expectations and η_{t+k} is a random forecast error, orthogonal to the information set. Relationship (3.81) is normally expressed in logarithms in order to circumvent the so-called 'Siegel paradox' (Siegel, 1972) that, because of a mathematical relationship known as Jensen's inequality, we cannot have simultaneously an unbiased expectation of, say the deutschmark–US dollar exchange rate (deutschmarks per dollar) and of the US dollar–deutschmark exchange rate (US dollars per deutschmark) because $1/\mathrm{E}(S) \neq \mathrm{E}(1/S)$. This problem does not arise if agents are assumed to form expectations of the *logarithm* of exchange rates, however, because $\mathrm{E}(-s) = -\mathrm{E}(s)$. McCulloch (1975) has investigated the empirical importance of this phenomenon (using 1920s data) and shown the operational importance of the Siegel paradox to be slight. Nevertheless, the literature has continued to work with logarithmic transformations of the data.

If agents are risk-neutral, then since a profit can be expected to be made when the forward rate differs from the expected future spot rate (by taking open forward positions), we might expect the forward rate for maturity k

periods ahead to be forced into equality with the market's expectation of the spot rate at time $t + k$:

$$f_t = s^e_{t+k} \qquad (3.82)$$

If agents are risk averse, however, the forward rate will not be driven to full equality with the expected future spot rate because of the risk involved in taking open forward positions. Thus a risk premium, λ_t say, might be expected to drive a wedge between f_t and s^e_{t+k}. Under this assumption, (3.82) can be rewritten, after subtracting s_t from both sides,

$$fp_t = \Delta s^e_{t+k} + \lambda_t \qquad (3.83)$$

where fp_t denotes the logarithm of the forward premium and λ_t represents a risk premium which is required to compensate agents from exposure to the risk involved in running open positions in the currency in question.

On using (3.81) and (3.83) we obtain the following statement of the EMH under risk aversion:

$$fp_t = \Delta s_{t+k} + \epsilon_{t+k} + \lambda_t \qquad (3.84)$$

where $\epsilon_{t+k} = -\eta_{t+k}$ of equation (3.81). As we shall see, in trying to interpret the often quoted finding that the forward premium is a biased predictor of the exchange rate depreciation researchers either assume that λ_t is zero, and conclude that rejection is attribute to 'irrationality', or assume that agents are rational and conclude that rejection is due to the presence of a statistically significant risk premium.

A popular way of testing the joint EMH is to regress the actual change in the exchange rate on the forward premium

$$\Delta s_{t+k} = \alpha + \beta fp_t + u_{t+k} \qquad (3.85)$$

and if agents are risk neutral and rational, we would expect $\alpha = 0$, $\beta = 1$ and, if non-overlapping data are being used ($k = 1$), the disturbance term to be a white noise process. If, however, agents are risk averse or 'irrational' (or both) then such conditions will be violated.

An alternative test of the optimality of the forward rate as a predictor of the change in exchange rate has been to conduct forecast error orthogonality tests. More specifically, a number of researchers (see below for details) estimate an equation of the form

$$s_{t+k} - f_t = \Gamma X_t + \omega_{t+k} \qquad (3.86)$$

where X_t is a vector of variables known at time t, which is the econometricians' observed portion of the 'true' information set I_t available to agents, Γ is a vector of parameters and ω_{t+k} is an error term. The null hypothesis of rational expectations and risk neutrality is equivalent to the hypothesis that Γ should equal the null vector, so that the error in forecasting the exchange rate using the current forward rate should be unforecastable using current information, i.e. it should be orthogonal to all elements of the information set available at time t. If this condition is significantly violated then information available to agents at time t has remained unexploited, contradicting rationality.

3.4.2 Tests of the Forward Premium as an Optimal Predictor of the Rate of Depreciation

A large number of researchers using a variety of currencies and time periods have implemented (3.85) for the recent floating experience, and report results which are unfavourable to the EMH under risk neutrality. For example, Bilson (1981), Longworth (1981), Fama (1984), Gregory and McCurdy (1984), Taylor (1988b) and Kearney and MacDonald (forthcoming) all report a result which seems to suggest a resounding rejection of the unbiasedness hypothesis, namely, a significantly negative point estimate of β. This result seems particularly robust given the variety of estimation techniques used by researchers and the mix of overlapping and non-overlapping data sets. A typical example of the kind of result obtained by researchers is (the result is from Fama (1984) and the currency is Swiss franc–US dollar):

$$\Delta s_{t+k} = \begin{array}{cc} 0.81 - & 1.15(f - s)_t \\ (0.42) & (0.50) \end{array} \tag{3.87}$$

where standard errors are in parentheses.

A large amount of research effort has been expended in trying to rationalize this finding. Perhaps the most popular explanation lies in the existence of a non-zero time-varying risk premium which drives a wedge between the forward rate and future spot rate (see Fama, 1984; Hodrick and Srivastava, 1986).

3.4.3 Error Orthogonality Tests of the Efficient Markets Hypothesis

Alternative tests of the EMH have relied on testing the second property, noted above, of the error term ϵ in (3.85), namely, that it should be orthogonal to information available to agents in period t. Tests of equation (3.86) can be split into those which include only lagged forecast errors in the conditioning information set (in terms of Fama's (1976) nomenclature such tests are weak form tests, which we categorize as type A tests) and those which include information additional to lagged forecast errors in the information set (semi-strong form tests, which we label type B tests).

Type A tests have been conducted by, *inter alia*, Geweke and Feige (1978), Frankel (1979b), MacDonald (1983b), Cumby and Obstfeld (1984), Gregory and McCurdy (1984) and MacDonald and Taylor (1989a). These authors use a variety of different sample periods (i.e. recent float and interwar float), exchange rates (usually bilateral dollar rates) and estimation techniques (OLS, generalized least squares (GLS), Zellner's 'seemingly unrelated regressions' technique (ZSURE) and the generalized method of moments (GMM)). Their basic finding is that the EMH is rejected for a number of currencies for the recent and interwar floating experiences. For example, Hansen and Hodrick (1980) estimate equation (3.86), using a weekly data base, for part of the recent float and find that the orthogonality property is violated for three currencies (the Swiss franc, the Italian lira and the deutschmark). Hansen and Hodrick estimate their version of equation (3.86), using OLS (since it is consistent), but correct the covariance matrix of standard errors for the implied moving-average error structure which is implied by overlapping data ($k > 1$) using Hansen's (1982) GMM procedure. MacDonald and Taylor (1989a) also use Hansen's GMM technique to conduct type A tests for the interwar period, but, in contrast with Hansen and Hodrick, MacDonald and Taylor use the GMM procedure to correct for both the implied moving-average error and conditional heteroscedasticity (Hansen and Hodrick assume conditional homoscedasticity); they find very strong rejection for US dollar–sterling, Swiss franc–sterling and French franc–sterling (this result contrasts with other tests of the EMH for this period).

Given the rejections of the null reported when researchers conduct type A tests, it is hardly surprising to find that type B tests result in even stronger rejections. Thus, Geweke and Feige (1978), Hansen and Hodrick (1980), Hakkio (1981a), Hsieh (1984) and MacDonald and Taylor (1989a) all test the orthogonality of the forward rate forecast error with respect to own lagged forecast errors and lagged forecast errors from other foreign exchange markets and find that the null hypothesis $\Gamma = 0$ is resoundingly rejected.

3.4.4 Rationalizing Inefficiency Findings

The rejection of the EMH noted above is usually explained in one of two ways. The EMH is a joint null hypothesis of rational expectations and an assumption concerning the attitude of agents towards risk. It has often been tested under the assumption of risk neutrality. Thus the first, and by far the most popular, explanation of the inefficiency finding is to argue that agents are risk averse and therefore that λ_t is non-zero in (3.83). For examples of attempts to model or test for the foreign exchange risk premium econometrically see, *inter alia*, Hansen and Hodrick (1983), Fama (1984),

Domowitz and Hakkio (1985), Wolff (1987) and Taylor (1988b). By and large, however, the risk premium has proved elusive in that few of these authors report satisfactory estimates of it. For extensive surveys of this issue see Hodrick (1987), MacDonald (1988, 1990) and MacDonald and Taylor (1989b).

Alternatively, researchers have sought to explain rejection in terms of a failure, in some sense, of the expectations component of the joint hypothesis. Examples in this group are the 'peso problem' suggested by Krasker (1980), the rational bubbles phenomenon, originally suggested by Flood and Garber (1980), and inefficient information processing, as suggested by Bilson (1981) (see MacDonald and Taylor (1989b) for a more detailed survey).

A problem with each of these possible rationalizations of the inefficiency finding is that in order to test for a failure in one leg of the EMH, the researcher must normally assume that the other component of the joint hypothesis is valid. For example, all the investigations of foreign exchange risk premiums cited above are conducted conditional on the assumption of rational expectations. Clearly we would like to be able to conduct tests of each component of the joint hypothesis in order to discern which component joint is at fault. The recent availability of survey data on exchange rate expectations, from a variety of sources, has allowed researchers to do just that. For example, Frankel and Froot (1987, 1989), MacDonald and Torrance (1988a, 1990) and Taylor (1989b) all use exchange rate survey data to this end. The broad conclusion to emerge from this research is that the joint hypothesis fails both because agents are risk averse and because their expectations do not conform to the rational expectations hypothesis (see MacDonald and Taylor 1989b).

3.4.5 The Efficient Markets Hypothesis: Anything Left?

There is now overwhelming evidence to suggest that the forward foreign exchange rate is a biased and inefficient predictor of the future spot rate. The simpler version of the EMH (i.e. assuming risk neutrality) thus seems to have been decisively rejected for the foreign exchange market.[17] This result is commonly explained in terms of either a time-varying risk premium or some problem with the expectations leg of the joint hypothesis of market efficiency. The time-varying risk premium story, although intuitively extremely plausible, receives rather mixed support from the data, and at best we must conclude that the jury is still out on this as an explanation. Furthermore, a number of researchers have argued that the use of a time-varying risk premium is a rather vacuous device which 'has no function but tautologically to save the theory' (Mankiw and Summers, 1984).[18] Perhaps then the failure of the joint efficiency hypothesis should be traced to the expectations leg of the joint hypothesis. The reported profitability of some simple trading rules would certainly seem to point in this direction. Indeed MacDonald and Young (1986), Frankel and Froot (1987), Goodhart (1988) and Allen and Taylor (1989) have recently argued that combining a chartist view of exchange rate determination with an equilibrium, or fundamentalist, view offers a much more realistic description of how exchange rates are actually determined and helps to explain why the forward rate is such a poor predictor of the future exchange rate.[19] This is a view with which we concur, and we believe that it offers a great deal of potential for future research on exchange rate economics.

Notes

1   Even if investors effect forward cover, i.e. sell the proceeds of their investment against their local currency in the forward market, the cost of this cover will be close to the expected rate of depreciation of the domestic currency (and exactly equal if the forward market is efficient and agents are risk neutral – see section 3.4).

2   There are in fact a number of reasons (such as differential tax risk, liquidity considerations, political risk, default risk and exchange risk) which suggest that non-money assets issued in different currencies are unlikely to be perfect substitutes.

3   Assuming that the Marshall–Lerner condition holds (see, for example, Cuthbertson and Taylor, 1987; MacDonald, 1988).

4   This abstracts from any short-run J-curve effects.

5   We have drawn figure 3.10 under the implicit assumption that F is positive. If F were negative then, since S must be positive, the $S = 0$ locus would be the branch of the rectangular hyperbola (3.28) located in the northwestern, rather than the northeastern quadrant. For the implications of this see Buiter (1984) for example.

6   That is, all variables except interest rates are in natural logarithms.

7   So that, as before, an increase in s denotes a depreciation of the domestic currency.

8   See MacDonald and Taylor (1990) for a discussion of the empirical evidence on international parity relationships. Note that in this section we explicitly work in discrete rather than continuous time in order to ease the transition from the theoretical to the empirical model – data are usually available in discrete form.

9   The application of rational expectations to exchange rates was first considered by Black (1973).

10   The long-run solution would be qualitatively similar if the forcing variables were allowed to enter long-run steady state growth.

11   To see this for the SPM model, substitute m_t' from (3.40) into (3.45).

12   See MacDonald and Taylor (1989b) for a fuller discussion.

13   Meese uses monthly data over the period October 1973 to November 1982.

14   Subject to a maintained hypothesis concerning expectations formation, e.g. rational expectations.
15   The forecasting performance of these equations is even better for the extended sample period when money market dynamics are allowed for.
16   See Pentecost (1988) for a useful survey of the out-of-sample forecasting performance of asset approach reduced forms.
17   The *Financial Times* noted (5 April 1988, p. 16): 'In the hurly-burly of City dealing rooms, where anomalous price movements are exploited daily, the [efficient markets] theory has always been dismissed as the product of remote academic theorising'.
18   See also Goodhart (1988) for a discussion along similar lines.
19   Frankel and Froot (1990) present the most complete and formal statement of this view.

Bibliography

Adler, M. and Lehmann, B. (1983) Deviations from purchasing power parity in the long run. *Journal of Finance* 38 (5), 1471–87.
Alexander, S. S. (1961) Price movements in speculative markets: trends or random walks. *Industrial Management Review* May, 7–26.
Aliber, R. Z. (1974) Attributes of national monies and the independence of national monetary policies. In R. Z. Aliber (ed.), *National Monetary Policies and the International System*. Chicago, IL: Chicago University Press.
Allen, H. and Taylor, M. P. (1989) Charts and fundamentals in the London foreign exchange market. *Bank of England Quarterly Bulletin* November.
—— and —— (1990) Charts, noise and fundamentals in the foreign exchange market. *Economic Journal (Supplement)* 49–59.
Allen, P. R. and Kenen, P. B. (1978) *The Balance of Payments, Exchange Rates and Economic Policy (A Survey and Synthesis of Recent Developments)*. Athens, GA: Centre of Planning and Economic Research.
Artis, M. J. and Lewis, M. K. (1981) *Monetary Control in the United Kingdom*. Oxford: Phillip Allan.
Artus, J. (1976) Exchange rate stability and managed floating: the experience of the Federal Republic of Germany. *IMF Staff Papers* 23, 312–33.
Backus, D. (1984) Empirical models of the exchange rate: separating the wheat from the chaff. *Canadian Journal of Economics* 17 (4), 824–46.
—— and Gregory, A. W. (1988) Risk premiums in asset prices and returns. Mimeo, Queen's University, Canada.
—— Gregory, A. W. and Zin, S. E. (1988) Risk premiums in the term structure: evidence from artificial economies. Mimeo, Queen's University, Canada.
Barr, D. (1989) Exchange rate dynamics: An empirical analysis. In R. MacDonald and M. P. Taylor (eds), *Exchange Rates and Open Economy Macroeconomics*. Oxford: Basil Blackwell.
Begg, D. K. H. (1982) *The Rational Expectations Revolution in Macroeconomics Theories and Evidence*. Oxford: Phillip Allan.
Bhandari, J., Driskell, R. D. and Frenkel, J. A. (1984) Capital mobility and exchange rate overshooting. *European Economic Review* 24, 309–20.

Bilson, J. F. O. (1978a) Rational expectations and the exchange rate. In J. A. Frankel and H. G. Johnson (eds), *The Economics of Exchange Rates*. Reading, MA: Addison-Wesley, pp. 75–96.

—— (1978b) The monetary approach to the exchange rate – some empirical evidence. *IMF Staff Papers* 25, 48–75.

—— (1979) Recent developments in monetary models of exchange rate determination. *IMF Staff Papers* 26, 201–23.

—— (1981) The speculative efficiency hypothesis. *Journal of Business* 54, 435–51.

—— (1985) Macro-economic stability and flexible exchange rates. *American Economic Review, Papers and Proceedings* 75, 62–7.

Bisignano, J. and Hoóver, K. (1982) Some suggested improvements to a simple portfolio balance model of exchange rate determination with special reference to the US dollar/Canadian dollar rate. *Weltwirtschaftliches Archiv* 119, 19–37.

Black, S. W. (1973) *International Money Markets and Flexible Exchange Rates*. Princeton, NJ: Princeton University Press, Princeton Studies in International Finance, no. 32.

Blanchard, O. (1981a) Output, the stock market and interest rates. *American Economic Review* 71, 132–43.

—— (1981b) Speculative bubbles, crashes and rational expectations. *Economic Letters* 4, 387–91.

—— and Dornbusch, R. (1984) *US Deficits, the Dollar and Europe*. Banca Nationale Del Lavoro, pp. 89–113.

—— and Kahn, C. M. (1980) The solution of linear difference models under rational expectations. *Econometrica* 48, 1305–11.

—— and Watson M. (1982) Bubbles, rational expectations and financial markets. In P. Wachtel (ed.), *Crises in the Economic and Financial Structure*. Lexington, MA: Lexington Books.

Bomhoff, E. S. and Korteweg, P. (1983) Exchange rate variability and monetary policy under rational expectations: some Euro-American experience 1973–1979. *Journal of Monetary Economics* 11 (2), 169–206.

Boothe, P. and Glassman, D. (1987) The statistical distribution of exchange rates: empirical evidence and economic implications. *Journal of International Economics* 22, 236–50.

—— and —— (1987) Off the mark: lessons for exchange rate modelling. *Oxford Economic Papers* 39, 443–57.

Boughton, J. M. (1984) Exchange rate movements and adjustment in financial markets: quarterly estimates for major currencies. *IMF Staff Papers* 31, 445–68.

Branson, W. H. (1977) Asset markets and relative prices in exchange rate determination. Reprint Series 98, Institute for International Economic Studies.

—— (1983) Macroeconomic determinants of real exchange risk. In R. J. Herring (ed.), *Managing Foreign Exchange Risk*. Cambridge: Cambridge University Press.

—— (1984) Exchange rate policy after a decade of 'floating'. In J. F. O. Bilson and R. C. Marston (eds), *Exchange Rate Theory and Practice*. Chicago, IL: University of Chicago Press.

—— and Halttunen, H. (1979) Asset-market determination of exchange rates: initial empirical and policy results. In J. P. Martin and A. Smith (eds), *Trade and Payments Adjustment under Flexible Exchange Rates*. London: Macmillan, pp. 55–85.

214   R. MacDonald and M. P. Taylor

—, — and Masson, P. (1977) Exchange rates in the short run: the dollar-Deutschemark rate. *European Economic Review* 10, 303–24.

—, — and — (1979) Exchange rates in the short run. *European Economic Review* 10, 395–402.

Buiter, W. H. (1984) Comment on Branson. In J. F. O. Bilson and R. C. Marston (eds), *Exchange Rate Theory and Practice*. Chicago, IL: University of Chicago Press.

— and Miller, M. H. (1981) Monetary policy and international competitiveness: the problem of adjustment. *Oxford Economic Papers* 33, 143–75.

— and Purvis, D. D. (1983). Oil, disinflation, and export competitiveness: a model of the 'Dutch Disease'. In J. S. Bhandari and B. H. Putnam (eds), *Economic Interdependence and Flexible Exchange Rates*. Cambridge, MA: MIT Press.

Campbell, J. Y. and Clarida, R. H. (1987) The term structure of euromarket interest rates: an empirical investigation. *Journal of Monetary Economics* 19, 25–44.

— and Shiller, R. (1987) Cointegration and tests of present value models. *Journal of Political Economy* 96, 1062–88.

Canova, F. and Ito, T. (1988) On time series properties of time-varying risk premium in the yen/dollar exchange market. NBER Working Paper 2678, National Bureau of Economic Research.

Caves, D. and Feige, E. L. (1980) Efficient foreign exchange markets and the monetary approach to exchange rate determination. *American Economic Review* 70 (1), 120–34.

Coghlan, R. T. (1978) A transactions demand for money. *Bank of England Quarterly Bulletin* 18, 1–115.

Copeland, L. (1984) The pound sterling/US dollar exchange rate and the 'news'. *Economics Letters* 15, 109–13.

Cornell, B. (1983) Money supply announcements and interest-rates: another view. *Journal of Business* 56, 1–23.

Cox, J., Ingersoll, J. and Ross, S. (1981) The relation between forward prices and future prices. *Journal of Financial Economics* 9, 321–46.

Cumby, R. E. and Obstfeld, M. (1984) International interest rate and price level linkages under flexible exchange rates: a review of the recent evidence. In J. F. O. Bilson and R. C. Marston (eds), *Exchange Rate Theory and Practice*. Chicago, IL: University of Chicago Press.

Cuthbertson, K. and Taylor, M. P. (1987) *Macroeconomic Systems*. Oxford: Basil Blackwell.

Danker, D. J., Haas, R. A., Henderson, D. W., Symansky, S. A. and Tyron, R. W. (1985) Small empirical models of exchange market intervention: applications to Germany, Japan, and Canada. Staff Studies 135, Board of Governors of the Federal Reserve System, Washington, DC.

Davidson, J. (1985) Econometric modelling of the sterling effective exchange rate. *Review of Economic Studies* 211, 231–40.

Dominguez, K. (1986) Are foreign exchange forecasts rational? New evidence from survey data. *Economics Letters* 21, 277–81.

Domowitz, I. and Hakkio, C. (1985) Conditional variance and the risk premium in the foreign exchange market. *Journal of International Economics* 19, 47–66.

Dooley, M., and Isard, P. (1982) A portfolio balance rational expectations model of the dollar mark exchange rate. *Journal of International Economics* 12, 257–76.

—— and —— (1987) Country preferences, currency values and policy issues. *Journal of Policy Modelling* 9.

—— and —— (1989a) Fiscal policy, locational decisions and exchange rates. *IMF Staff Papers* 35.

—— and —— (1989b) A note on fiscal policy, locational decisions and exchange rates. Mimeo, International Monetary Fund, Washington, DC.

Dooley, M. and Shafer, J.R. (1976) Analysis of short-run exchange rate behaviour, March 1973 to September 1975. *International Finance Discussion Papers* 76.

Dornbusch, R. (1976) Expectations and exchange rate dynamics. *Journal of Political Economy* 84, 1161–76.

—— (1979) Monetary policy under exchange rate flexibility. In *Managed Exchange Rate Flexibility: The Recent Experience*. Boston, MA: Federal Reserve Bank of Boston, pp. 90–122.

—— (1980) Exchange rate economics: where do we stand? *Brookings Papers on Economic Activity* 1, 143–85.

—— (1983) Flexible exchange rates and interdependence. *IMF Staff Papers* 31, 3–38.

—— (1987) Exchange rate economics: 1986. *Economic Journal* 97, 1–18.

—— and Fischer, S. (1980) Exchange rates and the current account. *American Economic Review* 70 (5), 960–71.

—— and Frankel, J.A. (1988) The flexible exchange rate system: experience and alternatives. NBER Working Paper 2464, National Bureau of Economic Research.

Driskell, R.A. (1981) Exchange rate dynamics: An empirical investigation. *Journal of Political Economy* 89 (2), 357–71.

—— and Sheffrin, S.M. (1981) On the mark: comment. *American Economic Review* 71 (5), 1068–74.

Eastwood, R.K. and Venables, A.J. (1982) The macroeconomic implications of a resource discovery in an open economy. *Economic Journal* 92, 285–99.

Edison, H.J. (1985) The rise and fall of sterling: testing alternative models of exchange rate determination. *Applied Economics* 17, 1003–21.

Edwards, S. (1982) Exchange rate market efficiency and new information. *Economics Letters* 9, 377–82.

—— (1983) Exchange rates and 'news': a multicurrency approach. *Journal of International Money and Finance* 1 (3), 211–24.

Engel, C. and Frankel, J.A. (1984) Why interest rates react to money announcements: an explanation from the foreign exchange market. *Journal of Monetary Economics* 13 (1), 31–46.

Engle, R. (1982) Autoregressive conditional heteroscedasticity with estimates of the variance of the United Kingdom rate of inflation. *Econometrica* 50, 987–1007.

—— and Granger, C.W.J. (1987) Cointegration and error correction: representation, estimation and testing. *Econometrica* 55, 251–76.

Evans, G.W. (1986) A test for speculative bubbles in the sterling–dollar exchange rate: 1981–84. *American Economic Review* 76, 621–36.

Fair, R. (1970) The estimation of simultaneous equation models with lagged endogenous variables and first order serially correlated errors. *Econometrica* 38, 507–16.

Fama, E. F. (1970) Efficient capital markets: A review of theory and empirical work. *Journal of Finance* 25, 383–417.

—— (1976) *Foundations of Finance.* New York: Basic Books.

—— (1984) Forward and spot exchange rates. *Journal of Monetary Economics* 14 (3), 319–38.

—— and Farber, A. (1979) Money, bonds and foreign exchange. *American Economic Review* 69, 639–49.

Feige, E. L. and Pearce, D. K. (1976) Economically rational expectations: are innovations in the rate of inflation independent of innovations in measures of monetary and fiscal policy? *Journal of Political Economy* 84, 499–522.

Finn, M. G, (1986) Forecasting the exchange rate: A monetary or random walk phenomenon? *Journal of International Money and Finance* 5, 181–220.

Fleming, J. M. (1962) Domestic financial policies under fixed and floating exchange rates. *IMF Staff Papers* 3, 369–80.

Flood, R. P. and Garber, P. M. (1980) Market fundamentals versus price level bubbles: The first tests. *Journal of Political Economy* 88, 745–70.

—— and Hodrick, R. (1990) Testable implications of indeterminacies in models with rational expectations. *Journal of Economic Perspectives* 4, 85–102.

Forsyth, P. J. and Kay, J. A. (1980) The economic implications of North Sea oil reserves. *Fiscal Studies* 1, 1–28.

Frankel, J. A. (1979a) On the mark: A theory of floating exchange rates based on real interest differentials. *American Economic Review* 69, 610–22.

—— (1979b) Test of rational expectations in the forward exchange market. *Southern Journal of Economics* 46, 103–1101.

—— (1982) In search of the exchange risk premium: a six-currency test assuming mean–variance optimisation. *Journal of International Money and Finance* 1, 255–74.

—— (1982a) The mystery of the multiplying marks: A modification of the monetary model. *Review of Economics and Statistics* August.

—— (1982b) A test of perfect substitutability in the foreign exchange market. *Southern Economic Journal* 49 (2), 406–16.

—— (1982c) In search of the exchange risk premium: a six-currency test assuming mean variance optimization. *Journal of International Money and Finance* 1, 255–74.

—— (1983) Monetary and portfolio balance models of exchange rate determination. In J. S. Bhandari and B. H. Putnam (eds), *Economic Interdependence and Flexible Exchange Rates.* Cambridge, MA: MIT Press, pp. 84–115.

—— (1984) Tests of monetary and portfolio balance models of exchange rate determination. In J. F. O. Bilson and R. C. Marston (eds), *Exchange Rate Theory and Practice.* Chicago, IL: University of Chicago Press, pp. 239–59.

—— (1985) The dazzling dollar. *Brookings Papers on Economic Activity* 1, 199–217.

—— and Engel, C. (1984) Do asset demands optimize over the mean and variance of real returns? a six-currency test. *Journal of International Economics* 17, 309–23.

—— and Froot, K. (1986a) Interpreting tests of forward discount bias using exchange rate survey data. NBER Working Paper 1963, National Bureau of Economic Research.

—— and —— (1986b) Short-term and long-term expectations of the yen/dollar exchange rate: evidence from survey data. *International Finance Discussion Papers* 292.

—— and —— (1986c) Under the US dollar in the eighties: the expectations of chartists and fundamentalists. *Economic Record (Special Issue)* 24–38.

—— and —— (1987) Using survey data to test some standard propositions regarding exchange rate expectations. *American Economic Review* 77 (1), 133–53.

—— and —— (1989) Interpreting tests of forward discount bias using survey data on exchange rate expectations. *Quarterly Journal of Economics* 104, 139–61.

—— and —— (1990) Chartists, fundamentalists and the demand for dollars. In A. S. Courakis and M. P. Taylor (eds), *Policy Issues for Interdependent Economies*. Oxford: Oxford University Press.

Frenkel, J. A. (1976) A monetary approach to the exchange rate: doctrinal aspects and empirical evidence. *Scandinavian Journal of Economics* 78 (2), 200–24.

—— (1980) Exchange rates, prices and money, lessons from the 1920's. *American Economic Association, Papers and Proceedings* 70, 235–42.

—— (1981) Flexible exchange rates, prices and the role of 'news': lessons from the 1970s. *Journal of Political Economy* 89 (4), 665–705.

—— and Johnson, H. G. (eds) (1976) *The Monetary Approach to the Balance of Payments*. London: Allen & Unwin.

—— and —— (1978) *The Economics of Exchange Rates*. Reading, MA: Addison-Wesley.

—— and Razin, A. (1982) Stochastic prices and tests of efficiency of foreign exchange markets. *Economics Letters* 6, 165–70.

—— and —— (1987) *Fiscal Policies and the World Economy*. Cambridge, MA: MIT Press.

Friedman, M. (1953) The case for flexible exchange rates. In *Essays in Positive Economics*. Chicago, IL: University of Chicago Press, pp. 157–203.

Froot, K. A. and Ito, T. (1988) On the consistency of short-run and long-run exchange rate expectations. NBER Working Paper 2577, National Bureau of Economic Research.

Genberg, H. (1981) Effects of central bank intervention in the foreign exchange market. *IMF Staff Papers* 30, 451–76.

—— and Kierzkowski, H. (1979) Impact and long run effects of economic disturbances in a dynamic model of exchange rate determination. *Weltwirtschaftliches Archiv* 115, 605–27.

Geweke, J. and Feige, E. L. (1978) Some joint tests of markets for forward exchange. *Review of Economics and Statistics* 61, 334–41.

Giddy, I. H. and Duffey, G. (1975) The random behaviour of flexible exchange rates. *Journal of International Business Studies* 6, 1–32.

Giovannini, A. and Jorion, P. (1987) Interest rates and risk premia in the stock market and in the foreign exchange markets. *Journal of International Money and Finance* 6.

Goldfeld, S. M. (1976) The case of the missing money. *Brookings Papers on Economic Activity* 3, 683–730.

Goodhart, C. A. E. (1988) The foreign exchange market: A random walk with a dragging anchor. *Economica* 55, 437–60.

Granger, C. W. and Newbold, P. (1974) Spurious regressions in econometrics. *Journal of Econometrics* 2, 111-20.

Grauer, F., Litzenberger, R. and Stehle, R. (1976) Sharing rules and equilibrium in an international capital market under uncertainty. *Journal of Financial Economics* 3, 233-56.

Gray, M. R. and Turnovsky, S. J. (1979) The stability of exchange rate dynamics under perfect myopic foresight. *International Economic Review* 20, 643-60.

Gregory, A. W. and McCurdy, T. H. (1984) Testing unbiasedness in the forward foreign exchange market: a specification analysis. *Journal of International Money and Finance* 3, 357-68.

Grossman, S. J. and Stiglitz, J. E. (1980) On the impossibility of informationally efficient markets. *American Economic Review* 70, 393-407.

Hacche, G. and Townend, J. (1981) Exchange rates and monetary policy: modelling sterling's effective exchange rate, 1972-80. In W. A. Eltis and P. J. N. Sinclair (eds), *The Money Supply and the Exchange Rate*. Oxford: Oxford University Press, pp. 201-47.

—— and —— (1983) Some problems in exchange rate modelling: the case of sterling. *Zeitschrift für Nationalökonomie* 3, 127-62.

Hakkio, C. S. (1981a) The term structure of the forward premium. *Journal of Monetary Economics* 8, 41-58.

—— (1981b) Expectations and the forward exchange rate. *International Economic Review* 22, 663-78.

Hannan, E. J. (1970) *Multiple Time Series Analysis*. London: Wiley.

Hansen, L. P. (1982) Large sample properties of generalised method of moments estimators. *Econometrica* 50, 1029-54.

—— and Hodrick, R. J. (1980) Forward exchange rates as optimal predictors of future spot rates: an econometric analysis. *Journal of Political Economy* 88, 829-53.

—— and —— (1983) Risk averse speculation in the forward foreign exchange market: an econometric analysis of linear models. In J. A. Frenkel (ed.), *Exchange Rates and International Macroeconomics*. Chicago, IL: University of Chicago Press for National Bureau of Economic Research.

—— and Richard, S. (1984) A general approach for deducing testable restrictions implied by asset pricing models. Mimeo, Carnegie–Mellon University.

—— and Singleton, K. J. (1982) Generalized instrumental variables estimation of nonlinear rational expectations models. *Econometrica* 50, 1269-86.

Hartley, P. R. (1983) Rational expectations and the foreign exchange market. In J. A. Frenkel (ed.), *Exchange Rates and International Macroeconomics*. Chicago, IL: University of Chicago Press for National Bureau of Economic Research.

Hausman, J. A. (1978) Specification tests in economics. *Econometrica* 46, 1251-72.

Haynes, S. E. and Stone, J. A. (1981) On the mark: comment, *American Economic Review* 71 (5), 1060-7.

Hendry, D. F., Pagan, A. R. and Sargan, J. D. (1984) Dynamic specification. In Z. Griliches and M. D. Intriligator (eds), *Handbook of Econometrics*, vol. 2. Amsterdam: North-Holland.

Hodrick, R. J. (1978) An empirical analysis of the monetary approach to the determination of the exchange rate. In J. A. Frenkel and H. G. Johnson (eds), *The*

Economics of Exchange Rates. Reading, MA: Addison-Wesley, pp. 97–128.

—— (1987) *The Empirical Evidence on the Efficiency of Forward and Futures Foreign Exchange Markets*. London: Harwood.

—— and Srivastava, S. (1984) An investigation of risk and return in forward foreign exchange. *Journal of International Money and Finance* 3, 1–29.

—— and —— (1986) The covariation of risk premiums and expected future spot exchange rates. *Journal of International Money and Finance* 5, S5–S22.

Hoffman, D. and Schlagenhauf, D. (1983) Rational expectations and monetary models of exchange rate determination: an empirical examination. *Journal of Monetary Economics* 11, 247–60.

Hooper, P. and Morton, J. (1982) Fluctuations in the dollar: a model of nominal and real exchange rate determination. *Journal of International Money and Finance* 1 (1), 39–56.

Hsieh, D. (1984) Tests of rational expectations and no risk premium in forward exchange markets. *Journal of International Economics* 17, 173–84.

Huang, R. D. (1981) The monetary approach to exchange rate in an efficient foreign exchange market: tests based on volatility. *Journal of Finance* 36 (1), 31–41.

—— (1984) Some alternative tests of forward exchange rates as predictors of future spot rates. *Journal of International Money and Finance* 3 (2), 157–67.

Isard, P. (1980) Expected and unexpected changes in exchange rates: the roles of relative price levels, balance of payments factors, interest rates and risk. *International Finance Discussion Papers* 156.

Ito, T. (1988) Foreign exchange rate expectations: micro survey data. NBER Working Paper 22679, National Bureau of Economic Research.

Johnson, H. G. (1958) Towards a general theory of the balance of payments. In H. G. Johnson (ed.), *International Trade and Economic Growth*. London, Allen & Unwin.

Kaminsky, G. L. and Peruga, R. (1988) Risk premium and the foreign exchange market. Mimeo, University of California, San Diego.

Kawai, M. (1985) Exchange rates, the current account and monetary fiscal policies in the short run and in the long run. *Oxford Economic Papers* 37.

Kearney, C. P. and MacDonald, R. (1985) Asset markets and the exchange rate: a structural model of the sterling–dollar rate 1972–1982. *Journal of Economic Studies* 12, 33–60.

—— and —— (1986) Intervention and sterilisation under floating exchange rates: the UK 1973–1983. *European Economic Review* 30, 345–64.

—— and —— (1990) Exchange rate volatility, news and bubbles. *Australian Economic Papers*, 1–20.

—— and —— (forthcoming) Tests of efficiency in the Australian forward foreign exchange market. *Economic Record*.

Kolhagen, S. (1975) The performance of the foreign exchange markets: 1971–1974. *Journal of International Business Studies* 6.

Korajczyk, R. A. (1985) The pricing of forward contracts for foreign exchange. *Journal of Political Economy* 93, 346–68.

Kouri, P. J. K. (1976) The exchange rate and the balance of payments in the short run and in the long run: A monetary approach. *Scandinavian Journal of Economics* 78 (2), 280–304.

—— (1977) International investment and interest rate linkages under flexible exchange rates. In R. Z. Aliber (ed.), *The Political Economy of Monetary Reform.* London: Macmillan.

Krasker, W. S. (1980) The 'peso problem' in testing the efficiency of forward exchange markets. *Journal of Monetary Economics* 6, 276–96.

Krueger, A. S. (1983) *Exchange Rate Determination.* Cambridge: Cambridge University Press.

Leroy, S. F. (1984) Efficiency and the variability of asset prices. *American Economic Review, Proceedings* 74, 183–7.

Levich, R. M. (1979) On the efficiency of markets for foreign exchange. In R. Dornbusch and J. Frenkel (eds), *International Economic Policy Theory and Evidence.* Baltimore, MD: Johns Hopkins University Press, pp. 246–67.

—— (1985) Empirical studies of exchange rates: price behaviour, rate determination and market efficiency. In R. W. Jones and P. B. Kenen (eds), *Handbook of International Economics.* Amsterdam: North-Holland, pp. 979–1040.

Levine, R. (1986) The pricing of forward exchange rates. *International Finance Discussion Papers* 312.

Levy, E. and Nobay, A. R. (1986) The speculative efficiency hypothesis: a bivariate analysis. *Economic Journal (Supplement)* 96, 109–21.

Lewis, K. K. (1989) Risk aversion and the effectiveness of sterilised intervention. Mimeo.

Logue, D. E. and Sweeney, R. J. (1977) White noise in imperfect markets: The case of the franc/dollar exchange rate. *Journal of Finance* 32, 761–8.

Longworth, D. (1981) Testing the efficiency of the Canadian–US exchange market under the assumption of no risk premium. *Journal of Finance* 36, 43–9.

——, Boothe, P. and Clinton, K. (1983) *A Study of the Efficiency of the Foreign Exchange Market.* Ottawa: Bank of Canada.

Lucas, R. E. (1976) Econometric policy evaluation: a critique. In K. Brunner and A. H. Meltzer (eds), *The Phillips Curve and Labour Markets.* Amsterdam: North Holland. Carnegie Rochester Conference Series on Public Policy, vol. 1, pp. 19–46.

—— (1982) Interest rates and currency prices in a two-country world. *Journal of Monetary Economics* 10, 335–60.

MacDonald, R. (1983a) Some tests of the rational expectations hypothesis in the foreign exchange market. *Scottish Journal of Political Economy* 30 (3), 235–50.

—— (1983b) Tests of efficiency and the impact of news in three foreign exchange markets: The experience of the 1920s. *Bulletin of Economic Research* 35 (2), 123–44.

—— (1983c) Our experience with floating exchange rates: a survey of the empirical evidence on exchange rate models, news and risk. Discussion Paper 74, Loughborough University.

—— (1985a) 'News' and the 1920's experience with floating exchange rates. *Economics Letters* 17, 379–83.

—— (1985b) Do deviations of the real effective exchange rate follow a random walk? *Economic Notes* 14 (1), 63–9.

—— (1985c) Are deviations from purchasing power parity efficient? Some further answers. *Weltwirtschaftliches Archiv* 121 (4), 638–45.

—— (1988) *Floating Exchange Rates: Theories and Evidence*. London: Unwin Hyman.

—— (1990) Exchange rate economics: An empirical perspective. In G. Brid (ed.), *The International Financial Regime*. Guildford: Surrey University Press.

—— (forthcoming) Are foreign exchange market forecasters 'rational'? Some survey based tests. *Manchester School*.

—— and Taylor, M. P. (1987) On unit root tests in exchange rates, spot market efficiency and cointegration: some evidence from the recent float. Discussion Paper 87–16, Aberdeen University.

—— and Taylor, M. P. (1989a) Risk, efficiency and speculation in the interwar foreign exchange market. Discussion Paper, City University Business School, London.

—— and —— (1989b) The economic analysis of foreign exchange markets: an expository survey. In R. MacDonald and M. P. Taylor (eds), *Exchange Rates and Open Economy Macroeconomics*. Oxford: Basil Blackwell.

—— and —— (1989c) Foreign exchange market efficiency and cointegration: some evidence from the recent float. *Economics Letters* 29, 63–8.

—— and —— (1990) International parity conditions. In A. S. Courakis and M. P. Taylor (eds), *Policy Issues for Interdependent Economies*. Oxford: Oxford University Press.

—— and —— (1990) The term structure of forward foreign exchange premia: the interwar experience. *Manchester School* 58, 54–65.

—— and Torrance, T. S. (1988a) Exchange rates and the news: some evidence using UK survey data. *Manchester School* 56 (1), 69–76.

—— and —— (1988b) On risk, rationality and excessive speculation in the deutschemark–US dollar exchange market: some evidence using survey data. *Oxford Bulletin of Economics and Statistics* 50, 107–24.

—— and —— (1990) Expectations formation and risk in four foreign exchange markets. *Oxford Economic Papers*.

—— and Young, R. (1986) Decision rules, expectations and efficiency in two foreign exchange models. *De Economist* 134 (1), 42–60.

Mankiw, H. G. and Summers, L. H. (1984) Do long-term interest rates over-react to short-term interest rates? *Brookings Papers on Economic Activity* 1, 223–47.

Mark, N. C. (1985) Some evidence on the international inequality of real interest rates. *Journal of International Money and Finance* 4, 189–208.

Masson, P. and Knight, M. (1986) International transmission of fiscal policies in major industrial countries. *IMF Staff Papers* 33.

—— and —— (1990) Economic interactions and the fiscal policies of major industrial countries: 1980–1988. In A. S. Courakis and M. P. Taylor (eds), *Policy Issues for Interdependent Economies*. Oxford: Oxford University Press.

McCallum, B. T. (1976) Rational expectations and the estimation of econometric models: An alternative procedure. *International Economic Review* 17, 484–90.

McCormick, F. (1971) Covered interest arbitrage: Unexploited profits? Comment. *Journal of Political Economy* April, 418–22.

McCulloch, J. H. (1975) Operational aspects of the Siegal paradox. *Quarterly Journal of Economics* 89, 170–2.

McKinnon, R. I. (1976) Floating exchange rates 1973–74; the emperor's new clothes.

Journal of Monetary Economics, Carnegie-Rochester Supplement 3.

Meese, R. A. (1987) Testing for bubbles in exchange markets: a case of sparkling rates. *Journal of Political Economy* 94 (2), 345-73.

—— and Rogoff, K. (1983) Empirical exchange rate models of the seventies: do they fit out of sample? *Journal of International Economics* 14, 3-24.

—— and —— (1984) The out of sample failure of empirical exchange rate models: sampling error or misspecification? In J. A. Frenkel (ed.), *Exchange Rates and International Macroeconomics*. Chicago, IL: University of Chicago Press for National Bureau of Economic Research.

—— and Singleton, K. J. (1982) On unit roots and the empirical modelling of exchange rates. *Journal of Finance* 37 (4), 1029-35.

Mehra, R. and Prescott E. (1985) The equity premium: a puzzle. *Journal of Monetary Economics* 15, 145-62.

Minford, P. and Peel, D. A. (1983) *Rational Expectations and the New Macroeconomics*. Oxford: Martin Robertson.

Mundell, R. (1968) *International Economics*. New York: Macmillan.

Mussa, M. (1976) The exchange rate, the balance of payments, and monetary policy under a regime of controlled floating. *Scandinavian Journal of Economics* 78, 229-48.

—— (1979) Empirical regularities in the behaviour of exchange rates and theories of the foreign exchange market. *Journal of Monetary Economics, Carnegie-Rochester Supplement* 11, 9-57.

—— (1981) The role of intervention. Group of Thirty Occasional Papers 6, New York.

Nelson, C. R. and Plosser, C. (1982) Trends and random walks in macroeconomic time series: some evidence and implications. *Journal of Monetary Economics* 10, 139-62.

Nerlove, M., Diebold, F. X., Van Beeck, H. and Cheung, Y. (1988) A multivariate ARCH model of foreign exchange rate determination. Mimeo.

Obstfeld, M. (1983) Exchange rates, inflation and the sterilisation problem: Germany 1975-1981. *European Economic Review* 21, 161-89.

Papell, D. H. (1988) Expectations and exchange rate dynamics after a decade of floating. *Journal of International Economics* 25, 303-17.

Pentecost, E. J. (1988) The out-of-sample forecasting performance of exchange rate models: an appraisal of the recent evidence. Mimeo.

Polak, J. J. (1957) Monetary analysis of income formation and payments problems. *IMF Staff Papers* 4, 1-50.

Poole, W. (1967) Speculative prices as random walks: an analysis of ten time series of flexible exchange rates. *Southern Economic Journal* 33, 4.

Putnam, B. H. and Woodbury, J. R. (1979) Exchange rate stability and monetary policy. *Review of Business and Economic Research* 15 (2), 1-10.

Rasulo, J. and Wilford, D. (1980) Estimating monetary models of the balance of payments and exchange rates: a bias. *Southern Economic Journal* 47, 136-46.

Richard, S. and Sundaresan, S. (1981) A continuous time equilibrium model of forward prices and future prices in a multigood economy. *Journal of Financial Economics* 9, 347-72.

Rogoff, K. (1984) On the effects of sterilised intervention: an analysis of weekly data. *Journal of Monetary Economics* 14 (2), 133–50.

Roll, R. (1979) Violations of purchasing power parity and their implications for efficient international commodity markets. In M. Sarnat and G. Szego (eds), *International Finance and Trade I*. Cambridge, MA: Ballinger, pp. 133–76.

Salemi, M.K. (1984) Comment. In J.A. Frenkel (ed.), *Exchange Rates and International Macroeconomics*. Chicago, IL: University of Chicago Press for the National Bureau of Economic Research.

Samuelson, P.A. (1965) Proof that properly anticipated prices fluctuate randomly. *Industrial Management Review* 6, 41–9.

Sargent, T.J. (1979) A note on maximum likelihood estimation of the rational expectations model of the term structure. *Journal of Monetary Economics* 5, 133–43.

Schinasi, G.J. and Swamy, P.A.V.B. (1987) The out-of-sample forecasting performance of exchange rate models when coefficients are allowed to change. *International Finance Discussion Papers* 301.

Shiller, R.J. (1978) Rational expectations and the dynamic structure of macroeconomic models. *Journal of Monetary Economics* 4, 1–44.

—— (1979) The volatility of long-term interest rates and expectations models of the term structure. *Journal of Political Economy* 87, 1190–219.

Siegel, J. (1972) Risk interest rates and the forward exchange. *Quarterly Journal of Economics* 86, 303–19.

Smith, P. and Wickens, M. (1988) A stylised econometric model of an open economy: UK 1973–1981. Mimeo.

—— and —— (1990) Assessing monetary shocks and exchange rate variability with a stylised econometric model of the UK. In A.S. Courakis and M.P. Taylor (eds), *Policy Issues for Interdependent Economies*. Oxford: Oxford University Press.

Somanath, V.S. (1986) Efficient exchange rate forecasts: lagged models better than the random walk. *Journal of International Money and Finance* 5, 195–220.

Stockman, A.C. (1978) Risk, information, and forward exchange rates. In J.A. Frenkel and H.G. Johnson (eds), *The Economics of Exchange Rates*. Reading, MA: Addison-Wesley.

Sweeney, R.J. (1986) Beating the foreign exchange market. *Journal of Finance* 41, 163–82.

Taylor, J.B. (1977) Conditions for unique solutions in stochastic macroeconomic models with rational expectations. *Econometrica* 45, 1377–85.

Taylor, M.P. (1987a) Expectations, risk and uncertainty in the foreign exchange market: Some results based on survey data. Bank of England Discussion Paper.

—— (1987b) The role of speculation in the forward exchange market: some consistent estimates assuming rational expectations. *Oxford Bulletin of Economics and Statistics* 49, 323–33.

—— (1987c) Risk premia and foreign exchange: a multiple time series approach to testing uncovered interest parity. *Weltwirtschaftliches Archiv* 123, 579–91.

—— (1988a) An empirical examination of long-run purchasing power parity using cointegration techniques. *Applied Economics* 20, 1369–82.

—— (1988b) A DYMIMIC model of forward foreign exchange risk, with estimates for three major exchange rates. *Manchester School* 56, 55–68.

—— (1988c) What do investment managers know? An empirical study of practitioners' predictions. *Economica* 55, 185–202.

—— (1988d) Covered interest parity: a high-frequency, high-quality data study. *Economics* 54, 429–38.

—— (1989a) Covered interest arbitrage and market turbulence. *Economica Journal* 99, 376–91.

—— (1989b) Expectations, risk and uncertainty in the foreign exchange market: some results based on survey data. *Manchester School* 57, 142–53.

—— (1990a) On unit roots and real exchange rates: empirical evidence and Monte Carlo analysis. *Applied Economics.*

—— (1990b) Testing *ex ante* purchasing power parity using vector autoregressions in the time domain. *Empirical Economics.*

—— and McMahon, P.C. (1988) Long-run purchasing power parity in the 1920s. *European Economic Review* 32, 179–97.

Tobin, J. (1969) A general equilibrium approach to monetary theory. *Journal of Money, Credit and Banking* 1, 15–29.

Urich, T.J. and Wachtel, P. (1981) Market response to weekly money supply announcements in the 1970's. *Journal of Finance* 36, 1063–72.

Vaubel, R. (1980) International shifts in the demand for money, their effects on exchange rates and price levels and their implications for the pre-announcement of monetary expansion. *Wertwirthschaftliche Archiv 116, 1–44.*

Wadhwani, S.B. (1984) Are exchange rates excessively volatile?' Discussion Paper 198, Centre for Labour Economics, London School of Economics.

—— (1987) Are exchange rates excessively volatile? *Journal of International Economics* 22, 339–48.

Wallace, M.S. (1979) The monetary approach to flexible exchange rates in the short run: an empirical test. *Review of Business and Economic Research* 23, 98–102.

West, K.D. (1986) A specification test for speculative bubbles. Working paper 2067, National Bureau of Economic Research.

Wilson, C.A. (1979) Anticipated shocks and exchange rate dynamics. *Journal of Political Economy* 87 (3), 639–47.

Wolff, C.P. (1987) Forward foreign exchange rates, expected spot rates, and premia: a signal-extraction approach. *Journal of Finance* 42, 395–406.

Woo, W.T. (1985) The monetary approach to exchange rate determination under rational expectations. *Journal of International Economics* 18, 1–16.

4 The Money Transmission Mechanism

David K. Miles and Joe Wilcox

4.1 INTRODUCTION

In this chapter our aim is to survey some of the work undertaken over the last 30 years to describe the transmission mechanism. We discuss empirical and theoretical research and try to relate the literature to developments in the UK economy. In recent years the most important differences between economists who have analysed the impact of monetary policy upon prices and output have stemmed from differences in views about labour and goods markets. Indeed, in the 1970s and 1980s there has been much less emphasis than in the 1960s on the links between changes in the money stock and the level of nominal demand and more on the impact of changes in aggregate nominal demand upon wages, goods prices and quantities. In much theoretical work in macroeconomics nominal demand is modelled in a particularly simple way with aggregate demand depending on the money stock. These kinds of reduced form equations explicitly pass over the issue of the transmission mechanism from money to demand in order to concentrate on modelling factor and product markets. As devices to assess the impact of monetary policy such models are limited, for the influence of policy depends on the relative importance and the stability of various transmission mechanisms – from money to nominal demand and from demand to prices

The views expressed in this chapter are those of the authors and not necessarily those of the Bank of England. The authors are grateful to members of the Economics Division of the Bank of England, Christopher Green, and Patrick McMahon for comments on the previous draft. Final responsibility for the contents rests solely with the authors.

and output. In particular, the way in which a given change in nominal demand, induced by some change in monetary conditions, will be split between price and quantity responses will itself often depend on how monetary conditions are altered. The most obvious example of the dependence of the price/output effects upon the way in which the level of aggregate nominal demand is changed stems from the important distinction between expected and unexpected changes in macroeconomic policy. For the purposes of practical policy advice it is also important to analyse how a change in monetary policy – say an increase in nominal interest rates – impinges on particular elements of demand; an aggregate reduced form link from money to total demand is simply too crude to be helpful here.

In this chapter we shall assess the relative importance and the stability of various monetary transmission mechanisms in the light of money, price and output trends in the UK. Part of the value of such an exercise was described by Milton Friedman some 20 years ago when he argued that: 'However consistent may be the relation between monetary changes and economic changes and however strong the evidence for the autonomy of monetary changes, we shall not be persuaded that the monetary changes are the source of the economic changes unless we can specify in some detail the mechanism that connects the one with the other' (Friedman, 1969, p. 229). As Friedman implies, without a plausible description of the transmission mechanism one is left puzzling quite how to interpret the enormous outpouring of results reporting correlations of prices, output and money. (On the much discussed empirical issue of money -income causality see the classic articles by Granger (1969) and Sims (1972). For UK evidence see Williams et al. (1976) and for a review of more recent literature see Saunders (1988). On the theoretical issues of money income causality see Tobin (1970) and Kaldor (1980, 1982.)

4.2 MONEY A VEIL

It has never been denied that in antiquity the rapid development of the argentiferous lead mines of Laurium raised the price of a medimnus of wheat from 1 to 3 drachmas in the interval between Solon and Aristophanes.

(Walras, *Elements of Pure Economics*)

Despite Walras' observation there is no consensus amongst economists on the relation between the aggregate stock of money, however measured, and the levels of output and prices. Nonetheless, the idea that changes in the level of money lead to equiproportionate changes in prices, at least in the long run, has a long history going back at least to David Hume. The hypothesis has most usually been expressed using the Fisher equation

$$MV = PT \qquad\qquad\qquad (4.1)$$

and the auxiliary hypotheses of (a) the independence of T (real transactions or output) from M ('the' money stock), (b) the stability of the velocity of circulation V and (c) the exogeneity of money. The equation, allied with this set of assumptions, yields the strong neutrality result – money only affects nominal magnitudes and does so in a one-for-one way – but it cannot be taken as a theory of monetary policy and nor is it helpful to describe the equation as a model. What is missing is any description of the process whereby changes in money, or more generally in monetary policy, come to impact upon prices and or quantities. Developing models which spell out a transmission mechanism inevitably raises further issues: How is money defined? How is the stock of money changed? Is the relation between money, quantities and prices one which suggests a particular policy rule?

4.3 EARLY KEYNESIAN AND MONETARIST MODELS

The formalization of the basic Keynesian model undertaken by Hicks, and the detailed consideration of various extensions by Patinkin (1956), spelt out several channels by which changes in the stock of money – assumed to be exogenous – influence the demand for goods. Summarizing these mechanisms Goodhart (1975) says: 'Monetary policy affects expenditure decisions by causing changes in (these) relative yields and also by causing variations in people's wealth through altering the market value of outstanding assets'.

In the standard IS–LM framework, increases in money (usually interpreted as exogenous changes in the quantity of non-interest-bearing outside money) cause a shift in the interest rate on financial assets (bonds) which are money substitutes. The reduction in the return on bonds changes the attractiveness of holding real, compared with financial, assets and in the consequent transition to a new equilibrium increases the flow of investment expenditure. If, in equilibrium, gross investment is assumed to be an increasing function of the desired capital stock, then gross investment is higher in the new equilibrium. In this simple story the transmission mechanism runs from (outside) money to prices of financial assets (bond yields) to investment expenditure. The difference between nominal and real yields on assets is often handled by assuming zero (or at least fixed) inflation, and more direct effects of changing money stocks on expenditure, via wealth effects, are ignored in simple models. Neither of these restrictions is essential. The transmission mechanism in the simple IS–LM framework can be made richer by allowing a direct wealth effect upon consumption and the story, although more complex, is not in principle changed when prices can move. Richer portfolio models with more assets can allow the impact of changes in money to reverberate throughout the financial system in rather complex ways (see Tobin, 1952, 1961, 1969; Tobin and Brainard, 1968). For example, allowing for less than perfect substitutability between bonds and capital goods, which would imply that the return on these assets will generally differ, adds greater complexity and can generate counter-intuitive comparative statics results depending on the assumed substitutabilities between money, bonds and capital goods (see Tobin, 1961, 1969; B. Friedman, 1978).

However, despite the great scope for disagreement about price elasticities of demand for various assets, the very different monetary policy proposals advanced by monetarists, New Classicists and Keynesians (to use convenient labels) remain more a reflection of disagreements about the structure of labour and goods markets. Indeed, in some ways there is nothing fundamental about the differences between those economists who in the 1960s believed that the substitutability between money and bonds, and the interest rate elasticity of real expenditures, were such as to make money transmission mechanisms running through such channels weak and those who believed that such mechanisms, and more direct real-balance-type effects, were strong. Although the monetarist–Keynesian debate of the 1960s did appear to revolve around disagreements over the substitutability of different assets, the different views on the operation of goods and labour markets which determined how a change in nominal expenditure might he reflected in prices and quantities were much more fundamental.

Thus, what gives the policy recommendations in Friedman's 1968 Presidential address their strength is not so much a detailed defence of the hypothesis that the relevant degrees of substitution are such as to make a money to nominal income channel 'powerful', but more a series of simple arguments to show that changes in nominal demand can only effect nominal magnitudes, at least in the longer term (Friedman, 1968). Friedman argued that since uncertainty about the price level was itself an economic bad and given that money affects, and in the longer term only affects, prices then a stable path for the money supply was an essential element in macroeconomic policy. He went on to argue that a rate of inflation which was positive encouraged people to economize on holding non-interest-bearing money and that since the production of such money was not costly a low (indeed a negative) rate of money growth was optimal.

What was crucial about Friedman's argument was that a unique equilibrium level of real output existed which was independent of nominal magnitudes. His reference to the levels of trade 'ground out' by the operation of the Walrasian auctioneer is important just because in the Walrasian fiction of the auction there is no role for money and the only prices which are determined are relative. Money is really only important in the Friedman model because its quantity ties down the price level.

4.4 THE DEFINITION OF MONEY AND ITS CONTROL

Before focusing on the different assumptions about the operation of labour and goods markets, it is important to be clear about just how much is passed over by simply assuming that aggregate nominal demand is a stable, increasing and, in the most restrictive case, proportional function of the supply of nominal money. Two major difficulties can be illustrated using the basic Fisher equation. The first is the definition of money and corresponding transactions; the second is the control of the stock of money, however defined.

4.4.1 The Definition of Money and its Control

If equation (4.1), where money holdings are made a proportion of the level of transactions, is to capture the demand for money it would seem essential that money should be used primarily for transactions. The broader is the definition of money the smaller is the proportion used for transactions and the greater for savings. The narrowest monetary aggregate M0 is mainly notes and coin, and hence transactions balance. When the velocity relative to GDP is considered (figure 4.1) there is a continuous increase over the

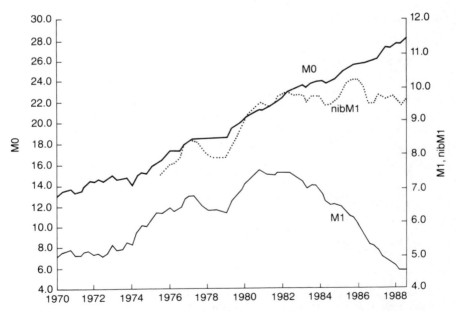

Figure 4.1 Velocity of M0, M1 and non-interest-bearing M1 (nibM1)

past 20 years. This illustrates the problem that the velocity of circulation of money, however defined, is unlikely to be constant even when money is used primarily for transactions. Increasing use of bank and building society accounts and credit cards helps explain the increasing velocity of M0. Although the velocity has altered over the period it has changed in one direction – a steady increase as cash-saving payments methods have been introduced. The velocity of other measures of narrow money have followed a more erratic course, (figure 4.1). The relatively rapid growth of interest-bearing M1 since 1980 is particularly noticeable, with the growth of interest-bearing chequing accounts increasing the problems in distinguishing between savings and transactions balances. The velocity of broader measures of money relative to GDP (figure 4.2) reflects the heterogeneity of transactions underlying the broader aggregates and the influence of savings balances. But, as with the narrower aggregates, technological developments and other forms of innovation have caused dramatic changes in the velocity of broad money. This would have come as no surprise to the Keynes of the *Treatise*: 'But the relationship between the total annual receipts of income receivers and the average stock of money held for all purposes is a hybrid conception having no particular significance, (Keynes, 1930, Ch. 24). Not only was Keynes anxious to separate out savings deposits from transactions deposits but he also stressed the distinction between transactions arising from per-

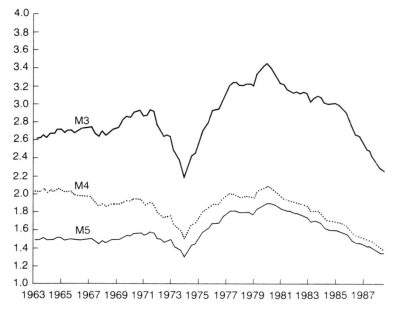

Figure 4.2   Velocity of broad money

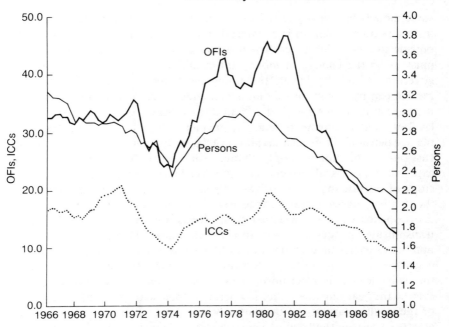

Figure 4.3   Velocity of sectoral M4 relative to GDP (ICCs, industrial and commercial companies; OFIs, other financial intermediaries)

sonal income and those from business, with the latter split between industrial circulation and financial circulation (see Keynes, 1930, Ch. 15, 1936).

A breakdown of broad money holdings by sector is available, however. Sectoral velocities (relative to GDP) are shown in figure 4.3. The change in these velocities reflect important changes in the financial markets over this period (for a detailed description see Bank of England (1986). We shall return to this topic when considering credit constraints in section 4.10. The point to note here is that technological and institutional changes in financial markets can alter the properties of various monetary aggregates and raise difficult problems in the measurement of money.

4.4.2 Control of the Money Supply

Many specifications of the transmission mechanism make sense only if the stock of money is a liability of the government and does not include inside money. The process whereby the stock of outside money is changed then becomes important. Helicopter drops of money may be a useful fiction in some models but clearly they leave a lot to be desired if an analysis of the transmission mechanism is of interest in itself. The simplest stories of how outside money is increased which are at least institutionally recognizable must make the change in money the result of some transaction between government and the private (including the financial) sector. The simplest mechanism by which outside money changes is as a result of government net purchases (or net sales) of commodities or as a result of a change in the level of transfer payments (e.g. the payment of a £10 Christmas bonus to old age pensioners). In this case it is crucial to distinguish the demand repercussions of the money supply change from that of the direct government expenditure, or fiscal, effects. The non-fiscal direct effects of changes in the stock of outside money on private expenditure, via changes in wealth, are the familiar Pigovian real balance effects. There are theoretical and empirical problems with the idea that such effects are an important element in transmitting changes in money to demand. Stiglitz (1982) has developed a number of irrelevance propositions which show that in an explicitly dynamic general equilibrium model with rational expectations public finance structure is irrelevant. Furthermore, as noted by Greenwald and Stiglitz (1987), even if the real balance effect is operative then with plausible magnitudes of the wealth elasticity of demand it would have taken a century for such effects to restore the level of demand to pre-depression levels in the USA, given even the fastest rates of price deflation in the 1920s and 1930s.

A more unambiguously monetary mechanism for changing the stock of money is where the government buys bonds from the public with money (this transaction can work through financial intermediaries without changing the essentials). Exactly how this money for bonds switch will affect demand will in this case depend crucially upon whether private sector net wealth is seen as having changed. If government bonds are not considered net wealth, because, as noted first by Ricardo, the private sector may discount the future tax charges needed to service the debt, the money for bonds swap may increase nominal, although in a classical framework not real (see Barro, 1974), wealth by the full extent of the swap. If bonds are seen as being as valuable as currency then the money–bonds switch will only tend to have effects inasmuch as portfolio reallocation changes the equilibrium pattern of yields on assets.

In practice, the stock of outside money is comparatively small in most Western economies and the idea that monetary policy works in any simple way via manipulation of the stock of such money is hard to accept. However, central bank influence over interest rates is founded on the monopoly of supply of the ultimate means of payment – outside or high powered money. In the UK it is the knowledge that the Bank of England could make shortages in the money markets bite that gives it such power to move short-term interest rates. A key point here is that because of the potential to make money shortages bite in financial markets it is not, in fact, necessary to initiate major changes in the quantity of outside money via significant open market operations in order to move interest rates. Expectations of central bank reactions to a failure of interest rates to respond to signs from the authorities that some change is desired can act as a powerful lever for the authorities. What this means is that reduced form relations between the level of aggregate demand and the stock of outside money are rather misleading in suggesting that fluctuations in the quantity of money generate either direct wealth effects or adjustments in the pattern of interest rates, for in practice direct wealth effects[1] are not likely to be very significant and interest rates may move significantly with little immediate change in the quantity of outside money. Provided, however, that the demand for outside money is not completely inelastic there will be some effect upon the private (financial and non-financial) sector's holding of money when interest rates change. But if the interest elasticity of demand for outside money is low and the adjustment of portfolios to the new pattern of rates is slow, then we could not expect to find any strong relation between changes in nominal interest rates and the stock of outside money. Certainly it would not be possible to identify a causal relation running from changes in the stock of exogenously supplied outside money to subsequent movements in the pattern of interest rates.

Nonetheless it is common in theoretical work to see a simple aggregate demand function depending only on the money stock used as a model simplification. Such a simplification – which leaves out any details of the transmission mechanism of which it is a reduced form and which does not specify the relative importance of induced interest rate changes and wealth – real balance effects – should not in itself be taken as an indication that a model is monetarist, New Classical or Keynesian. In fact, the key distinction between these broad classes of model is in the structure of the goods and labour markets which determines how changes in nominal demand feed through to prices and output. We might call these mechanisms – from aggregate demand to prices and output – the second part of the money transmission mechanism; it is to this link in the transmission mechanism that we now turn.

4.5 NATURAL RATE MODELS WITH AND WITHOUT RATIONAL EXPECTATIONS

Early monetarist work (the classic exposition of which is still Friedman (1968)) saw the transmission process from higher nominal money running, initially, through higher prices (or higher inflation if prices were already moving). With unchanged nominal wages, higher prices encourage producers to increase output. In the short term more labour is supplied as workers are slow to perceive the decline in real wages. In time, wage bargains come to reflect the higher prices, and unless nominal demand and prices continue to increase real wages will rise and desired output will fall. If wage bargainers come to expect an increase in prices equal to that experienced in recent years, and if equilibrium real wages need to rise to bring forth extra labour supply, then nominal demand needs to rise at ever faster rates in order to keep real output above its initial (equilibrium) value. This is the now familiar story of a long-run vertical Phillips curve. If we append to this goods and labour markets theory a reduced form aggregate demand relation making real demand a function of real (outside) money, the simple monetarist result of long-run equality of money and price changes can follow under further strong conditions. If, however, the real interest rate depends upon the growth of the money supply, the superneutrality of money – the invariance of any real magnitude to changes in the growth of money – is lost. The standard IS–LM model does, in fact, generally make the real interest rate depend negatively on the rate of growth of money, at least along a transition from one steady state growth path to another. This is the so-called Mundell–Tobin effect whereby a rise in the growth of money initially causes a less than equal rise in the nominal interest rate and a more than equal rise in prices so that the real supply of (outside) money is reduced in line with the fall in demand for it induced by higher nominal interest rates. If the long-run capital stock is altered as a result of this transition, then the long-run real interest rate may also be affected. However, the Mundell–Tobin effect will be quantitatively small if the demand for outside money is highly interest inelastic, in which case the superneutrality result will still hold approximately.

The most influential theoretical development of the 1970s was to take this model but make price and wage bargains more forward looking. In the limit an assumption of superneutrality for correctly perceived changes in money and perfect foresight would make any deviation of real magnitudes from equilibrium values as a result of monetary policy impossible. More plausible, and now widely used, are rational expectations models which make agents' expectation-generating mechanisms consistent with the true structure of the economy; agents make mistakes but not in any systematic way, which reflects an inability to learn about the non-random components of economic time series. (See Muth (1961) for the original contribution.) With some randomness in processes generating prices, deviations between actual and predicted paths for those exogenous variables which determine aggregate nominal demand cause real magnitudes to deviate from equilibrium values as individuals mistake nominal for real shocks, but with the underlying assumption of a vertical Phillips curve and a unique real economy equilibrium such deviations will only result from unexpected monetary or fiscal developments (see Lucas, 1972; Sargent and Wallace, 1975, 1976). More recently, real business cycle models have been developed which, unlike the earlier New Classical models, can generate persistence in the deviations of real magnitudes from equilibrium values. The invariance of real magnitudes to systematic macroeconomic policy is common to both the first and this second generation of New Classical models.

A simple New Classical model which shows how the neutrality results are derived is the following three-equation structure used by Sargent (1973) in his paper on interest rates and the natural rate of unemployment. He assumes that the macroeconomy can be described by

$$y_t = k_t + a(p_t - {}_tp_{t-1}) + u_t \tag{4.2}$$

$$y_t = k_t + b[r_t - ({}_{t+1}p_t - p_t)] + eZ_t + e_t \tag{4.3}$$

$$m_t = p_t + y_t + dr_t + v_t \tag{4.4}$$

where y_t, p_t and m_t are the natural logarithms of real national income, the price level and the exogenous money supply respectively, r_t is the nominal rate of interest, Z_t is a vector of exogenous variables, u_t, e_t and v_t are mutually uncorrelated random variables and ${}_{t+1}p_t$ is the public's expectation at time t of p_{t+1}. The variable k_t is a measure of normal productive capacity (e.g. the logarithm of the stock of labour or capital, or of some linear combination of the two); it is assumed to be exogenous. Equation (4.2) is an aggregate supply schedule making the deviation of output from normal productive capacity depend only on the forecast error for current prices and a random element. This is a Lucas type supply curve which makes supplies of factors of production differ from equilibrium levels only inasmuch as agents misperceive factor prices. Equation (4.3) is an aggregate demand or IS schedule making the deviations of output from capacity inversely related to the real rate of interest and also dependent on a vector of exogenous variables which includes government expenditure and tax rates. Equation (4.4) is a simple portfolio balance equation where bonds and equities are assumed to be perfect substitutes and are alternative assets to real money balances. The demand for money depends on the return on the other assets and upon real income; thus equation (4.4) is the familiar LM relation.

If agents have rational expectations, a number of powerful results emerge from this simple model. First, a natural rate of output exists in the sense that the deviation of output from its normal level is statistically independent of the systematic (and hence forecastable) parts of monetary and fiscal policy. Second, the real rate of interest is independent of the systematic part of the money supply – only random movements in the money supply have effects on both aggregate supply and the real rate of interest. These results depend crucially upon the form of the aggregate supply relation (2.2); they do not rely upon the relative magnitudes of parameters of the IS or LM curves nor do the results depend upon the simplifying assumption that bonds and equities are perfect substitutes. Indeed any macromodel with rational expectations and a supply function like (2.2) is almost certain to yield ineffectiveness results for systematic monetary policy and, depending on the exact assumptions about the form of money demand functions and the exogeneity of money, will make inflation and the price level depend on the path of the money stock.

The key feature of these models is in bringing out the difference between anticipated and unanticipated changes in monetary policy. In drawing this distinction the models reveal that it can be misleading to talk about the transmission mechanism, for even in the simplest models there are now two transmission mechanisms for monetary policy: one for anticipated monetary policy and a potentially quite distinct mechanism for unanticipated policy. In the New Classical models anticipated policy will generally only influence nominal magnitudes (ignoring Mundell–Tobin type effects as at most second order); unanticipated policy will influence both real and nominal variables.

Further, the added emphasis on the importance of expectations which has followed the New Classical 'revolution' has prompted economists to take seriously the impact of announcements of future policy. Such effects, stemming from the credibility of a statement about future changes in monetary conditions, could be viewed as another element of the transmission mechanism but one which works before any monetary policy levers are pulled.

Indeed, recent empirical work suggests that announcements of future policy can have effects, especially in financial markets (see Goodhart and Smith, 1985; MacDonald and Torrance, 1988a, b). As yet, convincing evidence that announcements have significant effects in the wider economy has not appeared. A much larger literature exists on the empirical evidence for the differential impact of anticipated and unanticipated monetary developments. For the UK there is strong evidence against the New Classical proposition that only unanticipated monetary policy affects real variables (see Garner, 1982; Alogoskoufis and Pissarides, 1983; Fitzgerald and Pollio, 1983; Symons, 1983; Bean, 1984).

As a theory of the transmission mechanism from monetary or fiscal policy to prices and output the new classical models have been widely criticized for failing to account for several clear features of the aggregate time series data for money, output, prices and employment. Most fundamentally, the theories seem hard to reconcile with very high serial correlation in deviations of output from trend and the apparent high correlation in the USA between nominal money and real output (see Blanchard, 1987). Our earlier discussion of the problems of measuring money presage the difficulty encountered in any attempt to relate the predictions of New Classical theoretical models with data for the UK. In the models the money stock is generally exogenously determined by the authorities. In practice the monetary authorities do not have such control over monetary aggregates. In the UK interest rates and various credit restrictions have been used to influence the path of monetary aggregates, although there has always been great uncertainty about how changes in the instruments of monetary policy would impinge on particular measures of the money stock. The problem of predicting how changes in interest rates and credit restrictions will affect monetary aggregates has been particularly acute over recent years when the pace of financial innovation has been rapid. Innovation has made it difficult to gauge the rate of growth of monetary aggregates compatible with low inflation – any correlation between broad money growth and inflation in the 1970s and 1960s has certainly changed since the early 1980s (figure 4.4 shows the change in one of the broadest definitions of money M4 and the change in prices over the past 25 years); it also makes it hard to isolate those parts of the growth in money which are forecastable by private agents and this makes an assessment of the New Classical theory problematic.

However, it is difficult to reconcile the theories outlined above, which make unexpected money supply changes a key determinant of deviations of output from trend, with the fact that changes in the money supply, interest rates or credit restrictions are promptly and widely publicized.

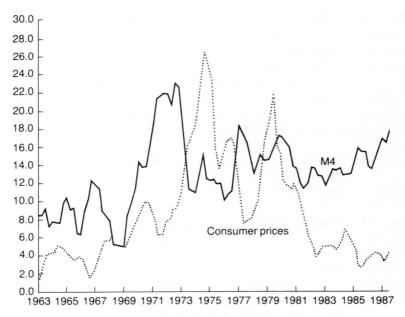

Figure 4.4 Annual change in M4 and consumer prices

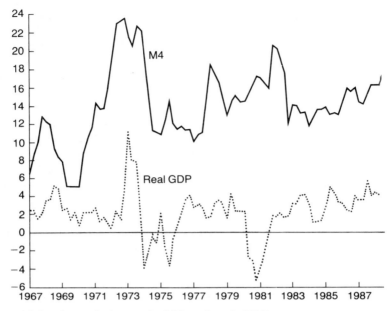

Figure 4.5   Annual change in M4 and real GDP

Time series data on money, output and prices in the UK also seem hard to reconcile with New Classical models. Figure 4.5 illustrates the growth of broad money (again we use M4) and real GDP. As a first approximation deviations from recent trend growth rates could be taken as unanticipated movements. The period from late 1971 to early 1973 might then be analysed as an apt illustration of the effect of unanticipated movements in money supply. However, closer examination of this episode indicates that the transmission mechanism at work during that period is unlikely to be accurately represented by the models considered so far. Competition and credit control removed restrictions on the financial system, and in particular on the supply of credit, in 1971. Thus, the transmission mechanism at this time partly worked through the removal of credit restrictions, which we examine in more detail in section 4.9 and 4.10. Furthermore, it is clear that over long periods of time deviations in output from trend have been highly persistent in the UK. As noted above, this is also not easy to reconcile with simple New Classical models.

However, theories which are consistent with the New Classical policy ineffectiveness result and are also consistent with the type of correlations between macroaggregates noted above have been constructed, most notably by Lucas (1975, 1977, 1980). According to Lucas (1977) unsystematic monetary–fiscal shocks lead to serially correlated deviations in output from trend because of information lags and an accelerator effect. Irreversibility of investment decisions is enough to generate persistence in output movements from trend if an initial one-off shock is misinterpreted by agents as a signal for a higher level of the optimal capital stock. Other mechanisms which generate persistence working through inventories (Sargent, 1979; Blinder and Fisher, 1981) and which build upon institutional features of labour markets, in particular the existence of long-term overlapping wage contracts (see Taylor, 1979) have been developed. If information about nominal shocks was not even available *ex post*, the changes in the money stock (with the simple reduced form aggregate nominal demand equations used in such models) could cause misperceptions about relative price changes for a long period and persistence in deviations of output and employment from trend would occur even if capital stock and inventory decisions were easily reversible (see Lucas, 1975; Taylor, 1975).

The plausibility of these mechanisms for persistence of the effects of monetary policy is not high. A theory which, for example, makes large sustained movements in output, employment and the capital stock depend on unexpected money supply movements is surely undermined by the fact that measures of the money stock are widely published in the press and broadcast on radio and television with a lag of only a few weeks.

4.6 FIXED PRICE MODELS

At the other extreme, in terms of price flexibility, from the New Classical models of the 1970s are the fixed price models (see Benassy, 1975; Barro and Grossman, 1976; Grandmont, 1977; Malinvaud, 1977). The assumption that, at least in the short run, prices are fixed clearly gives a very different transmission mechanism from aggregate demand to output than in the flexible price New Classical models. The fix price models have the implication that in some cases increases in nominal demand, linked as in the New Classical models to increases in the money supply, result in increases in output; in other cases (of repressed inflation) higher stocks of money have no positive, although sometimes a negative, impact on output. In states of repressed inflation factor prices are such as to make higher output unprofitable.

The fix price models showed clearly how monetary and fiscal policies could have real effects out of Walrasian equilibria. Nor were they as restrictive as the name 'fix price' suggests, for the results on the effectiveness of deterministic macropolicy are not nullified if the simplifying assumption that prices do not move at all is dropped. All that need be ruled out was that prices jump to (new) Walrasian levels when exogenous variables change. Thus, if the economy were in a Keynesian underemployment regime with constant prices where expansionary policy would increase output, the real effects of a loosening of monetary conditions would not necessarily disappear if prices started to move towards their market-clearing levels. If and when such price movements do take the economy to Walrasian equilibria further, expansionary monetary policy will have no effect on output and employment.

What was missing from the fix price literature were plausible theories of how prices would move away from market-clearing equilibria. As a general theory of the transmission mechanism from money to prices and output these models have not, therefore, proved very helpful. We consider some recent developments in imperfect competition, where price-setting behaviour is explicitly modelled, and in the analysis of out-of-equilibrium dynamics in section 4.11.

4.7 THE ROLE OF THE RATE OF INTEREST AND FUNDING POLICY

We noted above that New Classical models have the implication that systematic changes in money stocks have no impact upon real interest rates. The implications of assuming rational expectations and efficient capital markets are far reaching and can make other aspects of monetary and fiscal policy irrelevant to real outcomes. In an important paper, which drew on arguments going back to Ricardo, Barro (1974) showed that under conditions where individuals rationally look to government funding requirements into the distant future current funding of the public sector borrowing requirement (PSBR) is irrelevant for real magnitudes and government bonds are not net wealth. But while the rational expectations model where agents are certain of the economic environment and act as if they lived indefinitely and in which it becomes irrelevant whether the government finances expenditure through taxation, printing money or issuing bonds is a useful benchmark, in practice the importance of the method of financing the PSBR is widely accepted. Whether this is due to a failure of the assumption that individuals are sufficiently forward looking or that their expectations are irrational, or that some other assumption of the irrelevance models is seriously at odds with the world, is unclear. What is relevant is that funding policy may have an impact on the real returns on various assets and that fluctuations in real returns are an important channel through which monetary policy works. In this section we consider movements in interest rates and the impact of changes in rates on expenditure. Having up to now considered some classes of theoretical models, we shall concentrate more on empirical findings here. We first consider funding policy.

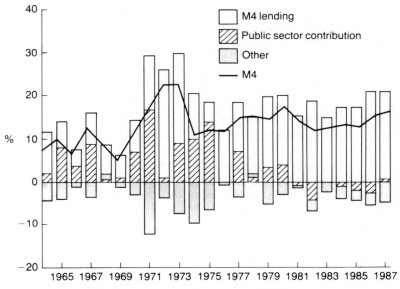

Figure 4.6   Contributions to annual growth of M4

4.7.1 Funding and Overfunding

If we are to consider changes in methods of financing the PSBR we must move away from the simplification that increases in money arise 'from the printing press'. If by 'money' we mean a broad measure of the money supply such as M4, then, in practice, government funding of the PSBR by borrowing from the banks and building societies is what people now mean by 'printing money'. This public sector counterpart to broad money growth is shown in figure 4.6. It accounted for a significant proportion of broad money growth during the 1960s and 1970s, but since 1981 it has been a contractionary influence on money. Thus there has been a dramatic change in the way in which the PSBR has been funded. At times during the first half of the 1980s the PSBR was heavily overfunded, i.e. sales of public sector debt to the domestic private sector other than banks substantially exceeded the PSBR in most years, in contrast with the (at times) heavy underfunding of the previous decade. Overfunding increased during the early 1980s as companies resorted more heavily to bank financing (partly as a response to pressure on their finances resulting from fiscal tightening), the deposit counterpart of which in banks' balance sheets would have represented monetary growth in excess of the M3 target had it not been sterilized by additional debt sales.

An indirect consequence of overfunding was that the Bank, through its market assistance to relieve consequent cash shortages in the banking system, repaid government debt held by banks (largely as treasury bills) and later bought substantial quantities of commercial bills from them. We can think of this as a process in which company borrowing was ultimately financed increasingly by the non-bank private sector holding long-term debt rather than liquid M3 deposits, with the Bank of England acting as an intermediary (and maturity transformer) between the public and the banks. The effects of the overfunding policy on money and interest rates are not easy to assess.

Other things being equal, a change in the proportion of the PSBR financed through gilt sales, or a change in the size of the PSBR with a fixed level of gilt sales, will have a one-for-one impact on M3.[2] But, as numerous commentators have pointed out, the identity which links the PSBR, gilt sales and movements in M3 has, like all identities, no behavioural content and an inference that changes in the PSBR will have a one-for-one effect on M3 is not valid. Indeed, the empirical evidence on the link between the PSBR and the growth of broad money reveals no clear relation (see, in particular, Kaldor, 1980, 1982).

However, the substitution of government debt for bank deposits in the hands of the public, which was a repercussion of the policy of overfunding, and the subsequent money market intervention possibly led to a steepening of the yield curve compared with what it would otherwise have been although, once again, empirical evidence on the effect of funding policy on bond yields suggests that if effects do exist they are not strong (see Goodhart and Gowland, 1977, 1978). Even the direction of any effect on the general level of interest rates is hard to predict; to the extent that lower monetary growth led to lower inflation expectations, nominal bond yields (and other longer-term rates) may eventually have been generally lower than otherwise as a result of the policy, whereas real longer-term rates may have been either higher or lower. Figure 4.7 shows non-bank private sector holdings of public debt as a proportion of total gross wealth. *Ex post* real yields are plotted on the same figure (gross redemption yields on 20 year government bonds less actual retail price inflation). No simple relation between the two is apparent; in practice the reduction of inflation and the decline in the gap between actual price changes and expectations has more to do with the rise in real government bond yields in the 1980s than any change in outstanding stocks of long-term public debt. The net effect of changes in real government debt on real yields remains hard to identify.

Overall, it is clear that the effects on M3 of overfunding were probably less than one-for-one, since some additional bank borrowing by companies may well have been induced by relatively lower short-term rates; however,

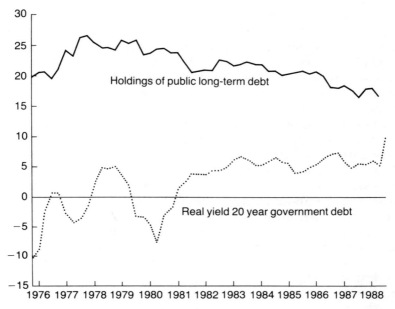

Figure 4.7   Public debt in wealth of the non-bank private sector and real yields

the growth of M3 was almost certainly lower than it would otherwise have been (Wright, 1984).

The policy of systematically overfunding the PSBR was abandoned in 1985. It had become apparent by then that much of the fall in broad money velocity during the 1980s was due to financial innovation, that the link between broad money and nominal income was highly uncertain and that it was possible for broad money growth to give misleading signals. Over-funding also raised concerns over the growing scale of money market assistance and the associated allegations about round-tripping. However, the adverse effects of overfunding have never been convincingly demonstrated.

4.7.2 Money Market Intervention and Short-term Interest Rates

The authorities also influence rates through operations in the money markets. In principle, it is as a monopolist supplier of high powered money that the authorities have significant influence on rates of interest through the discount market. (But, as noted above, in practice it is not accurate to see the influence of the authorities working through the engineering of significant changes in high powered money which lead to changes in nominal interest rates.) Nevertheless, models which assume that the authorities can choose any level of the rate independent of market sentiment ascribe too great a degree of control: '. . . if we sought to impose a level of rates against strong market opposition we are liable to be forced to change our stance' (Bank of England, 1987). What would make the authorities change their stance is not so much an inability to make a particular short-term nominal interest rate stick, for technically it would always be possible to engineer the conditions to make any rate hold, but more the cost in terms of other objectives of moving rates to 'extreme' regions.

The authorities' influence over long-term rates, which may be more relevant than short-term rates for decisions about expenditure on durable commodities, is far from complete. This contrasts with standard macromodels where, through changing the stock of money, a variable assumed to be in the power of the monetary authorities to vary exogenously, any level of interest rates can be achieved. Standard macromodels also assume that changes in interest rates brought about by the monetary authorities have an impact upon real expenditure. This link between interest rates and real expenditures is clearly a crucial chain in the transmission mechanism.

4.7.3 The Impact of Changes in Interest Rates

It has proved difficult to identify significant stable interest rate responses on expenditure.[3] Channels which run through the cost of capital are generally slow and have proved hard to model. One reason for the apparent weakness of such effects may well be that the true cost of capital and stocks is not easy to calculate. But perhaps more importantly the time lag between changes in the cost of capital and any impact of expenditure is likely to be long, even if such effects are eventually significant, and it is nominal interest rates which monetary policy affects but it is the real cost of funds which is relevant for expenditure decisions. Conditional on given inflation expectations, a change in nominal rates does, of course, change real rates. But the impact of changes in nominal rates on inflation expectations (even the direction of which is by no means clear) and the effects of the tax system make the link between nominal interest rate changes and the real cost of capital hard to predict. More significant may be the fact that the long lags between decision-making and implementation of expenditure, and the long life of many capital projects, make it inevitable that decision-makers must look at the cost of capital many periods ahead; changes in interest rates which are thought to be temporary are therefore unlikely to have much effect on investment and expenditure on consumer durables. Furthermore, anticipated changes in interest rates, if realized, may have little apparent effect on expenditure as past investment plans, and hence the capital stock, will have already taken them into account.

The introduction of the supply side now means that there is a cost of capital effect on investment and stockbuilding in some models. Most macro-models find that short-term interest rates have a negative impact on consumers' expenditure and a powerful depressing effect on house building. Furthermore, there is reason to expect that the effects of changing interest rates on consumers' expenditure may have increased in the 1980s as the debt of the personal sector has risen sharply (see Dicks, 1988). In the course of 1988 the personal sector's holdings of liquid liabilities exceeded their holdings of liquid assets for the first time in at least 20 years. Thus income effects of interest rate changes will enhance substitution effects.

Another important channel through which interest rate changes influence demand, and especially prices, works through induced movements in the exchange rate and in real competitiveness. This mechanism has been of great significance since capital controls were removed in the late 1970s. We now consider in some detail the important issues in the links between monetary policy and the exchange rate.

4.8 THE EXCHANGE RATE

In traditional models of the transmission mechanism with fixed exchange rates, an increase in the supply of money results in a balance of payments deficit and outflows of money which may eventually return the money supply to its original level. Figure 4.8 shows that over the period 1967–71, when sterling was on a fixed exchange rate, the external counterpart to broad money moved closely with the current account. This association between trade deficits and external influences on money growth did not break down until early in 1977, several years after sterling was floated. An important step in the evolution of monetary policy occurred in the autumn of 1977 (end October) when, in the face of continued strong upward pressure on sterling, exchange market intervention to hold the exchange rate down was abandoned and the currency was left to find its free-market level. This step was taken because the domestic monetary consequences of intervention were seen as a threat to the monetary target; attempts to sterilize through extra gilts sales would have put such a heavy burden on funding policy that UK interest rates might have had to rise, thereby inducing further upward pressure on sterling. More fundamentally it was seen that if a non-accommodating monetary policy was to be effective in reducing inflation, it would have to work in part by raising the exchange rate. With a freely floating exchange rate and the abolition of exchange controls in September 1979 the channels through which monetary policy worked altered. Attention

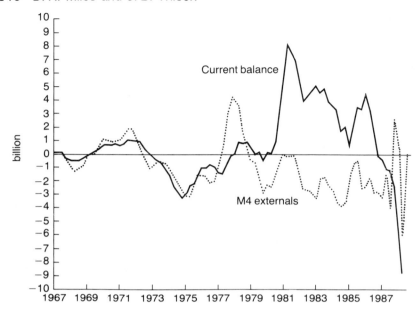

Figure 4.8   Annual change in the M4 external counterpart and current balance.

has been particularly focused on the link between interest rates and the exchange rate, which is now seen as one of the most powerful transmission mechanisms between monetary policy and prices and output.

One important set of theoretical models which analyse the responses to changing monetary conditions in an open economy with a flexible exchange rate were developed from Dornbusch's seminal paper of the mid-1970s (Dornbusch, 1976). In the original Dornbusch model important distinctions were drawn between commodities which were traded on internationally competitive markets and those produced only in the home country. The significance of free-capital movements and close (in simple cases perfect) substitutability between assets denominated in different currencies was analysed. The original model, with forward-looking agents and some prices able to adjust instantaneously to changed conditions, showed that a key mechanism from monetary policy to prices and output would work through the exchange rate. If domestic nominal interest rates were to rise as a result of some tightening in monetary policy, then with foreign rates constant and perfect substitutability between foreign and domestic assets the interest rate differential would need to be offset by an expectation of depreciation of the home currency. If long-run purchasing power parity also held and the tightening of monetary conditions implied lower long-term traded goods prices, in domestic currency, then the exchange rate would initially need to jump beyond its higher long-term value. The implications of this mechanism in models with fast-moving asset prices (interest rates and exchange rates) but more slowly moving goods prices have been analysed in several papers (see Eltis and Sinclair, 1981; Buiter and Miller, 1982, 1983).

The analysis of the inflation, output and employment trends in the early 1980s by Buiter and Miller (1981, 1983) was particularly influential. The argument here was that by far the most significant transmission mechanism for monetary policy ran from interest rate changes to sharp movements in the exchange rate and competitivenes and then to domestic activity and prices. The sharp rise in the UK real interest rates in 1980 and the rapid deterioration, and subsequent gradual recovery, in real competitiveness seemed to be consistent with exchange rate overshooting (figures 4.9 and 4.10). The empirical significance of some of the key elements in the over-shooting story have been questioned, however. In particular, the claim that dramatic exchange rate movements follow movements in differentials between domestic and foreign interest rates has been questioned (see for example Beenstock et al., (1981). The degree of substitutability between foreign and domestic assets is central to this issue; the original paper by Dornbusch which derived the overshooting result assumed perfect sub-titutability. However, whilst perfect substitutability is unlikely, a high

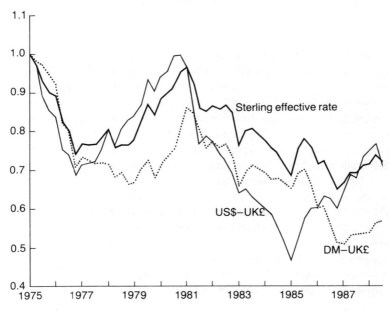

Figure 4.9 Exchange rates (1975 = 1)

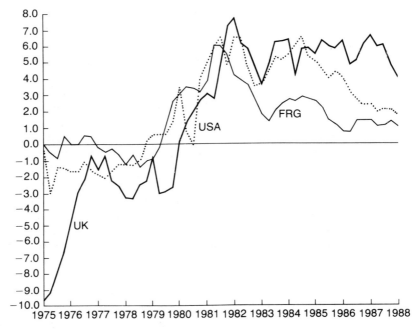

Figure 4.10   Real rates to lenders: gross nominal rate to lender minus proxy for expected rate of change of GDP price inflation (see Lomax, 1988)

degree of substitutability is not; in fact the overshooting result only requires the latter. In one of the few attempts to test for the possibility of overshooting by estimating structural equations and testing the (complex) parameter restrictions which would generate such behaviour, Barr (1982) found that the possibility of overshooting could not be ruled out for the UK.

However, empirical evidence here is not decisive; attempts to model the exchange rate have not been successful enough to judge whether overshooting is merely a theoretical possibility. The dramatic rise in sterling in the early 1980s, which Buiter and Miller ascribe largely to domestic monetary policy, coincided with the growing contribution of North Sea oil which in itself would have put upward pressure on the pound; disentangling the influence of these financial and real developments has proved difficult. However, even if overshooting does not occur, the impact of interest rate changes upon the exchange rate can be of key importance; furthermore, the link to the rest of the economy from exchange rate movements is rapid inasmuch as the cost of commodities priced in foreign currencies moves instantly.

4.9 THEORIES OF CREDIT RATIONING

It is by no means clear that all the major impacts of monetary policy are transmitted through changes in interest rates. In the 1950s both the Radcliffe Report in the UK and the 'availability doctrine' in the USA stressed that the government could influence expenditure through monetary policy without large changes in the rate of interest even if desired expenditure was interest inelastic. The policy was conjectured to work through the availability of funds rather than through changes in interest rates. This hypothesis stimulated research into the effects of credit rationing (see Baltensperger (1978) and for an excellent and recent review of the literature see Blinder (1987)).

Credit rationing may arise because of the imposition of restrictions on interest rates or loan quantities, because financial institutions pursue objectives other than profit maximization or because of information problems. Situations in which credit rationing resulted from restrictions on the rate of interest, such as interest rate ceilings, were explored by Jaffee and Modigliani (1969) and Jaffee (1971). Controls on lending have been exercised by, for example, the system of Supplementary Special Deposits in the UK (see Bank of England, 1982). The third rationale for credit rationing given above is thought to have applied to building societies in the UK up to the 1980s. Anderson and Hendry (1984), for example, provide evidence to support the proposition that the building societies did not maximize profits during the period up to the early 1980s but pursued more general objectives. Imposed controls which lead to suboptimal lending by suppliers of credit create an incentive for them to avoid the controls. Such difficulties are clearly greater now than during the earlier period, with barriers between different financial functions disappearing, particularly in an open financial system like that in the UK.

A difficulty in the early literature was in finding the appropriate definition of rationing. Confusion arose from the treatment of loans as homogeneous goods; however, the good being traded in loan markets is an agent's promise to pay a specified sum at some future date. The value of this good depends on characteristics such as the value of collateral and the probability distribution of returns. When considered in this way, the appropriate definition of rationing for loans is analogous to that of any other differentiated commodity (Stiglitz and Weiss, 1981). Stiglitz and Weiss illustrated ways in which credit rationing may result from informational asymmetries. An example is the case in which in the face of excess demand a financial institution may not increase expected profits by increasing the rate of interest if it is unable to monitor the riskiness of customers. The result follows as raising the rate will, under certain conditions, worsen the mix of customers. The type of credit rationing which emerges from this type of model, where borrowers with similar characteristics are treated differently, is equilibrium rationing. This can be contrasted with disequilibrium rationing where a discrepancy between the demands and supplies of funds in a market is not closed because of either controls over the price of funds or other forms of price inertia.

A model illustrating a feedback from interest rate changes to the real economy, given imperfect capital markets, was provided by Jackman and Sutton (1982). In the model credit-constrained consumers have a higher marginal propensity to consume than those who do not face constraints. The transmission mechanism may then work through redistribution between the two sets of consumers leading to changes in net consumption.

A quite distinct branch of literature which analyses the transmission mechanism from money to prices and output has been stressed in a series of recent papers (Stiglitz, 1985; Greenwald and Stiglitz, 1986, 1987). This work shares some important features with the models of Hart, Fisher and Hahn which focus on deviations in the microstructure of markets from perfect competition and which generate non-Walrasian results (see section 4.11). Of central importance in the analysis of Stiglitz's transmission mechanism is the pervasive influence of information problems in financial markets. What is also distinctive about the mechanisms which Stiglitz describes for the transmission of monetary policy changes to real and nominal variables is that they work through credit markets in ways which reflect the particular forms of financial intermediation which exist in most developed economies. We noted above that much of the theoretical literature in macroeconomies relies on very simple relations, generally reduced form, between nominal money and aggregate nominal demand which omit details of the transmission mechanism. The information-based theories which Greenwald and Stiglitz have developed are firmly rooted in the detailed microstructure of credit markets, structures which themselves reflect important asymmetries of information.

The theory is premised on the existence of a close link between money and credit creation, and between credit creation and the level of economic activity. A key part of the story is that many firms are credit constrained. Such constraints are not merely assumed but are derived from theoretical models where asymmetries of information between lenders (banks) and borrowers (firms) can make rationing efficient (see Stiglitz and Weiss, 1981, 1983). If firms find their access to credit with a particular bank reduced they find it hard to obtain funds elsewhere; other banks will be reluctant to lend to a relatively unknown entity and use of equity markets will be unattractive if potential investors interpret a new issue as a sign that a firm is having problems raising funds elsewhere. Thus restrictions in the supply of bank credit can force cutbacks in real expenditure. The argument is that the transmission mechanism then runs from (perhaps short-term) restrictions on high powered money, or direct controls on bank deposits, to reductions in the availability of credit which, with no close substitutes available to firms, hits real output via inventory reductions and lower investment. The process is cumulative because of important multiplier effects arising from credit constraints. A significant feature of this process is that changes in interest rates do not play an important role. Because of information problems interest rates do not clear credit markets and quantities of credit may move with no price change. Furthermore, the flexibility of output prices, which it is often argued should prevent any real effects of monetary policy, can, in the Stiglitz models, exacerbate problems; falling prices increase the real value of liabilities, increase bankruptcy risks and further tighten credit constraints. (On the potentially destabilizing impact of flexible prices see Neary and Stiglitz (1983) and, in very different models, Flemming (1987) and de Long and Summers (1986)).

It is hard to assess the importance of the credit driven transmission mechanism outlined in the persuasively written papers cited above. There are many sectoral links in the proposed chain which connects money shocks, or planned monetary policy changes, to prices and output. This is one of the strengths of the theory in that the mechanisms work through recognizable institutions; there is no black box. The difficulty is that, although the phenomena which Stiglitz describes certainly exist (asymmetric information, an apparent reluctance of firms to use equity markets to raise funds and periodic, though hard to measure, credit constraints) the extent of their overall impact remains unclear. Indeed, some of the key features of Stiglitz's model, e.g. the prevalence of credit rationing of firms, do not find clear support in the limited amount of empirical work in the area (see, in particular, the Wilson Committee, 1977). Nor are testable implications of the theory clear, although Bernanke undertook some rather crude tests of a related set of hypotheses which give some weight to the idea that the disruption of credit relations were important in one particular episode of US economic history – the Great Depression (see Bernanke (1983) and, for related arguments, Bernanke and Gertler (1985)).

For the UK there is clear evidence that in one particular financial market – that for mortgages – there have been long periods of quantity rationing. It is less clear, however, that this was equilibrium rationing of the type analysed by Stiglitz and Weiss (1981). In fact institutional changes in the late 1970s and 1980s, which brought banks and building societies into greater competition in the market for lending, saw mortgage rationing decline. This increasing competition between financial institutions and the clear reductions in queues for mortgages has occurred at a time when house price inflation has been high, although regional variations are dramatic. This gives some support to the link from credit constraints to nominal demand, although convincing evidence has yet to be produced.[4]

Development in credit markets are reviewed in more detail in the next section; one point to note here is that if a key transmission mechanism for monetary policy runs through variations in the supply of credit, such demand effects that result are not likely to be spread evenly across the economy, for, to the extent that credit restrictions bite, they do so in particular markets and induced changes in demand may be tied to particular commodities such as housing. The price and quantity responses to nominal demand changes triggered by changes in credit availability are, in turn, likely to vary significantly depending on which class of credit relations are affected since elasticities of supply vary hugely for different goods. To predict the effect of changes in monetary conditions on aggregate prices and output it will therefore be essential to go beyond simple highly aggregated models which limit the transmission mechanism to run from a change in money markets conditions to changes in total nominal demand and hence to prices and output in a way which depends only on aggregate labour and goods market conditions. In the next section therefore we consider how changes in the availability of credit have affected different groups of agents in the UK over the past decade.

4.10 THE IMPACT OF THE REMOVAL OF RESTRICTIONS ON UK FINANCIAL SYSTEM

Credit controls of one form on another were operated for much of the period 1964–81. The growth of the lending counterpart to broad money is illustrated in figure 4.6. We shall not document in detail the various periods of imposition and removal of restrictions. However, it is worth noting some of the largest changes. The most noticeable accelerations of the lending series follow the relaxation of restrictions, for example, the advent of competition and credit control in 1971. In late 1972 restrictions were re-imposed in the form of a call for special deposits applying to the whole banking sector. A further sharp acceleration in lending followed a temporary release of special deposits early in 1976 and the abolition of the corset in 1980.

The mortgage market was most noticeably affected by the restrictions on credit. Figure 4.11 shows percentage changes in mortgage lending by banks and building societies and percentage change in real house prices. By influencing the demand for housing relative to other demand, mortgage rationing may have influenced relative prices. Developments in the mortgage market were an important influence on people holding deposits with, and borrowing from, the monetary sector over the period. The profile of M4 mortgage lending relative to total personal income is shown in figure 4.12. The overall trend is somewhat misleading as an indicator of the ratio for a typical individual as owner occupation has grown significantly over the

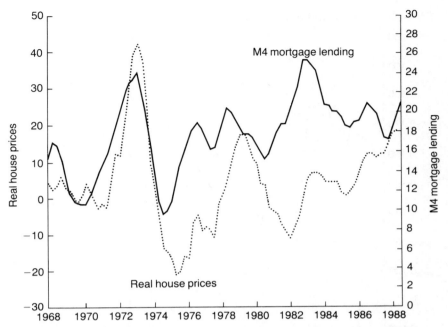

Figure 4.11 Annual growth rate of M4 mortgage lending and real house prices

Figure 4.12 M4 mortgage lending relative to personal income

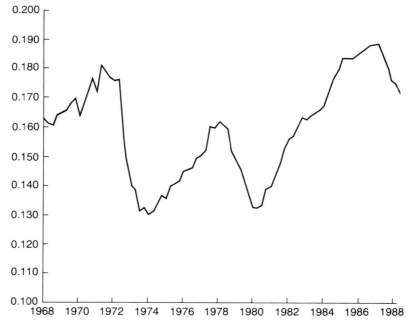

Figure 4.13   M4 mortgage lending relative to the value of owner-occupied housing

period. An alternative is to consider the ratio of mortgage lending to the value of the stock of owner-occupied housing (figure 4.13). The striking fall during the 1970s and recovery in the 1980s may be attributable to credit rationing and the long lags of adjustment in the mortgage market. High levels of inflation during the 1970s eroded the real value of the mortgage stock; households were unable to restore debt levels in part because debt was usually changed only when moving house and partly because of credit rationing. These adjustment problems also implied that households were unable to obtain the capital gains which arose in the housing market. This rundown in real borrowing (see figure 4.13) appears to have had an important effect on people's expenditure and asset accumulation. Households facing such constraints would have run down liquid assets in order to maintain desired consumption levels.

4.11 RECENT THEORETICAL DEVELOPMENTS

We have considered theoretical models where prices move instantly to clear all markets, where prices do not move at all and where some prices may jump and others are sluggish. The effects of monetary policy are, in theory, very different in these models. But two features common to all the models discussed above stand out. First, the size and speed of adjustment of prices in the models is not derived from analysis of the decisions of individual agents. Second, the models generally have unique equilibria which are independent of adjustment paths. Recent theoretical work has aimed at building models where pricing decisions reflect agents' optimizing decisions in disequilibrium states; the possibility of multiplicity and path dependence of equilibria have also been the focus of much work. The effects of monetary policy in such models are of particular interest.

4.11.1 Price Setting Agents

Analysis of the macroeconomic implications of the existence of price-setting power by agents has a long history. Arrow (1959) pointed out 30 years ago that if prices are not always somehow equal to their Walrasian market clearing levels then even an economy with many buyers and sellers in each market will be one where agents find the hypothesis that they can buy and sell as much as they want at current prices falsified. Koopmans (1957) made the same point when he wondered how, if agents all take prices as given, prices ever change. Furthermore, under imperfect competition, as in the fixed price models, each agent's actions will generally depend on the realized transactions of others. Clower (1965) observed that this seems a crucial feature of any Keynesian model.

Modelling how prices and quantities move from one equilibrium to another as a result of optimizing decisions by individual agents conditional on their expectations of others' decisions has been the aim of a huge amount of research, starting with the seminal paper of Negishi (1960). The existence of price-setting, or monopolistic, power does not in itself have any obvious implication for the way in which changes in aggregate nominal demand are transmitted to prices and quantities. (It is a well-known result that optimal pricing with constant elasticity demand curves makes equilibrium prices set by imperfect competitors a fixed mark-up on costs; this is quite consistent with Friedmanesque results for the ineffectiveness of monetary policy to change output in the long run.) What has been important in the literature is the idea that how prices set by agents should respond to demand changes depends upon what they perceive the responses of other agents will be. In many models a multiplicity of equilibria exists, some with higher levels of output than others; the economy may become stuck in a low output equilibrium and no un-co-ordinated actions by individuals will drive it to a higher output equilibrium (see Hahn (1977, 1978, 1982) where the notion of conjectural equilibria is discussed and in particular the multiplicity of such equilibria).

One example of such a model where monetary policy might be used to move the economy from alow to a high output equilibrium at unchanged prices is developed in an important paper by Hart (1982). The paper is Keynesian in spirit, in that a co-ordinated reduction in the prices of produced goods and of labour, with a constant stock of Hart's non-produced good (the numeraire), could give higher output which is welfare improving, but on one agent perceives it as in his/her interest to initiate such a price cut. An increase in aggregate demand resulting from government policy can, however, achieve the same goal. The robustness of the result, however, is not strong. With essentially similar models Snower (1983) and Dixon (1986) show that monetary policy can often only lead to price changes; there are natural rates of unemployment. In a more recent paper, however, Dixon (1988) develops a model where imperfect competition generates non-Walrasian equilibria where government policy is effective. More fundamentally, the seminal volume edited by Phelps (1970) showed that it was possible to develop a range of models with non-co-ordinated price setting by individual agents which generated classical results.

4.11.2 Multiple Equilibria

It remains, however, a feature of rational expectations models that there generally exist multiple, and often a continuum, of equilibria and that without some restrictions on paths to, or points of, convergence the responses in such models to monetary or fiscal changes are not classical. This is a point stressed in much of the work of Hahn (1978, 1982) and Fisher (1983). Fisher, in a series of important papers summarized and extended in Fisher (1983), derives several results on paths of adjustment in monetary economies where trades take place out of equilibrium and where prices are set by individual agents conditional on their (rational) expectations. He finds the following general results. First, when trade out of equilibrium takes place then if the process of adjustment does converge the final equilibrium of the economy is not independent of the path travelled. Such path dependence, or hysteresis, means that comparative static results are seriously misleading and that policies which appear to have no real effects when attention is focused only on equilibrium states can have lasting real effects when plausible disequilibrium processes are explicitly modelled. Fisher says:

> The question of whether the economy converges to a quantity-constrained equilibrium, possibly with underemployment *à la* Keynes, has been seen intimately to involve the question of how perceptions of demand and supply

change. Such questions cannot be answered by looking only at the existence of such equilibria; they depend on the specifics of the adjustment process – specifics that are sadly lacking in the present state of the art.

His conclusion on price dynamics and on adjustment paths of prices to external (e.g. monetary) shocks also warns against reliance on simple results from models where out-of-equilibrium behaviour is either ignored or assumed away:

> The way in which prices are formed and the role which they play in the allocation of resources is the central topic of economic analysis. It is no small thing that we are uncertain as to how this takes place. In more specific terms, the answer to the question of how perceived demand and supply change – which, as we have seen, is also the questions of how prices are set – determines whether or not equilibria will be Walrasian.

These are not reassuring conclusions and yield no easy results on how, in particular, changes in the stance of monetary policy will affect prices and quantities; indeed, no explicit analysis of the transmission mechanism is given in Fisher's models. The positive message of the disequilibrium modelling is more to expose the fragility of results on transmission processes derived from models where adjustment paths are ignored or where the economy is assumed to be in a state of perpetual equilibrium with discontinuous jumps in free variables following unforecastable shocks.

4.12 CONCLUSION

The relative importance of the various channels of influence from monetary policy to prices and output which we have described remains unclear. This reflects uncertainty both about the importance of particular transmission mechanisms from money to elements of nominal aggregate demand, and uncertainty about the way in which such changes in nominal demand are transmitted to prices and quantities. What is clearly crucial is the way in which changes in monetary policy impact upon the prices of a whole range of financial assets and liabilities – currency, equities, bonds – and on the impact upon the availability of credit. Two points arise from this. First, any impact will almost certainly depend upon whether a given change in monetary conditions is perceived as being temporary or permanent and on whether the authorities, even if they should wish to sustain a particular policy stance, are thought able to do so. Expectations of future policy and the credibility of an announced policy to attain particular goals will be central in assessing the impact of any policy. We have not tried to summarize the huge and rapidly growing literature on credibility, time consistency and the game-theoretical aspects of macropolicy design. In some ways this literature is peripheral to the transmission mechanism as narrowly defined. At the same time issues of credibility and expectations are obviously crucial in many aspects of government and private sector behaviour.

The second point is that both substitutability between various assets, which will determine how far the portfolio reallocation impacts of monetary policy go, and credit restrictions – two factors which we noted were central to the transition mechanism – are strongly dependent on institutional developments. For example, competition between banks and non-bank financial intermediaries affects both credit availability and the number and nature of assets which are close substitutes to those offered by banks. Financial deregulation, removal of exchange controls and the increasing internationalization of financial markets have had, and will have, dramatic effects on how monetary policy operates. It is impossible to assess the changing nature of the transmission mechanism without reference to the partly endogenous evolution of financial institutions and markets, within which the process must be worked out. The perception of this may lead to a shift of emphasis in modelling. Reduced form type models may increasingly be replaced by institutional-based models where the way in which the transmission mechanism operates will depend on the detailed structure of financial markets. Empirical work is likely to remain more traditional, largely because the empirical modelling of the process of financial innovation – especially changes in the scope of, and competitive pressures on, financial institutions – is problematic. The tractability of this empirical problem is still hard to gauge; this makes the extent to which more institutional models will be empirically testable equally hard to assess.

Notes

1 That is, wealth effects which result from changes in money or bond stocks rather than from revaluations due to changes in interest rates.
2 Greater money market assistance by the Bank of England to relieve a cash shortage in the banking system will in practice be needed if, other things being equal, there are more gilt sales.
3 For useful sources on the interest rate properties of large models of the UK see Chouraqui et al. (1988) and Fisher et al. (1989).
4 For a discussion of further links from asset prices to labour markets see Bover et al. (1988).

References

Alogoskoufis, G. and Pissarides, C. (1983) A test of price sluggishness in the simple rational expectations model: UK 1950–1980. *Economic Journal* 93, 616–28.

Anderson, G. and Hendry, D. (1984) An econometric model of United Kingdom building societies: *Oxford Bulletin of Economics and Statistics* 46, 185–211.

Arrow, K. (1959) Towards a theory of price adjustment. In M. Abramowitz (ed.), *The Allocation of Economic Resources*. Stanford, CA: Stanford University Press.

Baltensperger, E. (1978) Credit Rationing: issues and questions. *Journal of Money, Credit and Banking* 10, 170–83.

Bank of England (1982) The Supplementary Special Deposits scheme. *Bank of England Quarterly Bulletin* 22 (1), 74–85.

—— (1986) Financial change and broad money. *Bank of England Quarterly Bulletin* 26 (4), 499–507.

—— (1987) The instruments of monetary policy. *Bank of England Quarterly Bulletin* 27 (3), 365–70.

Barr, D. (1982) Exchange rate dynamics: an empirical analysis. Discussion Paper 200, Centre for Labour Economics.

Barro, R. (1974) Are government bonds net wealth. *Journal of Political Economy* 88, 1095–118.

—— and Grossman, H. (1976) *Money, Employment and Inflation*. Cambridge: Cambridge University Press.

Bean, C. (1984) A little bit more evidence on the natural rate hypothesis from the UK. *European Economic Review* 25, 279–92.

Beenstock, M., Budd, A. and Warburton, P. (1981) Monetary policy, expectations and real exchange rate dynamics. In W. Eltis and P. Sinclair (eds), *The Money Supply and the Exchange Rate*. Oxford: Oxford University Press.

Benassy, J.-P. (1975) Neo-Keynesian disequilibrium theory in a monetary economy. *Review of Economic Studies* 42, 503–24.

Bernanke, B. (1983) Non-monetary effects of the financial crisis in the propogation of the great depression. *American Economic Review*, 73, 257–76.

—— and Gertler, M. (1985) Banking and macroeconomic equilibrium. NBER Discussion Paper 1647, National Bureau of Economic Research.

Blanchard, O. (1987) Why does money affect output? A survey. NBER Discussion Paper 2285, National Bureau of Economic Research, June.

Blinder, A. (1987) Credit rationing and effective supply failures. *Economic Journal*, 97, 327–52.

—— and Fisher, S. (1981) Inventories, rational expectations and the business cycle. *Journal of Monetary Economics* 8, 277–304.

Bover, O., Muellbauer, J. and Murphy, A. (1988) Housing, wages and UK labour markets. CEPR Discussion Paper, Centre for Economic Policy Research.

Buiter, W. and Miller, M. (1981) The Thatcher experiment: an interim report. Discussion Paper 106, Centre for Labour Economics, London School of Economics, December.

—— and —— (1982) Exchange rate overshooting and the real cost of bringing down inflation. *European Economic Review* 18, 85–124.

—— and —— (1983) The macroeconomic consequences of a change in regime: the UK under Mrs Thatcher. *Brookings Papers on Economic Activity* 2, 305–80.

Chouraqui, J.-C. Driscoll, M. and Strauss-Kahn, M.O. (1988) The effects of monetary policy on the real sector: an overview of empirical evidence for selected OECD economies. Working Paper, OECD Department of Economics and Statistics.

Clower, R. (1965) The Keynesian counter-revolution: A theoretical appraisal. In F. Hahn and F. P. R. Brechling (eds), *The Theory of Interest Rates*. London: Macmillan.

de Long, J. and Summers, L. (1986) Is increased price flexibility stabilising? *American Economic Review* 76, 1031–44.

Dicks, M. (1988) The interest elasticity of consumers' expenditure. Bank of England Technical Series Paper 20.

Dixon, H. (1986) A simple model of imperfect competition with Walrasian features. Discussion Paper in Economics 186, Birkbeck College, April.

—— (1988) Unions, oligopoly and the natural rate of employment. *Economic Journal* 98, 1127–48.

Dornbusch, R. (1976) Expectations and exchange rate dynamics. *Journal of Political Economy* 84, 1161–76.

Eltis, W. and Sinclair, P (eds) (1981) *The Money Supply and the Exchange Rate*. Oxford: Oxford University Press.

Fisher, F. (1983) *Disequilibrium Foundations of Equilibrium Economics*. Cambridge: Cambridge University Press.

Fisher, P. G , Tanna, S. K., Turner, D. S., Wallis, K. F. and Whitley, J. D., (1989) Comparative properties of models of the UK economy. *National Institute Economic Review* 129, 69–87.

Fitzgerald, M. and Pollio, G. (1983) Money, activity and prices: some inter-country evidence. *European Economic Review* 23, 279–314.

Flemming, J. (1987) Wage flexibility and employment stability. *Oxford Economic Papers* 39, 161–74.

Friedman, B (1978) Crowding out or crowding in? *Brookings Papers on Economic Activity* 3, 593–655.

Friedman, M. (1968) The role of monetary policy. *American Economic Review* 58, 1–17.

—— (1969) *The Optimum Quantity of Money*. London: Macmillan.

Garner, C. (1982) Tests of monetary neutrality for the United Kingdom. *Quarterly Review of Economics and Business* 22, 81–95.

Goodhart, C (1975) *Money, Information and Uncertainty*. London, Macmillan.

—— and Gowland, D. (1977) The relationship between yields on short and long-dated gilt edged stocks. *Bulletin of Economic Research* 29, 96–106.

—— and —— (1978) The relationship between long-dated gilt yields and other variables. *Bulletin of Economic Research* 30, 59–70.

—— and Smith, R. (1985) The relationship between exchange rate movements and monetary surprises: results for the United Kingdom and United States compared and contrasted. *Manchester School* 53, 2–22.

Grandmont, J. (1977) Temporary general equilibrium theory. *Econometrica* 43 535–72.

Granger, C. (1969) Investigating causal relations by econometric models and cross-spectral methods. *Econometrica* 37, 424–38.

Greenwald, B. and Stiglitz, J. (1986) Imperfect information, credit markets and unemployment. NBER Discussion Paper 2093, National Bureau for Economic Research, December.

—— and —— (1987) Money, imperfect information and economic fluctuations. NBER Discussion Paper 2188, National Bureau of Economic Research, March.

Hahn, F. (1977) Exercises in conjectural equilibria. *Scandinavian Journal of Economics* 79, 210–26.

—— (1978) On non-Walrasian equilibria. *Review of Economic Studies* 45, 1–18.

—— (1982) *Money and Inflation*. Oxford: Basil Blackwell.

Hart, O. (1982) A model of imperfect competition with Keynesian features. *Quarterly Journal of Economics* 97, 109–38.

Jackman, R. and Sutton, J. (1982) Imperfect capital markets and monetarist black box: liquidity constraints, inflation, and the asymmetric effects of interest rate policy. *Economic Journal* 92, 108–28.

Jaffee, D. M. (1971) *Credit Rationing and the Commercial Loan Market*. New York: Wiley.

—— and Modigliani, F. (1969) A theory and test of credit rationing. *American Economic Review* 59, 850–72.

Kaldor, N. (1980) *Evidence to the Treasury and Civil Service Committee*. London: HMSO.

—— (1982) *The Scourge of Monetarism*. Oxford: Oxford University Press.

Keynes, J. (1930) *A Treatise on Money*. London: Macmillan.

—— (1936) *The General Theory of Employment, Interest and Money*. London: Macmillan.

Koopmans, T. (1957) *Three Essays on the State of Economic Science*. Cambridge, MA: Harvard University Press.

Lomax, J. W. (1988) Trends in real interest rates. *Bank of England Quarterly Bulletin* 28(2), 225–31.

Lucas, R. (1972): Expectations and the neutrality of money. *Journal of Economic Theory* 4, 103–24.

—— (1975) An equilibrium model of the business cycle. *Journal of Political Economy* 83, 1113–44.

—— (1977) Understanding business cycles. In K. Brunner and A. Meltzer (eds), *Stabilisation of Domestic and International Economy*. Amsterdam: North-Holland, pp. 7–31.

—— (1980) Methods and problems in business cycle theory. *Journal of Money Credit and Banking* 12, 696–713.

MacDonald, R. and Torrance, T. (1988a) Monetary policy and the real interest rate: some UK evidence. *Scottish Journal of Political Economy* 35, 361–71.

—— and —— (1988b) Exchange rates and news: some evidence using UK survey data: *Manchester School* 56, 69–76.

Malinvaud, E. (1977) *The Theory of Unemployment Reconsidered*. Oxford: Basil Blackwell.

Miller, M. (1985) Monetary stabilisation policy in an open economy. *Scottish Journal of Political Economy* 32, 220–33.

Muth, J. (1961) Rational expectations and the theory of price movements. *Econometrica* 29, 315–35.

Neary, P. and Stiglitz, J. (1983) Towards a reconstruction of Keynesian economics: expectations and constrained equilibria. *Quarterly Journal of Economics* 98, 199–228.

Negishi, T. (1960) Monopolistic competition and general equilibrium. *Review of Economic Studies* 28, 196–201.

Patinkin, D. (1956) *Money, Interest and Prices*. Evanston, IL: Row, Peterson.

Phelps, E. ed.) (1970) *Microeconomic Foundations of Employment and Inflation Theory* New York: Norton.

Sargent, T. 1973) Rational expectations, the real rate of interest and the natural rate of unemployment. *Brookings Papers on Economic Activity* 2, 429–72.

—— (1979) *Macroeconomic Theory*. New York: Academic Press.

—— and Wallace, N. (1975) Rational expectations, the optimal monetary instrument, and the optimal money supply rule. *Journal of Political Economy* 83, 241–54.

—— and —— (1976) Rational expectations and the theory of economic policy. *Journal of Monetary Economics* 2, 169–83.

Saunders, F. (1988) An empirical investigation of the effects of monetary changes on the U economy. *Scottish Journal of Political Economy* 35, 372–86.

Sims, C. (1972) Money, income and causality. *American Economic Review* 62, 540–52.

Snower, D. (1983) Imperfect competition, underemployment and crowding-out. *Oxford Economic Papers* 35, 245–70.

Stiglitz, J. (982) On the relevance or irrelevance of public financial policy: indexation, price rigidities and optimal monetary policy. In R. Dornbusch and M. Simonsen (eds), *Inflation, Debt and Indexation*. Cambridge, MA: MIT Press.

—— (1985) Credit markets and the control of capital. *Journal of Money, Credit and Banking* 7, 133–52.

—— and Weiss, A. (1981) Credit rationing in markets with imperfect information. *American Economic Review* 71, 393–410.

—— and —— (1983) Incentive effects of termination: applications to the credit and labour markets. *American Economic Review* 72, 912–27.

Symons, J. 1983) Money and the real interest rate in the UK. *Manchester School* 51, 250–6.

Taylor, J. 1975) Monetary policy during a transition to rational expectations. *Journal of Political Economy* 83, 1009–21.

—— (1979) Staggered price setting in a macro model. *American Economic Review* 83, 108–1.

Tobin, J. (1952) Asset holdings and spending decisions. *American Economic Review* 42, 109–2.

—— (1961) Money, capital and other stores of value. *American Economic Review* 51, 26–37

—— (1969) a general equilibrium approach to monetary theory. *Journal of Money, Credit and Banking* 1, 15–29.

—— (1970) Money and Income: *Post hoc ergo propter hoc. Quarterly Journal of Economics* 84, (2), 301–30.

—— and Brainard, W. (1968) Pitfalls in financial model building. *American Economic Review* 58, 99–122.

Williams, D, Goodhart, C. and Gowland, D. (1976) Money, income and causality: the UK experience. *American Economic Review* 66, 417–24.

Wilson Committee (1977) *Committee to Review the Functioning of Financial Institutions*, London: HMSO cmmd 7937.

Wright, P. (984) Funding the public sector borrowing requirement 1952-1983. *Bank of England Quarterly Bulletin* December, 482–92.

5   The Conduct of Monetary Policy

Charles Goodhart

Nowadays the central bank is the monopoly supplier of legal tender currency. The commercial banks are committed to making their deposits convertible at par into such currency. Therefore the banks need to keep reserves in the form of currency and deposits at the central bank. The central bank primarily conducts its policy by buying and selling financial securities, e.g. treasury bills or foreign exchange, in exchange for its own liabilities, i.e. open market operations. Academic economists generally regard such operations as adjusting the quantitative volume of the banks' reserve base, and hence of the money stock, with rates (prices) in such markets simultaneously determined by the interplay of demand and supply. Central bank practitioners almost always view themselves as unable to deny the banks the reserve base that the banking system requires, and see themselves as setting the level of interest rates at which such reserve requirements are met, with the quantity of money then simultaneously determined by the portfolio preferences of private sector banks and non-banks. This difference in perceptions is discussed again in section 5.3.

Whether the monetary policy operations of central banks should be viewed primarily in terms of quantity-setting, or rate-setting, actions (although, of course, one is the dual of the other), these had allowed inflation and inflationary expectations to become entrenched by the end of the

My thanks for help and suggestions in the compilation of this paper go to Mike Artis, John Black, Peter Bull, Victoria Chick, Jean-Claude Chouraqui, Keith Cuthbertson, Dick Davis, Hermann-Joseph Dudler, Kim Frame, Chuck Freedman, Eric Hansen, David Hendry, Richard Jackman, David Laidler, David Lindsey, Ian Macfarlane, Gordon Midgley, Mark Mullins, Peter Nicholl, Andrew Oswald, Robert Raymond, Yoshio Suzuki, Richard Urwin and my referees, none of whom should be held responsible for my opinions or remaining errors.

1970s. A selection of representative statistics for a number of the leading industrialized countries is given in table 5.1.

This table indicates a common pattern among the countries of interaction between interest rates, inflation and the growth of output. The first period, 1969-78, is marked by high inflation, negative real interest rates and slightly above average growth; the second period, 1979-82, is marked by very high nominal, and high real, interest rates, high (but falling) inflation and very low output growth. The final period, 1983-7, is marked by much lower inflation, lower nominal, but still high real, interest rates and a recovery in output growth, in some cases to above average rates. In contrast, the relationship in these countries between the growth of their chosen key monetary aggregate and nominal incomes appears much weaker (see also Clinton and Chouraqui, 1987, especially p. 7).

Whether measured in terms of monetary growth or in terms of 'real' interest rates, i.e. after adjustment for prospective future inflation, policy during the 1970s had become quite slack. Such accommodative policy had been accompanied by higher inflation than in previous decades, but not by

Table 5.1

		1969(1)–1987(4)	1969(1)–1978(4)	1979(1)–1987(4)	1979(1)–1982(4)	1983(1)–1987(4)
UK						
A	(£M3)	12.3	12.3	13.6	13.1	14.1
B	(Y)	11.9	14.0	9.6	11.6	8.0
C	(y)	2.1	2.1	2.1	0.3	3.5
D	(P)	9.8	11.9	7.6	11.4	4.5
E	(i_s)	10.7	9.4	12.2	14.1	10.6
F	(i_l)	11.7	11.6	11.8	13.6	10.3
USA						
A	(M1)	7.4	6.2	8.9	7.8	9.6
B	(Y)	9.0	10.0	7.9	8.0	7.8
C	(y)	2.7	3.0	2.5	−0.1	4.5
D	(P)	6.2	6.9	5.3	8.1	3.2
E	(i_s)	8.5	6.9	10.4	13.1	8.2
F	(i_l)	9.0	7.2	10.9	12.0	10.1
FRG						
A	(CBM)	7.6	9.3	5.8	4.9	6.2
B	(Y)	7.3	9.3	5.0	5.0	4.8
C	(y)	2.7	3.6	1.8	0.7	2.5

Table 5.1 *continued*

		1969(1)–1987(4)	1969(1)–1978(4)	1979(1)–1987(4)	1979(1)–1982(4)	1983(1)–1987(4)
D	(P)	4.5	5.6	3.2	4.3	2.3
E	(i_s)	6.9	6.7	7.0	9.3	5.2
F	(i_l)	7.8	7.8	7.7	8.8	6.8
Japan						
A	(M2)	12.7	16.4	8.7	8.7	8.9
B	(Y)	10.4	14.4	5.9	6.5	5.4
C	(y)	4.9	5.7	4.0	3.8	4.4
D	(P)	5.2	8.4	1.8	2.6	1.0
E	(i_s)	7.0	7.5	6.5	7.8	5.5
F	(i_l)	7.3	7.6	7.0	8.4	5.9
France						
A	(M2)	12.2	14.7	9.2	11.3	7.2
B	(Y)	11.8	13.4	10.0	13.1	7.4
C	(y)	3.1	4.2	1.8	1.9	1.9
D	(P)	8.5	8.9	8.0	10.9	5.4
E	(i_s)	9.7	8.4	11.1	12.6	10.0
F	(i_l)	10.3	8.7	12.1	13.5	11.0
Canada						
A	(M1)	8.2	10.3	6.1	5.3	6.4
B	(Y)	11.1	12.6	9.4	10.7	8.5
C	(y)	4.0	4.8	3.1	0.5	4.9
D	(P)	6.9	7.5	6.2	10.1	3.4
E	(i_s)	9.7	7.7	11.8	14.5	9.6
F	(i_l)	10.0	8.3	11.9	13.1	11.0
Australia						
A	(M2)	12.9	12.9	12.9	11.6	13.7
B	(Y)	13.2	14.4	11.6	12.0	11.6
C	(y)	3.5	3.2	3.7	3.1	4.6
D	(P)	9.5	11.0	7.7	8.8	6.8
E	(i_s)	9.4	6.6	12.6	11.9	13.1
F	(i_l)	10.6	8.1	13.3	12.7	13.9

A, annualized mean percentage growth of key monetary aggregate; B, annualized mean percentage growth of nominal income; C, annualized mean percentage growth of real output; D, annualized mean percentage growth of inflation; E, annualized mean level of representative short-term (three-month) interest rate; F, annualized mean level of representative long-term (ten-year) interest rate.

particularly strong output growth. While it remained possible to argue, and was often so argued in the UK during the 1970s, that this conjuncture was caused by the adverse oil related supply-side shocks of 1973 and 1979, the combination of the stagflation of this decade, together with the Lucas (1976) critique of Keynesian macromodels, as exemplified in the M. Friedman (1968)–Phelps (1968) analysis of the irrationality – and probable disappearance – of a downward-sloping Phillips curve, led to a downgrading of Keynesian demand management and associated monetary policy strategies (Mankiw, 1988). In addition, the demonstration effect of the comparative success of the German and Swiss economies, which first adopted overtly quasi-monetarist policies, in reviving from the 1973 crisis led to a shift towards targetry and monetary rules. Therefore by the close of the 1970s most major industrialized countries had committed themselves to following targets, sometimes stretching into the medium term, for a selected monetary aggregate, a particular definition of the domestic money stock. With each country choosing its separate domestic target, the international relationship between the currencies was, perforce, flexibly determined through the foreign exchange market.

The power to conduct such monetary policy is not, however, concentrated solely in the central bank. In many countries, such as the UK, Australia and France, the central bank acts as the executive agent to carry out the strategic policy decisions of the Chancellor or Minister of Finance; meanwhile the Treasury and/or Ministry of Finance as well as the central bank plays a major role in the formulation of such policy. Even where the central bank is constitutionally independent of the Executive, as in the USA and the FRG, the decisions of the central bank are not, and can hardly be, taken in a political vacuum. Havrilesky (1988) provides a recent example (and an excellent reading list) of the entertaining US literature examining the degree to which the Federal Reserve's actions are affected by pressure from the Executive or Congress. Two more substantial works on this politico-economic borderline are, for the USA, Wooley (1984) and, for the UK, Moran (1984). Greider (1988) has written a more popular recent book about the Federal Reserve; for the UK see Fay (1987) and for a survey of several countries see Hodgman (1983).

In practice, the balance of power to determine monetary policy between the political minister, the Ministry of Finance or the Treasury and the central bank varies both between countries, depending often as much on the wider political context as on the precise constitutional position of the central bank – e.g. the comparatively powerful role of the Banca d'Italia and Banca d'Espana – and also over time, depending strongly on the accident of personalities. Nevertheless, there has been some interest in the question of whether the comparative susceptibility of central banks to political pressures has been a factor in their performance, e.g. in combating inflation (see Frey and Schneider, 1981; Burdekin, 1986; Mayer, 1987). For the purpose of this survey, we shall not pursue this question further; instead we shall explore the acts of the monetary authorities, without too much concern for the internal balance between central bank and the Treasury.

Nevertheless the failure of the monetary authorities, whether central bankers or ministers of finance, to stem inflation in the 1970s led to reconsideration of whether they were selflessly working for the public good – as implicit in much Keynesian theory – or might be swayed by other political and bureaucratic objectives. Such public choice theorizing about the incentives affecting the decision-making process of the authorities was for many monetarists (M. Friedman, 1984a) at the root of their preference for 'rules' rather than discretion.

A more analytically rigorous and persuasive reformulation of the arguments against discretionary intervention appeared somewhat later, in the guise of the 'rules versus discretion' literature initially developed by Kydland and Prescott (1977) and Calvo (1978), and made more accessible to the generality of economists by Barro and Gordon (1983a, b) and Barro (1986); see also Isard and Rojas-Suarez (1986) and McCallum (1987, 1988). In such models, if the authorities either assume (incorrectly) that expectations are relatively inflexible or place excessive weight upon the short run, e.g. because of approaching elections, they will be led to introduce an expansionary (inflationary) policy which they would have previously pledged to abjure (time inconsistency). Unless the authorities are deterred from such actions by penalties arising from a loss of reputation in the future, leading to a reputational equilibrium, the ultimate outcome of discretion will be a higher inflation – same unemployment (time-consistent) equilibrium than could be achieved by sticking to a monetary rule. It is doubtful how far those in charge of monetary policy followed the finer points of this analysis. But the general thrust of the importance of credibility, commitment and sticking to (simple) rules undoubtedly struck a resonant chord among them at the end of the 1970s.

Therefore at the outset of this decade (1980s) there was a considerable degree of concordance between (most) policy-makers and (most) academic economists. Monetary policy should be based on the achievement of monetary targets predicated on an assumed long-term stable relationship between the money stock and nominal incomes. Apart from setting and maintaining such quantitative monetary targets, the authorities should refrain from market intervention, e.g. in the foreign exchange market, since in conditions of efficient financial markets, in which agents were informed by rational expectations, such intervention could only destabilize the market to no good end.

By the latter part of the 1980s, however, the more technical elements (as contrasted with the broader politico-economic ends) of this experiment were deemed, by the generality of policy-makers, to have comprehensively failed. However, the policies adopted in the early 1980s did allow the authorities freedom to raise interest rates to levels that subdued inflation, and the accompanying check to output growth, although severe, was indeed temporary. In terms of the mechanics, as contrasted with the ultimate objectives, of the policy, however, the crucial long-term relationships, i.e. the relationships between the money stock and nominal incomes (velocity), and between prices in two countries and their nominal exchange rate (purchasing power parity), appeared far more fragile than expected.[1] The extraordinary movements (misalignments) in foreign exchange markets and the crash of October 1987 put major question marks over the rational expectations efficient markets hypothesis.

Yet a large wing of mainstream (mostly US) macrotheoretical economists appear to have taken little notice of such historical experience in recent years, driving ever deeper into an artificial (Arrow–Debreu) world of perfectly clearing (complete) markets, in which money and finance do not matter, and business cycles are caused by real phenomena (e.g. Kydland and Prescott, 1982; Long and Plosser, 1983; King and Plosser, 1984). Moreover, in a number of analytical studies of this kind (e.g. Lucas, 1972; Sargent and Wallace, 1975), the only reason why monetary policy may affect real variables is owing to an informational imperfection, which would seem simple and worthwhile to overcome. This leaves something of a gap between state of the art macrotheory and practical policy analysis (see Laidler, 1988a, b).

It is not the function, or purpose, of this chapter to examine the recent development of macroeconomic theory, on which two recent surveys (Fischer, 1988; Mankiw, 1988) can be consulted. Both note the increasing divorce between theory and current practice. Thus Fischer (1988, p. 331) comments that 'there is greater not less confusion at the business end of macroeconomics in understanding the actual causes of macroeconomic fluctuations, and in applying macroeconomics to policy-making'. Instead, the main aim of this chapter is to document how, and why, policy-makers in the main moved decisively away from the ideological (pragmatic monetarist) position adopted at the outset of the decade.

For this latter exercise we shall begin by examining the actual historical record of what policy-makers have said and done (section 5.1). In this section we shall somewhat arbitrarily divide up the recent decade into four periods: (a) the shift of policy towards monetarism up till 1979; (b) the high tide of monetarism, 1979–82; (c) the return to pragmatism, 1982–5; (d) the increasing concern with exchange rate regimes from 1985 onwards.

A severe problem, occasioned by space limitations, concerns which countries' experiences to record. Naturally, we focus primarily on the UK, but we must also review developments in the USA, not only since it has remained the central economic power but also because US experience shapes the views of the dominant body of (US) monetary theorists.[2]

The main reason for the progressive withdrawal of the monetary authorities from a public commitment to a preset monetary target was that such targetry was predicated on the existence of a predictable, and preferably stable, relationship between monetary growth and (subsequent) growth of nominal incomes. The previously estimated econometric relationships between movements in the money stock and in nominal incomes increasingly came apart at the seams during the 1980s, although less dramatically in some countries, such as the FRG and France, than in others, such as the UK, the USA and Canada. Since the purpose of monetary targetry was to seek to compress the rate of growth of nominal incomes (to a rate in line with the underlying potential rate of real growth) (see Lawson, 1986), the inability to predict what rate of growth of money would be consistent with the preferred path of nominal incomes removed the rationale for the authorities choosing, and seeking to maintain, some particular numerical target for monetary growth (Leigh-Pemberton, 1986). We record the main features of this story in section 5.2.

The breakdown of existing econometric relationships, e.g. in the form of demand for money functions, and the difficulties of replacing these earlier relationships with superior, and *credible*, more stable alternatives can easily be retold. What remains much harder is to explain just how, and why, such breakdowns occurred. During the last two decades, however, theoretical economists have emphasized that statistically estimated equations, such as demand for money functions, are not true 'deep' structural equations, but are conditioned on the institutional structures and policy regimes – and the behaviour and expectations that these induce. The last decade has seen a wave of financial innovations (Solomon, 1981), again more so in the Anglo-Saxon countries than in continental Europe, in part in response to the various pressures within the financial system brought about by the earlier policy regime switch towards monetary targetry and 'practical monetarism' (as described by Richardson (1978)). This is discussed in section 5.2.2.

One of the more important of such financial innovations was the spreading practice of banks offering market related interest rates on deposits that had earlier borne zero interest (i.e. sight/demand deposits) or whose interest rates had been administratively constrained. The increasing scope for liability management limited the authorities' capacity to control the volume of bank deposits by varying the general level of short-term interest rates, since they could no longer thereby control the relative differential between rates on deposits and on non-monetary assets. At the outset of the 1980s the ability of the authorities to control the money stock by this traditional method (interest rate adjustment) was the subject of sharp debate, and the alternative policy of monetary base control (MBC) was strongly advocated, and, subject to some qualifications, partially adopted in the USA. We discuss such control issues in section 5.3. As policy-makers came to place less weight on the achievement of monetary targets, public concern with the techniques of monetary control abated. Even so, reliance on interest rate adjustments (whether occasioned directly by the authorities or indirectly through the market under MBC) in order to stabilize monetary growth appeared to entail sizeable fluctuations in such rates. There remained, therefore, some interest in other possible methods of monetary control, notably the policy of 'overfunding' which was peculiar to the UK.

Nevertheless, especially following the removal of exchange controls (abolished in the UK in October 1979 – see Lawson (1980) for the rationale) and other barriers to the free movement of capital between countries, it became generally accepted that adjustments to the general level of short-term interest rates formed just about the only effective monetary instrument (Lawson, 1986, 1988; Leigh-Pemberton, 1987). With monetary targets falling out of favour as key intermediate objectives, concern shifted away from the question of how interest rate adjustments might affect the monetary aggregates back towards the more traditional question of how they might affect nominal incomes and inflation.

This latter is considered in section 5.4, but only briefly and mainly by reference to other survey papers. The subject of the transmission mechanism of monetary policy is both too large and impinges too much on general macroeconomic issues to cover adequately here. Even so, we regard it as important to distinguish in this respect between the standard Keynesian IS–LM approach (which views the transmission mechanism as being restricted to a limited channel running from short-term interest rates to long-term interest rates and equity prices, and hence to expenditures) and both the monetarist and neo-Keynesian approaches, wherein monetary/credit shocks can directly affect expenditure, e.g. by relaxing market imperfections. While most economists would probably now accept some aspects of this latter position, there remains great uncertainty on the relative importance of credit and monetary shocks.

Therefore this chapter has the following structure: section 5.1, historical overview; section 5.2, demand for money; section 5.3, supply of money; section 5.4, transmission mechanism.

The chapter is intended for the general non-technical reader. Some technical references to current econometric methodology creep into section 5.2, but, even so, the literary description is meant to give everyone some understanding of what is afoot.

As evidenced in section 5.1, as the 1980s progressed, policy-makers became increasingly concerned with the wayward behaviour of the foreign exchange market and concerned to re-establish co-operative exchange rate regimes, either regionally (European Monetary System: EMS) or internationally (e.g. at the meetings of the Group of Seven (G7) finance ministers), to restore some 'order' to the international system. Although germane, and indeed increasingly central, to the story of the conduct of monetary policy in these years, space limitations have regretfully precluded a satisfactory coverage of this further extensive subject here.

5.1 A HISTORICAL OVERVIEW

The 1970s – The Policy Shifts

During the mid-1970s, the monetary authorities in a growing number of countries adopted published monetary targets, starting with the FRG late in 1974, and then quite rapidly followed by the USA, Switzerland and Canada in 1975, and the UK, France and Australia in 1976 (see Foot, 1981; Hoskins, 1985; Chouraqui et al., 1988, table 3, p. 45). Nevertheless the commitment of the authorities in a number of these countries was still doubted by sceptical commentators. Indeed, 'Judged solely by whether or not the targets were met, the results [in the earlier years were] generally poor' (Foot, 1981, p. 28). In the USA the authorities initially shifted the target period forward a quarter at a time until the end of 1978, when, under the terms of the Humphrey–Hawkins Act of that year, targets were generally set for a full year at a time. The earlier approach in particular proved fertile ground for 'base drift', the practice of starting the new target from the actual (higher) money stock obtaining at the end of each quarter, rather than from the previously desired objective position (Wang, 1980; M. Friedman, 1982; Broaddus and Goodfriend, 1984). In the UK, the authorities had been required by the International Monetary Fund (IMF) to accept ceilings on domestic credit expansion in the course of dealing with the exchange rate crisis of 1976; while the associated adoption of published monetary objectives by the UK government was an independent decision, it is doubtful whether they would have taken that step without the external pressures. Moreover, whereas the Prime Minister (Callaghan) and Chancellor (Healey) did appreciate that the pursuit of some level of employment, or output growth, beyond that consistent with equilibrium would lead to accelerating and unacceptable inflation, it was doubtful how far the Labour Party as a whole was willing to absorb that argument, or still believed that some refurbished incomes policy could reconcile both nominal and real objectives. The Bank of England's wavering attitude to the proper balance between monetary targets and incomes policies is apparent in Lord Richardson's Mais Lecture (Richardson, 1978).

Be that as it may, the second half of the 1970s saw only limited further improvements in the reduction of inflation, following those achieved in the post-1973 deflation. In many countries nominal interest rates remained below the concurrent rate of inflation, and even reached the ridiculously low figure of 5 per cent in the autumn of 1977 in the UK as the authorities strove to maintain the competitive advantage for their manufacturing industry of the low exchange rate occasioned by the crisis in 1976 – a scenario that was to be replayed with a different cast in 1987–8. Inflationary expectations remained entrenched.

The overthrow of the Shah of Iran, causing fears of a shortage of oil, then led to the second oil shock in 1979, with crude oil prices more than doubling to about $29 a barrel by the beginning of 1980. Besides the direct effect of this on prices, the apparent weakness of President Carter led to growing fears about US policies more generally, and for the longer-term outlook for US inflation. The dollar had weakened sharply in 1978, and remained weak, despite official support in 1979; moreover, during 1979 there was a remarkable surge in the prices of precious metals (gold and silver) which, following the Russian intervention in Afghanistan, reached an extraordinary peak in early 1980.

This was the backdrop to the announcement on Saturday 6 October 1979 by Paul Volcker, the newly appointed Chairman of the Federal Reserve Board, of a new approach to monetary control. Previously, the Federal Reserve had operated by controlling the level of the Federal Reserve Funds rate. While they could hit their chosen rate virtually exactly, various pressures, such as the natural tendency to limit changes under conditions of uncertainty and the political unpopularity of upward movements in interest rates, had limited the flexibility with which the Federal Reserve felt able to vary such rates. From 6 October the Federal Reserve moved to control non-borrowed reserves – a modified form of MBC (see section 5.3) – allowing interest rates to vary within wide and unpublished limits as market forces might dictate. This single step transformed monetary conditions around the world and was quite largely responsible, along with concurrent shifts to more deflationary policies in other major countries, for the shift from the generally inflationary conditions of the 1970s to the generally deflationary conditions of the 1980s.

Meanwhile, in the UK the General Election of May 1979 had led to a Conservative victory. The new Conservative leaders had interpreted the inflationary upsurge of 1974–5 as being the direct consequence of the explosive increase in the broad money stock (sterling M3) in 1972–3. From the outset, in his first Budget on 12 June 1979, the Chancellor, Sir Geoffrey Howe, reaffirmed the government's commitment to controlling the growth of the monetary aggregates as the centrepiece of monetary policy (Howe, 1979). At the same time, however, he presided over measures that would make such control more problematical. First, he raised the general level of value added tax (VAT) sharply, from 8 to 15 per cent, thereby at a stroke increasing the margin between the current rate of increase of prices and of nominal expenditures on the one hand, and the target rate of monetary growth on the other. Second, he set in motion the removal of exchange controls, which was fully effected in October 1979; this allowed such obvious possibilities of disintermediation from the direct control over monetary growth then in operation, the 'corset' – for an account see Bank of England (1982a) – that there was no alternative but its speedy abandonment, which occurred in June 1980.

5.1.2 1979–1982: The High Water Mark of National Monetarism

In the face of the upsurge of prices and nominal incomes in 1979, with the year-on-year retail price index (RPI) reaching a peak of 21.9 per cent in May 1980, the Bank of England ran into immediate problems in trying to hold sterling M3 down to the reaffirmed target of 7–11 per cent. Bank lending rates were increased to 17 per cent in November. Despite such operational problems, the Chancellor adopted a medium-term financial strategy (MTFS), announced in the March 1980 Budget, in which a pre-set declining target path for sterling M3 was made the centrepiece of the government's strategy, and whereby the fiscal policy decision on the size of the Budget deficit, the public sector borrowing requirement (PSBR), was subordinated to the need to achieve the monetary target at acceptable interest rate levels.[3] Thus 'there would be no question of departing from the money supply policy, which is essential to the success of any anti-inflationary strategy' (*FSBR*, 1980–1, p. 19, para 16).

Given the extent of instability already evident in UK demand for money studies (e.g. Hacche, 1974), there were grounds for concern whether the relationships between (any particular definition of) monetary growth and nominal incomes were too fragile a basis for such a long-term commitment. A number of commentators, e.g. the Treasury and Civil Service Committee (1981), expressed such doubts. Perhaps because of differing views about the existing evidence, but more likely because of a belief that it was worth taking risks in order to establish a convincing picture of credible commitment, such worries were brushed aside by the Government. Such commitment was welcomed by a number of influential commentators (e.g. Brittan, 1980), who believed that it could so alter expectations as to allow a decline in inflation with less associated unemployment. The *locus classicus* wherein the authorities' strategy was outlined was the speech given in Zurich on 14 January 1981 by Nigel Lawson, then the Financial Secretary (Lawson, 1981; see also Lawson, 1980, 1982, 1985), who is generally held to be the architect of the MTFS.

In that summer, June 1980, the corset control ended. An immediate upsurge in bank deposits and bank lending had been forecast, as reinter-mediation became possible. In the event the upsurge was over twice what had been expected, and the growth of sterling M3 shot through its upper limit, causing considerable embarrassment and annoyance (mostly aimed at the Bank) in the Government, especially coming so shortly after its prior public commitment. Interest rates were kept at the high level of 16 per cent, and there was intensive consideration of the merits of moving to MBC.

At the same time (in 1980), however, the combination of the UK's new found role as a major oil producer, the high level of interest rates and the credibility of Mrs Thatcher's anti-inflation commitment, led to a dramatic rise in the UK's nominal exchange rate, and even more in its real exchange rate[4] (Buiter and Miller, 1982, 1983).

Despite the embarrassment of accepting a large overshoot in the first year of the MTFS, a further tightening of monetary policy, in the form of higher interest rates (beyond 16 per cent), at such a time was unacceptable, and indeed rates were reduced to 14 per cent in November 1980.[5] Even so, the deflationary pressure from the increased real exchange rate was intense, with industrial production falling by 10 per cent (1980(4) on 1979(4)) and unemployment rising by over a half, from 1.3 to 2.2 million during 1980 (January to January).

Moreover, during the autumn of 1980 Alan Walters took up the position of economic adviser to the Prime Minister. He doubted, on analytical grounds, whether sterling M3 was the most appropriate monetary aggregate to target, and noted that the stance of monetary policy appeared much tighter if one looked at narrower aggregates (M1 or M0) instead (Walters, 1986). A colleague from Johns Hopkins University, Professor J. Niehans, was encouraged to perform an academic study of this issue. His paper (Niehans, 1981), which was widely circulated though not subsequently pub-lished in a journal, was influential.

Nevertheless, if monetary and nominal income growth were to be reduced in line with the target, without any further upward ratchet in interest and exchange rates, it was thought that the PSBR had to be kept tight. The conti-nuing commitment of the Chancellor to the MTFS, and his refusal to allow even the automatic stabilizers to bring about an increase in the PSBR at a time of severe cyclical downturn, brought down upon his head the outrage of the (Keynesian) economic establishment in the UK as the famous letter from 364 economists, organized by Hahn and Nield, attests (*The Times*, 31 March 1981) (see also Healy, 1987). The publication date of the letter coincided fairly closely with the low point in the cycle. A combination of world-wide deflation and, beyond that, the rise in the UK exchange rate was helping to bring about a sharp decline in import prices,[6] which began to feed through into declining levels for the RPI and nominal wage increases. Moreover, the latter did appear sensitive to movements in (short-term) unemployment (Layard and Nickell, 1986; Hall and Henry, 1987). It is also arguable that the 1981 Budget decision, whether or not strictly necessary within the MTFS framework, provided a dramatic manifestation of the Government's shift to counter-inflationary commitment away from Keynesian demand management, and hence helped to break the inflationary psychology of the time.

During the first half of fiscal 1981, a Civil Service strike led to delays in the receipt of certain taxes, and so the course of monetary growth was distorted. With the rate of growth of nominal incomes declining quite sharply, while monetary growth remained quite strong, and with sterling M3 growing by about 14.5 per cent in 1981–2, the pressures imposed on the system by the MTFS were somewhat relieved, and interest rates, having been raised sharply in the autumn of 1981 to counteract downward pressure on sterling, were steadily reduced in 1982 to a trough of 9 per cent in November.

5.1.3 1982–1985: The Return to Pragmatism

Apart from 1972 and 1973, the years of the Barber 'boom' and monetary surge, the path of velocity of sterling M3 in the UK remained steadily upwards, i.e. nominal incomes grew faster than sterling M3, from the 1960s through till 1979. This historical trend quite naturally provided the main basis for choosing the target rates of growth of sterling M3 in June 1979 and March 1980. Initially the overshoots in 1980–1 and 1981–2 led to fears that there was a resulting excess 'overhang' of money which would lead to a subsequent re-emergence of inflation.

On the other hand more immediate measures of inflationary pressure, such as the exchange rate, asset prices, wage increases and various measures of inflation itself, e.g. RPI or GDP deflator, let alone real variables such as output and unemployment, were indicating the continuing presence of deflation. Initially, up till March 1982, an uneasy compromise resulted. The target for sterling M3 was extended on the assumption that the historic trend in velocity would be re-established, but no attempt was made to claw back prior overshoots, despite initial hopes/intentions of doing so (*FSBR*, 1981–2, p. 16, para 11; Lawson, 1982). Meanwhile, pressure was maintained on the Bank of England to achieve the target growth rate, but interest rates were not allowed to vary without limit in pursuit of that target.

However, as time went by, it became increasingly difficult for the authorities to believe that they fully understood, or could predict, the path of velocity and/or the demand for money (see section 5.2). This erosion of confidence in their ability to interpret the signals given by their prior chosen main target and indicator, sterling M3, led the authorities to extend the range of monetary and other variables, including notably the exchange rate, that they would consult in assessing the stance of policy[7] and hence in deciding how to vary interest rates. Thus, in the March 1982 Budget (*FSBR*, 1982–3) targets were set for two additional monetary aggregates: M1, a narrow definition, and PSL2 (private sector liquidity, second definition), an even broader aggregate than sterling M3. (For an account of UK monetary statistics, see Bank of England (1982b, 1987)).) Outside commentators complained that this would give the authorities a greater chance to hit at least one target: insiders worried that the markets would concentrate on whichever indicator/target was currently doing worst.

Meanwhile, the demand by the private sector for bank loans continued to grow at persistently high levels, due initially to the needs of industry to overcome the financial squeeze in 1980–1 and then increasingly to the (apparently almost insatiable) demand for mortgage finance from the personal sector. From both casual and econometric evidence (Goodhart, 1984; Moore and Threadgold, 1985) such demand for bank loans appeared to be highly interest inelastic. Even as early as the autumn of 1980, the Government shrunk from the option of pushing up interest rates high enough (and what level would that be?) to close off such lending directly. In order then to prevent such rapid increases in bank lending coming through in a commensurate increase in bank deposits, the authorities had to reduce bank lending to the public sector (see note 3); they did so by selling more public sector debt to the non-bank private sector than necessary to finance the PSBR, i.e. 'overfunding'. They achieved this in part by a number of innovations which made public sector debt more attractive to the private sector, e.g. part paid issues, convertibles and index-linked issues, and in part by an assiduous concern with maximizing sales in the light of existing market conditions. At no time did the authorities seek to force some prearranged quantum of gilts upon an unwilling market. Moreover, while overfunding may have resulted in some twist to the yield curve (although no rigorous evidence to that effect is available), it was not brought about by the authorities acting directly on the yield curve for that purpose.

In practice, the Bank of England was remarkably successful in this exercise. But with bank credit continuing to grow at a very rapid pace, some commentators wondered whether mopping up bank deposits by selling a larger volume of gilts (public sector bonds) was a somewhat contrived, even artificial, way of holding monetary growth nearer to its target level. With growing uncertainty about the central relevance of sterling M3, and with its control in the years 1982–5 more subject to the influence of 'overfunding' than of interest rate changes, this then left the question of what factors determined the choice of short-term interest rates during this period. The latter became increasingly pragmatic, involving a combined assessment of a range of monetary indicators and of direct measures of domestic inflation, even on occasions with a glance at real variables, but increasingly attention became drawn in practice to exchange rate fluctuations. It was no accident that the main occasions from 1981 through to 1986 on which interest rates were jerked upwards (October 1981, January 1983, July 1984, January 1985 and January 1986) all coincided with periods of sterling weakness on the foreign exchange (forex) market.

Whereas some aspects of this story are peculiar, even unique, to the UK, e.g. the use of 'overfunding' to seek to attain a broad monetary target, other aspects were also reflected abroad. In particular the timing and scale of the bend in the trend in the growth of the key monetary aggregate (M1) in the USA and Canada coincides very closely with UK experience, even though the coverage of the monetary aggregate concerned differed. Possible causes for this are discussed further in section 5.2.

The consequences and reactions were, not surprisingly, much the same in the USA and Canada as in the UK. Until 1982 (see Lindsey, 1986), the US authorities kept M1 as the main target, viewing disturbances to the demand for money function as possibly temporary or resulting from transitory shocks such as the introduction of NOW (Negotiable Order of Withdrawal) accounts nation-wide in 1981 (see the series of papers by Wenninger and associates in the 1980s, e.g. Radecki and Wenninger (1985)). Then, in the face of the continuing unpredictability of velocity (while some considerable success and credibility had been achieved in the containment of inflation), the Federal Reserve moved, at broadly the same speed as the UK, down the road of widening the range of monetary targets/indicators and returning to a more discretionary and pragmatic mode of determining money market rates. In Canada the switch from the regime of monetary targeting to discretionary interest rate adjustment appeared rather more abrupt (Bouey, 1982; Freedman, 1983), as was also the case in Australia (R. A. Johnston, 1985; Keating, 1985).

5.1.4 1985 Onwards: Increasing Concern with Exchange Rate Regimes

The misalignment of sterling during the years 1980–2 had had a devastating impact on the UK manufacturing sector, but had not impinged seriously on the Western world more widely. However, the subsequent misalignment of the US dollar, which reached its apogee in early 1985, greatly affected all the major countries. This latter experience led to growing doubts among policy-makers whether it really was the case that the forex market did adjust prices efficiently (or at least more efficiently than policy-makers could) and rapidly into line with some 'fundamental equilibrium'. 'Governments have to come to terms with the behaviour of the foreign exchange market. Left entirely to its own devices, we have seen in recent years how destabilising and destructive that behaviour can at times be' (Lawson, 1988).

The combination of growing doubts about the predictability of domestic velocity, and increasing concern about medium-term forex misalignments, led to a tendency for medium-sized countries, e.g. Sweden, Canada, the UK and Australia, to conduct their own monetary policy in practice[8] largely with a view to stabilizing their exchange rate, in some cases bilaterally with a larger neighbour, such as the USA or the FRG (Crow, 1988), but on occasion against a basket of currencies (for Australia, see Hogan (1986); for a more general assessment, see Atkinson and Chouraqui (1987)).

This option was not really open to the three main economies, the USA, Japan and the FRG. In this case academic interest turned to the possibility of applying co-operative monetary policies (among the three major economies) for the joint purpose of stabilizing both international exchange rates and world inflation. Suggestions to this end were put forward by Williamson (1983), McKinnon (1984), Edison et al. (1987) and McKinnon and Ohno (1988), among others. For a commentary and a critique, see Frenkel and Goldstein (1988). Although a series of meetings of finance ministers, starting with that at the Plaza in New York in September 1985, was held with the aim of establishing whether there was scope for enhanced international co-ordination, it is debatable how much actual difference such meetings have made to the policy steps that the protagonists would have adopted independently anyhow (Feldstein, 1988). This should not be read as implying that exchange rate movements had no influence on the domestic monetary policy decisions in the FRG and Japan; clearly the German and Japanese authorities adjusted the fervour with which they pursued their domestic monetary targets in the light of external developments, but such adjustments were autonomously decided and not undertaken in order to preserve international co-operation and amity.

Be that as it may, doubts about the central significance of sterling M3, and concern whether 'overfunding' was leading to some artificial distortions in both relative interest rates and in the growth of the aggregates, led the Chancellor to aim at 'full funding' – but not overfunding of the PSBR – and to downgrade sterling M3 as a target variable during 1985 (Lawson, 1985). The virtual abandonment by 1985 of the monetary variable chosen to be the centre piece of policy in 1979–80 represented a considerable *volte-face*. It was, however, too much for the Chancellor, who in 1980–1 had opposed virtually any intervention to check the giddy rise of sterling, to take the further step of linking monetary policy formally to exchange rate developments (Lawson, 1986, 1988), and also politically difficult for him to do so in the context of the Prime Minister's opposition to the UK's joining the Exchange Rate Mechanism (ERM) of the EMS.

In any case financial innovations, which were held to be largely responsible for the breakdown in the statistical relationships between the various monetary aggregates on the one hand and nominal incomes and interest rates on the other (see section 5.2 and Leigh-Pemberton (1986)), appeared to be causing relatively less disturbance to the relationship between the monetary base M0 and nominal incomes in the UK (R.B. Johnston, 1984); nevertheless, technological and social changes, e.g. the spread of automated teller machines (ATMs), electronic funds transfers (EFTPOS) (point of sale, place of work etc.), home banking etc. threatened potential instability here too (Hall et al., 1988).

Moreover, M0 is overwhelmingly (99 per cent) represented by currency outstanding in the hands of the public (84 per cent) or in banks' vaults/tills (15 per cent). Such currency is provided automatically on demand by the Bank of England. While there *are* reasons why one might believe (see section 5.4.2) that monetary/credit shocks would have subsequent effects on the economy, most outside commentators in the UK reckoned that movements in M0 were no more than a concurrent measure, with additional noise, of consumer expenditures. The Chancellor disagreed, and he emphasized that he regarded M0 as an '*advance* indicator' of money GDP (Lawson, 1986, p. 12); the econometric basis for this claim is uncertain (and is not to be found in R.B. Johnston (1984)).

Nonetheless, perhaps out of a belief in its economic significance, perhaps out of a presentational desire to stick with *some* monetary target aggregate (and one for which technological/social changes were still leading to comparatively low growth figures), the Chancellor and the Treasury have since maintained an annual target for M0 as *the* monetary target[9] for the conduct of monetary policy. In practice, however, interest rate adjustments during the course of 1986 appeared to depend on the same pragmatic blend of discretionary response to monetary developments (more generally than just M0), on current domestic inflationary indicators and on exchange rate developments, as already described.

Then, some time in the early spring (March?) of 1987, policy appeared to shift, in part perhaps influenced by the understandings reached between Finance Ministers at the Louvre meeting in February, though without any formal, public announcement – indeed, the monetary target set out in the FSBR (1987) continued to be expressed in terms of a growth rate for M0. However, from March 1987 to March 1988 the value of the pound remained held in a narrow trading range against the deutschmark, and whenever the pound tended to rise above 3.00 DM[10] overt policy action, either in the form of intervention or reductions in interest rates, was taken to prevent it breaking that limit. There was still room for intramarginal interest rate adjustments, e.g. the upward hike in August 1987 owing to general concern with inflation and the post-October-crash (internationally concerted) reductions. Even so, the parameters within which such discretion could operate appeared to have become more closely restricted by this new policy of 'shadowing' the deutschmark in the forex market.

Early in 1988 this caused a problem. Boom conditions in the UK gave rise to fears about incipient worsening inflation, such that higher interest rates appeared domestically prudent. But there was already a yield differential *vis-à-vis* German interest rates that made capital inflows profitable as long as the expectation remained that the peg to the deutschmark would remain in place. The scale of capital inflows put upward pressure on sterling sufficient to force large intervention by the Bank of England to maintain the peg, and this in turn tended to expand the money stock even faster.

This gave rise to a policy dilemma (a dilemma condition that Walters (1986) had warned would be endemic in such instances): hold the external peg and suffer worse short-term inflationary pressures, or abandon the peg and lose the medium-term (counter-inflationary) support of maintaining a deutschmark peg. There were reports in the newspapers of high level ministerial conflict over which choice to make; in the event the second was adopted. Thereafter, for some 3½ months, policy seemed to move onto a new tack of varying the balance between the exchange rate and interest rates so as to maintain a constant pressure upon nominal incomes. The (econometric) finding of the Treasury's forecasting model, whereby a 4 per cent appreciation of sterling, e.g. from 3.00 DM to 3.12 DM, would have its deflationary effect on nominal incomes offset by a 1 per cent reduction, e.g. from 9.5 to 8.5 per cent, in short-term interest rates, found its way into the press. Whether or not this was an accurate report, from March until July 1988 it was noted that every 5–7 pfennig appreciation (depreciation) in the sterling–deutschmark spot exchange rate was counterbalanced by a 0.5 per cent cut (hike) in interest rates.

In turn, this period of appearing to balance interest rate adjustments against exchange rate adjustments, so as to achieve a constant pressure (of demand) on nominal incomes, seemed to conclude in early July. A series of indicators revealed continuing strong output, worsening inflationary pressure and a weakening balance of payments. The authorities then raised interest rates (though initially in steps of only 0.5 per cent at a time) quite sharply through the summer: the strength of the US dollar and some appalling UK trade figures enabled the authorities to do so without incurring any further appreciation of sterling, which became increasingly subject to weakness.

With national monetarism plus flexible exchange rates having effectively broken down in the first half of the 1980s, the Chancellor appeared to be looking for an alternative (coherent) strategy of international monetary co-operation and co-ordination involving more or less formal linkages within regions, e.g. the ERM in Europe and closer co-operation between the the Group of Three (G3) – the USA, the FRG and Japan. In the event, in early 1988 this objective conflicted with the Government's overriding commitment to contain domestic inflation, causing a policy dilemma. The latter objective took priority (as it also has in similar dilemmas in the FRG), but exactly how the conduct of monetary policy can best be calibrated under present conditions to achieve this objective remains a subject for debate.

5.2 THE UNSTEADY RELATIONSHIP BETWEEN MONEY AND NOMINAL INCOMES

5.2.1 The Demand for Money

Studies of the demand for money usually start from a presumption that there exists a long-term equilibrium relationship between private sector money holdings and certain other aggregate macroeconomic variables, such as the price level, real incomes (or expenditures), (some set of) interest rates and, perhaps, wealth and the rate of inflation. The relevant variables to appear as arguments in this long-run (equilibrium) relationship are normally initially chosen on the basis of *a priori* theory, whether deriving from Keynes' suggested motives for holding money (i.e. transactions, precautionary, speculative), from a Tobin–Baumol inventory theoretical analysis or from Friedman's more general portfolio choice approach (M. Friedman, 1956). In most earlier studies the variables considered to be relevant in the long-term equilibrium relationship were then embedded in a short-run demand for money function via some, often *ad hoc*, partial adjustment mechanism and tested directly against the data. Indeed, this is still the most usual approach in the USA; for recent surveys see Judd and Scadding (1982) and Roley (1985).

More recently econometricians have sought to examine and test directly for the presence of such a long-run equilibrium relationship between variables (*before* imbedding them in equations which also explore short-run dynamic adjustments) by determining whether such variables are cointegrated. If such a long-run relationship does exist between variables X and Y, which may well be both non-stationary and trended in levels, but stationary in differenced form, i.e. they are both $I(1)$ series, then in the simple linear relationship between the series in levels

$$Z_t = X_t - aY_t,$$

the residual Z_t from an ordinary least squares (OLS) regression of X on Y will be stationary (i.e. an $I(0)$ series), and this can be easily tested (see Engle and Granger, 1987) although problems may still arise since the cointegrating vector need not be unique. However, it is minimal information to know that X and Y are cointegrated. We do not know why and in what relationship it appears; in a multi-equation context it would not even tell us which linear combinations of which cointegrated variables constituted the long-run relationship of interest. Therefore, as Hendry (1985, 1988) argues, it is necessary to model the long run and the short run jointly to establish in which equations the error corrections appear and hence to identify them.

In more behavioural terms, if an equilibrium long-run relationship exists between variables X and Y, say of the linear form $X = aY$, then any deviation from this relationship will induce pressures to drive X or Y or both back towards the equilibrium. The implication of this is that equations to examine short-run adjustment should include an error correction mechanism, along the lines proposed by Granger (1981) in more theoretical work and by Hendry (1979, 1985, 1988) in a series of more applied studies.

This approach involves no preconditions about the nature of the shocks that may disturb the long-run equilibrium relationship, or whether the resumption of the equilibrium involves a readjustment primarily in X or Y, or whether they both adjust. Thus, in the context of the relationship between money holdings and nominal incomes, the existence, if indeed it does still exist (see further below), of a long-run relationship between them (i.e. a predictable and stable velocity) implies no prior conditions on whether the shocks that disturb the relationship occur primarily to money holdings or to nominal incomes, or on whether the subsequent return to equilibrium occurs via an adjustment in money holdings or in nominal incomes. In particular, the money stock may well be largely endogenously determined, as economists such as Moore (1988a, b) and Kaldor (1982) have argued, and it can still be the case that shocks to the money stock, which disturb the long-term equilibrium, may lead to subsequent adjustments in nominal incomes. The latter is an empirical question, which does *not* depend on the money stock's being exogenous with respect to nominal incomes.

There is quite a close connection, although it has not been widely recognized, between the cointegration/error correction mechanism and the buffer stock approach to monetary analysis (see Laidler, 1983b, 1986). Like the former, the latter depends on the existence of a stable long-term relationship between money holdings and nominal incomes. Various shocks, especially those affecting bank credit expansion, e.g. on the occasion of deregulation, then drive actual money balances away from their long-term equilibrium level, a divergence that people are willing to tolerate temporarily because money balances are particularly well suited to act as a buffer to such shocks. But this divergence (from long-term equilibrium) then sets up forces that will affect both monetary variables (i.e. the demand for both loans and deposits) *and* nominal expenditures. Models along this line began with 1976 Reserve Bank of Australia model (Jonson et al., 1977) and (generally small) models have since been constructed for several countries, including the USA (Laidler and Bentley, 1983), the Netherlands (Knoester and van Sinderen,

1982) and the UK (Davidson, 1987; Davidson and Ireland, 1987). The literature on buffer stock money is now becoming large: for recent contributions see Cuthbertson and Taylor (1987) and Muscatelli (1988). Again, this approach has not been widely adopted in the USA, with certain exceptions (e.g. Carr and Darby (1981) and Judd and Scadding (1981)), in part because critics such as Milbourne (1987) have queried the microfoundations of the approach, and in part because the concept that agents may allow themselves to be driven temporarily off their demand function is alien to the dominant US model of (relatively) perfect clearing markets.

Be that as it may, early empirical work (see Goldfeld (1973) for the USA, and Laidler and Parkin (1970) and Goodhart and Crockett (1970) for the UK) soon established that money holdings appeared to adjust to the arguments in the long-run relationship rather slowly, i.e. with long lags. In most US literature such lags were modelled by the adoption of a partial adjustment mechanism applied to either real or nominal money balances (see Roley (1985) and the comment thereon by Hafer (1985)). In the UK, again under the influence of David Hendry, the recent tendency in such econometric work has been to put as few prior restrictions as possible on the form of the dynamic adjustment model, and to test down from very general models to more 'parsimonious' equations using restrictions, e.g. excluding variables, that are data consistent. Therefore there is quite a marked disparity between the Granger–Engle–Hendry approach (i.e. start by examining the stationarity characteristics of the time series, next test for cointegration and then embed the resulting error correction variable(s) into a general short-term adjustment model, which is tested down to a more parsimonious version) and the more common single-equation partial-adjustment standard demand for money function.

Either approach, however, is liable to leave one with a 'preferred' equation including lags of the monetary aggregate serving as dependent variable and, possibly, lagged values of the other arguments, which generally imply a lengthy adjustment period. This has been criticized on several scores. First, it would seem to suggest that, should there be 'exogenous' shocks to the money stock, certain other variables, e.g. interest rates, would have to overshoot. Second, the length of adjustment seems to be too long to be readily accounted for by costs of adjustment (see Goodfriend, 1985; Laidler, 1985). Third, it is not generally clear whether these lags and the error correction feedback mechanism are consistent with rational expectations. Lane (1984), Cuthbertson and Taylor (1987), Cuthbertson (1988a), and Dutkowsky and Foote (1988), among others, have explored a two-stage approach whereby a 'model-consistent' estimate of expectations is constructed in the first stage and these forward-looking variables are then entered into a demand for money function in conjunction with backward looking variables including error correction mechanisms.

Hendry (1988) has argued that, should the expectations-generating process shift during the data period, it should be possible to discriminate between feedback and 'feedforward' mechanisms (see also Hendry and Neale, 1988). While he clearly demonstrates that interest rates and real output movements are so hard to predict, as they are close to random walks, that there can be little power to feedforward mechanisms, even he expresses surprise that the data apparently suggest that agents 'ignore the predictability of inflation in adjusting their M1 balances' (Hendry, 1988, p. 146). Cuthbertson (1988b) has responded by arguing that Hendry's assessment, and claimed refutation, of the Lucas critique is weakened by the fact that in a finite sample the marginal model for the forward-looking variables is likely to be highly inefficient. But if such marginal models, including in this case Cuthbertson's own equations, are so inefficient how can any *confident* forward-looking expectation be established?

However, this is not a survey of demand for money studies, even less of their econometric technicalities. Policy-makers were, in the main, less concerned with the academic details of the studies than with the question of whether the relationships uncovered were sufficiently robust to serve as a basis for conducting monetary policy. As already noted, the early work on such relationships, undertaken in the years until 1973, did in the main appear to demonstrate, around the end of the 1960s, that the demand for money was a predictable function of a few variables. However, that predictability then suffered some knocks during the disturbed years in the early mid-1970s notably with 'the case of the missing money' (Goldfeld, 1976) in the USA.

Nowhere else, however, did the prior stability of the (short-run) demand for money function exhibit such a comprehensive collapse as in the case of sterling M3 in the UK in 1972–3. A surge in bank lending to the private sector (and a large PSBR) was funded by a huge increase in wholesale bank deposits as the banks bid aggressively for funds. This drove sterling M3 far beyond the level that would have been predicted on the basis of previously calculated equations; even when attempts (Hacche, 1974; Smith, 1978, 1980) were made to account for the banks' new liability management practices, the refitted equations could not account satisfactorily for the monetary surge in 1972–3 (for an exception see Taylor (1987)). The consensus remains that the demand for money function for sterling M3 broke down in 1972–3 and has remained unstable ever since (this breakdown is most evident in the case of company sector holdings of sterling M3; indeed, Lubrano et al. (1986) report that the *long-term* relationship for the *personal* sector remained fairly stable, at least until 1981). At one time a study by Grice *et al.* (1981) (see also Grice and Bennett, 1984) suggested that a stable function for sterling M3 could be obtained by relating it to a measure of gross financial wealth and an estimate of expected returns on gilts (i.e. government bonds), but not only did this formulation entail some inherent problems (e.g. in taking bank lending as exogenously determined), but its out-of-sample forecasting properties soon disappointed. For a recent survey, see Holtham *et al.* (1988).

This might provoke the question why this breakdown did *not* discourage UK policy-makers from placing so much reliance on sterling M3. The crucial reason is that the subsequent upsurge in prices and nominal incomes in 1974–5 appeared to confirm the monetarists' historical/policy claim that major monetary shocks caused subsequent nominal income changes. Thus the breakdown of the (short run) demand for money function in the UK signalled to many monetarist economists (and policy-makers) that the UK had been running these regressions the wrong way around, rather than that the long-run money–nominal income nexus was fragile and unreliable.

First steps at transforming the equation to make sterling M3 into an independent right-hand-side variable were taken Artis and Lewis (1976), but initially they took the level of interest rates, rather than nominal incomes as their dependent variable (see also Andersen, 1985). Subsequently Mills (1983b) examined the extent to which various measures of the UK money stock appeared to be able to predict movements in nominal incomes, once the pattern of autoregression in nominal incomes had been taken into consideration, and concluded that sterling M3 represented the best guide.

The UK experience in the mid-1970s was unusual, however. In several other countries the earlier fitted equations had had some predictive problems in the mid-1970s, but these had been quite minor, relative to the shock in the UK, and normal econometric running repairs had encouraged central banks in most major countries to base the technical choice of their chosen money stock target numbers on their preferred demand for money function.

As recorded in section 5.1, policy shifted in late 1979 onto a much more deflationary tack, initiated by the major change in the monetary control regime in the USA. From that point onwards, velocity trends shifted and the monetary aggregates grew more rapidly relative to nominal incomes than in the past. This experience occurred at roughly the same time, although to different degrees, in most Western countries and in Japan (Ueda, 1988).

Lucas (1976) had earlier demonstrated why a regime change might well lead to instability and parameter shifts in previously estimated 'structural' equations. The adoption of new operating procedures in the USA on 6 October 1979 represented a major policy regime change. American economists soon noted that the prediction errors in the demand for money functions could have resulted from such regime changes (Judd and Scadding, 1982). Indeed, Gordon (1984) called for the abandonment of efforts to estimate short-term demand for money functions, since the appropriate form of short-run relationships that can be estimated between the monetary base, the money stock, interest rates and nominal incomes may depend more on the (changing) form of the policy regime than on the (changing) nature of behavioural responses of the private sector.

Even though a number of economists, especially in the USA, have continued to argue that (at least some definitions, especially the monetary base, of) the money stock still exhibits a well-behaved demand for money function,[11] the extent of predictive failure subsequently went beyond the ability of most (US) economists to explain in terms of regime change or of (UK) economists to explain in terms of a buffer stock (disequilibrium) response to monetary shocks. The inherent problem with these approaches has been that they seek to, and can only, explain *short-term* deviations of velocity. Thus a monetary surge, caused say by the abolition of the corset control in the UK in 1980, will lead to a temporary fall in velocity, or alternatively the changed monetary regime, as in the USA in 1979, could lead people to expect an initial monetary overshoot, relative to the target, to provoke a future rise in interest rates as the authorities react and hence cause the private sector to wish to hold more, not less, monetary balances on speculative grounds (see Vaciago, 1985).

Therefore there are quite a number of (partly related) grounds for explaining short-term fluctuations in velocity and short-term instability in the demand for money function. But such approaches (notably including the buffer stock–disequilibrium models) generally incorporate an assumption of a stable long-run equilibrium relationship between money holdings and nominal incomes. Indeed, it is the divergence of the short-run (credit counterpart determined) money stock from the stable long-run desired level that drives expenditures in these models. In more policy-oriented terms, economic advisers in the UK were waiting with trepidation for the built-up 'overhang', or excess money balances, to spill over into higher expenditures in 1981, 1982, 1983 and 1984. Eventually they grew tired of waiting and accepted that there must have been some change to the underlying long-term demand for money (though see Artis and Lewis (1984) and Budd and Holly (1986) for a graphical illustration of its prior stability). Similarly, in the USA and Canada, the change in the trend since 1979 has gone on too long to explain as a purely short-run phenomenon. For an illustration of the long-run changes in velocity in the various countries discussed in this chapter, see figures 5.1 and 5.2.

Put in more formal terms, both Engle and Granger (1987) and Miller (1988) have demonstrated that, over the last couple of decades in the USA, the various monetary aggregates, with the possible exception of M2, have not been cointegrated with nominal incomes, i.e. velocity has been generally non-stationary. The latest empirical studies undertaken within the Federal Reserve Board now also lead to a preference for M2 over M1 as a monetary target (Moore et al., 1988); the same preference also currently holds in Canada (Crow, 1988). This longer-term departure of velocity for US M1 from prior trends has been nicely illustrated by B. Friedman (1988a); see also Wenninger (1988).

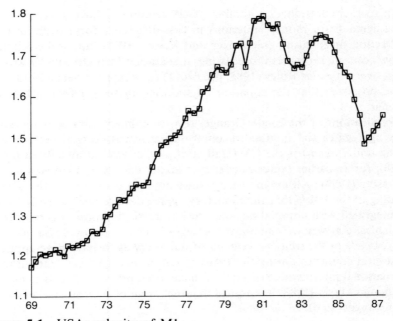

Figure 5.1 USA: velocity of M1

Figure 5.2 UK: velocity of M3

In such circumstances a number of US economists have advocated running demand for money equations in first-difference form (without error correction mechanism) (see Cover and Keeler, 1987) but, while this may allow accurate short-term forecasting, it enables velocity to wander without limit over time. See Roley (1985, pp. 620–1) for a review of economists who have proposed that the equation be specified in such a first-differenced format.

Replications of the Engle–Granger tests of cointegration between monetary aggregates and nominal incomes during recent decades are currently being undertaken for the UK (Hall et al., 1988; Ireland and Wren-Lewis, 1988); for an earlier exercise covering a longer data period see Hendry and Ericsson (1983). Although these results are still provisional, the general finding in the UK is that the monetary aggregates are not currently simply cointegrated with nominal incomes; however, the addition of certain other variables, e.g. wealth, can allow cointegration to be restored. Be that as it may, bends in the trend of velocity of monetary aggregates have appeared in several countries during the 1980s, often in that aggregate chosen to be *the* national intermediate target, and have often proved difficult to explain (although Mayer (1988) has argued that the extent of such 'breaks' has often been exaggerated).

5.2.2 Some Explanations of the Shifting Path of Velocity

So, why did the trend bend? There are a variety of suggested answers, none of them fully satisfactory, although all of them may possess some validity. First, it may be that econometricians had previously failed to estimate the effect of certain interest rate relativities correctly. As already noted, the period 1979–82 was marked by extreme interest rate volatility in the USA. We would expect an increase in the variance of key asset prices, around a given mean level, to raise the (speculative and precautionary) demand for money (Tobin, 1958; Buiter and Armstrong, 1978; Walsh, 1984). There is some econometric evidence to this effect (e.g. Baba et al., 1987; Ueda, 1988), but the decline in velocity continued after 1982 whereas interest rate volatility reverted to lower levels.

Second, the 1980s represented a period of declining inflation and (rather more slowly) declining nominal interest rates. It may be that earlier studies underestimated the elasticity of response of desired money balances to inflation and/or nominal interest rates. In those cases where financial innovation led to the payment of interest rates that were either fixed or had an upper ceiling on certain monetary aggregates – as with NOW accounts in the USA until January 1986 – it is possible that the elasticity of such balances to changes in market interest rates increased (Simpson, 1984; Heller, 1988).

The question of whether financial innovations led to an increase in interest elasticity has provoked a sizeable literature in the USA (see for example Akhtar, 1983; Brayton et al., 1983; Hafer and Hein, 1984; Wenninger, 1986; Darby et al., 1987). Greenspan (1988) appears confident that 'the aggregates have become more responsive to interest rate changes in the 1980s'.

If such elasticities were higher than previously thought, this would then intensify certain consequential problems for monetary targetry, commonly described as 'the re-entry problem' (see Simpson, 1984; Budd and Holly, 1986; Blundell-Wignall and Thorp, 1987). The difficulty is that a successful counter-inflationary policy would entail lower inflation and nominal interest rates; this would so raise the demand for money that either the resulting target values would *look* lax or, if a continuing hold was kept on the target numbers, the intermediate target objective could prove unduly restrictive.

Third, the increase in competitive pressures in the financial system, among banks and between banks and other financial intermediaries in the 1980s has led to a paring of spreads between lending and deposit rates, with interest rates on deposits being made more attractive, while the cost of borrowing to the personal sector, e.g. on mortgages, has been reduced in a number of countries, notably in the UK. The private sector, both the company and the personal sectors, has enormously increased both its indebtedness to and claims upon the banking sector. Although the microlevel data make it hard to estimate whether the borrowers are the same or different entities as the depositors (note, though, that more assured access to bank borrowing facilities could have been expected to reduce precautionary holdings of deposits), there is no question but that the scale of bank intermediation has increased dramatically; for an analysis of the UK personal sector see R.B. Johnston (1985), and for the UK company sector see Chowdhury et al. (1986). The best measure of the cost of intermediating through (some part of) the financial system is the spread charged therein (see Miller and Sprenkle, 1980; R.B. Johnston, 1983). As Miller and Sprenkle argued, the scale of intermediation may respond elastically to reductions in the spread.

A further factor tending to raise the demand for liquid assets in general will have been the enormous increase in the value of non-human wealth, e.g. equities and houses, during the bull market of the early 1980s (up till 1987–8) and an associated upsurge in the volume of financial transactions (see Grice and Bennett, 1984; Ueda, 1988), although Wenninger and Radecki (1986) doubt whether the growth of financial transactions had much effect on M1's growth in the USA.

This first set of suggestions all point to the possibility that the response of desired money balances to certain interest rate relativities may have been underestimated. The second set of suggestions, *not* in any way mutually exclusive with the first, cover the possibility that the characteristics of bank liabilities and assets were upgraded by financial innovation making them more attractive to hold (Hester, 1981; Akhtar, 1983; Leigh-Pemberton, 1986; Artus, 1987; de Cecco, 1987; Tamura, 1987). The term 'financial innovation' tends to make most people think of exotic new instruments, e.g. options, futures, options on futures, forward rate agreements, swaps etc., but the financial innovations of key importance for the conduct of monetary policy have been rather more prosaic. The controls imposed by the authorities, both 'prudential' and direct credit controls, and the oligopolistic nature of the banking industry in several countries had restricted the range and variety of lending facilities and the payment of interest on deposits available to the private sector *retail* customer; from the 1960s onwards the *wholesale* customer had benefited from the benchmark competition provided by the Eurocurrency markets.

Anyhow, the extension of variable-rate lending in mortgage form made relatively much cheaper credit available to personal sector borrowers in the United Kingdom. The rapid expansion of bank credit to the private sector in most countries throughout the 1980s, in part a supply-side shock, required the banks to act more aggressively to fund the additional demand for loans, and the continuing process of de-regulation allowed them to do so. This need for funds, the increasing competition in the industry and the trend towards de-regulation[12] then combined to induce banks to pay higher interest rates than previously, often market related, on categories of deposit that had previously borne zero interest by custom or by regulation, e.g. checkable sight deposits, or where the rates had been administratively pegged.

The payment of market-related interest rates on certain categories of checkable deposits naturally made them much more attractive to hold. Assets jointly held in a portfolio will provide the same utility at the margin. If one asset offers the same rate of interest as another safe but non-monetary asset, but also provides certain extra liquidity or transaction services, then both assets will only be held simultaneously if the demand for the transactions–liquidity services of the first asset is completely satiated. Therefore the provision of market-related interest rates on a wider range of bank deposits would lead to a surge in demand for them, until the demand for their extra liquidity services became approximately satisfied and, at the margin, such deposits were held as interest-bearing safe assets rather than as 'money'.

In that case the rate of growth of the monetary aggregates will have overstated, possibly considerably, the rate of growth of true 'money' since the money-like characteristics of the interest-bearing deposits will have declined. This is the argument and analysis preferred by those who advocate the use of a Divisia index, whereby the 'moneyness' of a deposit is represented by the divergence between its own rate and that on a non-monetary safe asset. There is now quite a large literature on this topic: see Barnett (1982) and Barnett et al. (1984); for the US see Mills (1983a). The use of a Divisia index to measure money can go some way to explain recent trends in velocity, in so far as the innovation process is reflected in shifts in relative interest rates. While in principle this approach would seem to have much to recommend it in a period of rapid shifts in deposit characteristics, in practice the use of such monetary indices in the USA would have provided 'little clear improvement in terms of either demand equation or reduced-form equation performance' in the 1980s (Lindsey and Spindt, 1986). Despite much of the academic research on this having been done under the aegis of central banks, senior officials have been reluctant to give the concept much public prominence or any policy role.

Competition may well drive banks towards offering a fully market-related interest rate for deposits, while at the same time charging full economic costs for their payments and transactions services. If so, the above analysis would suggest that deposit holdings would increase until the demand for liquidity was satiated and would be perfectly substitutable for non-monetary assets of the same maturity. If so, what, if anything, would remain of the distinction between money and other assets of a similar maturity? Is one particular characteristic of money, as Tobin (1963) has earlier suggested, that the interest payable on it is externally restricted? Could the distinction between monetary and non-monetary assets become further blurred by an extension in the range of assets that can be monetized and/or the range of intermediaries offering perhaps limited payments services on the back of electronic technology? It might seem that, with the extension of market-related interest rates to a wider range of deposits, the only essential 'money' left might be currency outstanding or the monetary base (see Solomon, 1981). However, demand for such currency is affected by cross-border holdings (e.g. for deutschmarks in Eastern Europe and for dollars around the world (Board of Governors, 1988, Appendix on Monetary Base; Greenspan, 1988)) and by the 'black economy' (Thomas, 1988). Thus surveys of currency holdings can only account for a fraction of the amount outstanding (see Porter and Bayer, 1983; Avery et al., 1987) although econometric studies for the UK (R. B. Johnston, 1984) and for the USA (Dotsey, 1988) have continued to show generally stable demand for currency functions, unlike the FRG where the demand for currency function has recently become unstable (see Deutsche Bundesbank, 1988; Holtham et al., 1988). Moreover, techniques are available whereby interest could be paid even now on currency (McCulloch, 1986), although they are unlikely to be adopted, since seignorage represents an attractive and simple source of taxation. While such receipts are small in most developed non-inflationary countries (Buiter, 1985), they are large enough in several southern European countries to cause certain problems in the process of convergence to a unified non-inflationary EMS (see, for example, Grilli, 1988).

5.3 MONETARY CONTROL METHODS

5.3.1 The Debate over Monetary Base Control

The advent of liability management weakened the ability of the authorities to use their traditional mechanism of interest rate adjustment to control monetary growth, because the banks would compete with the central bank for funds, leading to an upward spiral in interest rates, as long as they could continue to intermediate profitably, i.e. to lend out such funds to borrowers at a margin above (wholesale) deposit rates (Moore, 1989). In addition, the demand for bank loans has proved notably interest inelastic. Moreover, there have always been certain other difficulties in using this approach.

Even before the adoption of liability management, the interest elasticity of demand for bank deposits was subject to considerable uncertainty so that the authorities could not calibrate at all exactly how much interest rates had to change to bring about a desired adjustment in the money stock. Moreover, the authorities only had occasional, once a month or once a quarter in most countries, snapshots of the money stock, which were frequently distorted by temporary disturbances, e.g. a large new issue, or a take-over bid, or a strike or even bad weather disrupting the normal course of bank clearing, so that it was always hard to distinguish temporary from more permanent monetary movements. Given such uncertainty, and the 'political' dislike of raising interest rates – interestingly enough more clearly apparent in the USA where the Federal Reserve is independent of the Executive than in the UK where the Bank of England is not – there was a natural tendency for interest rate adjustments to be (or to be perceived to be) 'too little and too late', as was recognized in the Green Paper on Monetary Control (HM Treasury and Bank of England, 1980; see also M. Friedman, 1982, 1984b).

Therefore there were inherent reasons to suspect that the central banks' traditional methods of interest rate adjustments would not operate satisfactorily to achieve adequate monetary control, and that such deficiencies would be particularly marked at times of severe inflationary pressures when lags in the process of interest rate adjustment would induce the authorities temporarily to accommodate each inflationary shock to the demand for money until they had managed both to observe it and to come to a decision to offset it. With monetary control becoming the centrepiece of many governments' policies at the end of the 1970s, it was therefore inevitable that intensive consideration would be given to an alternative method of monetary control, namely MBC.

Banks need to maintain high-powered cash reserves R in order to honour their commitment to maintain the convertibility of their deposits D into currency C. If the ratio of such reserves to deposits which they maintain is stable, and if the general public maintains a stable currency-to-deposit ratio, then the multiplier linking the money stock M to the high powered reserve base H will also remain stable via the identity

$$M = H \frac{C/D + 1}{C/D + R/D}$$

Empirical work tended to demonstrate that these ratios were generally stable and quite closely predictable for the USA (Johannes and Rasche, 1979, 1981; Dewald and Lai, 1987) but less so in the UK in recent years (Capie and Wood, 1986). Therefore the argument was straightforward. The central bank can control H, which incidentally represents its own liabilities, by open market operations. Given the predicted values for the two key ratios (which might, indeed, be sensitive to interest rates, but we could attempt to measure such sensitivity), the authorities could set H in a manner that would deliver any desired M. Of course, the determination of a quantity M implies the determination of a dual. In the short term, while the general level of prices is slowly adjusting, this would be reflected in changes of flexible asset prices, in particular of nominal interest rates. But it was the excessively sluggish adjustment of nominal interest rates that was (it was claimed) part of the problem with the traditional mechanism, and much more variable short-term interest rates would be an acceptable price to pay for better monetary control, especially since longer term asset prices might show *greater* stability than in the past because inflationary expectations would be stabilized.

After a pre-emptive counter-attack by the Bank of England on these arguments (Foot et al., 1979), the Government established a Bank–Treasury working party to study the issue, and their report, in effect, was published in the Green Paper on *Monetary Control* (HM Treasury and Bank of England, 1980). In this, the working party accepted much of the case against MBC. Briefly it runs as follows. The historical stability of the banks' reserve ratio had depended on the willingness of the authorities always to supply extra cash on demand at an interest rate chosen by the authorities. If the authorities should shift the operational form of the system, by refusing banks' free access to cash at any price, the banks' desired reserve ratio might experience a major shift and could then become much more variable. There would be a long transition period from regime to regime in which it would be hard to select an appropriate level of base money, and the variability of the banks' reserve-to-deposit ratio under the new system could be so large as to prevent any improvement in monetary control, while at the same time losing grip on interest rates.

The above arguments referred essentially to a system of MBC operated without any mandatory controls on required bank reserves. If, however, the banks were required to hold a mandatorily required reserve ratio, then there would be a (somewhat) firmer fulcrum, with a more stable reserve-to-deposit ratio. But this alternative option ran into some technical problems over the accounting base for the required reserves that has plagued the Americans in practice. If the required reserves were to be based on a previous known deposit base – a lagged accounting rule – then there would be nothing the banks could do by their own actions, e.g. by running down current assets, to lessen their need for reserves. Under such circumstances the authorities really have no alternative to giving them the reserves that the banks require, as in the case, for example, of the FRG (see Kloten, 1987); they can only choose the interest rate or penalty for providing the required reserves (for an authoritative account of the operational practices of the Bundesbank, see Deutsche Bundesbank (1987)). However, this would then just be a throwback to the traditional system (see M. Friedman, 1982). Owing to the difficulty of estimating deposit levels, except at the close of business, operational lags etc., moving to a current-accounting basis does not really avoid this prior difficulty.

A more radical solution to this problem, advocated in a few quarters (see Laurent, 1979; Kopecky, 1984), was to move to a system of forward accounting whereby the permissible volume of deposits at future date $t + x$ would be dependent on the volume of reserves held at time t. An inherent problem with this approach, as with the even more radical suggestion (Duck and Sheppard, 1978) of selling the commercial banks (non-monetary) permits to expand deposits, is that it would have the effect of artificially raising the cost of *banks'* intermediation, when restrictive pressure was applied, relative to costs via other financial channels and would thus promote large-scale ('cosmetic') disintermediation.

Since the arguments, pro and con, in the UK depended largely on claims about how banks and other agents in the financial system might behave in the hypothetical conditions of a change in the regime to (some version of) MBC, it was not really possible to demonstrate the superiority of one set of arguments over the other. The protagonists on either side in the UK, who met to discuss it under official auspices in the improbable venue of Church House in Westminster on 29 September 1980, generally stuck to their prejudices. One argument that did sway some of those in positions of power and influence, however, was that it would be difficult to steer the system clearly through the transitional learning period; thus 'we in the UK have very little idea of the size of cash balances the banks would wish to hold if we were to move to a system of monetary base control' (Lawson, 1981); moreover the ratio of sterling M3 to base money was not stable or predictable, so that there was 'little or no point in trying to use the MBC system to control £M3' (Walters, 1986, p. 123). These considerations, combined with the convinced opposition to MBC from the Bank of England, the commercial bankers and the City of London, persuaded the monetarists not to push more strongly for MBC, although remaining unpersuaded of the contrary case, in the early years of the MTFS (i.e. 1980, 1981 and 1982). Thereafter, the progressive withdrawal from monetary targetry has relegated the associated/subsidiary issue of MBC to the very back of the policy burner.

In the USA the constraints on a flexible use of traditional interest rate adjustments were even more severe than in the UK. Accordingly, on 6 October 1979 the authorities *did* decide to shift their operating procedures, into a form with a number of the characteristics of MBC. The approach adopted to control *non-borrowed reserves* was ingenious. Although the accounting system remained on a lagged basis, so that the banks had to obtain a given total of required reserves, they could do so by borrowing reserves from the Federal Reserve, given the volume of non-borrowed reserves. The US system of borrowing at the discount window is such that additional borrowing would be stimulated by a rise in the margin between market rates and the (administratively pegged) discount rate, although the relationship involved some intertemporal complexities (see Goodfriend, 1983). Hence an expansionary monetary shock impinging on an unchanged total of non-borrowed reserves would lead to a quasi-automatic market increase in interest rates until enough extra borrowing was induced to allow the banks to satisfy their required ratio (Axilrod and Lindsey, 1981; Federal Reserve Staff Studies, 1981). Thus interest rates would adjust much more rapidly and flexibly in the face of monetary shocks, but would not spiral away without limit; as a further safety measure the Federal Reserve set (unpublished) interest rate bands, whereby at the upper (lower) limit it would intervene directly to inject (withdraw) reserves to prevent excessively wild interest rate movements.

In the event, however, these bands were set quite widely and often adjusted in line with market movements, so that they only rarely came into play, (Sternlight and Axilrod, 1982). The change in policy increased both the level and volatility of market interest rates immediately and dramatically, with volatility in the period 1979–82 being some four or five times greater than before 1979 (see Evans, 1981, 1984; Walsh, 1982; Mascaro and Meltzer, 1983). The effect of such high and variable interest rates, and the determination of Paul Volcker to continue with the medicine, undoubtedly played a major role both in shifting the US and world economy from a generally inflationary to a generally deflationary tack and in stemming inflationary expectations and psychology.

However, a number of technical operating problems did arise (see the papers presented at the Conference on Current Issues in the Conduct of U.S. Monetary Policy, republished in the *Journal of Money, Credit and Banking*, November 1982). First, although the Federal Reserve did broadly achieve its annual M1 targets, the shorter-term quarter-to-quarter time path of M1 became even more variable than before 1979. Second, whereas some greater variability of short-term interest rates had been expected (although no one was sure in advance of the scale of the increase; see Walsh (1982) for a comparison of the outcome with earlier studies), the concomitant increase in volatility of longer-term bond yields had not been predicted (Volcker, 1978; Spindt and Tarhan, 1987). Monetarists ascribed both failings to a lack of zeal in the Federal Reserve and to the modifications from full MBC out-lined above, and advocated such measures as a shift to current accounting (adopted in 1984) and closure of the discount window, or greater penalties from using it, and/or a shift from using non-borrowed reserves to a total reserves or monetary base operating target (M. Friedman, 1982, 1984a, b; Poole, 1982; Rasche and Meltzer, 1982; Brunner and Meltzer, 1983; Mascaro and Meltzer, 1983; McCallum, 1985; Rasche, 1985). The Federal Reserve often advanced particular conjunctural explanations for each short-term surge, or fall, in M1 (see the studies by Wenninger and associates from 1981 onwards, e.g. Radecki and Wenninger (1985), and Bryant (1982) provided econometric evidence to support the claim that little or no improvement in monetary control could have been obtained by changing the operational basis, e.g. to a total reserves target, see Tinsley et al. (1982) and Lindsey et al. (1984). Others regarded such fluctuations as the inevitable result of trying (too hard) to impose short-term control on a monetary system wherein there were lengthy lags in the adjustment of the demand of both deposits and advances to interest rates (instrument instability) (e.g. White, 1976; Radecki, 1982; Cosimano and Jansen, 1987); however, see Lane (1984) and McCallum (1985) for an attempted rebuttal.

Be that as it may, the adoption of this operating procedure led to a very bumpy ride over the period 1979–82.[13] In the summer of 1982, a combination of falling inflation in the USA and the onset of the debt crisis in the less-developed countries (LDCs) (in some large part triggered by the change in US monetary policy (see Congdon, 1988)) induced the Federal Reserve to move away from MBC. This took the form of shifting from a target for *non-borrowed* reserves to a target for *borrowed* reserves (see Wallich, 1984). At a superficial glance this still sounds like a reserve base objective. However, as already noted, the demand for borrowed reserves is a function of the margin between market interest rates and the discount rate, so that a target for borrowed reserves implicitly represents an interest rate objective and also implies that monetary shocks would be accommodated by accompanying movements in non-borrowed reserves at given borrowed reserve/interest rate levels. As in the UK and elsewhere, the withdrawal from monetary targetry in the USA has meant that this area of argument has gone quiet there also, though not as moribund as in the UK.

5.3.2 Subsequent UK History

Although in 1980 the UK Government did not seek to impose MBC on a banking community that deeply opposed the idea, one of the features of MBC that had attracted the Government was that it removed the determination of nominal interest rates from the hands of the authorities and gave it to the market. At that time it was one of the tenets of the Conservative Government that prices were set much more efficiently in markets than by the decision of some group of policy-makers. Therefore, even though the Government did not insist on MBC, they wanted to introduce a system which gave more scope to the market, and equivalently less to the Bank of England, to set interest rates.

Previously, the Bank of England had organized the pattern of the weekly treasury bill issue so as to leave the market normally slightly short of its desired cash reserve levels (Bank of England, 1984b, ch. 6). Since the market would then regularly have to sell paper to the Bank to obtain cash, it would facilitate the Bank's control over the price that the market would receive for such paper, i.e. over nominal interest rates. In mid-1981 the Government and the Bank agreed that this practice would henceforth cease. At its weekly treasury bill tender the Bank would aim to leave the market in balance. On those days, expected to be in the majority, when the market was roughly in balance the Bank could withdraw, leaving rates to be determined in the free market. However, the authorities remained concerned not to allow freedom to become entirely untrammelled, and thus stated that they would set (unpublished) bands which would represent those levels of interest rates beyond which the authorities would intervene to prevent further market-driven movement of interest rates.

In the event, however, this system never came into operation, and the concept of market freedom within unpublished bands proved chimerical. The reason was as follows. During the years 1981–5, the authorities continued to aim to achieve a target for sterling M3. But at the same time the authorities had lost faith in their ability to achieve such a target by an (acceptable) adjustment in the level of nominal interest rates and were beginning to vary interest rates in the light of the (pragmatic) blend of concern with monetary conditions, domestic indicators of inflation and exchange rates described earlier. Meanwhile, with interest rates thus determined, bank lending to the private sector continued to grow at around 20 per cent per annum compared with a target for sterling M3 nearer 10 per cent per annum. The authorities, with the Bank taking the lead, sought to resolve this conundrum by offsetting the faster rate of growth of bank lending to the private sector by inducing a fall in bank lending to the public sector. They did this by selling more public sector debt to the non-bank private sector than needed to fund the PSBR, thus making the banks systematically short of cash in their transactions with the Government via the Bank. The commercial banks then relaxed their cash shortage by allowing their short-dated public sector debt to run off, or by selling their longer-dated public sector debt. But this effectively forced the Bank again to determine the interest rate level at which it would resolve the systematic cash shortage by buying in the banks' paper, (Bank of England, 1984a).

This policy was remarkably successful in reconciling continuing extremely rapid creation of bank credit with a much lower monetary target. By about 1981, however, a technical problem ensued. The commercial banks effectively ran out of public sector debt to sell back or run off. This problem was then resolved by the Bank of England's buying private sector commercial bills from the commercial banks. This resolved the problem, but only temporarily until the bills matured, when the whole process had to be rolled over. Therefore on each occasion of overfunding, the 'bill mountain' steadily grew, leading in time to an almost farcical situation of vast quantities of bills maturing on each day, huge resulting cash shortages in the banking system and the Bank needing to purchase 'wheelbarrow loads' of further commercial bills from the market to balance the books. This raised numerous questions. The authorities were selling long-dated securities and buying back short-dated bills. Did this make commercial sense?[14] In order to generate the wheelbarrow loads of commercial bills they needed to buy (to square the books),[5] interest rates on commercial bills were reduced below interest rates on alternative assets. This led to some arbitrage opportunities. Indeed, the authorities aimed to induce borrowers to shift to bill finance out of loan finance. But it was claimed that the need to generate the vast additional amounts of bills at times caused bill rates to fall to a level that could encourage various undesirable forms of 'hard' arbitrage, which could inflate both bank lending and deposits. More generally, did a programme of selling longer-dated debt and buying shorter-dated bills tilt the yield curve in a way that would encourage private sector borrowers to seek funds from banks rather than from capital markets, which was one cause of the original problem? More fundamentally yet, was a technique that allowed bank credit expansion to continue roaring ahead, but restrained the growth of bank deposits, achieving any proper purpose, or was it just another 'cosmetic' device?

It has never been easy to answer these questions, and they continued to raise nagging doubts at the time. As the emphasis given to controlling sterling M3 lapsed (and such control was largely achieved by overfunding), so the Chancellor decided in mid-1985 to abandon the policy of overfunding and to shift to a policy of fully funding the (rapidly falling) PSBR outside the banking system (Lawson, 1985); a similar full-fund policy was also adopted in Australia (Johnston, 1985) and New Zealand (Reserve Bank,

1987a). Quite how this (full-fund) policy might be operated now that the public sector has moved into increasing surplus[16] remains to be seen. In the event, the abandonment of overfunding did have the predicted effect of producing a jump in the growth rate of sterling M3 bringing it broadly into line with that of bank lending, at about 20 per cent per annum in 1987–8, compared with a growth of nominal incomes of about half as much.

Whereas the Government, which had claimed in 1980–1 that sterling M3 was the absolute centrepiece of policy, treated such expansion with apparent unconcern, the Bank remained concerned that, although the messages from the broad monetary aggregates might be hard to decipher, it was wrong to ignore them entirely.

5.4 MONETARY TRANSMISSION MECHANISMS

5.4.1 The Effect of Interest Rates on the Domestic Economy

The unification of financial markets, especially following the abolition of exchange controls, has lessened the efficacy of direct credit controls or other constraints on intermediation imposed on one segment of that (international) market. In any case the conventional wisdom is that such direct controls on financial markets are generally undesirable. This has left the authorities' discretionary determination of (short-term) market interest rates as the chief, virtually the sole, instrument of monetary policy[17] (Leigh-Pemberton, 1987).

The main effect of interest rate adjustment probably works through its influence on external capital flows and exchange rates, but space limitation precludes us from considering that here. Instead, in the remainder of this subsection, we shall review briefly how interest rate adjustments are perceived to affect domestic nominal expenditures and incomes. However, this topic is, perhaps, more a part of general applied macroeconomics; although it is a subject of major concern to monetary policy-makers, it is one where they turn mainly to specialist economic advisors for advice and assistance, rather than a subject where they feel responsible for reaching and defending a conclusion themselves. Accordingly we shall refer briefly to some general surveys, rather than more specialized papers.

A suitable starting point is the OECD paper by Chouraqui et al. (1988) on 'The effects of monetary policy on the real sector: an overview of empirical evidence for selected OECD economies', which explores the evidence from some 30 large-scale national and international macromodels. For a recent study concentrating on the effect of changes in interest rates in UK macroeconomic models see Easton (1985), and for a review of such effects in the USA see Akhtar and Harris (1987).

Chouraqui et al. begin by noting that an initial decline in interest rates, associated with a rise in the monetary base, can lead to such flexible adjustments in inflationary expectations and in prices that any systematic, or anticipated, monetary policy becomes impotent to affect real output, following the arguments of the New Classical economics, of which Sargent and Wallace (1975) represents the prototype. They then examine the evidence whether rational expectation structurally neutral (RESN) conditions appeared to hold in practice. One of the tests of this, following Barro (1977, 1978), is whether real output reacts to unanticipated monetary changes but not to anticipated monetary movements. They survey some 70 empirical studies of this question, covering seven countries (Chouraqui et al., 1988, table 13), and note that 'the number of studies claiming refutation of the proposition that only unanticipated monetary policy matters is running ahead of corroborative ones' (p. 27). For this, and other reasons, e.g. 'the apparent dependence of the current price level on its own past values' (p. 24) and that 'Evidence from survey data on expectations does not generally support the idea that expectations are formed rationally' (referring to Holden et al. (1985) for a comprehensive survey of studies of data on expectations surveys), they reach the conclusion that 'On the whole, the evidence on models which combined market clearing and rational expectations is not favourable to their relevance in current circumstances. Market clearing and rational expectations have little or no empirical foundation, the weight of evidence providing more support for a macroeconomic framework in which prices adjust slowly.'

Be that as it may – and it is not a function of this survey to attempt further adjudication – the major macroeconomic models, to which policy-makers turn for a quantification of the effect of interest rates changes, do incorporate a sluggish adjustment of prices and of future inflationary expectations. Although this does imply that administered interest rate adjustments, whether anticipated or not, would not be impotent, the effect of such changes on the various categories of (domestic) expenditures, e.g. business fixed investment, residential investment, consumption and inventory investment, varies quite widely not only between countries but even more markedly between models. Even so, Chouraqui et al. comment that 'One thing that does emerge from recent evidence compared with studies of earlier vintage is the finding of significant interest rate effects' (p. 13) (on domestic expenditures) perhaps because the recent high level of real interest rates has made agents more conscious of interest costs and because the more competitive and more nearly perfect financial markets spread their effects more widely. Even so, 'The diversity in the size of the reported multipliers and the widely varying structure of the models, the parameters of which are often subject to large revisions, means that the short-run response of real sector variables to changes in financial conditions cannot be known with any degree of confidence' (p. 22).

Even though both the strength of the effect of interest rates on domestic expenditures and the time lags involved are uncertain, at least the direction of effect appears unambiguous.

In the short run, however, the relationship between increases in interest rates and in price levels can be ambiguous, in part because interest rates represent a business cost – and pricing may be of the cost plus form – and in part because of the curious manner in which mortgage interest rates enter into the RPI in the UK. As already noted, however, the main impact of changes in interest rates is perceived to work through its effect on international capital flows and hence on the exchange rate. 'More immediate, and more powerful, channels through which interest rate changes influence demand work through induced movements in real competitiveness' (Miles and Wilcox, 1988). If this latter channel is allowed to work freely, any short-term adverse domestic effect on inflation of higher interest rates should be more than countered by an appreciation in the exchange rate.

5.4.2 Other Possible Channels

An unhelpful dichotomy between the theory and the reality of central bank operations was introduced into macroeconomics by the IS–LM codification of Keynes' *The General Theory* (1936), and has been continued by M. Friedman (1970, 1971) among others. When either of these two great economists would discuss practical policy matters concerning the level of short-term interest rates, they had no doubt that these were normally determined by the authorities, and could be changed by them, and were not freely determined in the market (putting the US experience in 1979–82 on one side). Whether or not this was the most appropriate operating procedure is another question; this was how it has worked in practice. However, when they came to their more theoretical papers, they often reverted to the assumption that the central bank sets the nominal money stock, or alternatively fixes the level of the monetary base. If then the goods and labour markets were somewhat sticky, so that the general level of prices did not adjust immediately, the demand and supply of money would be equilibrated in the short run in this theoretical framework by market-led adjustments in nominal interest rates. With equilibrium between the demand and supply of money thus being restored by adjustments in nominal interest rates, subsequent effects on nominal incomes/expenditures would seem to have to work entirely via such interest rate movements (see for example Crow (1988) for a restatement of this 'mainline' view) unless we make some auxiliary assumption, e.g. using the buffer stock/disequilibrium money type approach, that the equilibrium achieved in the money market was less than perfect.

All that remains a subject of continuing debate. If, however, we stick to the real world in which the authorities set the level of nominal interest rates, then the question of the additional effects of monetary and credit shocks on the economy, beyond that working via adjustments in interest rates, is much easier to comprehend. With a given discretionarily determined level of short-term interest rates, there can, of course, be all kinds of shocks to the credit and money markets which will cause the aggregates to change without there being any (necessary) change in short-term money market rates. How much do these latter changes in the aggregates matter? Moreover, in section 5.3. we noted how 'overfunding' could divorce bank credit shocks from monetary changes. Although money and (bank) credit usually vary together, they need not do so, and as Brunner and Meltzer (1972a, b, 1988) have continued to argue they are not the same thing. On this same subject see also Greenfield and Yeager (1986) and Kohl (1988). Which matters most?

In a world characterized by perfect markets, expenditure decisions would be determined by the budget constraint in the form of the present value of human and non-human wealth, the current and expected future levels of prices etc. It is not clear why monetary, or various credit, aggregates should play a strategic role. Thus Gertler (1988) comments that 'Most of macro-economic theory presumes that the financial system functions smoothly – and smoothly enough to justify abstracting from financial considerations ... The currently popular real business cycle paradigm proceeds under the working hypothesis that financial structure is irrelevant.'[18] Indeed, in a world of perfect markets, which presumably implies costless information, complete trust etc., it is dubious whether there is any need for money in its role as a means of exchange (without the introduction of *ad hoc* imperfections, such as a cash in advance constraint, which would be inconsistent with the conditions otherwise allowing perfect markets to exist), although there would still be a need for intertemporal stores of value. The literature on all this is, of course, vast; for a formal treatment see Gale (1982, 1983).

Accordingly, a key function of credit/monetary expansion, given the level of interest rates, may be in allowing certain market imperfections to be overcome owing to imperfect or asymmetric information (Kohn and Tsiang, 1988). There has been considerable theoretical interest in the question of whether credit rationing may exist when the financial system is in 'equilibrium' (e.g. Jaffee and Russell 1976; Stiglitz and Weiss, 1981; Gale and Helwig, 1985) as well as when such rationing occurs as a result of slow or restricted adjustment of interest rates (McKinnon, 1973; Shaw, 1973; Fry, 1988). Such studies, to which Stiglitz has been a major contributor, have extended to both theoretical and empirical analyses of how changes in credit conditions can affect the economy (Bernanke and Gertler, 1987; Blinder, 1987; Gertler, 1988; Gertler and Hubbard, 1988; Greenwald and Stiglitz, 1988; Woodford, 1988 etc.).

A practical current example of this in the UK has been the move of banks into mortgage lending,[19] the greater competition between banks and building societies in (mortgage-backed) personal lending and the surge in such lending following the end of the building societies' cartel (Meen, 1985). The effect of this can be seen in table 5.2. This has raised the question of what effect this supply-side shock has had on the real economy, e.g. consumer demand, house construction, housing prices etc. (Drayson, 1985).

During the early 1980s, the effect of this credit surge on the broad money supply was offset by the policy of overfunding. As noted in section 5.1, this involved offering terms on gilt-edged securities that would shift wealth holders out of bank deposits into gilts. Whereas it is comparatively easy to see how certain market imperfections may be assuaged by relaxations in credit market conditions (or vice versa following the imposition of credit controls), it is somewhat harder to see why expenditures should respond directly to portfolio shifts between monetary deposits and other assets, except in response to the shift in wealth and in the pattern of interest rates thereby generated. Now that proviso is, of course, of vital importance. Friedman has argued that the linkage between (some definition of) the monetary aggregates and nominal incomes and expenditures has been sufficiently stable and strong that no significant extra explanatory power would be achieved by considering the nature of the credit counterparts to that expansion. For example, in the context of the policy-oriented discussion of overfunding, it is arguable that, had that been continued after 1985, with sterling M3 correspondingly lower, there would have been less money directed towards UK housing, property and equity markets, so that non-human wealth, expenditure and nominal incomes would all now have been lower.

All this is now a subject of both theoretical and empirical debate. In his survey paper, Gertler (1988) notes that earlier 'the theory of liquidity preference and the time series work of Friedman and Schwartz (1963 and 1982) provided motivation for the preoccupation with money'. Moreover 'the widespread use of vector autoregressions to analyse time series shifted the focus back to money as the key financial aggregate' (e.g. Sims, 1972). But now, Gertler claims, there is a revival of interest in studying the financial, and especially the credit-related, aspects of the business cycle, at both the theoretical level (e.g. Williamson, 1987) and the empirical level (e.g. Bernanke, 1983; Hamilton, 1987; Gertler and Hubbard, 1988), but for doubts about the empirical relevance of the credit view see King (1986).

Although B. Friedman (1980a, 1982) had reported that a credit aggregate could be found in the USA which gave just as stable a relationship with

Table 5.2

	1976	1977	1978	1979	1980	1981	1982	1983	1984	1985	1986	1987
Increase in lending (%)	15.9	17.7	19.6	20.1	17.8	21.1	24.1	21.1	18.6	17.8	18.7	18.2
to persons (£billion)	4.1	5.3	6.9	8.5	9.0	12.6	18.0	19.5	20.7	24.8	29.4	33.8
Of which												
Building societies (£billion)	3.6	4.1	5.1	5.3	5.7	6.3	8.1	10.9	14.5	14.6	19.4	15.3
Banks (£billion)	0.5	1.2	1.8	3.2	3.3	6.3	9.8	8.6	6.2	10.2	10.0	18.5
Of which latter,												
mortgage-based (£billion)	0.1	0.1	0.3	0.6	0.5	2.3	5.1	3.5	2.0	4.2	4.7	10.0

nominal incomes as did M1 for example, the weight of argument in the 1970s persuaded most central bankers that it was indeed the (most appropriate definition of the) money stock that should be the centre of policy, rather than some more pragmatic blend of concern with interest rates, monetary and credit expansion, asset prices etc. Now, of course, that earlier (always somewhat fragile) confidence in the stability (predictability) of the velocity of money has gone, and central bankers' traditional concern with credit (see M. Friedman, 1982), rather than or as well as money, has resurfaced, even though the stability of the credit aggregate relationship has fared no better econometrically (B. Friedman, 1988a).

But in this somewhat confused state (of economic argumentation), what exactly, besides the level of nominal (and real) interest rates does/should a policy-maker look at, and how does he arrive at a policy judgement?[20]

To conclude and summarize, the (pure Keynesian) route for assessing the effect of money upon the economy using the IS–LM paradigm usually has money market interest rates determined by the interaction of the demand for and the (central bank determined) supply of the (high powered) money base; then short-term interest rates affect longer-term rates, equity yields, etc., and hence, via Tobinesque q effects and standard interest elasticities, affect expenditures and thereby influence nominal expenditures. This approach ignores the effects of credit and monetary shocks, at given levels of interest rates, in relaxing certain market imperfections, as even erstwhile committed Keynesians now accept (e.g. Dow and Saville, 1988). *Per contra*, the monetarist approach wrapped up all the various channels of possible influence in its concentration on the direct (econometric) relationship between money and nominal incomes. The weakening in the predictability of such relationships has now made policy-makers reluctant to continue to base policy on any further revised and warmed-up econometric findings in this field.

Instead, policy-makers are tending to look directly at domestic indicators of nominal incomes and of inflation and to vary nominal interest rates in the light of these, while continuing to cast a rather anxious glance at both credit and monetary aggregates, and also at asset prices (e.g. mainly equities and houses). This is sometimes partially formalized into a 'check-list' approach (R. A. Johnston, 1985; Reserve Bank of New Zealand, 1987) whereby central bankers record the list of indicators which they take into account. Supporters would describe it as sensible pragmatism; detractors would describe it as a reversion to a muddled discretion which, once again, allows the authorities more rope than is good for them or us.

5.5 CONCLUSIONS

During the course of the 1970s, economists and policy-makers came to view the economic system as based on a number of long-run equilibrium conditions. Among the most important were (a) the natural (equilibrium) level of output and unemployment, (b) the long-run relationship between the money stock and nominal incomes, a predictable long-term velocity, and (c) the long-run relationship between prices of tradeable goods among pairs of countries and their bilateral exchange rate, i.e. purchasing power parity (PPP).

A whole variety of shocks on the demand or supply side, induced by natural causes or by human agents, could divert the economy temporarily from its long-term equilibrium but market forces would tend to restore it to that equilibrium. The speed with which market forces would operate to restore the economy to its full equilibrium would depend on the extent of market imperfection and consequential price sluggishness, and there was, and remains, considerable debate on how extensive such imperfections might be. Nevertheless, given that agents could anchor their longer-term expectations on the restoration of such fundamental equilibria (a transversality condition) and dependent on the assumed extent of shorter-run price stickiness, it should, in principle, be possible to trace out the (rationally expected) intervening future path for the economy in response to current shocks. In this context it was hard to see any useful role for the authorities apart from setting a medium-term target (rule) for monetary growth, so as to anchor long-term expectations of price inflation, and also acting to eliminate current market imperfections (supply-side economics).

The main problem with this view of the economic system is that experience in the 1980s has demonstrated that there appears to be little tendency for the economy to revert with any perceptible speed to a (unique) equilibrium. Unemployment in the UK rose sharply at the start of the 1980s, and remained high – only falling markedly in 1987–8 – without apparently causing much sustained downward pressure on wages and prices. More important for our own story, previously predictable long-term relationships between the money stock and nominal incomes appeared to fall apart, while exchange rates proved capable of diverging from PPP both substantially and for long periods.

Under these circumstances the anchor given to forward expectations by such long-term equilibrium conditions or by the (in the event temporary) adoption of monetary targets by the authorities in the early 1980s was not firmly set. During this last decade speculation based on an expectation of a (rapid) reversion of velocity or exchange rates to their prior norm would not have been generally financially rewarding, and indeed speculation based on such longer-term fundamentals was rarely visible.

If the natural forces driving the economy back to a (unique) equilibrium are, in practice, much weaker than earlier expected – or even at times non-existent or offset by other market considerations – then there is much more room for intervention and much more need for discretion by the authorities, since they cannot just sit back and leave affairs to rational agents operating in efficient markets.

In the main, policy-makers, even some of those most captivated by the earlier vision such as Lawson, have accepted that practical lesson. We do not live in a world in which we can confidently rely on market forces to restore the economy to a stable (unique) equilibrium as long as the authorities themselves do not rock the boat. In this context, the authorities have reverted to discretionary intervention. Their current main problem is how to operate so as to balance the (occasionally conflicting) objectives of external and internal price stability, but that is another continuing story.

Many macrotheorists are apparently loathe to accept any dilution of their earlier image of the economy, partly because it raises questions about the adequacy of their models and the meaning of such accepted concepts as rational expectations. As noted in the introduction, this has led to an increasing divide between state of the art macrotheory and practical policy analysis. On this my own sympathies are firmly on the side of the policy-maker, who has to cope with reality and cannot retreat to the more tractable and elegant models of the theorist.

Notes

1 For a reconsideration of rules for targetry in these new circumstances, and an advocacy of their reformulation in terms of a feedback rule from nominal incomes (or some combination of price and output behaviour) to base money, see Hall (1986) and McCallum (1988). For a continuing critique of such rules, see Lamfalussy (1981), Tobin (1983) and Summers (1988).

2 The continental parochialism of US economists is remarkable. Purely as an example, without wishing to impugn an otherwise admirable paper, B. Friedman's (1988b) bibliography of approximately 100 citations has no reference to experience outside North America, and cites, by my count, only a couple of economists not primarily resident there.

3 The association between monetary and fiscal policy can be most easily seen via the credit counterparts approach. Assume that, with flexible exchange rates, the expected change in banks' net foreign assets is zero, and also ignore any possible change in banks' non-deposit liabilities. Then, the following accounting identities will hold: $\Delta D = \Delta A$, $\Delta A = \Delta BLPub + \Delta BLPS$ and $\Delta BLPub = PSBR - DS, NBPS$, where D is sterling M3, A is the banks' holdings of domestic assets, BLPub is the bank lending to the public sector,

BLPS is the bank lending to the private sector and DS, NBPS are (net) public sector debt sales to the non-bank private sector.

Since both BLPS and DS, NBPS are functions of interest rates and a vector of other assets, so that ΔBLPS $= F(i, X)$, then, given X, a desire to achieve both the target for ΔD and some preferred level of i constrains the size of the PSBR. 'Too high a PSBR requires either that the Government borrow heavily from the Banks – which adds directly to the money supply; or, failing this, that it borrows from individuals and institutions, but at ever-increasing rates of interest, which places an unacceptable squeeze on the private sector. From these two facts comes one conclusion, and one conclusion only – that the PSBR is too large' (Lawson, 1980); see also *FSBR*, 1980-1, p. 16, para 4. For a more sceptical view of the strength of the behavioural relationships involved, see Treasury and Civil Service Committee (1981), and Dow and Saville (1988). Indeed, despite these accounting identities, the strength of the relationship between public sector deficits and interest rates, and between public sector deficits and the growth of monetary aggregates, has usually been found to be weak when the data are tested (see Dwyer, 1985). This finding caused this aspect of the MTFS to be criticized by both British Keynesians, e.g. Kaldor (1982), and US monetarists, e.g. M. Friedman in his evidence to the above Committee.

4   It proved remarkably difficult to sort out the proportional responsibility of these different factors, and none of the attempts appears really convincing; see Niehans (1981) and Bean (1987) among others.

5   The Bank of England's minimum lending rate (MLR) was suspended in August 1981; thereafter interest rates in the UK refer to the London clearing bank base rates, unless otherwise specified.

6   Papers arguing that the reduction in inflation in the 1980s has been largely due to a fall in commodity prices, and not to the (direct) effect of monetary restriction (Beckerman, 1985), can be misleading in so far as such declines are themselves the indirect consequence of monetary tightness (see Lawson, 1986).

7   There was some subsequent reinterpretation of the degree to which the government had tied itself to the single target of sterling M3, (Lawson, 1982), together with the beguiling concept (later formalized in some of the academic literature on policy games (e.g. Driffill, 1988; Persson, 1988)) that the more committed the authorities appeared to be to monetarism in theory, the more discretionary they could be in practice. Thus, 'If, on the other hand, the discretion is being exercised by those whose commitment to the policy, and to the overriding need to maintain financial discipline is beyond doubt, then there is no cause for such misgivings' Lawson, 1982, p. 5).

8   In principle, however, some of these countries, e.g. the UK and France, retained domestic monetary targets as their formally declared intermediate objective.

9   There was no suggestion in the latter period, however, that the authorities should also shift their control mechanism and adopt MBC. Indeed, the latter option was publicly dismissed (Lawson, 1983).

10   Because sterling remained generally strong during this period, the associated (unpublished) lower limit could not be so easily ascertained.

11   For a recent example see Rasche (1988) who states that: 'The research cited here suggests strongly that a very simple demand function specification can account

for a large portion of the observed variation in all of these [monetary] aggregates, and that with only two exceptions this function appears very robust over the entire post accord period. The two exceptions are the monetary base and M1 for which there is a significant change in the constant term of the first difference specification around the beginning of 1981' (p. 58). See also Hamburger (1983) and Baba et al. (1987).

12 A dramatic switch occurred in New Zealand in 1984–5 (see Reserve Bank of New Zealand, 1986; Spencer and Carey, 1988).

13 For an analysis of some of the consequences of greater interest rates volatility, see B. Friedman (1982) for its effects in US capital markets, Enzler and Johnson (1981) for its effects on output and prices, Black (1982) for its effects on exchange rates and Walsh (1984) for its effects on the demand for money.

14 In fact the yield curve was downward sloping for much of the period, and the authorities may well have made a commercial profit from the exercise.

15 By this time the authorities' effective money market dealing was almost entirely in commercial bills. Treasury bills could have been completely phased out. The only reason for continuing with a residual treasury bill market and weekly tender was the educational function of keeping market-makers familiar with an instrument which might some day regain an important role.

16 In the introduction, we described how the adoption of the MTFS led the fiscal decision on the size of the PSBR to be subordinated to the requirements of monetary policy. With the progressive abandonment of monetary targetry, the influence of such monetary considerations on the fiscal decision weakened. Indeed, exactly what balance of Keynesian, monetarist, long-term structural or yet other concepts and ideas either does or should now influence the choice of the size of public sector deficit/surplus in the UK remains unclear, but to follow that murky issue further would take us outside the scope of this chapter.

17 Some economists worry over the question of whether, and how, the central bank can set interest rates (e.g. Dow and Saville, 1988). In practice, on a day-to-day basis the central bank's monopoly control over the high powered monetary base enables it to dictate the price – the short-term interest rate – at which it will provide the banking system with the cash that it requires (Bank of England, 1984b, ch. 6). In the medium and longer term, however, the central bank's ability to determine the nominal, and even more the real, interest rate is constrained by a wide range of both political and economic considerations.

18 In this same paper, Gertler (1988, p. 10) commented that 'the methodological revolution in macroeconomics in the 1970s also helped shift attention away from financial factors, in a less direct but probably more substantial way. The resulting emphasis on developing macroeconomic models explicitly from individual optimization posed an obstacle. At the time, the only available and tractable model suitable for pursuing this methodological approach – the stochastic competitive equilibrium growth model, developed by Brock and Mirman (1972) and others – was essentially an Arrow–Debreu model, and thus had the property that financial structure was irrelevant'.

19 For practical examples concerning the USA see Wojnilower (1980).

20 A good example of such uncertainty can be found in the policy-makers' reaction to the crash of 19 October 1987. It was argued that the fall in asset prices might

have a deflationary effect for various reasons: first, it might cause insolvencies and a contagious collapse in the financial system; second, and related to the first, it might cause a weakening in 'confidence' and hence in both business and personal expenditure; third, through the wealth effect, it would cause some reduction in consumers' expenditures. With the benefit of hindsight the (rather slight) effect of the last factor appears to have been well captured by the models. But was the subsequent absence of the first two effects due to a (correctly) expansionary monetary policy then adopted by the authorities, or were the fears always exaggerated?

References

Akhtar, M. A. (1983) Financial innovations and their implications for monetary policy: an international perspective. *Bank for International Settlements Economic Papers* 9.

—— and Harris, E. S. (1987) Monetary policy influence on the economy – an empirical analysis. *Federal Reserve Bank of New York Quarterly Review* Winter, 19–32.

Andersen, P. S. (1985) The stability of money demand functions: an alternative approach. *Bank for International Settlements Economic Papers* 14.

Artis, M. J. and Lewis, M. K. (1976) The demand for money in the United Kingdom, 1963–73. *Manchester School* 44 (2), 147–81.

—— and —— (1984) How unstable is the demand for money in the United Kingdom? *Economica* 51, 473–6.

Artus, P. (1987) La politique monetaire en France dans un contexte d'innovation financière de dereglementation et de plus grande mobilité des capitaux. Working Paper 87-36/2, Banque de France, Direction Générale des Etudes, March.

Atkinson, P. and Chouraqui, J.-C. (1987) Implications of financial innovation and exchange rate variability on the conduct of monetary policy. *Journal of Foreign Exchange and International Finance* 1 (1), 64–84.

Avery, R. B., Elliehausen, G. E., Kennickell, A. B. and Spindt, P. A. (1987) Changes in the use of transaction accounts and cash from 1984 to 1986. *Federal Reserve Bulletin* 73, 179–96.

Axilrod, S. H. and Lindsey, D. E. (1981) Federal Reserve System implementation of monetary policy: analytical foundations of the new approach. *American Economic Review* 71 (2), 246–52.

Baba, Y., Hendry, D. F. and Starr, R. M. (1987) US money demand, 1960-1984. Discussion Paper 27, Nuffield College, Oxford.

Bank of England (1982a) The supplementary special deposits scheme. *Bank of England Quarterly Bulletin* 22 (1), 74–85.

—— (1982b) Composition of monetary and liquidity aggregates, and associated statistics. *Bank of England Quarterly Bulletin* 22 (4), 530–7.

—— (1984a) Funding the public sector borrowing requirement: 1952-83. *Bank of England Quarterly Bulletin* 24 (4), 482–92.

—— (1982b) *The Development and Operation of Monetary Policy, 1960-1983*. Oxford: Clarendon Press.

—— (1987) Measures of broad money. *Bank of England Quarterly Bulletin* 27 (2), 212–19.

Bank for International Settlements (1986) *Recent Innovations in International Banking* (report of a committee of central bankers chaired by Samuel Cross). Basle: Bank of International Settlements.

Barnett, W. A. (1982) The optimal level of monetary aggregation. *Journal of Money, Credit and Banking* 14 (4), 687–710.

——, Offenbacher, E. K. and Spindt, P. A. (1984) The new Divisia monetary aggregates. *Journal of Political Economy* 92(6), 1049–85.

Barro, R. J. (1977) Unanticipated money growth and unemployment in the United States. *American Economic Review* 67(2), 101–15.

—— (1978) Unanticipated money output and the price level in the United States. *Journal of Political Economy* 86 (4), 549–80.

—— (1986) Recent developments in the theory of rules versus discretion. *Economic Journal (Supplement)* 96, 23–37.

—— and Gordon, D. B. (1983a) Rules, discretion and reputation in a model of monetary policy. *Journal of Monetary Economics* 12 (1), 101–21.

—— and —— (1983b) A positive theory of monetary policy in a natural rate model. *Journal of Political Economy* 91 (4), 589–610.

Bean, C. (1987) The impact of North Sea oil. In R. Dornbusch and R. Layard (eds), *The Performance of the British Economy*. Oxford: Clarendon Press, ch. 3.

Beckerman, W. (1985) How the battle against inflation was really won. *Lloyds Bank Review* January, 1–12.

Bernanke, B. S. (1983) Non-monetary effects of the financial crisis in the propagation of the Great Depression. *American Economic Review* 73, 257–76.

—— and Gertler, M. (1987) Banking and macroeconomic equilibrium. In W. A. Barnett and K. Singleton (eds), *New Approaches to Monetary Economics*. New York: Cambridge University Press.

Black, S. W. (1982) The effects of alternative monetary control procedures on exchange rates and output. *Journal of Money, Credit and Banking* 14 (4), 746–60.

Blinder, A. S. (1987) Credit rationing and effective supply failures. *Economic Journal* 97 (386), 327–52.

Blundell-Wignall, A. and Thorp, S. (1987) Money demand, own interest rates and deregulation. Research Discussion Paper 8703, Reserve Bank of Australia, May.

Board of Governors of the Federal Reserve System (1988) Monetary policy report to Congress pursuant to the full employment and balanced growth [Humphrey-Hawkins] Act of 1978. Federal Reserve Board Press Release, 13 July.

Bouey, G. K. (1982) Recovering from inflation. Notes for Remarks to the Canadian Club, Toronto, Ontario, 29 November. Reprinted in *Bank of Canada Review* December.

Brayton, F., Farr, T. and Porter, R. (1983) Alternative money demand specifications and recent growth in M1. Mimeo, Board of Governors of the Federal Reserve System, May.

Brittan, S. (1980) A coherent budget at last. *Financial Times*, 27 March, p. 24.

Broaddus, A. and Goodfriend, M. (1984) Base drift and the longer run growth of M1: experience from a decade of monetary targeting. *Federal Reserve Bank of Richmond Economic Review* 70 (6), 3–14.

Brock, W. A. and Mirman, L. J. (1972) Optimal economic growth and uncertainty: the discounted cases. *Journal of Economic Theory* 4, 479–513.

Brunner, K. and Meltzer, A. H. (1972a) Money, debt, and economic activity. *Journal of Political Economy*. 80 (5), 951–77.

—— and —— (1972b) A monetarist framework for aggregative analysis. *Proceedings of the First Konstanzer Seminar, Kredit und Kapital*, Beideft I. Berlin: Duncker and Humblot.

—— and —— (1983) Strategies and tactics for monetary control. In K. Brunner and A. H. Meltzer (eds), *Money, Monetary Policy, and Financial Institutions*. Amsterdam: North Holland, Carnegie–Rochester Conference Series on Public Policy, vol. 19.

—— and —— (1988) Money and credit in the monetary transmission process. *American Economic Review* 78 (2), 446–51.

Bryant, R. C. (1982) Federal Reserve control of the money stock. *Journal of Money, Credit and Banking* 14 (4), 597–625.

Budd, A. and Holly, S. (1986) Does broad money matter? *London Business School Economic Outlook* 10 (9), 16–22.

Buiter, W. H. (1985) A guide to public sector debt and deficits. *Economic Policy* 1, 14–79

—— and Armstrong, C. A. (1978) A didactic note on the transaction demand for money and behavior towards risk. *Journal of Money, Credit and Banking* 10, 529–38.

—— and Miller, M. H. (1982) Real exchange-rate overshooting and the output cost of bringing down inflation. *European Economic Review* 18 (1–2), 85–123.

—— and —— (1983) Changing the rules – economic consequences of the Thatcher regime. *Brookings Papers on Economic Activity* 2, 305–79.

Burdekin, R. C. K. (1986) Cross-country evidence on the relationship between central banks and governments. Research Paper 8603, Federal Reserve Bank of Dallas.

Calvo, G. A. (1978) On the time consistency of optimal policy in a monetary economy. *Econometrica* 46, 1411–28.

Capie, F. H. and Wood, G. E. (1986) The long-run behaviour of velocity in the UK. Discussion Paper 23, Centre for Banking and International Finance, Centre for the Study of Monetary History, The City University, May.

Carr, J. and Darby, M. (1981) The role of money supply shocks in the short-run demand for money. *Journal of Monetary Economics* 8, 183–200.

de Cecco, M. (ed.) (1987) *Changing Money: Financial Innovation in Developed Countries*. Oxford: Basil Blackwell.

Chouraqui, J.-C., Driscoll, M. and Strauss-Kahn, M.-O. (1988) The effects of monetary policy on the real sector: an overview of empirical evidence for selected OECD economies. *OECD Working Papers 51*, April.

Chowdhury, G., Green, C. J. and Miles, D. K. (1986) An empirical model of company short-term financial decisions: evidence from company accounts data. *Bank of England Discussion Papers 26*.

Clinton, K. and Chouraqui, J.-C. (1987) Monetary policy in the second half of the 1980s: how much room for manoeuvre? Working Paper 39, OECD Department of Economics and Statistics, February.

Congdon, T. (1988) *The Debt Threat*. Oxford: Basil Blackwell.

Cosimano, T. F. and Jansen, D. W. (1987) The relation between money growth variability and the variability of money about target. *Economics Letters* 25, 355–8.

Cover, J. P. and Keeler, J. P. (1987) Estimating money demand in log-first-difference form. *Southern Economic Journal* 53 (3), 751–67.

Crow, J. W. (1988) The work of Canadian monetary policy. Paper presented at the Eric S. Hanson Lecture, University of Alberta, 18 January. Mimeo, Bank of Canada.

Cuthbertson, K. (1988a) The demand for M1: a forward-looking buffer stock model. *Oxford Economic Papers* 40, 110–81.

—— (1988b) The encompassing implications of feedforward versus feedback mechanisms: a comment. Mimeo, Newcastle University, July.

—— and Taylor, M. P. (1987) Buffer-stock money: an appraisal. In C. Goodhart, D. Currie and D. Llewellyn (eds), *The Operation and Regulation of Financial Markets*. London: Macmillan, ch. 5.

Darby, M. R., Poole, W., Lindsey, D. E., Friedman, M. and Bazdarich, M. J. (1987) Recent behavior of the velocity of money. *Contemporary Policy Issues* 5, 1–32.

Davidson, J. E. H. (1987) Disequilibrium money: some further results with a monetary model of the UK. In C. Goodhart, D. Currie and D. Llewellyn (eds), *The Operation and Regulation of Financial Markets* London: Macmillan, ch. 6.

—— and Ireland, J. (1987) Buffer stock models of the monetary sector. *National Institute Economic Review* 121, 67–71.

Deutsche Bundesbank (1987) *The Deutsche Bundesbank: Its Monetary Policy Instruments and Functions*. Deutsche Bundesbank Special Series, no. 7.

—— (1988) Methodological notes on the monetary target variable. 'M3'. *Monthly Report* 40 (3), 18–21.

Dewald, W. G. and Lai Tsung-Hui (1987) Factors affecting monetary growth: ARIMA forecasts of monetary base and multiplier. *Kredit und Kapital* 20 (3), 303–16.

Dotsey, M. (1988) The demand for currency in the United States. *Journal of Money, Credit and Banking* 20 (1), 22–40.

Dow, C. and Saville, I. (1988) *A Critique of Monetary Policy*. Oxford: Clarendon Press.

Drayson, S. J. (1985) The housing finance market: recent growth in perspective. *Bank of England Quarterly Bulletin* 25 (1), 80–91.

Driffill, J. (1988) Macroeconomic policy games with incomplete information. *European Economic Review* 32, 533–41.

Duck, N. W. and Sheppard, D. K. (1978) A proposal for the control of the UK money supply. *Economic Journal* 88 (349), 1–17.

Dutkowsky, D. H. and Foote, W. G. (1988) The demand for money: a rational expectations approach. *Review of Economics and Statistics* 70 (1), 83–92.

Dwyer, G. P., Jr (1985) Federal deficits, interest rates and monetary policy. *Journal of Money, Credit and Banking* 17 (4), 655–81.

Easton, W. W. (1985) The importance of interest rates in five macroeconomic models. *Bank of England Discussion Papers* 24, October.

Edison, H. J., Miller, M. H. and Williamson, J. (1987) On evaluating and extending the target zone proposal. *Journal of Policy Modelling* 9 (1), 199–224.

Engle, R. F. and Granger, C. W. J. (1987) Cointegration and error correction:

314 C. Goodhart

representation, estimation and testing. *Econometrica* 55 (2), 251–76.

Enzler, J.J. and Johnson, L. (1981) Cycles resulting from money stock targeting. In *New Monetary Control Procedures*. Washington, DC: Board of Governors of the Federal Reserve System, Federal Reserve Staff Study, vol. 1.

Evans, P. (1981) Why have interest rates been so volatile? *Federal Reserve Bank of San Francisco Economic Review* Summer, 7–20.

—— (1984) The effects on output of money growth and interest rate volatility in the United States. *Journal of Political Economy* 92 (2), 204–20.

Fay, S. (1987) *Portrait of an Old Lady*. Harmondsworth: Viking.

Federal Reserve Staff Studies (1981) *New Monetary Control Procedures*. Washington, DC: Board of Governors of the Federal Reserve System, 2 vols.

Feldstein, M. (1988) Rethinking international economic coordination. *Oxford Economic Papers* 40 (2) 205–19.

Fischer, S. (1988) Recent developments in macroeconomics. *Economic Journal* 98 (391), 294–339.

Foot, M.D.K.W. (1981) Monetary targets: their nature and record in the major economies. In B. Griffiths and G.E. Wood (eds), *Monetary Targets*. London: Macmillan.

——, Goodhart, C.A.E. and Hotson, A.C. (1979) Monetary base control. *Bank of England Quarterly Bulletin* 19 (2), 149–59.

Freedman, C. (1983) Financial innovation in Canada: causes and consequences. *American Economic Review* 73 (2), 101–6.

Frenkel, J.A. and Goldstein, M. (1988) Exchange rate volatility and misalignment: evaluating some proposals for reform. Paper presented at Federal Reserve Bank of Kansas City Conference on Financial Market Volatility, 17–19 August.

Frey, B. and Schneider, F. (1981) Central bank behavior: a positive empirical analysis. *Journal of Monetary Economics* 7, 291–316.

Friedman, B.M. (1980a) Debt and economic activity in the United States. In B.M. Friedman (ed.), *The Changing Roles of Debt and Equity in Financing US Capital Formation*. Chicago, IL: University of Chicago Press, pp. 91–110.

—— (1980b) Postwar changes in the American financial markets. In M. Feldstein (ed.), *The American Economy in Transition*. Chicago, IL: University of Chicago Press, pp. 9–78.

—— (1982) Federal Reserve policy, interest rate volatility, and the US capital raising mechanism. *Journal of Money, Credit and Banking* 14 (4), 721–45.

—— (1988a) Monetary policy without quantity variables. *American Economic Review Proceedings* 78 (2), 440–5.

—— (1988b) Targets and instruments of monetary policy. NBER Working Paper 2668, National Bureau of Economic Research, July.

Friedman, M. (1956) The quantity theory of money – a restatement. In M. Friedman (ed.), *Studies in the Quantity Theory of Money*. Chicago, IL: University of Chicago Press.

—— (1968) The role of monetary policy. *American Economic Review* 58, 1–17.

—— (1970) A theoretical framework for monetary analysis. *Journal of Political Economy* 78, 193–228.

—— (1971) A monetary theory of nominal income. *Journal of Political Economy* 79, 323–37.

—— (1982) Monetary theory: policy and practice. *Journal of Money, Credit and Banking* 14 (1), 98–118.

—— (1984a) Monetary policy of the 1980s. In J. Moore (ed.), *To Promote Prosperity*. Stanford, CA: Hoover Institute Press, ch. 2.

—— (1984b) Lessons from the 1979–82 monetary policy experiment. *American Economic Review* 74 (2), 397–400.

—— and Schwartz, A. J. (1963) *A Monetary History of the United States, 1867–1960*. Princeton, NJ: Princeton University Press for the National Bureau of Economic Research.

—— and —— (1982) *Monetary Trends in the United States and the United Kingdom*. Chicago, IL: University of Chicago Press.

Fry, M. J. (1988) *Money, Interest, and Banking in Economic Development*. Baltimore, MD: Johns Hopkins University Press.

FSBR (Financial Statement and Budget Report). London: HMSO, annually. Also known as the *Budget Redbook*.

Gale, D. (1982) *Money: In Equilibrium*. Cambridge: Cambridge University Press.

—— (1983) *Money: In Disequilibrium*. Cambridge: Cambridge University Press.

—— and Hellwig, M. (1985) Incentive-compatible debt contracts: the one-period problem. *Review of Economic Studies* 52 (4), 647–64.

Gertler, M. (1988) Financial structure and aggregate economic activity: an overview. *Journal of Money, Credit and Banking* 20 (3), 559–89.

—— and Hubbard, G. R. (1988) Financial factors and business fluctuations. Paper presented at Federal Reserve Bank of Kansas City Conference on Financial Volatility, Jackson Hole, WY, 17–19 August.

Goldfeld, S. M. (1973) The demand for money revisited. *Brookings Papers on Economic Activity* 3, 577–638.

—— (1976) The case of the missing money. *Brookings Papers on Economic Activity* 3, 683–730.

Goodfriend, M. (1983) Discount window borrowing, monetary policy, and the post-October 6, 1979, Federal Reserve operating procedure. *Journal of Monetary Economics* 12, 343–56.

—— (1985) Reinterpreting money demand regressions. In K. Brunner and A. H. Meltzer (eds),. *Understanding Monetary Regimes*. Amsterdam: North-Holland, Carnegie-Rochester Conference Series on Public Policy, vol. 22.

Goodhart, C. (1984) *Monetary Theory and Practice*. London: Macmillan.

—— and Crockett, A. D. (1970) The importance of money. *Bank of England Quarterly Bulletin* 10 (2), 159–98.

Gordon, R. J. (1984) The short run demand for money: a reconsideration. *Journal of Money, Credit and Banking* 16 (1), 403–34.

Granger, C. W. J. (1981) Some properties of time series data and their use in econometric model specification. *Journal of Econometrics* 16 (1).

Greenfield, R. L. and Yeager, B. (1986) Money and credit confused: an appraisal of economic doctrine and Federal Reserve procedure. *Southern Economic Journal* 53 (2), 364–73.

Greenspan, A. (1988) Statement before the US Senate Committee on Banking, Housing and Urban Affairs. Press Release, Federal Reserve Board, 13 July.

Greenwald, B. C. and Stiglitz, J. E. (1988) Imperfect information, finance constraints, and business fluctuations, and Money, imperfect information, and economic fluctuations. In M. Kohn and S-C. Tsiang (eds), *Finance Constraints, Expectations, and Macroeconomics*. Oxford: Clarendon Press, chs 7, 8.

Greider, W. (1988) *Secrets of the Temple*. New York: Simon & Schuster.

Grice, J., Bennett, A. and Cumming, N. (1981) The demand for sterling £M3 and other aggregates in the United Kingdom. Working Paper 20, HM Treasury, August.

—— and —— (1984) Wealth and the demand for £M3 in the United Kingdom, 1963–1978. *Manchester School* 52 (3), 239–71.

Grilli, V. (1988) Exchange rates and seignorage. Unpublished manuscript.

Hacche, G. (1974) The demand for money in the United Kingdom: experience since 1971. *Bank of England Quarterly Bulletin* 14 (3), 284–305.

Hafer, R. W. (1985) Comment on 'Money demand predictability'. *Journal of Money, Credit and Banking* 17 (4), 642–6.

—— and Hein, S. E. (1984) Financial innovations and the interest elasticity of money demand: some historical evidence. *Journal of Money, Credit and Banking* 16 (2), 247–52.

Hall, R. E. (1986) Optimal monetary institutions and policy. In C. D. Campbell and W. R. Dougan (eds), *Alternative Monetary Regimes*. Baltimore, MD: Johns Hopkins University Press.

Hall, S. and Henry, B. (1987) Wage models. *National Institute Economic Review* 119, February.

——, —— and Wilcox, J. (1988) The long run determination of the UK monetary aggregates. Mimeo, Bank of England, April.

Hamburger, M. J. (1983) Recent velocity behavior, the demand for money and monetary policy. Presented at a Conference on Monetary Targetting and Velocity, Federal Reserve Bank of San Francisco.

Hamilton, J. (1987) Monetary factors in the Great Depression. *Journal of Monetary Economics* 19(2), 145–70.

Havrilesky, T. (1988) Monetary policy signalling from the administration to the Federal Reserve. *Journal of Money, Credit and Banking* 20 (1), 83–101.

Healy, N. M. (1987) The UK 1979–82 'monetarist experiment': why economists will still disagree. *Banca Nazionale del Lavoro Quarterly Review* 163, 471–99.

Heller, H. R. (1988) Implementing monetary policy. *Federal Reserve Bulletin* 74 (7), 419–29.

Hendry, D. F. (1979) Predictive failure and econometric modelling in macro-economics: the transactions demand for money. In P. Ormerod (ed.), *Economic Modelling*. London: Heinemann, ch. 9.

—— (1985) Monetary economic myth and econometric reality. *Oxford Review of Economic Policy* 1(1), 72–84.

—— (1988) The encompassing implications of feedback versus feedforward mechanisms in econometrics. *Oxford Economic Papers* 40, 132–49.

—— and Ericsson, N. R. (1983) Assertion without empirical basis: an econometric appraisal of Monetary Trends in . . . the United Kingdom' by Milton Friedman and Anna Schwartz. Panel Paper 22, Bank of England Panel of Academic Consultants, October.

—— and Neale, A. J. (1988) Interpreting long-run equilibrium solutions in conventional macro models: a comment. *Economic Journal* 98 (392) 808–17.

Hester, D. D. (1981) Innovations and monetary control. *Brookings Papers on Economic Activity* 1, 141–89.

Hodgman, D. R. (1983) *The Political Economy of Monetary Policy: National and International Aspects.* Boston, MA: Federal Reserve Bank of Boston.

Hogan, L. I. (1986) A comparison of alternative exchange rate forecasting models. *Economic Record* 62 (177), 215–23.

Holden, K., Peel, D. and Thompson, J. (1985) *Expectations: Theory and Evidence.* London: Macmillan.

Holtham, G., Keating, G. and Spencer, P. (1988) Developments in the demand for liquid assets in Germany and the UK. Paper presented at the Conference on Monetary Aggregates and Financial Sector Behavior in Interdependent Economies, Board of Governors of the Federal Reserve System, Washington, DC, 26–7 May.

Hoskins, W. L. (1985) Foreign experiences with monetary targeting: a practitioner's perspective. *Contemporary Policy Issues* 3, 71–83.

Howe, Sir Geoffrey (1979) Budget Statement. *Hansard* 968, 241–4.

Ireland, J. and Wren-Lewis, S. (1988) Buffer stock money and the company sector. Paper presented at the Money Study Group Conference, Oxford, 23 September.

Isard, P. and Rojas-Suarez, L. (1986) Velocity of money and the practice of monetary targeting: experience, theory, and the policy debate. In *Staff Studies for the World Economic Outlook.* Washington, DC: International Monetary Fund, ch. 3, pp. 73–112.

Jaffee, D. M. and Russell, T. (1976) Imperfect information and credit rationing. *Quarterly Journal of Economics* 90 (4), 651–66.

Johannes, J. M. and Rasche, R. H. (1979) Predicting the money multiplier. *Journal of Monetary Economics* 5, 301–25.

—— (1981) Can the reserves approach to monetary control really work? *Journal of Money, Credit and Banking* 13, 298–313.

Johnston, R. A. (1985) Monetary policy – the changing environment. T. A. Coghlan Memorial Lecture, University of New South Wales, May; reprinted in *Reserve Bank of Australia Bulletin* June.

Johnston, R. B. (1983) *The Economics of the Euro-Market.* London: Macmillan.

—— (1984) The demand for non interest bearing money in the United Kingdom. *Working Paper* 28, HM Treasury.

—— (1985) The demand for liquidity aggregates by the UK personal sector. *Working Paper* 36, HM Treasury.

Jonson, P. D., Moses, E. R. and Wymer, C. R. (1977) The RBA76 model of the Australian economy. *Conference in Applied Economic Research.* Reserve Bank of Australia.

—— and Rankin, R. W. (1986) On some recent developments in monetary economics. *Economic Record* 62 (179) 257–67.

Judd, J. P. and Scadding, J. L. (1981) The search for a stable money demand function: a survey of the post-1973 literature. *Journal of Economic Literature* 20, 993–1023.

—— and —— (1982) Liability management, bank loans, and deposit 'market' disequilibrium. *San Francisco Federal Reserve Bank Review* Summer, 21–44.

—— and Motly, B. (1984) The 'Great Velocity Decline' of 1982–83: a comparative analysis of M1 and M2. *Federal Reserve Bank of San Francisco Economic Review* Summer, 56–74.

Kaldor, N. (1982) *The Scourge of Monetarism*. Oxford: Oxford University Press.

Keating, P. (1985) Statement by the Treasurer, The Hon. Paul Keating, M.P. *Reserve Bank of Australia Bulletin* February, 507–9.

Keynes, J.M. (1936) *The General Theory of Employment, Interest and Money*. London: Macmillan, reprinted in 1973 for the Royal Economic Society.

King, R.G. and Plosser, C.I. (1984) Money, credit and prices in a real business cycle. *American Economic Review* 74, 363–80.

King, S.R. (1986) Monetary transmission: through bank loans and bank liabilities? *Journal of Money, Credit and Banking* 18 (3), 290–303.

Kloten, N. (1987) The control of monetary aggregates in West Germany under changing conditions: the impact of innovations, the internationalisation of financial markets and the EMS. Paper presented at the Second Surrey Monetary Conference on Financial Innovation, Deregulation and the Control of Monetary Aggregates, University of Surrey, Guildford, 8–10 April.

Knoester, A. and van Sinderen, J. (1982) Economic policy and unemployment. In A. Maddison and B.S. Wilpstra (eds), *Unemployment: a Dutch Perspective*. The Hague: Ministry of Social Affairs.

Kohn, M. (1988) The finance constraint theory of money: a progress report. Working Paper, Dartmouth College, August.

—— and Tsiang Sho-Chieh (1988) *Financial Constraints, Expectations, and Macroeconomics*. Oxford: Clarendon Press.

Kopecky, K.J. (1984) Monetary control under reverse lag and contemporaneous reserve accounting: a comparison, and A reply, by R.D. Laurent. *Journal of Money, Credit and Banking* 16 (1), 81–92.

Kydland, F.E. and Prescott, E.C. (1977) Rules rather than discretion: the inconsistency of optimal plans. *Journal of Political Economy* 85, 473–91.

—— and —— (1982) Time to build and aggregate fluctuations. *Econometrica* 50, 1345–70.

Laidler, D.E.W. (1983a) *Monetarist Perspectives*. Oxford: Phillip Allan.

—— (1983b) The buffer stock notion in monetary economics. *Economic Journal (Supplement)* 94, 17–34.

—— (1985) Comment on 'Money Demand Predictability'. *Journal of Money, Credit and Banking* 17 (4), 647–53.

—— (1986) What do we really know about monetary policy? *Australian Economic Papers* 25 (46), 1–16.

—— (1988a) Taking money seriously. Report 9904, Department of Economics Research, University of Western Ontario.

—— (1988b) Monetarism, microfoundations and the theory of monetary policy. Working Paper 8807c, Centre for the Study of International Economic Relations; paper presented at a Conference on Monetary Policy, Free University of Berlin, 31 August–2 September.

—— and Bentley, B. (1983) A small macro-model of the post-war United States 1953–72. *Manchester School* 51, 317–40.

—— and Parkin, M.J. (1970) The demand for money in the United Kingdom, 1956-1967: some preliminary estimates. *Manchester School* 38 (3), 187-208.

Lamfalussy, A. (1981) 'Rules vs. discretion': an essay on monetary policy in an inflationary environment. Economic Paper 3, Bank of International Settlements.

Lane, T.D. (1984) Instrument instability and short-term monetary control. *Journal of Monetary Economics* 14, 209-24.

Lawson, N. (1980) Britain's policy and Britain's place in the international financial community. Speech at the *Financial Times* 1980 Euromarket Conference, 21 January. Press Release, HM Treasury.

—— (1981) Thatcherism in practice: a progress report. Speech to the Zurich Society of Economics, 14 January. Press Release, HM Treasury.

—— (1982) Financial discipline restored. Pamphlet, Conservative Political Centre, May.

—— (1983) Mansion House Speech. Press Release, HM Treasury, October.

—— (1985) Mansion House Speech. Press Release, HM Treasury, 17 October.

—— (1986) Monetary policy. Lombard Association Speech. Press Release, HM Treasury, 16 April.

—— (1988) The state of the market. Speech to the Institute of Economic Affairs. Press Release, HM Treasury, 21 July.

Layard, R. and Nickell, S. (1986) Unemployment in Britain. *Economica (Supplement)* 33, 121-70.

Leigh-Pemberton, R. (1986) Financial change and broad money. Loughborough University Banking Centre Lecture in Finance. *Bank of England Quarterly Bulletin* 26 (4), 499-507.

—— (1987) The instruments of monetary policy. Seventh Mais Lecture, City University Business School, 13 May. *Bank of England Quarterly Bulletin* 27 (3), 365-70.

Lindsey, D.E. (1986) The monetary regime of the Federal Reserve System. In C.D. Campbell and W.R. Dougan (eds), *Alternative Monetary Regimes* Baltimore, MD: Johns Hopkins University Press.

—— and Spindt, P. (1986) An evaluation of monetary indices. Special Studies Paper 195, Division of Research and Statistics, Federal Reserve Board.

——, Farr, H.T., Gillum, G.P., Kopecky, K.J. and Porter, R.D. (1984) Short-run monetary control. *Journal of Monetary Economics* 13, 87-111.

Long, J.B., Jr, and Plosser, C.I. (1983) Real business cycles. *Journal of Political Economy* 91, 39-69.

Lubrano, M., Pierse, R.G. and Richard, J.F. (1986) Stability of a UK money demand equation: a Bayesian approach to testing exogeneity. *Review of Economic Studies* 53, 603-34.

Lucas, R.E., Jr. (1972) Expectations and the neutrality of money. *Journal of Economic Theory* 4, 103-24.

—— (1976) Econometric policy evaluation: a critique. In K. Brunner and A.H. Meltzer (eds), *The Phillips Curve and Labor Markets*. Amsterdam: North Holland, Carnegie-Rochester Conference Series on Public Policy, vol. 1, pp. 19-46.

Mankiw, N.G. (1988) Recent developments in macroeconomics: a very quick refresher course. *Journal of Money, Credit and Banking* 20 (3), 436-49.

Mascaro, A. and Meltzer, A. H. (1983) Long-and short-term interest rates in a risky world. *Journal of Monetary Economics* 12, 485–518.

Mayer, T. (1987) The debate about monetarist policy recommendations. *Kredit und Kapital* 20, 281–302.

—— (1988) Monetarism in a world without 'money'. Working Paper 56, Research Program in Applied Macroeconomics and Macro Policy, University of California, Davis.

McCallum, B. T. (1985) On consequences and criticisms of monetary targeting. *Journal of Money, Credit and Banking* 17 (4), 570–97.

—— (1987) The case for rules in the conduct of monetary policy: a concrete example. *Weltwirtschaftliches Archiv* 123, 415–28.

—— (1988) Postwar developments in business cycle theory: a moderately classical perspective. *Journal of Money, Credit and Banking* 20 (3), 459–71.

McCulloch, J. H. (1986) Beyond the historical gold standard. In C. D. Campbell and W. R. Dougan (eds), *Alternative Monetary Regimes*. Baltimore, MD: Johns Hopkins University Press, pp. 73–81.

McKinnon, R. I. (1973) *Money and Capital in Economic Development*. Washington, DC: Brookings Institution.

—— (1984) *An International Standard for Monetary Stabilisation*. Washington, DC: Institute for International Economics.

—— and Ohno, K. (1988) Purchasing power parity as a monetary standard. Paper presented at a Conference on the Future of the International Monetary System, York University, Toronto.

Meen, G. P. (1985) An econometric analysis of mortgage rationing. Working Paper 79, UK Government Economic Service.

Milbourne, R. (1987) Re-examining the buffer-stock model of money. *Economic Journal (Conference Supplement)* 97, 130–42.

Miles, D. K. and Wilcox, J. B. (1988) The transmission mechanism. Mimeo, Bank of England.

Miller, M. H. and Sprenkle, C. M. (1980) The precautionary demand for narrow and broad money. *Economica* 47 (188), 407–22.

Miller, S. M. (1988) Long-run and short-run money demands: an application of co-integration and error-correction modelling. Mimeo, June.

Mills, T. C. (1983a) Composite monetary indicators for the United Kingdom: construction and empirical analyses. *Bank of England Discussion Paper, Technical Series*, 3.

—— (1983b) The information content of the UK monetary components and aggregates. *Bulletin of Economic Research* 35 (1), 25–46.

Moore, G. R., Porter, R. D. and Small, D. H. (1988) Modeling the disaggregated demands for M2 and M1 in the 1980's: the US experience. Paper presented to the Federal Reserve Board Conference on Monetary Aggregates and Financial Sector Behavior in Interdependent Economies, 26 May.

Moore, B. J. (1988a) The endogenous money supply. *Journal of Post Keynesian Economics* 10 (3), 372–85.

—— (1988b) *Horizontalists and Verticalists: The Macroeconomics of Credit Money*. Cambridge: Cambridge University Press.

—— (1989) A simple model of bank intermediation. *Journal of Post Keynesian Economics* 12 (1), 10–28.

—— and Threadgold, A. (1985) Corporate bank borrowing in the UK, 1965–1981 *Economica* 52, 65–78.

Moran, M. (1984) *The Politics of Banking*. London: Macmillan.

Muscatelli, V. A. (1988) Alternative models of buffer stock money: an empirical investigation. *Scottish Journal of Political Economy* 35 (1), 1–21.

Niehans, J. (1981) The appreciation of sterling – causes, effects, policies. Discussion Paper, Money Study Group, February.

Persson, T. (1988) Credibility of macroeconomic policy: an introduction and a broad survey. *European Economic Review* 32, 519–32.

Phelps, E. S. (1968) Money wage dynamics and labor market equilibrium. *Journal of Political Economy* 76, 678–711.

Poole, W. (1982) Federal Reserve operating procedures: a survey and evaluation of the historical record since October 1979. *Journal of Money, Credit and Banking* 14 (4), 576–96.

Porter, R. D. and Bayer A. (1983) A monetary perspective on underground economic activity in the United States. *Federal Reserve Bulletin* 70, 177–89.

Radecki, L. (1982) Short-run monetary control: an analysis of some possible dangers. *Federal Reserve Bank of New York Quarterly Review* 7, 1–10.

—— and Wenninger J. (1985) Recent instability in M1's velocity. *Federal Reserve Bank of New York Quarterly Review* 10 (3), 16–22.

Rasche, R. H. (1985) Interest rate volatility and alternative monetary control procedures. *Federal Reserve Bank of San Francisco Economic Review* Summer, 46–63.

—— (1988) Demand functions for US money and credit measures. Paper presented at the Conference on Monetary Aggregates and Financial Sector Behavior in Interdependent Economies, Federal Reserve Board, Washington, DC, 26–27 May.

—— and Meltzer, A. H. (1982) Is the Federal Reserve's monetary control policy misdirected? *Journal of Money, Credit and Banking* 14 (1), 119–47.

Reserve Bank of New Zealand (1986) *Financial Policy Reform*. Wellington, New Zealand: RBNZ.

—— (1987) Post-election briefing paper to the Minister of Finance. Special Paper, Reserve Bank of New Zealand, Wellington, August.

Richardson, G. (1978) Reflections on the conduct of monetary policy. *Bank of England Quarterly Bulletin* 18 (1), 51–8.

Roley, V. V. (1985) Money demand predictability. *Journal of Money, Credit and Banking* 17 (4), 615–41.

Sargent, T. J. and Wallace, N. (1975) 'Rational' expectations, the optimal monetary instrument, and the optimal money supply rule. *Journal of Political Economy* 83 (2), 241–54.

Shaw, E. S. (1973) *Financial Deepening in Economic Development*. New York: Oxford University Press.

Simpson, T. D. (1984) Changes in the financial system: implications for monetary policy. *Brookings Papers on Economic Activity* 1, 249–65.

Sims, C. A. (1972) Money, income and causality. *American Economic Review* 62 (4), 540–52.

Smith, D. (1978) The demand for alternative monies in the UK, 1924–77. *National Westminster Bank Quarterly Review* November, 35–49.

—— (1980) The monetary conundrum. *London Business School Economic Outlook* 5, (2), 1–2.

Solomon, A. M. (1981) Financial innovation and monetary policy. Paper presented before the Joint Luncheon of the American Economic and American Finance Associations, 28 December. Mimeo, Federal Reserve Bank of New York.

Spencer, G. and Carey, D. (1988) Financial policy reform: the New Zealand experience. Discussion Paper. G88/1, Reserve Bank of New Zealand, April.

Spindt, P. A. and Tarhan, V. (1987) The Federal Reserve's new operating procedures: a post mortem. *Journal of Monetary Economics* 19, 107–23.

Sternlight, P. D. and Axilrod, S. H. (1982) Is the Federal Reserve's monetary control policy misdirected? *Journal of Money, Credit and Banking* 14 (1), 119–47.

Stiglitz, J. E. and Weiss, A. (1981) Credit rationing in markets with imperfect information. *American Economic Review* 71 (3), 393–410.

Summers, L. H. (1988) Comment on B. T. McCallum (1988). *Journal of Money, Credit and Banking* 20 (3), 472–6.

Tamura, T. (1987) Monetary control in Japan. Paper presented at the Second Surrey Monetary Conference on Financial Innovation, Deregulation and the Control of Monetary Aggregates, University of Surrey, Guildford, 8–10 April.

Taylor, M. P. (1987) Financial innovation, inflation and the stability of the demand for broad money in the United Kingdom. *Bulletin of Economic Research* 39 (3), 225–33.

Thomas, J. J. (1988) The politics of the black economy. *Work, Employment and Society* 2, 169–90.

Tinsley, P. A., Farr, H. T., Fries, G., Garrett, B. and Von Zur Muehlen, P. (1982) Policy robustness: specification and simulation of a monthly money market model. *Journal of Money, Credit and Banking* 14 (4), 829–56.

Tobin, J. (1958) Liquidity preference as behavior towards risk. *Review of Economic Studies* 25, 65–86.

—— (1963) Commercial banks as creators of 'money'. In D. Carson (ed.), *Banking and Monetary Studies*. Homewood, IL: Richard Irwin, ch. 22.

—— (1983) Monetary policy: rules, targets and shocks. *Journal of Money, Credit and Banking* 15 (4), 506–18.

HM Treasury and Bank of England (1980) *Monetary Control*. London: HMSO, Cmnd 7858.

Treasury and Civil Service Committee (1981) *Monetary Policy: Report*. London: HMSO.

Ueda, K. (1988) Financial deregulation and the demand for money in Japan. Paper presented at the Conference on Monetary Aggregates and Financial Sector Behavior in Interdependent Economics, Federal Reserve Board, Washington, DC, 26–27 May.

Vaciago, G. (1985) Financial innovation and monetary policy: Italy *versus* the United States. *Banca Nazionale del Lavoro Quarterly Review* 155, 309–26.

Volcker, P. A. (1978) The role of monetary targets in an age of inflation. *Journal of Monetary Economics* 4, 329–39.

Wallich, H. C. (1984) Recent techniques of monetary policy. *Federal Reserve Bank of Kansas City Economic Review* May, 21–30.

Walsh, C. E. (1982) The Federal Reserve's operating procedures and interest rate fluctuations. *Federal Reserve Bank of Kansas City Economic Review* May, 8–18.

—— (1984) Interest rate volatility and monetary policy. *Journal of Money, Credit and Banking* 16 (2), 133–50.

Walters, A. (1986) *Britain's Economic Renaissance*. New York: Oxford University Press.

Wang, R. W. (1980) The FOMC in 1979: introducing reserve targetting. *Federal Reserve Bank of St Louis Review* 62 (3), 2–25.

Wenninger, J. (1986) Responsiveness of interest rate spreads and deposit flows to changes in market rates. *Federal Reserve Bank of New York Quarterly Review* Autumn, 1–10.

—— (1988) Money demand – some long-run properties. *Federal Reserve Bank of New York Quarterly Review* Spring, 23–40.

—— and Radecki, L. J. (1986) Financial transactions and the demand for M1. *Federal Reserve Bank of New York Quarterly Review* Summer, 24–9.

White, L. H. (1984) *Free Banking in Britain*. New York: Cambridge University Press.

White, W. R. (1976) The demand for money in Canada and the control of monetary aggregates. Mimeo, Bank of Canada.

Williamson, J. (1983) *The Exchange Rate System*. Washington, DC: Institute for International Economics (revised).

Williamson, S. D. (1987) Financial intermediation, business failures, and real business cycles. *Journal of Political Economy* 95 (6), 1196–216.

Wojnilower, A. M. (1980) The central role of credit crunches in recent financial history. *Brookings Papers on Economic Activity* 2, 277–339.

Woodford, M. (1988) Expectations, finance and aggregate instability. In M. Kohn and Tsiang Sho-Chieh (eds), *Finance Constraints, Expectations, and Macroeconomics*. Oxford: Clarendon Press, ch. 12, pp. 230–61.

Wooley, J. (1984) *Monetary Politics: The Federal Reserve and the Politics of Monetary Policy*. New York: Cambridge University Press.

6 Modelling the Monetary Sector

Kent Matthews

6.1 INTRODUCTION

In this chapter we are concerned with surveying the models of the UK monetary sector. A considerable amount of research has gone into this area. In the main, this has been the province of the major macroeconomic model builders and in this survey we shall concentrate on the monetary sectors contained in their respective models. However, the modelling of the monetary sector of the UK has not been the exclusive domain of the major macromodel builders. The late 1970s saw the development of 'small monetary models' as a means of modelling the effects of monetary policy, and the modelling of subsectors of the monetary sector such as the banking sector has always been the subject of continuing interest in academic circles. Some of these developments will be surveyed in this chapter but to examine each in detail would be to burden unnecessarily both the reader and the writer of this chapter. The best way of studying models of the monetary sector is to examine their assumed interaction with the rest of the economy, i.e. the transmission mechanism. An examination of a monetary model in isolation from the real sector is of interest only if it adds to our understanding of economic behaviour within the sector, but again this will be of interest only if it has implications for the rest of the economy. The major macroeconomic models have the advantage of containing relatively sophisticated monetary sectors which interact with the rest of the model, allowing for an examination of the effects of monetary policy.

The monetary sectors of the major macroeconomic models have undergone a considerable transformation over the past 20 years. In the early years of UK macroeconomic models, monetary sectors were noticeable only by their absence. One of the earliest macroeconomic models (Surrey, 1971) allowed for the exogenous effects of bank advances and personal credit on household expenditure, but no other route for the effects of interest rates or money was modelled. The development of monetary sectors in macro-models during the late 1960s and 1970s paralleled the revival in interest in monetary economics, beginning with the foundation of the Money Study Group. The economic events of the past 20 years have also provided a fertile background to this development, starting with the upsurge in infla-tion, through deregulation of the banking system and the switch to floating exchange rates, and ending with the adoption of monetary targets and the medium-term financial strategy. To a large extent the pace of development of monetary sector models has been dictated by changes in monetary policy, advances in monetary theory and innovation in econometric methods.

In surveying the monetary sectors of the current macroeconomic models it is important to realize that a macroeconomic model is the outcome of a dynamic research strategy. By the time the reader reaches the end of this chapter it is possible that the models discussed will have changed. Equations will have been adjusted, added to or removed. However, the structure and philosophy of these models will not have changed dramatically. In this chapter therefore we shall be concerned with taking a broad look at the monetary process in the major macromodels rather than the detailed struc-ture. The models that will be examined will be the major forecasting models of the UK. These are the Treasury (HMT) model, the London Business School (LBS) model, the National Institute of Economic and Social Research (NIESR) model, the Bank of England (BE) model and the Liver-pool (LVPL) model.

The attempt to model the impacts of monetary policy directly without the detail of a complex monetary interaction has been the primary objective of the development of 'small monetary models'. The models that fall into this category are the small monetary buffer stock models, the Bank of England small monetary model and the St Louis type reduced form model.

6.2 THE MONETARY SECTOR – A MODELLING STRATEGY

The detailed monetary sectors of the various macroeconomic models differ according to levels of disaggregation and modelling philosophy. However, the common features that exist across all the models stem from theoretical developments in monetary economics which have played a part in modelling strategy. We can distinguish five separate areas where the development of monetary theory has contributed to the modelling of the monetary sector.

First, there is the distinction made by Gurley and Shaw (1960) between 'inside' and 'outside' wealth and the economics of the Radcliffe Committee

(1959). This has received greater credence since the switch to M0 as an official target and the use of M3, M4 and M5 as target indicators. Money as the liabilities of the government sector (outside money) is distinguished from money which includes deposits held within the banking system (inside money). Monetary sectors distinguish between gross and net financial wealth and its effects on expenditure. Similarly models of the monetary sector distinguish between the different measures of money, from its narrowest measure (currency) to broader measures (M4, M5). At one end the HMT model includes all the various measures, while at the other end the LVPL model includes only M0.

Second, there has been the development of portfolio theory which has contributed to the understanding of asset markets and the implicit modelling of the demand for money (Tobin, 1958). The demand for money is a demand for an asset determined in conjunction with the demand for other financial assets. Wealth effects in the demand for money and the long-run homogeneity of the price level are now accepted modelling restrictions. In the case of the broad measures of money, the 'opportunity cost' of holding money as measured by the rate of interest on an alternative asset is complemented with 'own interest' rate effects and in some cases the direct cost of holding money is proxied by inflation or expected inflation.

Third, balance sheet and 'adding up' constraints on the lines of Tobin and Brainard (1968) are at least implicitly if not explicitly incorporated in models of the monetary sector.

Fourth, there has been the contribution of the monetary theory of the balance of payments,[1] international monetary theory as in the portfolio theory of exchange rate determination (Branson, 1977) and the theory of efficient financial markets.[2] These developments have added further routes to the transmission mechanism in monetary models, in particular, the linking of international monetary developments and the effects of domestic monetary shocks on the exchange rate through portfolio effects and forward expectations.

Finally, the most significant recent development has been the application of the theory of rational expectations (RE) to forward expectations. The LVPL model was the first to pioneer the application of rational expectations in a macroeconomic model of the UK (Minford et al., 1980). The revolution of yesterday is the common practice of today with the NIESR and LBS models including forward rational expectations in the monetary sectors of their respective forecasting models. The HMT model has a rational expectations capability, used currently for simulation purposes only, and the application of rational expectations in the BE model is an active research programme.

The specification of most models of the demand for money follow that of the textbook Keynesian model. The basic specification is altered to include own interest rate effects depending on the monetary aggregate that is modelled and wealth effects. Although the functional form of these models resembles the Keynesian framework, their underpinnings derive from portfolio considerations rather than the motives approach of Keynes. As a modelling strategy, the favoured approach has been to specify a utility function which includes as its arguments real balances and real bonds (Patinkin, 1965) and to derive implicit money demand functions. This defines the long-run equilibrium demand for money which then leaves the modeller free to investigate the precise functional form and appropriate dynamics as popularized in the general to specific approach[3] to econometric model building. This has been the approach taken by the BE and HMT macromodels.

However, this particular innovation in econometric practice has not been as universal as the developments in monetary theory. Some modellers have taken the strong *a priori* approach in the specification of both the functional form and the dynamics. A more restrictive and theoretically richer approach (in the Popperian sense of refutability) than the loose general to specific methodology is to specify the utility function explicitly and derive the explicit functional form with all the relevant restrictions. This is the approach taken by the LBS model and to a lesser extent the LVPL and NIESR models.

However, the common ground that exists between the models regarding the modelling of the demand for money in general terms gives way to differing modelling strategies when modelling other key monetary aggregates. For example, the NIESR and BE models determine the stock of broad money (M3) from the counterparts to the PSBR. That is, M3 is treated as the residual asset in the counterparts identity which links the public sector borrowing requirement to the increase in sales of gilt-edged stock plus the increase in M3 less the increase in bank advances. While the broad money stock is determined by the private sector's demand for bank advances and government bonds, the stock of M1 is determined from a dynamic specification of a demand for money. The NIESR model differs from the BE model in its explicit treatment of forward expectations terms as consistent or rational, in the sense of Muth (1961), in the specification of the demand for M1. In contrast with the BE and NIESR models, the stock of broad money (M3) in the HMT model is determined from an explicit demand for money function. Similarly, the narrow monetary aggregates are obtained from separate demand functions. The monetary sector of the LVPL model differs from all others not in terms of specification but in terms of theory and parsimony. The only monetary variable that matters in the LVPL model is M0.

Interest rates in all of the models except LVPL are determined as fixed or variable mark-ups on the administered base or short-term rate of interest. In the LVPL model interest rates are determined by a term structure that links domestic rates to international interest rates through the 'efficient markets condition'.

The specification of key behavioural relationships that underpin the monetary sector and its broad structure for each model is described in the following section.

6.3 A STYLIZED MODEL

This section details a textbook type stylized model of the monetary sector incorporating the points made in the previous section. The most important of these, following Friedman (1956), is that the demand for money cannot be determined independently of the demand for other financial assets. Financial assets are held by the non-bank private sector (NBPS) and the banking sector. The decision to accumulate financial assets by the various sectors and the particular structure of the asset–liability framework is the remit of the monetary sector model. The financial balance sheet of the private sector is outlined below:

Private sector financial balance

Assets	Liabilities
Currency	
Deposits	Loans
Government bonds	
Foreign assets	Foreign liabilities

The banking sector

Assets	Liabilities
Currency reserves	
Loans	Deposits
Government bonds	
Foreign currency	
Foreign assets	

The organization of the NBPS asset holdings is that of an optimal portfolio framework along the following lines:

$$C_p = c(r_d, r_l, r_f, r_b) W \tag{6.1}$$

$$D = e(r_d, r_l, r_f, r_b) W \tag{6.2}$$

$$L = n(r_c, r_l, r_f, r_b) W \tag{6.3}$$

$$B = b(r_c, r_l, r_f, r_b) W \tag{6.4}$$

$$F/S = f(r_d, r_l, r_f, r_b) W \tag{6.5}$$

where C_p is the NBPS holding of currency, D is bank deposits, L is bank advances to the NBPS, B is the holding of government bonds, F is the net foreign asset position of the NBPS valued in foreign currency and S is the exchange rate described as foreign currency per unit of domestic. The rates of interest are the deposit rate r_d, the loan rate r_1, the bond rate r_b and the covered foreign rate r_f where

$$r_f = r^* + \frac{S - S^e}{S} \tag{6.6}$$

and S^e is the expected exchange rate. The wealth W is defined as

$$W = C_p + D + B - L + F/S \tag{6.7}$$

Equation (6.7) defines the private sector's balance sheet identity which in turn implies the following adding up constraints:

$$c + e + b - n + f = 1$$

$$\frac{\partial c}{\partial r_d} + \frac{\partial e}{\partial r_d} + \frac{\partial b}{\partial r_d} - \frac{\partial n}{\partial r_d} + \frac{\partial f}{\partial r_d} = 0$$

$$\frac{\partial c}{\partial r_1} + \frac{\partial e}{\partial r_1} + \frac{\partial b}{\partial r_1} - \frac{\partial n}{\partial r_1} + \frac{\partial f}{\partial r_1} = 0$$

$$\frac{\partial c}{\partial r_f} + \frac{\partial e}{\partial r_f} + \frac{\partial b}{\partial r_f} - \frac{\partial n}{\partial r_f} + \frac{\partial f}{\partial r_f} = 0$$

$$\frac{\partial c}{\partial r_b} + \frac{\partial e}{\partial r_b} + \frac{\partial b}{\partial r_b} - \frac{\partial n}{\partial r_b} + \frac{\partial f}{\partial r_b} = 0$$

This system provides a framework for the allocation of financial assets within the private sector. This directly affects spending decisions via credit demand and the holding of liquid assets. The banking sector and the supply of outside financial assets could be assumed to be passive, in which case interest rates are determined as mark-ups on an exogenous control rate of interest such as the base rate. Alternatively, the banking sector can be assumed to be active, in which case interest rates are determined by the interaction of the supply and demand for financial assets. For example, the profit-maximizing bank would determine its asset–liability structure on similar portfolio principles to the non-bank sector. The supply of loans would depend on the 'margin of intermediation', i.e. the spread between loan and deposit rates:

$$L^s = h(r_1 - r_d) \qquad \frac{\partial h}{\partial r_1} > 0 \tag{6.8}$$

Similarly, the banking sector's holdings of government bonds and foreign assets will depend in turn on relative returns adjusted for risk:

$$\frac{F_B}{S} = n(r_f - r_d) \qquad \frac{\partial m}{\partial r_f} > 0 \tag{6.9}$$

$$B_B = v(r_b - r_d) \qquad \frac{\partial p}{\partial r_b} > 0 \tag{6.10}$$

where F_B/S is the net foreign asset position of the banking sector and B_B is bank lending to the public sector (holding of government bonds). The supply of deposits will be residually determined from the bank's balance sheet:

$$L + B_B + F_B/S = D(1 - k) \tag{6.11}$$

where k is the ratio of reserves to deposits.

In practice, most macroeconomic models assume that the banking sector is passive, which means that the banking sector sets its deposit rate and loan rate as a fixed mark-up on the administered base or minimum lending rate. This amounts to the assumption that $\partial h/\partial r_1 = \infty$. Similarly, the spread between loan and deposit rate is also assumed to be constant.

Two remaining identities determine the supply of outside assets to the private sector. The public sector budget constraint determines the supply of base money and bonds and the external balance sheet determines the supply of net foreign assets. Basically,

$$PSBR = (1 - g)B + (1 - g)B_B + (1 - g)C_p + (1 - g)C_B \tag{6.12}$$

where PSBR is the public sector borrowing requirement, C_B is the bank's holding of reserve currency, which is assumed to be a fraction k of deposits in the textbooks, and g is the lag operator ($gX_t = X_{t-1}$, $g^2 X_t = X_{t-2}$ etc.) and

$$CA + (1 - g)R = (1 - g)F/S + (1 - g)F_B/S \tag{6.13}$$

where CA is the current account and R is the stock of foreign currency reserves.

Models that treat interest rates and/or the exchange rate as exogenous are clearly placing limits on the transmission mechanism. Models that allow for interest rates and the exchange rate to be determined endogenously provide a richer interaction both within the monetary sector and with the rest of the model.

6.4 EXPECTATIONS

Differences can also occur on the assumptions relating to expectations.[4] There are three areas in which expectations figure in the monetary sector. These are the exchange rate, interest rates and inflation. From equations (6.5) and (6.13) it is clear that the exchange rate is partially determined by the expected future exchange rate. In the special case when $\partial f/\partial r_f = \infty$ (domestic and foreign financial assets are perfect substitutes) the domestic rate of interest is equated with the foreign rate plus the expected change in the exchange rate over a common maturity (see the next section). Similarly, liquidity preference and the portfolio behaviour of the private sector will in part be determined by the expected capital gains on assets. Finally, expectations of inflation will also matter to asset holders. Interest rates would be adjusted in line with changes in inflation expectations.

Expectations can be assumed to be modelled as adaptive or according to some other mechanical dynamic rule, as a quasi-reduced form – which can allow for monetary and other policy influences – or as a rational expectation. The adaptive expectations model is essentially a dynamic error learning mechanism in which expectations are adjusted by a fraction of the previous period's expectational error. The expectation X_t^e of X_t is given by

$$X_t^e - X_{t-1}^e = \phi(X_{t-1} - X_{t-1}^e) \qquad 0 < \phi \le 1 \tag{6.14}$$

By continuous back substitution equation (6.14) can be written as a continuous distributed lag in X with geometrically declining weights:

$$X_t^e = \phi \sum_{i=0}^{\infty} (1 - \phi)^i X_{t-i-1} \tag{6.15}$$

The quasi-reduced form model relates the expectation of X to a vector of current and past exogenous variables, similar in kind to the method of McCallum (1976) and Wickens (1982) in the first stage of the rational expectations estimation. This can be viewed as a halfway stage between adaptive and rational expectations. It allows for changes in policy variables to influence expectations but does not allow for expectations of future policy (announcements).

Rational expectations is based on the notion that economic agents exploit all available relevant information in deriving expectations and that these expectations are unbiased. This implies that the expectations are generated from the true economic model. From an operational viewpoint, what this means is that the expectation of X for a particular time horizon is the same as that of the model prediction for the same time horizon, so that the expectation is consistent with the model used to describe economic behaviour. This method has also been referred to as consistent expectations. The term consistent expectations disguises the tacit assumption that the model may not be the 'true model', in which case its predictions (expectations) would not be unbiased. However, from a model operational standpoint, there is no difference between the two terms.

The application of rational expectations to a model that previously employed the adaptive expectations assumption, dramatically alters its dynamic properties (see, for example, Anderson, 1979). Forward-looking behaviour replaces backward-looking behaviour. The result is that variables that react to expectations (jump variables) respond more strongly to shocks and also react to expected future changes in exogenous variables. This is most obvious in the case of the exchange rate determined by the interest parity condition. In the case of adaptive expectations, a change in the interest rate differential between the world rate and the domestic rate would not affect the expected exchange rate in the first period. Consequently, the current exchange rate would adjust according to the current interest differential. In the case of rational expectations, the expected future exchange rate would adjust in line with all future interest rate differentials, forcing the current exchange rate to adjust even more. An example will illustrate the case.

Consider the following simplified model consisting of an aggregate demand schedule, given by a demand for money m^d and an aggregate supply schedule of the Sargent and Wallace (1975) type:

$$m^d_t - p_t = y_t - \alpha(p^e_{t+1} - p^e_t) \tag{6.16}$$

$$m^s_t = m^* + \epsilon_t \tag{6.17}$$

$$y_t - y^* = \beta(p_t - p^e_t) + \phi(y_{t-1} - y^*) \tag{6.18}$$

All variables are in terms of natural logarithms. The endogenous variables are the (log) price level p_t and (log) output y_t. The exogenous variables are the underlying level of the (log) money supply m^*, the equilibrium level of output y^* and the stochastic term ϵ_t.

The model will be solved for adaptive expectations (AE)

$$p^e_{t+1} = p_t \qquad \text{and} \qquad p^e_t = p_{t-1}$$

and rational expectations (RE)

$$p^e_{t+1} = E_{t-1}p_{t+1} \qquad \text{and} \qquad p^e_t = E_{t-1}p_t$$

The solution for the AE case is

$$p_t = \frac{\phi + \beta - \alpha(1 + \phi)}{1 + \beta - \alpha}p_{t-1} + \frac{\alpha\phi}{1 + \beta - \alpha}p_{t-2} + \frac{1}{1 + \beta - \alpha}m^s_t - \frac{\phi}{1 + \beta - \alpha}m^s_{t-1}$$

and that for the RE case is (Minford and Peel, 1983)

$$p_t = \phi p_{t-1} + (1 - \phi)m^* + \pi_0 \epsilon_t + \pi_1 \epsilon_{t-1}$$

where

$$\pi_0 = \frac{1}{1 + \beta}$$

$$\pi_1 = -\frac{\phi\beta}{(1 + \beta)[1 + \alpha(1 - \phi)]}$$

Let $\alpha = 0.5$, $\phi = 0.5$ and $\beta = 1.0$ and let $y^* = 0$. We can distinguish between a temporary and permanent shock to the money supply by operating on m^* or ϵ_t. Figures 6.1 and 6.2 show the dynamic properties of the two models in the case of a permanent one-off increase in the money supply from 0.0 to 1.0.

With the permanent shock, the jump in p in the RE case is greater than in the AE case and the approach to the equilibrium level is faster. This is because the forward-looking property of the RE has the effect of shortening the time taken to reach the long run. With the temporary increase in money, the effects are the opposite. The jump in p in the RE case is less than in the AE case because the long-run equilibrium has not altered and this is registered in the forward expectations process. Again, the path to equilibrium is faster in the RE case than in the AE case. These differences become more apparent when we come to examine the properties of models that allow for rational or consistent expectations, but before examining the monetary sector of each model in turn we present a textbook model of the monetary transmission mechanism.

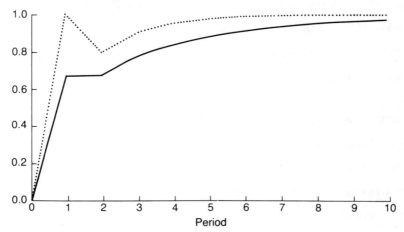

Figure 6.1   Permanent shock: —, AE; ---, RE.

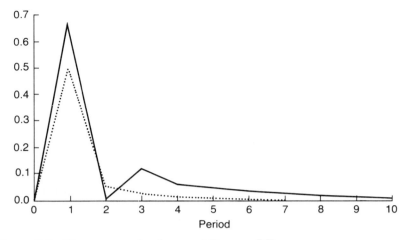

Figure 6.2 Temporary shock: —, AE; ---, RE.

6.5 THE TEXTBOOK TRANSMISSION MECHANISM

The textbook transmission mechanism, as presented in the standard IS–LM
Keynesian–neoclassical synthesis framework, still remains the best way of
understanding the interaction between the monetary and real sectors of the
economy. In this section we outline a simple textbook model which consists
of wealth-augmented IS–LM schedules, a balance of payments equilibrium
(BB) schedule and an expectations-augmented supply curve. The effects of
monetary and fiscal shocks are outlined in a brief diagrammatic representation. The following is an illustration of the type of model:

$$\text{LM}\quad M/P = L(R, Y, W)\qquad L_R < 0,\ L_Y > 0,\ L_W > 0 \tag{6.19}$$

$$\text{IS}\qquad Y = I(R, G, e, W)\qquad I_R < 0,\ I_G > 0,\ I_e < 0,\ I_W > 0 \tag{6.20}$$

$$\text{BB}\qquad H = H[R - R_f - (S - S^e)/S, e, Y]\qquad H_r > 0,\ H_e < 0,\ H_y < 0 \tag{6.21}$$

$$\text{WW}\quad \dot{W} = (G - T + cRW) + eX(e, Y) \tag{6.22}$$

balance sheet constraint

$$M/P + B + F/S = W \tag{6.23}$$

expectations – augmented supply curve

$$P = \phi(Y/Y^*) + P^e \tag{6.24}$$

Fisher equation

$$R = r + \pi^{\varepsilon} \qquad (6.25)$$

real exchange rate

$$e = PS/P_{\mathrm{f}} \qquad (6.26)$$

All variables have their conventional meanings: Y, real gross domestic product (GDP); P, price level; P^{e}, expected price level; π, rate of inflation; π^{e}, expected rate of inflation; R, nominal rate of interest; W, real value of financial wealth; r, real rate of interest; G, real government expenditure; e, real exchange rate (rise is an appreciation); S, nominal exchange rate (foreign currency per unit of domestic currency); B, real value of the stock of bonds; F, real value of the stock of net foreign assets (foreign currency); Y^*, real equilibrium output; M, nominal stock of money; R_{f}, foreign nominal rate of interest; P_{f}, foreign price level; S^{e}, expected exchange rate; X, net trade; cRW, debt interest, where c is the proportion of W that consists of interest-bearing public sector debt.

The stylized model is presented in Figure 6.3(a). The northeast quadrant depicts the conventional IS schedule, drawn in nominal interest space and defines equilibrium in the goods market; the LM schedule defines equilibrium in the money market and the BB schedule defines equilibrium in the external sector. By Walras' law the bond market can be excluded. The slope of the BB schedule relative to the LM schedule depends on the elasticity of capital mobility, which is empirically determined within each model. The greater the degree of capital mobility the flatter is the BB schedule. Perfect capital mobility implies a horizontal BB schedule (e.g. Parkin and Bade, 1988). An appreciation of the exchange rate shifts the BB schedule up to the left while an expected appreciation will cause it to move down to the right. The PP schedule in the southeast quadrant depicts the short-run trade-off between the price level and output described by the supply curve of equation (6.24). As the expectation of the price level adjusts to an initial price shock, the PP schedule shifts. An increase in expected prices pushes the PP schedule down. The expectations-augmented supply curve ensures a short-run trade-off between output and the price level in all the models. However, with the exception of the LVPL model, the long-run properties of the major macroeconomic models have not been fully explored. In practice, homogeneity, long-run neutrality or a vertical aggregate supply curve cannot be assumed. The simulation results refer only to short-run effects.

The northwest quadrant shows the relationship between the exchange rate and the rate of interest which equilibrates the external sector. Setting $H = 0$ in (6.21) and taking a linear representation, we obtain

$$H_R\left(R - R_{\mathrm{f}} - \frac{S - S^{\mathrm{e}}}{S}\right) + H_e e + H_Y \qquad Y = 0 \qquad (6.27)$$

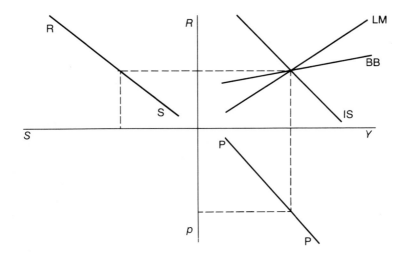

(a)

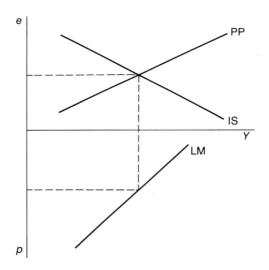

(b)

Figure 6.3 The stylized models

so that

$$R = R_f + \frac{S - S^e}{S} - \frac{H_e}{H_R}e - \frac{H_Y}{H_R}Y \qquad (6.28)$$

If it is assumed that the expected appreciation/depreciation of the exchange rate follows a stable path around its equilibrium value S^* as in Dornbusch (1976), we have

$$S^e - S = -k(S - S^*) \qquad k > 0 \qquad (6.29)$$

Substituting (6.29) in (6.30) yields

$$R = R_f + k\frac{(S - S^*)}{S} - \frac{H_e}{H_R}e - \frac{H_Y}{H_R}Y \qquad (6.30)$$

which reduces to

$$R = R_f + k(S - S^*)/S \qquad (6.30a)$$

in the case of perfect capital mobility ($H_R = \infty$).

This is the modelling assumption used in the LVPL and NIESR models, where the interest parity condition of (6.30a) is written in terms of domestic and foreign real interest rates and expected changes in the real exchange rate. The SR schedule moves down to the left with a rise in the equilibrium exchange rate S^* and up for a fall in S^*.

In the LVPL model, long-run equilibrium is ensured by the method of terminal conditions. This forces the model to solve along the stable minimum variance path of Taylor (1977). This means that the path for the expected real exchange rate will be given by its deviation from long-run equilibrium e^*. Thus

$$E(e_{+1}) - e = -q(e - e^*) \qquad q > 0 \qquad (6.31)$$

which can be substituted into the efficient markets condition

$$r = r_f + e - E(e_{+1}) \qquad (6.32)$$

to yield

$$r = r_f + q(e - e^*) \qquad (6.32a)$$

This simplification means that the real exchange rate can replace the real interest rate in the IS function. The aggregate supply function has also to be modified in the LVPL case which has an explicit open economy specification. This can be seen as an inverted supply curve with real exchange rate responses:

$$Y = Y^* - d(P - P^e) + g(e) \qquad (6.33)$$

The stylized version of the LVPL model is shown in figure 6.3(b). The IS schedule is drawn in real exchange rate–output space. The PP schedule represents the open economy supply curve and the LM schedule is depicted in price–income space. An increase in government spending will cause a temporary upward shift in the IS schedule while unanticipated changes in the price level cause shifts in the PP schedule. An unanticipated rise in the price level would cause a temporary shift of the PP schedule down to the right.

In the case of the NIESR model, the terminal condition determines the value of the forward exchange rate at the terminal date. However, the terminal condition itself is given by the solution path of the model rather than by an equilibrium condition.

6.6 THE MONETARY SECTORS

6.6.1 The HMT Model (HM Treasury, 1987)

The HMT model is the largest and most disaggregated of all the macro-models.[5] It contains about 200 variables relating to the domestic financial system. The monetary sector alone contains about 30 behavioural relationships and 130 identities or technical relationships. The monetary submodel determines private sector wealth, liquid assets, bank lending, M3, government bonds, M0 and expected capital gains. Interest rates can be exogenous, in which case the money supply is demand determined, or they are endogenous when monetary targets are in operation. The basic structure of the HMT monetary sector is outlined graphically in figure 6.4. The private sector is made up of the personal sector, industrial and commercial companies and financial companies.

The monetary model essentially determines the allocation of the non-bank private sector's financial wealth. The apex of the monetary system is the decision to accumulate financial wealth which arises out of the private sector surplus. This is the familiar flow of funds statement that equates the private sector's financial transactions (net acquisition of financial assets (NAFA)) to savings S less private investment I. The liabilities of the private sector are mainly sterling bank borrowing and foreign currency liabilities, the latter being determined within the capital flows sector of the model. Given the net worth of the private sector, the demand for bonds acts as the residual asset to give the balance sheet identity. Formally,

$$S - I = \text{NAFA}$$
$$(1 - g)W = \text{NAFA} + (1 - g)L - \phi R_L W_{t-1}$$
$$(1 - g)B = (1 - g)W - (1 - g)\text{M3} + (1 - g)L$$

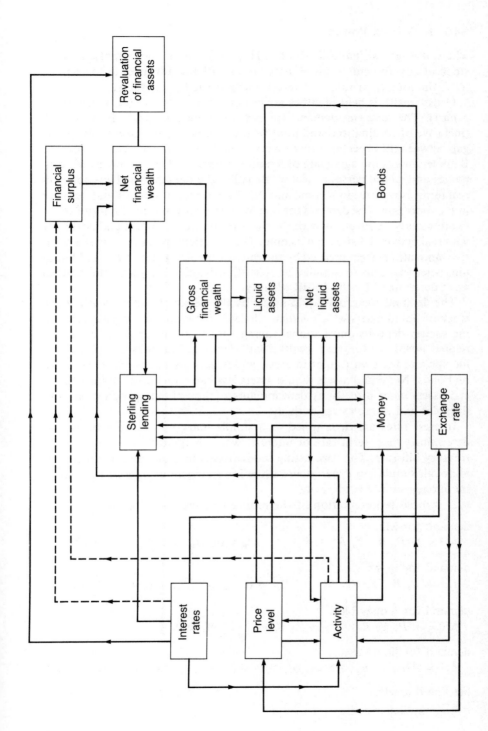

Figure 6.4 HMT model; financial sector.

where W is gross financial wealth, M3 is the broad money supply, B is the stock of government bonds, L is the stock of bank advances to the NBPS, R_L is the long-term rate of interest and g is the lag operator.

Gross wealth is held in either government bonds or M3 (of which M0 is a part). The long-run demand for real M3 depends positively on wealth (inclusive of revaluation) and total final expenditure, and negatively on the gap between the expected return on bonds and the short-term rate of interest. Bank lending is the aggregate of lending to industrial and commercial companies and to the personal sector. Broadly, the demand for bank loans in real terms is positive in income and the foreign rate of interest and negative in the short rate. The demand for real M0 has a conventional long-run specification, varying inversely with the short-term rate of interest and positively with real personal disposable income. The specification also includes a negative innovation effect proxied by the ratio of the number of bank and building society deposits to population. The flow demand for gilts is the residual asset determined by the PSBR identity.

The demand for gross liquid assets by the personal sector identifies the stock of liquid assets which is then allocated between bank deposits, building society deposits and national savings. Personal sector liquid assets are related positively to gross wealth, bank lending, real personal disposable income and the own rate of interest, and negatively to the expected return on bonds. Net liquid assets (liquid assets less bank advances) and net financial assets enter directly as determinants of household spending on nondurables and durables respectively.

Interest rates are determined as a simple mark-up on the exogenously determined short-term rate of interest, which is typically the three month treasury bill rate. The forecasting model treats interest rates as exogenous although simulation experiments allow for endogenous interest rates when the money supply is targeted.

A stylized representation of the monetary sector is as follows:

demand for M3
$$M3 = M(P,\ W,\ Y,\ R_L^* - R_S) \qquad M_P > 0,\ M_W > 0,\ M_Y > 0,\ M_R < 0$$

demand for loans
$$L = L(P,\ W,\ Y,\ R_S,\ R_F) \qquad L_P > 0,\ L_W > 0,\ L_Y > 0,\ L_{R_s} < 0,\ L_{R_f} > 0$$

demand for money base
$$M0 = m(P,\ Y,\ R_S) \qquad m_P > 0,\ m_Y > 0,\ m_R < 0$$

demand for liquid assets
$$LA = A(L,\ Y,\ R_S,\ R^*,\ R_A) A_L > 0,\ A_Y > 0,\ A_{R_s} < 0,\ A_{R^*} < 0,\ A_{R_A} > 0$$

net liquid assets

$$NLA = \frac{LA - L}{P}$$

expected returns on bonds
$$R^* = R_L + \mu^e$$

where P is the price level, Y is income, R_S is the short rate, R_A is the own rate on liquid assets, R_L is the long rate, R_F is the foreign rate of interest and μ^e is expected capital gains on bonds. Details of the key behavioural equations contained in the HMT monetary sector are presented in appendix 1.

The discussion of the HMT monetary sector is made complete with an explanation of its interaction with the exchange rate. The theory that underpins the determination of the exchange rate is a mixture of the Mundell–Fleming imperfect capital mobility model with the monetary theory of the balance of payments. The determination of the exchange rate can be broken down into components of the determination of the equilibrium exchange rate and the expected exchange rate, where both the actual and equilibrium exchange rates have domestic and foreign money supply as co-determinants. The following stylized model describes the determination of the exchange rate:

$$S^e = E(\text{NSO}^e, M/M_f, R_S - R_F, \text{RULC}, S^*)$$
$$E_N > 0, \ E_M < 0, \ E_{R_S} > 0, \ E_{\text{RULC}} < 0, \ E_S > 0$$

$$S^* = Q(\text{NSO}^e, M/M_F, R_S - R_F, \text{RULC})$$
$$Q_N > 0, \ Q_M < 0, \ Q_{R_S} > 0, \ Q_{\text{RULC}} < 0$$

$$S = S(S^e, R_S - R_F, \text{BB}/M) \qquad S_{S^e} > 0, \ S_R > 0, \ S_B > 0$$

$$M = \text{M3} + \text{M0}$$

where NSO^e is the real value of the expected stock of North Sea oil, RULC refers to relative unit labour costs, BB is the basic balance of payments, S^e is the one-quarter-ahead expected exchange rate, S^* is the expected long-run sustainable exchange rate and S is the sterling effective exchange rate. The model for the expected exchange rate is a quasi-reduced form, which allows interest rates and the money supply to influence it directly. This can be viewed as a half-way stage between the AE and RE models. According to this model, current monetary policy affects expectations but not future expected monetary policy. Also, the response of expectations is not consistent with the full model.

The actual exchange rate has a unit response to a change in the expected exchange rate, and a 1 per cent change in the interest rate differential produces an equivalent 1 per cent change in the exchange rate in the long run.

The degree of imperfect capital mobility is measured by the coefficient S_B. If $S_B = 0$, this implies perfect capital mobility.

Recently, the Treasury has announced the arrival of an updated but smaller version of the HMT model to be used for forecasting and simulation (Mellis et al., 1989). The model structure and properties are broadly similar to the HMT model but one additional characteristic is that the new model (the SLIM model) can be solved for rational expectations. The monetary sector of the new Treasury model is examined briefly in appendix 2.

6.6.2 The NIESR Model (NIESR, 1986)

The monetary sector plays only a minor role in the NIESR model (Wallis et al., 1988) with some effects from interest rates on private expenditure. The starting point for the monetary sector is the PSBR. By definition, the PSBR is financed by bank lending to the public sector, by debt sales to the private sector, by the issue of currency and by borrowing from the overseas sector. The latter source of finance is treated as exogenous in the NIESR monetary sector model. The broad money supply is explained as the residual from the counterparts to the PSBR identity, while bank lending, the demand for gilts and currency are explained by behavioural equations. Unlike the approach of the HMT model, the demand for M1 is obtained from an explicit optimizing framework. Agents are assumed to minimize a quadratic cost function which minimizes the costs of current and future discrepancies between actual and desired money holdings. This results in a specification for the demand for money which relates the current demand for money to expected future demands. The forward recursive nature of the specification leads to testable restrictions between the determinants of forward money demand and the lagged level of money balances (Artis and Cuthbertson, 1985).

The final specification relates the demand for money to its lagged level, expected future levels of real income, interest rate, the price level and current innovations in the price level, output and interest rates. This somewhat sophisticated approach is in stark contrast to the rest of the monetary sector which turns out to be unexcitingly conventional. The demand for gilts by the non-bank private sector is related to the stock demand for national savings which in turn is related to the local authority three month rate and the own rate on national savings. Bank advances to the private sector are made up of sterling lending to the company sector and to other financial institutions, lending to the personal sector for house purchases and lending to the personal sector for non-house purchases.

A stylized representation begins with the PSBR financing identity from which the broad money supply can be derived:

$$(1 - g)L_B = - (1 - g)C - (1 - g)B + \text{PSBR}$$

$$(1 - g)\text{M3} = (1 - g)C + (1 - g)L_B + \text{PSBR} + (1 - g)L$$

$$L = L(Y, P) \qquad L_Y > 0$$

$$C/P = C(Y) \qquad C_Y > 0$$

$$\text{M1} = M(Y^e, R^e, P^e, U_R, U_P, U_Y) \qquad M_Y > 0, M_R < 0,$$
$$M_P > 0, M_{U_R} < 0, M_{U_P} > 0, M_{U_Y} > 0$$

$$B = B(R_S, R_B, P) \qquad B_{R_S} < 0, B_{R_B} > 0$$

where L_B is sterling lending to the public sector, C is currency, L is bank advances to the private sector, B is the stock of government bonds, R_S is the short-term rate of interest, R_B is the rate of interest on bonds, Y^e is expected real income, R^e is the expected interest rate, P^e is the expected price level and the U_i are innovations in the rate of interest, price level and real income respectively (see appendix 3 for details).

The most important variable that the monetary sector impinges on is the exchange rate. The exchange rate in the NIESR model is given from the real exchange rate which is itself determined by a dynamic form of an open arbitrage interest parity condition. The real interest rate is defined as the nominal rate minus the rate of inflation π:

real interest rate
$$r = R - \pi$$

real exchange rate
$$ln\ e = a \ln e_{-1} + (1 - a)\ \text{E} \ln e_{+1} + (1 - g)(r - r^*)$$

nominal exchange rate
$$S = e/P$$

The term E $\ln e_{+1}$ is the one-period-ahead rationally expected real exchange rate. Despite the sparseness of monetary interaction in the model, monetary shocks can have significant effects through the exchange rate mechanism.

6.6.3 The LBS Model

The monetary sector of the LBS model represents the most sophisticated attempt to date at a modelling strategy (Keating, 1985). In a bold break with the traditionally *ad hoc* or implicit theorizing strategy, the LBS opted for a model that was first ambitious in the level of disaggregation, second derived from explicit optimizing behaviour and third assumed to be rational

344 K. G. P. Matthews

in its treatment of expectations. The financial sector is distinguished by nine subsectors. These are the personal sector, industrial and commercial companies (ICCS), pension funds and insurance companies, banks, building societies, unit and investment trusts, other financial institutions, the public sector and the overseas sector. The set of assets open to these sectors are bonds, equities, treasury bills, local authorities (LA) bills and certificates of deposit (CDs), time deposits, sight deposits, mortgage loans, other bank loans, notes and coin, national savings certificates, building society shares, hire purchase loans, foreign currency short-term assets and foreign currency long-term assets.

Asset demands are based on a modified Parkin (1970) type mean–variance model in which agents maximize an exponential utility function with respect to the expected return on their portfolio subject to a balance sheet constraint and adjustment costs. The objective function is further modified to allow for choice between equally non-risky assets by allowing for utility from certain assets. The exercise involves the maximization

$$\max \ Y_t' X_t - \frac{\beta}{2} X_t' \Sigma X_t - (X_t - P_t P_{t-1}^{-1} X_{t-1})' \frac{\theta}{2} (X_t - P_t P_{t-1}^{-1} X_{t-1})$$
$$\text{subject to } i'X_t = W_t$$

where Y is an $n \times 1$ vector of expected asset yields (coupon plus expected capital gain/loss), X is an $n \times 1$ vector of assets at real market prices, Σ is an $n \times n$ covariance matrix of asset returns, i is an $n \times 1$ unit vector, W is a scalar stating the agent's real wealth and θ is an $n \times n$ matrix measuring costs of adjustment. This yields the following set of asset demands:

$$X_t = A Y_t + bW_t + A\theta P_t P_{t-1}^{-1} X_{t-1} \tag{6.34}$$

where A is an $n \times n$ matrix of parameters of rates of return Y and $A = (\beta\Sigma + \theta)^{-1}(I - ib')$ (see Keating, 1985). Additional restrictions on the model were imposed by assuming that all stochastic returns are independently distributed (and cross-partial utility terms are zero). This yields the empirical restriction that Σ is diagonal. Second, costs of adjustment were considered independent between assets, which yields the restriction that θ is diagonal.

The optimizing framework outlined above was applied to three sectors: the personal sector, the company sector and the pension fund and insurance company sector. No explicit optimizing framework was posited for the rest of the financial sector. Banks were assumed to set interest rates on deposits and loans at fixed mark-ups.

The asset demand equations for the personal, company and pension fund and insurance sectors take the form

$$A(i) = L(i)[R(i) - C + M/K]$$

where C is the average return over all assets, K is the sum over all assets, M is the sector budget constraint and $L(i)$ is the risk aversion parameter for the ith asset. The return $R(i)$ on the ith asset is given by the nominal interest rate, the expected capital gain, tax rates and revaluations to asset stock:

$$R(i) = I(i)t + D(i)t_g + k(i) + h(i)A(i, -1)\frac{P(i)}{P(i, -1)}$$

where $I(i)$ is the nominal interest rate on the ith asset, $D(i)$ is the expected capital gain on the ith asset, $P(i)$ is the price of the ith asset, $k(i)$, $h(i)$ are parameters and t, t_g are the retention rates for income tax and capital gains tax respectively.

The expected capital gain is the rationally expected one-period-ahead increase in the asset price. Asset prices are determined by the full financial sector model and resemble the theoretical framework of the stylized model above. The three sets of assets and asset prices relate to equities, gilts and overseas assets; the exchange rate is the inverse of the price of overseas assets. The supply of equities is assumed to be exogenous. The supply of gilt-edged stock can be treated as exogenous, in which case it is assumed that the monetary authorities supply commercial and treasury bills at a given short-term rate of interest as a residual source of finance. The model also allows for funding policy to vary to meet a particular monetary target by varying short-term rates of interest. The external balance determines the supply of net foreign assets.

Such a specific modelling strategy is of course likely to draw specific criticism. A comprehensive critique of the modelling framework and empirical results is provided by Courakis (1988). The critique concentrates on the theoretical implications of the diagonality of Σ and θ and the implications of the estimated parameters for the relative returns of assets and the costs of adjustment.[6] However, this does not detract from the analytical framework which aims to develop a model of financial asset demands which, together with supplies, determine asset prices. The forward component in asset prices is solved as a rational expectation which means that the current asset price discounts expected future disturbances.

The empirical results are not reproduced here mainly for reasons of space; we refer to Keating (1985) for partial results and Budd et al. (1984) for a full listing. The empirical results for the personal sector are summarized in appendix 4 as an illustration.

6.6.4 The Liverpool Model

The Liverpool model differs from all other macroeconomic models in terms of structure, theory and treatment of expectations. In terms of structure it is much more aggregative. In terms of theory it is classical, equilibrium in nature, dichotomized in the long run and supply driven. In its treatment of expectations it is comprehensively new classical (Minford et al., 1984). The monetary sector of the model consists of one equation for the demand for money in terms of M0. Earlier versions (Munford et al., 1980) derived the demand for money (M1) within a portfolio framework in which the demand for an asset is derived from a nested multilevel constant elasticity of substitution utility function. The first stage separates physical assets from financial assets and, given the demand for total financial assets, the second stage separates money from other financial assets (domestic and foreign financial assets are assumed to be perfect substitutes). The current demand for money represents a return to implicit theorizing. Its functional form is much more conventional but includes variables not usually associated with the demand for money:

$$M0/P = M(R_s, Y_d, b, t_e, t_y) \qquad M_R < 0, M_Y > 0, M_b, M_{t_e}, M_{t_y} > 0$$

where R_s is the short-term rate of interest, Y_d is disposable income, b is the real value of unemployment benefits, t_e is employer's contributions and t_y is the average tax rate. The first two terms are readily explicable; the last three terms are included to capture aspects of the 'black economy'.[7]

The rest of the financial sector refers to the supply of domestic and foreign financial assets from the consolidated public and external sector balance sheets and the term structure derived from the efficient markets condition:

$$(1 - g)F = \frac{PSBR + CBAL}{P} - \delta(1 - g)R_L F_{t-1} - \pi F_{t-1}$$

$$r_n = r_n^* + \ln e - E \ln e_{+n}$$

$$r = r^* + \ln e - E \ln e_{+1}$$

$$R_n = r_n + E\pi_{+n}$$

$$R = r + E\pi_{+1}$$

The first equation is the consolidation of external and domestic balance sheets, where F refers to the real market value of total financial assets and CBAL is the current balance. The last two terms on the right-hand side of the expression refer to capital and real valuation effects, where π is the rate of inflation and R_L is the long-term rate of interest. The next two equations are derived from the efficient markets condition for maturities of one year and n years, where r_n is the real rate of interest of maturity n, r is the real rate of interest on one year holdings and the asterisk indicates foreign real rates. The final two equations are the familiar Fisher conditions. The demand for M0 equation of the LVPL model is presented in appendix 5.

6.6.5 The BE Model (Patterson et al., 1987)

Like the Treasury model, the financial sector of the BE model takes as its basis the sector flow of funds, with sectoral surpluses being generated in the real sector and allocated across varying financial assets.[8] The financial sector is comprehensive in its construction, the basis of which is the full flow of funds matrix. The matrix describes the acquisition of financial assets and liabilities by each sector. The model identifies six sectors: the personal sector, ICCs, other financial institutions (OFIs) public sector, banking and overseas sector. Each column of the matrix represents a particular sector, while the row refers to an asset/liability. By construction, the row sum of elements in the matrix will sum to zero. Some of the elements are determined behaviourally, others are treated as exogenous and the rest are determined residually.

The most important behavioural relationship in the personal sector refers to the determination of real net liquid assets. Its importance is underlined by its interrelationship with the real sector in which real net liquid assets enter as a determinant of consumer durable spending. The specification is of an 'error correction' type in which the change in real net liquid assets is related to the change in real net financial assets, the acceleration in inflation, real net wealth including physical assets and the discrepancy between equilibrium real net liquid assets and actual real net liquid assets in the previous quarter. In its stylized format, the function can be described in the following way:

$$(\text{NLA}/P)_H = N\{\text{NAFA}_H/P, \pi, W, [(\text{NLA*}/P) - (\text{NLA}/P)]_H\}$$

$$N_{\text{NAFA}} > 0, \ N_\pi < 0, \ N_W > 0, \ N_{\text{NLA*}} > 0$$

where NLA_H is net liquid assets of the personal sector, NFA_H is net acquisition of financial assets by the personal sector, π is the rate of inflation, W is real personal sector wealth and $\text{NLA*}/P$ is equilibrium net liquid assets. The latter variable is given by the function J:

$$(\text{NLA*}/P) = J(W, \text{NAFA}_H/P, R_S - R_L, \pi_d, \pi_n)$$

$$J_W > 0, \ J_{\text{NAFA}} > 0, \ J_R > 0, \ J_{\pi_d} > 0, \ J_{\pi_n} < 0$$

where π_d is the price inflation of durables and π_n is the price inflation of non-durables. The positive response of durable goods inflation reflects the notion that durables are substitutes to liquid assets in the consumer's overall wealth portfolio. The interest rate differential captures differential yields between liquid and non-liquid financial assets.

The demand for bank advances is separated into the various sectoral components with behavioural functions specified for the personal and company sectors. The specification for the demand for bank credit is conventional in so far as it consists of a scale variable and a relative cost–price variable. In the personal sector the scale variable is given by consumers' current and capital spending, whereas for the company sector this is given by the firms' working capital (Moore and Threadgold, 1985) and for OFIs it is given by GDP. The relative cost–price term is taken as the rate of inflation in the case of the personal sector and the real cost of borrowing in the case of the corporate sector and OFIs. The latter sector also includes the long-term rate as a negative determinant of bank lending. The demand for bank lending by the corporate sector also includes a variable to capture the opportunity for round-tripping, which is taken as the non-negative differential between the CD rate and a 1 per cent point margin on the clearing banks' base rate.

The banking sector is entirely passive in the sense that the supply of deposits and loans is made up of the sum of the sectoral demands for each. Additional currency holdings by the personal sector are assumed to account for 90 per cent of the change in currency supplied through the financing implication of the public sector balance sheet. Similarly, the demand for public sector debt by the personal sector is derived as a constant relationship to the PSBR or, in the case of short-term debt, the existing stock of bonds. Deposits held by the personal sector are derived as a residual. It follows that no one specific behavioural or technical relation can be identified as the determinant of the stock of M3 or any other monetary variable. M3 is derived from the total of bank deposits held by each sector and the net issue of currency. The private sector demand for the stock of currency is modelled as positive in consumer spending, negative in the building society rate of interest and negative in the rate of unemployment.

Interest rates in the BE model are given as reaction functions to various presures from the real and financial sectors of the economy. Interest rates and the exchange rate are assumed to interact. The exchange rate depends on relative rates of interest in the UK and the USA, relative unit labour costs in the UK and the USA, oil prices, North Sea output and the basic balance of payments (current balance plus outward investment flows):

$$S = S(R_S - R_F, \text{ULC} - \text{ULC}_F, P_{oil}, \text{BAL})$$

$$S_R > 0, \ S_U < 0, \ S_P > 0, \ S_B > 0$$

The short-term interest rate reacts to changes in the exchange rate, the acceleration in the money supply, capacity utilization, a weighted sum of past PSBR-to-GDP ratios and the acceleration in producer price inflation. The long-term rate is derived from the short rate, expected inflation π^e and supply pressure from the gilt-edged market measured by the PSBR-to-GDP ratio:

$$R_S = K[R_F, (1 - g)S, CU, (1 - g)^2 M3, PSBR/Y, (1 - g)\pi]$$

$$K_{R_F}, K_{CU}, K_{PSBR/Y}, K_\pi, K_M > 0, K_S < 0$$

$$R_1 = H(R_S, PSBR/Y, \pi^e)$$

$$H_R > 0, H_{PSBR/Y} > 0, K_\pi > 0$$

Expected inflation is modelled as a weighted average of past inflation rates. Other remaining rates of interest in the model are derived as mark-ups on the pivotal short-term rate of interest, which is taken to be the local authority three month rate.

The monetary sectors of the major macroeconomic models have been outlined within a stylized framework. This sector includes the determination of the range and structure of financial assets as well as interest rates and the exchange rate. The transmission of monetary shocks to the rest of the economy is more easily appreciated within such a stylized framework. We now turn to the simulation properties of the models so far reviewed with the aid of the stylized model.

6.7 THE TRANSMISSION MECHANISM

6.7.1 The HMT Model

The transmission mechanism in the HMT model follows three principle routes: the wealth effect, the direct interest rate effect and the indirect interest rate effect. Household spending is influenced directly by the stock of private sector financial assets. Stock building and capital formation are both influenced directly by changes in short and long rates. Competitiveness changes through the consequent effect on the exchange rate following a change in domestic interest rates.

Domestic prices are modelled on a 'normal cost' hypothesis which relates the price level to wage costs, import prices and capacity. Wages respond to prices (with long-run homogeneity), output and the retention ratio. In terms of the stylized IS–LM framework above, the supply curve equation would be augmented with an import price effect as follows.

$$P = F(Y/Y^*) + aP_F/S + (1 - a)P^e \tag{6.35}$$

Notice that this can also be inverted to obtain the open economy supply curve in the LVPL model.

6.7.2 The NIESR Model

The NIESR model contains few direct monetary effects. The real value of financial wealth enters into non-durable consumption and residential fixed investment is affected by the mortgage rate, but the bulk of the expenditure side of the model is demand driven, with forward expectations of demand playing the most important role. Like the HMT model prices depend on import prices and labour costs; consequently the open economy version of the Phillips curve given above is equally appropriate in any stylized representation.

6.7.3 The LBS Model

Like the HMT and NIESR models, the LBS model is based around an income–expenditure framework, but unlike the other two models it has often been referred to as an international monetarist model. Household spending is directly affected by the rate of interest and real financial wealth. The former term is supposed to capture the substitution effect between current and future consumption, while the income effect is included in real disposable income through net receipts of interest and dividends. The latter term responds to interest rate changes through changes in valuation. As in the HMT model, stockbuilding and investment are directly affected by the rate of interest, and prices are a mark-up on labour costs and raw material costs. Like the NIESR model prices can respond to changes in the monetary environment through the exchange rate mechanism.

6.7.4 The LVPL Model

The LVPL model identifies three areas through which the monetary sector interacts with the rest of the economy. These are wealth effects, direct monetary shocks and through expectations. Financial wealth plays a powerful role in private sector demand. Inflation and interest rate changes affect private demand indirectly through real and capital valuation changes to financial assets. The direct effect on private expenditure comes through unanticipated changes to inflation. This affects real interest rates which enter the determination of non-durable consumption, durables, inventories and private gross domestic fixed capital formation (GDFCF). Inflation is determined in the money market; thus higher expected monetary growth fuels inflation expectations which, through the Fisher condition, drive up interest rates. Higher interest rates reduce the demand for real balances so that for any given current money supply the price level jumps up to equilibrate the money market.

6.7.5 The BE Model

Like the HMT model, the transmission mechanism follows the interest rate and net wealth route. Personal real net financial wealth is a direct determinant of non-durable spending, while real net liquid assets, mortgage lending and the real rate of interest determine durables spending. Real interest rates influence investment, both residential as well as manufacturing and inventory accumulation.

6.8 SIMULATIONS

In the following section we describe the effects of three standard simulations of the models which will be analysed with the aid of the stylized model. The effects of an increase in government spending is analysed using first fixed monetary targets and second fixed interest rates. Third, a monetary shock is simulated by examining the effects of an interest rate cut.[9] The results of a permanent increase in government spending are shown in tables 6.1 and 6.2. In the first simulation, the LBS, NIESR and BE models exhibit roughly the same properties with output expanding, prices rising and the exchange rate depreciating. The intermediate effects are shown in figure 6.5. The results are conventional and conform closely to the textbook result. The increase in government spending shifts the IS schedule up to the right to IS′, pushing up interest rates, output and the price level. The response of the exchange rate differs depending on the model. In the case of the LBS model the expected deficit on the current balance depresses the equilibrium exchange rate, causing the SR schedule to move up to SR′ and the BB schedule up to the left to BB′. The rise in the interest rate is insufficient to offset the arbitrage gap caused by the fall in the expected exchange rate, thus causing the spot rate to decline. The second-round effect of this is to expand demand further through a fall in the real exchange rate, but the rise in the price level would produce counteracting real effects on spending through the wealth effect and also the rise in prices would set off a wage–price chain causing the PP schedule to move down. A similar transmission story can be related in the case of the NIESR model, with the exception that the reduction in the expected exchange rate follows a fall in the expected real exchange rate caused by a reduction in real interest rates (price level rises faster than interest rates). The HMT model has the exchange rate appreciating. This is because the expected exchange rate which responds to money

Table 6.1 Permanent increase in government current expenditure of £1 billion: fixed money

Year	HMT	LBS	NIESR	LVPL	BE
GDP (%)					
1	0.18	0.08	0.36	0.20	0.22
2	0.13	0.11	0.37	0.16	0.22
3	0.05	0.20	0.41	0.17	0.23
4	−0.04	0.33	0.42	0.17	0.24
5	−0.09	0.45	0.42	0.17	0.22
6	−0.11	0.58		0.17	
7		0.69		0.16	
Consumer prices (%)					
1	0.04	0.00	0.13	−0.16	0.04
2	0.15	0.04	0.33	−0.21	0.10
3	0.24	0.18	0.50	−0.24	0.21
4	0.32	0.34	0.67	−0.25	0.35
5	0.38	0.50	0.80	−0.26	0.50
6	0.45	0.79		−0.25	
7		1.13		−0.23	
Nominal exchange rate (%)					
1	0.14	−0.36	−1.03	0.39	0.02
2	0.13	−0.76	−0.95	0.43	−0.19
3	0.27	−1.16	−1.20	0.44	−0.40
4	0.33	−1.49	−1.29	0.45	−0.53
5	0.33	−2.12	−1.43	0.46	−0.56
6	0.22	−2.41		0.46	
7		−2.68		0.46	
Current balance (£billion)					
1	−0.2	−0.5	−0.7	−0.8	−0.2
2	−0.3	−0.7	−0.5	−0.7	−0.3
3	−0.3	−1.0	−0.6	−0.8	−0.2
4	−0.3	−1.2	−0.5	−0.9	−0.2
5	−0.4	−1.7	−0.6	−0.9	−0.3
6	−0.6	−2.1		−1.0	
Short-term rate of interest					
1	0.12	0.07	0.05	0.0	0.07
2	0.29	0.07	0.07	0.0	0.09
3	0.37	0.07	0.09	0.0	0.12
4	0.41	0.07	0.10	0.0	0.14
5	0.42	0.07	0.10		0.20
6	0.42	0.09			

Table 6.2 Permanent increase in government current expenditure of £1 billion: fixed interest rates

Year	HMT	LBS	NIESR	LVPL	BE
GDP (%)					
1	0.25	0.23	0.36	−0.18	0.22
2	0.25	0.32	0.37	0.14	0.26
3	0.24	0.37	0.41	0.00	0.27
4	0.22	0.39	0.42	0.00	0.25
5	0.20	0.41	0.42	−0.06	0.21
6		0.42		−0.13	
7		0.41		−0.20	
Consumer prices (%)					
1	0.06	0.05	0.13	1.08	0.04
2	0.23	0.24	0.33	2.05	0.11
3	0.43	0.48	0.50	3.15	0.24
4	0.62	0.71	0.67	4.28	0.39
5	0.80	0.97	0.80	5.46	0.55
6		1.31		6.68	
7		1.70		7.94	
Nominal exchange rate (%)					
1	−0.13	−1.22	−1.03	−2.41	−0.06
2	−0.28	−1.52	−0.95	−3.05	−0.28
3	−0.41	−1.88	−1.20	−3.86	−0.48
4	−0.57	−2.26	−1.29	−4.74	−0.59
5	−0.73	−2.81	−1.42	−5.71	−0.59
6		−3.12		−6.77	
7		−3.36		−7.88	
Current account balance (£billion)					
1	−0.3	−0.7	−0.7	1.5	−0.2
2	−0.5	−0.7	−0.5	0.4	−0.3
3	−0.5	−1.0	−0.6	0.6	−0.2
4	−0.5	−1.2	−0.5	0.7	−0.2
5	−0.5	−1.7	−0.6	0.6	−0.2
6		−2.1		0.9	
7		−2.2		1.2	

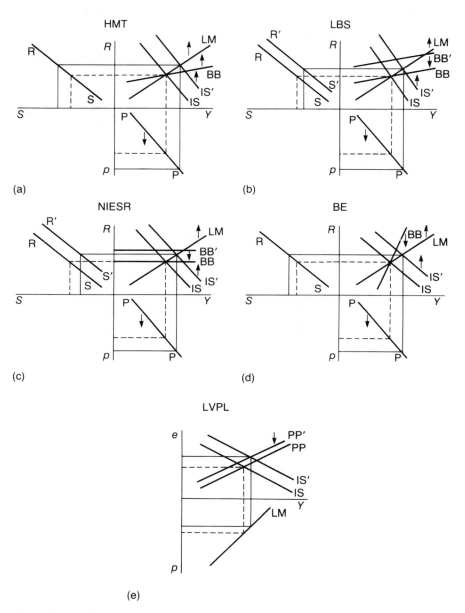

Figure 6.5 Fiscal expansion with fixed money supply rule: (a) HMT; (b) LBS; (c) NIESR; (d) BE; (e) LVPL

supply growth is unaffected by a pure fiscal shock. Thus the increase in demand (IS shifts up to IS') induces a capital inflow putting upward pressure on the exchange rate.

While all the large macromodels show a positive response in the price level to the expansionary fiscal shock, the LVPL model has the price level declining. The increase in government spending, assuming bond financing (holding money supply constant), shifts the IS schedule out to IS', raising the real exchange rate and output. The increase in demand increases the demand for real balances, which can only be satisfied through a decline in the price level.

A fiscal expansion with fixed interest rates produces a stronger output increase in the case of the HMT, NIESR, LBS and BE models. Table 6.2 outlines the effects. The transmission mechanism, which is broadly similar, is shown in figures 6.6(a)–6.6(d). The fiscal expansion (IS shifts up to IS') is matched by an expansionary monetary policy (LM shifts down to LM'). The LBS and NIESR models show a sharper depreciation of the exchange rate compared with the HMT or BE models. This is primarily because the former models incorporate forward expectations of the exchange rate which is modelled as rational. The reduction in real interest rates in the case of NIESR and the decline in the current account lead to a depreciation of the forward exchange rate which translates cumulatively into the current rate (BB moves to BB' and SR moves to SR'). In the case of the LVPL model the increase in government spending is balanced financed (money and bonds). The increase in money raises inflation which, through a deflationary wealth effect, reduces private spending. This counteracts the expansionary effect of the increase in government spending; thus IS shifts down to IS' (figure 6.6(e)). The increase in inflation is unexpected, and reduces real wages temporarily and increases supply (PP shifts down to PP'). The overall effect is to depress output in the first period. The fall in the exchange rate (compounded by a fall in the real exchange rate in response to unanticipated inflation) and the rise in the price level is stronger in the LVPL model.

Finally we examine the effects of a monetary shock. The rate of interest is depressed by 1 per cent. Since interest rates are endogenous in the LVPL model, in the first year this was translated into a temporary increase in the money supply sufficient to produce a temporary depression of 1 per cent in the short-term rate of interest. Table 6.3 presents the results. According to the textbook transmission mechanism a reduction in the rate of interest is represented by a downward shift of the LM schedule (expansionary monetary policy), which expands output, increases prices and depreciates the exchange rate. This is generally confirmed by the simulation results in the case of the quarterly models (figures 6.7(a)–6.7(d)). A sharper depreciation of the exchange rate is noticeable in the LBS and NIESR models. The odd one out is the LVPL model which shows output declining in the first year.

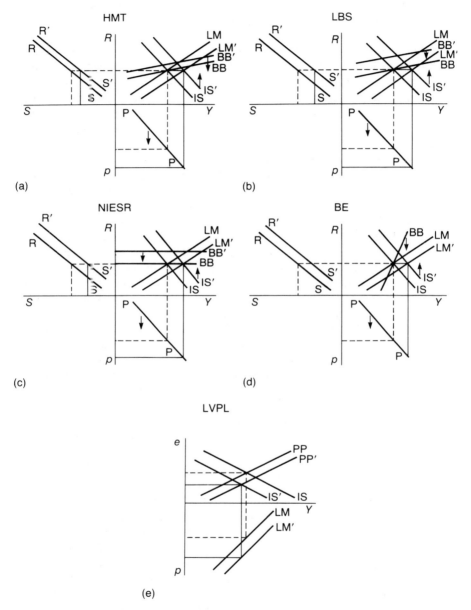

Figure 6.6 Fiscal expansion with fixed interest rates: (a) HMT; (b) LBS; (c) NIESR; (d) BE; (e) LVPL

Table 6.3   Effect of a 1 per cent reduction in nominal short rates

	HMT	LBS	NIESR	LVPL	BE
GDP (%)					
1	0.38	0.36	0.67	−0.19	0.24
2	0.68	0.72	0.95	−0.03	0.49
3	0.76	0.77	1.09	−0.11	0.29
4	0.73	0.65	1.14	−0.08	0.00
5	0.71	0.50	1.13	−0.06	−0.27
6	0.71	0.31		−0.05	
7		0.12		−0.03	
Consumer prices (%)					
1	0.07	0.22	0.21	2.07	0.05
2	0.31	0.90	0.70	2.12	0.21
3	0.70	1.45	1.23	2.32	0.36
4	1.02	1.95	1.87	2.47	0.48
5	1.17	2.40	2.42	2.58	0.46
6	1.17	2.82		2.58	
		3.09		2.56	
Nominal exchange rate (%)					
1	−1.54	−4.14	−1.54	−3.82	−1.39
2	−2.15	−4.07	−2.16	−2.80	−0.85
3	−2.34	−3.85	−2.41	−2.52	−0.32
4	−2.51	−3.68	−2.63	−2.51	0.23
5	−2.62	−3.56	−2.80	−2.58	0.69
6	−2.61	−3.05		−2.60	
7		−2.31		−2.60	
Current balance (£billion)					
1	−0.7	−1.9	−1.6	1.9	0.1
2	−1.0	−1.4	−0.4	0.6	0.2
3	−0.5	−1.6	−0.4	0.5	0.4
4	0.1	−1.9	0.3	0.3	0.3
5	0.5	−2.4	0.9	0.1	−0.0
6	0.8	−2.4		0.1	
7		−1.9		0.1	

The reduction in interest rates is obtained through an unanticipated expansion in the money stock resulting in unanticipated inflation which shifts the PP schedule down to PP'. The rise in inflation reduces the real value of wealth which induces a contraction in private sector spending (IS shifts down

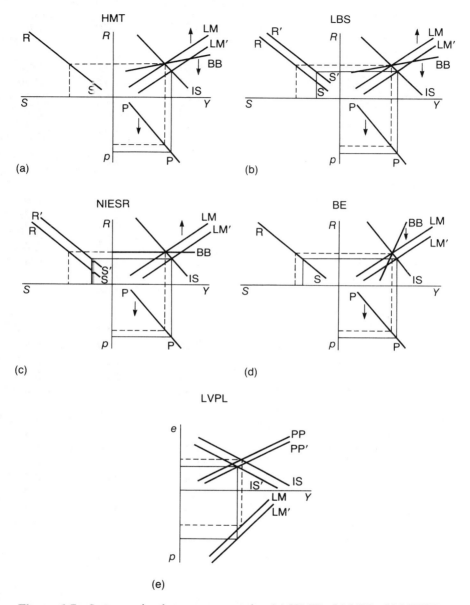

Figure 6.7 Increase in the money supply: (a) HMT; (b) LBS; (c) NIESR; (d) BE; (e) LVPL

to IS'). On balance the net effect is contradictionary, with a sharper effect on the nominal and real exchange rates. The increase in the money stock is a one-off event which has little effect on real variables after the first few years.

In summary, an examination of the monetary sectors of the various models shows that there is broad consensus regarding the principal routes of the transmission mechanism. Real interest rates and financial wealth impinge on spending decisions directly. Indirect effects of changes in interest rates on aggregate demand follow from changes in competitiveness from the exchange rate and from capital valuation effects on financial wealth. Expectations enter implicitly or explicitly in the determination of exchange rates, capital gains on financial assets, investment and consumption functions through real interest rates and in the wage–price block. There is a broad consensus also as to the modelling of expectations and its speed of adjustment. Rational expectations is favoured only in asset markets, principally the forward exchange rate. Models which include expectations of capital gains and forward pricing of financial assets (LBS and HMT) allow for the possibility of rational expectations solution. On the whole, inflation expectations are modelled as an adaptive framework. This reflects the accepted view that rational expectations is useful in the context of auction markets such as asset markets but not in the context of labour and goods markets. On this score the LVPL model, where all expectations are modelled as rational but sluggishness is introduced into the labour market through the fixed term non-contingent contracts, stands apart.

Despite differences in modelling strategy, the simulation experiments show that on the whole model properties are not dissimilar with respect to monetary and monetary-constrained fiscal shocks. Models with explicit rational forward expectations of the exchange rate tend to exhibit a faster reaction of this variable, to shocks. The LVPL and HMT models exhibit more powerful crowding out properties but, except for LVPL, the major models show broadly similar properties for monetary and fiscal policy shocks.

6.9 SMALL MODELS: AN ALTERNATIVE STRATEGY

An alternative to the detailed structure of the monetary sectors of the major macroeconomic models (LVPL excepted) has been developed in the framework of small monetary models. The philosophy of this approach is to minimize the details of the transmission mechanism, concentrating rather on the overall effects of monetary policy. An extreme case is the approach adopted by the Federal Reserve Bank of St Louis which attempts to cut out the transmission mechanism by appealing to a reduced form specification.[10]

Other models that fall into the small monetary model paradigm have typically taken the disequilibrium buffer stock approach as their modelling strategy. Such models see the stock of money acting as an absorber of unanticipated shocks. Costs of portfolio adjustment can produce large deviations between desired and actual money holding. Hence the buffer stock model is viewed as a disequilibrium monetary adjustment process.

The reduced form approach has not been popular in the UK. The first attempt to estimate a Federal Reserve Bank of St Louis type model for the UK met with only limited success (Artis and Nobay, 1969). Unlike the results for the USA, Artis and Nobay found that monetary policy had weak impacts on nominal income while fiscal policy had strong impacts. The basic model related the change in nominal income Y to distributed lags of changes in the money supply and changes to a measure of fiscal policy, as in the following specification where D is the difference operator $(Dx = (1 - g)x_t = x_t - x_{t-1})$.

$$DY = \sum_{i=0}^{k} \beta_i DM_{t-i} + \sum_{i=0}^{m} \delta_i DG_{t-i} \qquad (6.36)$$

A further examination by Matthews and Ormerod (1978) found that once the fiscal variable G was adjusted for cyclical effects and base money M0 was used for the monetary variable M, the estimated relation bore a close resemblance to the US findings. In particular, it was found that $\Sigma_{i=0}^{4}\beta_i = 4.7$ and $\Sigma_{i=0}^{4}\delta_j = -0.02$. At a first glance this may appear to give strong support to a short-run quantity theory interpretation of the transmission mechanism but, as critics of the St Louis approach note, the reduced form model is equally consistent with a non-monetarist structure. Other criticisms focus on the econometric results and the potential for bias in the parameters from estimating a truncated reduced form of an alternative but equally valid structural model (Gordon, 1976). The zero fiscal impact is explained by the perfect stabilizing power of fiscal policy, while the positive monetary multipliers are explained by the interest-rate-stabilizing reaction of monetary policy to real shocks (Gordon, 1976). The result of both theoretical and empirical criticism of the approach have led to neglect of the reduced form paradigm in the UK.

The notion of disequilibrium money has its roots in the microtheoretical precautionary type demand for money (Miller and Orr, 1966). The demand for money adjusts to the desired or optimum level when the stock of money breaches a theoretically determined upper or lower bound. Within this range, the actual stock of money can systematically deviate from the desired level. The adjustment of the actual stock of money towards the desired level will prompt adjustments in other economic variables. An example of this kind of adjustment effect is given by Archibald and Lipsey (1958). Excess money holdings are rundown in each time period by acquiring goods. In principle the adjustment of excess money holdings will impinge on all the endogenous variables that make up the demand for money. Furthermore, portfolio theory states that an excess supply of money will activate adjustments to the demands for other financial assets. the conventional transmission mechanism is through changes in interest rates and wealth, but the buffer stock model suggests that part of the excess money would feed directly into asset demands. The buffer stock paradigm recognizes that in a monetary economy, as money enters into all exchanges, an excess stock of money would bring about adjustments to expenditure, prices and asset stocks.

The following structure is typical of the modelling strategy used in empirical work in this area (Cuthbertson and Taylor, 1987; Davidson and Ireland, 1987):

$$DM^s = \text{PSBR} + \text{CA} - \text{D}B + \text{D}L - \text{D}F \tag{6.37}$$

$$\Gamma(g)X = \Omega(g)Z + \phi(g)(M^s - M^d) \tag{6.38}$$

$$M^d/P = M(R, Y, W) \qquad M_R < 0, M_Y, M_W > 0 \tag{6.39}$$

$$W = M + B + F - L \tag{6.40}$$

where M^s is the money supply derived from the consolidated public and external sector balance sheets, PSBR is the public sector borrowing requirement, CA is the current balance, B is the stock of government bonds, L is the stock of bank advances, F is the stock of net foreign assets, D is the difference operator, M^d is the demand for money, Y is the level of output, R is the rate of interest, W is the stock of financial wealth, X is a vector of real and nominal endogenous variables such as output, prices, asset stocks, exchange rate etc., z is a matrix of predetermined variables, $\phi(g)$ is a vector polynomial in the lag operator, and $\Gamma(g)$ and $\Omega(g)$ are suitably conformable polynomial matrices in the lag operator.

Models of this type have been successfully estimated for the USA (Laidler and Bentley, 1983) and for the UK (Coghlan, 1979; Davidson, 1987). The first equation is the familiar counterparts identity for M3 (see *Bank of England Quarterly Bulletin* or *Financial Statistics*). In this framework, the money supply is supply driven and is treated as endogenous. The money supply is determined as the residual item of the counterparts equation. Thus shocks to the demand for loans by the NBPS or the PSBR would be fully reflected in the money supply. However, because money is also a buffer asset, the supply or money does not necessarily equal the demand for money that is consistent with full portfolio equilibrium. As asset prices alter and, importantly, the absolute price level adjusts, the demand for money (and the demand for other financial assets) adjust so that full equilibrium is obtained in the long run. This way, the adjustment is on both the demand side and the supply side – the adjustment in the demand for other financial assets feeds back into the money supply through the counterparts equation. This is the approach taken by Coghlan (1979) and Davidson (1984, 1987), whereas in a similar study for the USA, Laidler and Bentley (1983) assume that the money supply is exogenous. This fits in with the institutional set-up in the USA. The Federal Reserve is largely independent of the Treasury and determines monetary policy, at least in the short run, independently of fiscal policy. Therefore, the adjustment to the discrepancy between supply and demand for money occurs entirely on the demand side by the movement of interest rates, the price level and the level of economic activity.

The second equation represents the adjustment of expenditure, asset holdings and prices, including interest rates and the exchange rate, as a response to disequilibrium money. The problem for estimation is that of consistency; the specification implies a series of cross-equation restrictions such that the implied values of the money demand parameters are the same within the full set of equations for X. This means that the full system has to be estimated jointly. This is the approach taken by Davidson (1987). The Coghlan model was estimated using single-equation techniques and without the imposition of cross-equation restrictions.

The third equation is the long-run or equilibrium demand for money implied from an estimated equation. In Coghlan's model the target or equilibrium model is described by a quantity theory specification. The Davidson model imposes a long-run unit income elasticity but includes a proxy for the real interest rate and the long–short interest rate differential.

The buffer stock paradigm has generated a considerable amount of research output[11] and appears to be the most promising route for the future of monetary modelling.

Criticism of the buffer stock approach is primarily concerned with the assumed costs of portfolio adjustment that allow for sustained monetary disequilibrium. The existence of near monies and the continued decline in the costs of transfer between assets initiated by advances in financial innovation undermines the basis of such models. The development of interest-bearing sight deposits and the continued trend towards cashless spending reduces the 'medium of exchange' function associated with concrete money and highlights the 'store of value' function. The property of 'jointness' in the Friedman and Schwartz (1969) sense recedes as the store of value function comes to dominate. Hence, broad measures of money become more influenced by savings and portfolio decisions than by transactions decisions.

In the parlance of Pesek and Saving (1968), deposits lose their 'moneyness'. In the limit we can envisage a world in which abstract money exists only as a 'unit of account' and all concrete money is a 'store of value' (see for instance Sargent and Wallace, 1982). In such a world the property of liquidity associated with money and the buffer stock model would be irrelevant. The implication of all this is that the buffer stock model may have been useful in modelling the past but in the context of the Lucas critique it may prove to be of less value in the future.

The general acceptance of the buffer stock approach has also been hindered by the econometric implications of the strategy which appeals more to the small model approach than to that of the large macroeconomic forecasting models reviewed earlier. However, there are signs that model proprietors are beginning to experiment with the single-equation specification.[12] The direction of this research programme is as yet an open question.

6.10 CONCLUSION

Several conclusions can be drawn from this survey. On the whole modellers are content with implicit theorizing. To the modeller, the macroeconomic model is not merely a forecasting tool but also an aid to analytical thinking. In that respect the model has to be viewed as an approximation to the truth. As an approximation, few modellers have attempted to construct models based on explicit microfoundations. Notable exceptions have been the LBS monetary sector, the LVPL model and, to a lesser extent, the demand for money in the NIESR model. However, modelling practice tends to follow innovations in theory with something of a lag. The current major innovation in monetary theory is the attempt to build monetary theory up from 'solid microfoundations' on the lines of the research programme led by Minnesota and Chicago (see Kareken and Wallace, 1980). If a prediction on the direction which modelling strategy takes is called for, the most likely direction, spurred on by the Lucas critique, is towards a more microtheoretical approach for specification of behavioural functions and the modelling of expectations as model consistent.[13]

To date, the consensus regarding 'rational' or 'model-consistent' expectations is that such a modelling strategy is appropriate to asset markets but not to product or labour markets. Forward, rational or consistent expectations in the LBS model is confined to expectations of capital gains in asset markets and to the exchange rate; in the NIESR model it is used only to model the future real exchange rate. This represents the accepted or received view that not all markets behave as auction markets; in particular, the labour market is assumed to exhibit sluggishness not consistent with instantaneous market clearing. This has led to the adoption of *ad hoc* specification of expectations determination functions for labour and product markets. However, if in the future the macromodeller is likely to pay greater attention to microfoundations, a stronger case would have to be put up for the retention of adaptive or mechanical rules of expectations adjustment. If it is the case that product and labour markets appear to behave sluggishly, one interpretation which does not give up the consistent expectations formulation is to embed the models of those markets in an optimum contracts framework which yields sluggish price behaviour but is in principle derivable from optimizing behaviour.

The simulations reveal that models with detailed structures of the monetary sector do not necessarily produce stronger real side interactions. Note that the NIESR model exhibits powerful monetary effects in the case of an interest rate change. Specifically, the NIESR model had a low level of interaction with the real sector, compared with the effects of the more detailed HMT model which has a richer interaction. In the case of the NIESR model, this occurs because of the consistent expectations model of the exchange rate based on the open arbitrage–efficient markets condition. Small changes to the domestic real rate of interest causes sharp changes to the spot real exchange rate and to net trade.

The application of rational expectations and the greater attention that is likely to be paid to microfoundations suggests that in the future modellers are likely to opt for simplicity in modelling the transmission mechanism. Smaller models will be likely to include stronger interest rate effects, wealth effects and expectations effects. The tendency towards models of more manageable size with stronger monetary interactions is evidenced in the Treasury's replacement of its current model with the much smaller SLIM model. Academic work on the effects of domestic and global monetary policies will be based on smaller models with readily understood transmission mechanisms (e.g. Buiter and Miller, 1981; Currie and Levine, 1985; Levine and Currie, 1987; Smith and Wickens, 1989). The consequence of this is that the study of monetary systems and aspects of applied monetary economics will become more the province of academic research than part of a modeller's research strategy.[14] Financial innovation has already blurred the conventional transmission mechanism by heightening the store of value function of money which has developed without altering the medium of exchange function. Since financial innovation is a dynamic process, models of wider monetary structures are unlikely to exhibit stable properties for forecasting and simulation analysis. The theory of financial innovation also suggests that the link between the wider monetary aggregates and nominal income would weaken. In the extreme case when the banking sector is fully deregulated and competitive, the bank's supply of deposits and loans becomes perfectly interest elastic as in Fama (1981, 1983). This means that the transmission mechanism with the broad monetary aggregates could become increasingly irrelevant. The official enhancement of MO as an indicator adds further force to the development of simpler transmission processes. Simpler but tighter and more rigorously based monetary models are not developments that occur overnight. The macromodeller is going to be fully employed in the future.

Appendix 1   The HMT Model

The HMT model is the only model to include an explicit function determining the demand for M3. The detailed specification is outlined below, where ln refers to the natural logarithm and L is the lag operator.

$$\ln M3 = \ln PTFE + (0.87 - 0.89L + 0.15L^2)$$

$$\ln\left(\frac{GROSWPR - CUMREV}{PTFE}\right) + (0.29 - 0.23L + 0.035L^2$$

$$+ 0.035L^3)\ \ln\left(1 + \frac{CUMREV}{GROSWPR - CUMREV}\right)$$

$$+ \sum_{i=0}^{3}(L^i)a_i RGM + \sum_{i=0}^{3}(L^i)b_i\ \ln TFE - 0.00096537T$$

$$+ (1.057 - 0.179L^2)L\ \ln\left(\frac{M3}{PTFE}\right)$$

i	a	b
0	− 0.0035	− 0.2500
1	0.0035	− 0.2230
2	− 0.0005	0.0110
3	− 0.0004	− 0.0075
Sum	− 0.0009	0.0305

The elasticities are as follows:

	Impact	*Long run*
Real wealth	0.9	1.1
TFE	0.3	0.2
Long rate	− 0.4	− 0.7

The terms used are defined as follows: PTFE, total financial expenditure deflator; GROSW, gross wealth of the non-bank private sector (NBPS); CUMREV, accumulated revaluations in NBPS gilt and other public sector debt; RGFM, post-tax yields on gilts relative to M3; TFE, total final expenditure (1980 prices); TIME, time trend.

The specification draws on the earlier work of Grice and Bennett (1981) of HM Treasury. The model exhibits both short-run and long-run homogeneity in the price level and a dynamic structure that suggests an unusually lengthy adjustment process exhibiting an initial overshoot in response to shocks. The response of money demand to gross wealth is little different between the short run and the long run. Importantly, the demand for money is shown to react differently to changes in gross wealth depending on whether the change comes from a change in the stock or a change in its value. The near unitary long-run wealth elasticity can be defended on theoretical grounds, but the low income elasticity indicating strong economies of scale in the use of cash in lower than even that predicted from inventory theory (as in Baumol, 1952).

In contrast, the specification of the demand for non-interest-bearing M1 is much more conventional in terms of the Keynes–New Classical synthesis and, except for the dynamics, contains few empirical surprises. The detailed specification is described below.

$$\ln\left(\frac{\text{NIM1}}{\text{PC}}\right) = -0.88 + 0.578L \ln\left(\frac{\text{NIM1}}{\text{PC}}\right) + (0.0045 - 0.005L^4)L \text{ PC}$$
$$+ 0.333 \ln C - (0.0055 + 0.00402L^2 + 0.0061L^5)\text{RSHRT}$$
$$- 0.00107L^3 \text{ INNOV}$$

where NIM1 is non-interest-bearing M1, PC is the consumer price deflator, C is consumer spending (1980 prices) and INNOV is the number of bank accounts and building society accounts per capita. The elasticities are as follows (the asterisk denotes semi-elasticity):

	Impact	Long run
Real consumption	0.333	0.789
Annual inflation	0.0045	− 0.0011
Short rate*	− 0.0055	− 0.0382

The demand for narrow money was included in the HMT model following the switch of emphasis towards targeting M0. The most recent equation, which refers to notes and coin held by the private sector and banks' till money, was included in August 1987. This replaced the earlier estimated equation describing the demand for notes and coin by the NBPS which was reported by Johnston (1984):

$$\ln\left(\frac{CASH}{PC}\right) = 0.5 \ln L \frac{CASH}{PC} + 0.5 \ln CNDI - 0.416\, L(1 - L^4)\ln PC$$

$$- \frac{7.9866}{106CDISP} + 1.970\, PROPM - 3.433$$

$$+ \sum_{i=0}^{3} L^i[0.01a_i RBDEP(1 - TPBK)]$$

i	a
0	-0.125
1	-0.250
2	-0.083
3	-0.042
Sum	-0.500

The terms are defined as follows: CASH, notes and coin held by the private sector; PC, consumer price index; CNDI real consumption of non-durables excluding services; CDISP, number of cash dispenser; PROPM, proportion of manual workers; TPBK, banks' tax rate; RBDEP, rate of interest on bank deposits.

The elasticities are as follows (the asterisks denote semi-elasticities):

	Impact	*Long run*
Non-durable consumption	0.5	1.0
PROPM	1.97	3.94
Inflation*	-0.416	-0.83
Deposit rate*	-0.125	-1.0
CDISP	-7.99×10^{-6}	-1.6×10^{-5}

The unitary elasticity effects on the rate of interest, non-durable consumption and the price level were imposed but were not rejected by the data on conventional criteria.

Appendix 2   The Treasury SLIM Model

The new Treasury model SLIM identifies two monetary aggregates, M0 and M4. The broader measure of money M4 recognizes the breakdown in the traditional demarcation between the banks and building societies and replaces M3 used in the previous version of the model. Except for the definitional change in the money supply and the consequent change in the definition of wealth of the private sector (non-bank and building society private sector), the broad structure of the financial model remains the same. The demand for notes and coin remains much the same as in the HMT model.

The personal sector allocates assets across three classes, namely bank deposits, building society deposits and National Savings. The apex of the decision-making process is the personal sector's demand for liquid assets which can be characterized as follows.

$$\text{LIQPE} = g[(1 - g)\text{GWER, GFWPE, YPDY, RLIQ, RS, RL} + \mu_e]$$

where LIQPE is the total stock of personal sector liquid assets, GWER is acquisitions of gross wealth, excluding revaluation, GFWPE is the gross financial wealth of the private sector, YPDY is personal disposable income, RLIQ is the return on holding liquid assets, RS are short rates and RL $+ \mu_e$ is the return on holding gilts including expected revaluation.

A portfolio structure is used to allocate LIQE along the following lines:

$$A_i = h(gA_i, gA_j, \text{LIQPE}, R_i, R_j)$$

where A_i is the ith liquid asset, A_j are all other liquid assets j/i, R_i are own rates of return and R_j are cross-rates of return. The allocation of personal sector liquid assets between bank and building society deposits are given by estimated functions of the type described above, with National Savings being determined as the residual asset.

A demand for M4 by the company sector determines the total M4 by adding to personal sector bank and building society deposits and notes and coin. Company sector M4 is given by an estimated function specified as follows:

$$\ln\left(\frac{\text{M4}_{\text{CO}}}{\text{P}}\right) = (g)k\left[\ln\left(\frac{\text{GW}_{\text{CO}}}{\text{P}}\right), \ln Y, DP, r_{\text{M4}} - r_i, \text{FLOW}\right]$$

where M4_{CO} is company sector M4, GW_{CO} is gross financial wealth of company sector, P is the TFE deflator, Y is the measure of activity, $r_{\text{M4}} - r_i$ is the interest differential and FLOW are inflows and outflows to the portfolio. Equations for bank lending to people, ICCs and OFIs were re-estimated but contained principally the same arguments as the previous model.

Consistent expectations are introduced in the determination of the forward expected exchange rate and the expected capital gains on gilts. With the latter, the associated arbitrage condition ensures that the holding period yields (including expected capital gains) on short- and long-term bonds are equalized. The terminal condition is that expected capital gain in equilibrium is zero. With the exchange rate, the terminal condition is that exchange rate consistent with a zero basic balance (current balance plus capital flows).

Table 6.A1 highlights the difference between the AE and RE simulations, of the SLIM model. The pivotal short-term rate of interest is raised by one percentage point. In the case of the RE simulation, the announcement of a permanent change in short-term interest rates would not be viewed as credible by financial markets. Consequently, interest rates are raised for two years only. In the case of the AE simulation, the short-term rate is permanently raised by one percentage point.

The introduction of consistent or rational expectations in the determination of the exchange rate has dramatically altered its dynamic properties. In the AE case the exchange rate rises sluggishly in response to the rise in the short-term interest rate, whereas in the RE case all the adjustment occurs in the first period.

Table 6.A1 Interest rate simulation

Year	Adaptive RS + 1% permanently	Consistent RS + 1% for 2 years
GDP (%)		
1	−0.4	−0.7
2	−0.8	−1.2
3	−1.1	−0.7
4	−1.1	−0.1
5	−1.0	0.5
RPI (%)		
1	0.4	0.1
2	0.2	−0.7
3	−0.4	−2.0
4	−1.4	−2.9
5	−2.5	−3.3
Ex rate (%)		
1	1.4	5.0
2	1.8	3.8
3	2.6	3.0
4	3.6	2.6
5	4.7	2.1

Appendix 3   The NIESR Model

The demand for M1 is the NIESR model is based on the buffer stock principle (Artis and Cuthbertson, 1985). The demand for money is made up of two components – a planned component M_p and an unplanned component M_u. The planned component is modelled by the application of a multiperiod costs of adjustment framework. The familiar quadratic cost function which underlies much of the work on the demand for money is generalized to many periods:

$$C = E_{-1} \sum_{t=0}^{T} [D^t a (M_t - M_t^*)^2 + b(M_t - M_{t-1})^2]$$

The first-order conditions for $t < T$ are

$$\frac{\partial C_t}{\partial M_t} = 2a(M_t - M_{t-1}^*) + 2b(M_t - M_{t-1}) - 2b(M_{t+1} - M_t)$$
$$= 0$$

$$M_t = A_1 M_t^* + B_1 M_{t-1} + B_1 M_{t+1}$$

where $A_1 = a/(a + 2b)$, $B_1 = b/(a + 2b)$ and $A_1 + 2B_1 = 1$, and for the terminal date

$$\frac{\partial C_T}{\partial M_T} = 2a(M_T - M_T^*) + 2b(M_T - M_{T-1})$$
$$= 0$$

$$M_T = A_2 M_T^* + B_2 M_{T-1}$$

where $A_2 = a/(a + b)$ and $A_2 + B_2 = 1$.

The following specification is obtained after applying the Sargent (1979) method of forward operators (the details are given by Cuthbertson (1985, pp. 136–8):

$$M_t = q M_{t-1} + \frac{a}{b} q \sum_{i=0}^{\infty} q^i M_{t+i}^*$$

The unplanned component of the demand for money is modelled as dependent on innovations in prices output and interest rates, where expectations are the predictions from autoregressive equations.

The estimated demand for M1 (narrow money) obtained using this methodology is as follows:

$$\ln M1 = 0.105 + 0.913 \ln M1_{-1} + 0.608 \ln \left(\frac{CPI}{CPI^e}\right)$$

$$+ 0.0846 \ln \left(\frac{QRDY}{QRDY^e}\right) - 0.042 \ln \left(\frac{RLA}{RLA^e}\right) - 0.0002Q_1$$

$$- 0.0000028Q_Z + 0.028Q_3 + 0.0128\sum_{i=0}^{4} 0.913^i \ln (QRDY)_{+i}$$

$$- 0.0168\sum_{i=0}^{3} 0.913^i \ln(RLA)_{+i} + (1 - 0.913)\frac{2}{1 - 0.9135}$$

$$\sum_{i=0}^{4} 0.93^i \ln(CPI)_{+i}$$

where M1 is the money supply M1 definition, QRDY is the real personal disposable income, CPI is the consumer price deflator and RLA is the three month local authority debt. The elasticities are as follows:

	Short run		Long run
	Anticipated	Unanticipated	
CPI	0.0207	0.6287	1.0000
QRDY	0.0128	0.0974	0.6183
RLA	− 0.0168	− 0.0588	− 0.0589

Appendix 4   The London Business School Model

The estimated functions for the personal sector of the LBS financial sector model are presented in table 6.A2.

Table 6.A2   Personal sector (plus unit and investment trusts)

Asset	Coefficient on				
	Relative return and budget constraint	Lagged depend	Constant	Std error	Durbin's H
Equities	4.07 (3.9)	0.97 (0.03)	—	115.4	0.71
Gilts	2.28 (0.42)	0.95[a]	—	31.7	1.96

continued

Table 6.A2 *continued*

| | Coefficient on | | | | |
| | Relative return and budget | Lagged depend | Constant | | |
Asset	constraint			Std error	Durbin's H
Bank loans	1.43 (0.93)	0.96[a]	−38.5 (8.2)	30.6	1.04
Time deposits	0.26 (0.74)	0.95[a]	40.3 (7.3)	20.4	1.04
Overseas shorts'	0.66 (0.22)	0.84 (0.09)	—	2.52	−1.89
Overseas securities	2.42 (0.79)	0.94 (0.05)	—	10.8	−1.33
Sight deposits	2.59 (1.87)	—	383.4 (15.5)	36.5	0.94
Notes and coin	3.53 (1.65)	—	182.0 (13.7)	32.2	1.68
Savings certificates	0.75 (0.10)	0.95[a]	—	7.74	1.38
Building society shares	0.50[a]	0.987 (0.018)[a]	16.94 (17.96)	16.3	4.32
Hire purchase	1.00[a]	0.35 (0.14)[a]	−64.5 (11.8)	18.0	2.26
Mortgages	4.41 (1.34)	0.974 (0.009)	−100[a]	21.6	.36

Standard errors in parentheses.
*[a] Imposed coefficient.

Appendix 5 The Liverpool Model

The monetary sector of the LVPL model is the most sparse of all the major macroeconomic models. It consists of one estimated function, the demand for M0:

$$\ln\left(\frac{M0}{P}\right) = -2.77 - 0.54R_s + 0.635 \ln \text{RDY} + 0.1137 \ln B$$
$$+ 0.332T_Y + 0.1878T_e - 0.01\text{TIME} + 0.598 \ln \left(\frac{M0}{P}\right)_{-1}$$

where M0 is the stock of M0 money, R_S is the three month treasury bill yield, RDY is real disposable income, B are real unemployment benefits, T_Y is the average income tax rate, T_Y is the average percentage employer's contributions and TIME is the time trend. Both the unemployment benefit and income tax rates refer to a married man with two children.

The elasticities are as follows (the asterisk indicates semi-elasticity):

	Impact	Long run
R_S^*	-0.545	-1.355
RDY	0.635	1.580
B	0.1137	0.2828
T_Y	0.332	0.826
T_e	0.1878	0.467

Appendix 6 The Bank of England Model

The broad money measure M3 in the BE model is derived from the counter-parts identity, while M1 and notes and coin are obtained from estimated demand functions. The equation for notes and coin is given by

$$\ln NC = 0.281 \ln (NC)_{-1} + 0.659 \ln (\pounds CE) - 0.0057RZSN$$

$$- 0.0071RZSN_{-1} - 1.305\left(\frac{POWA\text{-}LE}{POWA}\right) + 0.238$$

where NC is notes and coin in circulation, £CE is the total consumer expenditure (current prices), RZSN is the net rate of interest on building society shares, POWA is the population of working age excluding those in full-time education and LE are employees in employment.

The elasticites are as follows (the asterisk indicates semi-elasticity):

Variable	Impact	Long run
£CE	0.659	0.958
RZSN*	-0.0057	-0.0178
UNEMP	-1.305	-1.815

The demand for M1 is given by the following equation:

$$\ln M1 = 0.855 \ln(M1)_{-1} + 0.145 \ln TFE + 0.139 \ln PTFE - 0.005RLA$$

where M1 is M1, TFE is the total final expenditure in 1980 prices, PTFE is the deflator for TFE and RLA is the local authority three month rate. The elasticities are as follows (the asterisk indicates semi-elasticity):

Variable	Impact	Long run
TFE	0.145	1.000
PTFE	−0.139	0.959
RLA*	−0.005	−0.034

Notes

1 See Frenkel and Johnson (1976) for a collection of essays on this subject.
2 For a survey of efficient markets theory and evidence see Fama (1970).
3 On the general to specific methodology see Mizon (1977), Mizon and Hendry (1980) and Hendry and Richard (1982).
4 For a good discussion of models of expectations, see Holden et al. (1985).
5 For a recent description see Mellis (1988).
6 Courakis (1988) notes that the implied parameter values of the estimated model for the personal sector suggest that time deposits are the most costly asset to adjust in the personal sector's portfolio whereas, in contrast, mortgages have the lowest adjustment cost. Other implausible properties are that equities, gilts and overseas securities are considered low risk or low other disutility features, while notes and coin and sight deposits are considered the riskiest. For a discussion of the implications of the restrictions of the model see also Green (1984).
7 For an explanation see Matthews and Rastogi (1985). Other researchers who have employed tax variables in the demand for money as a proxy for evasion or black economy effects are Cagan (1958), Sheppard (1977) and Tanzi (1983).
8 See Patterson et al. (1987) for a recent description.
9 The simulations are repetitions of those reported by Fisher et al. (1988).
10 See Anderson and Carlson (1970) and for a critique see Modigliani and Ando (1976).
11 See Milbourne (1988) for a recent survey.
12 The NIESR has already included an explicit buffer stock specification for the demand for narrow money and the application of disequilibrium money is an active research programme.
13 Some work is already under way at the Bank of England to model the monetary sector from a strong consumer – theoretical perspective (see for instance Barr and Cuthbertson, 1988).
14 The critique of the LBS model by Courakis (1988) is an example of this development.

References

Anderson, L. and Carlson, K. (1970) A monetarist model for economic stabilisation. *Federal Reserve Bank of St Louis Review* April, 7–21.

Anderson, P. A. (1979) Rational expectations forecasts from non-rational models. *Journal of Monetary Economics* January, 67–80.

Archibald, G. and Lipsey, D. (1958) Monetary and value theory: A critique of Lange and Patinkin. *Review of Economic Studies* 26, 1–22.

Artis, M. and Cuthbertson, K. (1985) The demand for M1: A forward-looking buffer stock model. Discussion Paper 87, National Institute of Economic and Social Research, April.

—— and Nobay, A. R. (1969) Two aspects of the monetary debate. *National Institute Economic Review* 49, 33–50.

Barr, D. G. and Cuthbertson, K. (1988) Neoclassical consumer demand theory and the demand for financial assets. Mimeo, Bank of England, September.

Baumol, W. (1952) The transactions demand for cash: an inventory theoretic approach. *Quarterly Journal of Economics* 66, 545–56.

Branson, W. H. (1977) Asset markets and relative prices in exchange rate determination *Sozialwissenschaftliche Annalen des Instituts für Hovere Studien.* 1 69–89.

Budd, A., Dicks, G., Holly, S., Keating, G. and Robinson, B. (1984) The London Business School model of the UK. *Economic Modelling* 1, 355–420.

Buiter, W. and Miller, M. (1981) Monetary policy and international competitiveness: the problem of adjustment. *Oxford Economic Papers (Supplement)* 33, 143–75.

Cagan, P. (1958) The demand for currency relative to the total money supply. *Journal of Political Economy* 66, 303–28.

Coghlan, R. (1979) A small monetary model of the UK economy. Bank of England Discussion Paper 3.

Courakis, A. (1988) Modelling portfolio selection. *Economic Journal 1* 98 (392), 619–42.

Currie, D. and Levine, P. (1985) Simple macroeconomic rules for the open economy. *Economic Journal (Supplement)* 95, 60–70.

Cuthbertson, K. (1985) *The Demand and Supply of Money*. Oxford: Basil Blackwell.

—— and Taylor, M. (1987) Buffer stock money: An appraisal. In C. Goodhart, D. Currie and D. Llewellyn (eds), *The Operation and Regulation of Financial Markets*, London: Macmillan.

Davidson, J. (1984) Money disequilibrium: an approach to modelling monetary phenomena in the UK. ICERD Econometric Discussion Paper 84/96, London School of Economics.

—— (1987) Disequilibrium money: some further results with a monetary model of the UK. In C. Goodhart, D. Currie and D. Llewellyn (eds), *The Operation and Regulation of Financial Markets*. London: Macmillan.

—— and Ireland, J. (1987) Buffer stock models of the monetary sector. *National Institute Economic Review* 121, 67–71.

Dornbusch, R. (1976) Expectations and exchange rate dynamics. *Journal of Political Economy* 84, 1611–76.

Fama, E. (1970) Efficient capital markets – A review of theory and empirical work. *Journal of Finance* 25, 384–417.

—— (1980) Banking in the theory of finance. *Journal of Monetary Economics* 6(1), 39–58.

—— (1983) Financial intermediation and price level control. *Journal of Monetary Economics* 12(1), 6–28.

Fisher, P., Tanna, S., Turner, D., Wallis, K. and Whitley, J. (1988) Comparative properties of models of the UK economy. *National Institute Economic Review* 125, 69–87.

Frenkel, J. and Johnson, H. (eds) (1976) *The Monetary Theory of the Balance of Payments*. London: Allen & Unwin.

Friedman, M. (1956) The quantity theory of money: a restatement. In M. Friedman (ed.), *Studies in the Quantity Theory of Money*. Chicago, IL: University of Chicago Press.

—— and Schwartz, A. (1969) The definition of money: net wealth and neutrality as criteria. *Journal of Money, Credit and Banking* 1, 1–14.

Gordon, R. (1976) Comments on Modigliani and Ando. In J. Stein (ed.), *Monetarism*. Amsterdam: North-Holland.

Green, C. J. (1984) Expectations, adjustment costs and equilibrium asset prices: an analytical note on the financial sector of the London Business School model. Mimeo, Bank of England, September.

Grice, J. and Bennett, A. (1981) The demand for sterling M3 and other aggregates in the United Kingdom. Working Paper 45, Government Economic Service, August.

Gurley, G. and Shaw, E. S. (1960) *Money in a Theory of Finance*. Washington, DC: Brookings Institution.

Hendry, D. F. and Richard, J. F. (1982) On the formulation of empirical models in dynamic econometrics. *Journal of Econometrics* 20, 3–33.

HM Treasury (1987) Macroeconomic model, list of equations and variable definitions, 26 October.

Holden, K., Peel, D. A. and Thompson, J. L. (1985) *Expectations: Theory and Evidence*. London: Macmillan.

Johnston, R. B. (1984) The demand for non-interest-bearing money in the UK, Working Paper 28, HM Treasury.

Kareken, J. and Wallace, N. (eds) (1980) *Models of Monetary Economies*. Minneapolis, MN: Federal Reserve Bank of Minneapolis.

Keating, G. (1985) The financial sector of the London Business School model. In D. Currie (ed.), *Advances in Monetary Economics*. London: Croom-Helm.

Laidler, D. and Bentley, B. (1983) A small macro-model of the post-war United States. *Manchester School* December, 317–40.

Levine, P. and Currie, D (1987) Does international macroeconomic policy coordination pay and is it sustainable? A two country analysis. *Oxford Economic Papers* 39, 38–74.

McCallum, B. T. (1976) Rational expectations and the natural rate hypothesis. *Econometrica* January, 43–52.

Matthews, K. and Ormerod, P. (1978) St. Louis models of the UK economy. *National Institute Economic Review* 84, 65–9.

—— and Rastogi, A. (1985) Little M0 and the moonlighters. *Quarterly Economic Bulletin, Liverpool Research Group in Macroeconomics* 6, 21–4.

Mellis, C. (1988) HM Treasury macroeconomic model 1986. *Economic Modelling* 5(3), 237–60.

——, Meen, G., Pain, N. and Whittaker, R. (1989) The New Treasury Model Project. Working Paper 54, HM Treasury, June.

Milbourne, R. (1988) Disequilibrium buffer stock models: a survey. Institute for Economic Research, Queens University, Discussion Paper 715, February.

Miller, M. and Orr, D. (1966) A model of the demand for money by firms. *Quarterly Journal of Economics* 79, 413–35.

Minford, P. and Peel, D. (1983) *Rational Expectations and the New Macroeconomics*. Oxford: Martin Robertson.

——, Brech, M. and Matthews, K. (1980) A rational expectations model of the UK under floating exchange rates. *European Economic Review* September, 189–220.

—— Marwaha, S., Matthews, K. and Sprague, A. (1984) The Liverpool macroeconomic model of the United Kingdom. *Economic Modelling* January, 24–62.

Mizon, C. (1977) Model selection procedures. In M. J. Artis and A. R. Nobay (eds), *Studies in Modern Economic Analysis*. Oxford: Blackwell.

—— and Hendry, D. F. (1980) An empirical application and Monte Carlo analysis of tests of dynamic specification. *Review of Economic Studies* 47, 21–46.

Modigliani, F. and Ando, A. (1976) Impacts of fiscal actions on aggregate income and the monetarist controversy: theory and evidence. In J. Stein (ed.), *Monetarism*. Amsterdam: North-Holland.

Moore, B. and Threadgold, A. (1985) Corporate borrowing in the UK, 1965–1982. *Economica* 52, 65–78.

Muth, J. F. (1961) Rational expectations and the theory of price movements. *Econometrica* 29, 315–35.

NIESR (1986) National Institute Model 9. National Institute of Economic and Social Research, November.

Parkin, M. (1970) Discount house portfolio and debt selection. *Review of Economic Studies* 37, 469–97.

—— and Bade, R. (1988) *Modern Macroeconomics*. Oxford: Phillip Allan, 2nd edn.

Patinkin, D. (1965) *Money, Interest and Prices*. New York: Harper & Row, 2nd edn.

Patterson, K., Harnett, I., Robinson, G. and Ryding, J. (1987) The Bank of England quarterly model of the UK economy. *Economic Modelling* 4(4), 398–529.

Pesek, B. and Saving, N. (1965) *Money, Wealth and Economic Theory*. New York: Macmillan.

Radcliffe Committee (1959) *Committee on the Working of the Monetary System: Report*. London: HMSO, Cmnd 827.

Sargent, T. (1979) *Macroeconomic Theory*. New York: Academic Press.

—— and Wallace, N. (1975) Rational expectations, the optimum monetary instrument and the optimal money supply rule. *Journal of Political Economy* 83, 241–54.

—— and —— (1982) The real bills doctrine versus the quantity theory: a reconsideration. *Journal of Political Economy* 90(6), 122–36.

Sheppard, D. (1977) *The Growth and Role of UK Financial Institutions 1880–1962*. London: Methuen.

Smith, P. N. and Wickens, M. R. (1989) Assessing the effects of monetary shocks on exchange rate variability with a stylised econometric model of the UK. *Greek Economic Review* June, 76–94.

Surrey, M. (1971) The analysis and forecasting of the British economy. Occasional paper 25, National Institute of Economic and Social Research.

Tanzi, V. (1983) The underground economy in the United States: Annual estimates 1930–80. *IMF Staff Papers* 30, 283–305.

Taylor, J. (1977) Conditions for unique solutions in stochastic macroeconomic models with rational expectations. *Econometrica* 45(6), 1377–86.

Tobin, J. (1958) Liquidity preference as a behaviour towards risk. *Review of Economic Studies* 25, 65–86.

—— and Brainard, W.C. (1968) Pitfalls in financial model building. *American Economic Review, Papers and Proceedings* 58, 99–122.

Wallis, K.F., Fisher, P.F., Longbottom, J.A., Turner, D.S. and Whitley, J.D. (1988) *Models of the UK Economy Fourth Review by the ESRC Macroeconomic Modelling Bureau.* Oxford: Oxford University Press.

Wickens, M.R. (1982) The efficient estimation of econometric models with rational expectations. *Review of Economic Studies* 49, 55–68.

7 The International Co-ordination of Monetary Policy: A Survey

David Currie and Paul Levine

7.1 INTRODUCTION

International economic policy co-ordination is the process whereby 'countries modify their economic policies in what is intended to be a mutually beneficial manner, taking account of international economic linkages' (Group of Thirty, 1988). This is a broad definition, encompassing a spectrum of forms of co-ordination ranging from the rather limited to the ambitious. At the ambitious end is the Bonn economic summit of 1978, where the Group of Seven (G7) countries agreed to a full blown package deal on macroeconomic and trade policies (Putnam and Bayne, 1987). At the more limited end is the multilateral surveillance process carried out by the International Monetary Fund under the Bretton Woods fixed exchange rate system.

Recent years have seen a resurgence of interest in international policy co-ordination, particular in the monetary sphere which is the concern of this survey.

The first half of the 1980s saw a period when governments were primarily concerned to 'put their own house in order', combating inflation by means of tight monetary policy. In this period, which saw a large and sustained appreciation of the dollar, international policy co-ordination was out of favour. But, by 1985, concern over the substantial misalignment of the dollar led to renewed interest in monetary co-ordination, particularly on the part of the USA. The Plaza Agreement of September 1985 was to co-ordinate monetary policy actions to manage the steady decline of the dollar from its peak of February 1988. A series of G7 summits since then have reaffirmed co-operation over monetary policy. The most significant of these was the Louvre Accord, which agreed to 'cooperate closely to foster stability of exchange rates around current levels' (For a review of this period, see Funabashi (1988).) This set in place a loose arrangement of unannounced exchange rate zones that since then has influenced policy, particularly amongst the Group of Three (G3) countries (the USA, the FRG and Japan), despite particular episodes when these informal zones have been threatened by foreign exchange market pressure. This period of co-ordination may provide the basis for a move towards a more formalized system of monetary co-ordination based on exchange rate targeting (see Group of Thirty, 1988), although many obstacles may impede that development (Currie et al., 1989).

These developments have given rise to a number of questions concerning monetary policy co-ordination. Is co-ordination desirable in principle? Can co-operative agreements be sustained or are they vulnerable to reneging by one or more of the countries participating in the arrangement. How large are the co-ordination gains in practice? Does model uncertainty undermine the case for co-ordination? What is the scope for limited forms of co-operation such as agreements focusing on the exchange rate or on simple rules which assign monetary policy to stabilizing specified target macroeconomic variables?

In the following, we survey the existing on monetary policy co-ordination and consider what answers, possibly partial, can be provided to these questions. In section 7.2, we set out the basic theoretical framework, deriving from Hamada, for analysing the potential inefficiency of non-co-ordinating policy-making, using an illustrative model that we also draw on in later sections. In section 7.3, we extend the analysis using the model to take account of issues of reputation and credibility; the recent literature has demonstrated that in an interdependent world the benefits of reputation and co-ordination are interlinked. In section 7.4 we consider the vital issue of whether co-ordinated policies are sustainable and which types of policies are vulnerable to reneging. In section 7.5 we consider the analysis of fixed exchange rate regimes, notably the European Monetary System (EMS). In section 7.6 we review the empirical literature on measuring the gains from policy co-ordination. Since this literature is typically concerned with the gains from the joint use of monetary and fiscal policy, this section has a scope broader than that of monetary policy alone. In section 7.7 we examine whether these benefits of co-ordination are lost if there is considerable uncertainty about the way in which the international economy operates. In section 7.8 we consider the benefits from adopting simple rules for the conduct of monetary, and more general macroeconomic, policies. Sections 7.6 and 7.8 are based on material presented by Currie et al (1989).

One area that we neglect wholly is the developing literature on North–South interactions and policy co-ordination (Currie and Vines, 1988). This is an important area, but one that is less crucial for our topic of international monetary co-operation.

The field that we have covered is a fast-moving one, where many issues remain the subject of active research. Inevitably, therefore, this survey is a snapshot, and intermediate in character. Therefore the conclusions that we draw in the final section 7.9 are preliminary, and may be overturned by subsequent research. Reflecting this activity, we seek in the conclusion to point to research issues that merit greater attention in future work.

7.2 THE INEFFICIENCY OF NON-CO-OPERATIVE POLICIES

In this section we begin the survey of the analysis literature dealing with international monetary policy issues. In general terms the case for policy co-ordination arises because of policy spill-overs between countries which results in the potential of Pareto inefficient non-co-operative outcomes. In a series of seminal articles Hamada (1974, 1976, 1979, 1985) demonstrated the gains from both full and partial co-operation in the form of internationally agreed 'rules of the game'. We examine Hamada's contribution using a simple two-country model which will also serve to demonstrate the more recent contributions to the literature.

Hamada adopts a stylized game-theoretical framework which others have subsequently followed. Each country or bloc is regarded as one entity or 'player' in an international macroeconomic policy game and each has a number of macroeconomic policy objectives such as targets for gross domestic product (GDP), inflation and the current account balance. To achieve these objectives the government of each country has a small number of instruments, say one fiscal instrument and one monetary instrument. In order to assess policies each policy-maker adopts a welfare measure (or welfare loss function) which penalizes deviation of target variables and instruments about desired values.

In a two-country world, Hamada then examines how successful the countries would be if they co-operated in pursuit of their objectives. This requires countries to agree to co-ordinate their policies in an appropriate manner to minimize a joint welfare loss function. This joint welfare function is a weighted average of the two individual welfare functions, with the weight being determined by relative bargaining power. (It should be noted that this does not require countries to share common objectives; indeed there is nothing to prevent the individual objectives of countries being totally at odds with one another.)

At the polar extreme of this framework is independent non-co-operative decision-making. Here, Hamada considers two non-co-operative alternatives. In the first, countries act independently, taking the actions of the other as given. This gives a Nash equilibrium outcome. In the second alternative, countries still act independently but one country (the leader) anticipates how the other country reacts to its policy. This leads to a Stackelberg equilibrium.

The general approach can be illustrated with the following two-country model. The countries have identical economies and pursue symmetrical objectives. On the demand side the model is given by

$$y_t = a_1 e_t - a_2 r_t + a_3 y_t^* \tag{7.1}$$

$$y_t^* = -a_1 e_t - a_2 r_t^* + a_3 y_t \tag{7.2}$$

where y_t denotes output at time t, e_t is the real exchange measured so that a rise represents a depreciation and r_t is the expected real interest rate. Asterisks denote country 2; all variables except the interest rate are in logarithms and all measured in deviation from about an equilibrium in which output is at its natural rate.

The supply side of the model is given be

$$y_t = -b_1 e_t - b_2 r_t + b_3 (\pi_t - \pi_{t,t}^e) \tag{7.3}$$

$$y_t^* = b_1 e_t - b_2 r_t^* + b_3 (\pi_t^* - \pi_{t,t}^{*e}) \tag{7.4}$$

where $\pi_{t,t}^e$ is denotes expectations of inflations π_t based on information available at the beginning of period t. Hereafter, $\pi_{\tau,\tau}^e$ is abbreviated to π_t^e. Equations (7.3) and (7.4) are Lucas supply curves augmented with real exchange rate and real interest rate effects. The former arises in an open economy because a real exchange rate appreciation (a reduction in e_t) drives a wedge between the producer and consumer real wage (see, for example, Artis and Currie, 1981). An increase in the expected real interest rate reduces output because it depresses the desired level of capital stock.

The model is completed with the uncovered interest rate parity condition which, in terms of the real exchange rate and the expected real interest rate, implies that

$$e_t = r_t^* - r_t + e_{t+1,t}^e \tag{7.5}$$

where $e_{t+1,t}^e$ denotes expectations of e_{t+1} formed at time t.

For the first policy-maker we assume an intertemporal welfare loss function at time t of the form

$$W_t = \frac{1}{2} \sum_{i=0}^{\infty} \lambda^i \left[(y_{t+i} - \hat{y})^2 + a\pi_{t+i}^2 \right] \tag{7.6}$$

with a similar expression with variables marked with asterisks for country 2; λ, where $0 < \lambda \leq 1$, is a discount factor assumed to be the same for both countries. The quadratic function penalizes output deviations around a target $\hat{y}$ and non-zero inflation. The monetary instrument is taken to be the rate of inflation π_t.

Following Aoki (1981), it is analytically convenient to consider separately the 'aggregate system' and the 'divergence system'. Let $y_t^a = \frac{1}{2}(y_t + y_t^*)$ and $y_t^d = \frac{1}{2}(y_t - y_t^*)$ with similar definitions for other variables. Then the aggregate demand and supply-side functions are given by

$$y_t^a = -(1 - a_3)^{-1} a_2 r_t^a \tag{7.7}$$

and

$$y_t^a = -b_2 r_t^a + b_3 (\pi_t^a - \pi_t^{ae}) \tag{7.8}$$

whilst the corresponding divergence system is given by

$$y_t^d = (1 + a_3)^{-1} (a_1 e_t - a_2 r_t^d) \tag{7.9}$$

$$y_t^d = -b_1 e_t - b_2 r_t^d + b_3 (\pi_t^d - \pi_t^{de}) \tag{7.10}$$

$$e_t = -2 r_t^d + e_{t+1,t}^e \tag{7.11}$$

Equating supply and demand gives the reduced form of the model as

$$y_t^a = \gamma^a (\pi_t^a - \pi_t^{ae}) \tag{7.12}$$

$$y_t^d = \gamma^d (\pi_t^d - \pi_t^{de}) - \xi e_{t+1,t}^e \tag{7.13}$$

$$r_t^a = -a_2^{-1} (1 - a_3) \gamma^a (\pi_t^a - \pi_t^{ae}) \tag{7.14}$$

$$r_t^d = -(2a_1 + a_2)^{-1} \gamma^d \{(1 + a_3)(\pi_t^d - \pi_t^{de}) - b_3^{-1}[a_1 + b_1(1 + a_3)] e_{t+1,t}^e\} \tag{7.15}$$

where

$$\gamma^a = [a_2 - b_2(1 - a_3)]^{-1} a_2 b_3$$

$$\gamma^d = [2a_1 + a_2 + (2b_1 - b_2)(1 + a_3)]^{-1} (2a_1 + a_2) b_3$$

$$\xi = (1 + a_3)^{-1} \{a_1 - \gamma^d b_3^{-1} [a_1 + b_1(1 + a_3)]\}$$

and e_t is given by (7.11). Equations (7.11) and (7.12)–(7.15) then express the real exchange rate and the aggregate and divergence values of output and real interest rates in terms of the monetary instruments π_t and π_t^* and the expectations of inflation and the future real exchange rate. The subsequent analysis will be conducted using these reduced form equations.

In order to demonstrate Hamada's analysis we first consider a non-rational expectations version of the model treating expectations variables as exogenous. For convenience we put $\pi_t^e = \pi_t^{*e} = e_{t+1,t}^e = 0$. Then adding (7.12) and (7.13) we obtain

$$y_t = y_t^a + y_t^d = \frac{1}{2}\left[(\gamma^a + \gamma^d)\pi_t + (\gamma^a - \gamma^d)\pi_t^*\right] \tag{7.16}$$

which highlights the nature of the policy spill-overs for this model. We assume that $a_2 > b_2(1 - a_3)$ so that $\gamma^a > 0$ and surprise inflation in (7.12) has the appropriate positive effect on output. We further assume that $2b_1 > b_2$. Then $\gamma^a > b_3$ but $\gamma^d < b_3$. Hence $\gamma^a > \gamma^d$ and inflation in country 2 has a positive effect on output in country 1. There are two channels through which monetary policy in country 2 effects output in country 1. The first is that monetary expansion lowers the real interest rate of country 2 and the real exchange rate depreciates (i.e. e_t rises). This represents an appreciation for country 1 which tends to increase its output. At the same time the real interest rate differential for country 2 decreases, which may imply an increase in the real interest rate of country 1 (although the average rate falls). This tends to decrease the output of country 1 but provided that parameter values are as stated this effect will be dominated by the exchange rate effect.

Now consider the regimes examined by Hamada. Under co-operation the symmetry of the problem implies that governments would minimize a simple average $\frac{1}{2}(W_t + W_t^*) = W_t^a + W_t^d$, where W_t^a is as in (7.6) with y_t and π_t replaced by y_t^d and π_t^a respectively and W_t^d is similarly obtained but with y replaced by half the difference between output objectives, i.e. equal to zero. Thus the global welfare loss can be expressed as an 'aggregate loss' and a 'divergence loss'. But again by symmetry $W_t^d = 0$. The model is also static so that minimizing the intertemporal loss function reduces to a single-period minimization of

$$z_t^a = \frac{1}{2}\left[(\gamma^a \pi_t^a - \hat{y})^2 + a\pi_t^{a2}\right] \tag{7.17}$$

which by symmetry gives the co-operative inflation rate as

$$\pi_t = \pi_t^* = \frac{\gamma^a \hat{y}}{(\gamma^a)^2 + a} = \pi^C \tag{7.18}$$

say.

For the Nash non-co-operative solution each country minimizes its welfare loss given the inflation rate of the other country. There is no agreement that inflation rates should be equal, although in fact this turns out to be the outcome. Then (from (7.16)) country 1 minimizes its single-period welfare loss

$$z_t = \frac{1}{2}\left[(\theta_1 \pi_t + \theta_2 \pi_t^* - \hat{y})^2 + a\pi_t^2\right] \tag{7.19}$$

given π_t^* where $\theta_1 = (\gamma^a + \gamma^d)/2$ and $\theta_2 = (\gamma^a - \gamma^d)/2$. This gives country 1's *reaction function*

$$\pi_t = (\theta_1^2 + a)^{-1}\theta_1(\hat{y} - \theta_2\pi_t^*) \tag{7.20}$$

By symmetry the reaction function of country 2 is

$$\pi_t^* = (\theta_1^2 + a)^{-1}\theta_1(\hat{y} - \theta_2\pi_t) \tag{7.21}$$

Thus, solving these two equations, we obtain the Nash non-co-operative solution as

$$\pi_t = \pi_t^* = \frac{(\gamma^a + \gamma^d)\hat{y}}{\gamma^a(\gamma^a + \gamma^d) + 2a} = \pi^{NC} \tag{7.22}$$

say (substituting back for θ_1 and θ_2).

Comparing (7.22) with the co-operative solution (7.18), it is straightforward to show that inflation rates under co-operation are higher than those under non-co-operation provided that $\gamma^a > \gamma^d$. Thus non-co-operation leads to the familiar contractionary bias: because some of the benefits of each country's monetary expansion are exported to the other country, both are inhibited in using their monetary instrument to the level that they would if the benefits were internalized.

These results are illustrated in diagrammatic form in figure 7.1. The loss function (7.19) for country 1 and its counterpart for country 2 are families

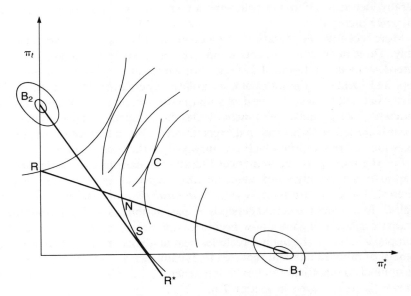

Figure 7.1   The gains from co-operation and leadership

of ellipses in the (π, π^*) plane. The bliss point B_1 for country 1 which results in zero welfare loss is at $\pi_t = 0$, $\pi_t^* = \theta_2^{-1} y$ with a symmetric result for the bliss point B_2 of country 2. The reaction function R of country 1 is obtained by treating π^* as parametric and is the locus of points where the welfare curve is tangential to the vertical lines $\pi_t^* = $ constant. Reaction function R^* follows similarly, and the Nash solution N lies at the intersection of the two reaction functions.

Pareto efficient combinations of policies lie along the contract curve which is the locus of tangencies between the welfare curves. The co-operative solution C is the symmetric point where $\pi_t = \pi_t^a$ on the contract curve. The diagram can also demonstrate a possible Stackelberg solution to the game. Suppose that country 1 is the leader. Then it chooses a point on country 2's reaction function which minimizes its welfare loss. The outcome is shown as point S in the figure. Compared with the Nash point N the inflation rate of the leader is less under this regime at the expense of a higher inflation rate in country 2.

The foregoing analysis serves to illustrate the general approach of Hamada's work. Much of his analysis takes place within a regime of fixed exchange rates in which the objectives of the countries are inflation rates, output and the balance of payments. We return to the question of fixed exchange rates as rules of the game in a later section. Canzoneri and Gray (1985) and Turnovsky and d'Orey (1986) adopt a similar framework to explore the games that may be played by monetary authorities in two structurally identical economies following a common external shock such as an oil price increase.

More recently, the literature on co-ordination issues has grown considerably. Three main developments stand out. First, whereas Hamada analysed interdependence in terms of a single-shot game, subsequent work considers repeated games or the international policy 'supergame'. We return to this theme in section 7.4 where we deal with the sustainability of the co-operative outcome. The second development tackles the issues raised by assuming that the private sector forms rational expectations. This in turn raises important questions of reputation which are surveyed in the next section.

For the most part the analytical literature is confined to static models. Repeated games introduce *strategic time dependence*. Of more general interest, however, are models with *structural time dependence* where the welfare loss in any one period depends on past actions as well as actions taken in that period. The games now become dynamic, which introduces greater complexity and, in the main, precludes neat analytical results. The principal benefit of proceeding from repeated to dynamic games is that the theory can be applied to empirical models which generally have high-order dynamics. This work is surveyed in section 7.6.

7.3 REPUTATION

The model employed in the previous section followed that of Hamada in that expectations (explicitly in our model and implicitly in Hamada's model) are non-rational. Introducing rational expectations means that the 'reputation' or 'credibility' problem needs to be addressed.

Notions of 'reputation' which relate to private sector beliefs regarding future government policy are now commonplace in the macroeconomic literature. At a more informal level these ideas frequently enter into discussions of policy effectiveness, especially relating to the disinflationary fiscal and monetary stances pursued by OECD countries in the early 1980s. At the theoretical level there has been much recent progress in developing and clarifying the issues (see the survey by Persson (1988) which emphasizes reputation in macroeconomic public finance and by Levine and Holly (1989) which focuses on reputation in structurally dynamic models).

What might be called the reputation problem was first highlighted by Kydland and Prescott (1977). They examined models where private agents are forward looking so that future government policies, if believed, can affect the present. The problem is that, with the passage of time, optimal policies formulated by minimizing some welfare loss function become suboptimal. The term *time inconsistency* is used to describe this property.

If governments are able to make binding commitments to their *ex ante* optimal policy, time inconsistency would not be a serious problem. In the absence of some institutional arrangements which, in the words of Kydland and Prescott, makes it a 'difficult and time-consuming process to change policy rules', an incentive to renege on the time-inconsistent policy occurs. This creates the reputation problem – the private sector with information on the government's optimization problem can anticipate future reneging so that time-inconsistent policies lack credibility. The only credible policies, or so it would appear, are those which are time consistent. Unfortunately, these can be severely suboptimal.

The main question posed by the literature is whether the *ex ante* optimal or 'ideal' policy can be made self-enforcing and therefore be sustained in the absence of binding commitments. In the Barro and Gordon (1983) policy game with complete information, it is shown that the policy-maker's concern for his or her reputation for precommitment can, in some circumstances, sustain the *ex ante* optimal policy or at least policies far superior to those which are time consistent.

The literature cited is concerned with the game between a single government and the private sector. International policy questions introduce a new set of strategic relationships – those between many policy-makers representing countries or blocs.

To explore how reputation transforms the nature of the international policy game let us consider the rational expectations variant of our model which in reduced form is given by equations (7.12)–(7.15). First consider co-operation with governments agreeing to minimize an average of their welfare losses jointly.

As before, the global single-period welfare loss function is given by

$$z_t^a = \frac{1}{2}\left[(y_t^a - \hat{y})^2 + a\pi_t^{a2})\right]$$ (7.17′)

and aggregate output is given by a Lucas supply curve

$$y_t^a = \gamma^a(\pi_t^a - \pi_t^{ae})$$ (7.12′)

The solution to this co-operative regime is identical with the closed economy problem considered by Barro and Gordon (1983). The best outcome or 'ideal rule' is zero inflation. Then a rational expectations solution is $\pi_t^a = \pi_t^{ae} = y_t^a = 0$ which, by symmetry, also holds for the inflation rates and outputs of each individual country.

However, given expectations of zero inflation there exists a temptation on the part of the policy-maker to choose a non-zero inflation obtained by minimizing (7.17′), treating private sector expectations π_t^{ae} as parametric. This results in

$$\pi_t^a = \frac{\gamma^a(\gamma^a\pi_t^{ae} + \hat{y})}{(\gamma^a)^2 + a} \qquad y_t^a > 0$$ (7.23)

If $\pi_t^{ae} = 0$ this results in the co-operative inflation rate (7.18) obtained for the non-rational expectations model. However, the private sector is assumed (in a rational expectations setting) to know the nature of the policy-maker's calculations. It will therefore form expectations in accordance with (7.23). This leads to

$$\pi_t^a = \pi_t^{ae} = \frac{\gamma^a\hat{y}}{a} \qquad y_t^a = 0$$ (7.24)

Thus output remains at the natural rate but inflation is higher.

As the problem has been posed, the ideal policy $\pi_t^a = 0$ lacks credibility because the private sector can anticipate that there exists an incentive to renege to π_t^a given by (7.23) (with $\pi_t^{ae} = 0$). Credibility may be achieved, however, if the policy-makers enjoy a reputation for precommitment. This may be achieved through one of two mechanisms. The first is through some binding institutional constraint which forces policy-makers to precommit. The second is the result of a private sector expectational mechanism whereby they only believe in the higher 'discretionary' inflation rate for some punishment period. We return to this question in the next section.

Whether credibility is achieved by postulating a legal constraint or by assuming an appropriate private sector response to reneging, we shall refer to the resulting policy as 'reputational'. Where neither mechanism exists or is ineffective the only policies open to the policy-makers are then 'non-reputational'. In analysing co-operation between governments in a two-country world, we can therefore distinguish between reputational and non-reputational policies. Allowing either government to pursue reputational or non-reputational policies gives rise to eight possible 'regimes'. Of these, four are symmetric and the other half are asymmetric in that only one country enjoys reputation. The four symmetric regimes are shown in figure 7.2.

Of these four regimes, the co-operative reputational (CR) policy cannot be improved upon. We have seen that

$$\pi_t = \pi_t^* = 0 \tag{7.25}$$

for regime CR whilst

$$\pi_t = \pi_t^* = \frac{\gamma^a \hat{y}}{a} = \pi^{CNR} \tag{7.26}$$

say, for co-operation without reputation (CNR). Consider next the two non-co-operative regimes NCR and NCNR.

Non-co-operation with reputation (NCR) can be dealt with in a straightforward fashion. If governments pursue reputational policies, they do not spring inflation surprises. But since anticipated monetary policy is neutral in our natural rate model, there is no other mechanism by which it can have real effects. Thus the chosen inflation rate must be zero. In other words, we have that for policy NCR both countries' inflation rates are zero.

Finally, consider non-co-operation without reputation (NCNR). Putting $y_t = y_t^a + y_t^d$ in the single-period welfare loss of country 1 and substituting y_t^a and y_t^d given by (7.12) and (7.13) gives

$$z_t = \frac{1}{2} \left\{ [\gamma^a(\pi_t^a - \pi_t^{ae}) + \gamma^d(\pi_t^d - \pi_t^{de}) - \xi e_{t+1,t}^e - \hat{y}]^2 + a\pi_t^2 \right\} \tag{7.27}$$

Relations between governments

		Co-operation (C)	Non-co-operation (NC)
Relations between governments and private sector	Reputation (R)	CR	NCR
	Non-reputational (NR)	CNR	NCNR

Figure 7.2 Four symmetric regimes

Country 1, acting independently and without reputation, minimizes z_t given by (7.27) with respect to π_t taking π_t^* and all expectations variables as given. This leads to an inflation choice

$$\pi_t = -\frac{\gamma^a + \gamma^d}{2a}(y_t^a + y_t^d - \xi e_{t+1,t}^e - \hat{y})$$ (7.28)

(noting that $\pi_t^a = \frac{1}{2}(\pi_t + \pi_t^*)$ and $\pi_t^d = \frac{1}{2}(\pi_t - \pi_t^*)$). For country 2 a similar result holds with the sign on $e_{t+1,t}^e$ reversed. In a rational expectations equilibrium $\pi_t^e = \pi_t$ and $\pi_t^{*e} = \pi_t^*$. Thus $y_t = y_t = y_t^a = y_t^d = 0$ and adding the two equations for the two countries gives

$$\pi_t + \pi_t^* = \frac{\gamma^a + \gamma^d}{a}\hat{y}$$ (7.29)

Thus, by symmetry,

$$\pi_t = \pi_t^* = \frac{\gamma^a + \gamma^d}{2a}\hat{y} = \pi^{NCNR}$$ (7.30)

say.

The important feature of this result is found by comparing π^{CNR} given by (7.26) with π^{NCNR} given by (7.30); we have

$$\pi^{NCNR} < \pi^{CNR}$$ (7.31)

provided that $\gamma^a > \gamma^d$ which holds given our assumptions about parameter values in the original structural model. Thus we have shown that co-operation without reputation may be counter-productive, a result first shown by Rogoff (1985) and confirmed by subsequent work (for dynamic models) by Miller and Salmon (1985), Levine and Currie (1987) and (for a static model) Canzoneri and Henderson (1988).

The intuition behind this result should be clear from our model. For $\gamma^a > \gamma^d$ part of the output gains from surprise inflation are exported through the depreciation of the exchange rate. This reduces the incentive for a country, acting individually, to engage in inflation surprises. With co-operation all gains are internalized and the incentive to spring inflation surprises increases, leading to a higher level of inflation in the rational expectations equilibrium.

Analogous to the Rogoff result that co-operation without reputation may not pay is the possibility that reputation without co-operation may also be counter-productive. In other words, the NCR regime may be inferior to the NCNR regime. This result has been shown by Oudiz and Sachs (1985) and Levine and Currie (1987). Both 'paradoxes' are discussed by Canzoneri and Henderson (1988).

In the essentially static model of this section the NCR regime in fact yields zero inflation for both countries as opposed to non-zero inflation for NCNR. Thus reputation without co-operation does pay in this case. However, in the models of Oudiz and Sachs and of Levine and Currie wage–price sluggishness is featured. The resulting dynamic models are then very prone to instability under the NCR regime because, with reputation, governments are more encouraged to manipulate the exchange rate to combat inflation using fiscal policy to avoid excessive output loss. This results in self-defeating competitive appreciations of the exchange rate which, for some combinations of model parameters and welfare criteria, can actually destabilize the economies.

To summarize this section, we have discussed four policy regimes: co-operation with and without reputation (CR and CNR) and non-co-operation with and without reputation (NCR and NCNR). For our illustrative model we have shown that the optimal choice of monetary policy gives the following inflation rates for each country:

$$0 = \pi^{CR} = \pi^{NCR} < \pi^{NCNR} < \pi^{CNR} \tag{7.32}$$

In other words reputation without co-operation does pay (and in fact renders co-operation unnecessary) but co-operation without reputation is counter-productive. Other work employing dynamic models has produced examples where reputation without co-operation may also be counter-productive. The outstanding issue that remains is how either co-operative or reputational policies may be sustained given the incentives to renege. This is the subject of the next section.

7.4 SUSTAINABILITY

There are two aspects of the sustainability problem to be considered. The first is whether the two countries will honour the co-operative agreement with each other. The second is the credibility problem familiar in the reputation literature: will governments cheat against the private sector? The sustainability of the 'ideal policy', co-operation with reputation, must address both forms of reneging.

If supranational bodies exist which can legally enforce precommitment by governments then the ideal policy will certainly be credible and sustainable. The outside agency can then prevent governments from reneging on each other or on the private sector. This approach is identified by Canzoneri and Henderson (1988) as a 'loss of sovereignty' and is contrasted with a form of sovereign policy-making whereby countries 'co-ordinate' rather than 'co-operate' on an agreed outcome (such as zero inflation in our example above) and employ trigger mechanisms to enforce that outcome.

The distinction between co-ordination between sovereign states and co-operation enforced by supranational institutions is a useful one. How-ever, both outcomes require agreement on some jointly chosen policies which in turn requires agreement on the appropriate global welfare mea-sure. The process by which countries bargain to arrive at a co-operative of co-ordinated agreement can be modelled in a number of ways (Hughes Hallet, 1986b). For identical economies, welfare criteria and shocks, the outcome of the bargain must by symmetrical as in our example. In what follows we shall continue to identify co-operation with mutually agreed policies (with or without some outside monitoring agency) and non-co-operation with independent policy-making.

Trigger mechanisms which may enforce efficient outcomes in the absence of legal constraints were introduced into oligopoly theory by Friedman (1971, 1977) and employed in a macroeconomic context by Barro and Gordon (1983). To illustrate the concept first consider the Hamada analysis using the non-rational expectations model.

The co-operative inflation rate $\pi^C = \gamma^a \hat{y}/((\gamma^a)^2 + a)$ (see (7.18)) is greater than the non-co-operative Nash inflation rate $\pi^{NC} = (\gamma^a + \gamma^d)\hat{y}$ $[\gamma^a(\gamma^a + \gamma^d) + 2a]$ (see 7.22)). But precisely because $\pi_t = \pi_t^* = \pi^C$ is not a Nash equilibrium there exists an incentive to renege on this co-operative agreement. Given that country 2 is sticking to inflation $\pi_t^* = \pi_t^C$, country 1 can improve its welfare by reneging to an inflation rate on its reaction function (7.20) given by

$$\pi_t = (\theta_1^2 + a)^{-1}\theta_1(\hat{y} - \theta_2\pi^C) = \pi^{REN} \tag{7.33}$$

say. A little algebra shows that $\pi^{REN} < \pi^C$ so that, given a co-operative agreement to pursue inflation rates $\pi_t = \pi_t^* = \pi^C$, each country will have an incentive to lower its inflation rate and free-ride on the higher inflation of the other country. In a one-period game both countries will switch to inflation rates along their own reaction function and the equilibrium out-come will be as in the familiar prisoner's dilemma – the Pareto inefficient non-co-operative inflation rate π^{NC}.

How then can the co-operative inflation rate be enforced? The answer is to consider repetitions of the single-period game or in other words to con-sider a *repeated game* with an intertemporal welfare loss given by (7.6). Suppose that country 1 employs the following trigger mechanism strategy:

$$\pi_{t+i} = \begin{cases} \pi^C & \text{if } \pi_t^* = \pi^C & i = 1,2,...,\infty \\ \pi^{NC} & \text{if } \pi_t \neq \pi^C & i = 1,2,...,P \\ \pi^C & & i = P+1, P+2,...,\infty \end{cases} \tag{7.34}$$

What this trigger mechanism says is that country 1 abides by the co-operative agreement if country 2 does likewise. If country 2 reneges then in the next period country 1 switches to the Nash non-co-operative policy for P periods and subsequently co-operation is restored. An identical strategy is employed by country 2.

Since in a Nash equilibrium both countries are on their reaction functions and hence are acting in an optimal way, the threat is credible. The equilibrium in which both countries pursue strategies described by (7.34) is then said to be *subgame perfect*. But will the outcome be the co-operative inflation rate π^C?

To answer this question we need to consider the one-period gains from reneging, or the *temptation*, and compare this with the costs of reneging, or the *enforcement*, which arises from the trigger strategy. Consider the single-period welfare loss for country 1 given by z_t which we write as

$$z_t = f(\pi_t, \pi_t^*) \tag{7.35}$$

The temptation for country 1 is then given by

$$\text{temptation} = z^C - z^{\text{REN}} \tag{7.36}$$

where $z^C = f(\pi^C, \pi^C)$ and $z^{\text{REN}} = f(\pi^{\text{REN}}, \pi^C)$ with π^{REN} given by (7.33). In other words the temptation is the welfare gain for country 1 from switching from $\pi_t = \pi^C$ to $\pi_t = \pi^{\text{REN}}$, assuming that country 2 still honours its commitment to $\pi_t^* = \pi^C$. This gain lasts for only one period after which the trigger mechanism (7.34) comes into operation.

Country 2 now switches to $\pi_t^* = \pi^{\text{NC}}$, in which case the optimal inflation for country 1 is also $\pi_t = \pi^{\text{NC}}$. The costs of reneging are then the increased welfare loss discounted for P periods or

$$\text{enforcement} = (z^{\text{NC}} - z^C)(\lambda + \lambda^2 + \ldots + \lambda^P) \tag{7.37}$$

where $z^{\text{NC}} = f(\pi^{\text{NC}}, \pi^{\text{NC}})$ and λ is the discount factor.

The co-operative inflation rate is sustainable if enforcement exceeds temptation, in which case there is no incentive to renege. From (7.36) and (7.37) this requires

$$(z^{\text{NC}} - z^C)\frac{\lambda(1 - \lambda^P)}{1 - \lambda} > z^C - z^{\text{REN}} \tag{7.38}$$

using $\lambda + \lambda^2 + \ldots + \lambda^P = \lambda(1 - \lambda^P)/(1 - \lambda)$.

Two extreme cases can now be distinguished. The first (assumed by Friedman) is to assume an infinite punishment period ($P = \infty$). Then the sustainability condition (7.37) becomes

$$\frac{\lambda}{1 - \lambda} > \frac{z^C - z^{\text{REN}}}{z^{\text{NC}} - z^C} \tag{7.39}$$

since $\lambda^P \to 0$ as $P \to \infty$ (assuming $\lambda < 1$). From (7.39) we arrive at Friedman's *balanced temptation theorem*: there exists a discount factor λ sufficiently close to unity for which enforcement exceeds temptation and $\pi_t = \pi_t^* = \pi^C$ is sustainable. This follows because the left-hand side of (7.39) can be made as large as is necessary by making λ approach unity. The other extreme is $P = 1$ in which case (7.38) becomes

$$\pi > \frac{z^C - z^{\text{REN}}}{z^{\text{NC}} - z^C} \tag{7.40}$$

Since $\lambda < 1$, (7.40) requires that the single-period gains from reneging $z^C - z^{\text{REN}}$ will not exceed the single-period gains from co-operation $z^{\text{NC}} - z^{\text{NC}}$. There is no reason why this condition should hold in general, and so there may be particular combinations of models and welfare criteria for which (7.40) can never hold. This does not mean that all is lost, however. Following Barro and Gordon (1983), in this case we can always find an intermediate inflation rate π_t between π^C and π^{NC} for which the temptation to renege is just exceeded by the enforcement effect.

One feature of the trigger mechanism approach to sustainability should now be apparent. A number of authors, including Rogoff (1987), Canzoneri and Henderson (1988) and Levine (1988) as well as Barro and Gordon themselves, have stressed the fact that there are many efficient solutions which can be supported depending on the length of the punishment period. This may not be a serious problem for countries acting strategically because we can envisage trigger strategies being chosen (possibly by a supranational agency) to be sufficiently damaging (i.e with P sufficiently large) to support the co-operative equilibrium. However, if we turn to the rational expectations model and consider co-operation with reputation, the choice of punishment period by the private sector becomes more problematic.

Now consider the rational expectations case. The question to examine is whether co-operation with reputation (policy CR) can be supported by appropriate trigger mechanisms by both the governments and the private sector. Suppose that the governments operate a trigger strategy as before except that the non-co-operative equilibrium may now be with or without reputation (NCR and NCNR). Following Barro and Gordon, the private sector adopts a trigger mechanism with respect to its beliefs about future policy. In particular for country 1

$$\pi_{t+i,t}^e = \begin{cases} \pi^{\text{CR}} & \text{if } \pi_t = \pi^{\text{CR}} & i = 1, 2, \ldots, \infty \\ \pi^{\text{NCNR}} & \text{if } \pi_t \neq \pi^{\text{CR}} & i = 1, 2, \ldots, P \\ \pi^{\text{CR}} & & i = P + 1, P + 2, \ldots, \infty \end{cases} \tag{7.41}$$

where $\pi_{t+i,t}^e$ denotes expectations of inflation in period $t + i$ formed on the basis of information available at time t. Clearly, in our symmetrical model an identical mechanism holds for country 2. It is now clear that the appropriate choice of non-co-operative equilibrium for the government's trigger strategy is π^{NCNR}. Reputation and co-operation both require a commitment to policy CR. If reneging occurs, both reputation and the co-operative agreement between governments break down when the two trigger mechanisms operate simultaneously.

The sustainability condition (analogous to (7.38)) now becomes

$$(z^{NCNR} - z^{CR})\frac{\lambda(1 - \lambda^{P})}{1 - \lambda} > z^{CR} - z^{REN} \tag{7.42}$$

For this case we shall pursue the matter further. Recall that $\pi^{CR} = 0$ and $\pi^{NCNR} = (\lambda^{a} + \lambda^{d})\hat{y}/2a$. The one-period reneging inflation rate assumes that $\pi_{t}^{*} = \pi_{t}^{*e} = \pi_{t}^{e} = 0$ and can therefore be obtained from the reaction function for the non-rational expectations model (7.33). Thus, if we put $\pi^{c} = 0$ in (7.33),

$$\pi^{REN} = \frac{\theta_{1}\hat{y}}{\theta_{1}^{2} + a} = \frac{2(\gamma^{a} + \gamma^{d})\,\hat{y}}{(\gamma^{a} + \gamma^{d})^{2} + 4a} \tag{7.43}$$

The corresponding single-period losses are given by

$$z^{CR} = \tfrac{1}{2}\hat{y}^{2} \tag{7.44}$$

$$z^{NCNR} = \frac{1}{2}\frac{(1 + (\gamma^{a} + \gamma^{d})^{2})\hat{y}^{2}}{4a} \tag{7.45}$$

and

$$z^{REN} = \frac{2a\hat{y}^{2}}{(\gamma^{a} + \gamma^{d})^{2} + 4a} < z^{CR} \tag{7.46}$$

Hence on substituting in (7.42) the sustainability condition becomes

$$\frac{\lambda(1 - \lambda^{P})}{1 - \lambda} > \frac{4a}{(\gamma^{a} + \gamma^{d})^{2} + 4a} \tag{7.47}$$

It emerges that factors which help sustainability are a discount factor close to unity, a long punishment interval and a high value of $\gamma^{a} + \gamma^{d}$ relative to a. The intuition behind the first two effects is obvious, but the last point is less so. The expression $\gamma^{a} + \gamma^{d}$ captures the output benefits of surprise inflation for country 1, taking all expectations and country 2's inflation as given. As $\gamma^{a} + \gamma^{d}$ increases, the benefits of surprise inflation increase but so does the non-reputational inflation rate π^{NCNR}. Thus both temptation and enforcement increase with $\gamma^{a} + \gamma^{d}$. For this model and choice of welfare loss function the latter dominates so that high values of $\gamma^{a} + \gamma^{d}$ relative to a help to achieve sustainability.

Suppose that we assume that a 1 per cent increase in output is associated with a 2 per cent inflation surprise (on an annual basis). Then
$\gamma^a + \gamma^d = 0.5$ and, if we put $a = 1$, (7.47) becomes

$$\frac{\lambda(1 - \lambda^P)}{1 - \lambda} > 0.94 \tag{7.48}$$

For the least effective trigger strategy, $P = 1$, this becomes $\lambda > 0.94$ or the
discount rate must be less than around 6 per cent per year which is not
implausible. At the other extreme $P = \infty$, (7.48) gives $\lambda > 0.48$ which is a
very lax restriction. The prospects for the trigger strategy supporting the co-
operative policy with reputation, zero inflation, seems good at least for this
model and choice of welfare criteria.

As we have mentioned, an important shortcoming of the trigger strategy
approach is that the choice of punishment period is indeterminate. This is
particularly serious for the private sector trigger mechanism if we assume
private agents to be atomistic. In this case there is no prospect for a strategic
choice of punishment period P. The determination of P becomes a postulate about private sector behaviour which may or may not be regarded as
empirically sound. However, large players such as the two policy-makers
can be assumed to make a strategic choice of P sufficient in length to support the optimal co-operative policy. The assumption about private sector
behaviour is then that they choose the same punishment period allowing the
strategic players to take the lead. The use of trigger mechanisms to support reputational policies then appears to be less problematic in the context of internationally co-ordinated policies, although the manner in which
players may choose punishment lengths strategically, weighing costs against
benefits, would benefit from being modelled in a game-theoretical way. This
in turn may require models with more explicit microfoundations as are
found in Kehoe (1987) and van der Ploeg (1988).

We conclude this section by briefly mentioning two developments in the
use of trigger mechanisms to establish sustainability. The first is the generalization of the preceding analysis to structurally dynamic models with price-
wage sluggishness, lagged responses of demand to competitiveness and so
on. The main changes lie in the added complexity of reputational and non-
reputational optimal policies and that the sustainability condition becomes
time varying and must be examined along all possible trajectories of the
regime to be sustained (see Levine (1988) for a single-country treatment and
Currie et al. (1988) for an application to international policy co-ordination
between two blocs).

The second development is to assume that stochastic shocks hit the
economy of either a demand-side or supply-side character. The principal
conceptual change is that temptation becomes stochastic in character so

that, for unbounded shocks, it is impossible to achieve sustainability for all realizations. However, in a dynamic context, enforcement, which now becomes the expected costs arising from the trigger strategy, also increases so that on average sustainability is improved but for some exceptional shock it breaks down. If the probability of this occurring is small it is then possible to assert that the ideal policy is an 'approximate' equilibrium in the sense used by Radner (1981). Canzoneri and Henderson (1988, 1989) for repeated games and Levine et al. (1989) for dynamic games apply this analysis to the policy co-ordination problem in a stochastic environment.

7.5 FIXED EXCHANGE RATE REGIMES

The EMS provides a notable example of international policy co-ordination in practice. A large literature exists on the empirical effects on inflation and exchange rate volatility in members (see for example, Giavazzi et al., 1988). We do not attempt to survey this work. The focus of this section is to survey the theoretical literature concerned with fixed exchange rate regimes.

Theoretical models of the EMS emphasize two broad features of EMS type arrangements. The first goes back at least as far as Hamada and points to the role of 'surrogate co-operation' in the form of fixed exchange rates which enable countries to avoid beggar thy neighbour attempts to export inflation by exchange rate appreciation or to import demand and output benefits by exchange rate depreciation. This feature is easily seen in the non-rational expectations model in section 7.2. If we interpret the 'fixed nominal exchange rate with regular alignments' description of the EMS as in effect fixing real exchange rates, then from equations (7.9)–(7.11) we can see that no divergence in outputs is possible. Under this constraint the two countries must therefore end up at the co-operative inflation rate π^C given by (7.18).

The other feature of the EMS which more recent literature has stressed is the reputational advantages that the arrangement brings to countries which lack reputation for low inflation when acting independently under flexible exchange rates. Thus inflation-prone countries such as Italy and France may within the EMS seek the benefits of a reputation for low inflation which previously only the FRG enjoyed. Our rational expectations model illustrates this point.

Suppose that country 2 enjoys a reputation for precommitment and sets $\pi_t^* = 0$. If country 1 acts independently with a flexible exchange rate, then it ends up with $\pi_t = \pi^{NCNR} > 0$ as before. Now suppose that country 1 is committed to setting its monetary policy so as to maintain a constant real exchange rate. Then $e_{t+1,t}^e = e_t = 0$, say, setting the constant agreed real exchange rate at the equilibrium co-operative level. For the rational expectations model the real exchange rate is given by

$$e_t = \frac{1 + a_3}{2(2a_1 + a_2)} \gamma^d (\pi_t^d - \pi_t^{de}) \qquad (7.49)$$

(from (7.11) and (7.15)). Since country 2 is committed to $\pi_t^* = \pi_t^{*e} = 0$, it follows that country 1 can only engage in surprise inflation if the real exchange rate is allowed to depreciate (i.e. e_t must rise). If this is ruled out by international agreement, then country 1 cannot renege on $\pi_t = 0$. Thus zero inflation also becomes credible and sustainable for the inflation-prone country.

It should be noted that this result only requires a commitment to keeping the real exchange fixed and therefore allows for realignment in the face of different inflation rates. This weak form of monetary discipline is still sufficient to give country 1 reputation on the back of country 2. The discipline derives from the demand side of the model where demand can only change if the real exchange rate e_t or the expected real interest rate is allowed to change. The commitment to a constant real exchange rate coupled with the credible commitment of country 2 to zero inflation rules out either of these possibilities. If, however, we supplement monetary with fiscal policy, then the extra policy instrument can be used to regulate demand in a manner consistent with a fixed real exchange rate and the argument then breaks down.

Giavazzi and Pagano (1988) show how a commitment to fixed nominal exchange rates can buy credibility for inflation-prone countries even where periodical realignments are allowed. The source of the discipline now is the extra penalty that the policy-maker attaches to real exchange rate appreciation which occurs between realignments. A difficulty with the model, which they attempt to address in further modifications, is that the real exchange rate fluctuates below its purchasing power parity level between realignments, therefore implying an ever-worsening trade balance.

The main insight provided by these simple models is that precommitment to a fixed, nominal or real exchange rate can act as a surrogate for binding agreements which focus directly on monetary policy itself. In both the forward- and backward-looking variants of our model this form of agreement leads to the Pareto efficient co-operative outcome. However, as Canzoneri and Henderson (1988) point out, in a sense this merely shifts the credibility problem from whether zero inflation is sustainable (given the incentive to engage in surprise inflation) to whether a constant real exchange rate is sustainable (given the incentive to appreciate or depreciate). At a formal level the analyses of both forms of reneging are equivalent and can be handled using the framework described in the previous section. At a less formal level (and going beyond the natural rate model) the benefits of agreements which focus on the exchange rate rather than national monetary policies are both the visibility and the mutuality of the commitment; for instance, the inflation-prone country's commitment to fixed exchange rates can be backed up by the intervention of the central bank of the country with reputation.

A number of problems remain unresolved by this analysis and have been addressed in the literature. The first is the source of the reputation enjoyed by the FRG. Melitz (1988) adopts the Barro – Gordon sustainability framework to explain German reputation as originating from the low rate of discount (i.e. a discount factor λ in (7.6) close to unity). We have seen how this can help to sustain a reputation for zero inflation. The reason for the low discount rate in the FRG is identified by Melitz as the independence of the Bundesbank which is not politically controlled as is the case for the Banque de France. Consequently, according to Melitz, 'the German monetary authorities can discount the future in the ordinary way . . . while the French ones cannot, but must assign unusual priority to all events prior to the next elections'.

A major problem with the analysis as it stands is that it cannot explain why the country with reputation should itself enter into a fixed exchange rate agreement. This brings us to some other ways in which the EMS is modelled. Many authors introduce an added asymmetry other than German reputation. Enjoying reputation means that precommitment is credible in the eyes of the private sector. But if a policy-maker can precommit himself/herself with respect to the private sector, it follows that he/she can do so with respect to the other countries as well and act as a Stackelberg leader. Thus Fischer (1987) writes that 'the EMS can be viewed as an agreement by France and Italy to accept German leadership in monetary policy, imposing constraints on domestic and fiscal policy'.

German leadership is modelled in different ways, some emphasizing fixed nominal exchange rates and others stressing realignment. The former applies to Canzoneri and Gray (1985), Oudiz (1985) and Roubini (1987), where it is assumed that the FRG sets monetary policy while the other members subordinate their monetary policies to maintain fixed nominal exchange rates. The latter is reflected in Giavazzi and Giovannini (1986) who assume that the FRG again sets monetary policy, but now the other members set their exchange rates relative to the deutschmark.

A comprehensive comparison of these alternative views of the EMS is provided by Collins (1988) using a non-rational expectations model which resembles the first of the models discussed in this chapter. The main result is that German leadership is inflationary compared with non-co-operation, but is not as inflationary as co-operation. There is little here to support the thesis that German leadership fosters monetary discipline.

Monetary discipline features in the rational expectations model employed in this survey: the inflation-prone country credibly committed to maintaining real exchange rates fixed earns a reputation for zero inflation. But the country initially with reputation does not benefit from this arrangement. A similar conclusion is reached by Canzoneri and Henderson (1988) in a rational expectations natural rate model.

An important limitation of the theoretical literature on the EMS and on policy co-ordination in general is the assumption of symmetrical, indeed identical, economies (although in a G3 context van der Ploeg (1987) examines interactions assuming real wage rigidity in Europe and Japan and nominal wage rigidity in the USA). Asymmetries in the economic structure, especially in the labour market, are clearly important in explaining the different inflationary experiences of countries within the EMS and hence the role of exchange rate management.

A satisfactory theoretical model of the EMS needs to explain how exchange rate co-operation reduces the scope for beggar thy neighbour exchange rate policies, induces monetary discipline in inflation-prone countries and benefits all members. Our main conclusion is that this literature can explain some but not all of these features. It would appear that more convincing models of the EMS require one to go beyond the two-country static symmetrical models that we have reviewed.

7.6 POLICY CO-ORDINATION: DOES CO-ORDINATION PAY?

In this section, we turn from theoretical analysis to consider the measurement of the benefits (or costs) to be derived from the co-ordination of monetary policy. In doing so, we broaden the areas of interest to consider also the benefits of monetary and fiscal policy co-ordination, not monetary policy alone. This is for the practical reason that most empirical studies of international policy co-ordination consider the benefits of co-ordinating both monetary and fiscal policy.

The approach to assessing the empirical gains from international policy co-ordination is to use the available international macroeconometric models. These models have the advantage of incorporating many important features of macroeconomies which the simplified models in the theoretical literature ignore, such as high-order structural dynamics and asymmetries in national economies. The empirical importance of asymmetries in the economic structures of the USA and Europe is highlighted by Karakitsos (1988). By comparing the outcome under co-operative decision-making with that under a non-co-operative benchmark, the benefits of co-ordination can be assessed. Since models are imperfect representations of the real world, the issue of model uncertainty is clearly crucial, and we address it in the following section.

Empirical studies which evaluate the potential gains from policy co-ordination have generally found the benefits to be significant but not large. In their pioneering study, Oudiz and Sachs (1984) estimated that the gains from co-operation among the G3 countries in the mid-1970s would be worth no more than 0.5 per cent of gross national product (GNP) to each country compared with the best non-co-operative outcomes.

Later studies have suggested that the gains from co-ordination among the OECD economies may be somewhat larger. In a more general analysis which allowed for dynamic decision-making, Hughes Hallett (1986a, b, 1987a) found that the gains became larger – between 0.5 and 1.5 per cent of GNP for the USA, the European Economic Community (EEC) and Japan. More recently, Canzoneri and Minford (1986), Currie et al. (1987) and Minford and Canzoneri (1987) have also suggested relatively small gains in the absence of major shocks, based on calculations from versions of the Liverpool and OECD models for the USA and the EEC or OECD respectively. However, those results turn out to vary significantly with the size and persistence of external shocks and the perceived reputations of the governments concerned. Persistent shocks and the existence of 'reputation' appreciably increases the relative value of co-ordination (Currie et al., 1987); governments with reputation may derive very large benefits for co-operation in the face of permanent shocks.

There has been little work on the probable distribution of co-operation gains between countries. Oudiz and Sachs (1984) found gains distributed roughly 2:1 in favour of the FRG relative to the USA for two different econometric models. Hughes Hallett's (1986b) study of the USA and EEC in the mid-1970s, using a wide range of bargaining models, suggests gains distributed 2:1 in favour of the EEC, which corroborates this finding. Later work showed this result to be somewhat sensitive to alternative types of exogenous shocks (Hughes Hallett, 1987b), although in no case was the position of the EEC as main gainer overturned. Hughes Hallett et al. (1989) examine surrogate co-operation in the form of agreed exchange rate paths. They find that the gains were asymmetrically distributed among the Group of Five (G5) countries in the late 1980s and that it is extremely difficult to find ways of improving the lot of those countries which benefit least under co-ordination. These are important but awkward results because they suggest that, whatever the overall gains, (a) it will be hard to secure *and maintain* a co-ordination agreement in the face of significant uncertainties, and (b) if those who make the gains and those who shoulder the burden of adjustment are different sets of people, there are going to be political difficulties in securing any agreement in the first place. However, it may well be that these distributional problems can be reduced by hierarchical approach to co-ordination, focusing first on co-ordination amongst the G3 countries and then subsequently within regional groupings.

These results have been drawn from empirical macromodels. They are not inconsistent with a separate strand of the literature which has sought to examine these findings from a theoretical vantage point, using small demonstration models in which each economy is represented by just a few simplified equations. Typically these equations restrict us to a world of two identically symmetric economies with either no dynamics or steady state dynamics, and in which the policy responses are known with certainty and there are no information innovations. These limitations reduce the interest of the resulting research findings. Nevertheless these simplified models also suggest that the gains from co-ordination are likely to be fairly small, but not insignificant; see, for example, the highly stylized models of Currie and Levine (1985), Miller and Salmon (1985), Oudiz and Sachs (1985), and Levine and Currie (1987), and the simple, but estimated, models of Carlozzi and Taylor (1985), Sachs and McKibbin (1985) and Taylor (1985).

The gains of co-ordination relative to non-co-ordination may well be substantially smaller than those of efficient non-co-operative policies over strategies which ignore predictable policy changes abroad. Thus co-ordination in the sense of information exchanges, rather than detailed co-ordination across all variables, may supply part of the improvements available from policy co-ordination. If this is so, an important function of international policy discussion is the exchange of information between policy-makers concerning policies and the state of their economies. Interestingly, this conclusion can hold even when the information exchanged was found to contain prediction errors (Hughes Hallett, 1987b). It has also been confirmed in a series of experiments carried out by Minford and Canzoneri (1987) using a very different model of the G7 countries over three different episodes in the 1980s.

Thus information exchanges appear to be a key part of the co-ordination process, irrespective of the model or time period. We might suppose that, the wider the range of policies reviewed, the greater are the benefits of information exchange to the decisions subsequently taken (Bryant, 1987). Certainly, prior consultation would alert policy-makers to potential and self-defeating conflicts, such as incompatible exchange rate or trade balance targets which would lead to competitive appreciations or depreciations, or inconsistent fiscal and monetary programmes. Prior consultation could also help policy-makers avoid any losses due to conditioning their own decisions on erroneous information about other policy-makers' intentions (e.g. what priorities they have, what target paths they aim at, what model they use for policy selection etc.). Whatever the difficulty of predicting the true state of the world, errors due to mistakes made about the information base being used by other decision-makers should be avoidable and there is no point in adding unavoidable (or genuinely random) errors. Information exchanges which take place through regular consultation may be routine, but we should not be surprised if they make significant contributions to improving policy choice.

None of the studies of policy co-ordination reviewed so far considered exchange rates to be a target of policy, either in their own right or as a surrogate target. Yet much of the recent policy debate has been concerned with exchange rate management, with the aim of either stabilizing exchange rates or of making controlled realignments. This may serve as a means of improving relative co-ordination between countries. The Hughes Hallett (1987c) study points out that although exchange rates will then be included among the targets during policy selection, they can either be included in the associated objective function evaluations (in which case exchange rate stability is a target in its own right) or excluded from those evaluations (in which case exchange rates are just an intermediate target, instrumental in securing improvements elsewhere). If the former holds, the gains from co-ordination appear larger than before, about 3–6 per cent of GNP as estimated across seven multicountry models. If exchange rates are treated merely as intermediate targets the gains are significantly smaller, much the same as in the earlier literature cited above. Later work which looked at the exchange rate targeting issue in more detail for the G5 countries (Hughes Hallett et al., 1989) generated the same findings: gains of 0.7–1.7 per cent of GNP, inclusive of exchange rate stability, were larger than others had estimated, but those figures were reduced by 0.3 per cent for each country when exchange rates were just taken as intermediate targets.

The point here is that an exchange rate is a shared variable, the domestic impact of which is the same whether exchange rate changes originate at home or abroad. In contrast, most other variables have impacts which are significantly smaller internationally than domestically. The need to limit exchange rate spill-overs is therefore greater than for other linkage variables, and the potential gains for co-ordination appear correspondingly larger when that is done. In fact, co-ordination itself appears to generate extra stability in the target variables and more continuity in the policy interventions – a characteristic which had already been noted in non-exchange-rate exercises (Hughes Hallett, 1986a). The explanation, according to Cooper (1969), is that ignoring independence within or between economies leads to oscillation and overshooting because the implied assignments (country by country) ignore the international side effects of decisions taken in the domestic interest until after they have appeared. Corrections then have to be applied. These are the costs of imposing policy assignments one to one by countries rather than for specific variables on a dynamic system. Target stability and policy continuity are therefore particularly sensitive to exchange rate management.

Success with shared targets, whether treated as intermediate or not, requires a measure of co-ordination of how they are controlled, and also some consensus about the target path which they should pursue. If that is missing, countries will inevitably waste policy power by pushing against each other in a vain attempt to achieve the impossible. This follows from the

$n - 1$ problem: there are one fewer independent exchange rates (or current accounts) than independent policy-makers. However, it does not follow that any agreed target path is better than none. Hughes Hallett et al. (1989) find that, among the G5 countries, jointly specifying exchange rate target paths independently of other objectives is frequently more damaging than moderate disagreement about what that target path should be as long as the suggested targets are not inconsistent with other objectives. Hence the problem appears to be one of choosing an appropriate set of target paths, not of securing precise agreement on some paths(s). Whether this conclusion is true of other shared variables, such as the current account, is an open question.

7.7 THE CONSEQUENCES OF MODEL UNCERTAINTY

The empirical results discussed up to now depend on the particular model that is used in the experiment. Important questions follow. How robust are the estimates of co-operation gains to the choice of model? Suppose that policy-makers design co-operative policies using one particular world model. How robust are the resulting policies if the 'correct' model turns out to be different?

The extent to which models offer quite different guidelines for policy-makers can be seen from the work of Frankel and Rockett (1988). Table 7.1 shows the estimates of 12 world models of the effects of a change in US monetary policy, keeping fiscal policy fixed. The disagreement is clearly substantial, particularly in the effect on the rest of the world. The effect in the second year on US output of a 4 per cent increase in the US money supply is estimated variously to range from 3.0 to 0.1 per cent. The effect on GDP in the rest of the world varies from -0.7 to 0.4 per cent. It is clear that there is not even agreement on the sign, let alone the magnitude, of relevant monetary spill-overs.

Frankel and Rockett's next step was to compare the effects of co-operative and non-co-operative policies under the assumption that policy-makers believe different models. Concentrating on six of the models and considering cooperation between the USA and the rest of the OECD bloc (ROECD), each of the two policy-makers has six choices of model on which to base policy decisions, givine $6 \times 6 = 36$ possible pairs of beliefs. Frankel and Rockett computed co-operative and non-co-operative policies for these 36 cases and constructed a payoff matrix which showed the gain from co-operation for each policy pair if each model in turn was correct.

There are now $6 \times 6 \times 6 = 216$ outcomes (co-operative versus non-co-operative) to examine. Frankel and Rockett showed that co-operation results in a welfare improvement in 62 per cent of these cases for both the USA

Table 7.1   Money multipliers in international models: effect of a 4 per cent increase in US money supply

Percentage difference after 2 years	USA GNP	ROECD GNP	Dollar
MCM	+1.5	−0.7	−6.0
EEC	+1.0	+0.2	−4.0
EPA	+1.2	−0.4	−6.4
LINK	+1.0	−0.1	−2.3
Liverpool	+0.1	−0.0	−3.9
MSG	+0.3	+0.4	−2.0
Minimod	+1.0	−0.2	−5.7
VAR	+3.0	+0.4	−22.9
OECD	+1.6	+0.3	−2.6
Taylor	+0.6	−0.2	−4.9
Wharton	+0.7	+0.4	−1.0
DRI	+1.8	−0.6	−14.6

MCM, US Federal Reserve Board's multicountry model; EEC, EEC Staff's Compact model; EPA, World Model of the Economic Planning Agency of the Japanese Government; Link, model of Project LINK; Liverpool, Liverpool University Model; MSG, McKibben–Sachs global model; Minimod, the model of Haas and Masson at the International Monetary Fund; VAR, the vector autoregressive model of Sims and Litterman; OECD, the OECD staff's interlink model; Taylor, the model of John Taylor, Stanford University; Wharton, Wharton World Econometric Model; DRI, the DATA Resources Inc. multicountry model.
Source: Frankel and Rockett, 1986

and ROECD. On the basis of this evidence the probability is that co-operation will benefit the world, but the risks of co-operation being counter-productive are substantial.

The pessimistic conclusion of the effects of model uncertainty on the gains from co-operation has been questioned by more recent work. Holtham and Hughes Hallett (1987) have pointed out an oddity in many of the failure of co-operation cases in the Frankel–Rockett work; in these cases, one or other party would be worse off as a result of the agreement. They refer to these as 'weak bargains'. Even in the absence of altruism, co-operating countries are likely to avoid weak bargains for one very good reason. In a weak bargain one party perceives that there is an incentive for the other to renege. In other words the agreement is not perceived to be sustainable.

As we have seen, sustainability is a crucial concept in considering agreements of any type. The ability to sustain a particular agreement depends on the nature of the bargain which is struck over the distribution of the gains. This involves the choice of weights used to average the individual welfare measures in arriving at the global welfare criterion.

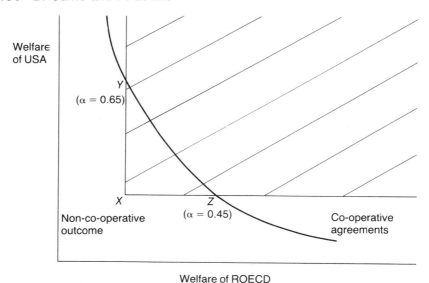

Figure 7.3   Sustainable co-operative agreements

Figure 7.3 shows a typical distribution of the welfare measure for each country under a co-operative agreement. The curve through points Y and Z plots the set of feasible co-operative agreements as the weight α varies. The shaded region is where the welfare for both blocs is higher than under the non-co-operative outcome (point X). In the hypothetical case shown all values of α between 0.45 and 0.65 result in co-operative agreement which benefits both blocs. Only these agreements are sustainable. The problem with many of the outcomes considered by Frankel and Rockett was that one or other party perceived the agreement as falling outside the sustainable region.

In 'strong bargains' both blocs believe that neither party is worse off under co-operation than under non-co-operation. Holtham and Hughes Hallett went on to re-examine the Frankel and Rockett payoff matrix, restricting possible agreements to 'strong bargains'. They found that within the smaller number of possible outcomes the success rate of co-operation increased significantly.

One interpretation of these studies is that they highlight the advantage of co-operative policy-making's being preceded by an agreement on the appropriate model on which to base the policies. But even if policy-makers can agree to use, say, the MCM model or some composite compromise model incorporating average behaviour, it would still be important that agreed policies are reasonably robust with respect to the choice of model.

Holtham and Hughes Hallett examined the case where policy-makers agree to use one of eight possible world models (including a composite model) to design a co-operative set of policies. They then calculated a payoff matrix in which one of these eight views of the world turns out to be correct. (This study overlaps with that of Frankel and Rockett. The main difference is that the latter only considered static optimization, whereas Holtham and Hughes Hallett considered optimal policies over a 6 year period.)

The payoff matrix is shown in table 7.2. The entries (USA, ROECD) show the percentage welfare gains from co-operation as compared with non-co-operation for the USA and ROECD respectively. Negative entries indicate that non-co-operation is best if the two blocs design policy on the basis of one model when the truth is captured by another model. There are 79 out of 128 negative entries. This proportion of failures is in fact higher than the Frankel and Rockett result and indicates that model uncertainty is as serious an obstacle to policy co-ordination as model disagreements.

The MCM is the only model for which policies give significant gains to co-operation whichever model turns out to be true. It would seem then that there is a strong argument for implementing a co-operative policy based on MCM. However, this conclusion requires qualification. If policy-makers are extremely risk averse, an alternative criterion is to examine the worst-case scenario for each policy from among all possible outcomes. A 'minimax' strategy then chooses the policy which gives the best worse-case outcome. This turns out to be the non-co-operative policy based on the LINK model. The argument for co-operative policy thus depends on the policy-makers' attitude to risk.

Do these studies across models undermine the case for policy co-ordination? There are a number of reasons for rejecting a pessimistic conclusion. First, the study by Holtham and Hughes Hallett included only two models which incorporate forward-looking expectations – the Taylor and MSG models. Only in these two cases can we consider the reputational effects discussed earlier. The consequence of this is that these studies do not fully capture the importance of combining reputation with co-operation highlighted in the Currie–Levine papers.

Second, Ghosh and Masson (1988) show that if policy-makers learn about the model (through observations of macroeconomic variables and Bayesian learning), then the performance of co-operative relative to non-co-operative policies substantially improves.

A third reason for not necessarily drawing an anti-co-operation conclusion from the multimodel studies is more technical. The policies designed by Holtham and Hughes Hallett are 'open loop' in character, i.e. fiscal and monetary policies take the form of paths over the 6 year period. Precommitment to these transition paths (for government spending and monetary growth) do not allow policy-makers to revise policy in the light of modelling errors which are discovered in the course of using one particular model. A

Table 7.2   Pay-off matrix: percentage gains to co-operation[a]

Reality	Link	OECD	EEC	MCM	Taylor	MSG	Minimod	Average
Link	33.6	−57.6	−0.2	88.9	87.7	75.9	66.1	5.2
	37.3	−33.6	−18.2	88.6	85.5	77.3	64.9	−42.2
OECD	−35.6	12.4	−133.7	93.5	94.3	91.6	62.1	−0.7
	−1193.2	57.6	−1107.2	64.0	−17.2	61.0	−13.9	−1115.1
EEC	−86.4	−855.0	20.4	78.5	65.5	7.6	1.4	−85.0
	−185.9	10.0	35.8	86.1	58.0	50.5	−6.8	27.9
MCM	−3218.4	−1488.3	−1698.2	52.3	−15.9	7.4	−844.6	−2894.7
	−1289.5	−366.2	−3831.3	66.5	51.3	−186.0	−272.9	−3353.4
Taylor	−1377.2	−603.4	−1035.2	40.7	93.1	−135.5	−2152.0	−2983.9
	−209.4	−160.0	−145.4	81.3	87.5	55.1	−152.3	−133.2
MSG	−593.4	−73.3	−31.9	34.2	83.3	81.9	−819.6	−531.5
	−1010.6	−433.7	−1192.2	33.4	−0.9	75.3	−81.7	−1400.8
Minimod	−152.6	−133.2	−509.6	52.0	83.5	81.3	70.7	−318.1
	−197.1	−44.6	−785.6	68.8	74.3	60.3	55.5	−532.9
Average	35.2	−92.7	−54.0	90.1	95.1	93.3	61.8	76.2
	−632.4	−44.6	−9.7	90.1	84.0	85.2	76.0	77.0
Minimax	−3218.4	−1488.3	−1698.2	34.2	−15.9	−135.5	−2152.0	−2983.9
	−1289.5	−433.7	−3831.3	33.4	−17.2	−186.0	−272.9	−3353.4

[a] The difference between the welfare loss under non-co-operation and co-operation as a percentage of the former; note that + implies a gain from co-operation and − implies a loss. The first line in each entry refers to the USA, and the second to the ROECD.

Source: Holtham and Hughes Hallett, 1987

more flexible form of precommitment would take the form of feedback rules which allow adjustments to be made as outturns differ from forecasts. It is a standard result from control theory that feedback rules improve robustness in the face of modelling uncertainties (and, incidentally, provide protection against exogenous shocks). In the next section we consider some recent work which approaches international policy co-ordination in the form of agreed feedback rules.

7.8 SIMPLE RULES

A difficulty with the empirical literature surveyed in sections 7.6 and 7.7

is that although policies can generally be formulated in terms of feedback rules, these turn out to involve extremely complex adjustments. (An exception is the study by Hughes Hallett et al. (1989) which formulates co-operative agreements in the form of agreed exchange rate paths.) It is often argued that policy needs to follow rules that are easily implemented, easily monitored and whose advantages are intuitively apparent if they are acceptable to policy-makers. The monitoring argument for simplicity carries particular force in the international sphere where the need to monitor policy commitments applies to both the private sector and the countries entering into agreements. It may well be that well-designed simple rules will increase the credibility of policy commitments in the eyes of the private sector and foreign governments. In that case, how far can simple policy rules be designed to replicate the gains from full co-ordination?

This raises the issue of what is meant by simplicity in this context. One aspect of simplicity is the need to ensure that policy rules have a simple dynamic structure. A second aspect is to restrict the range of variables or information to which policy instruments respond. If this goes together with a specialization whereby different instruments respond to distinct subsets of variables, then we arrive at assignment rules, which represent a specific form of simplification.

One system of simplified rules that has been proposed is the Williamson–Miller (1987) extended target zone proposal, which blends each of these elements of simplicity. They propose that fiscal policy should be used to manage internal nominal demand growth, while monetary policy is aimed at maintaining external balance by holding exchange rates within wide bands around equilibrium (fundamental equilibrium exchange rate (FEER)) levels. In addition, the absolute level of world interest rates is used to steer world nominal income growth. Objections to this policy are that monetary policy has rather limited effect on the current account, so that the scheme may be rather poor at dampening current account imbalances, and that fiscal policy is too inflexible for successful management of internal demand. An alternative scheme, proposed by Boughton (1989), suggests that fiscal policy should instead be assigned to achieving external current account balance in the medium term, while monetary policy steers internal demand growth.

Empirical testing of these simple policy rules is still fairly sparse. Currie and Wren-Lewis (1988, 1989), using the GEM model, find that the extended target zone scheme could well have improved on historical performance over the past decade, and that this conclusion is fairly robust with respect to changes in the objective function (including the implied flexibility of fiscal policy). Moreover, the extended target zone proposal is found to outperform the alternative scheme proposed by Boughton. These findings are for the G3 countries alone, supporting a hierarchical structure of co-ordination; it is not clear whether they would generalize to a larger group of countries adopting the target zone proposal in a non-hierarchical way. However, it should be said that these comparisons are with historical outcomes. Further work is required to show whether or not these schemes genuinely outperform non-co-operative decision-making and therefore help to contain the potential inefficiencies of non-co-operative outcomes.

Taylor (1989) uses his own model of the G7 countries to examine a number of simple monetary rules. A fixed exchange rate regime is compared with a flexible exchange rate in which monetary policy is assigned to stabilizing the price level or nominal income or both price and output with different elasticities. The general conclusion is that the latter mixed rule is likely to have superior stabilization properties in the face of exogenous shocks to the economy and that an agreement to fix nominal interest rates between the USA, or Japan and the FRG achieves little with respect to internal or external stability.

Frenkel et al. (1989) evaluate some simple rules for monetary and fiscal policy using MULTIMOD which include the Williamson–Miller target zone proposal and Boughton's reverse assignment. As with the Taylor exercise they considered stochastic exogenous shocks. Simulations of individual shocks emphasize a point in the theoretical literature going back to Poole (1970) that the performance of simple policy rules varies with the nature of the shocks facing the economy. Rules that perform best for some shocks may perform less well for others. The authors are cautious in drawing strong conclusions from the full stochastic simulations which attempt to meet this problem. However, there appears to be some indication that the Miller–Williamson proposal does better than the reverse assignment, providing some support for the findings of Currie and Wren-Lewis.

The studies so far examine the efficacy of co-ordinated simple rules by comparing one rule with another or with history. Levine et al. (1989) compare co-operative with non-co-operative regimes on the assumption that policy is conducted in terms of particular simple rules. The incentive compatibility problem that we have surveyed for optimal rules is extended to simple rules. Their main findings, using a reduced two-bloc version of the OECD Interlink model are as follows. First, policy co-ordination can be effective under the constraint that rules must be simple. This confirms the results of other studies that we have discussed. Second, there is considerable scope for using agreements in the form of simple rules as a surrogate for more far-reaching agreement on international policy co-ordination. Levine et al. find that if the USA and the rest of the world agree only on the assignment of fiscal and monetary policy instruments to targets (inflation and output in this study), then even if the decisions over the feedback parameters are made non-co-operatively, the outcome is far superior to non-co-operative decision-making with no agreement whatsoever.

The recent interest in simple feedback rules derives from their intuitive appeal, from the need for simplicity and credibility and from their relative ease of implementation. We also know that feedback rules are less sensitive than open loop policies to modelling errors. It has yet to be established that robust rules can be found that retain simplicity but perform reasonably well across a range of different views of the world economy. This remains a major challenge for economists working in this area.

7.9 CONCLUSIONS

7.9.1 What have we Learned about Monetary Policy Co-ordination?

The principal contribution of the theoretical literature is methodological; that is to say it provides a framework for analysing macroeconomic policy in interdependent economies in terms of a game in which the players are the policy-makers in different blocs or countries and an atomized private sector. By specifying policy-makers' objectives in terms of a welfare function, the gains from co-ordination can be assessed by comparing the values of the welfare criteria under co-operative and non-co-operative equilibria.

Using this framework, Hamada demonstrated the potential for inefficient non-co-operative outcomes between countries as a result of policy spillovers. His seminal studies were limited to simple symmetrical two-country models which lacked dynamics and implicitly assumed backward-looking expectations on the part of the private sector. By introducing strategic dynamics and rational expectations, subsequent literature has addressed issues to do with reputation and the incentive compatibility of co-operative agreements.

In the light of these developments, is co-ordination desirable in principle and can co-operative agreements be sustained? The unequivocal superiority of co-operation demonstrated by Hamada now needs careful qualification. Co-operation in a context where policy-makers lack reputation for precommitment may be counter-productive. Co-operation is only unambiguously superior to non-co-operative outcomes if policy-makers enjoy reputation. Co-operative agreements can in principle be sustained in the face of incentives to renege if both governments and the private sector adopt suitable trigger mechanisms. These specify switches in private sector expectations and switches in government policies if governments jointly or individually renege.

Turning to the empirical literature, how large are the gains in practice? The general consensus arising from a large number of studies is that the gains from the co-ordination of monetary and fiscal policy among the OECD countries may be quite small, though significant. However, this conclusion needs careful qualification. The outcome of these exercises is model dependent and depends on the choice of welfare function, the nature of the shocks and whether (in rational expectations models) the governments enjoy reputation for precommitment or not. In particular, if shocks are persistent, if policy-makers have conflicting objectives, particularly incompatible exchange rate targets, and if reputational policies can be pursued, then the gains from co-ordination increase appreciably.

A serious limitation of much of the literature is that it assumes that policy-makers know the global model. We have reviewed studies which alert us to the dangers of policy co-ordination where the model is unknown and different policy-makers may use different models. However, if policy-makers can agree on which model to use, then the literature suggests that a robust policy exists which gives co-operation gains irrespective of which model turns out to be correct. The effects of model uncertainty can be further ameliorated if learning is allowed and policy is formulated in terms of feedback rules.

Another limitation of the literature is that they assume full co-operation involving both monetary and fiscal policy and that the implied optimal rules are extremely complex. The theoretical literature on the EMS and fixed exchange rate regimes in general show that limited agreements which tie the hands of policy-makers by making them choose policies constrained to maintaining fixed nominal or real exchange rates can be useful forms of surrogate co-operation. Empirical work on agreed exchange rate paths as a form of co-operation is less encouraging. Co-operation gains are small and asymmetrically distributed between participating countries. A number of studies look at simple rules such as the extended target zone proposals of Williamson and Miller (1987) and the reverse assignment of Boughton (1989). The findings are favourable when outcomes are compared with history, but it has not been established whether these schemes outperform non-co-operative decision-making, possibly based on similar rules.

7.9.2 Future Research

The literature that we have surveyed in this chapter is, of course, in a continuing state of development, so that this survey represents an intermediate report. Therefore it may be helpful to conclude by pointing to issues that would merit greater attention in future work.

One of the considerable advances in this field has been the application of rigorous game-theoretical techniques to questions of policy co-ordination, following the innovative contribution of Hamada. However, much remains to be done to clarify and strengthen the game-theoretical foundations of this literature. In particular, the introduction of general trigger strategies greatly multiplies the number of admissible equilibria, and the multiplicity in turn generates an indeterminacy in the analysis of co-ordination. Recent advances in game theory have been in the direction of narrowing down the range of admissible equilibria by imposing stricter equilibrium conditions (see Abreu, 1988; Harsanyi and Selton, 1988). The introduction of this work into the analysis of co-ordination should be a fruitful line of research.

It seems likely that advances will be made in incorporating learning into models with forward-looking behaviour, relaxing the extreme assumptions of rational expectations. This will have important implications for the literature on policy co-ordination. In particular, it should allow a more developed analysis of the consequences of model uncertainty for policy co-ordination than that surveyed in section 7.7. It should also allow a rigorous analysis of the benefits of information exchanges and perhaps substantiate the suggestion in our survey that the benefit of information exchanges are at least as important as those of co-ordination *per se*.

More narrowly, we would expect the literature to continue the investigation of effective sustainable simple rules for policy co-ordination. This line of enquiry is important, because practical rules are likely to be simple in design. Yet advantages of simplicity should not be at the expense of sustainability, credibility or robustness. The systematic investigation of rules along these lines is likely to be a continuing area of productive research.

A notable advance is this area in the 1980s has been the increasing flow of empirically based results, making the theoretical research much more relevant to policy-makers. It is possible that the analysis is now outstripping the capabilities of our empirical macroeconometric models. There are two respects, in particular, where this may be so. First, the analysis of alternative regimes requires careful attention to issues concerning the Lucas critique which have been insufficiently addressed in the context of the international macroeconometric models used in this literature. Second, in assessing regimes and policy rules, notably the EMS and European monetary union, long-run relationships are of appreciable importance. The current state of empirical international macromodels is probably not sufficiently advanced to incorporate these adequately. The advance of this area of research, in particular in measuring the benefits or otherwise of co-ordination and in coming forward with practical policy advice, depends in a major way on improvements in empirical models.

References

Abreu, D. (1988) On the theory of infinitely repeated games with discounting. *Econometrica* 56, 383–96.

Aoki, M. (1981) *Dynamic Analysis of Open Economies* New York: Academic Press.

Artis, M. and Currie, D. (1981) Monetary targets and the exchange rate: a case for conditional targets. *Oxford Economic Papers* (*Supplement*) 33, 176–200.

Barro, R. J. and Gordon, D. A. (1983) Rules, discretion and reputation in a model of monetary policy. *Journal of Monetary Economics* 17, 101-22.

Boughton, J. (1989) Policy assignment strategies with somewhat flexible exchange rates. In M. Miller, B. Eichengreen and R. Portes (ed), *Blueprints for Exchange Rate Management*. New York: Academic Press.

Bryant, R. (1987) Intergovernmental coordination of economic policies: an interim stocktaking. In *International Monetary Cooperation: Essays in Honor of Hensy Wallich*. Princeton, NJ: Princeton University Press, Princeton Essays in International Finance 69.

Canzoneri, M. B. and Gray, J. (1985) Monetary policy games and the consequences of non-cooperative behavior. *International Economic Review* 26(3), 547-64.

—— and Henderson, D. W. (1988) Is sovereign policymaking bad? *Carnegie-Rochester Conference Series on Public Policy* 28, 93-140.

—— and —— (1989) *Noncooperative Monetary Policies in Interdependent Economics*.

—— and Minford, P. (1986) When policy coordination matters: an empirical analysis. Discussion Paper 119, Centre for Economic Policy Research, July.

Carlozzi, N. and Taylor, J. (1985) International capital mobility and the coordination of monetary rules. In J. Bhandari (ed.), *Exchange Rate Management under Uncertainty*. Cambridge, MA: MIT Press.

Collins, S. M. (1988) Inflation and the EMS. In F. Giavazzi, S. Micossi and M. Miller (eds), *The European Monetary System*. Cambridge: Cambridge University Press.

Cooper, R. N. (1969) Macroeconomic policy adjustment in interdependent economies. *Quarterly Journal of Economics* 83, 1-24.

Currie, D. A. and Levine, P. (1985) Macroeconomic policy design in an interdependent world. In W. H. Buiter and R. C. Marston (eds), *International Economic Party Coordination*. Cambridge: Cambridge University Press.

—— and Vines, D. (1988) *Macroeconomic Interactions between North and South*. Cambridge: Cambridge University Press.

—— and Wren-Lewis, S. (1988) Evaluating the extended target zone proposal for the G3. Discussion Paper 221, Centre for Eonomic Policy Research.

—— and —— (1989) Evaluating blueprints for the conduct of international macropolicy. *American Economic Review* 79(2), 264-9.

——, Levine, P. and Vidalis, N. (1987) Cooperative and noncooperative rules for monetary and fiscal policy in an empirical two-bloc model. In R. Bryant and R. Portes (eds), *Global Macroeconomics: Policy Conflict and Cooperation*. London: Macmillan.

—— Holtham, G. and Hughes Hallett, A. (1989) The theory and practice of international policy coordination: does coordination pay? In R. Bryant, D. A. Currie, J. A. Frenkel, P. Masson and R. Portes (eds), *Macroeconomic Policies in an Interdependent World*. Washington, DC: IMF.

Fischer, S. (1987) International macroeconomic policy coordination. In M. Feldstein (ed.), *International Economic Cooperation*. Chicago, IL: University of Chicago Press.

Frankel, J. A. and Rockett, K. E. (1988) International macroeconomic policy coordination when policy makers do not agree on the true model. *American Economic Review* 78, 318-40.

Frenkel, J.A., Goldstein, M. and Masson, P.R. (1989) Simulating the effects of some simple coordinated versus uncoordinated policy rules. In R. Bryant, D.A. Currie, J.A. Frenkel, P. Masson and R. Portes (eds), *Macroeconomic Policies in an Interdependent World*. Washington, DC: IMF.

Friedman, J.W. (1971) A non-cooperative equilibrium for supergames. *Review of Economic Studies* 38, 1–12.

—— (1977) *Oligopoly and the Theory of Games*. Amsterdam: North-Holland.

Funabashi, Y. (1988) *Managing the Dollar: From the Plaza to the Louvre*. Washington, DC: Institute for International Economics.

Ghosh, A. and Masson, P. (1988) Model uncertainty, learning and gains from policy coordination. Working Paper 88/114, IMF.

Giavazzi, F. and Giovannini, A. (1986) Monetary policy interactions under managed exchange rates. Discussion Paper 123, Centre for Economic Policy Research.

—— and Pagano, M. (1988) The advantage of tying one's hands: EMS discipline and central bank credibility. *European Economic Review* 32, 1055–82.

—— Micossi, S. and Miller, M. (eds) (1988) *The European Monetary System*. Cambridge: Cambridge University Press.

Group of Thirty (1988) *International Macroeconomic Policy Coordination*. London: Group of Thirty.

Hamada, K. (1974) Alternative exchange rate systems and the interdependence of monetary policies. In R.Z. Aliber (ed.), *National Monetary Policies and the International Financial System*. IL: University of Chicago Press.

—— (1976) A strategic analysis of monetary interdependence. *Journal of Political Economy* 84, 677–700.

—— (1979) Macroeconomic strategy and coordination under alternative exchange rates. In R. Dornbusch and J.A. Frenkel (eds), *International Economic Policy*. Baltimore, MD: Johns Hopkins University Press.

—— (1985) *The Political Economy of International Monetary Interdependence*. Cambridge, MA: MIT Press.

Harsanyi, J. and Selten, R. (1988) *A General Theory of Equilibrium Selection in Games*. Cambridge, MA: MIT Press.

Holtham, G. and Hughes Hallett, A. (1987) International policy cooperation and model uncertainty. In R. Bryant and R. Portes (eds), *Global Macroeconomics: Policy Conflict and Cooperation*. London: Macmillan. (An extended version appears in Discussion Paper 190, Centre for Economic Policy Research.)

Hughes Hallett, A.J. (1986a) Autonomy and the choice of policy in asymmetrically dependent economies. *Oxford Economic Papers* 38, 516–44.

—— (1986b) International policy design and the sustainability of policy bargains. *Journal of Economic Dynamics and Control* 10, 467–94.

—— (1987a) The impact of interdependence on economic policy design: the case of the US, EEC and Japan. *Economic Modelling* 4, 377–96.

—— (1987b) Robust policy regimes for interdependent economies: a new argument for coordinating economic policies. Discussion Paper 151, Centre for Economic Policy Research.

—— (1987c) How robust are the gains to policy coordination to variations in the model and objectives? *Ricerche Economiche* 41, 341–72.

—— Holtham, G. and Hutson, G. (1989) Exchange rate targetting as a surrogate for international policy coordination. In M. Miller, B. Eichengreen and R. Portes (eds), *Blueprints for Exchange Rate Management*. New York: Academic Press.

Karakitsos, E. (1988) Asymmetrical effects of monetary policy between the US and Europe. *Journal of Economic Dynamics and Control* 12(2), 79–84.

Kehoe, P. J. (1987) Coordination of fiscal policies in a world economy. *Journal of Monetary Economics* 19, 349–76.

Kydland, F. E. and Prescott, E. C. (1977) Rules rather than discretion: the inconsistency of optimal plans. *Journal of Political Economy* 85, 473–92.

Levine, P. (1988) Does time inconsistency matter? Discussion Paper 227, Centre for Economic Policy Research.

—— and Currie, D. A. (1987) Does international policy coordination pay and is it Sustainable? A two country analysis. *Oxford Economic Papers* 39, 38–74.

Levine, P. and Holly, S. (1989) The time inconsistency issue is macroeconomics: a survey. Discussion Paper 05–87, Centre for Economic Forecasting, London Business School.

Levine, P., Currie, D. A. and Gaines, J. (1989) The use of simple rules for international policy agreements. In M. Miller, B. Eichengreen and R. Portes (eds), *Blueprints for Exchange Rate Management*. London: Academic Press.

Melitz, J. (1988) Monetary discipline and cooperation in the European Monetary System: a synthesis. In P. Giavazzi, S. Micossi and M. Miller (eds), *The European Monetary System*. Cambridge: Cambridge University Press.

Minford, P. and Canzoneri, M. B. (1987) Policy interdependence: does strategic behaviour pay? Discussion Paper 201, Centre for Economic Policy Research.

Miller, M. H. and Salmon, M. H. (1985) Policy coordination and dynamic games. In W. M. Buiter and R. C. Marston (eds), *International Economic Policy Coordination*. Cambridge: Cambridge University Press.

Oudiz, G. (1985) European policy coordination: an evaluation. *Recherches Economiques de Louvain* 51, 301–9.

—— and —— (1984) Macroeconomic policy coordination among the industrial economies. *Brookings Papers on Economic Activity* 1, 1–64.

—— and —— (1985) International policy coordination in dynamic macroeconomic models. In W. H. Buiter and R. C. Marston (eds), *International Economic Policy Coordination*. Cambridge: Cambridge University Press.

Persson, T. (1988) Credibility of macroeconomic policy: an introduction and broad survey. *European Economic Review* 32(2–3), 519–32.

van der Ploeg, F. (1987) International interdependence and policy coordination in economies with real and nominal wage rigidity. Discussion Paper 217, Centre for Economic Policy Research.

—— (1988) International policy coordination in interdependent monetary economies. *Journal of International Economics* 25, 1–23.

Poole, W. (1970) Optimal choice of monetary policy instruments in a simple stochastic macro-model. *Quarterly Journal of Economics* 84, 197–216.

Putnam, R. and Bayne, N. (1987) *Hanging Together: Cooperation and Conflict in the Seven-Power Summits*. London: Sage, 2nd edn.

Radner, R. (1981) Monitoring cooperative agreements in a repeated principal–agent relationship. *Econometrica* 49(5), 1127–48.

Rogoff, K. (1985) Can international monetary policy coordination be counter-productive? *Journal of International Economics* 18, 199–217.

—— (1987) Reputational constraints on monetary policy. *Carnegie–Rochester Conference Series on Public Policy* 27, 141–81.

Roubini, N. (1987) Leadership and policy coordination in the EMS. Mimeo, Harvard University.

Sachs, J. and McKibbin, W. (1985) Macroeconomic policies in the OECD and LDC external adjustment. Discussion Paper 56, Centre for Economic Policy Research.

Taylor, J.B. (1985) International coordination in the design of macroeconomic policy rules. *European Economic Review* 28, 53–81.

Taylor, J.B. (1989) Policy analysis with a multi-country model. In R.C. Bryant, D.A. Currie, J.A. Frenkel, P.R. Masson and R. Portes (eds), *Macroeconomic Policies in an Interdependent World*. The Brookings Institution, Centre for Economic Policy Research, and International Monetary Fund.

Turnovsky, S.J. and d'Orey, V. (1986) Monetary policies in interdependent economies with stochastic disturbances: A strategic approach. *Economic Journal* 96, 696–721.

Williamson, J. and Miller, M.H. (1987) *Targets and Indicators: A Blueprint for the International Coordination of Economic Policy*. Washington, DC: Institute for International Economics.

Index